AMERICAN CONSTITUTIONAL LAW
Introduction and Case Studies

AMERICAN CONSTITUTIONAL LAW
Introduction and Case Studies

Robert J. Steamer
University of Massachusetts/Boston

Richard J. Maiman
University of Southern Maine

McGRAW-HILL, INC.

New York   St. Louis   San Francisco   Auckland   Bogotá   Caracas
Lisbon   London   Madrid   Mexico   Milan   Montreal   New Delhi   Paris
San Juan   Singapore   Sydney   Tokyo   Toronto

AMERICAN CONSTITUTIONAL LAW
Introduction and Case Studies

1 2 3 4 5 6 7 8 9 0 DOC DOC 9 0 9 8 7 6 5 4 3 2 1

ISBN 0-07-060916-0 {hard cover}
ISBN 0-07-060977-2 {soft cover}

This book was set in Aster by The Clarinda Company.
The editors were Bertrand W. Lummus and
Fred H. Burns;
the production supervisor was Leroy A. Young.
The cover was designed by Rafael Hernandez.
The photo editor was Anne Manning.
R. R. Donnelley & Sons Company was printer and
binder.

Photo credits

Collection of the Supreme Court of the United States: pages 1, 3, 4, 5, 6, 7, 8, 9, 10, 11, 13, 14, 16, 17, 18, 19, 20, 22, 24, and 26.

Supreme Court Historical Society: pages 2, 12, 15, 21, 23, and 25

Library of Congress Cataloging-in-Publication Data

Steamer, Robert J.
    American constitutional law: introduction and case studies /
  Robert J. Steamer, Richard J. Maiman.
        p.   cm.
    Includes index.
    ISBN 0-07-060916-0 (hc)—ISBN 0-07-060977-2 (sc)
    1. United States—Constitutional law—Cases.   I. Maiman, Richard
J.   II. Title.
KF4549.S7   1992
342.73—dc20
[347.302]   91-28100

About the Authors

ROBERT J. STEAMER is professor emeritus of political science at the University of Massachusetts, where he taught courses in constitutional law, civil liberties, and American politics. A former president of the New England Political Science Association, he is the author of several highly regarded books on the United States Supreme Court, including *The Supreme Court in Crisis* (University of Massachusetts Press, 1971). His most recent book, *Chief Justice: Leadership and the Supreme Court* (University of South Carolina Press, 1986) was selected by *Choice* as one of the "outstanding academic books" of 1986–1987. He has also contributed scores of articles and reviews to political science, history, and law journals.

RICHARD J. MAIMAN is professor of political science at the University of Southern Maine, where he teaches in the undergraduate college, the public policy and management graduate program, and the school of law. His areas of specialization include constitutional law, civil liberties, the American presidency, and dispute resolution. His seminal research on alternatives to court has been published in such scholarly journals as *Law and Society Review*, *Law and Policy*, and *Policy Studies Journal*.

Between them, the authors have some 60 years of experience as teachers of constitutional law. Both have won awards and recognition for teaching excellence and both have held academic appointments at several universities in the United States and in Great Britain.

To
JUSTIN, JILLIAN, BRUCE, AND DANIEL

CONTENTS

PREFACE

For the past several decades, most undergraduates have studied American Constitutional Law in a two-semester course sequence. The first semester typically is devoted to United States Supreme Court decisions on such subjects as judicial review, separation of powers, federalism, and economic regulation. Depending upon the instructor's orientation, there might also be coverage of institutional aspects of the court—such as internal decision making, the selection of justices, modes of constitutional interpretation, and debates about the Court's proper role in the American constitutional system. The second semester course usually focuses on civil rights and civil liberties, particularly freedom of speech, press, and religion, criminal procedure, and racial equality. This two-term approach assumes that the courses comprise two halves of a comprehensive whole; it usually takes for granted that most students will complete both courses.

In recent years, however, a growing number of political science departments have abandoned this traditional approach. In part this may reflect the increased competition from such relatively new political science offerings as public policy and area studies. Moreover, as colleges and universities move toward more elaborate core curricula, academic departments sometimes find it necessary to contract their major requirements to provide students with more flexibility in choosing their courses. Whatever the reasons, it is clear that the two-semester constitutional law sequence is no longer as dominant pedagogically as it once was. In fact, in a recent random survey of college and university catalogues, we found that about 40 percent of all political science or equivalent departments now offer only a single constitutional law course. Catalogue descriptions indicate that most such courses are hybrids of the traditional sequence—that is, they cover the most essential elements of the two-semester approach, including judicial review, separation of powers, civil rights and liberties, and Supreme Court decision making.

Despite these developments, constitutional law textbooks continue to be

written and published as if nothing had changed. Most of the books produced
for two-semester courses (still, of course, a sizable market) provide far too
much depth and detail for courses only half that length. Not surprisingly, students resent being required to buy an expensive textbook and then reading
only half of it. The other kind of casebook is written with only one-half of the
traditional sequence in mind. It may cover civil liberties quite admirably,
while ignoring governmental powers. And such books usually include little or
no coverage of institutional aspects of the Supreme Court. In sum, we believe
that neither the "long" nor the "short" casebooks now on the market are particularly well suited to one-semester constitutional law courses.

What we have produced, then, is a relatively compact, tightly organized
text/casebook that is both comprehensive and economical in its coverage of
constitutional law and the Supreme Court. Our goal has been to provide students with a solid grasp of the Supreme Court's work while introducing them
to major constitutional doctrines. This has been done through a technique of
selecting opinions to do double duty by simultaneously illustrating substantive constitutional development and judicial approaches to policy formulation. We have also tried to strike a reasonable balance between breadth and
depth by limiting the number of opinions we cover, but beginning each chapter with an expository essay and prefacing each case by an introductory nar-
rative. Following each edited opinion (except the most recent ones) is a discussion of the decision's aftermath. Typically this includes the impact of the
case on the litigants themselves (where this information is available) and,
more importantly, the effect of the case on future doctrinal development.

Within this framework we have devoted the first two chapters to discussion of crucial institutional matters—general legal concepts, the structure of
the judicial system, the Supreme Court's internal workings, conflicts about
the application of judicial review, and the Court's relationship with the presidency and Congress. The remaining five chapters deal with substantive issues
in constitutional law including federalism, separation of powers, due process
of law, freedom of speech and religion, and equal protection of the laws.
Although the book has been fashioned specifically for a one-semester course,
we believe that it would work equally well, with appropriate supplementary
materials, in either term of a year-long sequence.

Anyone who has ever written a book or designed a course will appreciate
that our most difficult task was to decide not what to put in, but what to
leave out. As experienced teachers, we were guided primarily by our convictions about what undergraduates must know to be conversant with the essentials of American constitutional law. We were also impelled by our experience of which Supreme Court cases are most likely to engage and interest
students. Thus, we have chosen what we consider a judicious mix of opinions
from different eras of the Court's history, organized topically to convey a
sense of the Court's influence upon the nation's political and legal structure.
Although we acknowledge some bias in our case selection toward the late
twentieth century and toward civil rights and liberties, our introductory
essays should make it abundantly clear that American constitutional history
did not begin with *Brown* v. *Board of Education* and end with *Roe* v. *Wade!*

We wish to express our gratitude to the following professional reviewers
whose cogent suggestions were, in large part, incorporated into the final

manuscript: Frank Anechiarico, Hamilton College; William Ansberry Southeast Missouri State University; Thomas Barth, University of Wisconsin–Eau Claire; Donald Dahlin, University of South Dakota; Dennis Goldford, Drake University; John O'Callaghan, Suffolk University; Samuel Ramsay, Bryant College; Susan Siggelakis, University of New Hampshire; Ron Stidham, Lamar University; and Robert Wood, North Dakota State University.

We would like to thank Senior Editor Bertrand Lummus and Senior Editing Supervisor Fred Burns, who helped guide the project from concept to typescript to textbook. We are also especially grateful to Karla Fuchs whose expertise with the word processor was invaluable.

ROBERT J. STEAMER
RICHARD J. MAIMAN

AMERICAN CONSTITUTIONAL LAW
Introduction and Case Studies

1 The Supreme Court in American Politics

The United States Congress may not authorize the comptroller general to make spending cuts as part of a statutory scheme to reduce the federal budget deficit . . . A state may not make it a crime to burn the American flag as an act of political protest . . . Congress may permit the detention of certain defendants without bail before trial . . . Military authorities may prohibit servicemen from wearing yarmulkas while in uniform . . . A public school principal may delete from a student newspaper articles he or she considers objectionable . . . A state may not mandate the death penalty for a murder committed by a prisoner already serving a life sentence without possibility of parole . . . Congress may withhold federal highway funds from states that set the legal drinking age at less than 21 years . . .

Scores of policy pronouncements like these are issued each year by the United States Supreme Court. Most meet the first test of political significance: they affect "who gets what, when and how" in the United States. Typically, the "who" in a Supreme Court case is a person, a private institution, a government agency, or a corporate enterprise, for whom the potential rewards of a favorable decision are sufficient to justify the considerable expense, time, and effort required to see a case through to the Supreme Court. Often these parties are supported financially by organizations representing others not directly involved in the case whose interests will be affected, for better or worse, by the Court's decision.

"What" is at stake is usually one of the conventional political resources of power, money, or freedom. In all likelihood the questions that come before the Supreme Court have been answered already by decision makers in the legislative and executive arenas. However, only the Court can determine that a particular outcome is required by the Constitution itself. Although a Supreme Court decision is not necessarily the last word on any given "what," it does lend tremendous legitimacy to a prevailing claim. Vindication by the Supreme Court is one of the greatest prizes available in American politics.

"When" a judgment occurs is a matter for the Supreme Court itself to decide, since it exercises extraordinary control over its own agenda. Generally it is several years between the initiation of a lawsuit and its resolution by the Supreme

Court, though in cases the Court deems especially important the waiting period can be reduced to a matter of a few weeks.

"How" Supreme Court decisions are made involves a unique combination of secrecy and public scrutiny. In each case the Court considers written and oral arguments, deliberates privately, and then issues its decision accompanied by a written explanation of the outcome. Members of the Court who disagree with the judgment are free to say so and to disclose their reasons in writing. Thus, despite the cloistered atmosphere in which it works, the Supreme Court engages in a continuing public dialogue about the major political issues of the day.

The famous (or infamous) Supreme Court ruling in *Roe* v. *Wade*, handed down in 1973, can be used to illustrate the Court's political decision-making role. Texas was one of about 20 states in the early 1970s with statutes dating from the nine-teenth century which prohibited abortions except when a woman's life would be endangered by continuing her pregnancy. An unmarried pregnant woman named Norma McCorvey, using the legal pseudonym Jane Roe to protect her anonymity, challenged the Texas law on the ground that it interfered with her personal priva-cy, which she claimed was protected by a number of provisions of the U.S. Constitution. In her complaint McCorvey specified that she was suing "on behalf of herself and all other women" similarly situated—all women, that is, who because of restrictive state laws were unable to obtain legal abortions. Thus the *who* in this case included the many thousands of persons who would be affected by the Court's decision. *What* the Court was asked to decide was whether the free-dom of reproductive choice that McCorvey believed the Texas law denied her was indeed protected by the American Constitution. While the Supreme Court had previously held that the Constitution protected "marital privacy," including the right of married persons to obtain contraceptives without state interference, it had not yet considered the question of abortion. In this respect the *Roe* case was rather unusual, since the Supreme Court generally prefers to take only small steps beyond its previous positions.

When Norma McCorvey's legal challenge was heard might have significantly affected its outcome, since the gestation period of a federal court case is consid-erably longer than that of a human fetus. To keep McCorvey's case alive, though she was no longer pregnant (she had had a child and given it up for adoption), the Court waived its usual procedural requirements regarding "mootness." Timing is a serious problem in judicial decision making, and particularly so in complex cases where the wheels of the legal process may move so slowly that pre-vailing parties are not able to enjoy the fruits of their eventual victories. Even after a decision is made, its implementation can be extremely time-consuming. For example, because of years of defiance and delay on the part of southern politicians and school officials, none of the black children who won the Supreme Court's landmark ruling in *Brown* v. *Board of Education* in 1954 ever benefited directly from the decision. Indeed, 35 years after *Brown* a federal court held that the Topeka, Kansas, school board still had not fully complied with the Supreme Court's mandate.

How the Supreme Court eventually responded to McCorvey's petition tells us a great deal about the Court's policy-making role. When the decision was announced in January 1973, a majority of the justices agreed with McCorvey's claim that she had a constitutionally protected right to obtain an abortion, and that state laws in Texas and elsewhere prohibiting the exercise of that right were therefore invalid. However, the seven justices in the majority based their decision not on a single explicit constitutional provision, but rather on a more generalized right of privacy which they found rooted variously in the First, Fourth, Fifth, Ninth, and Fourteenth Amendments. The two dissenting justices questioned the constitutional underpinnings of this right of privacy and severely criticized the Court's willingness to read into the Constitution a meaning that almost certainly was not intended by its authors. Implicit in their criticism was a question that the Court's critics often ask outright: why, in a nation that calls itself democratic, should a handful of judges with lifetime tenure be able to exercise such sweeping authority over their fellow citizens?

Why indeed? The role of the Supreme Court in the American political system is more widely debated than understood. To understand that role requires knowledge of the Constitution of the United States, of law and legal processes, of the structures and functions of courts, and of judicial behavior. It is simple enough to read a Supreme Court opinion and to understand in a literal sense what the Court has said. It is another matter to comprehend it fully, both as a decision which affects the legal rights of parties to a lawsuit, and as an authoritative pronouncement which may have a significant impact on the political system.

Each chapter of this book comprises a number of carefully selected and edited Supreme Court opinions covering many of the important issues in American constitutional law. These opinions, the basic units of Supreme Court decision making, normally consist of a ruling on the constitutional issues presented and the reasoning that supports it. The systematic study of judicial opinions makes it possible to grasp the fundamentals of American constitutionalism. However, to appreciate more fully the meaning of those opinions one must be conversant with the environment of judicial decision making. Thus in this book each set of Supreme Court opinions is preceded by an essay establishing the frameworks—historical, legal, and political—in which the opinions should be read. The remainder of this first essay will serve as a general introduction to the setting in which the Supreme Court operates.

WHAT IS LAW?

This question has been asked by the leading intellects of the day ever since humans have been capable of reasoning and communicating their thoughts to others. Yet even today, after centuries of probing, there is no definitive answer to what appears to be a perennially elusive question. We do know, however, that all societies live under rules. They may be relatively simple as in primitive societies, or they may be so complex that a professional class of lawyers is needed to interpret them for the general population. But whatever the nature or the number of the rules, their use is universal, a strong empirical indication that human beings cannot live together without them. In modern societies these rules are designated as law and are binding upon everyone, enforceable by the government through the threat of fine, imprisonment, or even death. And only the government, of all society's myriad institutions, possesses a legal monopoly of force. One may agree to be bound by the rules (law) of a church, a private club, or any number of organizations to which men and women gravitate, but one cannot be arrested or sent to jail by the Episcopal church, by the Elks club, or by the American Bar Association. Any attempt to punish members in a physically harmful way for not abiding by the organization's rules is itself subject to legal intervention by the state. Clearly, any discussion of law must include a discussion of the state, or politics, as well as philosophy, for law evolved and continues to grow and change only as humans reflect on their position in the universe and upon the best form of society.

Although scores of thinkers have pondered the fundamental issues surrounding the concept of law for centuries, neither the solutions for society's conflicts nor the basic problems themselves have changed much since the Greeks first grappled with them. It is, for example, difficult to improve upon Aristotle's formulations of the major themes and conflicts found in law. First is the concept of human beings as part of the universe, subject to its physical laws, and yet capable of dominating nature through a free will that can distinguish between good and evil. Second is Aristotle's distinction between distributive and remedial justice. The former concerns the distribution of goods and honors to each according to his place in the community, an ordering of equal treatment of equals before the law. This is much more complicated than appears at first glance as we shall see when we deal with "equal protection of the laws," a Fourteenth Amendment guarantee which the United States Supreme Court has construed broadly to ensure equal status of persons under the Constitution. Remedial or corrective justice relates to the redress of consequences of a person's action. Punishment redresses crime, and reparation redresses civil wrong. A thief may be sent to jail and a person whose automobile has been damaged may sue to collect the cost of repairs. In each instance it is the duty of the law to order a new arrangement which is objectively in balance with the old.

Aristotle's third contribution is his separation of legal from natural justice or, as moderns would state it, the difference between positive and natural law. This is essentially the distinction between man-made visible laws, enforceable as commands—in John Austin's phrase, "a rule laid down for the guidance of an intelligent being by an intelligent being having power over him"—and laws based on human nature, universally discoverable through reason, which dictate what human beings ought and ought not to do. Another of Aristotle's differentiations is that between law and equity. One of the most important characteristics of law is generality, a concept which maintains that laws must be phrased in broad language in order to apply to situations not contemplated by the legislators who write them. Courts apply laws written in general terms to concrete cases, or as Supreme Court Justice Felix Frankfurter once said, "Legislatures make law wholesale; courts make law retail." Generality makes possible impartiality in administration. At the same time a law may, if applied to an individual case, be unduly harsh, even unjust. Under such circumstances courts may apply a corrective, an equitable solution to a conflict by making an exception to the law. In its broadest sense equity denotes fairness. Equity also has a more technical meaning in Anglo-American law which we shall discuss below.

Aristotle's final contribution is a precursor of modern constitutionalism, namely, his definition of laws as a body of rules which bind the governors as well as the governed. "Laws," he wrote, "are the rules by which magistrates should exercise their powers, and should watch and check transgressors." American constitutional law is essentially concerned with rules by which magistrates exercise their powers, magistrates being an inclusive generic term embracing presidents, senators, congressmen, governors, legislators, bureaucrats, and judges as well as thousands upon thousands of local officials.

SOME WORKING DEFINITIONS

Although Aristotle's framework tells us that law cannot be defined neatly in a sentence or a paragraph, but must be viewed as a complex idea intertwined with the whole of human existence, it is appropriate to begin our study by defining the word "law" as it is prefaced by distinctive adjectives peculiar to American, and often Anglo-American, usage. This may be done by juxtaposing the six sets of terms which one encounters most often in any discussion of American law.

Public Law and Private Law

Public law embraces all questions and conflicts which arise as a result of the state acting in its sovereign capacity. Any lawsuit in which the government, or an agent of the government, is one of the parties is public. All criminal prosecutions, for example, fall into the category of public law as do cases involving a suit between two states, a dispute between the United States and a state, or an action brought against a local government by a citizen who is attempting to reduce tax assessments. Most acts of Congress, and all actions of the President and the executive bureaucracy, form a part of American public law. Private law, on the other hand, embraces private relationships which are defined primarily, although not exclusively, by state legislatures. The subject matter of statutes and lawsuits which may be deemed private include such human relationships as marriage, divorce, and contracts, and often involve actions for damages (torts) whether for personal physical assault, libel, or medical malpractice. The list of situations in which individuals come into conflict is almost endless, and legislatures and courts attempt to bring some order to the chaotic human struggle which the English philosopher Thomas Hobbes called "nasty, brutish, and short." The line between public and private law is somewhat blurred since the state furnishes not only the machinery for moderating private disputes but also fixes the ground rules governing the methods or procedure and modes of settlement. And in some instances a private controversy, such as a suit for money damages alleging defamation of character, becomes public because of the intrusion of the constitutionally guaranteed right of free speech. Or a divorce action in which one of the parties moves to a state other than that of the marriage domicile, may raise a public law question if the "full faith and credit clause" of Article IV of the Constitution becomes an issue. In spite of the imperfect line between public and private, there are broad areas of litigation in which the government itself is not directly involved.

Constitutional Law and Administrative Law

Public law has two major components: constitutional and administrative law. The latter encompasses the vast array of presidential edicts (executive orders) and rules and regulations promulgated by the executive departments, the independent regulatory commissions, and the armed forces. Given the growth of the federal bureaucracy in the twentieth century, Congress has had little choice but to permit the agencies to prescribe rules and regulations and to issue orders enforcing these rules. Any order issued by an administrative agency is subject to review in the courts, and a large body of law surrounds the process involving such matters as unfair labor practices dealt with by the National Labor Relations Board and the safety of aircraft supervised by the Federal Aviation Administration. If litigation raises constitutional questions, it may move into the category of constitutional law. More often than not, a corporation or an individual is merely challenging the agency's interpretation of an act of Congress and no constitutional question enters the case.

Constitutional law will, of course, be our main concern. In a phrase, it involves the interpretation and application of the Constitution by the Supreme Court as well as lower federal and state courts. In those nations in which the government is not bound by a single specific written instrument—England is the foremost example—constitutional law, while not ignoring court decisions, would find much of its significant material in acts of the parliament which are ipso facto constitutional. No court in the United Kingdom can declare them otherwise. In the United States, however, since the written Constitution is the "supreme law of the land," as it says with unvarnished clarity, and since the Supreme Court decides its final meaning, American constitutional law is primarily the study of Supreme Court decisions. Any action of any government official—federal, state, or local—must theoretically accord with the Constitution. When the Court is faced with a challenge to official action, it must first decide what the Constitution means, and very often the Court must determine the meaning of such inexact phrases as "due process," "equal protection," "interstate commerce," or "direct taxes." The Court gives definitive interpretation to the scope and limits of governmental power and at the same time guarantees the integrity of the system.

Statutory Law and Decisional Law

An important distinction must be made between *a* law and *the* law. The former refers to a written statute which has been formally enacted by a legislative body—Congress or a state legislature—and is known as *statutory law*. All statutes must conform to the Constitution of the United States and are subject to a challenge of unconstitutionality in a court of proper jurisdiction. When a court interprets and applies a law within the framework of a case, assuming the law is constitutional, the resulting decision then becomes *the* law on that particular subject. This is variously known as *decisional law* or *case law*. In practice there is an inevitable mixture of legislative statutes and court decisions, for sooner or later a statute will end up with a judge's view of its intent, a judicial gloss which may expand, contract, clarify, or even distort the original meaning of the legislature. If a legislative body disagrees with the judicial interpretation of a statute, it may reenact the legislation in language which will require a judicial reassessment of legislative intent. Thus, on matters of statutory interpretation, the legislative will is supreme, unlike questions of constitutionality on which the judicial word is final unless the Constitution is amended.

Common Law and Equity

This raises the controversial question: Who makes the law, the legislature or the courts? The answer is both. The American legal system is in the common law tradition and herein lies the root of judge-made law. The common law of England which developed over centuries was transplanted to most of the English-speaking world including the American colonies, and it is today the foundation of the

American legal system. It is the rule of decision in all state courts except Louisiana which has retained the Napoleonic code, or civil law, of its French heritage. Gradual changes in the law and in the courts of England took place under William the Conqueror and his immediate successors as the Norman influence began to affect Anglo-Saxon and Germanic practices, but it is Henry II, the king of England from 1154 to 1189, on whom the title, "Father of the Common Law," has been properly bestowed. His great contribution was the establishment of the first permanent system of national law courts with professional judges who were able to develop a body of national law common to the whole of England. They did so on a case-by-case basis in the absence of legislation, formulating the law as new controversies arose. In the present day when we turn primarily to legislatures to redress our grievances, and to the courts as a last resort, it is difficult to conceive of a time when changes in the law took place almost exclusively as a result of pronouncements of judges. Supreme Court Justice Oliver Wendell Holmes, Jr., traced the development of such legal concepts as liability, trespass, negligence, fraud, malice, contracts, succession, and possession, to their roots in the English common law. His work emphasized how incredibly complex human relationships are. For example, in discussing *possession,* a much older concept than *ownership,* Holmes asked: When does one become entitled to absolute protection of what one possesses? He then demonstrated how problems arise when one does not have a title to a particular piece of property, title normally being enough to retain possession under the common law. In whale fishing, if the harpoonist loses his hold on the whale and another comes along and kills the wounded creature, who can claim possession? Or supposing the first harpoon does not kill the whale but remains attached to the animal while a second harpoonist actually finishes it off? Who retains possession? Do the whalers split 50–50? Under English custom, confirmed by the common law courts, if the first striker lost his hold on the whale, and it was then killed by another, the first had no claims. If, however, the first harpoonist held fast to the whale until it was struck by another, but then lost his hold, he had possession of the entire whale.

Holmes also discussed a case in which a depositor in a bank left her pocketbook which was subsequently picked up by another customer. A reward was offered for the return of the pocketbook, but who might rightfully claim it? The owner of the bank or the finder? An English court said that the occupants of the banking house "were the proper depositories of the article so left," implying that a person has no rights in a commercial establishment except to transact the business which brought her there. In dealing with the conflicts of everyday life—from the simple to the complex—the common law judges created an entire legal system. In some instances common law judges simply confirmed custom, but in others they necessarily fashioned new rules when confronted with a human tangle which required authoritative straightening.

In addition to creating the substance of a legal system, the common law judges also formulated the procedures whereby courts bring litigation to an orderly conclusion. These include such matters as the issuance of writs, procedures surrounding arrests, or the initiation of a lawsuit, and the use of juries. Later, when the Bill of Rights was adopted, both the members of Congress who proposed the first 10 amendments and the state legislators who voted to ratify them assumed that the general language used would be defined in common law terms. For example, the word "jury" used in both the Sixth and Seventh Amendments was interpreted by American courts to mean a common law jury which consisted of

12 persons and required a unanimous verdict for guilt or acquittal. Although the Supreme Court has reinterpreted the constitutional meaning of jury trial so as to permit nonunanimous verdicts and the use of juries of less than 12 persons, the English common law definition was with us for almost two centuries.

Historically the common law became known as judge-made or unwritten law as opposed to codified or written law. The latter system grew out of the Roman tradition, which attempted to deal with latent conflicts through a comprehensive set of written rules. The concept of written as opposed to unwritten law is subject to some confusion. In a literal sense judges' decisions are written down and become a matter of record. This was in fact true in twelfth-century England when a record of legal proceedings was kept in yearbooks which were then used as a guide by legal practitioners. Moreover, Henry de Bracton, in his *De Legibus Angliae* published in the thirteenth century, compiled the great mass of law as it had developed in the English courts. And some 500 years later William Blackstone published his famous *Commentaries* on the common law. The appropriate distinction, therefore, between code law (known variously as civil law or Roman law) and common law is in the methods of determining what the law is, although in common parlance the common law is often spoken of as unwritten.

The main characteristic of common law is *stare decisis* (to stand by decided cases), or precedent, which means that once a point of law has been decided by the highest court of proper jurisdiction it is fixed law, and all judges are from that point on bound to apply it unless and until it is changed by legislation. While precedent is the key to an understanding of common law, giving Anglo-American law a measure of stability and predictability, the system has not been so rigid as to preclude change. *Stare decisis* does not imply that the law can never be altered, only that precedents are not to be discarded lightly. Thus paradoxically, the common law contained a balanced mixture of certainty and flexibility which afforded adaptation to new times, new places, and new conditions, from the twelfth century to the twentieth, from England to Africa, Australia, India, and America. Today the term *common law* as it is used in the United States refers to those legal principles developed in England from the time of the Norman conquest to the time of the American Revolution. Thus it makes more sense to differentiate statutory law from decisional (or case) law than from common law. In twentieth-century America, written statutes govern legal matters to such an extent that we approach a civil law system. Our courts act primarily as interpreters of legislative enactments rather than as initiators of legal rules. However, the influence of the common law on American judicial practice is pervasive and ineradicable. Many of its ancient forms and methods are still with us, and its spirit or mood seems destined to guide our legal system for generations to come.

Operating alongside and in conjunction with the common law is a somewhat different legal concept called *equity*. Although the principle of equity had been understood by legal philosophers for some time, at least since Aristotle, it was the English who developed it into a systematic procedure. English equity originated in the ancient concept that the king had the right to make rules of law where none existed, to exercise his "conscience" under special circumstances. In the fourteenth and fifteenth centuries these circumstances arose with such frequency that an entirely new system of courts came into being to dispense equity. Given the nature of the common law with its insistence on adherence to precedent—common law judges loved the maxim, "it is better that the law should be certain than that it should be just"—the law tended to injustice on occasion. If an aggrieved person could get no relief under the existing writs, he appealed to the king, or more likely to someone who was close to the king, to intercede in order to dispense justice or "do equity." These appeals to the king became so numerous that the king delegated them to the chancellor who became the "keeper of the king's conscience." Eventually the chancellor's court was formalized in a system of courts—courts of chancery—with rules of practice for granting equitable relief, and for centuries courts of law and courts of equity existed side by side.

Today, although the two procedures are still differentiated since they serve different purposes, judges in the United States and in England preside over proceedings of law and dispense equity in the same courtroom. Equity is used in modern times to prevent wrongs or to compel someone, either a private person or a public official, to live up to his or her obligations. A lawsuit can only redress wrongs by compensating for damages, but an equitable proceeding can prevent the wrong in the first place. For example, if a person were to sign a contract for the purchase of a home and the seller decided to withdraw, the buyer could bring suit for damages. Or the buyer might, in an equity proceeding, request a court to issue an injunction ordering the seller to live up to the contract. In the equity proceeding, the buyer could acquire the home for which he or she had contracted. In a lawsuit for damages this would not be possible. While suits at law involve a judge and a jury handing down a judgment, equity proceedings have no juries. The judge orders that something be done or not be done by issuing a decree, usually an injunction, violation of which results in a citation for contempt of court. Contempt is punishable by fine or imprisonment or both. Equity has important implications for constitutional law in that a person may request an injunction from a federal court to restrain a public official from enforcing a law on the ground that the law is unconstitutional. This has limited use, however, since courts will not enter a decree unless the challenger can show that he or she is personally in immediate danger of sustaining injury. In the usual course of events, it is impossible to demonstrate personal danger until the law has actually been applied, that is, until a person has been arrested and convicted. Then, of course, he or she can show the requisite harm, and may therefore challenge the constitutionality of the law, but this would be through the law and not through the equity route.

Civil Law and Criminal Law

This section might be titled civil and criminal *procedure* since the term, civil law, is used interchangeably with Roman law or code of law and thus may lead to some confusion. We are concerned with distinctions which the law makes between criminal offenses which involve violations of law, and civil suits which may or may not result from wrongdoing on the part of an individual.

Civil law embraces controversies between private parties, usually human beings, though sometimes the conflict involves the government, state, or nation, or corporations which may sue as "persons" in the courts. Civil litigation grows out of recurring and convenient relationships such as contracts, wills, marriage, divorce, patents, or copyrights, and often arises as a result of a private injury known legally as a "tort" action. Torts embrace such personal wrongs as assault, defamation of character, breach of contract, or any harm to persons or property which may result in a suit for damages. The government, whether or not it is one of the litigants, provides the machinery—the courts—through which an aggrieved party may attempt to remedy what he or she considers a wrongful act. In some instances a single incident may provoke both civil and criminal penalties. For example, one who believes that he or she is libeled by a television commentator may sue for damages in a civil proceeding, and the journalist may be prosecuted under state or federal criminal laws.

Criminal law deals with crimes which are defined as offenses against the state and are punishable by fine or imprisonment. Under federal law and under the constitution or laws of some states, acts are criminally punishable only if they are so defined in statutes. In other states acts are punishable if they were crimes under the common law of England. Both the common law and current statutes distinguish between major crimes known as felonies and petty crimes which are called misdemeanors. Felonies include such offenses as arson, murder, bribery, kidnapping, rape, and robbery and are punishable by no less than 1 year in the penitentiary and may include the death penalty. Misdemeanors may include any infractions of the public order which neither endanger life nor destroy property. Such acts as obstructing a public thoroughfare, making loud and boisterous noises, or public drunkenness are misdemeanors. Society has not yet found a way to keep some semblance of order without punishing defined wrongdoing or furnishing citizens with a vehicle (courts) to settle their inevitable conflicts.

Positive Law and Natural Law

Another distinction important for the student of constitutional law is that between positive and natural law. We alluded to this briefly in our discussion of Aristotle's major legal themes, but since Aristotle's day, these concepts have received extended treatment by legal philosophers throughout the western world. All of the aspects of law discussed above fall into the category of positive law, which embraces all law that has as its authority nothing beyond human will or human creation. In John Austin's words, "All positive law is deduced from a clearly determinable law-giver as sovereign." Positive law is "a species of commands" flowing "from a determinate source." Positive law does not include the laws of natural science, laws of morality, or any concept of universal or natural law. It is simply the total conglomerate of human rules to guide and to control individuals and societies.

Natural law, on the other hand, is a complex idea of ancient origin, which has had a commanding influence on American jurisprudence from the beginning. In the broadest sense natural law expresses the search for an ideal justice, a goal to which the positive law aspires but which it never quite attains. Although natural law theories have been used to support ideologies of varying kinds, its two great contributions which cannot be dismissed lightly are first, the idea of a universal order discoverable by reason which obligates human beings to act justly and decently, and second, the concept of inalienable rights possessed by everyone everywhere simply by virtue of being human. The natural rights idea of the seventeenth-century political theorist, John Locke, was written into the Declaration of Independence and later into the Bill of Rights of the Constitution, at which point certain natural law principles became the highest *positive* law of the United States. Justice Holmes dismissed natural law as a "brooding omnipresence in the sky" and yet he and most justices past and present have used such terms as "reasonableness," "fairness," "decency," or "common conscience of mankind" in filling out the content of constitutional rights. Such terms are essentially "natural law" concepts since they assume that reasonable persons can agree on an objective meaning of fairness or decency. Who, for example, would maintain that it is perfectly reasonable, fair, and decent for a police officer to beat a suspect with a club until he confessed to a crime? There is something inherently or "naturally" wrong with such brutality, and it is not simply a matter of what one person or even one society happens to prefer. There is, according to natural law, an injustice in certain acts that is clearly recognizable by all but those who refuse to make or are incapable of making a moral judgment.

While it may be possible for reasonable men and women to agree that some fundamental precepts are universal and natural in the sense that they are in tune with human nature or essence, it is also possible, in fact likely, that there may be reasonable disagreement as the universal descends into detail. Currently, for example, society is debating the question of when life begins and whether the abortion of a fetus is a violation of some fundamental decency; whether the death penalty is permissible in a just society; whether monogamous marriage and the family should continue to be sanctioned by society as the only legal method of propagation of the species. Whether there is an intrinsic right and wrong in these matters may be debatable, but the natural law theory will unquestionably have an impact on the outcome of the debate. Even the dedicated relativist cannot ignore the persistent idea that there are some universal rules governing human behavior, that what people prefer to do is not necessarily what they ought to do.

THE AMERICAN CONSTITUTION

Each year well over a million tourists file through the rotunda of the National Archives Building in Washington, D.C. For many, the Archives is simply one more stop on their patriotic pilgrimage, its contents barely distinguishable from those of the Museum of Natural History and the National Gallery of Art. For those with a somewhat better grasp of American history, the main attraction of the National Archives is likely to be the Declaration of Independence, which is dramatically displayed in a helium-filled, shatterproof glass case on a raised dais in the center of the rotunda. Also exhibited, slightly less prominently, are several of the original manuscript pages of the U.S. Constitution. The positions of the two documents probably reflects their relative importance in the minds of most Americans. Thomas Jefferson's ringing words—"We hold these truths to be self-evident: that all men are created equal . . . life, liberty, and the pursuit of happiness . . . our lives, our fortunes, and our sacred honor"—continue to echo in our minds years after we memorized them in school. The Constitution, by contrast, is full of obscure phrases like "advice and consent" and "full faith and credit," which mean little to anyone but the constitutional lawyers to whom they seem to mean everything. Relatively few Americans can quote accurately from the Constitution, much less explain its significance in any detail.

And yet undoubtedly the Constitution is the more important of the two documents. The Declaration was an eloquent political statement, though quite without legal force, giving the reasons why Americans wanted to be independent from Great Britain. The Constitution was—and is—a binding contract forging the people of the United States into a political union, specifying what they had won in their struggle with Britain, and what they intended to do with it.

The basic text of the Constitution was hammered out in secret over 13 intense weeks during the spring and summer of 1787. Twelve of the 13 states sent delegates to Philadelphia (Rhode Island, preoccupied with internal political strife, declined to participate), ostensibly to discuss possible changes in the Articles of Confederation that had loosely connected the states since 1781. After 6 troubled years, the Confederation was rapidly dissolving under the pressures of domestic economic competition and military threats from abroad. Quickly concluding that even radical surgery could not save the Articles, the delegates instead began consideration of a whole new document. As they worked their way through a succession of draft proposals, the delegates' fundamental challenge was to create "a more perfect union," a government strong enough to provide security and prosperity, but not so powerful as to threaten the American people's hard-won freedoms. Their final product, a 4000-word pastiche of high ideals and shrewd compromises, was influenced strongly by the works of John Locke and the French political theorist Charles de Secondat Montesquieu, both proponents of limited government.

Their work done, most of the delegates returned home from Philadelphia to play leading roles in securing approval of the Constitution by their own state legislatures. Over the next 2 years, the most influential arguments in favor of the new Constitution were marshaled by James Madison and Alexander Hamilton and published serially, with a few contributions by John Jay, in leading New York newspapers. Later these essays were collected—and immortalized—as the *Federalist Papers*, one of the classic works of American political thought. Despite vigorous opposition from the so-called Anti-Federalists, who saw the new document as a threat to state sovereignty and personal liberties, the Constitution was quickly approved by the required number of states, and became effective in 1788.

Although the Anti-Federalists failed to prevent the Constitution's ratification, they succeeded in raising a number of issues that its supporters felt compelled to address. When the United States Congress met for the first time in 1789, its first order of business was to consider a set of amendments to the Constitution proposed by James Madison, serving as a representative from Virginia. These amendments were essentially a list of individual liberties intended to be protected from interference by the new government of the United States. Some of these protections were quite sweeping: The First Amendment, for example, says that "Congress shall make *no* law . . . abridging the freedom of speech . . ." [emphasis added]. Others, however, were more limited in scope: the Fourth Amendment prohibits only ". . . *unreasonable* searches and seizures . . ." [emphasis added]. After some debate and considerable redrafting, 10 amendments, known collectively as the Bill of Rights, were approved by Congress. Ratification by the states was completed some 2 years later.

In its two centuries of existence, the U.S. Constitution has subsequently been amended only 16 times. In that sense the Constitution has been a remarkably stable instrument of government. Its principal features—government authority subject to popular consent, separate divisions of government sharing powers, and recognition of the sovereignty of the individual—have proven timeless and durable. However, those principles have survived in part because the actual language of the Constitution has been flexible enough to be given different meanings at different times. We shall return in Chapter 2 to the important role which the Supreme Court has played in interpreting the Constitution.

COURT STRUCTURE AND JURISDICTION

At the time the Constitution went into effect, 13 independent state court systems handled the judicial business of the nation. Under Article III, Congress was empowered to create a separate national structure of courts and did so when it enacted the Judiciary Act of 1789. Thus, from almost the moment the new Constitution became operative, a dual system of courts has existed in the United States, a situation that has required a careful delineation of powers and jurisdiction. Although the arrangement is a complex one, cases move relatively smoothly from the lower state or federal levels all the way to the Supreme Court. Delays in placing cases on the docket for trial or appeal are the result of defects that have very little to do with the dual structure.

State Courts

Although no two of the 50-state court systems are precisely alike, there is a uniformity of pattern in that each state has two or three tiers of courts which operate in roughly the same fashion. At the lowest level are the trial courts which have original jurisdiction over both civil and criminal cases. Most trial courts are presided over by appointed or elected judges who serve for terms ranging from 4 to 10 years or longer. They have civil and criminal jurisdiction over large metropolitan areas or serve a district consisting of one or more counties. Another category of courts at the trial level consists of tribunals which deal with special categories of litigation, including such matters as divorce, juvenile delinquency, small claims, probate (the administration of wills and estates), or even traffic offenses. The number and type of specialized courts vary greatly from state to state, depending upon the extent to which the legislature has seen the need to reduce the load of the regular trial courts by transferring a part of their work to new tribunals.

Most cases begin and end at the trial level, but in every state, the losing civil litigant or the convicted criminal may appeal the outcome to a higher court. Courts of appeals, or appellate courts, do not retry persons or issues, but simply determine whether the trial was conducted fairly and in accord with the laws and constitution of the state, and in some cases, of the United States. In about half of the states, the appeal must be taken first to an intermediate appellate court, and from there, at the losing party's discretion, to the state's supreme court. In the remaining states, only two tiers of courts—trial and supreme—exist, so the appeal goes directly to the supreme court. At the top of the hierarchy of courts in every state, then, is a supreme court, known variously as the court of appeals, the supreme judicial court, or supreme court of errors. Unlike trial courts which are presided over by a single judge, generally aided by a jury, state appellate courts consist of a panel of three or more judges who collectively decide cases and hand down written opinions which become precedents for use by other judges as well as for lawyers in future cases. State supreme court decisions are final unless the case involves a federal constitutional question, in which case it may be appealed directly to the United States Supreme Court. *Gideon* v. *Wainwright*, excerpted in this chapter, came to the Supreme Court in this fashion.

Federal Courts

Article III of the Constitution established "one Supreme Court" and authorized Congress to create "such inferior Courts" as it deemed necessary. The first law passed by Congress in 1789 established the initial judicial structure, a part of which remains intact today. The Judiciary Act staffed the Supreme Court with a chief justice and five associates (the number of justices fluctuated between 5 and 10 prior to its establishment at 9 in 1869). In addition, the act provided for district courts in every state. There are now 91 district courts, each state (plus Puerto Rico and the District of Columbia) having at least one. Some states have several district courts, the number depending upon the population and the corresponding amount of judicial business. Today there are 563 judges staffing the federal district courts, with another 85 judgeships to be added as the result of 1990 legislation.

District Courts

The district courts are the trial courts of the national judiciary, and they operate with a single judge plus a jury where called for by the Constitution and not waived by a defendant in a criminal trial or by the litigants in a civil suit. The two major areas of the district courts' jurisdiction are (1) federal questions, including all cases arising under the Constitution, treaties and laws of the United States; and (2) diversity of citizenship. (A third area of diminished importance embraces admiralty law.) Diversity of citizenship, the term used to describe suits between citizens from different states, makes up the largest single category of civil litigation in the district courts. Unlike the remainder of the federal courts' jurisdiction which is based on the nature of the subject matter, the diversity jurisdiction is based on the nature of the parties. The reason for its being placed in Article III of the Constitution was to protect a citizen of one state from being treated unfairly by the courts of a second state. Federal courts would theoretically provide a neutral forum for both parties, and such has been the case in practice. This provision has meant, however, that federal judges have spent much of their time deciding cases which turn exclusively on questions of state law, questions which might better be handled by the state courts. A plausible argument can be made that state courts no longer reflect the parochial tendencies of the past, and would not favor their own citizens against nonresidents, but the old system persists. In an effort to reduce the business of the federal courts, Congress in 1990 raised from $10,000 to $50,000 the minimum amount required for federal diversity of citizenship jurisdiction.

About 278,000 civil and criminal cases were filed in United States district courts in 1990, more than double the number filed in 1970. Partly because of the complexity of many civil cases, and partly because the Speedy Trial Act of 1978 imposed strict limits on the time that may pass between arrest, indictment, and trial in a federal criminal case, it often takes 2 years or more for civil cases to come to trial.

Courts of Appeals

The Judiciary Act of 1789 established three circuit courts to be staffed by the six Supreme Court justices who would "ride circuit," that is, sit as circuit court judges along with the judge in whose district the circuit court was being held. A century later, in the Courts of Appeals Act of 1891, Congress established a new level of intermediate courts consisting of 10 tribunals, one for each of nine circuits covering all the states and one for the District of Columbia. The act came about as a result of increasing national judicial business and the concomitant need to relieve the Supreme Court which in 1890 had a backlog of some 1800 cases. Appeals were now taken from the district courts to the new circuit courts, which cut the flow of business to the Supreme Court and permitted it for the first time in many years to catch up with its docket. It was not until 1911 that the old circuit courts were abolished, their jurisdiction being merged with the district courts.

The intermediate federal appellate courts have been called officially the United States Courts of Appeals since 1948. They have served well their intended function of relieving the Supreme Court of much of its appellate business, and the majority of all cases appealed from the district courts end at this level. The United States is now divided into 11 judicial circuits, plus a twelfth for the District of Columbia, each of which contains a court of appeals. In addition to the District of Columbia and the 11 circuits a thirteenth court of appeals has been in existence since 1981 when the Congress created the Court of Appeals for the Federal Circuit. It hears appeals from district courts in cases involving patents and monetary claims against the United States. The appeals courts are staffed by 156 judges who normally sit in panels of three when hearing cases. All decisions of the district courts are reviewable by these courts, although by no means does every litigant take an appeal. On the contrary, of the some 278,000 cases filed in the district courts in 1990, only 32,000 moved into the courts of appeals. Even so, the appellate caseload has grown much more quickly than the number of appellate judgeships, and most appeals courts have substantial case backlogs.

Legislative or Special Courts

Back in 1828 John Marshall wrote the opinion in *American Insurance Co.* v. *Cantor*, in which he announced the principle of legislative courts. Congress had created an admiralty court for the territory of Florida in which the judges' terms were limited to 4 years. Article III provides, however, that all federal judges are to be appointed for life or good behavior, so the law appeared to be in violation of the Constitution. Chief Justice Marshall ruled, however, that since Congress created the court under its power in Article I to govern territories belonging to the United States, the requirement of Article III did not apply. On the basis of this doctrine the judges of these specialized courts not only could be appointed for fixed terms, but presumably could be removed from office by methods other than impeachment, might have their salaries reduced while in office, and could be given jurisdiction other than that provided for in Article III. Courts of this nature became known as "legislative" courts because they were created under the legislative powers of Congress set forth in Article I rather than by the provision of Article III pertaining to judicial power. They are also known as "Article I" courts or "special" courts. Currently in existence in this category are territorial courts in Guam, the Virgin Islands, and the Northern Marianas, which handle litigation comparable to that of the federal district courts; the Temporary Court of Appeals which hears appeals under the economic stabilization laws; the Court of Claims which renders money judgments upon any claim against the United States; the Court of International Trade with jurisdiction over any civil action against the United States arising from import transactions; the Court of Military Appeals which reviews cases involving the death penalty and petitions from military personnel who have received a sentence of 1 year or more and/or a punitive discharge; and the Tax Court which has jurisdiction over controversies involving income, estate, gift, and excise taxes. Under certain circumstances cases may be appealed to the Supreme Court from these "Article I" courts.

The Supreme Court

The American system is a complex one with authority dispersed vertically between layers of local, state, and federal governments and also diffused horizontally among the branches of the national government. Since the entire scheme is controlled by a written constitution which enunciates general rules to guide and control those persons who wield power, there is a need for someone to see that the rules are followed. Very early in our history the Supreme Court assumed the role of referee or overseer. When a litigant who loses in a lower court wishes to take the case to the Supreme Court, he or she sends a request for a hearing to the office of the chief justice who circulates it among the eight associate justices. All nine justices take part from the beginning in the decision to hear the case, and this initial aspect of the Court's work is extremely time-consuming. The number of requests runs between 5000 and 5500 annually, of which over 95 percent will be denied, but every justice must review the records and decide which cases he or she believes should be heard. Under the Court's rules, if four justices are in favor of taking the case, it is placed on the docket. If the case is rejected, the decision of the last court in which the case was heard stands, though such a rejection does not, the Court maintains, indicate approval of the lower court's ruling.

Once the case is accepted for review, it is placed on one of two dockets, the *original,* or the *appellate.* Original jurisdiction cases—those in which the Supreme Court sits as a trial court—comprise only a minuscule portion of the Court's agenda, usually no more than a case or two each year. The bulk of the Court's workload falls under its appellate docket. Petitions for appellate review are divided by subject matter into two categories—*appeal* and *certiorari.* Cases brought to the Supreme Court on appeal theoretically must be heard, although the Court has developed ways of disposing of most of these cases without formal hearings and written opinions. *Certiorari* petitions are wholly within the Court's discretion to accept or reject. In practice, the Supreme Court has an extraordinary degree of control over its docket; it is the only federal court that can, in effect, decide what it wishes to decide. Each year the Supreme Court agrees to review and decide about 200 cases, of which some 150 are given its "full dress treatment" involving submission of written briefs and presentation of oral arguments by the petitioners' lawyers.

What criteria does the Court employ in selecting cases for review? Since the Court seldom gives explicit reasons for granting or denying review, the evidence is largely inferential. One important consideration in case selection appears to be the issue of "conflict among the circuits." When two or more federal appeals courts or state supreme courts have decided a constitutional or statutory question in different ways, the Supreme Court often agrees to review a case that will resolve the matter authoritatively. Another significant, if open-ended, criterion is whether a case raises an important enough federal question to require an answer by the Supreme Court. A recent example would be the 1986 decision, *Bowsher* v. *Synar* (excerpted in Chapter 3) in which the Court upheld a federal appeals court ruling that a provision of the Gramm-Rudman Act violated the constitutional doctrine of separation of powers. The law was the centerpiece of a concerted effort by the executive and legislative branches to reduce the federal budget deficit. Once the appeals court decision had thrown that effort into doubt, it became necessary for the Supreme Court to resolve the matter so that the law could either be implemented or redrafted. A similar sense of urgency impelled the Court in 1974 to hold an expedited hearing on President Nixon's claim that he was protected by the doctrine of executive privilege from being required to turn over his tape-recorded conversations to the Watergate special prosecutor. The Court's decision in *United States* v. *Nixon* (excerpted in Chapter 3) went against the President and prompted his resignation, thereby resolving a grave constitutional and political crisis in a way that only the Court could have done. *Must* cases like these are quite unusual, however. Typically there is little to prevent the Supreme Court from hearing only the cases it wants to hear, when it wants to hear them. The other side of this coin is that the Supreme Court, unlike the President and Congress, cannot create political issues of its own. It can only act on matters brought before it by parties to a legal dispute.

In spite of the fact that the Supreme Court necessarily must limit the number of cases it will accept for review, wealth and influence are definitely not among the criteria which the justices take into account in the selection process. However, the considerable expense involved in mounting an appeal undoubtedly prevents many persons of modest means from petitioning the High Court for review. Each year the Court dockets cases in which the appellant is penniless or serving time in prison and without adequate funds to pay for transcripts, filing fees, lawyers, or the myriad expenses connected with a lawsuit. The Court has held that indigents who wish to appeal a conviction must be provided with free transcripts of trial proceedings even when the appeal is a matter of discretion and not a matter of right. Most important, all indigent defendants must be provided with counsel unless they knowingly and intelligently waive the right. This very guarantee was made by the Court under its *certiorari* jurisdiction when it granted a hearing in 1962 to Clarence Earl Gideon, a Florida handyman, who, without a lawyer, had been convicted of robbing a poolroom. As in the case of Gideon, most litigation involving indigents originates with prison inmates who claim that they are illegally confined.

The Day-to-Day Operation

The Supreme Court opens its sessions on the first Monday of October each year and adjourns in early July. If a case of special importance arises in which a pronouncement from the high bench is needed immediately, it will hold a special session during the summer. It has done so only five times in this century. Although the Court is normally in session for about 40 weeks, the workload is so heavy that justices routinely review petitions throughout the summer months. During the term the Court usually devotes 2 weeks to oral argument in those cases that it has chosen for full treatment; it then spends 2 weeks in recess, devoted to researching and writing opinions. For 88 years prior to 1961 the Court's public sessions opened at 12 noon on Monday through Friday, with the conference (the meeting of the nine justices at which the cases are discussed) being held on Saturday. Since 1961 the Court has met Monday through Thursday from 10 a.m. until noon and from 1 to 3 p.m. Chief Justice Earl Warren early in his tenure changed the conference day from Saturday to Friday and this remains its current schedule.

Although the attorneys submit written briefs to the Court, oral argument gives the justices a chance to ask questions and to add to their knowledge of the case. The justices vary in the degree to which they participate in verbal give-and-take with attorneys, but all of them seem to prefer that lawyers not simply read their oral arguments. Dry recitations of facts and theories will usually be interrupted with questions intended to push the advocates' positions to their legal and practical limits. Oral arguments also give the public an opportunity to see the Court in action—175 seats are available on a first-come, first-served basis. In Chief Justice John Marshall's day lawyers might argue a case for days, but today attorneys are normally limited to a half hour, occasionally longer if the Court permits.

The Court's most important work is done behind closed doors. No decision is rendered until after the Court has met in conference and discussed the case. The conference is absolutely closed to all but the nine justices. Moreover, no official record is kept and whatever is said remains forever secret unless the justices wish to divulge its proceedings which, with rare exceptions, they do not. Justice Hugo Black believed so strongly in the principle of conference confidentiality that he insisted that the informal notes he took during conferences be destroyed on his retirement. Cases usually are decided, at least tentatively, in a single conference, but occasionally a discussion will continue for several conferences before a vote is taken. After *Brown* v. *Board of Education* had been argued in the fall of 1953, Chief Justice Warren, believing that a unanimous decision was crucial in such a controversial case, set aside time for the justices to discuss the case at each conference over a 6-month period. This allowed time for a consensus to build before a formal vote was taken, and the decision announced in May of 1954 was indeed unanimous.

Presiding over the conference is one of the most important tasks the chief justice performs, and it is in this role that he may exert a special influence over his brethren. The chief presents his view of the case first, and then proceeds to elicit the opinions and votes of the justices in order of seniority. If the chief is in the majority, he assigns the writing of the opinion; if he is in dissent, the most senior justice in the majority makes the assignment. Although, in part, the assigning of opinions is simply a fair division of labor, there can be some political strategy involved since the opinion of a particular justice may carry more weight on a given question than would that of any other. Some justices develop special expertise; some are more highly respected generally. During the Warren Court years, Justice William Brennan, after writing the opinion in *Roth* v. *United States* in 1957, became the Court's resident expert on obscenity and wrote the opinions in the significant obscenity cases which followed. Justice Tom Clark, a former United States attorney general, wrote several of the Court's important criminal procedure opinions in the 1950s and 1960s. However, it seemed most appropriate that Justice Hugo Black write the opinion in *Gideon* v. *Wainwright* in 1963 when the right to counsel was applied to the states through the Fourteenth Amendment, since Black had been advocating this move for a decade and a half. Chief justices often assign themselves opinions in the most important and controversial cases. Chief Justice Warren, for example, wrote the opinion in *Brown* v. *Board of Education* (excerpted in Chapter 7) holding that racial segregation in public schools violated the equal protection clause of the Fourteenth Amendment, and in *Miranda* v. *Arizona* (excerpted in Chapter 2) holding that the Fifth Amendment protection against self-incrimination extended to police interrogations. Chief Justice Warren Burger followed suit in such significant decisions as

United States v. *Nixon* and *Bowsher* v. *Synar,* hoping to give these landmark opinions greater prestige by clearly stamping the imprimatur of the chief justice on them.

Any justice may record a personal view of the case even though the opinion of the Court, the only official pronouncement of the law, has been assigned to another member of the Court. If a justice is among the majority, but disagrees with the reasoning supporting the decision, he or she may write a *concurring* opinion expressing the view that while the case was correctly decided, it should have been supported on different or additional constitutional or statutory grounds. Any or all of those who believe that the case was wrongly decided may write *dissenting* opinions in which they lay out the arguments for their position. Often justices will join in other concurring or dissenting opinions, rather than, or in addition to, writing an opinion of their own. Complicating matters even further, a justice will occasionally concur *and* dissent in the same case, agreeing with one part of the majority holding but disagreeing with another.

Until John Marshall became chief justice in 1801, the Court presented its opinion *seriatim,* that is, each justice wrote an opinion of the law in each case, an arrangement which placed a heavy burden on lawyers to determine precisely what had been decided. Marshall instituted the system described above, which has prevailed to this day. Although some critics of the Court bemoan the fact that so many of its decisions are split (nonunanimous), given the difficult and controversial nature of the cases they decide—the easier ones having been disposed of already by the lower courts—it is remarkable that the justices can agree to the extent that they do. Roughly 20 percent of the time decisions are unanimous, and it is a rare happenstance when so many opinions are written in a case that the constitutional question involved remains unsettled. A prominent example of such a situation was the 1971 *Pentagon Papers* case, *New York Times* v. *United States* (excerpted in this chapter), in which nine separate opinions were written. Although the Court decided in a brief *per curiam* (for the court) opinion that under the First Amendment *The New York Times* could not be restrained from publishing these classified government documents, each justice wrote his own view of the matter, leaving the law in a fragmented and uncertain state.

When a justice has completed a written opinion, it is circulated among the other justices for comment. This is done not only with the assigned majority opinion but with the concurrences and dissents as well. The final opinions that emerge from this interaction often differ significantly from the original versions as the authors take into account the critiques of their colleagues. Occasionally a vote is changed when a justice becomes convinced that the opposing side has the better of the argument (or manages to persuade a colleague of his or her point of view). Occasionally such a switch will affect the outcome of a case by converting a minority into a majority and vice versa. All of this negotiation, like the original discussion and voting, is done in private, unusual in this day of aggressive newspaper and television coverage of public affairs. Only very rarely has information about a pending decision been leaked before its announcement.

When the justices reach final agreement, the opinions are announced publicly from the bench. For many years the Court adhered to the tradition, originating in the nineteenth century, of issuing its decisions only on Mondays, but in 1965 Chief Justice Warren declared that in the future, cases would be reported as they became ready for decision at any session of the Court. Although no reason was given for this break with tradition, Warren said after his retirement that the new arrangement was for the benefit of the press, to give reporters more time to read and analyze opinions before filing them with their editors.

When the Court announces its decisions, the justice who authors the majority opinion, the opinion of the Court, delivers it from the bench. Tradition dictates that the most junior justice delivers his or her opinions first with a move up the line in accordance with seniority. Over the years the style of delivery has varied with the justice. A few read the opinion in full; most merely summarize the major points. Justice Frankfurter used to amaze onlookers by expounding his opinions from memory, including the citing of volumes and large numbers of pertinent cases bearing on the one at hand. On very rare occasions a justice may read a dissenting opinion as Justice John Paul Stevens did in the 1989 "flagburning" case about which he had particularly strong feelings. This procedure of "handing down" opinions may take from a matter of minutes to several hours, depending upon the number of decisions announced and the style of the justices involved in the announcing. It is a sober and dignified procedure throughout, from the moment the red velvet draperies are opened and the black-robed justices take their seats to the time the chief declares the session to be at an end.

Despite the aura of calm that surrounds the Court, a Supreme Court justice has one of the most demanding jobs in the world. Over half a century ago Chief Justice William Howard Taft—who rose at 5:15 a.m., worked for almost 4 hours before walking to the Capitol, and at the end of the Court session at 4:30 p.m., worked until 10 p.m. with an hour out for dinner—talked of the "exhausting character" of the judicial work. Charles Evans Hughes, who had been an active lawyer, an energetic governor of New York, and a vigorous presidential candidate, said that service on the Court was the toughest job of all. And today the justices are more hard-pressed than ever. They are able to handle the ever-increasing business in part by confining the number of cases with full opinion to a minimum, but they also manage reasonably well because of the help they receive, primarily from their law clerks. Each justice takes on top graduates from the nation's best law schools who serve for a year or two and do a great deal of the preliminary work leading to a final opinion or to a justice's decision to vote for or against granting review. Each justice generally has four law clerks. Throughout the Court's history law clerks have occasionally become justices themselves, including three on the present Court—Chief Justice William Rehnquist, Justice Byron White, and Justice John Paul Stevens—who served Justice Robert Jackson, Chief Justice Fred Vinson, and Justice Wiley Rutledge, respectively.

THE SUPREME COURT APPOINTMENT PROCESS

The Constitution in Article II divides the power to appoint Supreme Court justices between the President and the Senate. The President nominates a candidate and the Senate "advises and consents" by approving or rejecting the President's nomination. Prior to a vote by the full Senate, the nominee's record is evaluated by the American Bar Association, the FBI conducts a "background check," and the Senate Judiciary Committee holds a public hearing. Sometimes the hearing is strictly pro forma; at other times it becomes a searching inquiry into the candidate's political and judicial philosophies.

The Constitution is silent on the qualifications of Supreme Court justices. The one informal but seemingly iron-clad requirement is that justices be lawyers. Beyond that, presidents usually look for candidates whose political and judicial philosophies are consistent with their own, although a justice's behavior after joining the Court can be notoriously difficult to predict. President Eisenhower, for example, was bitterly disappointed in the liberal voting records of two of his appointees, Earl Warren and William Brennan. In times past, geography and religion were often important considerations, though they are much less so today. Beginning with Louis Brandeis's appointment in 1918 by President Wilson, there was a so-called "Jewish seat" on the Court until the resignation of Arthur Goldberg in 1965, and none has been appointed since. There are, however, two Roman Catholics—Justices Antonin Scalia and Anthony Kennedy—on the Court today.

Race and gender have become much more significant factors in Court nominations in recent years, and now that the Court's long-standing barriers have been broken (by Justices Thurgood Marshall and Sandra Day O'Connor, respectively), it is likely that the Court will never be without at least one black and one female justice. In 1986 Justice Scalia became the first Italian-American to serve on the Supreme Court. As racial and ethnic minorities grow in size and political importance, they can be expected to press for "representation" on the Supreme Court.

In the 200 years of our constitutional history, about one-quarter of all presidential nominations to the Supreme Court have been rejected or withdrawn in the face of opposition by the Senate. In the nineteenth century it was not unusual for the Senate to reject the President's Supreme Court nominees on partisan political grounds. However, in the twentieth century the Senate has been more deferential, usually approving the President's choice unless it could be shown that the nominee lacked proper personal or professional credentials. One recent exception to this modern rule of deference was President Reagan's unsuccessful effort to appoint federal appeals court judge Robert Bork to the Supreme Court in 1987. While no one questioned Bork's intellect or integrity, a substantial majority of senators voted against him because his politically conservative constitutional views on such matters as privacy and civil rights were characterized as "extreme." Three months later, however, another conservative, Anthony Kennedy, was confirmed unanimously by the Senate.

Excerpts of the four cases that follow are broadly illustrative of some important aspects of Supreme Court policy-making. In *Gideon* v. *Wainwright,* the Court unanimously overturned its own precedent in a decision that met with wide popular approval. *New York Times* v. *United States* is a case in which the Court moved quickly to address a fundamental constitutional issue, but its fragmented opinions left the state of the law in some doubt. The same can be said of the Court's decisions in *Furman* v. *Georgia,* except that subsequent cases have clarified considerably the Court's position. *Roe* v. *Wade* is an example of the judicial creation of a guaranteed right through an expansive reading of constitutional language.

Bibliography

ABRAHAM, HENRY. *The Judicial Process,* 4th ed. New York: Oxford University Press, 1980.

BAKER, LIVA. *Miranda: Crime, Law and Politics.* New York: Atheneum, 1983.

BAUM, LAWRENCE. *The Supreme Court.* Washington, D.C.: CQ Press, 1985.

BICKEL, ALEXANDER M. *The Least Dangerous Branch: The Supreme Court as the Bar of Politics.* Indianapolis: Bobbs-Merrill, 1963.

FAUX, MARIAN. *Roe* v. *Wade.* New York: New American Library, 1988.

FRIEDMAN, W. *Legal Theory,* 5th ed. London: Stevens & Sons, 1967.

HOLMES, OLIVER WENDELL, Jr. *The Common Law.* Boston: Little, Brown, 1881.

JACKSON, ROBERT H. *The Supreme Court in the*

American System of Government. Cambridge: Harvard University Press, 1955.

WASBY, STEPHEN L. *The Supreme Court in the Federal Judicial System.* New York: Holt, 1984.

WIECEK, WILLIAM M. *Liberty Under Law: The Supreme Court in American Life.* Baltimore: Johns Hopkins University Press, 1988.

Gideon v. *Wainwright*

372 U.S. 335(1963)

For many years the Supreme Court promulgated separate rules for the federal and state governments with respect to the Sixth Amendment's guarantee of the right to counsel to persons accused of a crime. Such a distinction was not without a reasonable constitutional foundation since, first, the language of the amendment was so general—"the accused shall . . . have the assistance of counsel for his defense"—that specific applications were appropriately a matter of judicial discretion; and second, under the rule established by John Marshall in 1833 *(Barron v. Baltimore)*, the provision, like all the provisions of the Bill of Rights, applied only to the national government. Thus the states were free to develop their own systems of criminal justice, subject only to the Fourteenth Amendment's requirement that they not deprive a person of life, liberty, or property without due process of law.

By the late 1930s, under the Court's interpretation of the Sixth Amendment, anyone accused of a federal crime was guaranteed the right to an attorney if the case went to trial. This included the right of an indigent to have a lawyer provided at public expense. At the state level, however, due process required only that a lawyer be made available to persons who had been indicted for a capital (possible death penalty) crime. The Court held in *Betts* v. *Brady* in 1942 that in all other state cases, a determination was to be made on an individual basis. In practice the justices, in hearing an appeal from a person convicted of a state crime who alleged that his trial was unfair because of the lack of counsel, decided each case on the basis of fairness in the entire trial record. If it were apparent that the absence of a lawyer was a crucial factor in the defendant's conviction, the Court reversed the conviction and ordered a new trial. On the other hand, if the defendant appeared to have been treated fairly at every step of the proceeding, the Court would uphold the conviction, thus rejecting the contention that the absence of counsel was in itself a denial of due process and grounds for granting a new trial. The dual system of assuring the right to counsel to a state defendant whose life was at stake and denying it for those who would receive lesser sentences persisted until 1963, when the Court accepted Clarence Gideon's appeal from his prison cell in Florida.

Clarence Earl Gideon was charged with breaking and entering a poolroom with intent to commit a crime, which was a felony under Florida law. At his trial Gideon, who had no money to hire a lawyer, asked the trial judge to appoint one for him. Declining to do so, the trial judge cited a Florida statute which permitted state-appointed counsel only in capital cases, a law that conformed to Supreme Court rules in effect at the time. Gideon conducted his own defense but was found guilty and sentenced to 5 years in prison. Eventually Gideon sought a writ of *habeas corpus* against Wainwright, the state director of corrections. After being denied relief by the Florida courts, he filed a handwritten petition for *certiorari* with the United States Supreme Court. The Court accepted Gideon's case and appointed Abe Fortas, one of the nation's most prominent attorneys (soon to be appointed a member of the Court himself) to represent Gideon. Twenty-two states filed *amicus curiae* briefs supporting Gideon's contention that the lack of counsel at his trial was, in itself, a denial of his rights under the Sixth and Fourteenth Amendments. The Court's decision, announced in 1963, was unanimous.

HUGO BLACK

A United States senator from Alabama at the time of his appointment to the Supreme Court by President Franklin D. Roosevelt in 1937, Hugo Black went on to have one of the longest (34 years) and most illustrious careers in the Court's history. Best known for his absolutist reading of the First Amendment and his total incorporation interpretation of the due process clause, Black's eloquent pen and combative personality inspired several generations of civil libertarians.

Mr. Justice **Black** delivered the opinion of the Court.

. . .

The Sixth Amendment provides, "In all criminal prosecutions, the accused shall enjoy the right . . . to have the Assistance of Counsel for his defence." We have construed this to mean that in federal courts counsel must be provided for defendants unable to employ counsel unless the right is competently and intelligently waived. Betts argued that this right is extended to indigent defendants in state courts by the Fourteenth Amendment. In response the Court stated that, while the Sixth Amendment laid down "no rule for the conduct of the states, the question recurs whether the constraint laid by the amendment upon the national courts expresses a rule so fundamental and essential to a fair trial, and so, to due process of law, that it is made obligatory upon the states by the Fourteenth Amendment." In order to decide whether the Sixth Amendment's guarantee of counsel is of

this fundamental nature, the Court in Betts set out and considered "[r]elevant data on the subject . . . afforded by constitutional and statutory provisions subsisting in the colonies and the states prior to the inclusion of the Bill of Rights in the national Constitution, and in the constitutional, legislative, and judicial history of the states to the present date." On the basis of this historical data the Court concluded that "appointment of counsel is not a fundamental right, essential to a fair trial." It was for this reason the Betts Court refused to accept the contention that the Sixth Amendment's guarantee of counsel for indigent federal defendants was extended to or, in the words of that Court, "made obligatory upon the states by the Fourteenth Amendment." Plainly, had the Court concluded that appointment of counsel for an indigent criminal defendant was "a fundamental right, essential to a fair trial," it would have held that the Fourteenth Amendment requires appointment of counsel in a state court, just as the Sixth Amendment requires in a federal court.

We think the Court in Betts had ample precedent for acknowledging that those guarantees of the Bill of Rights which are fundamental safeguards of liberty immune from federal abridgment are equally protected against state invasion by the Due Process Clause of the Fourteenth Amendment. This same principle was recognized, explained, and applied in Powell v. Alabama, a case upholding the right of counsel, where the Court held that despite sweeping language to the contrary in Hurtado v. California, the Fourteenth Amendment "embraced" those "'fundamental principles of liberty and justice which lie at the base of all our civil and political institutions,'" even though they had been "specifically dealt with in another part of the Federal Constitution." In many cases other than Powell and Betts, this Court has looked to the fundamental nature of original Bill of Rights guarantees to decide whether the Fourteenth Amendment makes them obligatory on the States. Explicitly recognized to be of this "fundamental nature" and therefore made immune from state invasion by the Fourteenth, or some part of it, are the First Amendment's freedoms of speech, press, religion, assembly, association, and petition for redress of grievances. For the same reason, though not always in precisely the same terminology, the Court has made obligatory on the States the Fifth Amendment's command that private property shall not be taken for public use without just compensation, the Fourth Amendment's prohibition of unreasonable searches and seizures, and the Eighth's ban on cruel and unusual punishment. On the other hand, this Court in Palko v. Connecticut, refused to hold that the Fourteenth Amendment made the double jeopardy provision of the Fifth Amendment obligatory on the States. In so refusing, however, the Court, speaking through Mr. Justice Cardozo, was careful to emphasize that "immunities that are valid as against the federal government by force of the specific pledges of particular amendments have been found to be implicit in the concept of ordered liberty, and thus, through the Fourteenth Amendment, become valid as against the states" and that guarantees "in their origin . . . effective against the federal government alone" had by prior cases "been taken over from the earlier articles of the Federal Bill of Rights and brought within the Fourteenth Amendment by a process of absorption."

We accept Betts v. Brady's assumption, based as it was on our prior cases, that a provision of the Bill of Rights which is "fundamental and essential to a fair trial" is made obligatory upon the States by the Fourteenth Amendment. We think the Court in Betts was wrong, however, in concluding that the Sixth Amendment's guarantee of counsel is not one of these fundamental rights. Ten years before Betts v. Brady, this Court, after full consideration of all the historical data examined in Betts, had unequivocally declared that "the right to the aid of counsel is of this fundamental character." Powell v. Alabama. While the Court at the close of its Powell opinion did by its language, as this Court frequently does, limit its holding to the particular facts and circumstances of that case, its conclusions about the fundamental nature of the right to counsel are unmistakable.

. . .

The fact is that in deciding as it did—that "appointment of counsel is not a fundamental right, essential to a fair trial"—the Court in Betts v. Brady made an abrupt break with its own well-considered precedents. In returning to these old precedents, sounder we believe than the new, we but restore constitutional principles established to achieve a fair system of justice. Not only these precedents but also reason and reflection require us to recognize that in our adversary system of criminal justice, any person haled into court, who is too poor to hire a lawyer, cannot be assured a fair trial unless counsel is provided for him. This seems to us to be an obvious truth. Governments, both state and federal, quite properly spend vast sums of money to establish machinery to try defendants accused of crime. Lawyers to prosecute are everywhere deemed essential to protect the public's interest in an orderly society. Similarly, there are few defendants charged with crime, few indeed, who fail to hire the best lawyers they can get to prepare and present their defenses. That government hires lawyers to prosecute and defendants who have the money hire lawyers to defend are the strongest indications of the widespread belief that lawyers in criminal courts are necessities, not luxuries. The right of one charged with crime to counsel may not be deemed fundamental and essential to fair trials in some countries, but it is in ours. From the very beginning, our state and national constitutions and laws have laid great emphasis on procedural and substantive safeguards designed to assure fair trials before impartial tribunals in which every defendant stands equal before the law. This noble ideal cannot be realized if the poor man charged with crime has to face his accusers without a lawyer to assist him. A defendant's need for a lawyer is nowhere better stated than in the moving words of Mr. Justice Sutherland in Powell v. Alabama:

"The right to be heard would be, in many cases, of little avail if it did not comprehend the right to be heard by counsel. Even the intelligent and educated layman has small and sometimes no skill in the science of law. If charged with crime, he is incapable, generally, of determining for himself whether the indictment is good or bad. He is unfamiliar with the rules of evidence. Left without the aid of counsel he may be put on trial without a proper charge, and convicted upon incompetent evidence, or evidence irrelevant to the issue or otherwise inadmissible. He lacks both the skill and knowledge adequately to prepare his defense, even though he have a perfect one. He requires the guiding hand of counsel at every step in the proceedings against him. Without it, though he be not guilty, he faces the danger of conviction because he does not know how to establish his innocence."

The Court in Betts v. Brady departed from the sound wisdom upon which the Court's holding in Powell v. Alabama rested. Florida, supported by two other states, has asked that Betts v. Brady be left intact. Twenty-two States, as friends of the Court, argue that Betts was "an anachronism when handed down" and that it should now be overruled. We agree.

The judgment is reversed and the cause is remanded to the Supreme Court of Florida for further action not inconsistent with this opinion.
Reversed.

Aftermath of Gideon *v.* Wainwright

Clarence Gideon was subsequently retried, this time with a court-appointed attorney representing him, and acquitted of the charges against him. Unlike many criminal defendants immortalized in Supreme Court cases bearing their names, Gideon managed to avoid further encounters with the law. When he died in 1972, he was buried by his family in Hannibal, Missouri, in an unmarked grave. In 1984 the American Civil Liberties Union paid tribute to the historical importance of Gideon's case by purchasing a headstone and holding a graveside ceremony which was attended by Hannibal's mayor, a state judge, the local public defender, and the president-elect of the state bar association.

An appellate court can only operate within the framework of the facts of the specific case before it, and when it decides to refashion the rules, it does so under constraints of constitutional language. When that language is fairly open-textured, as in the phrases "right to counsel" and "due process," the Supreme Court has considerable discretion in deciding what those words mean. But when and under what circumstances should the justices in the 1960s decide that those clauses have different meanings than those given by the justices in the 1930s or 1830s?

There is no easy answer, but it is clear that when the Supreme Court begins to alter the rules through the reinterpretation of constitutional language, it invites litigants to press for further changes. Such pressure was not long in coming when the Court in the year following the *Gideon* ruling decided the case of *Escobedo* v. *Illinois*. Prior to the decision in *Escobedo* it had been the presumption that when the government was mandated to provide the accused with an attorney, the lawyer

would be appointed after a person had been interrogated by the police and formally accused of a crime. At that point counsel would decide strategy for the
defense and follow through to final disposition of the case. But by the time the
machinery for the defense had been set in motion, the accused may already have
made incriminating statements to the police that might be used by the prosecuting attorney at his trial. In *Escobedo* the Court ruled by a 5–4 majority that when
a criminal suspect taken into custody by the police asks to see his own lawyer
prior to interrogation, the police must comply with the request. But what about
the more typical station house situation involving a suspect who has no lawyer
and has little or no understanding of the process or of his rights? The Court's
answer would come in *Miranda* v. *Arizona* in 1966 (excerpted in Chapter 2).

New York Times v. *United States*
403 U.S. 713(1971)

**When the Supreme Court decides a case unanimously, it is reasonably clear to every-
one who must apply the law or work within its framework—judges, lawyers, federal
and state administrators—what the Court intended, what the standards are, in short,
what the law is. If the Court is split, there is less certainty about the precise meaning
of the law, particularly when the majority is in disagreement, not over the disposition of the case but over the reasoning behind it—when for example, some of the justices support a broad construction of a rule and others maintain that it has a narrow
application. Ascertaining a precise rule of law when each of the nine justices writes
an opinion is extremely difficult. Lower courts are placed in an especially frustrating
situation since they are expected to follow the rules set by the Supreme Court, and
whatever guidance they have from nine separate opinions is so diffuse that all the
judges can do is seek a common denominator, if possible, within the disparate views
presented. Usually the Supreme Court itself is forced to come to terms with the issue
as new cases are bounced back up the line, seeking an authoritative pronouncement.
Unfortunately, no set of circumstances has arisen so far that has occasioned the
Court to reexamine various opinions in *New York Times* v. *United States* and to promulgate a more precise rule.**

**The *New York Times* case arose in the midst of the Vietnam War, one of the most
bitterly divisive periods in American history. It was at bottom a controversy over the
extent to which government censorship can coexist with the "freedom of the press"
clause of the First Amendment. Copies of a study classified as secret by the government entitled, "History of U.S. Decision-Making Process on Vietnam Policy," popularly known as "The Pentagon Papers," had been furnished to the press by Daniel
Ellsberg who had access to the documents through his employment with a private
research agency. The 47-volume, 7000-page study, which had been commissioned
during the Johnson administration by Defense Secretary Robert MacNamara, documented the origins and development of United States military involvement in
Vietnam. After holding the material for several months, *The New York Times*, as well
as other newspapers, began in June 1971 to publish excerpts from the study.
Bringing suit in federal district courts in New York and Washington, the Nixon
administration requested the courts to enjoin further publication of the materials by
The New York Times and *The Washington Post* on the ground that their disclosure
would seriously damage national security. After both district courts refused to halt**

publication, the government appealed unsuccessfully to the Court of Appeals for the District of Columbia, which affirmed the ruling of the lower court, and to the Court of Appeals for the Second Circuit encompassing New York, which remanded the case to the district court for further hearings. Both the government and *The New York Times* then sought review in the Supreme Court, which granted an expedited hearing. On June 30, just 2 weeks after *The Times* began publishing the material, the Court announced its decision in a brief *per curiam* order, to which each justice appended a separate concurring or dissenting opinion.

Per Curiam.

We granted certiorari in these cases in which the United States seeks to enjoin the New York Times and the Washington Post from publishing the contents of a classified study entitled "History of U.S. Decision-Making Process on Viet Nam Policy."

"Any system of prior restraints of expression comes to this Court bearing a heavy presumption against its constitutional validity." The Government "thus carries a heavy burden of showing justification for the imposition of such a restraint." The District Court for the Southern District of New York in the New York Times case and the District Court for the District of Columbia and the Court of Appeals for the District of Columbia Circuit in the Washington Post case held that the Government had not met that burden. We agree.

. . .

Mr. Justice **Black,** with whom Mr. Justice **Douglas** joins, concurring.

I adhere to the view that the Government's case against the Washington Post should have been dismissed and that the injunction against the New York Times should have been vacated without oral argument when the cases were first presented to this Court. I believe that every moment's continuance of the injunctions against these newspapers amounts to a flagrant, indefensible, and continuing violation of the First Amendment. . . .

In my view it is unfortunate that some of my Brethren are apparently willing to hold that the publication of news may sometimes be enjoined. Such a holding would make a shambles of the First Amendment.

Our Government was launched in 1789 with the adoption of the Constitution. The Bill of Rights, including the First Amendment, followed in 1791. Now, for the first time in the 182 years since the founding of the Republic, the federal courts are asked to hold that the First Amendment does not mean what it says, but rather means that the Government can halt the publication of current news of vital importance to the people of this country.

In seeking injunctions against these newspapers and in its presentation to the Court, the Executive Branch seems to have forgotten the essential purpose and history of the First Amendment. When the Constitution was adopted, many people strongly opposed it because the document contained no Bill of Rights to safeguard certain basic freedoms. They especially feared that the new powers granted to a central government might be interpreted to permit the government to curtail freedom of religion, press, assembly, and speech. In response to an overwhelming public clamor, James Madison offered a series of amendments to satisfy citizens that these great liberties would remain safe and beyond the power of government to abridge. . . .

In the First Amendment the Founding Fathers gave the free press the protection it must have to fulfill its essential role in our democracy. The press was to serve the governed, not the governors. The Government's power to censor the press was abolished so that the press would remain forever free to censure the Government. The press was protected so that it could bare the secrets of government and inform the people. Only a free and unrestrained press can effectively expose deception in government. And paramount among the responsibilities of a free press is the duty to prevent any part of the government from deceiving the people and sending them off to distant lands to die of foreign fevers and foreign shot and shell. In my view, far from deserving condemnation for their courageous reporting, the New York Times, the Washington Post, and other newspapers should be commended for serving the purpose that the Founding Fathers saw so clearly. In revealing the workings of government that led to the Viet Nam war, the newspapers nobly did precisely that which the Founders hoped and trusted they would do.

. . .

Mr. Justice **Douglas,** with whom Mr. Justice Black joins, concurring.

While I join the opinion of the Court I believe it necessary to express my views more fully.

It should be noted at the outset that the First Amendment provides that "Congress shall make no law . . . abridging the freedom of speech or of the press." That leaves, in my view, no room for governmental restraint on the press.

. . .

The dominant purpose of the First Amendment was to prohibit the widespread practice of governmental suppression of embarrassing information. It is common knowledge that the First Amendment was adopted against the widespread use of the common law of seditious libel to punish the dissemination of material that is embarrassing to the powers-that-be. The present cases will, I think, go down in history as the most dramatic illustration of that principle. A debate of large proportions goes on in the Nation over our posture in Vietnam. That debate antedated the disclosure of the contents of the present documents. The latter are highly relevant to the debate in progress.

Secrecy in government is fundamentally anti-democratic, perpetuating bureaucratic errors. Open debate and discussion of public issues are vital to our national health. On public questions there should be "open and robust debate."

. . .

Mr. Justice **Brennan,** concurring.

I write separately in these cases only to emphasize what should be apparent: that our judgment in the present cases may not be taken to indicate the propriety, in the future, of issuing temporary stays and restraining orders to block the publication of material sought to be suppressed by the Government. So far as I can determine, never before has the United States sought to enjoin a newspaper from publishing information in its possession. The relative novelty of the questions presented, the necessary haste with which decisions were reached, the magnitude of the interests asserted, and the fact that all the parties have concentrated their arguments upon the question whether permanent restraints were proper may have justified at least some of the restraints heretofore imposed in these cases. Certainly it is difficult to fault the several courts below for seeking to assure that the issues here involved were preserved for ultimate review by this Court. But even if it be assumed that some of the interim restraints were proper in the two cases before us, that assumption has no bearing upon the propriety of similar judicial action in the future. . . .

More important, the First Amendment stands as an absolute bar to the imposition of judicial restraints in circumstances of the kind presented by these cases.

The error which has pervaded these cases from the outset was the granting of any injunctive relief whatsoever, interim or otherwise. The entire thrust of the Government's claim throughout these cases has been that publication of the material sought to be enjoined "could," or "might," or "may" prejudice the national interest in various ways. But the First Amendment tolerates absolutely no prior judicial restraints of the press predicated upon surmise or conjecture that untoward consequences may result. . . .

Mr. Justice **Stewart,** with whom Mr. Justice **White** joins, concurring.

In the governmental structure created by our Constitution, the Executive is endowed with enormous power in the two related areas of national defense and international relations. This power, largely unchecked by the Legislative and Judicial branches, has been pressed to the very hilt since the advent of the nuclear missile age. For better or for worse, the simple fact is that a President of the United States possesses vastly greater constitutional independence in these two vital areas of power than does, say, a prime minister of a country with a parliamentary form of government.

In the absence of the governmental checks and balances present in other areas of our national life, the only effective restraint upon executive policy and power in the areas of national defense and international affairs may lie in an enlightened citizenry—in an informed and critical public opinion which alone can here protect the values of democratic government. For this reason, it is perhaps here that a press that is alert, aware, and free most vitally serves the basic purpose of the First Amendment. For without an informed and free press there cannot be an enlightened people.

Yet it is elementary that the successful conduct of international diplomacy and the maintenance of an effective national defense require both confidentiality and secrecy. Other nations can hardly deal with this Nation in an atmosphere of mutual trust unless they can be assured that their confidences will be kept. And within our own executive departments, the development of considered and intelligent international policies would be impossible if those charged with their formulation could not communicate with each other freely, frankly, and in confidence. In the area of basic national defense the frequent need for absolute secrecy is, of course, self-evident.

I think there can be but one answer to this dilemma, if dilemma it be. The responsibility must be where the power is. If the Constitution gives the Executive a large degree of unshared power in the conduct of foreign affairs and the maintenance of our national defense, then under the Constitution the Executive must have the largely unshared duty to determine and preserve the degree of internal security necessary to exercise that power successfully. It is an awesome responsibility, requiring judgment and wisdom of a high order. I should suppose that moral, political, and practical considerations would dic-

tate that a very first principle of that wisdom would be an insistence upon avoiding secrecy for its own sake. For when everything is classified, then nothing is classified, and the system becomes one to be disregarded by the cynical or the careless, and to be manipulated by those intent on self-protection or self-promotion. I should suppose, in short, that the hallmark of a truly effective internal security system would be the maximum possible disclosure, recognizing that secrecy can best be preserved only when credibility is truly maintained. But be that as it may, it is clear to me that it is the constitutional duty of the Executive—as a matter of sovereign perogative and not as a matter of law as the courts know law—through the promulgation and enforcement of executive regulations, to protect the confidentiality necessary to carry out its responsibilities in the fields of international relations and national defense.

. . .

But in the cases before us we are asked neither to construe specific regulations nor to apply specific laws. We are asked, instead, to perform a function that the Constitution gave to the Executive, not the Judiciary. We are asked, quite simply, to prevent the publication by two newspapers of material that the Executive Branch insists should not, in the national interest, be published. I am convinced that the Executive is correct with respect to some of the documents involved. But I cannot say that disclosure of any of them will surely result in direct, immediate, and irreparable damage to our Nation or its people. That being so, there can under the First Amendment be but one judicial resolution of the issues before us. I join the judgments of the Court.

Mr. Justice **White**, with whom Mr. Justice **Stewart** joins, concurring.

I concur in today's judgments, but only because of the concededly extraordinary protection against prior restraints enjoyed by the press under our constitutional system. I do not say that in no circumstances would the First

Amendment permit an injunction against publishing information about government plans or operations. Nor, after examining the materials the Government characterizes as the most sensitive and destructive, can I deny that revelation of these documents will do substantial damage to public interests. Indeed, I am confident that their disclosure will have that result. But I nevertheless agree that the United States has not satisfied the very heavy burden which it must meet to warrant an injunction against publication in these cases, at least in the absence of express and appropriately limited congressional authorization for prior restraints in circumstances such as these.

. . .

At least in the absence of legislation by Congress, based on its own investigations and findings, I am quite unable to agree that the inherent powers of the Executive and the courts reach so far as to authorize remedies having such sweeping potential for inhibiting publications by the press. Much of the difficulty inheres in the "grave and irreparable danger" standard suggested by the United States. If the United States were to have judgment under such a standard in these cases, our decision would be of little guidance to other courts in other cases, for the material at issue here would not be available from the Court's opinion or from public records, nor would it be published by the press. Indeed, even today where we hold that the United States has not met its burden, the material remains sealed in court records and it is properly not discussed in today's opinions. Moreover, because the material poses substantial dangers to national interests and because of the hazards of criminal sanctions, a responsible press may choose never to publish the more sensitive materials. To sustain the Government in these cases would start the courts down a long and hazardous road that I am not willing to travel at least without congressional guidance and direction.

. . .

What is more, terminating the ban on publication of the relatively few sensitive documents the Government now seeks to suppress does not mean that the law either requires or invites newspapers or others to publish them or that they will be immune from criminal action if they do. Prior restraints require an unusually heavy justification under the First Amendment; but failure by the Government to justify prior restraints does not measure its constitutional entitlement to a conviction for criminal publication. That the Government mistakenly chose to proceed by injunction does not mean that it could not successfully proceed in another way.

. . .

It is thus clear that Congress has addressed itself to the problems of protecting the security of the country and the national defense from unauthorized disclosure of potentially damaging information. It has not, however, authorized the injunctive remedy against threatened publication. It has apparently been satisfied to rely on criminal sanctions and their deterrent effect on the responsible as well as the irresponsible press. I am not, of course, saying that either of these newspapers has yet committed a crime or that either would commit a crime if they published all the material now in their possession. That matter must await resolution in the context of a criminal proceeding if one is instituted by the United States. In that event, the issue of guilt or innocence would be determined by procedures and standards quite different from those that have purported to govern these injunctive proceedings.

Mr. Justice **Marshall,** concurring.

The Government contends that the only issue in this case is whether in a suit by the United States, "the First Amendment bars a court from prohibiting a newspaper from publishing material whose disclosure would pose a grave and immediate danger to the security of the United States." With all due respect, I believe the ultimate issue in this case is even more basic than the one posed by the Solicitor General. The issue is whether this Court or the Congress has the power to make law.

. . .

It would be utterly inconsistent with the concept of separation of power for this Court to use its power of contempt to prevent behavior that Congress has specifically declined to prohibit. There would be a similar damage to the basic concept of these coequal branches of Government if when the Executive has adequate authority granted by Congress to protect "national security" it can choose instead to invoke the contempt power of a court to enjoin the threatened conduct. The Constitution provides that Congress shall make laws, the President execute laws, and courts interpret law. It did not provide for government by injunction in which the courts and the Executive can "make law" without regard to the action of Congress. It may be more convenient for the Executive if it need only convince a judge to prohibit conduct rather than to ask the Congress to pass a law and it may be more convenient to enforce a contempt order than seek a criminal conviction in a jury trial. Moreover, it may be considered politically wise to get a court to share the responsibility for arresting those who the Executive has probable cause to believe are violating the law. But convenience and political considerations of the moment do not justify a basic departure from the principles of our system of government.

. . .

Mr. Chief Justice **Burger,** dissenting.

. . . In this case, the imperative of a free and unfettered press comes into collision with another imperative, the effective functioning of a complex modern government and specifically the effective exercise of certain constitutional powers of the Executive. Only those who view the First Amendment as an absolute in all circumstances—a view I respect, but reject—can find such a case as this to be simple or easy.

. . .

Why are we in this posture, in which only those judges to whom the First Amendment is absolute and permits of no restraint in any circumstances or for any reason, are really in a position to act?

I suggest we are in this posture because these cases have been conducted in unseemly haste. Mr. Justice Harlan covers the chronology of events demonstrating the hectic pressures under which these cases have been processed and I need not restate them. The prompt setting of these cases reflects our universal abhorrence of prior restraint. But prompt judicial action does not mean unjudicial haste.

Here, moreover, the frenetic haste is due in large part to the manner in which the Times proceeded from the date it obtained the purloined documents. It seems reasonably clear now that the haste precluded reasonable and deliberate judicial treatment of these cases and was not warranted. The precipitous action of this Court aborting a trial not yet completed is not the kind of judicial conduct which ought to attend the disposition of a great issue.

The newspapers make a derivative claim under the First Amendment; they denominate this right as the public right-to-know; by implication, the Times asserts a sole trusteeship of that right by virtue of its journalist "scoop." The right is asserted as an absolute. Of course, the First Amendment right itself is not an absolute, as Justice Holmes so long ago pointed out in his aphorism concerning the right to shout of fire in a crowded theater. There are other exceptions, some of which Chief Justice Hughes mentioned by way of example in Near v. Minnesota. There are no doubt other exceptions no one has had occasion to describe or discuss. Conceivably such exceptions may be lurking in these cases and would have been flushed had they been properly considered in the trial courts, free from unwarranted deadlines and frenetic pressures. A great issue of this kind should be tried in a judicial atmosphere conducive to thoughtful, reflective deliberation, especially when haste, in terms of hours, is unwarranted in light of the long period the Times, by its own choice, deferred publication.

It is not disputed that the Times has had unauthorized possession of the documents for three to four months, during which it has had its expert analysts studying them, presumably digesting them and preparing the material for publication. During all of this time, the Times, presumably in its capacity as trustee of the public's "right to know," has held up publication for purposes it considered proper and thus public knowledge was delayed. No doubt this was for a good reason; the analysis of 7,000 pages of complex material drawn from a vastly greater volume of material would inevitably take time and the writing of good news stories takes time. But why should the United States Government, from whom this information was illegally acquired by someone, along with all the counsel, trial judges, and appellate judges be placed under needless pressure? After these months of deferral, the alleged right-to-know has somehow and suddenly become a right that must be vindicated instanter.

Would it have been unreasonable, since the newspaper could anticipate the government's objections to release of secret material, to give the government an opportunity to review the entire collection and determine whether agreement could be reached on publication? Stolen or not, if security was not in fact jeopardized, much of the material could no doubt have been declassified, since it spans a period ending in 1968. With such an approach—one that great newspapers have in the past practiced and stated editorially to be the duty of an honorable press—the newspapers and government might well have narrowed the area of disagreement as to what was and was not publishable, leaving the remainder to be resolved in orderly litigation if necessary. To me it is hardly believable that a newspaper long regarded as a great institution in American life would fail to perform one of the basic and simple duties of every citizen with respect to the discovery or possession of stolen property or secret government documents. That duty, I had thought—perhaps naively—was to report forthwith, to responsible public officers. This duty rests on taxi drivers, Justices and the New York Times. The course followed by the Times, whether so calculated or not, removed any possibility of orderly litigation of the issues. If the action of the judges up to now has been correct, that result is sheer happenstance.

. . .

The consequence of all this melancholy series of events is that we literally do not know what we are acting on. As I see it we have been forced to deal with litigation concerning rights of great magnitude without an adequate record, and surely without time for adequate treatment either in the prior proceedings or in this Court. It is interesting to note that counsel in oral argument before this Court were frequently unable to respond to questions on factual points. Not surprisingly they pointed out that they had been working literally "around the clock" and simply were unable to review the documents that give rise to these cases and were not familiar with them. This Court is in no better posture. I agree with Mr. Justice Harlan and Mr. Justice Blackmun but I am not prepared to reach the merits.

. . .

We all crave speedier judicial processes but when judges are pressured as in these cases the result is a parody of the judicial process.

Mr. Justice **Harlan,** with whom **The Chief Justice** and Mr. Justice **Blackmun** join, dissenting.

. . . With all respect, I consider that the Court has been almost irresponsibly feverish in dealing with these cases.

. . .

This frenzied train of events took place in the name of the presumption against prior restraints created by the First Amendment. Due regard for the extraordinarily important and difficult questions involved in these litigations should have led the Court to shun such a precipitate timetable. In order to decide the merits of these cases properly, some or all of the following questions should have been faced:

1. Whether the Attorney General is authorized to bring these suits in the name of the United States.

2. Whether the First Amendment permits the federal courts to enjoin publication of stories which would present a serious threat to national security.

3. Whether the threat to publish highly secret documents is of itself a sufficient implication of national security to justify an injunction on the theory that regardless of the contents of the documents harm enough results simply from the demonstration of such a breach of secrecy.

4. Whether the unauthorized disclosure of any of these particular documents would seriously impair the national security.

5. What weight should be given to the opinion of high officers in the Executive Branch of the Government with respect to questions 3 and 4.

6. Whether the newspapers are entitled to retain and use the documents notwithstanding the seemingly uncontested facts that the documents, or the originals of which they are duplicates, were purloined from the Government's possession and that the newspapers received them with knowledge that they had been feloniously acquired.

7. Whether the threatened harm to the national security or the Government's possessory interest in the documents justifies the issuance of an injunction against publication in light of—

a. The strong First Amendment policy against prior restraints on publication;

b. The doctrine against enjoining conduct in violation of criminal statutes; and

c. The extent to which the materials at issue have apparently already been otherwise disseminated.

These are difficult questions of fact, of law, and of judgment; the potential consequences of erroneous decision are enormous. The time which has been available to us, to the lower courts, and to the parties has been wholly inadequate for giving these cases the kind of consideration they deserve. It is a reflection on the stability of the judicial process that these great issues—as important as any that have arisen during my time on the Court—should have been decided under the pressures engendered by the torrent of publicity that has attended these litigations from their inception.

Forced as I am to reach the merits of these cases, I dissent from the opinion and judgments of the Court. Within the severe limitations imposed by the time constraints under which I have been required to operate, I can only state my reasons in telescoped form, even though in different circumstances I would have felt constrained to deal with the cases in the fuller sweep indicated above.

. . .

Mr. Justice **Blackmun.**

I join Mr. Justice Harlan in his dissent. I also am in substantial accord with much that Mr. Justice White says, by way of admonition, in the latter part of his opinion.

At this point the focus is on *only* the comparatively few documents specified by the Government as critical. So far as the other material—vast in amount—is concerned, let it be published and published forthwith if the newspapers, once the strain is gone and the sensationalism is eased, still feel the urge so to do.

. . .

Aftermath of New York Times *v.* United States

Although all six members of the majority in the Pentagon Papers case agreed that the government might not restrain publication of these particular documents under the circumstances, they were divided over what the government might or might not do in the future. Only two justices, Black and Douglas, maintained that *all* government censorship was a violation of the First Amendment. Justice Brennan differed slightly in that he would not preclude the possibility of the government's presenting proof of great danger to the national interest, thus justifying an injunction. Three of the justices, Marshall, Stewart, and White, argued that in the absence of congressional authorization, the executive lacked any inherent power to prohibit publication of official information unless it were shown that publication would result in "direct, immediate, and irreparable damage" to the United States or its people. This phrase, which appears almost offhandedly at the end of Justice Stewart's concurring opinion, was the closest thing to a rule of law to emerge from the case for resolving future First Amendment disputes. The three dissenters, Burger, Harlan, and Blackmun, objected to the speed with which the cases had been heard but reserved judgment on the main issue. On the peripheral issues of theft of documents and acceptance of stolen property, five of the justices, the three dissenters plus White and Stewart, hinted or implied that criminal proceedings might be brought. None was brought against the newspapers. In 1972 *The New York Times* received a Pulitzer Prize for its part in publishing the papers. Ellsberg, although indicted, was not convicted since some of the evidence against him was obtained illegally.

The Supreme Court has had no occasion since 1971 to either reapply or reconsider the *New York Times* test for determining when a prior restraint on publication of classified information might be acceptable. Both the government and the press generally prefer to avoid head-on confrontations over the First Amendment, each feeling that it has more to lose than to gain by submitting to the vagaries of the judicial process. However, one such confrontation did occur in 1979 when the publisher of a small leftist journal, *The Progressive,* announced that he was preparing to print an article entitled "The H-bomb Secret." The article's author, Howard Morland, had set out to show that while the official secrecy surrounding the nuclear weapons industry had successfully stifled public scrutiny and policy debate, it had not prevented a layperson like himself from piecing together the supposedly classified technical information necessary to build a hydrogen bomb. The United States government quickly went to court to request an order against publication of the article on the ground that disseminating such information would meet Justice Stewart's *New York Times* test—that is, it would result in "direct, immediate, and irreparable damage" to the nation by increasing the proliferation of nuclear weapons. The government's request was granted, marking the first time that an injunction had been issued in federal court imposing prior restraint on the press on national security grounds. *The Progressive* appealed the decision to the Court of Appeals. Before a hearing could occur, a letter containing essentially the same information as Morland's article, drawn entirely from public sources, was published in a Madison, Wisconsin, newspaper. Amid growing evidence that the "H-bomb secret" might not be such a secret after all, the government moved to have *The Progressive* case dismissed as moot. Despite the magazine's plea that the case be heard on its merits, the government's request was granted. Morland's article was published in November 1979 and no doubt enjoyed a much wider readership than would have been possible without the publicity it received from the government's efforts to suppress it.

Furman v. *Georgia*

408 U.S. 238(1972)

As in the Pentagon Papers case, *Furman* v. *Georgia* was a confusing decision in which the Court spoke with many voices on an issue of great public importance. Unlike the earlier case, however, subsequent litigation has clarified in part what the Constitution prohibits and what it requires. Over the years the Court had decided several cases in which a state was alleged to have violated the Eighth Amendment's prohibi-

tion against "cruel and unusual punishment" but the Court had always assumed, without ruling directly, that the words "cruel and unusual" were not intended to encompass the death penalty. Both public execution by a firing squad (*Wilkerson* v. *Utah*, 1878), and the then new method of electrocution (*In re Kemmler*, 1890) had been approved by the Court in the nineteenth century. In 1947 the Court even permitted the state of Louisiana to strap a prisoner into the electric chair a second time after a faulty system failed in the first attempt (*Louisiana ex rel Francis* v. *Resweber*). In the year prior to the *Furman* decision the Court upheld procedures in two states in which the jury, without statutory guidance, had complete discretion in rendering a death penalty verdict (*Mc Gautha* v. *California* and *Crampton* v. *Ohio*, 1971).

If nothing else, the Court in *Furman* v. *Georgia* wrote a comprehensive legal history of the death penalty as the opinions ran to 450 pages in the official reports. Along with *Furman* the Court heard two companion cases, *Jackson* v. *Georgia* and *Branch* v. *Texas*. William Henry Furman, a 26-year-old who had dropped out of school in the sixth grade, was convicted of killing a householder while seeking to enter his home at night. Lucius Jackson, who had escaped from a prison work gang, had entered the home of a woman and raped her while holding a scissors to her neck. Elmer Branch, mentally deficient with a 5$^1/_2$-year grade school education, had entered the home of a 65-year-old widow while she slept and raped her. Furman, Jackson, and Branch were black; all the victims were white. Each of the prisoners was sentenced to death after a jury trial and their sentences were upheld in the state appellate courts. They were represented in their Supreme Court appeals by lawyers from the Legal Defense Fund, an offshoot of the National Association for the Advancement of Colored People (NAACP), which since the early 1960s had been waging a legal battle against capital punishment.

Per Curiam.

. . . Certiorari was granted limited to the following question: "Does the imposition and carrying out of the death penalty in [these cases] constitute cruel and unusual punishment in violation of the Eighth and Fourteenth Amendments?" The Court holds that the imposition and carrying out of the death penalty in these cases constitutes cruel and unusual punishment in violation of the Eighth and Fourteenth Amendments. The judgment in each case is therefore reversed insofar as it leaves undisturbed the death sentence imposed, and the cases are remanded for further proceedings.

So ordered.

Mr. Justice Douglas, Mr. Justice Brennan, Mr. Justice Stewart, Mr. Justice White, and Mr. Justice Marshall have filed separate opinions in support of the judgments. The Chief Justice, Mr. Justice Blackmun, Mr. Justice Powell, and Mr. Justice Rehnquist have filed separate dissenting opinions.

. . .

Mr. Justice **Douglas,** concurring.

. . .

It has been assumed in our decisions that punishment by death is not cruel, unless the manner of execution can be said to be inhuman and barbarous. it is also said in our opinions that the proscription of cruel and unusual punishments "is not fastened to the obsolete but may acquire meaning as public opinion becomes enlightened by a humane justice." A like statement was made in Trop v. Dulles that the Eighth Amendment "must draw its meaning from the evolving standards of decency that mark the progress of a maturing society."

The generalities of a law inflicting capital punishment is one thing. What may be said of the validity of a law on the books and what may be done with the law in its application do or may lead to quite different conclusions.

It would seem to be incontestable that the death penalty inflicted on one defendant is "unusual" if it discriminates against him by reason of his race, religion, wealth, social position, or class, or if it is imposed under a procedure that gives room for the play of such prejudices.

. . .

The words "cruel and unusual" certainly include penalties that are barbaric. But the words, at least when read in light of the English proscription against selective and irregular use of penalties, suggest that it is "cruel and unusual" to apply the death penalty—or any other penalty—selectively to minorities whose numbers are few, who are outcasts of society, and who are unpopular, but whom society is willing to see suffer though it would not countenance general application of the same penalty across the boards. . . .

. . .

Those who wrote the Eighth Amendment knew what price their forebears had paid for a system based, not on equal justice, but on discrimination. In those days the target was not the Black's or the poor' but the dissenters, those who opposed absolutism in government, who struggled for a parliamentary regime, and who opposed government's recurring efforts to foist a particular religion on the people. But the tool of capital punishment was used with vengeance against the opposition and those unpopular with the regime. One cannot read this history without realizing that the desire for equality was reflected in the ban against "cruel and unusual punishments" contained in the Eighth Amendment.

In a Nation committed to Equal Protection of the laws there is no permissible "caste" aspect of law enforcement. Yet we know that the discretion of judges and juries in imposing the death penalty enables the penalty to be selectively applied, feeding prejudices against the accused if he is poor and despised, poor and lacking political clout, or if he is a member of a suspect or unpopular minority, and saving those who by social position may be in a more protected position.

. . .

The high service rendered by the "cruel and unusual" punishment clause of the Eighth Amendment is to require legislatures to write penal laws that are evenhanded, nonselective, and nonarbitrary, and to require judges to see to it that general laws are not applied sparsely, selectively, and spottily to unpopular groups.

. . .

Any law which is nondiscriminatory on its face may be applied in such a way as to violate the Equal Protection Clause of the Fourteenth Amendment. Such consequence might be the adding of a mandatory death penalty where equal or lesser sentences were imposed on the elite, a harsher one on the minorities or members of the lower castes. Whether a mandatory death penalty would otherwise be constitutional is a question I do not reach.

. . .

Mr. Justice **Brennan,** concurring.

. . .

Ours would indeed be a simple task were we required merely to measure a challenged punishment against those that history has long condemned. That narrow and unwarranted view of the Clause, however, was left behind with the 19th century. Our task today is more complex. We know "that the words of the [Clause] are not precise, and that their scope is not static." We know, therefore, that the Clause "must draw its meaning from the evolving standards of decency that mark the progress of a maturing society." That knowledge, of course, is but the beginning of the inquiry.

. . .

At bottom, . . . the Cruel and Unusual Punishments Clause prohibits the infliction of uncivilized and inhuman punishments. The State, even as it punishes, must treat its members with respect for their intrinsic worth as human beings. A punishment is "cruel and unusual," therefore, if it does not comport with human dignity.

. . .

In determining whether a punishment comports with human dignity, we are aided also by a second principle inherent in the Clause—that the State must not arbitrarily inflict a severe punishment. This principle derives from the notion that the State does not respect human dignity when, without reason, it inflicts upon some people a severe punishment that it does not inflict upon others. Indeed, the very words "cruel and unusual punishments" imply condemnation of the arbitrary infliction of severe punishments. And, as we now know, the English history of the Clause reveals a particular concern with the establishment of a safeguard against arbitrary punishments. . . .

. . .

In comparison to all other punishments today, then, the deliberate extinguishment of human life by the State is uniquely degrading to human dignity. I would not hesitate to hold, on that ground alone, that death is today a "cruel and unusual" punishment.

. . .

Mr. Justice **Stewart**, concurring.

The penalty of death differs from all other forms of criminal punishment, not in degree but in kind. It is unique in its total irrevocability. It is unique in its rejection of rehabilitation of the convict as a basic purpose of criminal justice. And it is unique, finally, in its absolute renunciation of all that is embodied in our concept of humanity.

For these and other reasons, at least two of my Brothers have concluded that the infliction of the death penalty is constitutionally impermissible in all circumstances under the Eighth and Fourteenth Amendments. Their case is a strong one. But I find it unnecessary to reach the ultimate question they would decide.

. . .

These death sentences are cruel and unusual in the same way that being struck by lightning is cruel and unusual. For, of all the people convicted of rapes and murders in 1967 and 1968, many just as reprehensible as these, the petitioners are among a capriciously selected random handful upon whom the sentence of death has in fact been imposed. . . .

. . .

Mr. Justice **White,** concurring.

The facial constitutionality of statutes requiring the imposition of the death penalty for first degree murder, for more narrowly defined categories of murder or for rape would present quite different issues under the Eighth Amendment than are posed by the cases before us. In joining the Court's judgment, therefore, I do not at all intimate that the death penalty is unconstitutional per se or that there is no system of capital punishment that would comport with the Eighth Amendment. . . .

. . .

The imposition and execution of the death penalty are obviously cruel in the dictionary sense. But the penalty has not been considered cruel and unusual punishment in the constitutional sense because it was thought justified by the social ends it was deemed to serve.

. . .

It is also my judgment that this point has been reached with respect to capital punishment as it is presently administered under the statutes involved in these cases. Concededly, it is difficult to prove as a general proposition that capital punishment, however administered, more effectively serves the ends of the criminal law than does imprisonment. But however that may be, I cannot avoid the conclusion that as the statutes before us are now administered, the penalty is so infrequently imposed that the threat of execution is too attenuated to be of substantial service to criminal justice.

. . .

I add only that past and present legislative judgment with respect to the death penalty loses much of its force when viewed in light of the recurring practice of delegating sentencing authority to the jury and the fact that a jury, in its own discretion and without violating its trust or any statutory policy, may refuse to impose the death penalty no matter what the circumstances of the crime. Legislative "policy" is thus necessarily defined not by what is legislatively authorized but by what juries and judges do in exercising the discretion so regularly conferred upon them. In my judgment what was done in these cases violated the Eighth Amendment.

. . .

Mr. Justice **Marshall,** concurring.

. . .

In order to assess whether or not death is an excessive or unnecessary penalty, it is necessary to consider the reasons why a legislature might select it as punishment for one or more offenses, and examine whether less severe penalties would satisfy the legitimate legislative wants as well as capital punishment. If they would, then the death penalty is unnecessary cruelty, and, therefore unconstitutional.

There are six purposes conceivably served by capital punishment: retribution, deterrence, prevention of repetitive criminal acts, encouragement of guilty pleas and confessions, eugenics, and economy.

. . .

. . . There is but one conclusion that can be drawn i.e., the death penalty is an excessive and unnecessary punishment which violates the Eighth Amendment. The statistical evidence is not convincing beyond all doubt, but it is persuasive. It is not improper at this point to take judicial notice of the fact that for more than 200 years men have labored to demonstrate that capital punishment serves no purpose that life imprisonment could not serve equally as well. And they have done so with great success. Little if any evidence has been adduced to prove the contrary. The point has now been reached at which deference to the legislatures is tantamount to abdication of our judicial roles as factfinders, judges, and ultimate arbiters of the Constitution. We know that at some point the presumption of constitutionality accorded legislative acts gives way to a realistic assessment of those acts. This point comes when there is sufficient evidence available so that judges can determine not whether the legislature acted wisely, but whether it had any rational basis whatsoever for acting. We have this evidence before us now. There is no rational basis for concluding that capital punishment is not excessive. It therefore violates the Eighth Amendment.

In addition, even if capital punishment is not excessive, it nonetheless violates the Eighth Amendment because it is morally unacceptable to the people of the United States at this time in their history.

. . .

At a time in our history when the streets of the Nation's cities inspire fear and despair, rather than pride and hope, it is difficult to maintain objectivity and concern for our fellow citizens. But, the measure of a country's greatness is its ability to retain compassion in time of crisis. No nation in the recorded history of man has a greater tradition of revering justice and fair treatment for all its citizens in times of turmoil, confusion, and tension than ours. This is a country which stands tallest in troubled times, a country that clings to fundamental principles, cherishes its constitutional heritage, and rejects simple solutions that compromise the values which lie at the roots of our democratic system.

In striking down capital punishment, this Court does not malign our system of government. On the contrary, it pays homage to it. Only in a free society could right triumph in difficult times, and could civilization record its magnificent advancement. In recognizing the humanity of our fellow beings, we pay ourselves the highest tribute. We achieve "a major milestone in the long road up from barbarism," and join the approximately 70 other jurisdictions in the world which celebrate their regard for civilization and humanity by shunning capital punishment.

. . .

Mr. Chief Justice **Burger,** with whom Mr. Justice **Blackmun,** Mr. Justice **Powell,** and Mr. Justice **Rehnquist** join, dissenting. . . .

If we were possessed of legislative power, I would either join with Mr. Justice Brennan and Mr. Justice Marshall or, at the very least, restrict the use of capital punishment to a small category of the most heinous crimes. Our constitutional inquiry, however, must be divorced from personal feelings as to the morality and efficacy of the death penalty and be confined to the meaning and applicability of the uncertain language of the Eighth Amendment. There is no novelty in being called upon to interpret a constitutional provision that is less than self-defining, but of all our fundamental guarantees, the ban on "cruel and unusual punishments" is one of the most difficult to translate into judicially manageable terms. The widely divergent views of the Amendment expressed in today's opinions reveals the haze that surrounds this constitutional command. Yet it is essential to our role as a court that we not seize upon the enigmatic character of the guarantee as an invitation to enact our personal predilections into law.

Although the Eighth Amendment literally reads as prohibiting only those punishments that are both "cruel" and "unusual," history compels the conclusion that the Constitution prohibits all punishments of extreme and barbarous cruelty, regardless of how frequently or infrequently imposed.

. . .

I do not suggest that the presence of the word "unusual" in the Eighth Amendment is merely vestigial, having no relevance to the constitutionality of any punishment that might be devised. But where, as here, we consider a punishment well known to history, and clearly authorized by legislative enactment, it disregards the history of the Eighth Amendment and all the judicial comment that has followed to rely on the term "unusual" as affecting the outcome of these cases. Instead, I view these cases as turning on the single question whether capital punishment is "cruel" in the constitutional sense. The term "unusual" cannot be read as limiting the ban on "cruel" punishments or as somehow expanding the meaning of the term "cruel." For this reason I am unpersuaded by the facile argument that since capital punishment has always been cruel in the everyday sense of the word, and has become unusual due to decreased use, it is, therefore, now "cruel and unusual."

. . .

Today the Court has not ruled that capital punishment is per se violative of the Eighth Amendment; nor has it ruled that the punishment is barred for any particular class or classes of crimes. The substantially similar concurring opinions of Mr. Justice Stewart and Mr. Justice White, which are necessary to support the judgment setting aside petitioners' sentences, stop short of reaching the ultimate question. The actual scope of the Court's ruling, which I take to be embodied in these concurring opinions, is not entirely clear. This much, however, seems apparent: if the legislatures are to continue to authorize capital punishment for some crimes, juries and judges can no longer be permitted to make the sentencing determination in the same manner they have in the past. This approach—not urged in oral arguments or briefs—misconceives the nature of the constitutional command against "cruel and unusual punishments," disregards controlling case law, and demands a rigidity in capital cases which, if possible of achievement, cannot be regarded as a welcome change. Indeed the contrary seems to be the case.

As I have earlier stated, the Eighth Amendment forbids the imposition of punishments that are so cruel and inhumane as to violate society's standards of civilized conduct. The Amendment does not prohibit all punishments the States are unable to prove necessary to deter or control crime. The Amendment is not concerned with the process by which a State determines that a particular punishment is to be imposed in a particular case. And the Amendment most assuredly does not speak to the power of legislatures to confer sentencing discretion on juries, rather than to fix all sentences by statute.

The critical factor in the concurring opinions of both Mr. Justice Stewart and Mr. Justice White is the infrequency with which the penalty is imposed. This factor is taken not as evidence of society's abhorrence of capital punishment—the inference that petitioners would have the Court draw—but as the earmark of a deteriorated system of sentencing. It is concluded that petitioners' sentences must be set aside, not because the punishment is impermissibly cruel, but because juries and judges have failed to exercise their sentencing discretion in acceptable fashion.

. . .

. . . The decisive grievance of the opinions—not translated into Eighth Amendment terms—is that the present system of discretionary sentencing in capital cases has failed to produce even-handed justice; the problem is not that too few have been sentenced to die, but that the selection process has followed no rational pattern. This claim of arbitrariness is not only lacking in empirical support, but it manifestly fails to establish that the death penalty is a "cruel and unusual" punishment. The Eighth Amendment was included in the Bill of Rights to assure that certain types of punishments would never be imposed, not to channelize the sentencing process. The approach of these concurring opinions has no antecedent in the Eighth Amendment cases. It is essentially and exclusively a procedural due process argument.

. . .

While I would not undertake to make a definitive statement as to the parameters of the Court's ruling, it is clear that if state legislatures and the Congress wish to maintain the availability of capital punishment, significant statutory changes will have to be made. Since the two pivotal concurring opinions turn on the assumption that the punishment of death is now meted out in a random and unpredictable manner, legislative bodies may seek to bring their laws into compliance with the Court's ruling by providing standards for juries and judges to follow in determining the sentence in capital cases or by more narrowly defining the crimes for which the penalty is to be imposed. If such standards can be devised or the crimes more meticulously defined, the result cannot be detrimental. . . .

. . .

Since there is no majority of the Court on the ultimate issue presented in these cases, the future of capital punishment in this country has been left in an uncertain limbo. Rather than providing a final and unambiguous answer on the basic constitutional question, the collective impact of the majority's ruling is to demand an undetermined measure of change from the various state legislatures and the Congress. While I cannot endorse the process of decisionmaking that has yielded today's result and the restraints which that result imposes on legislative action, I am not altogether displeased that legislative

bodies have been given the opportunity, and indeed unavoidable responsibility, to make a thorough re-evaluation of the entire subject of capital punishment. If today's opinions demonstrate nothing else, they starkly show that this is an area where legislatures can act far more effectively than courts.

The legislatures are free to eliminate capital punishment for specific crimes or to carve-out limited exceptions to a general abolition of the penalty, without adherence to the conceptual strictures of the Eighth Amendment. The legislatures can and should make an assessment of the deterrent influence of capital punishment, both generally and as affecting the commission of specific types of crimes. If legislatures come to doubt the efficacy of capital punishment, they can abolish it, either completely or on a selective basis. If new evidence persuades them that they have acted unwisely, they can reverse their field and reinstate the penalty to the extent it is thought warranted. An Eighth Amendment ruling by judges cannot be made with such flexibility or discriminating precision.

. . .

The highest judicial duty is to recognize the limits on judicial power and to permit the democratic processes to deal with matters falling outside of those limits. The "hydraulic pressures" that Holmes spoke of as being generated by cases of great import have propelled the Court to go beyond the limits of judicial power, while fortunately leaving some room for legislative judgment.

Mr. Justice **Blackmun,** dissenting.

I join the respective opinions of The Chief Justice, Mr. Justice Powell, and Mr. Justice Rehnquist, and add only the following, somewhat personal, comments.

Cases such as these provide for me an excruciating agony of the spirit. I yield to no one in the depth of my distaste, antipathy, and, indeed, abhorrence, for the death penalty, with all its aspects of physical distress and fear and of moral judgment exercised by finite minds. That distaste is buttressed by a belief that capital punishment serves no useful purpose that can be demonstrated. For me, it violates childhood's training and life's experiences, and is not compatible with the philosophical convictions I have been able to develop. It is antagonistic to any sense of "reverence for life." Were I a legislator, I would vote against the death penalty for the policy reasons argued by counsel for the respective petitioners and expressed and adopted in the several opinions filed by the Justices who vote to reverse these convictions.

. . .

Although personally I may rejoice at the Court's result, I find it difficult to accept or to justify as a matter of history, of law, or of constitutional pronouncement. I fear the Court has overstepped. It has sought and has achieved an end.

Mr. Justice **Powell,** with whom **The Chief Justice,** Mr. Justice **Blackmun,** and Mr. Justice **Rehnquist** join, dissenting.

. . .

. . . It is the judgment of five Justices that the death penalty, as customarily prescribed and implemented in this country today, offends the constitutional prohibition against cruel and unusual punishment. The reasons for that judgment are stated in five separate opinions, expressing as many separate rationales. In my view, none of these opinions provides a constitutionally adequate foundation for the Court's decision.

. . .

In terms of the constitutional role of this Court, the impact of the majority's ruling is all the greater because the decision encroaches upon an area squarely within the historic prerogative of the legislative branch—both state and federal—to protect the citizenry through the designation of penalties for prohibitable conduct. It is the very sort of judgment that the legislative branch is competent to make and for which the judiciary is ill-equipped. Throughout our history, Justices of this Court have emphasized the gravity of decisions invalidating legislative judgments, admonishing the nine

men who sit on this bench of the duty of self-restraint, especially when called upon to apply the expansive due process and cruel and unusual punishment rubrics. I can recall no case in which, in the name of deciding constitutional questions, this Court has subordinated national and local democratic processes to such an extent. . . .

. . .

With deference and respect for the views of the Justices who differ, it seems to me that . . . studies—both in this country and elsewhere— suggest that as a matter of policy and precedent this is a classic case for the exercise of our oft-announced allegiance to judicial restraint. I know of no case in which greater gravity and delicacy have attached to the duty that this Court is called on to perform whenever legislation—state or federal—is challenged on constitutional grounds. It seems to me that the sweeping judicial action undertaken today reflects a basic lack of faith and confidence in the democratic process. Many may regret, as I do, the failure of some legislative bodies to address the capital punishment issue with greater frankness or effectiveness. Many might decry their failure either to abolish the penalty entirely or selectively, or to establish standards for its enforcement. But impatience with the slowness, and even the unresponsiveness, of legislatures is no justification for judicial intrusion upon their historic powers. Rarely has there been a more appropriate opportunity for this Court to heed the philosophy of Mr. Justice Oliver Wendell Holmes. As Mr. Justice Frankfurter reminded the Court "the whole of [Mr. Justice Holmes'] work during his thirty years of service on this Court should be a constant reminder that the power to invalidate legislation must not be exercised as if, either in constitutional theory or in the act of government, it stood as the sole bulwark against unwisdom or excesses of the moment."

Mr. Justice **Rehnquist,** with whom **The Chief Justice,** Mr. Justice **Blackmun,** and Mr. Justice **Powell** join, dissenting.

The Court's judgment today strikes down a penalty that our Nation's legislators have thought

necessary since our country was founded. . . .
Whatever its precise rationale, today's holding
necessarily brings into sharp relief the fundamental question of the role of judicial review in
a democratic society. How can government by
the elected representatives of the people co-exist
with the power of the federal judiciary, whose
members are constitutionally insulated from
responsiveness to the popular will, to declare
invalid laws duly enacted by the popular branches of government?

The answer, of course, is found in Hamilton's
Federalist Paper No. 78 and in Chief Justice
Marshall's classic opinion in Marbury v.
Madison. An oft told story since then, it bears
summarization once more. Sovereignty resides
ultimately in the people as a whole, and by
adopting through their States a written Constitution for the Nation, and subsequently
adding amendments to that instrument, they
have both granted certain powers to the national
Government, and denied other powers to the
national and the state governments. Courts are
exercising no more than the judicial function
conferred upon them by Art. III of the Constitution when they assess, in a case before
them, whether or not a particular legislative
enactment is within the authority granted by
the Constitution to the enacting body, and
whether it runs afoul of some limitation placed
by the Constitution on the authority of that
body. For the theory is that the people themselves have spoken in the Constitution, and
therefore its commands are superior to the commands of the legislature, which is merely an
agent of the people.

The Founding Fathers thus wisely sought to
have the best of both worlds, the undeniable
benefits of both democratic self-government and
individual rights protected against possible
excesses of that form of government.

. . .

A separate reason for deference to the legislative judgment is the consequence of human
error on the part of the judiciary with respect
to the constitutional issue before it. Human

error there is bound to be, judges being men
and women, and men and women being what
they are. But an error in mistakenly sustaining
the constitutionality of a particular enactment,
while wrongfully depriving the individual of a
right secured to him by the Constitution, nonetheless does so by simply letting stand a
duly enacted law of a democratically chosen
legislative body. The error resulting from a
mistaken upholding of an individual constitutional claim against the validity of a legislative enactment is a good deal more serious.
For the result in such a case is not to leave
standing a law duly enacted by a representative
assembly, but to impose upon the Nation the
judicial fiat of a majority of a court of judges
whose connection with the popular will is
remote at best.

. . .

If there can be said to be one dominant
theme in the Constitution, perhaps more fully
articulated in The Federalist Papers than in the
instrument itself, it is the notion of checks and
balances. The Framers were well aware of the
natural desire of office holders as well as others
to seek to expand the scope and authority of
their particular office at the expense of others.
They sought to provide against success in such
efforts by erecting adequate checks and balances
in the form of grants of authority to each branch
of the government in order to counteract and
prevent usurpation on the part of the others.

. . .

The very nature of judicial review, as pointed
out by Justice Stone in his dissent in the Butler
case, makes the courts the least subject to
Madisonian check in the event that they shall,
for the best of motives, expand judicial authority
beyond the limits contemplated by the Framers.
It is for this reason that judicial self-restraint is
surely an implied, if not an expressed, condition
of the grant of authority of judicial review. The
Court's holding in these cases has been reached,
I believe, in complete disregard of that implied
condition.

Aftermath of Furman *v.* Georgia

What was the single common denominator of the nine opinions rendered in *Furman?* Only that the death penalty statutes under review constituted cruel and unusual punishment in violation of the Eighth Amendment. Three justices— Douglas, Stewart, and White—were concerned with the uneven application of the penalty. As stated by Justice Stewart, "These death sentences are cruel and unusual in the same way that being struck by lightning is cruel and unusual." Only Justices Brennan and Marshall declared flatly that the death penalty was in principle, under any and all circumstances, cruel and unusual punishment and therefore unconstitutional. Still, for Furman, Jackson, and Branch, as well as the 600 or so other prisoners then on death rows around the United States (a group which included such notorious murderers as Charles Manson and Richard Speck), the Court's decision amounted to a commutation of the death sentences they had been given under laws now found to be unconstitutional.

Chief Justice Burger's dissent was prophetic when he characterized the majority decision as leaving the future of capital punishment "in an uncertain limbo." What were the states and Congress to do? On the assumption that the Court had not declared the death penalty unconstitutional per se, state legislatures began to recast their statutes to conform to what they believed was the crux of the Court's ruling, that existing statutes allowed states excessive discretion in determining who would receive the death penalty. Two remedial approaches were followed. Some states removed *all* discretion from the sentencing process by making the death penalty mandatory for a few carefully specified crimes. Others decided to permit judges and juries to render a death sentence only after taking into account certain specified aggravating or mitigating circumstances, both with respect to the crime and the offender. Additionally, appellate courts were required to review all such cases "to ensure that similar results are reached in similar cases," in order to avoid racial or other discriminatory practices at the trial level.

In 1976 the Supreme Court handed down opinions in five cases, all of which attempted with limited success to bring some order out of the confusion created by *Furman*. Although the Court dealt with specific and often complex issues in each case, the questions most in need of answers were two: (1) Is the death penalty as punishment for murder under all circumstances, "cruel and unusual" in violation of the Eighth and Fourteenth Amendments of the Constitution? (2) Does a sentence "returned pursuant to a law imposing a mandatory death penalty for a broad category of homicidal offenses" constitute a cruel and unusual penalty?

In the leading case, *Gregg* v. *Georgia*, a majority of seven justices clearly held that capital punishment per se was not unconstitutional. In this instance Georgia's new statute was held to satisfy constitutional standards in that careful guidance was provided for juries. As Justice Stewart wrote for the majority, "The new Georgia sentencing procedures . . . focus the judiciary's attention on the particularized nature of the crime and the particularized characteristics of the individual defendant. While the jury is permitted to consider any aggravating or mitigating circumstances, it must find and identify at least one statutory aggravating factor before it may impose a penalty of death. In this way the jury's discretion is channeled."

Answering the second question was the accompanying decision in *Woodson* v. *North Carolina*. Unlike Georgia, North Carolina responded to the *Furman* decision by making death the mandatory sentence for all persons convicted of first-degree murder. A majority, again speaking through Justice Stewart, declared the mandatory death penalty unconstitutional, indicating that such a law did not "fulfill *Furman's* basic requirement by replacing arbitrary and wanton jury discretion with objective standards to guide, regularize and make rationally reviewable the process for imposing the death penalty."

Throughout the 1970s and 1980s the Supreme Court continued to hear cases involving new "guided discretion" laws and the application of such laws by judges and juries. In 1977, in *Coker* v. *Georgia*, the Court held by a 7–2 margin that the death penalty could be imposed only for first-degree murder. At this writing, however, the justices seem incapable of agreeing on more precise standards to guide the lower courts. For example, in *Lockett* v. *Ohio* (1978) a majority reversed the imposition of the death penalty of Sandra Lockett, who as one of four who devised and executed a murder, did not actually kill the victim, but drove the getaway car. Chief Justice Burger wrote that "the sentencers, in all but the rarest kind of capital case, [should] not be precluded from considering *as a mitigating factor* any aspect of a defendant's character or record or any of the circumstances of the offense that the defendant proffers as a basis for a sentence less than death." Justice White in dissent argued that the decision will "constitutionally compel a restoration of the state of affairs at the time *Furman* was decided, where the death penalty is imposed . . . erratically," and Justice Rehnquist observed that the Court's rule encouraging consideration of "anything under the sun" as a mitigating circumstance "will not guide sentencing discretion but will totally unleash it."

Since 1976, new death penalty statutes have been enacted in 37 states, though 22 of those states have yet to use them. (In 1989, when the state of Washington prepared to hang its first prisoner in 26 years, it was unable to find someone qualified to do the job, despite a nationwide search.) The appeals system continues to forestall most executions, and about 40 percent of all death sentences ultimately are overturned. Although a 6–3 decision in 1983 (*Barefoot* v. *Estelle*) approved the use of special speeded-up procedures to handle appeals by prisoners on death row, in 1990 more than 2100 prisoners were on death rows awaiting final determination of their fates. By the end of 1990 142 men and one woman had been put to death since the *Gregg* decision. Yet during the 1987 term alone, the Court reversed seven death sentences, four unanimously, and struck down the laws of 18 states allowing execution of persons for capital crimes committed at age 15 or younger (*Thompson* v. *Oklahoma*). In *Thompson* a majority of the justices, citing societal agreement that persons under the age of 16 lack sufficient maturity and moral responsibility to be subjected to capital punishment, concluded that executing such persons would offend civilized standards of decency.

Returning to the issue in 1989, the Court ruled that states are free to impose the death penalty on 16- and 17-year-olds, as well as on mildly retarded persons. Justice Sandra Day O'Connor's concurring opinion emphasized, however, that youth and mental capacity are legitimate "mitigating circumstances for juries to consider in imposing sentences" (*Wilkins* v. *Missouri*, *Stanford* v. *Kentucky*, and *Penry* v. *Lynaugh*).

Roe v. *Wade*

410 U.S. 11(1973)

Privacy was always implicit in the Fourth Amendment's prohibition against unreasonable searches and seizures, but it had been traditionally confined to a very narrow context, search of a person or dwelling, usually by law enforcement officers. However, in a 1965 decision, *Griswold* v. *Connecticut* (excerpted in Chapter 4), the Court for the first time spoke of a more generalized guarantee of privacy when it struck down a Connecticut statute prohibiting the use of contraceptive devices and the giving of information or instruction on the use of such devices. Writing the Court's opinion, Justice Douglas reasoned that "specific guarantees in the Bill of Rights have penumbras, formed by emanations from the guarantees" that create "zones of privacy," in this case the privacy of the marital relationship. Such "zones of privacy" are constitutionally protected from federal and state intrusion. From *Griswold*, it was but a short step to *Eisenstadt* v. *Baird* (1972), in which the Court extended the privacy right to unmarried persons.

Roe v. *Wade* arose under a Texas abortion law, which made it a criminal act for anyone to destroy a fetus except on "medical advice for the purpose of saving the mother." Although a number of states by the late 1960s had liberalized their abortion laws to permit abortions to preserve a woman's health as well as to save her life, about 20 states, including Texas, retained strong antiabortion statutes originally passed in the nineteenth century. At the time the *Roe* case began, between 500,000 and 600,000 legal abortions were being performed in the United States each year, and an estimated 1 million illegal abortions. Initially the Texas law was challenged in federal court by three plaintiffs—an unmarried pregnant woman, a licensed physician who was being prosecuted for performing abortions, and a childless married couple who for medical reasons could not use birth control but feared future pregnancy because of the woman's frail condition. Ultimately only the pregnant woman was deemed to have the requisite standing to challenge the state law. She alleged that the statute denied equal protection (poor women had to carry an unborn to term whereas those with money could afford abortions), that the phrase "preserving the life of the mother" was too vague and denied due process, and that the law violated the mother's right of privacy under the Fourteenth Amendment as it embraced the "emanations" from the First, Fourth, and Ninth Amendments.

The *Roe* case was initiated by two young Texas lawyers, Linda Coffee and Sarah Weddington, who viewed restrictive abortion laws as an affront to feminist principles. Deciding that an effort to have the Texas law changed by the state legislature would be futile, they began casting about for a plaintiff who would be willing to participate in a federal court case challenging the constitutionality of the law. They met Norma McCorvey in 1969. McCorvey, 21 years old, divorced, and with a 5-year-old child, was several months pregnant. She had been seeking an abortion but lacked the money to travel to a "liberal" state. (At the time she claimed her pregnancy had resulted from a rape, a story she later recanted.) After meeting several times with Coffee and Weddington, McCorvey decided to have the child and to become involved in their lawsuit. She was adamant, however, about retaining her privacy, and it was not until the early 1980s that Norma McCorvey emerged from behind the anonymity of the legal pseudonym, Jane Roe, by which she was identified in court.

The case was first argued before a three-judge federal court in Dallas, which unanimously declared the state law unconstitutional. An appeal was then taken to the Supreme Court, which granted *certiorari*. By this time the case had attracted interest and financial support from both sides of the issue, although the pro-choice forces were much better organized than their opponents. Ultimately, 42 *amicus curiae* briefs were filed with the Supreme Court supporting the constitutional challenge and four briefs were submitted defending the Texas law.

In a companion case, *Doe* v. *Bolton*, the Court also accepted for review a newly enacted Georgia statute which, while allowing abortions under certain conditions—danger to the life of the mother, pregnancy resulting from rape, or the probability of a child born with a severe and permanent defect—mandated that the surgery be performed only in special state-accredited hospitals, that the procedure be approved by a hospital abortion committee, and that two colleagues approve the attending physician's judgment. Again it was alleged that the statute violated the woman's right to privacy as well as the doctor's right to practice medicine.

HARRY BLACKMUN

At the time of his nomination to the Supreme Court by President Richard Nixon in 1970, Harry Blackmun was expected to be a solid member of the emerging conservative "Nixon majority." At first, Blackmun seemed prepared to fulfill that promise. However, Blackmun's voting record began to veer to the left in the late 1970s, and by the end of the 1980s he was one of the mainstays of the liberal bloc. Blackmun is known as a slow and careful craftsman as well as a prodigious worker. His experience as chief legal counsel to the Mayo Clinic led to his assignment as author of his best-known opinion, Roe v. Wade.

Mr. Justice **Blackmun** delivered the opinion of the Court.

This Texas federal appeal and its Georgia companion, Doe v. Bolton, present constitutional challenges to state criminal abortion legislation. The Texas statutes under attack here are typical of those that have been in effect in many States for approximately a century. The Georgia statutes, in contrast, have a modern cast and are a legislative product that, to an extent at least, obviously reflects the influences of recent attitudinal change, of advancing medical knowledge and techniques, and of new thinking about an old issue.

We forthwith acknowledge our awareness of the sensitive and emotional nature of the abortion controversy, of the vigorous opposing views, even among physicians, and of the deep and seemingly absolute convictions that the subject inspires. One's philosophy, one's experiences, one's exposure to the raw edges of human existence, one's religious training, one's attitudes toward life and family and their values, and the moral standards one establishes and seeks to observe, are all likely to influence and to color one's thinking and conclusions about abortion.

In addition, population growth, pollution, poverty, and racial overtones tend to complicate and not to simplify the problem.

Our task, of course, is to resolve the issue by constitutional measurement free of emotion and of predilection. We seek earnestly to do this, and, because we do, we have inquired into, and in this opinion place some emphasis upon, medical and medical-legal history and what that history reveals about man's attitudes toward the abortive procedure over the centuries. . . .

. . .

The principal thrust of appellant's attack on the Texas statutes is that they improperly invade a right, said to be possessed by the pregnant woman, to choose to terminate her pregnancy.

Appellant would discover this right in the concept of personal "liberty" embodied in the Fourteenth Amendment's Due Process Clause; or in personal, marital, familial, and sexual privacy said to be protected by the Bill of Rights or its penumbras, or among those rights reserved to the people by the Ninth Amendment. . . .

. . .

Three reasons have been advanced to explain historically the enactment of criminal abortion laws in the 19th century and to justify their continued existence.

It has been argued occasionally that these laws were the product of a Victorian social concern to discourage illicit sexual conduct. Texas, however, does not advance this justification in the present case, and it appears that no court or commentator has taken the argument seriously. The appellants and amici contend, moreover, that this is not a proper state purpose at all and suggest that, if it were, the Texas statutes are overbroad in protecting it since the law fails to distinguish between married and unwed mothers.

A second reason is concerned with abortion as a medical procedure. When most criminal abortion laws were first enacted, the procedure was a hazardous one for the woman. This was particularly true prior to the development of antisepsis. Antiseptic techniques, of course, were based on discoveries by Lister, Pasteur, and others first announced in 1867, but were not generally accepted and employed until about the turn of the century. Abortion mortality was high. Even after 1900, and perhaps until as late as the development of antibiotics in the 1940's, standard modern techniques such as dilation and curettage were not nearly so safe as they are today. Thus, it has been argued that a State's real concern in enacting a criminal abortion law was to protect the pregnant woman, that is, to restrain her from submitting to a procedure that placed her life in serious jeopardy.

Modern medical techniques have altered this situation. Appellants and various amici refer to medical data indicating that abortion in early pregnancy, this is, prior to the end of the first trimester, although not without its risk, is now relatively safe. Mortality rates for women undergoing early abortions, where the procedure is legal, appear to be as low as or lower than the rates for normal childbirth. Consequently, any interest of the State in protecting the woman from an inherently hazardous procedure, except when it would be equally dangerous for her to forgo it, has largely disappeared. Of course, important state interests in the area of health and medical standards do remain.

. . .

The third reason is the State's interest—some phrase it in terms of duty—in protecting prenatal life. Some of the argument for this justification rests on the theory that a new human life is present from the moment of conception. The State's interest and general obligation to protect life then extends, it is argued, to prenatal life. Only when the life of the pregnant mother herself is at stake, balanced against the life she carries within her, should the interest of the embryo or fetus not prevail. Logically, of course, a legitimate state interest in this area need not stand or fall on acceptance of the belief that life begins at conception or at some other point prior to live birth. In assessing the State's interest, recognition may be given to the less rigid claim that as long as at least *potential* life is involved, the State may assert interests beyond the protection of the pregnant woman alone.

. . .

The Constitution does not explicitly mention any right of privacy. In a line of decisions, however, going back perhaps as far as Union Pacific R. Co. v. Botsford, the Court has recognized that a right of personal privacy, or a guarantee of certain areas or zones of privacy, does exist under the Constitution. In varying contexts, the Court or individual Justices have, indeed, found at least the roots of that right in the First Amendment, in the Fourth and Fifth Amendments, in the penumbras of the Bill of Rights, in the Ninth Amendment, or in the concept of liberty guaranteed by the first section of the Fourteenth Amendment. These decisions make it clear that only personal rights that can be deemed "fundamental" or "implicit in the concept of ordered liberty," are included in this guarantee of personal privacy. They also make it clear that the right has some extension to activities relating to marriage, procreation, contraception, family relationships, and child rearing and education.

This right of privacy, whether it be founded in the Fourteenth Amendment's concept of personal liberty and restrictions upon state action, as we feel it is, or, as the District Court determined, in the Ninth Amendment's reservation of rights to the people, is broad enough to encompass a woman's decision whether or not to terminate her pregnancy. The detriment that the State would impose upon the pregnant woman by denying this choice altogether is apparent. Specific and direct harm medically diagnosable even in early pregnancy may be involved. Maternity, or additional offspring, may force upon the woman a distressful life and future. Psychological harm may be imminent. Mental and physical health may be taxed by child care. There is also the distress, for all concerned, associated with the unwanted child, and there is the problem of bringing a child into a family already unable, psychologically and otherwise, to care for it. In other cases, as in this one, the additional difficulties and continuing stigma of unwed motherhood may be involved. All these are factors the woman and her responsible physician necessarily will consider in consultation.

On the basis of elements such as these, appellant and some amici argue that the woman's right is absolute and that she is entitled to terminate her pregnancy at whatever time, in whatever way, and for whatever reason she alone chooses. With this we do not agree. Appellant's arguments that Texas either has no valid interest at all in regulating the abortion decision, or no interest strong enough to support any limitation upon the woman's sole determination, is unpersuasive. The Court's decisions recognizing a right of privacy also acknowledge that some state regulation in areas protected by that right is appropriate. As noted above, a State may properly assert important interests in safeguarding health, in maintaining medical standards, and in protecting potential life. At some point in pregnancy, these respective interests become sufficiently compelling to sustain regulation of the factors that govern the abortion decision. The

privacy right involved, therefore, cannot be said to be absolute. In fact, it is not clear to us that the claim asserted by some amici that one has an unlimited right to do with one's body as one pleases bears a close relationship to the right of privacy previously articulated in the Court's decisions. The Court has refused to recognize an unlimited right of this kind in the past.

We, therefore, conclude that the right of personal privacy includes the abortion decision, but that this right is not unqualified and must be considered against important state interests in regulation.

We note that those federal and state courts that have recently considered abortion law challenges have reached the same conclusion. A majority, in addition to the District Court in the present case, have held state laws unconstitutional, at least in part, because of vagueness or because of overbreadth and abridgment of rights.

. . .

Although the results are divided, most of these courts have agreed that the right of privacy, however based, is broad enough to cover the abortion decision; that the right, nonetheless, is not absolute and is subject to some limitations; and that at some point the state interests as to protection of health, medical standards, and prenatal life, become dominant. We agree with this approach.

Where certain "fundamental rights" are involved, the Court has held that regulation limiting these rights may be justified only by a "compelling state interest," and that legislative enactments must be narrowly drawn to express only the legitimate state interests at stake.

In the recent abortion cases, cited above, courts have recognized these principles. Those striking down state laws have generally scrutinized the State's interest in protecting health and potential life, and have concluded that neither interest justified broad limitations on the reasons for which a physician and his pregnant patient might decide that she should have an abortion in the early stages of pregnancy. Courts sustaining state laws have held that the State's determinations to protect health or prenatal life are dominant and constitutionally justifiable.

The District Court held that the appellee failed to meet his burden of demonstrating that the Texas statute's infringement upon Roe's rights was necessary to support a compelling state interest, and that, although the appellee presented "several compelling justifications for state presence in the area of abortions," the statutes outstripped these justifications and swept "far beyond any areas of compelling state interest." Appellant and appellee both contest that holding. Appellant, as has been indicated, claims an absolute right that bars any state imposition of criminal penalties in the area. Appellee argues that the State's determination to recognize and protect prenatal life from and after conception constitutes a compelling state interest. As noted above, we do not agree fully with either formulation.

The appellee and certain amici argue that the fetus is a "person" within the language and meaning of the Fourteenth Amendment. In support of this, they outline at length and in detail the well-known facts of fetal development. If this suggestion of personhood is established, the appellant's case, of course, collapses, for the fetus' right to life is then guaranteed specifically by the Amendment. The appellant conceded as much on reargument. On the other hand, the appellee conceded on reargument that no case could be cited that holds that a fetus is a person within the meaning of the Fourteenth Amendment.

The Constitution does not define "person" in so many words. Section 1 of the Fourteenth Amendment contains three references to "person." The first, in defining "citizens," speaks of "persons born or naturalized in the United States." The word also appears both in the Due Process Clause and in the Equal Protection Clause. "Person" is used in other places in the Constitution: in the listing of qualifications for Representatives and Senators, Art I, § 2, cl 2, and § 3, cl 3; in the Apportionment Clause, Art I, § 2, cl 3; in the Migration and Importation provision, Art I, § 9, cl 1; in the Emolument Clause, Art I, § 9, cl 8; in the Electors provisions, Art II, § 1, cl 2, and the superseded cl 3; in the provision outlining qualifications for the office of President, Art II, § 1, cl 5; in the Extradition provisions, Art IV, § 2, cl 2, and the superseded

Fugitive Slave Clause 3; and in the Fifth, Twelfth, and Twenty-second Amendments, as well as in §§ 2 and 3 of the Fourteenth Amendment. But in nearly all these instances, the use of the word is such that it has application only postnatally. None indicates, with any assurance, that it has any possible prenatal application.

All this, together with our observation, supra, that throughout the major portion of the 19th century prevailing legal abortion practices were far freer than they are today, persuades us that the word "person," as used in the Fourteenth Amendment, does not include the unborn. This is in accord with the results reached in those few cases where the issue has been squarely presented.

. . .

This conclusion, however, does not of itself fully answer the contentions raised by Texas, and we pass on to other considerations.

The pregnant woman cannot be isolated in her privacy. She carries an embryo and, later, a fetus, if one accepts the medical definitions of the developing young in the human uterus. The situation therefore is inherently different from marital intimacy, or bedroom possession of obscene material, or marriage, or procreation, or education, with which Eisenstadt, Griswold, Stanley, Loving, Skinner, Pierce, and Meyer were respectively concerned. As we have intimated above, it is reasonable and appropriate for a State to decide that at some point in time another interest, that of health of the mother or that of potential human life, becomes significantly involved. The woman's privacy is no longer sole and any right of privacy she possesses must be measured accordingly.

Texas urges that, apart from the Fourteenth Amendment, life begins at conception and is present throughout pregnancy, and that, therefore, the State has a compelling interest in protecting that life from and after conception. We need not resolve the difficult question of when life begins. When those trained in the respective disciplines of medicine, philosophy, and theology are unable to arrive at any consensus, the judiciary, at this point in the development of man's knowledge, is not in a position to speculate as to the answer.

It should be sufficient to note briefly the wide divergence of thinking on this most sensitive and difficult question. There has always been strong support for the view that life does not begin until live birth. This was the belief of the Stoics. It appears to be the predominant, though not the unanimous, attitude of the Jewish faith. It may be taken to represent also the position of a large segment of the Protestant community, insofar as that can be ascertained; organized groups that have taken a formal position on the abortion issue have generally regarded abortion as a matter for the conscience of the individual and her family. As we have noted, the common law found greater significance in quickening. Physicians and their scientific colleagues have regarded that event with less interest and have tended to focus either upon conception, upon live birth, or upon the interim point at which the fetus becomes "viable," that is, potentially able to live outside the mother's womb, albeit with artificial aid. Viability is usually placed at about seven months (28 weeks) but may occur earlier, even at 24 weeks. The Aristotelian theory of "mediate animation," that held sway throughout the Middle Ages and the Renaissance in Europe, continued to be official Roman Catholic dogma until the 19th century, despite opposition to this "ensoulment" theory from those in the Church who would recognize the existence of life from the moment of conception. The latter is now, of course, the official belief of the Catholic Church. As one of the briefs amicus discloses, this is a view strongly held by many non-Catholics as well, and by many physicians. Substantial problems for precise definition of this view are posed, however, by new embryological data that purport to indicate that conception is a "process" over time, rather than an event, and by new medical techniques such as menstrual extraction, the "morning-after" pill, implantation of embryos, artificial insemination, and even artificial wombs.

In areas other than criminal abortion, the law has been reluctant to endorse any theory that life, as we recognize it, begins before live birth or to accord legal rights to the unborn except in narrowly defined situations and except when the rights are contingent upon live birth.

. . .

In view of all this, we do not agree that, by adopting one theory of life, Texas may override the rights of the pregnant woman that are at stake. We repeat, however, that the State does have an important and legitimate interest in preserving and protecting the health of the pregnant woman, whether she be a resident of the State or a nonresident who seeks medical consultation and treatment there, and that it has still *another* important and legitimate interest in protecting the potentiality of human life. These interests are separate and distinct. Each grows in substantiality as the woman approaches term and at a point during pregnancy, each becomes "compelling."

With respect to the State's important and legitimate interest in the health of the mother, the "compelling" point, in the light of present medical knowledge, is at approximately the end of the first trimester. This is so because of the now-established medical fact that until the end of the first trimester mortality in abortion may be less than mortality in normal childbirth. It follows that, from and after this point, a State may regulate the abortion procedure to the extent that the regulation reasonably relates to the preservation and protection of maternal health. Examples of permissible state regulation in this area are requirements as to the qualifications of the person who is to perform the abortion; as to the licensure of that person; as to the facility in which the procedure is to be performed, that is, whether it must be a hospital or may be a clinic or some other place of less-than-hospital status; as to the licensing of the facility; and the like.

This means, on the other hand, that, for the period of pregnancy prior to this "compelling" point, the attending physician, in consultation with his patient, is free to determine, without regulation by the State, that, in his medical judgment, the patient's pregnancy should be terminated. If that decision is reached, the judgment may be effectuated by an abortion free of interference by the State.

With respect to the State's important and legitimate interest in potential life, the "compelling" point is at viability. This is so because the fetus then presumably has the capability of meaningful life outside the mother's womb. State regulation protective of fetal life after viability thus has both logical and biological justifications. If the State is interested in protecting fetal life after viability, it may go so far as to proscribe abortion during that period, except when it is necessary to preserve the life or health of the mother.

Measured against these standards, Art 1196 of the Texas Penal Code, in restricting legal abortions to those "procured or attempted by medical advice for the purpose of saving the life of the mother," sweeps too broadly. The statute makes no distinction between abortions performed early in pregnancy and those performed later, and it limits to a single reason, "saving" the mother's life, the legal justification for the procedure. The statute, therefore, cannot survive the constitutional attack made upon it here.

. . .

To summarize and to repeat:

1. A state criminal abortion statute of the current Texas type, that excepts from criminality only a *lifesaving* procedure on behalf of the mother, without regard to pregnancy stage and without recognition of the other interests involved, is violative of the Due Process Clause of the Fourteenth Amendment.

(a) For the stage prior to approximately the end of the first trimester, the abortion decision and its effectuation must be left to the medical judgment of the pregnant woman's attending physician.

(b) For the stage subsequent to approximately the end of the first trimester, the State, in promoting its interest in the health of the mother, may, if it chooses, regulate the abortion procedure in ways that are reasonably related to maternal health.

(c) For the stage subsequent to viability, the State in promoting its interest in the potentiality of human life may, if it chooses, regulate, and even proscribe, abortion except where it is necessary, in appropriate medical judgment, for the preservation of the life or health of the mother.

2. The State may define the term "physician," as it has been employed in the preceding numbered paragraphs of this Part XI of this opinion, to mean only a physician currently licensed by the State, and may proscribe any abortion by a person who is not a physician as so defined.

In Doe v. Bolton, procedural requirements contained in one of the modern abortion statutes are considered. That opinion and this one, of course, are to be read together.

This holding, we feel, is consistent with the relative weights of the respective interests involved, with the lessons and examples of medical and legal history, with the lenity of the common law, and with the demands of the profound problems of the present day. The decision leaves the State free to place increasing restrictions on abortion as the period of pregnancy lengthens, so long as those restrictions are tailored to the recognized state interests. The decision vindicates the right of the physician to administer medical treatment according to his professional judgment up to the points where important state interests provide compelling justifications for intervention. Up to those points, the abortion decision in all its aspects is inherently, and primarily, a medical decision, and basic responsibility for it must rest with the physician. If an individual practitioner abuses the privilege of exercising proper medical judgment, the usual remedies, judicial and intra-professional, are available.

. . .

Mr. Justice **White,** with whom Mr. Justice **Rehnquist** joins, dissenting.

At the heart of the controversy in these cases are those recurring pregnancies that pose no danger whatsoever to the life or health of the mother but are, nevertheless, unwanted for any one or more of a variety of reasons—convenience, family planning, economics, dislike of children, the embarrassment of illegitimacy, etc. The common claim before us is that for any one of such reasons, or for no reason at all, and without asserting or claiming any threat to life or health, any woman is entitled to an abortion at her request if she is able to find a medical advisor willing to undertake the procedure.

The Court for the most part sustains this position: During the period prior to the time the fetus becomes viable, the Constitution of the United States values the convenience, whim, or caprice of the putative mother more than the life or potential life of the fetus; the Constitution, therefore, guarantees the right to an abortion as against any state law or policy seeking to protect the fetus from an abortion not prompted by more compelling reasons of the mother.

With all due respect, I dissent. I find nothing in the language or history of the Constitution to support the Court's judgment. The Court simply fashions and announces a new constitutional right for pregnant mothers and, with scarcely any reason or authority for its action, invests that right with sufficient substance to override most existing state abortion statutes. The upshot is that the people and the legislatures of the 50 States are constitutionally disentitled to weigh the relative importance of the continued existence and development of the fetus, on the one hand, against a spectrum of possible impacts on the mother, on the other hand. As an exercise of raw judicial power, the Court perhaps has authority to do what it does today; but in my view this judgment is an improvident and extravagant exercise of the power of judicial review that the Constitution extends to this Court.

The Court apparently values the convenience of the pregnant mother more than the continued existence and development of the life or potential life that she carries. Whether or not I might agree with that marshaling of values, I can in no event join the Court's judgment because I find no constitutional warrant for imposing such an order of priorities on the people and legislatures of the States. In a sensitive area such as this, involving as it does issues over which reasonable men may easily and heatedly differ, I cannot accept the Court's exercise of its clear power of choice by interposing a constitutional barrier to state efforts to protect human life and by investing mothers and doctors with the constitutionally protected right to exterminate it. This issue, for the most part, should be left with the people and to the political processes the people have devised to govern their affairs.

. . .

Mr. Justice **Rehnquist,** dissenting.

The Court's opinion brings to the decision of this troubling question both extensive historical fact and a wealth of legal scholarship. While the opinion thus commands my respect, I find myself nonetheless in fundamental disagreement with those parts of it that invalidate the Texas statute in question, and therefore dissent.

. . .

If the Court means by the term "privacy" no more than that the claim of a person to be free from unwanted state regulation of consensual transactions may be a form of "liberty" protected by the Fourteenth Amendment, there is no doubt that similar claims have been upheld in our earlier decisions on the basis of that liberty. I agree with the statement of Mr. Justice Stewart in his concurring opinion that the "liberty," against deprivation of which without due process the Fourteenth Amendment protects, embraces more than the rights found in the Bill of Rights. But that liberty is not guaranteed absolutely against deprivation, only against deprivation without due process of law. The test traditionally applied in the area of social and economic legislation is whether or not a law such as that challenged has a rational relation to a valid state objective. The Due Process Clause of the Fourteenth Amendment undoubtedly does place a limit, albeit a broad one, on legislative power to enact laws such as this. If the Texas statute were to prohibit an abortion even where the mother's life is in jeopardy, I have little doubt that such a statute would lack a rational relation to a valid state objective under the test stated in Williamson. But the Court's sweeping invalidation of any restrictions on abortion during the first trimester is impossible to justify under that standard, and the conscious weighing of competing factors that the Court's opinion apparently substitutes for the established test is far more appropriate to a legislative judgment than to a judicial one.

The Court eschews the history of the Fourteenth Amendment in its reliance on the "compelling state interest" test. But the Court adds a new wrinkle to this test by transposing it from the legal considerations associated with the Equal Protection Clause of the Fourteenth Amendment to this case arising under the Due Process Clause of the Fourteenth Amendment. Unless I misapprehend the consequences of this transplanting of the "compelling state interest test," the Court's opinion will accomplish the seemingly impossible feat of leaving this area of the law more confused than it found it.

. . .

To reach its result the Court necessarily has had to find within the scope of the Fourteenth Amendment a right that was apparently completely unknown to the drafters of the Amendment. As early as 1821, the first state law dealing directly with abortion was enacted by the Connecticut Legislature. By the time of the adoption of the Fourteenth Amendment in 1868, there were at least 36 laws enacted by state or territorial legislatures limiting abortion. While many States have amended or updated their laws, 21 of the laws on the books in 1868 remain in effect today. Indeed, the Texas statute struck down today was, as the majority notes, first enacted in 1857 and "has remained substantially unchanged to the present time."

There apparently was no question concerning the validity of this provision or of any of the other state statutes when the Fourteenth Amendment was adopted. The only conclusion possible from this history is that the drafters did not intend to have the Fourteenth Amendment withdraw from the States the power to legislate with respect to this matter.

. . .

Aftermath of Roe *v.* Wade

Supreme Court decisions that break new ground generally do not settle the issue. In fact the more innovative the decision, the more likely the Court will be faced with additional litigation as legislatures attempt to bring the written laws into conformity with constitutional requirements or, in some instances, use various devices to negate or at least contravene the judicial mandate. *Roe* is a perfect example of this phenomenon. Scores of state and several federal laws have been passed in the 1970s and 1980s attempting to limit the holding in *Roe*. Nearly every one of these laws has been challenged by pro-choice groups in court, and a good many have found their way to the Supreme Court for further glosses on its *Roe* decision.

Three years after the decisions in *Roe* and *Doe*, the Court had to face logical corollaries arising out of its initial decision when it decided *Planned Parenthood of Central Missouri* v. *Danforth*. After affirming sections of a state law that required the informed, voluntary, and written consent of the woman seeking an abortion, and precise record-keeping of the entire proceeding, the Court then declared the following elements of the law unconstitutional: (1) the requirement of written consent from the husband of a married woman when the abortion was not necessary to save her life; (2) the requirement of written consent from a woman's parents if she were under 18 and unmarried except in a lifesaving situation; (3) prohibition of the use of saline amniocentesis as a means of inducing abortion; and (4) the imposition of criminal penalties on the attending physician for failure to exercise due care to preserve the life and health of the fetus.

Over the years the Court has also decided the following issues growing out of the original abortion decision:

1. Under the Social Security Act states participating in the federal grant-in-aid program are not required to pay for elective (nontherapeutic) abortions (*Beal* v. *Doe* [1977]).
2. States that subsidize therapeutic abortions are not constitutionally required under the equal protection clause to pay for elective abortions (*Maher* v. *Roe* [1977]).

3. A city hospital that provides for childbirth may refuse to perform elective abortions (*Poelker* v. *Doe* [1977]).
4. A state may not require, as a prerequisite to the performance of an abortion of an unmarried female minor, the consent of her parents or, if they refuse, a court order obtainable on a showing of good cause (*Bellotti* v. *Baird* [1979]).
5. Congress may prohibit the use of federal funds to pay for abortions except in cases of rape, incest, or where the life of the mother is endangered (*Harris* v. *McRae* [1980]).
6. A state may require a physician to "notify, if possible" the parents or guardian of a minor on whom an abortion is to be performed (*H. L.* v. *Matheson* [1981]).
7. A state may not require: (1) that all abortions performed after the first trimester of pregnancy be performed in a hospital; (2) that parental consent be obtained prior to performing an abortion on a minor under the age of 15; (3) that the attending physician inform the patient of the risks in abortion and of the availability of information on birth control, adoption, and childbirth; (4) that a 24-hour waiting period be observed after the pregnant woman signs a consent form; and (5) that fetal remains be disposed of in a "humane and sanitary manner" (*Akron* v. *Akron Center for Reproductive Health* [1983]).
8. A state may not require that all second trimester abortions be performed in a hospital, but may require that a second physician be present during abortions performed after viability and that a pathology report be made (*Planned Parenthood Association* v. *Ashcroft* [1983]).
9. A state may require that second trimester abortions be performed only in licensed clinics (*Simopoulos* v. *Virginia* [1983]).
10. A state may not require a doctor to provide information about the risks and alternatives to women seeking abortions, to file reports with the state, and to take steps to insure live births in late-term abortions (*Thornburgh* v. *American College of Obstetricians and Gynecologists* [1986]).

Another problem arising from the Court's articulation of a new right, in this instance the right of privacy, is the inability of the Court to limit the right without apparent inconsistency. This was clearly the case when the Court decided in *Bowers* v. *Hardwick* (excerpted in Chapter 4) in 1986 that a state law making it a crime for consenting adults to engage in certain homosexual acts did not contravene the Constitution, thus calling a halt to the expansion of the right to sexual privacy that had begun nearly two decades earlier with the *Griswold* decision.

In 1989 the Court retreated from its position in *Roe* v. *Wade* when in *Webster* v. *Reproductive Health Services* it upheld provisions of a Missouri statute (1) prohibiting the use of public facilities or employees to perform abortions, (2) prohibiting public funding of abortion counseling, and (3) requiring physicians to conduct a viability test prior to performing abortions. Although the basic principle of *Roe*—a woman's constitutional right to an abortion in the first trimester of pregnancy—remained intact, the decision seemed to open the door for state regulations of abortions that had previously been suspect. That promise seemed to be fulfilled the following year when the Court upheld laws in two states requiring that one or both parents be notified before an unmarried minor could obtain an abortion, provided that a "judicial bypass" option also existed (*Hodgson* v. *Minnesota* and *Ohio* v. *Akron Center for Reproductive Health*).

2 The Supreme Court and Judicial Review

JUDICIAL REVIEW IN THEORY

"Scarcely any political question arises in the United States that is not resolved, sooner or later, into a judicial question." So wrote Alexis de Tocqueville in 1835 in his political science masterpiece, *Democracy in America.* The closeness of this link between politics and law, which is a significant characteristic of the American system, is largely the product of the Supreme Court's authority to declare national or state laws and executive actions invalid if they conflict with the Constitution, a power known as judicial review. Of all the bold and imaginative principles of government contemplated by the Constitution's framers—federalism, the separation of powers, republicanism, a bill of rights—none has had a greater influence on the general ethos of the nation than judicial review.

Unlike most of the above-mentioned concepts, judicial review was not expressly provided for in the Constitution and had to arise, if at all, by implication. Much of what is done within the framework of the U.S. Constitution, or any constitution for that matter, is necessarily carried on without specific authorization in the document itself. No constitution can provide for the day-to-day operation of the government in detail. It must simply formulate in broad language the general principles on which the government is based, set forth powers, and perhaps most important, fix limits on the use of power by outlawing some actions altogether (no ex post facto laws), or by providing that power be used only under certain conditions (no suspension of the writ of habeas corpus except in times of invasion or insurrection). However, in spite of an essential looseness in the U.S. Constitution, its fundamental theory maintains that whenever an officer of the government performs an official act, it must conform to requirements of the Constitution. The governors as well as the governed must be limited by rules.

And how is this principle to be enforced against those in power? The obvious answer is the one given by the seventeenth-century English philosopher, John Locke, and later by Thomas Jefferson in the Declaration of Independence: government by consent of the governed. But even when the people elect their legislators and executives, they cannot, as a practical matter, consent to their every act. Furthermore, consent is never unanimous; it is in practice the agreement of a majority. And majorities may be every bit as tyrannical as a single despot. Thus, implicit in the idea of a written constitution is the principle that even majorities may not govern as they please. They, too, must stick to the rules. And how can majorities or their representatives be persuaded, or forced if need be, to measure up? There is no perfect answer to what is an insoluble dilemma in all democratic governments. It is possible, however, by devising institutional checks on power, to achieve a reconciliation between popular government and constitutional rule. Judicial review is one such institutional check.

But if judicial review is not written into the Constitution, by what right does the Supreme Court exercise it? Is not the Court itself acting arbitrarily by usurping a function to which the Constitution gives no sanction? Some distinguished scholars and statesmen have so argued for nearly two centuries, but for most, the predominant weight of the evidence falls on the other side.

In the first place, the idea of courts as a check on executive and legislative power had been a minor ingredient in Anglo-American political history for decades prior to the American Revolution. Acts of the colonial legislatures were subject to review in two separate procedures, either of which might result in the voiding of a legislative act. In the eighteenth century, the British Board of Trade examined some 8500 colonial statutes and recommended to the king that about 500 statutes be "disallowed" on the ground that they did not conform to acts of Parliament. In the second type of proceeding the Privy Council, sitting as the highest court in the British imperial system, heard several cases in which it was alleged that colonial statutes were in conflict with the original charters or with the terms of the governor's commission, although in only one case was a law actually voided judicially. Neither of these procedures was identical to the American practice of judicial review, but they do indicate that the idea, first expressed in 1610 by Sir Edward Coke, the Lord Chancellor of England, that courts might invalidate legislative acts if such acts run contrary to a higher law, had its historical roots in England. It could not flourish in the United Kingdom itself since no higher law—no written constitution—existed against which parliamentary enactments might be measured. This remains the case in Great Britain to this day. With the advent of the written constitution in America, however, judicial review was a natural concomitant.

Between the break with England in 1776 and the founding of the United States in 1789, there are a few scattered instances of state courts declaring state laws to be in conflict with their constitutions. Between 1789 and 1803 the courts in 10 states were requested to exercise judicial review, but in only three instances were laws declared unconstitutional. However, as we indicated above, the Constitution does not explicitly grant the power to the Supreme Court or to any federal court. Nevertheless, the records of the Constitutional Convention indicate beyond doubt that all but a tiny minority of the delegates were in favor of it in principle and fully expected that it would be used. Three of the most influential of the framers, Gouverneur Morris, James Madison, and Alexander Hamilton, strongly defended the judicial prerogative, the latter in his famous essay (no. 78) in *The Federalist*. And prior to the appointment of John Marshall as chief justice, pronouncements by federal judges in isolated cases suggested that it was only a matter of time before judicial review would become a full-fledged component of the system of checks and balances. In 1792 in *Hayburn's Case*, several Supreme Court justices on circuit duty refused to enforce an act of Congress because it saddled judges with nonjudicial duties. In this instance, the justices had been directed to pass judgment on disputed pension claims of war veterans, their decisions being subject to final review by the secretary of war and Congress. The issue moved to the Supreme Court but Congress revised the law before a decision was rendered. Meanwhile some of the justices decided to certify the claims to the secretary of war, not in their capacity as judges, but in their unofficial roles as commissioners. In 1794 the full Court in *United States* v. *Yale Todd* decided that the law could not be construed to permit judges to act as commissioners and that their adjudications in that capacity were invalid. It has been suggested by some historians that the Court actually declared the law unconstitutional, but the evidence is vague, particularly since the case was not even reported at the time. However, the series of judicial pronouncements on the pension claims law form a link in the chain leading to *Marbury* v. *Madison* (excerpted in this chapter), decided by the Supreme Court in 1803.

In *Marbury,* Chief Justice John Marshall seized upon a relatively trivial case to fashion a powerful—if not logically airtight—argument that laws found by the Supreme Court to be in conflict with the Constitution must be considered invalid. Because the law in question was in fact a grant of power to the Supreme Court, Marshall's opponents found it impossible to challenge the outcome. Even President Jefferson, whose attitude toward judicial review was less than friendly, could not take issue with the Court's assertion that it was protecting its own jurisdiction, protecting it, moreover, by telling the Congress that it was giving the Court *too much* power. Marshall's sweeping language justifying judicial review of acts of Congress was a strategic victory for judicial authority and a pronouncement of enduring significance for the future of the republic. By rejecting Congress's effort to confer upon it a relatively minor power because it had not been explicitly authorized by the Constitution, the Supreme Court assumed for itself an infinitely more important prerogative—determining the very meaning of the Constitution itself.

JUDICIAL REVIEW IN PRACTICE: AN OVERVIEW

With some allowance for overlapping and oversimplification, we can divide America's two centuries of national history into three roughly equal historical periods, with each period dominated by a different overarching constitutional question. In each era judicial review has allowed—indeed required—the Supreme Court to play an important part in helping resolve the dominant issue.

From the founding of the republic until the 1860s, the United States was preoccupied with defining itself as a nation, chiefly by working out the proper relationship between the central government and the states. It was not a task that the political system handled well, as the Civil War confirms, and the Supreme Court shares some of the blame for hastening that bloody conflict by its disastrous *Dred Scott* decision (excerpted in this chapter). Prior to that tragic misstep, however, the Court had played a creative role in the development of the federal system. It did so first under Chief Justice Marshall, a strong advocate of nationalism who nonetheless was willing to compromise with his more states-rights-oriented colleagues for the sake of a unified Supreme Court, and then under Marshall's successor Roger Taney, who helped expand the states' "police powers" under the doctrine of "dual federalism" (for a fuller discussion of federalism, see Chapter

3). By the time of the Civil War, the Court had overturned just two federal statutes and about a dozen state laws on constitutional grounds (one of these state cases, *Fletcher* v. *Peck,* is excerpted in this chapter). Until *Dred Scott,* the Court enjoyed considerable popular respect for the creative and pragmatic role it had played in the development of the American political and economic system. As a political institution the Court had managed to pull off the difficult feat of self-legitimation. By the mid-nineteenth century it was simply impossible to imagine the American political system functioning effectively without the Supreme Court.

When the smoke of the Civil War finally cleared, it was apparent that the American political landscape had been fundamentally changed. No longer were the states serious rivals of the national government for power. But another competitor—the corporate-industrial sector—now loomed on the horizon demanding a response from the political system. The next half century was dominated by the efforts of government at all levels to rein in the forces of industrialism. In this struggle, unlike the earlier one over the nature of federalism, the Supreme Court eventually staked out a highly visible, and partisan, role, using its power of judicial review much more expansively than it had in the past against both national and state regulation. Nearly 200 state laws were declared unconstitutional between 1899 and 1937, and several dozen congressional statutes as well. In the 1930s alone, a dozen federal laws were struck down as President Franklin D. Roosevelt's New Deal was challenged before the Court by his political opponents. This proved to be too active a role for the Court to sustain, however, and by the end of the 1930s political forces and events forced it back into line with prevailing opinion.

As a result of this strategic retreat, the Court did not suffer the kind of political isolation that it had experienced for two decades after *Dred Scott.* Thus it was well positioned to play a leading role in post–World War II American politics, which have been dominated down to the present day by the debate over the proper relationship between the individual and government. In at least four separate areas of this relationship—civil rights, criminal procedure, legislative reapportionment, and church-state relations—the Supreme Court has played a prominent, and often solitary, leadership role. More often than not the Court has found the Constitution to support the individual rather than the government, and in doing so has frequently run afoul of public opinion. Most of the resulting criticism, though, has been aimed at individual justices rather than at the Court as a whole. Ironically, as many of the Court's libertarian positions were slowly being woven into the fabric of the nation's political culture in the 1970s and 1980s, the Court itself was beginning to show greater sympathy for the prerogatives of government. The Court's record over the last decade serves as a reminder that there is nothing inherently conservative or liberal about judicial review.

That, in the final analysis, may be the single most important point about the enduring nature of judicial review. By definition, each Supreme Court case has two sides, and thus each Court decision will have both supporters and detractors. But except for the few occasions when the Court has persistently challenged passionately held majority opinions, it has managed to maintain its reservoir of public goodwill. For all of their pomp and gravity, Supreme Court pronouncements are rarely definitive or final. The Court's decisions inevitably produce new laws, new cases, and ultimately new decisions. Thus when the Court exercises judicial review it is engaging in a kind of dialogue with the American people, a dialogue in which no one person or institution has the last word.

JUDICIAL RESTRAINT AND ACTIVISM

By assuming the role of the final authority on constitutional questions, the Supreme Court could become, and did become, a policy-making body. Traditionally, this was not what courts were supposed to be, but the American system had already shattered some time-honored precedents regarding sound government, and judicial review was one more innovation. But to those who believe in democracy, even in modified republican form, there are always nagging doubts about the propriety of a handful of judges appointed for life commanding a veto over public policy questions of great moment. As Thomas Jefferson wrote: "To consider the judges as the ultimate arbiters of all constitutional questions [is] a very dangerous doctrine indeed, and one which would place us under the despotism of an oligarchy." Justice John B. Gibson of the Pennsylvania Supreme Court delivered a dissenting opinion in 1825 in the case of *Eakin* v. *Raub* in which he effectively answered Marshall's arguments in the Jeffersonian style:

> The oath to support the Constitution is not peculiar to the judges, but is taken indiscriminately by every officer of the government, and is designed rather as a test of the political principles of the man, than to bind the officer in the discharge of his duty. . . . it must be understood in reference to supporting the Constitution, only as far as that may be involved in his official duty; and consequently, if his official duty does not comprehend an inquiry into the authority of the legislature, neither does his oath. . . .
>
> But do not the judges do a positive act in violation of the Constitution when they give effect to an unconstitutional law? Not if the law has been passed according to the forms established in the Constitution. The fallacy of the question is, in supposing that the judiciary adopts the acts of the legislature as its own; whereas, the enactment of a law and the interpretation of it are not concurrent acts, and as the judiciary is not required to concur in the enactment, neither is it in the breach of the Constitution which may be the consequence of the enactment; the fault is imputable to the legislature, and on it the responsibility exclusively rests.

Gibson sets forth the typical majoritarian position. Members of the legislature (Congress) as well as judges take an oath to support the Constitution, and so long as they enact legislation in accord with the proper constitutional forms, it is not within the competence of the judiciary to call the legislature to account.

These arguments are echoed in the contemporary debates over the propriety of the Supreme Court's reversal of legislative policies in such areas as race relations, criminal procedure, and abortion. The heirs of Jefferson and Gibson, known today as advocates of "judicial restraint," typically accept the legitimacy of judicial review itself, but argue that it should be exercised much more sparingly than it has been in the past, especially in the recent past. Restraintists see in judicial review an inherent threat to democracy, a power whose overuse can sap the impulse for self-government on which democracy depends. They warn that the temptation to "let the judges do it," to allow courts to function as "super legislatures," must be resisted if democracy is to survive. Moreover, because judges often lack training and experience in dealing with complex social problems, judicial fiats will not only be less representative than legislative enactments, but less effective as well. For restraintists, the only permissible exceptions to the rule of judicial deference to elected officials occur when those officials have obviously transgressed commonly accepted constitutional boundaries.

Judicial restraintists also fear that, paradoxically, the exercise of judicial review may undermine the authority of the Court itself. Unpopular decisions may be ignored or defied by the legislative and executive branches. With neither "the sword nor the purse" at its command, the Court must depend upon its reservoir of public good will to ensure compliance with its judgments. Rather than risk the loss of that good will by drawing upon it too frequently, the Supreme Court should conserve its strength for the relatively few cases in which judicial review is necessary to correct a serious injustice.

On the other side of the debate over the Supreme Court's proper political role are the "judicial activists" who believe that it is not only acceptable but essential that the Supreme Court deal with controversial issues which for various reasons Congress and state legislatures often fail to address, or address in ways that satisfy public opinion at the expense of constitutional principles. Far from threatening self-government, activists maintain, judicial review strengthens democracy by ensuring that groups ignored or oppressed by electoral majorities have a voice in policy making. Democratic majorities may act arbitrarily and judicial review is, as one activist has put it, "democracy's way of covering its bet."

Responding to the restraintists' fears that overreliance on judicial review can undermine the Supreme Court's authority, activists argue that an even greater danger lies in its underuse. A political institution overly concerned with maintaining its popularity may find—too late—that it has lost its power.

During the chief justiceship of Earl Warren from 1953 to 1969 the Supreme Court was both the target of criticism and the object of praise for its judicial activism. To its critics, the Court had entered a preserve where it did not belong, particularly in reversing public policy in such areas as race relations, legislative apportionment, and criminal procedure. Solutions to these problems, it was said, went beyond the competence of courts and rested more properly with the legislative and executive branches of the government. On the other hand, defenders of the Warren Court argued that it was not only acceptable but essential that the Court deal with controversial issues which, because of their difficulty, Congress and the state legislatures had failed to address.

The terms *restraintist* and *activist* describe opposing conceptions of the Supreme Court's proper role in American government. We refer to these differences as matters of "judicial philosophy." One must take care not to confuse these labels with the terms "conservative" and "liberal," which are attached to more general political or economic views. During the early New Deal period (1933–1937), for example, Justices George Sutherland, Pierce Butler, Willis Van Devanter, and James McReynolds (and Owen Roberts and Chief Justice Charles Evans Hughes to a lesser extent) disagreed emphatically with President Roosevelt's philosophy of federal regulation and control of the economy. When cases came before them, they consistently found such laws unconstitutional. In their opposition to government regulation these justices were political conservatives, but their ability to find support for such principles in the Constitution, and their willingness to use them to invalidate federal and state laws made them judicial activists.

During the Warren Court era the chief justice and such justices as Hugo Black, William Douglas, William Brennan, Arthur Goldberg, Abe Fortas, and Thurgood

Marshall disagreed with state and federal laws that restricted personal liberty, such as enforced segregation or interference with freedom of speech. These positions qualified them as political liberals. What identified them as judicial activists was their willingness to use the power of judicial review to declare such laws unconstitutional. When, incidentally, these same justices voted to *uphold* acts of Congress or of state legislatures regulating the economy, they were judicial restraintists because they were deferring to legislative policy; but here, too, their positions were politically liberal.

During his 1968 presidential campaign Richard Nixon often criticized the liberal activism of the Warren years and expressed his desire to appoint judicial restraintists to the Supreme Court. Nixon was able to appoint four justices during his first term, but the result was a shift not to restraintism but to *conservative* activism. Chief Justice Warren Burger and Justices Harry Blackmun (who has subsequently become much more liberal), Lewis Powell, and William Rehnquist were in varying degrees political conservatives who were not reluctant to express their political ideas in judicial terms. On the whole, the Burger Court years (1969–1986) were marked by a policy of judicial activism, predominantly conservative politically but occasionally—as in the abortion decision in 1973 in which Burger, Blackmun, and Powell voted to strike down state laws making abortion illegal—decidedly liberal.

In recent years the argument between judicial restraintists and activists has been played out in the highly publicized debate over the appropriateness of "original intention" as the principal standard for constitutional interpretation. Some critics of activism have contended that in deciding the meaning of a particular constitutional provision, judges ought to be guided as much as possible by the expressed or implied intentions of the drafters and ratifiers of that provision. One of the most prominent advocates of this view is Robert Bork, whose nomination to the Supreme Court was rejected by the Senate in 1987. Opponents of "originalism," led by Justice William Brennan, argue that such an approach errs in treating the Constitution as a historical artifact rather than as an organic instrument of government. In the contemporary context, originalism is almost exclusively associated with political conservatism, although in theory the approach might be used to achieve liberal results as well.

For most, though not all, justices, judicial philosophy usually takes a back seat to political and economic views. That is, whether one is an activist or a restraintist is usually determined by whether one's preferred interpretation of the Constitution will be served by upholding or striking down legislative actions. A prominent exception to this rule was Justice Felix Frankfurter, whose belief in the restraintist position proved far stronger than his commitment to liberal political principles. Time and again through the 1940s and 1950s, Frankfurter voted to uphold conservative state and federal laws with which he personally disagreed because he believed that the Supreme Court should defer to legislatures unless the violation of constitutional norms was unmistakably clear. Frankfurter had learned his judicial philosophy from Justice Oliver Wendell Holmes, Jr., a political conservative who in the early twentieth century had voted consistently to uphold liberal legislation because of his overriding commitment to judicial restraint.

It must be stressed that neither position in this debate is an absolute one. No judicial restraintist today suggests that judicial review should *never* be used against laws or executive actions, nor would an activist argue that *every* policy issue is appropriate for judicial intervention. The difference between the two sides is one of degree: given that the institution of judicial review has secured the Supreme Court a role in the American governmental process, just how large should that role be? The continued vigor of the debate between restraintists and activists after nearly two centuries is a reflection of the nation's commitment to two inherently contradictory values: *popular sovereignty*—the idea that power properly lies in the hands of the people through their elected representatives— and *fundamental law*—the notion that such power should be limited by certain overarching principles. The tension between these two ideas can never be wholly reconciled without doing violence to the essential character of the American political enterprise.

Even if we admit that courts generally attempt to make reasoned judgments— as opposed to legislatures which tend to respond to pressures with barely controlled emotion—Justice Gibson's criticism remains. Judicial review *is* inherently antimajoritarian and undemocratic. It does not operate in aid of majority rule; it works against it. This in spite of the fact that majority will or the "voice of the people" is reflected imperfectly in Congress and in the presidency. But impurities in one part of the system are no argument for total rejection of the professed norm in another part. Judicial review is a departure from what Americans say they believe in, namely, majority rule institutionalized in popularly elected assemblies. Such a belief cannot square with an arrangement in which an oligarchy of nine men and women, not elected for fixed terms, but appointed for life, make final decisions on public policies including vital matters of freedom, property rights, and even life and death.

Undemocratic as judicial review may be, however, it is consistent with a system based on a rule of law. In both its origins and in its growth, the American system has been predicated on the assumption that rules of law limit everyone including majorities themselves, and majorities, by acquiescing in the Supreme Court's extraordinary function, have democratically consented to be undemocratically restrained.

But Supreme Court justices are human beings like the rest of us, and it is logical to ask what restraints prevent them from usurping power, from creating a directorate of nine authoritarians running the government of the United States. In the following section we consider the institutional restraints that historically have worked to prevent such a judicial dictatorship from occurring.

LIMITATIONS ON JUDICIAL REVIEW

Jurisdiction

At first glance it may seem paradoxical that the very instrument of government which the Supreme Court interprets is also a limit on the Court's own powers. And yet the U.S. Constitution presupposes that all public officials are bound by its terms, and the judiciary is no exception. The first major limitation on any court is its jurisdiction, that is, the defined area of litigation which it is authorized to hear and upon which it may render judgment. The Constitution clearly delineates the Supreme Court's jurisdiction, dividing it into original and appellate. Article III specifically limits the original jurisdiction to only two categories: those cases involving foreign ambassadors and ministers to the United States and those in which a state is a party and the adversary is another state, a foreign nation, or a citizen of another state or of a foreign state. The judiciary article then declares that the Supreme Court shall have appellate jurisdiction in all other cases "with such exceptions, and under such regulations as Congress shall make." As we know from *Marbury* v. *Madison*, the Congress may not alter the Court's original jurisdiction, but the Court has also held that Congress may enlarge, minimize, or even abolish its appellate jurisdiction, the area which accounts for more than 90 percent of its work. Over the years scores of bills have been introduced in Congress which would have curtailed the Court's jurisdiction—at one point in the early 1980s there were some thirty "court-curbing" bills pending in Congress, covering such issues as school prayer, abortion, and busing to achieve school desegregation—but so far no significant limitations have been passed. If the Court and Congress were to move on a collision course in the matter, it seems doubtful that the Court would emerge the winner. Congress does, in the final analysis, reflect public opinion, and if the public mood is strong enough to support a congressional attack on the Court, the judiciary will acquiesce. Generally, the view has prevailed in Congress that it is wise to avoid legislative intrusion into the Court's jurisdiction, but the incipient threat is always present.

Adversary Parties

Another constitutional limit on the Supreme Court is the language of Article III which declares that "judicial power shall extend to all cases" arising under the Constitution, laws, or treaties of the United States. It is clear that courts are empowered to hear and to decide "cases" and nothing more. But what constitutes a case? Although undefined by the Constitution, the term, case (or controversy), has been held by the Supreme Court to embrace several elements. First, there must be adverse parties; that is, there must be a genuine argument between at least two persons, or between a government (state or federal) and a person, or between two governments. It is essential that the parties actually be in conflict. If the Court suspects collusion or a trumped-up arrangement in which the litigants are really on the same side in the sense that both will emerge either the winners or the losers, it will not take jurisdiction. There are, however, exceptions to this rule (see, for example, *Fletcher* v. *Peck*, excerpted in this chapter); if the Court wants badly enough to hear a case, it is not likely to allow the suggestion of collusion to stop it.

Advisory Opinions

The Court will not give advice on legal questions to private citizens, to the President, to the Congress, or to any public official. At first glance, it might seem prudent and expedient for the President or Congress to seek the Court's opinion on proposed legislation, for if the Court were to say that in its view the proposal was unconstitutional, it might forestall expensive litigation at a later date. The problem is that in such circumstances the Court has no authority to render advisory opinions because there is no actual case or lawsuit involved. As a practical matter, the Court, in rendering a judgment, would need to hypothesize a set of facts and then rule on its own hypothesis, something entirely different from ruling on a concrete factual controversy. Federal courts, including the Supreme Court, do render declaratory judgments, but they are made when there is an actual controversy, although neither party has committed a legal wrong. The court decides what the rights of the parties are without granting relief. Unlike an advisory opinion, a declaratory judgment involves a real set of facts and not merely an abstraction.

Mootness

Another requirement is that moot cases be beyond judicial power, that is, there is no case once the issue has been resolved. An example of mootness arose in *Johnson* v. *New York Education Department* decided in 1972.

An action had been instituted in federal district court challenging a New York law which required local schools to furnish free textbooks to students in grades 7 to 12, but authorized free books to students in grades 1 to 6 only if a majority of a school district's voters consented to a special tax assessment. The law's challengers, indigent recipients of public assistance, argued that their children in the lower grades were being discriminated against on the basis of wealth, in violation of the Fourteenth Amendment's equal protection clause. Both the district court and the federal court of appeals had upheld the constitutionality of the New York law. Meanwhile the voters had elected to assess a tax for the purchase of books for grades 1 to 6, but the litigation moved to the Supreme Court which had the option of reversing the lower courts and invalidating the New York law. In the Court's view, however, the issue seemed to have been resolved, so it chose not to decide the constitutional question.

Mootness is not, however, an ironclad principle. In *Roe* v. *Wade,* for example, the Supreme Court chose to ignore the question of mootness, reasoning that if the requirement were mechanically applied, no pregnant woman would ever be able to challenge an antiabortion statute. Thus by the time the Court vindicated Norma McCorvey's constitutional right to an abortion in Texas, she had long since given birth to a child. In recent years the Court has relaxed the mootness doctrine somewhat, and today tends to invoke it only when one of the parties to the case presses the point.

Standing and Ripeness

Assuming that the elements described above have been met, two additional obstacles need to be surmounted before the Supreme Court will decide a case. First, it must be determined that the person asserting the claim is the proper person to do so. This is called "standing" to sue. Second, a determination is made on the question whether the claim is being pressed at the proper time; that is, does the controversy possess the requisite "ripeness"? Has it developed to the point where the Court can make an informed choice between two opposing arguments? These rules have some flexibility, and whether standing and ripeness have been satisfied in a given case is often a matter of dispute among the justices themselves. When a person is challenging the constitutionality of a law, it is not enough to present logical arguments to the Court; the challenger must show that as a result of the operation of the statute he or she is in immediate personal danger of sustaining financial injury or the loss of a constitutionally guaranteed right. Thus, a person has no standing to sue on the ground that a law is injurious to the public generally or to the people of his or her state or town. One must have a personal stake in the outcome. If one cannot show the requisite personal injury, no case exists, and if there is no case, the Court will dismiss the proceeding for lack of standing. On the other hand, even if a party can show a real or potential injury from a law, the Court may dismiss a challenge to its constitutionality because in the Court's opinion, the issues in the case are not sufficiently "ripe" to allow for a definitive decision.

Political Questions and Justiciability

Of all the limits on judicial review the doctrine of political questions is the most difficult to define. When the Supreme Court says that a case is "nonjusticiable" because it is a "political question," it argues essentially that the subject matter of the controversy should not be resolved judicially since the text of the Constitution places final authority over the matter in the political branches of the government, namely, the presidency or Congress, and at the state level, the legislature or the governor. Certainly this idea lends itself to abuse, since the justices theoretically can dismiss many cases on the grounds that the President and Congress are the proper authorities for final decision. It will be recalled, however, that judicial review is not mandated by the Constitution. It is a creature of the Court itself, and at times it may be prudent for the justices to refuse to exert power beyond the bounds of practical necessity. The political question doctrine is most frequently invoked on behalf of judicial restraint. Some commentators suggest that political questions are simply those which the Court decides not to decide. The principle, it is argued, is nothing more than a dodge, a cop-out. Regardless of one's perspective, political questions are a significant limiting factor in the exercise of judicial power.

The following excerpted opinions have been chosen to illustrate or exemplify a number of aspects of judicial review. *Marbury* v. *Madison* is the "cornerstone" of judicial review cases, the first case in which the Supreme Court declared an act of Congress unconstitutional. In *Fletcher* v. *Peck* the Court further expanded judicial review by holding a state law unconstitutional. *Dred Scott* v. *Sanford* shows quite vividly the intensely political nature of judicial review. The majority and dissenting opinions in *Home Building and Loan Association* v. *Blaisdell* are good examples of the debate among Supreme Court justices regarding the proper role of the Court in exercising its power of judicial review. The remaining cases—*Schechter Poultry Corp.* v. *United States, Heart of Atlanta Motel* v. *United States, Miranda* v. *Arizona,* and *San Antonio Independent School District* v. *Rodriguez*—have been included as illustrations of conservative activism, liberal restraint, liberal activism, and conservative restraint, respectively.

Bibliography

COX, ARCHIBALD. *The Court and the Constitution.* Boston: Houghton Mifflin, 1982.

FORTE, DAVID, ed. *The Supreme Court in American Politics.* Lexington, Mass.: Heath, 1972.

HOPKINS, VINCENT C. *Dred Scott's Case.* New York: Atheneum, 1967.

LEVY, LEONARD W., ed. *Judicial Review and the Supreme Court.* New York: Harper & Row, 1986.

SIEGAN, BERNARD. *The Supreme Court's Constitution.* New Brunswick, N.J.: Transaction Books, 1987.

WOLFE, CHRISTOPHER. *The Rise of Modern Judicial Review.* New York: Basic Books, 1986.

Marbury v. Madison

1 CRANCH 137(1803)

Thomas Jefferson's victory over the incumbent John Adams in the presidential election of 1800 was a watershed in America's political history, marking the end of the Federalists' brief reign as the nation's dominant party. Jefferson's Republicans would occupy the presidency and command congressional majorities for the next two decades.

The Federalists did not go quietly, however. In the waning days of the Adams administration, Congress passed the Judiciary Act of 1801, creating 42 new federal judgeships which Adams hastened to fill with loyal Federalists. Some of these were lifetime judicial appointments; having lost control of the executive and legislative branches, the Federalist party hoped to extend its influence through the judiciary. The new judicial posts also included a number of less important 5-year justice of the peace appointments in the District of Columbia, which likewise went to faithful party supporters, including one William Marbury.

Following Senate confirmation of the judicial appointments, President Adams signed the commission papers and his secretary of state, John Marshall, who had already been nominated and confirmed as chief justice, affixed the United States seal to them as required by law. Marshall's brother James was apparently responsible for delivering the commissions to the new appointees, but in the last hectic hours of the Adams presidency, four of the commissions, including Marbury's, were overlooked. The incoming President discovered them in the State Department the next day, signed, sealed, but undelivered. Angered by Adams' *coup* in appointing his so-called midnight judges, Jefferson ordered that these commissions be treated as "mere nullities." Marbury and the other presumptive appointees then brought suit in the United States Supreme Court under a provision of the Judiciary Act of 1789 which gave the Court the authority under its original jurisdiction to issue writs of mandamus ordering public officials to perform a legal duty. By today's standards of judicial conduct, it would be unthinkable for a Supreme Court justice (or any judge for that matter) to hear a case in which he or she had been previously involved. Nevertheless, Marshall wrote the Court's opinion in *Marbury v. Madison*, which was handed down in 1803.

JOHN MARSHALL

John Marshall, appointed by President John Adams in 1801, served for 35 years, longer than any other chief justice. Generally held to be the greatest justice ever to sit on the Supreme Court, Marshall molded the judiciary into a powerful third branch of government, after its inauspicious beginning under his three predecessors, John Jay, Oliver Ellsworth, and John Rutledge. Emphasizing the primacy of the Constitution and the supremacy of national over state power, Marshall and his Court gave permanent life to the major clauses of the Constitution.

Chief Justice **Marshall** delivered the opinion of the Court.

. . .

In the order in which the court has viewed this subject, the following questions have been considered and decided.

1st. Has the applicant a right to the commission he demands?

2dly. If he has a right, and that right has been violated, do the laws of his country afford him a remedy?

3dly. If they do afford him a remedy, is it a *mandamus* issuing from this court?

The first object of enquiry is,

1st. Has the applicant a right to the commission he demands?

. . .

In order to determine whether he is entitled to this commission, it becomes necessary to enquire whether he has been appointed to the office. For if he has been appointed, the law continues him in office for five years, and he is entitled to the possession of those evidences of office, which, being completed, became his property.

. . .

This is an appointment made by the President, by and with the advice and consent of the senate, and is evidenced by no act but the commission itself. In such a case therefore the commission and the appointment seem inseparable; it being almost impossible to shew an appointment otherwise than by proving the existence of a commission. . . .

. . .

The last act to be done by the President, is the signature of the commission. He has then acted on the advice and consent of the senate to his own nomination. The time for deliberation has then passed. He has decided. His judgment, on the advice and consent of the senate concurring with his nomination, has been made, and the officer is appointed. This appointment is evidenced by an open, unequivocal act; and being the last act required from the person making it, necessarily excludes the idea of its being, so far as respects the appointment, an inchoate and incomplete transaction.

. . .

The transmission of the commission, is a practice directed by convenience, but not by law. It cannot therefore be necessary to constitute the appointment which must precede it, and which is the mere act of the President. If the executive required that every person appointed to an office, should himself take means to procure his commission, the appointment would not be the less valid on that account. The appointment is the sole act of the President; the transmission of the commission is the sole act of the officer to whom that duty is assigned, and may be accelerated or retarded by circumstances which can have no influence on the appointment. A commission is transmitted to a person already appointed; not to a person to be appointed or not, as the letter enclosing the commission should happen to get into the post-office and reach him in safety, or to miscarry.

. . .

It is therefore decidedly the opinion of the court, that when a commission has been signed by the President, the appointment is made; and that the commission is complete, when the seal of the United States has been affixed to it by the secretary of state.

. . .

Mr. Marbury, then, since his commission was signed by the President, and sealed by the secretary of state, was appointed; and as the law creating the office, gave the officer a right to hold for five years, independent of the executive, the appointment was not revocable; but vested in the officer legal rights, which are protected by the laws of his country.

To withhold his commission, therefore, is an act deemed by the court not warranted by law, but violative of a vested legal right.

This brings us to the second enquiry; which is,

2dly. If he has a right, and that right has been violated, do the laws of his country afford him a remedy?

. . .

The government of the United States has been emphatically termed a government of laws, and not of men. It will certainly cease to deserve this high appellation, if the laws furnish no remedy for the violation of a vested legal right.

. . .

The power of nominating to the senate, and the power of appointing the person nominated, are political powers, to be exercised by the President according to his own discretion. When he has made an appointment, he has exercised his whole power, and his discretion has been completely applied to the case. If, by law, the officer be removable at the will of the President, then a new appointment may be immediately made, and the rights of the officer are terminated. But as a fact which has existed cannot be made never to have existed, the appointment cannot be annihilated; and consequently if the officer is by law not removable at the will of the President; the rights he has acquired are protected by the law, and are not resumable by the President. They cannot be extinguished by executive authority, and he has the privilege of asserting them in like manner as if they had been derived from any other source.

The question whether a right has vested or not, is, in its nature, judicial, and must be tried by the judicial authority. If, for example, Mr. Marbury had taken the oaths of a magistrate, and proceeded to act as one; in consequence of which a suit had been instituted against him, in which his defence had depended on his being a magistrate; the validity of his appointment must have been determined by judicial authority.

So, if he conceives that, by virtue of his appointment, he has a legal right, either to the commission which has been made out for him, or to a copy of that commission, it is equally a question examinable in a court, and the decision of the court upon it must depend on the opinion entertained of his appointment.

That question has been discussed, and the opinion is, that the latest point of time which can be taken as that at which the appointment was complete, and evidenced, was when, after the signature of the president, the seal of the United States was affixed to the commission.

It is then the opinion of the court,

1st. That by signing the commission of Mr. Marbury, the president of the United States appointed him a justice of peace, for the county of Washington in the district of Columbia; and that the seal of the United States, affixed thereto by the secretary of state, is conclusive testimony of the verity of the signature, and of the completion of the appointment; and that the appointment conferred on him a legal right to the office for the space of five years.

2dly. That, having this legal title to the office, he has a consequent right to the commission; a refusal to deliver which, is a plain violation of that right, for which the laws of his country afford him a remedy.

It remains to be enquired whether,

3dly. He is entitled to the remedy for which he applies. This depends on,

1st. The nature of the writ applied for, and, 2dly. The power of this court. 1st. The nature of the writ.

. . .

If one of the heads of departments commits any illegal act, under color of his office, by which an individual sustains an injury, it cannot be pretended that his office alone exempts him from being sued in the ordinary mode of proceeding, and being compelled to obey the judgment of the law. How then can his office exempt him from this particular mode of deciding on the legality of his conduct, if the case be such a case as would, were any other individual the party complained of, authorize the process?

It is not by the office of the person to whom the writ is directed, but the nature of the thing to be done that the propriety or impropriety of issuing a mandamus, is to be determined. Where the head of a department acts in a case, in which executive discretion is to be exercised; in which he is the mere organ of executive will; it is again repeated, that any application to a court to control, in any respect, his conduct, would be rejected without hesitation.

But where he is directed by law to do a certain act affecting the absolute rights of individuals, in the performance of which he is not placed under the particular direction of the President, and the performance of which the President cannot lawfully forbid, and therefore is never presumed to have forbidden; as for example, to record a commission, or a patent for land, which has received all the legal solemnities; or to give a copy of such record; in such cases, it is not perceived on what ground the courts of the country are further excused from the duty of giving judgment, that right be done to an injured individual, than if the same services were to be performed by a person not the head of a department.

. . .

This, then, is a plain case for a mandamus, either to deliver the commission, or a copy of it from the record; and it only remains to be enquired,

Whether it can issue from this court.

The act to establish the judicial courts of the United States authorizes the supreme court "to issue writs of mandamus, in cases warranted by the principles and usages of law, to any courts appointed, or persons holding office, under the authority of the United States."

The secretary of state, being a person holding an office under the authority of the United States, is precisely within the letter of the description; and if this court is not authorized to issue a writ of mandamus to such an officer, it must be because the law is unconstitutional, and therefore absolutely incapable of conferring the authority, and assigning the duties which its words purport to confer and assign.

The constitution vests the whole judicial power of the United States in one supreme court, and such inferior courts as congress shall, from time to time, ordain and establish. This power is expressly extended to all cases arising under the laws of the United States; and consequently, in some form, may be exercised over the present case; because the right claimed is given by a law of the United States.

In the distribution of this power it is declared that "the supreme court shall have original jurisdiction in all cases affecting ambassadors, other public ministers and consuls, and those in which a state shall be a party. In all other cases, the supreme court shall have appellate jurisdiction."

It has been insisted, at the bar, that as the original grant of jurisdiction, to the supreme and inferior courts, is general, and the clause, assigning original jurisdiction to the supreme court, contains no negative or restrictive words; the power remains to the legislature, to assign original jurisdiction to that court in other cases than those specified in the article which has been recited; provided those cases belong to the judicial power of the United States.

If it had been intended to leave it in the discretion of the legislature to apportion the judicial power between the supreme and inferior courts according to the will of that body, it would certainly have been useless to have proceeded further than to have defined the judicial power, and the tribunals in which it should be vested. The subsequent part of the selection is mere surplussage, is entirely without meaning, if such is to be the construction. If congress remains at liberty to give this court appellate jurisdiction, where the constitution has declared their jurisdiction shall be original; and original jurisdiction where the constitution has declared it shall be appellate; the distribution of jurisdiction, made in the constitution, is form without substance.

. . .

When an instrument organizing fundamentally a judicial system, divides it into one supreme, and so many inferior courts as the legislature may ordain and establish; then enumerates its powers, and proceeds so far to distribute them, as to define the jurisdiction of the supreme court by declaring the cases in which it shall take original jurisdiction, and that in others it shall take appellate jurisdiction; the plain import of the words seems to be, that in one class of cases its jurisdiction is original, and not appellate; in the other it is appellate, and not original. If any other construction would render the clause inoperative, that is an additional reason for rejecting such other construction, and for adhering to their obvious meaning.

To enable this court then to issue a mandamus, it must be shewn to be an exercise of appellate jurisdiction, or to be necessary to enable them to exercise appellate jurisdiction.

It has been stated at the bar that the appellate jurisdiction may be exercised in a variety of forms, and that if it be the will of the legislature that a mandamus should be used for that purpose, that will must be obeyed. This is true, yet the jurisdiction must be appellate, not original.

It is the essential criterion of appellate jurisdiction, that it revises and corrects the proceedings in a cause already instituted, and does not create that cause. Although, therefore, a mandamus may be directed to courts, yet to issue such a writ to an officer for the delivery of a paper, is in effect the same as to sustain an original action for that paper, and therefore seems not to belong to appellate, but to original jurisdiction. Neither is it necessary in such a case as this, to enable the court to exercise its appellate jurisdiction.

The authority, therefore, given to the supreme court, by the act establishing the judicial courts of the United States, to issue writs of mandamus to public officers, appears not to be warranted by the constitution; and it becomes necessary to enquire whether a jurisdiction, so conferred, can be exercised.

The question, whether an act, repugnant to the constitution, can become the law of the land, is a question deeply interesting to the United States; but, happily, not of an intricacy proportioned to its interest. It seems only necessary to recognise certain principles, supposed to have been long and well established, to decide it.

That the people have an original right to establish, for their future government, such principles as, in their opinion, shall most conduce to their own happiness, is the basis, on which the whole American fabric has been erected. The exercise of this original right is a very great exertion; nor can it, nor ought it to be frequently repeated. The principles, therefore, so established, are deemed fundamental. And as the authority, from which they proceed, is supreme, and can seldom act, they are designed to be permanent.

This original and supreme will organizes the government, and assigns, to different departments, their respective powers. It may either stop here; or establish certain limits not to be transcended by those departments.

The government of the United States is of the latter description. The powers of the legislature are defined, and limited; and that those limits may not be mistaken, or forgotten, the constitution is written. To what purpose are powers limited, and to what purpose is that limitation committed to writing, if these limits may, at any time, be passed by those intended to be restrained? The distinction, between a government with limited and unlimited powers, is abolished, if those limits do not confine the persons on whom they are imposed, and if acts prohibited and acts allowed, are of equal obligation. It is a proposition too plain to be contested, that the constitution controls any legislative act repugnant to it; or, that the legislature may alter the constitution by an ordinary act.

Between these alternatives there is no middle ground. The constitution is either a superior, paramount law, unchangeable by ordinary means, or it is on a level with ordinary legislative acts, and like other acts, is alterable when the legislature shall please to alter it.

If the former part of the alternative be true, then a legislative act contrary to the constitution is not law: if the latter part be true, then written constitutions are absurd attempts, on the part of the people, to limit a power, in its own nature illimitable.

Certainly all those who have framed written constitutions contemplate them as forming the fundamental and paramount law of the nation, and consequently the theory of every such government must be, that an act of the legislature, repugnant to the constitution, is void.

This theory is essentially attached to a written constitution, and is consequently to be considered, by this court, as one of the fundamental principles of our society. It is not therefore to be lost sight of in the further consideration of this subject.

If an act of the legislature, repugnant to the constitution, is void, does it, notwithstanding its invalidity, bind the courts, and oblige them to give it effect? Or, in other words, though it be not law, does it constitute a rule as operative as if it was a law? This would be to overthrow in fact what was established in theory; and would seem, at first view, an absurdity too gross to be insisted on. It shall, however, receive a more attentive consideration.

It is emphatically the province and duty of the judicial department to say what the law is. Those who apply the rule to particular cases, must of necessity expound and interpret that rule. If two laws conflict with each other, the courts must decide on the operation of each.

So if a law be in opposition to the constitution; if both the law and the constitution apply to a particular case, so that the court must either decide that case conformably to the law, disregarding the constitution; or conformably to the constitution, disregarding the law; the court must determine which of these conflicting rules governs the case. This is of the very essence of judicial duty.

If then the courts are to regard the constitution; and the constitution is superior to any ordinary act of the legislature; the constitution, and not such ordinary act, must govern the case to which they both apply.

Those then who controvert the principle that the constitution is to be considered, in court, as a paramount law, are reduced to the necessity of maintaining that courts must close their eyes on the constitution, and see only the law.

This doctrine would subvert the very foundation of all written constitutions. It would declare that an act, which, according to the principles and theory of our government, is entirely void; is yet, in practice, completely obligatory. It would declare, that if the legislature shall do what is expressly forbidden, such act, notwithstanding the express prohibition, is in reality effectual. It would be giving to the legislature a practical and real omnipotence, with the same breath which professes to restrict their powers within narrow limits. It is prescribing limits, and declaring that those limits may be passed at pleasure.

That it thus reduces to nothing what we have deemed the greatest improvement on political institutions—a written constitution—would of itself be sufficient, in America, where written constitutions have been viewed with so much reverence, for rejecting the constitution. But the peculiar expressions of the constitution of the United States furnish additional arguments in favour of its rejection.

The judicial power of the United States is extended to all cases arising under the constitution.

Could it be the intention of those who gave this power, to say that, in using it, the constitution should not be looked into? That a case arising under the constitution should be decided without examining the instrument under which it arises?

This is too extravagant to be maintained.

In some cases then, the constitution must be looked into by the judges. And if they can open it at all, what part of it are they forbidden to read, or to obey?

There are many other parts of the constitution which serve to illustrate this subject.

It is declared that "no tax or duty shall be laid on articles exported from any state." Suppose a duty on the export of cotton, of tobacco, or of flour; and a suit instituted to recover it. Ought judgment to be rendered in such a case? ought the judges to close their eyes on the constitution, and only see the law.

The constitution declares that "no bill of attainder or *ex post facto* law shall be passed."

If, however, such a bill should be passed and a person should be prosecuted under it; must the court condemn to death those victims whom the constitution endeavours to preserve?

"No person," says the constitution, "shall be convicted of treason unless on the testimony of two witnesses to the same overt act, or on confession in open court."

Here the language of the constitution is addressed especially to the courts. It prescribes, directly for them, a rule of evidence not to be departed from. If the legislature should change that rule, and declare *one* witness, or a confession *out* of court, sufficient for conviction, must the constitutional principle yield to the legislative act?

From these, and many other selections which might be made, it is apparent, that the framers of the constitution contemplated that instrument, as a rule for the government of *courts*, as well as of the legislature.

Why otherwise does it direct the judges to take an oath to support it? This oath certainly applies, in an especial manner, to their conduct in their official character. How immoral to impose it on them, if they were to be used as the instruments, and the knowing instruments, for violating what they swear to support!

The oath of office, too, imposed by the legislature, is completely demonstrative of the legislative opinion on this subject. It is in these words, "I do solemnly swear that I will administer justice without respect to persons, and do equal right to the poor and to the rich; and that I will faithfully and impartially discharge all the duties incumbent on me as according to the best of my abilities and understanding, agreeably to *the constitution*, and laws of the United States."

Why does a judge swear to discharge his duties agreeably to the constitution of the United States, if that constitution forms no rule for his government? if it is closed upon him, and cannot be inspected by him?

If such be the real state of things, this is worse than solemn mockery. To prescribe, or to take this oath, becomes equally a crime.

It is also not entirely unworthy of observation, that in declaring what shall be the *supreme* law of the land, the *constitution* itself is first mentioned; and not the laws of the United States generally, but those only which shall be made in *pursuance* of the constitution, have that rank.

Thus, the particular phraseology of the constitution of the United States confirms and strengthens the principle, supposed to be essential to all written constitutions, that a law repugnant to the constitution is void; and that *courts*, as well as other departments, are bound by that instrument.

The rule must be discharged.

Aftermath of Marbury *v.* Madison

Marshall's decision in *Marbury* took nearly everyone by surprise. It had been assumed that Marshall would throw the weight of the Supreme Court, such as it was at the time, behind Marbury's effort to collect his commission from the Republicans, and Jefferson apparently was fully prepared to defy such an order. But Marshall's decision avoided such a confrontation by holding that despite Marbury's legal (and, by implication, moral) right to his commission, the Court had no power to order its delivery because the Judiciary Act of 1789, on which Marbury had relied, had given the Court original jurisdiction beyond what was authorized by the Constitution. Thus the law was invalid—unconstitutional—and could not be enforced. Marshall had cleverly traded an insignificant power—that of issuing writs of mandamus—for a vastly more important one—the power to declare acts of Congress unconstitutional if, in the Court's opinion, they conflicted with the Constitution. Jefferson and Madison understood immediately the real meaning of *Marbury*, that henceforth the Supreme Court would play an important political role alongside the executive branch and legislature by determining the meaning and application of the Constitution. But because Marshall had chosen a case that required no response from the executive branch or legislature, there was no practical opportunity for Marshall's opponents to challenge the Court's assumption of this power of judicial review.

William Marbury never received his commission and had to settle instead for being the most famous "loser" in Supreme Court history. Today his portrait hangs in a Supreme Court conference room, the gift of a descendant who in the mid-nineteenth century married a descendant of John Marshall.

Fletcher v. Peck
6 CRANCH 87(1810)

In the late 1700s the state of Georgia claimed title to about 35 million acres of land covering most of what is now the states of Alabama and Mississippi. Parts of this huge tract, known as the Yazoo lands, were also claimed by the federal government, Spain, and numerous Indian tribes. The land was much coveted by land speculators. One such group was led by James Gunn, a United States senator from Georgia and a staunch Federalist. In 1795 the Georgia legislature passed a law allowing Gunn's company to purchase the Yazoo lands for $500,000. Other speculators had offered the state larger sums, but nearly all of the legislators voting to sell the land to Gunn had been bribed with shares of the company or direct cash payments. A public outcry followed, some of it fomented by Georgia's other senator, James Jackson, a Jeffersonian Republican. Jackson led a movement to purge the state legislature of those who had taken bribes and to nullify the land sale act. In 1796 a virtually new legislature was elected and an act was quickly passed repealing the Yazoo land sale.

Meanwhile about one-third of the Yazoo lands had been resold to the New England Mississippi Land Company for over $1 million returning a profit to the original purchasers of some 650 percent. This land in turn was divided up and resold, some of it to small investors who claimed to have no knowledge of the fraudulent circumstances of the sale, or of the repeal legislation. The United States government was soon drawn into the dispute because of its own interest in acquiring the Yazoo lands. But acquire it from whom?

Federalists in Congress, strong believers in the sanctity of private property, argued that the original sale was valid and that the government ought to negotiate with its new owners. Republicans, committed to states' rights, held that Georgia owned the land because the repeal legislation was a proper exercise of state authority. In 1802 a compromise of sorts was struck: Georgia transferred ownership of the Yazoo lands to the federal government for $1,250,000, with 5 million acres set aside to settle claims by private purchasers. The New England Mississippi Land Company then began to lobby Congress for compensation for their lost property. From 1804 to 1807 their efforts were thwarted almost single-handedly by Representative John Randolph of Virginia, a sworn defender of state sovereignty and enemy of land capitalists.

Seeking ways of strengthening their case for compensation, the Yazoo speculators turned to the federal courts, which were still dominated by the Federalist party. They reasoned that Federalist judges would respond positively to the argument that Georgia's repeal legislation had been an impairment of contract, violating Article I, Section 10 of the United States Constitution. A "friendly lawsuit" was duly arranged, one that would be heard in federal court under the "diversity of citizenship" jurisdiction—that is, a citizen of one state suing a citizen of another state. In 1803 Robert Fletcher of New Hampshire sued John Peck of Massachusetts for selling him 15,000 acres of Georgia land that were not legally his because of the repeal act. Despite their ostensibly adversary relationship, Fletcher and Peck had much in common: both were land speculators with large Yazoo holdings, and both therefore had an interest in seeing the repeal act declared invalid so they could demand compensation from the federal government. After the circuit court upheld the original sale, the case languished for 3 years while the speculators pressed their claim unsuccessfully in Congress. Deciding that a more definitive court decision was needed, Fletcher (acting, of course, on behalf of the speculators) took an appeal to the United States Supreme Court in 1809. The decision was announced the following year.

Chief Justice **Marshall** delivered the opinion of the Court:

. . .

[In the first and second parts of his opinion, Marshall states that Georgia had the authority under its constitution to sell the Yazoo lands and that the corruption of the legislature did not render the 1795 sale invalid.]

The lands in controversy vested absolutely in James Gunn and others, the original grantees, by the conveyance of the governor, made in pursuance of an act of assembly to which the legislature was fully competent. Being thus in full possession of the legal estate, they, for a valuable consideration, conveyed portions of the land to those who were willing to purchase. If the original transaction was infected with fraud, these purchasers did not participate in it, and had no notice of it. They were innocent. Yet the legislature of Georgia has involved them in the fate of the first parties to the transaction, and, if the act be valid, has annihilated their rights also.

The legislature of Georgia was a party to this transaction; and for a party to pronounce its own deed invalid, whatever cause may be assigned for its invalidity, must be considered as a mere act of power which must find its vindication in a train of reasoning not often heard in courts of justice.

. . .

If the legislature be its own judge in its own case, it would seem equitable that its decision should be regulated by those rules which would have regulated the decision of a judicial tribunal. The question was, in its nature, a question of title, and the tribunal which decided it was either acting in the character of a court of justice, and performing a duty usually assigned to a court, or it was exerting a mere act of power in which it was controlled only by its own will.

If a suit be brought to set aside a conveyance obtained by fraud, and the fraud be clearly proved, the conveyance will be set aside, as between the parties; but the rights of third persons, who are purchasers without notice, for a valuable consideration, cannot be disregarded. Titles, which, according to every legal test, are perfect, are acquired with that confidence which is inspired by the opinion that the purchaser is safe. If there be any concealed defect, arising from the conduct of those who had held the property long before he acquired it, of which he had no notice, that concealed defect cannot be set up against him. He has paid his money for a title good at law, he is innocent, whatever may be the guilt of others, and equity will not subject him to the penalties attached to that guilt. All titles would be insecure, and the intercourse between man and man would be very seriously obstructed, if this principle be overturned.

A court of chancery, therefore, had a bill been brought to set aside the conveyance made to James Gunn and others, as being obtained by improper practices with the legislature, whatever might have been its decision as respected the original grantees, would have been bound, by its own rules, and by the clearest principles of equity, to leave unmolested those who were purchasers, without notice, for a valuable consideration.

If the legislature felt itself absolved from those rules of property which are common to all the citizens of the United States, and from those principles of equity which are acknowledged in all our courts, its act is to be supported by its power alone, and the same power may devest any other individual of his lands, if it shall be the will of the legislature so to exert it.

It is not intended to speak with disrespect of the legislature of Georgia, or of its acts. Far from it. The question is a general question, and is treated as one. For although such powerful objections to a legislative grant, as are alleged against this, may not again exist, yet the principle, on which alone this rescinding act is to be supported, may be applied to every case to which it shall be the will of any legislature to apply it. The principle is this; that a legislature may, by its own act, devest the vested estate of any man whatever, for reasons which shall, by itself, be deemed sufficient.

In this case the legislature may have had ample proof that the original grant was obtained by practices which can never be too much reprobated, and which would have justified its abrogation so far as respected those to whom crime was imputable. But the grant, when issued, conveyed an estate in fee-simple to the grantee, clothed with all the solemnities which law can bestow. This estate was transferrable; and those who purchased parts of it were not stained by that guilt which infected the original transaction. Their case is not distinguishable from the ordinary case of purchasers of a legal estate without knowledge of any secret fraud which might have led to the emanation of the original grant. According to the well known course of equity, their rights could not be affected by such fraud. Their situation was the same, their title was the same, with that of every other member of the community who holds land by regular conveyances from the original patentee.

Is the power of the legislature competent to the annihilation of such title, and to a resumption of the property thus held?

The principle asserted is, that one legislature is competent to repeal any act which a former legislature was competent to pass; and that one legislature cannot abridge the powers of a succeeding legislature.

The correctness of this principle, so far as respects general legislation, can never be controverted. But, if an act be done under a law, a succeeding legislature cannot undo it. The past cannot be recalled by the most absolute power. Conveyances have been made, those conveyances have vested legal estates, and, if those estates may be seized by the sovereign authority, still, that they originally vested is a fact, and cannot cease to be a fact.

When, then, a law is in its nature a contract, when absolute rights have vested under that contract, a repeal of the law cannot devest those rights; and the act of annulling them, if legitimate, is rendered so by a power applicable to the case of every individual in the community.

It may well be doubted whether the nature of society and of government does not prescribe some limits to the legislative power; and, if any be prescribed, where are they to be found, if the property of an individual, fairly and honestly acquired, may be seized without compensation.

To the legislature all legislative power is granted; but the question, whether the act of transferring the property of an individual to the public, be in the nature of the legislative power, is well worthy of serious reflection.

It is the peculiar province of the legislature to prescribe general rules for the government of society; the application of those rules to individuals in society would seem to be the duty of other departments. How far the power of giving the law may involve every other power, in cases where the constitution is silent, never has been, and perhaps never can be, definitely stated.

The validity of this rescinding act, then, might well be doubted, were Georgia a single sovereign power. But Georgia cannot be viewed as a single, unconnected, sovereign power, on whose legislature no other restrictions are imposed than may be found in its own constitution. She is a part of a large empire; she is a member of the American union; and that union has a constitution the supremacy of which all acknowledge, and which imposes limits to the legislatures of the several states, which none claim a right to pass. The constitution of the United States declares that no state shall pass any bill of attainder, *ex post facto* law, or law impairing the obligation of contracts.

Does the case now under consideration come within this prohibitory section of the constitution?

In considering this very interesting question, we immediately ask ourselves what is a contract? Is a grant a contract?

A contract is a compact between two or more parties, and is either executory or executed. An executory contract is one in which a party binds himself to do, or not to do, a particular thing; such was the law under which the conveyance was made by the governor. A contract executed is one in which the object of contract is performed; and this, says Blackstone, differs in nothing from a grant. The contract between Georgia and the purchasers was executed by the grant. A contract executed, as well as one which is executory, contains obligations binding on the parties. A grant, in its own nature, amounts to an extinguishment of the right of the grantor, and implies a contract not to reassert that right. A party is, therefore, always estopped by his own grant.

Since, then, in fact, a grant is a contract executed, the obligation of which still continues, and since the constitution uses the general term contract, without distinguishing between those which are executory and those which are executed, it must be construed to comprehend the latter as well as the former. A law annulling conveyances between individuals, and declaring that the grantors should stand seized of their former estates, notwithstanding those grants, would be as repugnant to the constitution as a law discharging the vendors of property from the obligation of executing their contracts by conveyances. It would be strange if a contract to convey was secured by the constitution, while an absolute conveyance remained unprotected.

If, under a fair construction the constitution, grants are comprehended under the term contracts, is a grant from the state excluded from the operation of the provision? Is the clause to be considered as inhibiting the state from impairing the obligation of contracts between two individuals, but as excluding from that inhibition contracts made with itself?

The words themselves contain no such distinction. They are general, and are applicable to contracts of every description. If contracts made with the state are to be exempted from their operation, the exception must arise from the character of the contracting party, not from the words which are employed.

Whatever respect might have been felt for the state sovereignties, it is not to be disguised that the framers of the constitution viewed, with some apprehension, the violent acts which might grow out of the feelings of the moment; and that the people of the United States, in adopting that instrument, have manifested a determination to shield themselves and their property from the effects of those sudden and strong passions to which men are exposed. The restrictions on the legislative power of the states are obviously founded in this sentiment; and the constitution of the United States contains what may be deemed a bill of rights for the people of each state.

No state shall pass any bill of attainder, *ex post facto* law, or law impairing the obligation of contracts.

A bill of attainder may affect the life of an individual, or may confiscate his property, or may do both.

In this form the power of the legislature over the lives and fortunes of individuals is expressly restrained. What motive, then, for implying, in words which import a general prohibition to impair the obligation of contracts, an exception in favour of the right to impair the obligation of those contracts into which the state may enter?

The state legislatures can pass no *ex post facto* law. An *ex post facto* law is one which renders an act punishable in a manner in which it was not punishable when it was committed. Such a law may inflict penalties on the person, or may inflict pecuniary penalties which swell the public treasury. The legislature is then prohibited from passing a law by which a man's estate, or any part of it, shall be seized for a crime which was not declared, by some previous law, to render him liable to that punishment. Why, then, should violence be done to the natural meaning of words for the purpose of leaving to the legislature the power of seizing, for public use, the estate of an individual in the form of a law annulling the title by which he holds that estate? The court can perceive no sufficient grounds for making this distinction. This rescinding act would have the effect of an *ex post facto* law. It forfeits the estate of Fletcher for a crime not committed by himself, but by those from whom he purchased. This cannot be effected in the form of an *ex post facto* law, or bill of attainder; why, then, is it allowable in the form of a law annulling the original grant?

. . .

It is, then, the unanimous opinion of the court, that, in this case, the estate having passed into the hands of a purchaser for a valuable consideration, without notice, the state of Georgia was restrained, either by general principles which are common to our free institutions, or by the particular provisions of the constitution of the United States, from passing a law whereby the estate of the plaintiff in the premises so purchased could be constitutionally and legally impaired and rendered null and void. . . .

Aftermath of Fletcher *v.* Peck

Fletcher v. *Peck* was the first important Supreme Court decision holding a state law invalid for violating the United States Constitution. (The previous year, in *United States* v. *Judge Peters,* the Court had overturned a Pennsylvania law nullifying a federal court decision.) Thus *Fletcher* v. *Peck* stands with *Marbury* v. *Madison* as one of the foundation cases of American constitutional law. The decision also marked the Court's first use of the contract clause (Article I, Section 10) as a limitation on state authority. For most of the nineteenth century, until it was displaced by the Fourteenth Amendment's due process clause, the contract clause was the Supreme Court's chief means of limiting state interference with capitalist enterprises. Of the approximately 160 Supreme Court decisions between 1810 and 1889 declaring state laws unconstitutional, nearly half were based on the contract clause.

Although the Yazoo speculators were arguably the first organized interest group to use the judiciary to help achieve a political reward, they were not particularly interested in either the institutional or the constitutional significance of *Fletcher* v. *Peck.* From the beginning of their case, they had sought a favorable court decision simply to improve their bargaining position in the congressional debate over compensation. Despite Marshall's powerful opinion, it was not until 1814, with Mississippi's campaign to enter the Union stalled by the unresolved land claims, that Congress finally voted to pay the Yazoo purchasers up to $5 million in return for legal releases of their claims to the land.

Dred Scott v. Sanford

60 U.S. 393(1856)

The Louisiana Purchase of 1803 expanded by some four times the territory of the United States, opening vast areas of land to exploration, settlement, and eventually statehood. As the process of clearing the territory unfolded, however, the inability of the north and the south to reach consensus on the "peculiar institution" of slavery transformed a national blessing into a curse. Would the states that were carved out of western lands be admitted to the Union as free or slave states? Should the territories themselves be free or slave? Underlying these questions were hard choices about the nation's economic and political future. As sectional positions hardened and the slavery issue became more intractable, Congress attempted a solomonic solution through the Missouri Compromise of 1820, splitting the Louisiana Territory at the latitude of 36° 30', north of which slavery would be prohibited and south of which it would be allowed. Like most compromises, this solution pleased no one but at least permitted western expansion to continue while postponing a final resolution of the slavery question.

In 1834 Dr. John Emerson, a United States Army physician stationed in St. Louis, purchased for $500 a black slave by the name of Dred Scott. In the next 2 years Scott and his wife Harriet accompanied Emerson first to Illinois, a free state, and then to Fort Snelling, part of the Upper Louisiana Territory in what is now Minnesota, where slavery was prohibited under the terms of the Missouri Compromise. In 1838 the Scotts returned to St. Louis where they were hired out as servants. After Emerson

died in 1843, Dred Scott tried to buy his family's freedom from Emerson's widow but was refused. In 1846, with the help of the family which had sold him to Emerson, Scott sued Mrs. Emerson for his freedom on the ground that his residence in Illinois and Fort Snelling had made him a free man. A Missouri trial court upheld Scott's claim, but the judgment was reversed on appeal by the state supreme court. By this time Scott's case had attracted the attention of abolitionists who saw in it an opportunity to establish two important legal principles: that a slave could gain freedom by living in a free territory, and that such a claim was enforceable in the federal courts. With the apparent acquiescence of all parties, it was arranged that Scott would become the property of John Sanford, the brother of Emerson's widow. Sanford resided in the state of New York, which meant that Dred Scott could bring a lawsuit against him in federal court under the "diversity of citizenship" rule. This Scott did in 1854, and when his claims were denied in the federal district court an appeal was filed with the United States Supreme Court.

Dred Scott's case was heard in 1856, in an atmosphere of increasing polarization both inside and outside the Supreme Court. The Court's membership represented a wide range of opinion on the key political issue of the day, states' rights versus national authority. Five of the justices were from the south and were strongly opposed to congressional meddling in state and territorial affairs. One of these was the aged Chief Justice Roger Taney, a Maryland Democrat who had been appointed in 1836 by Andrew Jackson. Taney, though he had freed his own slaves many years before, identified strongly with southern culture and values and embraced the states' rights position on slavery. Taney had also become convinced that a definitive statement from the Supreme Court on the slavery question would steer the north and south away from their moral and political collision course. At the other end of the political spectrum was Associate Justice John McLean, a member of the Court since 1829, who had become increasingly supportive of the Unionist position that slavery could and should be prohibited by an act of Congress. McLean had been encouraged by abolitionists to think that he might be their candidate for president in 1860, and he saw *Dred Scott* v. *Sanford* as an opportunity to make an unequivocal statement of his position.

Dred Scott presented the Supreme Court with three major questions: (1) Was a black man like Scott a United States citizen with the right to sue in federal court? (2) Was Scott now a free man because of his residence in a free state and territory? (3) Had Congress acted constitutionally by prohibiting slavery in the Louisiana Territory north of 36°30'? At first the five southern justices were inclined to dispose of the case on narrow grounds by simply answering the second question negatively, since they could not secure at least one vote of a northern justice for a more comprehensive opinion. Then Justices McLean and Benjamin Curtis announced that they intended to answer all three questions in the affirmative and to file elaborate opinions to that effect. The majority justices then decided to expand the scope of their decision as well and with the highly improper assistance of President-elect James Buchanan, succeeded in persuading Justice Robert Grier of Pennsylvania to join the sweeping opinion written by Chief Justice Taney.

ROGER BROOKE TANEY

Roger B. Taney was appointed chief justice as John Marshall's successor by President Andrew Jackson in 1836. He had previously served as Jackson's attorney general. Taney's views embraced a curious mixture of Jeffersonian agrarianism, Jacksonian opposition to special privilege, and a state-based Madisonian federalism. Until the unfortunate opinion in Dred Scott, *the Supreme Court under Taney's leadership was held in high esteem by the American public. Today Taney is generally regarded by Court historians as a talented jurist and a skillful chief justice.*

Chief Justice **Taney** delivered the opinion of the Court:

. . .

The question is simply this: can a negro, whose ancestors were imported into this country and sold as slaves, become a member of the political community formed and brought into existence by the Constitution of the United States, and as such become entitled to all the rights, and privileges, and immunities, guarantied by that instrument to the citizen. One of these rights is the privilege of suing in a court of the United States in the cases specified in the Constitution.

It will be observed, that the plea applies to that class of persons only whose ancestors were negroes of the African race, and imported into this country, and sold and held as slaves. The only matter in issue before the court, therefore, is, whether the descendants of such slaves, when they shall be emancipated, or who are born of parents who had become free before their birth, are citizens of a state, in the sense in which the word "citizen" is used in the Constitution of the United States. And this being the only matter in dispute on the pleadings, the court must be understood as speaking in this opinion of that class only; that is, of those persons who are the descendants of Africans who were imported into this country and sold as slaves.

The words "people of the United States" and "citizens" are synonymous terms, and mean the same thing. They both describe the political body, who, according to our republican institutions, form the sovereignty, and who hold the power and conduct the government through their representatives. They are what we familiarly call the "sovereign people," and every citizen is one of this people, and a constituent member of this sovereignty. The question before us is, whether the class of persons described in the plea in abatement compose a portion of this people, and are constituent members of this sovereignty. We think they are not, and that they are not included, and were not intended to be included, under the word "citizens" in the Constitution, and can, therefore, claim none of the rights and privileges which that instrument provides for and secures to citizens of the United States. On the contrary, they were at that time considered as a subordinate and inferior class of beings, who had been subjugated by the dominant race, and whether emancipated or not, yet remained subject to their authority, and had no rights or privileges but such as those who held the power and the government might choose to grant them.

. . .

It is very clear . . . that no State can, by any Act or law of its own, passed since the adoption of the Constitution, introduce a new member into the political community created by the Constitution of the United States. It cannot make him a member of this community by making him a member of its own. And for the same reason it cannot introduce any person, or descriptions of persons, who were not intended to be embraced in this new political family, which the Constitution brought into existence, but were intended to be excluded from it.

. . .

It becomes necessary, therefore, to determine who were citizens of the several States when the Constitution was adopted. And in order to do this, we must recur to the governments and institutions of the thirteen Colonies, when they separated from Great Britain and formed new sovereignties, and took their places in the family of independent nations. We must inquire who, at that time, were recognized as the people or citizens of a State, whose rights and liberties had been outraged by the English Government; and who declared their independence, and assumed the powers of government to defend their rights by force of arms.

In the opinion of the court, the legislation and histories of the times, and the language used in the Declaration of Independence, show, that neither the class of persons who had been imported as slaves, nor their descendants, whether they had become free or not, were then acknowledged as a part of the people, nor intended to be included in the general words used in that memorable instrument.

It is difficult at this day to realize the state of public opinion in relation to that unfortunate race, which prevailed in the civilized and enlightened portions of the world at the time of the Declaration of Independence, and when the Constitution of the United States was framed and adopted. But the public history of every European nation displays it, in a manner too plain to be mistaken.

They had for more than a century before been regarded as beings of an inferior order; and altogether unfit to associate with the white race, either in social or political relations; and so far inferior, that they had no rights which the white man was bound to respect; and that the negro might justly and lawfully be reduced to slavery for his benefit. He was bought and sold, and treated as an ordinary article of merchandise and traffic, whenever a profit could be made by

it. This opinion was at that time fixed and universal in the civilized portion of the white race. It was regarded as an axiom in morals as well as in politics, which no one thought of disputing, or supposed to be open to dispute; and men in every grade and position in society daily and habitually acted upon it in their private pursuits, as well as in matters of public concern, without doubting for a moment the correctness of this opinion.

And in no nation was this opinion more firmly fixed or more uniformly acted upon than by the English government and English people. They not only seized them on the coast of Africa, and sold them or held them in slavery for their own use; but they took them as ordinary articles of merchandise to every country where they could make a profit on them, and were far more extensively engaged in this commerce than any other nation in the world.

The opinion thus entertained and acted upon in England was naturally impressed upon the colonies they founded on this side of the Atlantic. And, accordingly, a negro of the African race was regarded by them as an article of property, and held, and bought and sold as such, in every one of the thirteen Colonies which united in the Declaration of Independence, and afterwards formed the Constitution of the United States. The slaves were more or less numerous in the different Colonies, as slave labor was found more or less profitable. But no one seems to have doubted the correctness of the prevailing opinion of the time.

. . .

No one, we presume, supposes that any change in public opinion or feeling in relation to this unfortunate race, in the civilized nations of Europe or in this country, should induce the court to give to the words of the Constitution a more liberal construction in their favor than they were intended to bear when the instrument was framed and adopted. Such an argument would be altogether inadmissible in any tribunal called on to interpret it. If any of its provisions are deemed unjust, there is a mode prescribed in the instrument itself by which it may be amended; but while it remains unaltered, it must be construed now as it was understood at the time of its adoption. It is not only the same in words, but the same in meaning, and delegates the same powers to the government, and reserves and secures the same rights and privileges to the citizen; and as long as it continues to exist in its present form, it speaks not only in the same words, but with the same meaning and intent with which it spoke when it came from the hands of its framers, and was voted on and adopted by the people of the United States. Any other rule of construction would abrogate the judicial character of this court, and make it the mere reflex of the popular opinion or passion of the day. This court was not created by the Constitution for such purposes. Higher and graver trusts have been confided to it, and it must not falter in the path of duty.

And upon a full and careful consideration of the subject, the court is of opinion that, upon the facts stated in the plea in abatement, Dred Scott was not a citizen of Missouri within the meaning of the Constitution of the United States, and not entitled as such to sue in its courts; and, consequently, that the Circuit Court had no jurisdiction of the case, and that the judgment on the plea in abatement is erroneous.

. . .

It is true that the result either way, by dismissal or by judgment for the defendant, makes very little, if any difference in a pecuniary or personal point of view to either party. But the fact that the result would be very nearly the same to the parties in either form of judgment, would not justify this court in sanctioning an error in the judgment which is patent on the record, and which, if sanctioned, might be drawn into precedent, and lead to serious mischief and injustice in some future suit.

We proceed, therefore, to inquire whether the facts relied on by the plaintiff entitled him to his freedom. . . .

In considering this part of the controversy, two questions arise: 1st. Was he, together with his family, free in Missouri by reason of the stay in the territory of the United States hereinbefore mentioned? And 2d. If they were not, is Scott himself free by reason of his removal to Rock Island, in the State of Illinois, as stated in the above admissions?

We proceed to examine the first question.

The Act of Congress, upon which the plaintiff relies, declares that slavery and involuntary servitude, except as a punishment for crime, shall be forever prohibited in all that part of that territory ceded by France, under the name of Louisiana, which lies north of thirty-six degrees thirty minutes north latitude, and not included within the limits of Missouri. And the difficulty which meets us at the threshold of this part of the inquiry is, whether Congress was authorized to pass this law under any of the powers granted to it by the Constitution; for if the authority is not given by that instrument, it is the duty of this court to declare it void and inoperative, and incapable of conferring freedom upon one who is held as a slave under the laws of any one of the States.

. . .

This brings us to examine by what provision of the Constitution the present Federal Government under its delegated and restricted powers, is authorized to acquire territory outside of the original limits of the United States, and what powers it may exercise therein over the person or property of a citizen of the United States, while it remains a territory, and until it shall be admitted as one of the States of the Union.

. . .

. . . The power to expand the territory of the United States by the admission of new States is plainly given; and in the construction of this power by all the departments of the government, it has been held to authorize the acquisition of territory, not fit for admission at the time, but to be admitted as soon as its population and situation would entitle it to admission. It is acquired to become a State, and not to be held as a colony and governed by Congress with absolute authority. . . .

. . . And when the territory becomes a part of the United States, the Federal Government enters into possession in the character impressed upon it by those who created it. It enters upon it with its powers over the citizen strictly defined, and limited by the Constitution, from which it derives its own existence, and by virtue of which alone it continues to exist and act as a government and sovereignty. It has no power of any kind beyond it; and it cannot, when it enters a territory of the United States, put off its character, and assume discretionary or despotic powers which the Constitution has denied to it. . . .

A reference to a few of the provisions of the Constitution will illustrate this proposition.

For example, no one, we presume, will contend that Congress can make any law in a territory respecting the establishment of religion or the free exercise thereof, or abridging the freedom of speech or of the press, or the right of the people of the territory peaceably to assemble and to petition the government for the redress of grievances.

Nor can Congress deny to the people the right to keep and bear arms, nor the right to trial by jury, nor compel anyone to be a witness against himself in a criminal proceeding.

These powers, and others in relation to rights of person, which it is not necessary here to enumerate, are, in express and positive terms, denied to the general government; and the rights of private property have been guarded with equal care. Thus the rights of property are united with the rights of person, and placed on the same ground by the fifth amendment to the Constitution, which provides that no person shall be deprived of life, liberty and property, without due process of law. And an Act of Congress which deprives a citizen of the United States of his liberty or property, merely because he came himself or brought his property into a particular Territory of the United States, and who had committed no offense against the laws, could hardly be dignified with the name of due process of law. . . .

Now, as we have already said in an earlier part of this opinion, upon a different point, the right of property in a slave is distinctly and expressly affirmed in the Constitution. The right to traffic in it, like an ordinary article of merchandise and property, was guaranteed to the citizens of the United States, in every State that might desire it, for twenty years. And the government in express terms is pledged to protect it in all future time, if the slave escapes from his owner. This is done in plain words—too plain to be misunderstood. And no word can be found in the Constitution which gives Congress a greater power over slave property, or which entitles property of that kind to less protection than property of any other description. The only power conferred is the power coupled with the duty of guarding and protecting the owner in his rights.

Upon these considerations, it is the opinion of the court that the Act of Congress which prohibited a citizen from holding and owning property of this kind in the territory of the United States north of the line therein mentioned, is not warranted by the Constitution, and is therefore void; and that neither Dred Scott himself, nor any of his family, were made free by being carried into this territory; even if they had been carried there by the owner, with the intention of becoming a permanent resident. . . .

But there is another point in the case which depends on state power and state law. And it is contended, on the part of the plaintiff, that he is made free by being taken to Rock Island, in the State of Illinois, independently of his residence in the territory of the United States; and being so made free he was not again reduced to a state of slavery by being brought back to Missouri.

Our notice of this part of the case will be very brief; for the principle on which it depends was decided in this court, upon much consideration, in the case of Strader et al. v. Graham [1850]. In that case, the slaves had been taken from Kentucky to Ohio, with the consent of the owner, and afterwards brought back to Kentucky. And this court held that their status or condition, as free or slave, depended upon the laws of Kentucky, when they were brought back into that State, and not of Ohio; and that this court had no jurisdiction to revise the judgment of a state court upon its own laws. This was the point directly before the court, and the decision that this court had not jurisdiction, turned upon it, as will be seen by the report of the case.

So in this case: as Scott was a slave when taken into the State of Illinois by his owner, and was there held as such, and brought back in that character, his status, as free or slave, depended on the laws of Missouri, and not of Illinois. . . .

Upon the whole, therefore, it is the judgment of this court, that it appears by the record before us that the plaintiff in error is not a citizen of Missouri, in the sense in which that word is used in the Constitution; and that the Circuit Court of

the United States, for that reason, had no jurisdiction in the case, and could give no judgment
in it.

Its judgment for the defendant must, consequently, be reversed, and a mandate issued
directing the suit to be dismissed for want of
jurisdiction.

Mr. Justice **Curtis** dissented:

To determine whether any free persons, de-
scended from Africans held in slavery, were citizens of the United States under the Confederation, and consequently at the time of the
adoption of the Constitution of the United
States, it is only necessary to know whether any
such persons were citizens of either of the States
under the Confederation at the time of the adoption of the Constitution.

Of this there can be no doubt. At the time of
the ratification of the Articles of Confederation,
all free native-born inhabitants of the States of
New Hampshire, Massachusetts, New York,
New Jersey and North Carolina, though de-
scended from African slaves, were not only citi-

zens of those States, but such of them as had the
other necessary qualifications possessed the
franchise of electors on equal terms with other
citizens. . . .

Did the Constitution of the United States
deprive them or their descendants of citizenship?

That Constitution was ordained and established by the people of the United States through
the action, in each State, of those persons who
were qualified by its laws to act thereon, in
behalf of themselves and all other citizens of
that State. In some of the States, as we have
seen, colored persons were among those qualified by law to act on this subject. These colored
persons were not only included in the body of
"the people of the United States by whom the
Constitution was ordained and established," but
in at least five of the States they had the power
to act, and doubtless did act, by their suffrages,
upon the question of its adoption. It would be
strange, if we were to find in that instrument
anything which deprived of their citizenship any
part of the people of the United States who were
among those by whom it was established.

Aftermath of Dred Scott *v.* Sanford

Taney's majority opinion in *Dred Scott* is by common consensus the most damaging decision ever made by the Supreme Court, inflicting great harm on both the
country and the Court itself. What Taney had intended as a comprehensive constitutional pronouncement that would settle the slavery question once and for all,
instead helped to widen the sectional conflict until it was all but unbridgeable. The
antislavery organs of the northern press vilified Taney and his colleagues in the
majority as corrupt, treasonous, and sinful, and the opinion was denounced in
Congress as a "wicked stump speech." For the Court to declare an act of Congress
unconstitutional was treachery enough, but to deny all blacks, freemen as well as
slaves, the rights of American citizenship was nothing short of depraved. Though
Dred Scott was acclaimed in the south, such support counted for little as the
Confederacy edged closer to abandoning the Union. Thus the Supreme Court,
which had played a creative and respected role in national policy-making throughout the first half of the nineteenth century, went into a political eclipse from which
it would not emerge for several decades.

Dred Scott's putative owner, John Sanford, had died before the Court's decision. Arrangements were made to transfer ownership of Scott and his family to the
son of his original owner so that they could be manumitted in Missouri, where
Scott worked as a hotel porter and helped his wife run her laundry business. The
necessary papers were filed, and less than 3 months after the United States
Supreme Court had declared Dred Scott to be a slave, a municipal court in St.
Louis set him free. He died the following year of consumption.

Home Building and Loan Association v. Blaisdell
290 U.S. 398(1934)

The *Blaisdell* case presented what appeared to be a clear-cut violation of the Constitution since the law in question was the very kind that the contract clause was meant to forbid. It is also an example of judicial caution during a time of national emergency and, while not a conflict in federalism in the classic sense of national versus state policies, it does demonstrate the potential standoff between a powerful arm of the national government, the Supreme Court, and the state governments when the latter attempt to finesse the Constitution itself.

At issue in *Blaisdell* was the Minnesota Mortgage Moratorium Act, a measure that granted relief to farmers who found themselves in an alarming financial bind as a result of the collapse of the nation's economy in 1929. By 1932 farm income had dropped from $12 billion to just over $5 billion with a corresponding decline in agricultural prices. About half the land was subject to mortgages, most of which had been incurred when the farm price level was four times as high as at the close of 1932. Many farms were foreclosed and placed on the market at rock-bottom prices and it became clear to the legislatures of Minnesota and other farm states that if action were not forthcoming, large numbers of people would lose their homes, their land, and their only means of support. Given these conditions Minnesota enacted a mortgage moratorium law providing that foreclosure of mortgages and execution of sales thereunder might be postponed and periods of exemptions extended "for such additional time as the court may deem just and equitable." Courts were to determine a reasonable rental value of the property and to permit the mortgagor to retain possession while paying a reasonable amount toward taxes, insurance, interest, and principal. Before the Supreme Court the Home Building and Loan Association argued that this law violated the contract clause by clearly interfering with John Blaisdell's written promise to pay off his loan under specified agreed-to conditions under an executory contract.

CHARLES EVANS HUGHES

Charles Evans Hughes was appointed to the Supreme Court as an associate justice by President William Howard Taft in 1910 and resigned in 1916 to make an unsuccessful run for the presidency against Woodrow Wilson. He returned to the Court in 1929 when President Hoover named him chief justice. During his two terms of service Hughes, a political conservative, wrote for the Court in several landmark cases which laid the foundation for a permanent and broad protection of civil liberties. He is also remembered for his effective leadership of the Supreme Court when it was under attack by President Franklin Roosevelt in 1937.

Mr. Chief Justice **Hughes** delivered the opinion of the Court.

. . .

The state court upheld the statute as an emergency measure. Although conceding that the obligations of the mortgage contract were impaired, the court decided that what it thus described as an impairment was, notwithstanding the contract clause of the Federal Constitution, within the police power of the State as that power was called into exercise by the public economic emergency which the legislature had found to exist. . . .

. . .

In determining whether the provision for this temporary and conditional relief exceeds the power of the State by reason of the clause in the Federal Constitution prohibiting impairment of the obligations of contracts, we must consider the relation of emergency to constitutional power, the historical setting of the contract clause, the development of the jurisprudence of this Court in the construction of that clause, and the principles of construction which we may consider to be established.

Emergency does not create power. Emergency does not increase granted power or remove or diminish the restrictions imposed upon power granted or reserved. The Constitution was adopted in a period of grave emergency. Its grants of power to the Federal Government and its limitations of the power of the States were determined in the light of emergency and they are not altered by emergency. What power was thus granted and what limitations were thus imposed are questions which have always been, and always will be, the subject of close examination under our constitutional system.

While emergency does not create power, emergency may furnish the occasion for the exercise of power. "Although an emergency may not call into life a power which has never lived, nevertheless emergency may afford a reason for the exertion of a living power already enjoyed." The constitutional question presented in the light of an emergency is whether the power possessed embraces the particular exercise of it in response to particular conditions. Thus, the war power of the Federal Government is not created by the emergency of war, but it is a power given to meet that emergency. It is a power to wage war successfully, and thus it permits the harnessing of the entire energies of the people in a supreme coöperative effort to preserve the nation. But even the war power does not remove constitutional limitations safeguarding essential liberties. When the provisions of the Constitution, in grant or restriction, are specific, so particularized as not to admit of construction, no question is presented. Thus, emergency would not permit a State to have more than two Senators in the Congress, or permit the election of President by a general popular vote without regard to the number of electors to which the States are respectively entitled, or permit the States to "coin money" or to "make anything but gold and silver coin a tender in payment of debts." But where constitutional grants and limitations of power are set forth in general clauses, which afford a broad outline, the process of construction is essential to fill in the details. . . .

In the construction of the contract clause, the debates in the Constitutional Convention are of little aid. But the reasons which led to the adoption of that clause, and of the other prohibitions of Section 10 of Article I, are not left in doubt and have frequently been described with eloquent emphasis. The widespread distress following the revolutionary period, and the plight of debtors, had called forth in the States an ignoble array of legislative schemes for the defeat of creditors and the invasion of contractual obligations. Legislative interferences had been so numerous and extreme that the confidence essential to prosperous trade had been undermined and the utter destruction of credit was threatened. "The sober people of America" were convinced that some "thorough reform" was needed which would "inspire a general prudence and industry, and give a regular course to the business of society." It was necessary to interpose the restraining power of a central authority in order to secure the foundations even of "private faith." . . .

But full recognition of the occasion and general purpose of the clause does not suffice to fix its precise scope. Nor does an examination of the details of prior legislation in the States yield criteria which can be considered controlling. To ascertain the scope of the constitutional prohibition we examine the course of judicial decisions in its application. These put it beyond question that the prohibition is not an absolute one and is not to be read with literal exactness like a mathematical formula. . . .

. . .

[Here follows a lengthy examination of case law supporting the proposition that private contracts are subject to the authority of the state "to secure the peace and good order of society."]

It is manifest from this review of our decisions that there has been a growing appreciation of public needs and of the necessity of finding ground for a rational compromise between individual rights and public welfare. The settlement and consequent contraction of the public domain, the pressure of a constantly increasing density of population, the interrelation of the activities of our people and the complexity of our economic interests, have inevitably led to an increased use of the organization of society in order to protect the very bases of individual opportunity. Where, in earlier days, it was thought that only the concerns of individuals or of classes were involved, and that those of the State itself were touched only remotely, it has later been found that the fundamental interests of the State are directly affected; and that the question is no longer merely that of one party to a contract as against another, but of the use of reasonable means to safeguard the economic structure upon which the good of all depends.

It is no answer to say that this public need was not apprehended a century ago, or to insist that what the provision of the Constitution meant to the vision of that day it must mean to the vision of our time. If by the statement that what the Constitution meant at the time of its adoption it means to-day, it is intended to say that the great clauses of the Constitution must be confined to the interpretation which the framers, with the conditions and outlook of their time, would have placed upon them, the state-

ment carries its own refutation. It was to guard against such a narrow conception that Chief Justice Marshall uttered the memorable warning—"We must never forget that it is a *constitution* we are expounding" *(McCulloch* v. *Maryland)*—"a constitution intended to endure for ages to come, and consequently, to be adapted to the various *crises* of human affairs." When we are dealing with the words of the Constitution, said this Court in *Missouri* v. *Holland,* "we must realize that they have called into life a being the development of which could not have been foreseen completely by the most gifted of its begetters. . . . The case before us must be considered in the light of our whole experience and not merely in that of what was said a hundred years ago."

. . .

Undoubtedly, whatever is reserved of state power must be consistent with the fair intent of the constitutional limitation of that power. The reserved power cannot be construed so as to destroy the limitation, nor is the limitation to be construed to destroy the reserved power in its essential aspects. They must be construed in harmony with each other. This principle precludes a construction which would permit the State to adopt as its policy the repudiation of debts or the destruction of contracts or the denial of means to enforce them. But it does not follow that conditions may not arise in which a temporary restraint of enforcement may be consistent with the spirit and purpose of the constitutional provision and thus be found to be within the range of the reserved power of the State to protect the vital interests of the community. It cannot be maintained that the constitutional prohibition should be so construed as to prevent limited and temporary interpositions with respect to the enforcement of contracts if made necessary by a great public calamity such as fire, flood, or earthquake. The reservation of state power appropriate to such extraordinary conditions may be deemed to be as much a part of all contracts, as is the reservation of state power to protect the public interest in the other situations to which we have referred. And if state power exists to give temporary relief from the enforcement of contracts in the presence of disasters due to physical causes such as fire, flood or earthquake, that power cannot be said to be non-existent when the urgent public need demanding such relief is produced by other and economic causes.

. . .

Nor is it helpful to attempt to draw a fine distinction between the intended meaning of the words of the Constitution and their intended application. When we consider the contract clause and the decisions which have expounded it in harmony with the essential reserved power of the States to protect the security of their peoples, we find no warrant for the conclusion that the clause has been warped by these decisions from its proper significance or that the founders of our Government would have interpreted the clause differently had they had occasion to assume that responsibility in the conditions of the later day. The vast body of law which has been developed was unknown to the fathers, but it is believed to have preserved the essential content and the spirit of the Constitution. With a growing recognition of public needs and the relation of individual right to public security, the court has sought to prevent the perversion of the clause through its use as an instrument to throttle the capacity of the States to protect their fundamental interests. This development is a growth from the seeds which the fathers planted. It is a development forecast by the prophetic words of Justice Johnson in *Ogden* v. *Saunders,* already quoted. And the germs of the later decisions are found in the early cases of the *Charles River Bridge* and the *West River Bridge,* which upheld the public right against strong insistence upon the contract clause. The principle of this development is, as we have seen, that the reservation of the reasonable exercise of the protective power of the State is read into all contracts and there is no greater reason for refusing to apply this principle to Minnesota mortgages than to New York leases.

Applying the criteria established by our decisions we conclude:

1. An emergency existed in Minnesota which furnished a proper occasion for the exercise of the reserved power of the State to protect the vital interests of the community. The declarations of the existence of this emergency by the legislature and by the Supreme Court of Minnesota cannot be regarded as a subterfuge or as lacking in adequate basis. The finding of the legislature and state court has support in the facts of which we take judicial notice. . . .

2. The legislation was addressed to a legitimate end, that is, the legislation was not for the mere advantage of particular individuals but for the protection of a basic interest of society.

3. In view of the nature of the contracts in question—mortgages of unquestionable validity—the relief afforded and justified by the emergency, in order not to contravene the constitutional provision, could only be of a character appropriate to that emergency and could be granted only upon reasonable conditions.

4. The conditions upon which the period of redemption is extended do not appear to be unreasonable. . . .

5. The legislation is temporary in operation. It is limited to the exigency which called it forth. While the postponement of the period of redemption from the foreclosure sale is to May 1, 1935, that period may be reduced by the order of the court under the statute, in case of a change in circumstances, and the operation of the statute itself could not validly outlast the emergency or be so extended as virtually to destroy the contracts.

We are of the opinion that the Minnesota statute as here applied does not violate the contract clause of the Federal Constitution. Whether the legislation is wise or unwise as a matter of policy is a question with which we are not concerned.

. . .

The judgment of the Supreme Court of Minnesota is affirmed.

Mr. Justice **Sutherland,** with whom Mr. Justice **Van Devanter,** Mr. Justice **McReynolds,** and Mr. Justice **Butler** concurred, dissenting.

Few questions of greater moment than that just decided have been submitted for judicial inquiry during this generation. He simply closes his eyes to the necessary implications of the decision who fails to see in it the potentiality of future gradual but ever-advancing encroachments upon the sanctity of private and public contracts. The effect of the Minnesota legislation, though serious enough in itself, is of trivial significance compared with the far more serious and dangerous inroads upon the limitations of the Constitution which are almost certain to ensue as a consequence naturally following any step beyond the boundaries fixed by that instrument. And those of us who are thus apprehensive of the effect of this decision would, in a matter so important, be neglectful of our duty should we fail to spread upon the permanent records of the court the reasons which move us to the opposite view.

A provision of the Constitution, it is hardly necessary to say, does not admit of two distinctly opposite interpretations. It does not mean one thing at one time and an entirely different thing at another time. If the contract impairment clause, when framed and adopted, meant that the terms of a contract for the payment of money could not be altered *in invitum* by a state statute enacted for the relief of hardly pressed debtors to the end and with the effect of postponing payment or enforcement during and because of an economic or financial emergency, it is but to state the obvious to say that it means the same now. This view, at once so rational in its application to the written word, and so necessary to the stability of constitutional principles, though from time to time challenged, has never, unless recently, been put within the realm of doubt by the decisions of this court. The true rule was forcefully declared in *Ex parte Milligan*, in the face of circumstances of national peril and public unrest and disturbance far greater than any that exist today. In that great case this court said that the provisions of the Constitution there under consideration had been expressed by our ancestors in such plain English words that it would seem the ingenuity of man could not evade them, but that after the lapse of more than seventy years they were sought to be avoided. "Those great and good men," the court said, "foresaw that troublous times would arise, when rulers and people would become restive under

restraint, and seek by sharp and decisive measures to accomplish ends deemed just and proper; and that the principles of constitutional liberty would be in peril, unless established by irrepealable law. The history of the world had taught them that what was done in the past might be attempted in the future." And then, in words the power and truth of which have become increasingly evident with the lapse of time, there was laid down the rule without which the Constitution would cease to be the "supreme law of the land," binding equally upon governments and governed at all times and under all circumstances, and become a mere collection of political maxims to be adhered to or disregarded according to the prevailing sentiment or the legislative and judicial opinion in respect of the supposed necessities of the hour:

"The Constitution of the United States is a law for rulers and people, equally in war and in peace, and covers with the shield of its protection all classes of men, at all times, and under all circumstances. No doctrine, involving more pernicious consequences, was ever invented by the wit of man than that any of its provisions can be suspended during any of the great exigencies of government. Such a doctrine leads directly to anarchy or despotism. . . ."

The provisions of the Federal Constitution, undoubtedly, are pliable in the sense that in appropriate cases they have the capacity of bringing within their grasp every new condition which falls within their meaning. But, their *meaning* is changeless; it is only their *application* which is extensible. . . .

. . .

The whole aim of construction, as applied to a provision of the Constitution, is to discover the meaning, to ascertain and give effect to the intent, of its framers and the people who adopted it. The necessities which gave rise to the provision, the controversies which preceded, as well as the conflicts of opinion which were settled by its adoption, are matters to be considered to enable us to arrive at a correct result. The history of the times, the state of things existing when the provision was framed and adopted, should be looked to in order to ascertain the mischief and the remedy. As nearly as possible we should place ourselves in the condition of those who framed and adopted it. And if the meaning be at all doubtful, the doubt should be resolved, wherever reasonably possible to do so, in a way to forward the evident purpose with which the provision was adopted.

An application of these principles to the question under review removes any doubt, if otherwise there would be any, that the contract impairment clause denies to the several states the power to mitigate hard consequences resulting to debtors from financial or economic exigencies by an impairment of the obligation of contracts of indebtedness. A candid consideration of the history and circumstances which led up to and accompanied the framing and adoption of this clause will demonstrate conclusively that it was framed and adopted with the specific and studied purpose of preventing legislation designed to relieve debtors *especially* in time of financial distress. Indeed, it is not probable that any other purpose was definitely in the minds of those who composed the framers' convention or the ratifying state conventions which followed. . . .

. . .

[Here follows an analysis of the Constitutional Convention of 1787 showing that the purpose of the contract clause was precisely to prohibit the abrogation of private contracts by state legislatures during times of economic crisis. This is followed by a discussion of case law upholding the sanctity of contract against usurpation by state legislative actions.]

The present exigency is nothing new. From the beginning of our existence as a nation, periods of depression, of industrial failure, of financial distress, of unpaid and unpayable indebtedness, have alternated with years of plenty. The vital lesson that expenditure beyond income begets poverty, that public or private extravagance, financed by promises to pay, either must end in complete or partial repudiation or the promises be fulfilled by self-denial and painful effort, though constantly taught by bitter experience, seems never to be learned; and the attempt by legislative devices to shift the misfortune of the debtor to the shoulders of the creditor with-

out coming into conflict with the contract impairment clause has been persistent and oft-repeated.

The defense of the Minnesota law is made upon grounds which were discountenanced by the makers of the Constitution and have many times been rejected by this court. That defense should not now succeed, because it constitutes an effort to overthrow the constitutional provision by an appeal to facts and circumstances identical with those which brought it into existence. With due regard for the processes of logical thinking, it legitimately cannot be urged that conditions which produced the rule may now be invoked to destroy it.

. . .

A statute which materially delays enforcement of the mortgagee's contractual right of ownership and possession does not modify the remedy merely; it destroys for the period of delay, *all* remedy so far as the enforcement of that right is concerned. The phrase, "obligation of a contract," in the constitutional sense imports a legal duty to perform the specified obligation of *that* contract, not to substitute and perform, against the will of one of the parties, a different, albeit equally valuable, obligation. And a state, under the contract impairment clause, has no more power to accomplish such a substitution than has one of the parties to the contract against the will of the other. It cannot do so either by acting directly upon the contract, or by bringing about the result under the guise of a statute in form acting only upon the remedy. If it could, the efficacy of the constitutional restriction would, in large measure, be made to disappear. . . .

. . .

I quite agree with the opinion of the court that whether the legislation under review is wise or unwise is a matter with which we have nothing to do. Whether it is likely to work well or work ill presents a question entirely irrelevant to the issue. The only legitimate inquiry we can make is whether it is constitutional. If it is not, its virtues, if it have any, cannot save it; if it is, its faults cannot be invoked to accomplish its destruction. If the provisions of the Constitution be not upheld when they pinch as well as when they comfort, they may as well be abandoned. Being unable to reach any other conclusion than that the Minnesota statute infringes the constitutional restriction under review, I have no choice but to say so.

Aftermath of Home Building and Loan *v.* Blaisdell

No permanent damage to the stability of private contracts appears to have occurred as a result of the *Blaisdell* case. It was the Court's emphatic position that the decision in this particular instance was based primarily on the existence of an emergency, and once the emergency was over, the *status quo ante* of the contract clause was reinstated. What the case does demonstrate, however, is that the Supreme Court is not averse to suspending a clause in the Constitution under conditions of extreme economic crisis. Of course the opinion of Chief Justice Charles Evans Hughes did not admit that the Constitution was being suspended or superseded by the emergency, only that it might be subject to varying interpretations to fit the needs of the times. What would have happened to the nation's economy had the Court ruled differently is difficult to say, but perhaps one should keep in mind that "permanence" is a vital necessity if the fundamental law of a nation is to be respected by its people. Thus, we should not dismiss out of hand the warning in Justice George Sutherland's dissent as he answered Hughes' reliance on Justice Oliver Wendell Holmes' dictum that the "case before us must be considered in the light of our whole experience and not merely in that of what was said a hundred years ago." Sutherland replied that the Constitution is not a "mere collection of political maxims to be adhered to or disregarded according to the prevailing sentiment," that circumstance cannot change the Constitution, for "if the provisions . . . be not upheld when they pinch as well as when they comfort, they may as well be abandoned."

Schechter Poultry Corp. v. *United States*

295 U.S. 495(1935)

In 1932, in the midst of the most severe economic depression in the nation's history, the Democratic party, with a dynamic standard bearer, captured the White House and the Congress with the overwhelming support of the American people. President Franklin D. Roosevelt had immediate success in persuading the Congress to implement his program—the New Deal—with various regulatory measures designed to move the nation on the path of economic recovery. For well over half a century the nation had been governed by conservative presidents who had, in general, appointed politically conservative judges. The new legislative construct that made up the New Deal was destined to face a hostile Supreme Court, most of whose members were believers in a laissez-faire economy and had little sympathy with government regulation.

The centerpiece of the early New Deal period was the National Industrial Recovery Act of 1933, the purpose of which was to promote industrywide arrangements on wages, hours, and trade practices in an effort to restore economic stability and to prevent cutthroat competition. Under its terms the various trade associations proposed agreements to the President who then promulgated a code of fair competition for governing a given industry. If an industry could not or did not offer an acceptable agree-

ment, the President could prescribe a governing code and, in either case, violation of the code was made a punishable offense. In the first test of the NIRA, *Panama Refining Co. v. Ryan,* in 1935, the Court voted 8–1 to declare Section 9(c) of the act unconstitutional on the ground that Congress had improperly delegated excessive discretion to the President who was empowered to prohibit the production of oil in whatever amounts he chose that were in excess of state-authorized levels. This, said the Court, was a violation of the constitutional principle of separation of powers.

Involved in the *Schechter* case was a small poultry business run by the Schechter brothers in New York City which purchased chickens from outside the state and then killed and prepared them for resale to local butchers. They were convicted in a federal district court for violating the Live Poultry Code of the NIRA, a conviction that was upheld in the Court of Appeals. The Schechters contended in the Supreme Court that the legislation authorizing the codes was unconstitutional on two grounds: (1) that it represented an invalid delegation of legislative power to the executive; and (2) that it went beyond permissible congressional regulation of interstate commerce under the commerce clause of the Constitution.

Chief Justice **Hughes** delivered the opinion of the Court:

. . .

. . . We are told that the provision of the statute authorizing the adoption of codes must be viewed in the light of the grave national crisis with which Congress was confronted. Undoubtedly, the conditions to which power is addressed are always to be considered when the exercise of power is challenged. Extraordinary conditions may call for extraordinary remedies. But the argument necessarily stops short of an attempt to justify action which lies outside the sphere of constitutional authority. Extraordinary conditions do not create or enlarge constitutional power. The Constitution established a national government with powers deemed to be adequate, as they have proved to be both in war and peace, but these powers of the national government are limited by the constitutional grants. Those who act under these grants are not at liberty to transcend the imposed limits because they believe that more or different power is necessary. Such assertions of extraconstitutional authority were anticipated and precluded by the explicit terms of the Tenth Amendment—"The powers not delegated to the United States by the Constitution, nor prohibited by it to the States, are reserved to the States respectively, or to the people."

. . . The Constitution provides that "All legislative powers herein granted shall be vested in a Congress of the United States, which shall consist of a Senate and House of Representatives." Article I, Section I. And the Congress is authorized "To make all laws which shall be necessary and proper for carrying into execution" its general powers. Article I, Section 8, par. 18. The Congress is not permitted to abdicate or to transfer to others the essential legislative functions with which it is thus vested. . . .

Accordingly, we look to the statute to see whether Congress has overstepped these limitations—whether Congress in authorizing "codes of fair competition" has itself established the standards of legal obligation, thus performing its essential legislative function, or, by the failure to enact such standards, has attempted to transfer that function to others. . . .

The Government urges that the codes will "consist of rules of competition deemed fair for each industry by representative members of that industry—by the persons most vitally concerned and most familiar with its problems." . . . Such a delegation of legislative power is unknown to our law and is utterly inconsistent with the constitutional prerogatives and duties of Congress.

The question, then, turns upon the authority which Section 3 of the Recovery Act vests in the President to approve or prescribe. If the codes have standing as penal statutes, this must be due to the effect of the executive action. But Congress cannot delegate legislative power to the President to exercise an unfettered discretion to make whatever laws he thinks may be needed or advisable. . . .

For the legislative undertaking, Section 3 sets

up no standards, aside from the statement of the general aims of rehabilitation, correction, and expansion described in Section 1. In view of the scope of that broad declaration, and of the nature of the few restrictions that are imposed, the discretion of the President in approving or prescribing codes, and thus enacting laws for the government of trade and industry throughout the country, is virtually unfettered. We think that the code-making authority thus conferred is an unconstitutional delegation of legislative power.

. . .

This aspect of the case presents the question whether the particular provisions of the Live Poultry Code, which the defendants were convicted for violating and for having conspired to violate, were within the regulating power of Congress.

These provisions relate to the hours and wages of those employed by defendants in their slaughterhouses in Brooklyn and to the sales there made to retail dealers and butchers.

(1) Were these transaction *"in"* interstate commerce? Much is made of the fact that almost all the poultry coming to New York is sent there from other States. But the code provisions, as here applied, do not concern the transportation of the poultry from other States to New York, or the transactions of the commission men or others to whom it is consigned, or the sales made by such consigners to defendants. When defendants had made their purchases, whether at the West Washington market in New York City or at the railroad terminals serving the City, or elsewhere, the poultry was trucked to their slaughterhouses in Brooklyn for local disposition. The interstate transactions in relation to that poultry then ended. Defendants held the poultry at their slaughterhouse markets for slaughter and local sale to retail dealers and butchers, who in turn sold directly to consumers. Neither the slaughtering nor the sales by defendants were transactions in interstate commerce.

The undisputed facts thus afford no warrant for the argument that the poultry handled by defendants at their slaughterhouse markets was in a *"current"* or *"flow"* of interstate commerce and was thus subject to congressional regula-

tion. The mere fact that there may be a constant flow of commodities into a State does not mean that the flow continues after the property has arrived and has become commingled with the mass of property within the State and is there held solely for local disposition and use. So far as the poultry here in question is concerned, the flow in interstate commerce had ceased. The poultry had come to a permanent rest within the State. . . .

(2) Did the defendants' transactions directly *"affect"* interstate commerce so as to be subject to federal regulation? The power of Congress extends not only to the regulation of transactions which are part of interstate commerce, but to the protection of that commerce from injury. . . .

. . .

In determining how far the federal government may go in controlling intrastate transactions upon the ground that they "affect" interstate commerce, there is a necessary and well-established distinction between direct and indirect effects. . . . But where the effect of intrastate transactions upon interstate commerce is merely indirect, such transactions remain with the domain of state power. If the commerce clause were construed to reach all enterprises and transactions which could be said to have an indirect effect upon interstate commerce, the federal authority would embrace practically all the activities of the people, and the authority of the State over its domestic concerns would exist only by sufferance of the federal government. . . .

We are of the opinion that the attempt through the provisions of the Code to fix the hours and wages of employees of defendants in their intrastate business was not a valid exercise of federal power.

. . .

On both the grounds we have discussed, the attempted delegation of legislative power, and the attempted regulation of intrastate transactions which affect interstate commerce only indirectly, we hold the code provisions here in question to be invalid and that the judgment of conviction must be reversed. . . .

Aftermath of Schechter Poultry Corp. v. United States

The *Schechter* case was one in a series of 12 conservative activist decisions that, taken together in the brief period between January 1935 and June 1936, frustrated President Roosevelt and persuaded him that the Court would not look favorably on any future regulatory legislation. Four of the sitting justices were irrevocably committed to an economic and political philosophy that would permit little, if any, compromise with the President's New Deal, and much of the time they were joined in their opinions by a fifth, and some of the time by a sixth, Chief Justice Hughes. In a bold move following his landslide reelection in 1936, the President sent a bill to Congress, the main feature of which would have permitted him to appoint an additional justice to the Court when any member with at least 10 years of service had served 6 months after reaching the age of 70 and failed to resign or retire. The size of the Court would have been limited to 15 and, had the measure become law, it would have permitted counterappointments for those justices who had been voting against the President's program. In defense of the proposal the President alluded to old men out of step with the times, but his main theme was the need for more judges to handle the Court's work load, an argument which the chief justice was able to refute point by point. President Roosevelt was never able to translate his political popularity into public support for the bill, which was dubbed by its opponents a "court-packing" plan. After a fierce debate both in and out of Congress, the measure was effectively killed in July 1937 when the Senate voted 70–20 to recommit the bill to the Judiciary Committee. By that time, however, a new liberal restraintist majority had emerged on the Court in two decisions upholding a state minimum wage law (*West Coast Hotel* v. *Parrish*) and the National Labor Relations Act, a centerpiece of the "Second New Deal" (*National Labor Relations Board* v. *Jones & Laughlin Steel Corporation,* excerpted in Chapter 3).

Heart of Atlanta Motel v. United States

379 U.S. 241(1964)

In the early 1960s the civil rights movement was shifting from the courts to the streets. After decades of legal victories by the National Association for the Advancement of Colored People, which thanks to the stratagems of state and local officials and the indifference of the national government were largely unenforced, black Americans were turning to more direct action. Led by Dr. Martin Luther King and his Southern Christian Leadership Conference, thousands took part in acts of civil disobedience throughout the south, inviting arrest and risking assault to demonstrate their opposition to racially discriminatory laws and practices. President John F. Kennedy was sympathetic to civil rights but wished to put off major legislative initiatives until after the 1964 election. Meanwhile he signed executive orders prohibiting racial discrimination in federal employment and federally funded housing and sent national guard troops to the universities of Mississippi and Alabama to ensure that black students would be allowed to enroll and attend classes. By 1963, however, it was clear that Kennedy's schedule had been overtaken by events, and on June 19 he sent Congress legislation outlawing racial discrimination in education and public accommodations which, if enacted, would put the muscle of the federal government behind the enforcement of racial equality. Later that summer several hundred thou-

sand people staged a "march on Washington" to demonstrate support for the legislation and heard King deliver his famous "I Have a Dream" speech at the Lincoln Memorial. After Kennedy's assassination in November, President Lyndon B. Johnson gave the civil rights bill his strongest support and it was passed in June 1964, exactly 1 year after its submission to Congress.

Support for the Civil Rights Act was strong but not unanimous. Many southerners and political conservatives viewed the legislation as an encroachment on the rights of states to govern their own affairs. They also opposed the law's ban on private discrimination. Much of their ire was directed at Title II, the public accommodations section, which prohibited racial discrimination by restaurants, hotels and motels, sports and entertainment establishments, and gasoline service stations—in short, all businesses licensed to serve the public. The congressional authors of the Civil Rights Act had grounded this authority in the interstate commerce clause of Article I, a constitutional provision which the Supreme Court since the days of John Marshall had interpreted as a broad grant of congressional power (with a single exception in 1918 and another more sustained interruption in the 1930s when the Court tried to scuttle President Franklin Roosevelt's New Deal). Although the Court had previously ruled that the commerce clause covered the movement of people in interstate travel, opponents of the law were determined to press their case in court. President Johnson's signature on the act was barely dry before a suit was filed in federal court by Heart of Atlanta Motel, a large motel with an interstate clientele that wished to maintain its policy of refusing to serve blacks. It was the motel owners' contention that the Civil Rights Act should be held unconstitutional on the ground that Congress had overstepped its authority to regulate interstate commerce. They were essentially asking the judges to use judicial activism to achieve a politically conservative result. The motel's challenge was rejected by a three-judge court and the Supreme Court expedited a direct appeal. Just how important the Court thought the issue to be (and how easily it was resolved) is shown by the fact that the *Heart of Atlanta* decision was handed down within 5 months of the law's passage.

TOM C. CLARK

Tom C. Clark, appointed by President Harry S Truman in 1949, had served in the Department of Justice for 8 years, 4 as attorney general. His nomination was greeted with strong opposition from political liberals, but as a justice he proved to be surprisingly sympathetic to civil rights and civil liberties. Clark resigned from the Court in 1966 when his son Ramsey was named attorney general and in an "active retired" status continued to participate in federal district and appeals court decisions for another decade.

Mr. Justice **Clark** delivered the opinion of the Court.

. . .

It is admitted that the operation of the motel brings it within the provisions of § 201 (a) of the

[Civil Rights] Act and that appellant refused to provide lodging for transient Negroes because of their race or color and that it intends to continue that policy unless restrained.

The sole question posed is, therefore, the constitutionality of the Civil Rights Act of 1964 as applied to these facts. The legislative history of the Act indicates that Congress based the Act on § 5 and the Equal Protection Clause of the Fourteenth Amendment as well as its power to regulate interstate commerce under Art. I, § 8, cl. 3, of the Constitution.

The Senate Commerce Committee made it quite clear that the fundamental object of Title II was to vindicate "the deprivation of personal dignity that surely accompanies denials of equal access to public establishments." At the same time, however, it noted that such an objective has been and could be readily achieved "by congressional action based on the commerce power of the Constitution." Our study of the legislative record, made in the light of prior cases, has brought us to the conclusion that Congress possessed ample power in this regard, and we have therefore not considered the other grounds relied upon. . . .

. . .

While the Act as adopted carried no congressional findings the record of its passage through each house is replete with evidence of the burdens that discrimination by race or color places upon interstate commerce. This testimony included the fact that our people have become increasingly mobile with millions of people of all races traveling from State to State; that Negroes in particular have been the subject of discrimination in transient accommodations, having to travel great distances to secure the same; that often they have been unable to obtain accommodations and have had to call upon friends to put them up overnight; and that these conditions had become so acute as to require the listing of available lodging for Negroes in a special guidebook which was itself "dramatic testimony to the difficulties" Negroes encounter in travel. These exclusionary practices were found to be nationwide, the Under Secretary of Commerce testifying that there is "no question that this discrimination in the North still exists to a large degree" and in the West and Midwest as well. This testimony indicated a qualitative as well as quantitative effect on interstate travel by Negroes. The former was the obvious impairment of the Negro traveler's pleasure and convenience that resulted when he continually was

uncertain of finding lodging. As for the latter, there was evidence that this uncertainty stemming from racial discrimination had the effect of discouraging travel on the part of a substantial portion of the Negro community. This was the conclusion not only of the Under Secretary of Commerce but also of the Administrator of the Federal Aviation Agency who wrote the Chairman of the Senate Commerce Committee that it was his "belief that air commerce is adversely affected by the denial to a substantial segment of the traveling public of adequate and desegregated public accommodations." We shall not burden this opinion with further details since the voluminous testimony presents overwhelming evidence that discrimination by hotels and motels impedes interstate travel.

. . .

The power of Congress to deal with these obstructions depends on the meaning of the Commerce Clause. Its meaning was first enunciated 140 years ago by the great Chief Justice John Marshall in *Gibbons* v. *Ogden* (1824), in these words:

"The subject to be regulated is commerce; and . . . to ascertain the extent of the power, it becomes necessary to settle the meaning of the word. The counsel for the appellee would limit it to traffic, to buying and selling, or the interchange of commodities . . . but it is something more: it is intercourse . . . between nations, and parts of nations, in all its branches, and is regulated by prescribing rules for carrying on that intercourse.

. . .

"To what commerce does this power extend? The constitution informs us, to commerce 'with foreign nations, and among the several States, and with the Indian tribes.'

"It has, we believe, been universally admitted, that these words comprehend every species of commercial intercourse. . . . No sort of trade can be carried on . . . to which this power does not extend.

. . .

"The subject to which the power is next applied, is to commerce 'among the several States.' The word 'among' means intermingled. . . .

. . .

". . . [I]t may very properly be restricted to that commerce which concerns more States than one. . . . The genius and character of the whole government seem to be, that its action is to be applied to all the . . . internal concerns [of the Nation] which affect the States generally; but not to those which are completely within a particular State, which do not affect other States, and with which it is not necessary to interfere, for the purpose of executing some of the general powers of the government.

. . .

"We are now arrived at the inquiry—What is this power?

"It is the power to regulate; that is, to prescribe the rule by which commerce is to be governed. This power, like all others vested in Congress, is complete in itself, may be exercised to its utmost extent, and acknowledges no limitations, other than are prescribed in the constitution. . . . If, as has always been understood, the sovereignty of Congress . . . is plenary as to those objects [specified in the Constitution], the power over commerce . . . is vested in Congress as absolutely as it would be in a single government, having in its constitution the same restrictions on the exercise of the power as are found in the constitution of the United States. The wisdom and the discretion of Congress, their identity with the people, and the influence which their constituents possess at elections, are, in this, as in many other instances, as that, for example, of declaring war, the sole restraints on which they have relied, to secure them from its abuse. They are the restraints on which the people must often rely solely, in all representative governments." In short, the determinative test of the exercise of power by the Congress under the Commerce Clause is simply whether the activity sought to be regulated is "commerce which concerns more States than one" and has a real and substantial relation to the national interest. Let us now turn to this facet of the problem.

That the "intercourse" of which the Chief Justice spoke included the movement of persons through more States than one was settled as early as 1849, in the *Passenger Cases*. . . . Again in 1913 Mr. Justice McKenna, speaking for the Court, said: "Commerce among the States, we have said, consists of intercourse and traffic between their citizens, and includes the transportation of persons and property." *Hoke* v. *United States*. . . .

Nor does it make any difference whether the transportation is commercial in character. . . .

The same interest in protecting interstate commerce which led Congress to deal with segregation in interstate carriers and the white-slave traffic has prompted it to extend the exercise of its power to gambling; to criminal enterprises; to deceptive practices in the sale of products; to fraudulent security transactions; to misbranding of drugs; to wages and hours; to members of labor unions; to crop control; to discrimination against shippers; to the protection of small business from injurious price cutting; to resale price maintenance; to professional football; and to racial discrimination by owners and managers of terminal restaurants.

That Congress was legislating against moral wrongs in many of these areas rendered its enactments no less valid. In framing Title II of this Act Congress was also dealing with what it considered a moral problem. But that fact does not detract from the overwhelming evidence of the disruptive effect that racial discrimination has had on commercial intercourse. It was this burden which empowered Congress to enact appropriate legislation, and, given this basis for the exercise of its power, Congress was not restricted by the fact that the particular obstruction to interstate commerce with which it was dealing was also deemed a moral and social wrong.

It is said that the operation of the motel here is of a purely local character. But, assuming this to be true, "[i]f it is interstate commerce that feels the pinch, it does not matter how local the operation which applies the squeeze." *United States* v. *Women's Sportswear Mfrs. Assn.* (1949). . . . Thus the power of Congress to promote interstate commerce also includes the power to regulate the local incidents thereof, including local activities in both the States of origin and destination, which might have a substantial and harmful effect upon that commerce. One need only examine the evidence which we have discussed above to see that Congress may—as it has—prohibit racial discrimination by motels serving travelers, however "local" their operations may appear.

Nor does the Act deprive appellant of liberty or property under the Fifth Amendment. The commerce power invoked here by the Congress is a specific and plenary one authorized by the Constitution itself. The only questions are: (1) whether Congress had a rational basis for finding that racial discrimination by motels affected commerce, and (2) if it had such a basis, whether the means it selected to eliminate that evil are reasonable and appropriate. If they are, appellant has no "right" to select its guests as it sees fit, free from governmental regulation.

There is nothing novel about such legislation. Thirty-two States now have it on their books either by statute or executive order and many cities provide such regulation. Some of these Acts go back fourscore years. It has been repeatedly held by this Court that such laws do not violate the Due Process Clause of the Fourteenth Amendment. . . .

. . .

We find no merit in the remainder of appellant's contentions, including that of "involuntary servitude." . . .

We, therefore, conclude that the action of the Congress in the adoption of the Act as applied here to a motel which concededly serves interstate travelers is within the power granted it by the Commerce Clause of the Constitution, as interpreted by this Court for 140 years. It may be argued that Congress could have pursued other methods to eliminate the obstructions it found in interstate commerce caused by racial discrimination. But this is a matter of policy that rests entirely with the Congress not with the courts. How obstructions in commerce may be removed—what means are to be employed—is within the sound and exclusive discretion of the Congress. It is subject only to one caveat—that the means chosen by it must be reasonably adapted to the end permitted by the Constitution. We cannot say that its choice here was not so adapted. The Constitution requires no more.

Affirmed.

Mr. Justice **Douglas,** concurring.

Though I join the Court's opinions, I am somewhat reluctant . . . to rest solely on the Commerce Clause. My reluctance is not due to any conviction that Congress lacks power to regulate commerce in the interests of human rights. It is rather my belief that the right of people to be free of state action that discriminates against them because of race, like the "right of persons to move freely from State to State" (*Edwards* v. *California*), "occupies a more protected position in our constitutional system than does the movement of cattle, fruit, steel and coal across state lines." Moreover, when we come to the problem of abatement . . . the result reached by the Court is for me much more obvious as a protective measure under the Fourteenth Amendment than under the Commerce Clause. For the former deals with the constitutional status of the individual not with the impact on commerce of local activities or vice versa.

Hence I would prefer to rest on the assertion of legislative power contained in § 5 of the Fourteenth Amendment which states: "The Congress shall have power to enforce, by appropriate legislation, the provisions of this article"—a power which the Court concedes was exercised at least in part in this Act.

A decision based on the Fourteenth Amendment would have a more settling effect, making unnecessary litigation over whether a particular restaurant or inn is within the commerce definitions of the Act or whether a particular customer is an interstate traveler. Under my construction, the Act would apply to all customers in all the enumerated places of public accommodation. And that construction would put an end to all obstructionist strategies and finally close one door on a bitter chapter in American history.

Aftermath of Heart of Atlanta Motel *v.* United States

In a companion case heard and decided with *Heart of Atlanta,* the Court made clear that it was not a business's patronage alone which justified its inclusion under the Civil Rights Act. In *Katzenbach* v. *McClung* the Court held, also unanimously, that an Alabama restaurant which bought foodstuffs out of state was covered by Title II as well. Since by this standard virtually no business would be considered to operate entirely "intrastate," the Court had in short order disposed of any doubts about the constitutionality and sweeping authority of the Civil Rights Act. Over the next decade the Justice Department would bring more than 400 lawsuits against business establishments for racial discrimination, virtually all of them ending with an agreement or a court order to serve black customers. The Justice Department also filed hundreds of lawsuits against school districts (in both the north and the south) for failing to meet desegregation guidelines specified in the law. However, the pace of school desegregation did not begin to quicken until the act was amended to require the Department of Health, Education, and Welfare (now Health and Human Services) to withhold federal education funds from school districts that discriminated racially.

Miranda v. *Arizona*

384 U.S. 436(1966)

At issue in this case was the admissibility of evidence obtained from persons being interrogated by the police. Two constitutional provisions were involved: the Sixth Amendment's guarantee of the assistance of counsel and the Fifth Amendment's prohibition against self-incrimination. The two are connected by the claim that if a suspect in custody is not provided with a lawyer early in the criminal process, all of his rights may be in jeopardy, including the right not to make possibly incriminating statements.

On March 3, 1963, an 18-year-old woman was abducted and raped near Phoenix, Arizona, Ten days later, on the basis of information from the victim about the automobile in which she had been attacked, police detectives arrested Ernest Miranda, a 23-year-old high school dropout with a police record. At the police station Miranda was interrogated for 2 hours, after which he signed a statement written in his own hand describing and admitting to the crime. He was subsequently arraigned on charges of kidnapping and rape and an attorney was appointed to represent him at trial. After a brief trial Miranda was found guilty and sentenced to 20 to 30 years in the Arizona State Prison.

At the trial and again in his appeal to the Arizona Supreme Court, Miranda's lawyer raised questions about the voluntariness of his client's confession. It was true that Miranda had signed a typed statement that he understood his rights, but exactly what he understood those rights to be was not clear from the record, nor was it clear what, if anything, his interrogators had told him. The Arizona Supreme Court unanimously rejected Miranda's appeal, reasoning that anyone with the defendant's courtroom experience must have known that he had the right to have his lawyer present at the station house. There was no indication, said the court, that Miranda had made such a request.

By all odds, that should have been the end of Ernest Miranda's case. Several thousand state prisoners file *certiorari* petitions with the United States Supreme Court each year, but only a handful of these are chosen for review. However, unbeknownst

to Miranda, in 1965 the Supreme Court was especially anxious to address some of the constitutional issues left unresolved the previous year in *Escobedo* v. *Illinois*. There the Court had held that a criminal suspect who had previously retained a lawyer could not be prevented from consulting that lawyer prior to police interrogation. Sticking closely to the facts of the case, the Court in *Escobedo* did not address the more common situation involving a suspect without a lawyer.

At the same time the American Civil Liberties Union was looking for cases through which it might persuade the Court to expand its ruling in *Escobedo*. Two prominent Phoenix attorneys with ACLU connections agreed to represent Miranda *pro bono* (without pay) in his Supreme Court appeal. One of these attorneys, John Frank, was a former Supreme Court clerk and a well-known constitutional historian, a fact that probably helped Miranda's chances of having his petition chosen from among the approximately 150 Escobedo-type appeals that had flooded the Court that year. Eventually the Court selected *Miranda* v. *Arizona*, along with three "companion cases," to be heard in February 1966. Despite some significant factual differences, the four cases shared several salient features, including the absence of a "full and effective warning" of the defendant's rights by police interrogators, and a police station confession that had been admitted as evidence at the defendant's trial. Like *Escobedo*, *Miranda* was decided by a narrow 5–4 majority. Unlike the earlier case, however, the *Miranda* decision was sweeping, indeed revolutionary, in its implications for law-enforcement practices.

Mr. Chief Justice **Warren** delivered the opinion of the Court.

The cases before us raise questions which go to the roots of our concepts of American criminal jurisprudence: the restraints society must observe consistent with the Federal Constitution in prosecuting individuals for crime. More specifically, we deal with the admissibility of statements obtained from an individual who is subjected to custodial police interrogation and the necessity for procedures which assure that the individual is accorded his privilege under the Fifth Amendment to the Constitution not to be compelled to incriminate himself.

. . .

Our holding will be spelled out with some specificity in the pages which follow but briefly stated it is this: the prosecution may not use statements, whether exculpatory or inculpatory, stemming from custodial interrogation of the defendant unless it demonstrates the use of procedural safeguards effective to secure the privilege against self-incrimination. By custodial interrogation, we mean questioning initiated by law enforcement officers after a person has been taken into custody or otherwise deprived of his freedom of action in any significant way. As for the procedural safeguards to be employed, unless other fully effective means are devised to inform accused persons of their right of silence and to assure a continuous opportunity to exercise it, the following measures are required. Prior to any questioning, the person must be warned that he has a right to remain silent, that any statement he does make may be used as evidence against him, and that he has a right to the presence of an attorney, either retained or appointed. The defendant may waive effectuation of these rights, provided the waiver is made voluntarily, knowingly and intelligently. If, however, he indicates in any manner and at any stage of the process that he wishes to consult with an attorney before speaking there can be no questioning. Likewise, if the individual is alone and indicates in any manner that he does not wish to be interrogated, the police may not question him. The mere fact that he may have answered some questions or volunteered some statements on his own does not deprive him of the right to refrain from answering any further inquiries until he has consulted with an attorney and thereafter consents to be questioned.

The constitutional issue we decide in each of these cases is the admissibility of statements obtained from a defendant questioned while in custody and deprived of his freedom of action. In each, the defendant was questioned by police officers, detectives, or a prosecuting attorney in a room in which he was cut off from the outside world. In none of these cases was the defendant given a full and effective warning of his rights at the outset of the interrogation process. In all the cases, the questioning elicited oral admissions, and in three of them, signed statements as well which were admitted at their trials. They all thus share salient features—incommunicado interrogation of individuals in a police-dominated atmosphere, resulting in self-incriminating statements without full warnings of constitutional rights.

An understanding of the nature and setting of this in-custody interrogation is essential to our decisions today. The difficulty in depicting what transpires at such interrogations stems from the fact that in this country they have largely taken place incommunicado. From extensive factual studies undertaken in the early 1930's, including the famous Wickersham Report to Congress by a Presidential Commission, it is clear that police violence and the "third degree" flourished at that time. In a series of cases decided by this Court long after these studies, the police resorted to physical brutality—beatings, hanging, whipping—and to sustained and protracted questioning incommunicado in order to extort confessions. The 1961 Commission on Civil Rights found much evidence to indicate that "some policemen still resort to physical force to obtain confessions." The use of physical brutality and violence is not, unfortunately, relegated to the past or to any part of the country. Only recently in Kings County, New York, the police brutally beat, kicked and placed lighted cigarette butts on the back of a potential witness under interrogation for the purpose of securing a statement incriminating a third party.

The examples given above are undoubtedly the exception now, but they are sufficiently widespread to be the object of concern. Unless a proper limitation upon custodial interrogation is achieved—such as these decisions will advance—there can be no assurance that practices of this nature will be eradicated in the foreseeable future. The conclusion of the Wickersham Commission Report, made over 30 years ago, is still pertinent:

"To the contention that the third degree is necessary to get the facts, the reporters aptly reply in the language of the present Lord Chancellor of England (Lord Sankey): 'It is not admissible to do a great right by doing a little wrong. . . . It is not sufficient to do justice by obtaining a proper result by irregular or improper means.' Not only does the use of the third degree involve a flagrant violation of law by the officers of the law, but it involves also the dangers of false confessions, and it tends to make police and prosecutors less zealous in the search for objective evidence. As the New York prosecutor quoted in the report said, 'It is a short cut and makes the police lazy and unenterprising.' Or, as another official quoted remarked: 'If you use your fists, you are not so likely to use your wits.' We agree with the conclusion expressed in the report, that 'The third degree brutalizes the police, hardens the prisoner against society, and lowers the esteem in which the administration of justice is held by the public.'"

Again we stress that the modern practice of in-custody interrogation is psychologically rather than physically oriented. As we have stated before, "Since Chambers v. Florida, this Court has recognized that coercion can be mental as well as physical, and that the blood of the accused is not the only hallmark of an unconstitutional inquisition." Blackburn v Alabama (1960). Interrogation still takes place in privacy. Privacy results in secrecy and this in turn results in a gap in our knowledge as to what in fact goes on in the interrogation rooms. A valuable source of information about present police practices, however, may be found in various police manuals and texts which document procedures employed with success in the past, and which recommend various other effective tactics. These texts are used by law enforcement agencies themselves as guides. It should be noted that these texts professedly present the most enlightened and effective means presently used to obtain statements through custodial interrogation. By considering these texts and other data, it is possible to describe procedures observed and noted around the country.

. . .

From . . . representative samples of interrogation techniques, the setting prescribed by the manuals and observed in practice becomes clear. In essence, it is this: To be alone with the subject is essential to prevent distraction and to deprive him of any outside support. The aura of confidence in his guilt undermines his will to resist. He merely confirms the preconceived story the police seek to have him describe. Patience and persistence, at times relentless questioning, are employed. To obtain a confession, the interrogator must "patiently maneuver himself or his quarry into a position from which the desired object may be obtained." When normal procedures fail to produce the needed result, the police may resort to deceptive stratagems such as giving false legal advice. It is important to keep the subject off balance, for example, by trading on his insecurity about himself or his surroundings. The police then persuade, trick, or cajole him out of exercising his constitutional rights.

Even without employing brutality, the "third degree" or the specific stratagems described above, the very fact of custodial interrogation exacts a heavy toll on individual liberty and trades on the weakness of individuals.

. . .

It is obvious that such an interrogation environment is created for no purpose other than to subjugate the individual to the will of his examiner. This atmosphere carries its own badge of intimidation. To be sure, this is not physical intimidation, but it is equally destructive of human dignity. The current practice of incommunicado interrogation is at odds with one of our Nation's most cherished principles—that the individual may not be compelled to incriminate himself. Unless adequate protective devices are employed to dispel the compulsion inherent in custodial surroundings, no statement obtained from the defendant can truly be the product of his free choice.

From the foregoing, we can readily perceive an intimate connection between the privilege against self-incrimination and police custodial questioning.

. . .

The question in these cases is whether the privilege is fully applicable during a period of custodial interrogation. In this Court, the privilege has consistently been accorded a liberal construction.

. . .

We are satisfied that all the principles embodied in the privilege apply to informal compulsion exerted by law-enforcement officers during in-custody questioning. An individual swept from familiar surroundings into police custody, surrounded by antagonistic forces, and subjected to the techniques of persuasion described above cannot be otherwise than under compulsion to speak. As a practical matter, the compulsion to speak in the isolated setting of the police station may well be greater than in courts or other official investigations, where there are often impartial observers to guard against intimidation or trickery.

. . .

Today, then, there can be no doubt that the Fifth Amendment privilege is available outside of criminal court proceedings and serves to protect persons in all settings in which their freedom of action is curtailed from being compelled to incriminate themselves. We have concluded that without proper safeguards the process of in-custody interrogation of persons suspected or accused of crime contains inherently compelling pressures which work to undermine the individual's will to resist and to compel him to speak where he would not otherwise do so freely. In order to combat these pressures and to permit a full opportunity to exercise the privilege against self-incrimination, the accused must be adequately and effectively apprised of his rights and the exercise of those rights must be fully honored.

It is impossible for us to foresee the potential alternatives for protecting the privilege which might be devised by Congress or the States in the exercise of their creative rule-making capacities. Therefore we cannot say that the Constitution necessarily requires adherence to any particular solution for the inherent compulsions of the interrogation process as it is presently conducted. Our decision in no way creates a constitutional straitjacket which will handicap sound efforts at reform, nor is it intended to have this effect. We encourage Congress and the States to continue their laudable search for increasingly effective ways of protecting the rights of the individual while promoting efficient enforcement of our criminal laws. However, unless we are shown other procedures which are at least as effective in apprising accused persons of their right of silence and in assuring a continuous opportunity to exercise it, the following safeguards must be observed.

At the outset, if a person in custody is to be subjected to interrogation, he must first be informed in clear and unequivocal terms that he has the right to remain silent. For those unaware of the privilege, the warning is needed simply to make them aware of it—the threshold requirement for an intelligent decision as to its exercise. More important, such a warning is an absolute prerequisite in overcoming the inherent pressures of the interrogation atmosphere. It is not just the subnormal or woefully ignorant who succumb to an interrogator's imprecations, whether implied or expressly stated, that the interrogation will continue until a confession is obtained or that silence in the face of accusation is itself damning and will bode ill when presented to a jury. Further, the warning will show the individual that his interrogators are prepared to recognize his privilege should he choose to exercise it.

The Fifth Amendment privilege is so fundamental to our system of constitutional rule and the expedient of giving an adequate warning as to the availability of the privilege so simple, we will not pause to inquire in individual cases whether the defendant was aware of his rights without a warning being given. Assessments of the knowledge the defendant possessed, based on information as to his age, education, intelligence, or prior contact with authorities, can never be more than speculation; a warning is a clearcut fact. More important, whatever the background of the person interrogated, a warning at the time of the interrogation is indispensable to overcome its pressures and to insure that the individual knows he is free to exercise the privilege at that point in time.

The warning of the right to remain silent must be accompanied by the explanation that anything said can and will be used against the individual in court. This warning is needed in order to make him aware not only of the privilege, but also of the consequences of forgoing it. It is only through an awareness of these conse-

quences that there can be any assurance of real understanding and intelligent exercise of the privilege. Moreover, this warning may serve to make the individual more acutely aware that he is faced with a phase of the adversary system— that he is not in the presence of persons acting solely in his interest.

The circumstances surrounding in-custody interrogation can operate very quickly to overbear the will of one merely made aware of his privilege by his interrogators. Therefore, the right to have counsel present at the interrogation is indispensable to the protection of the Fifth Amendment privilege under the system we delineate today. Our aim is to assure that the individual's right to choose between silence and speech remains unfettered throughout the interrogation process. A once-stated warning, delivered by those who will conduct the interrogation, cannot itself suffice to that end among those who most require knowledge of their rights. A mere warning given by the interrogators is not alone sufficient to accomplish that end. Prosecutors themselves claim that the admonishment of the right to remain silent without more "will benefit only the recidivist and the professional."

Thus, the need for counsel to protect the Fifth Amendment privilege comprehends not merely a right to consult with counsel prior to questioning, but also to have counsel present during any questioning if the defendant so desires.

The presence of counsel at the interrogation may serve several significant subsidiary functions as well. If the accused decides to talk to his interrogators, the assistance of counsel can mitigate the dangers of untrustworthiness. With a lawyer present the likelihood that the police will practice coercion is reduced, and if coercion is nevertheless exercised the lawyer can testify to it in court. The presence of a lawyer can also help to guarantee that the accused gives a fully accurate statement to the police and that the statement is rightly reported by the prosecution at trial.

An individual need not make a pre-interrogation request for a lawyer. While such request affirmatively secures his right to have one, his failure to ask for a lawyer does not constitute a waiver. No effective waiver of the right to counsel during interrogation can be recognized unless specifically made after the warnings we here delineate have been given. The accused who does not know his rights and therefore does not make a request may be the person who most needs counsel.

. . .

Accordingly we hold that an individual held for interrogation must be clearly informed that he has the right to consult with a lawyer and to have the lawyer with him during interrogation under the system for protecting the privilege we delineate today. As with the warnings of the right to remain silent and that anything stated can be used in evidence against him, this warning is an absolute prerequisite to interrogation. No amount of circumstantial evidence that the person may have been aware of this right will suffice to stand in its stead. Only through such a warning is there ascertainable assurance that the accused was aware of this right.

. . .

The principles announced today deal with the protection which must be given to the privilege against self-incrimination when the individual is first subjected to police interrogation while in custody at the station or otherwise deprived of his freedom of action in any way. It is at this point that our adversary system of criminal proceedings commences, distinguishing itself at the outset from the inquisitorial system recognized in some countries. Under the system of warnings we delineate today or under any other system which may be devised and found effective, the safeguards to be erected about the privilege must come into play at this point.

Our decision is not intended to hamper the traditional function of police officers in investigating crime. When an individual is in custody on probable cause, the police may, of course, seek out evidence in the field to be used at trial against him. Such investigation may include inquiry of persons not under restraint. General on-the-scene questioning as to facts surrounding a crime or other general questioning of citizens in the fact-finding process is not affected by our holding. It is an act of responsible citizenship for individuals to give whatever information

they may have to aid in law enforcement. In such situations the compelling atmosphere inherent in the process of in-custody interrogation is not necessarily present.

. . .

To summarize, we hold that when an individual is taken into custody or otherwise deprived of his freedom by the authorities and is subjected to questioning, the privilege against self-incrimination is jeopardized. Procedural safeguards must be employed to protect the privilege, and unless other fully effective means are adopted to notify the person of his right of silence and to assure that the exercise of the right will be scrupulously honored, the following measures are required. He must be warned prior to any questioning that he has the right to remain silent, that anything he says can be used against him in a court of law, that he has the right to the presence of an attorney, and that if he cannot afford an attorney one will be appointed for him prior to any questioning if he so desires. Opportunity to exercise these rights must be afforded to him throughout the interrogation. After such warnings have been given, and such opportunity afforded him, the individual may knowingly and intelligently waive these rights and agree to answer questions or make a statement. But unless and until such warnings and waiver are demonstrated by the prosecution at trial, no evidence obtained as a result of interrogation can be used against him.

A recurrent argument made in these cases is that society's need for interrogation outweighs the privilege. This argument is not unfamiliar to this Court. The whole thrust of our foregoing discussion demonstrates that the Constitution has prescribed the rights of the individual when confronted with the power of government when it provided in the Fifth Amendment that an individual cannot be compelled to be a witness against himself. That right cannot be abridged.

. . .

In announcing these principles, we are not unmindful of the burdens which law enforcement officials must bear, often under trying circumstances. We also fully recognize the obligation of all citizens to aid in enforcing the criminal laws. This Court, while protecting individual rights, has always given ample latitude to law enforcement agencies in the legitimate exercise of their duties. The limits we have placed on the interrogation process should not constitute an undue interference with a proper system of law enforcement. As we have noted, our decision does not in any way preclude police from carrying out their traditional investigatory functions. Although confessions may play an important role in some convictions, the cases before us present graphic examples of the overstatement of the "need" for confessions. In each case authorities conducted interrogations ranging up to five days in duration despite the presence, through standard investigating practices, of considerable evidence against each defendant.

. . .

It is also urged upon us that we withhold decision on this issue until state legislative bodies and advisory groups have had an opportunity to deal with these problems by rule making. We have already pointed out that the Constitution does not require any specific code of procedures for protecting the privilege against self-incrimination during custodial interrogation. Congress and the States are free to develop their own safeguards for the privilege, so long as they are fully as effective as those described above in informing accused persons of their right of silence and in affording a continuous opportunity to exercise it. In any event, however, the issues presented are of constitutional dimensions and must be determined by the courts. The admissibility of a statement in the face of a claim that it was obtained in violation of the defendant's constitutional rights is an issue the resolution of which has long since been undertaken by this Court. Judicial solutions to problems of constitutional dimension have evolved decade by decade. As courts have been presented with the need to enforce constitutional rights, they have found means of doing so. That was our responsibility when Escobedo was before us and it is our responsibility today. Where rights secured by the Constitution are involved, there can be no rule making or legislation which would abrogate them.

Because of the nature of the problem and because of its recurrent significance in numerous cases, we have to this point discussed the relationship of the Fifth Amendment privilege to police interrogation without specific concentration on the facts of the cases before us. We turn now to these facts to consider the application to these cases of the constitutional principles discussed above. In each instance, we have concluded that statements were obtained from the defendant under circumstances that did not meet constitutional standards for protection of the privilege.

. . .

Mr. Justice **Harlan,** whom Mr. Justice **Stewart** and Mr. Justice **White** join, dissenting.

I believe the decision of the Court represents poor constitutional law and entails harmful consequences for the country at large. How serious these consequences may prove to be only time can tell. But the basic flaws in the Court's justification seem to me readily apparent now once all sides of the problem are considered.

At the outset, it is well to note exactly what is required by the Court's new constitutional code of rules for confessions. The foremost requirement, upon which later admissibility of a confession depends, is that a four-fold warning be given to a person in custody before he is questioned: namely, that he has a right to remain silent, that anything he says may be used against him, that he has a right to have present an attorney during the questioning, and that if indigent he has a right to a lawyer without charge. To forgo these rights, some affirmative statement of rejection is seemingly required, and threats, tricks, or cajolings to obtain this waiver are forbidden. If before or during questioning the suspect seeks to invoke his right to remain silent, interrogation must be forgone or cease; a request for counsel brings about the same result until a lawyer is procured. Finally, there are a miscellany of minor directives, for example, the burden of proof of waiver is on the State, admissions and exculpatory statements are treated just like confessions, withdrawal of a waiver is always permitted, and so forth.

While the fine points of this scheme are far

less clear than the Court admits, the tenor is quite apparent. The new rules are not designed to guard against police brutality or other unmistakably banned forms of coercion. Those who use third-degree tactics and deny them in court are equally able and destined to lie as skillfully about warnings and waivers. Rather, the thrust of the new rules is to negate all pressures, to reinforce the nervous or ignorant suspect, and ultimately to discourage any confession at all. The aim in short is toward "voluntariness" in a utopian sense, or to view it from a different angle, voluntariness with a vengeance.

To incorporate this notion into the Constitution requires a strained reading of history and precedent and a disregard of the very pragmatic concerns that alone may on occasion justify such strains.

. . .

Viewed as a choice based on pure policy, these new rules prove to be a highly debatable if not one-sided appraisal of the competing interests, imposed over widespread objection, at the very time when judicial restraint is most called for by the circumstances.

Having decided that the Fifth Amendment privilege does apply in the police station, the Court reveals that the privilege imposes more exacting restrictions than does the Fourteenth Amendment's voluntariness tests. It then emerges from a discussion of Escobedo that the Fifth Amendment requires for an admissible confession that it be given by one distinctly aware of his right not to speak and shielded from "the compelling atmosphere" of interrogation. From these key premises, the Court finally develops the safeguards of warning, counsel, and so forth. I do not believe these premises are sustained by precedents under the Fifth Amendment.

. . .

Without at all subscribing to the generally black picture of police conduct painted by the Court, I think it must be frankly recognized at the outset that police questioning allowable under due process precedents may inherently entail some pressure on the suspect and may seek advantage in his ignorance or weaknesses.

The atmosphere and questioning techniques, proper and fair though they be, can in themselves exert a tug on the suspect to confess, and in this light "[t]o speak of any confessions of crime made after arrest as being `voluntary' or `uncoerced' is somewhat inaccurate, although traditional. A confession is wholly and incontestably voluntary only if a guilty person gives himself up to the law and becomes his own accuser." Until today, the role of the Constitution has been only to sift out *undue* pressure, not to assure spontaneous confessions.

The Court's new rules aim to offset these minor pressures and disadvantages intrinsic to any kind of police interrogation. The rules do not serve due process interests in preventing blatant coercion since, as I noted earlier, they do nothing to contain the policeman who is prepared to lie from the start. The rules work for reliability in confessions almost only in the Pickwickian sense that they can prevent some from being given at all. In short, the benefit of this new regime is simply to lessen or wipe out the inherent compulsion and inequalities to which the Court devotes some nine pages of description.

What the Court largely ignores is that its rules impair, if they will not eventually serve wholly to frustrate, an instrument of law enforcement that has long and quite reasonably been thought worth the price paid for it. There can be little doubt that the Court's new code would markedly decrease the number of confessions. To warn the suspect that he may remain silent and remind him that his confession may be used in court are minor obstructions. To require also an express waiver by the suspect and an end to questioning whenever he demurs must heavily handicap questioning. And to suggest or provide counsel for the suspect simply invites the end of the interrogation.

How much harm this decision will inflict on law enforcement cannot fairly be predicted with accuracy. Evidence on the role of confessions is notoriously incomplete, and little is added by the Court's reference to the FBI experience and the resources believed wasted in interrogation. We do know that some crimes cannot be solved without confessions, that ample expert testimony attests to their importance in crime control, and that the Court is taking a real risk with society's welfare in imposing its new regime on the country. The social costs of crime are too great to call the new rules anything but a hazardous experimentation.

While passing over the costs and risks of its experiment, the Court portrays the evils of normal police questioning in terms which I think are exaggerated. Albeit stringently confined by the due process standards interrogation is no doubt often inconvenient and unpleasant for the suspect. However, it is no less so for a man to be arrested and jailed, to have his house searched, or to stand trial in court, yet all this may properly happen to the most innocent given probable cause, a warrant, or an indictment. Society has always paid a stiff price for law and order, and peaceful interrogation is not one of the dark moments of the law.

This brief statement of the competing considerations seems to me ample proof that the Court's preference is highly debatable at best and therefore not to be read into the Constitution.

In conclusion: Nothing in the letter or the spirit of the Constitution or in the precedents squares with the heavy handed and one-sided action that is so precipitously taken by the Court in the name of fulfilling its constitutional responsibilities. The foray which the Court takes today brings to mind the wise and farsighted words of Mr. Justice Jackson in Douglas v Jeannette. . . . "This Court is forever adding new stories to the temples of constitutional law, and the temples have a way of collapsing when one story too many is added."

Mr. Justice **White,** with whom Mr. Justice **Harlan** and Mr. Justice **Stewart** join, dissenting.

The proposition that the privilege against self-incrimination forbids in-custody interrogation without the warnings specified in the majority opinion and without a clear waiver of counsel has no significant support in the history of the privilege or in the language of the Fifth Amendment. As for the English authorities and the common-law history, the privilege, firmly established in the second half of the seventeenth century, was never applied except to prohibit compelled judicial interrogations. The rule excluding coerced confessions matured about 100 years later, "[b]ut there is nothing in the reports to suggest that the theory has its roots in the privilege against self-incrimination. And so far as the cases reveal, the privilege, as such, seems to have been given effect only in judicial proceedings, including the preliminary examinations by authorized magistrates."

Our own constitutional provision provides that no person "shall be compelled in any criminal case to be a witness against himself." These words, when "[c]onsidered in the light to be shed by grammar and the dictionary . . . appear to signify simply that nobody shall be compelled to give oral testimony against himself in a criminal proceeding under way in which he is defendant."

. . .

That the Court's holding today is neither compelled nor even strongly suggested by the language of the Fifth Amendment, is at odds with American and English legal history, and involves a departure from a long line of precedent does not prove either that the Court has exceeded its powers or that the Court is wrong or unwise in its present reinterpretation of the Fifth Amendment. It does, however, underscore the obvious—that the Court has not discovered or found the law in making today's decision, nor has it derived it from some irrefutable sources; what it has done is to make new law and new public policy in much the same way that it has in the course of interpreting other great clauses of the Constitution. This is what the Court historically has done. Indeed, it is what it must do and will continue to do until and unless there is some fundamental change in the constitutional distribution of governmental powers.

But if the Court is here and now to announce new and fundamental policy to govern certain aspects of our affairs, it is wholly legitimate to examine the mode of this or any other constitutional decision in this Court and to inquire into the advisability of its end product in terms of the long-range interest of the country. At the very least the Court's text and reasoning should withstand analysis and be a fair exposition of the constitutional provision which its opinion interprets.

Decisions like these cannot rest alone on syllogism, metaphysics or some ill-defined notions of natural justice, although each will perhaps play its part. In proceeding to such constructions as it now announces, the Court should also duly consider all the factors and interests bearing upon the cases, at least insofar as the relevant materials are available; and if the necessary considerations are not treated in the record or obtainable from some other reliable source, the Court should not proceed to formulate fundamental policies based on speculation alone.

. . .

Much of the trouble with the Court's new rule is that it will operate indiscriminately in all criminal cases, regardless of the severity of the crime or the circumstances involved. It applies to every defendant, whether the professional criminal or one committing a crime of momentary passion who is not part and parcel of organized crime. It will slow down the investigation and the apprehension of confederates in those cases where time is of the essence, such as kidnaping, . . . and some organized crime situations. In the latter context the lawyer who arrives may also be the lawyer for the defendants' colleagues and can be relied upon to insure that no breach of the organization's security takes place even though the accused may feel that the best thing he can do is to cooperate.

At the same time, the Court's per se approach may not be justified on the ground that it provides a "bright line" permitting the authorities to judge in advance whether interrogation may safely be pursued without jeopardizing the admissibility of any information obtained as a consequence. Nor can it be claimed that judicial time and effort, assuming that is a relevant consideration, will be conserved because of the ease of application of the new rule. Today's decision leaves open such questions as whether the accused was in custody, whether his statements were spontaneous or the product of interrogation, whether the accused has effectively waived his rights, and whether nontestimonial evidence introduced at trial is the fruit of statements made during a prohibited interrogation, all of which are certain to prove productive of uncertainty during investigation and litigation during prosecution. For all these reasons, if further restrictions on police interrogation are desirable at this time, a more flexible approach makes much more sense than the Court's constitutional straitjacket which forecloses more discriminating treatment by legislative or rule-making pronouncements.

Applying the traditional standards to the cases before the Court, I would hold these confessions voluntary.

Aftermath of Miranda *v.* Arizona

Despite the protestations of local police departments, the *Miranda* rule went into effect and soon became a routine part of police arrest procedures. Nevertheless, criticism of the decision, which came to be seen as the archetypal liberal-activist ruling, was unceasing. President Richard Nixon promised during his 1968 campaign that his appointees to the Supreme Court would be much tougher on criminals than the justices who had fashioned the *Miranda* rule. The implication was that the decision would eventually be overturned. By 1972 four justices had either died or resigned, permitting President Nixon to fill the vacancies with relatively conservative appointees. By the end of President Reagan's tenure in 1989, the Supreme Court had been largely reconstituted with only one of the original *Miranda* majority, Justice Brennan, and one of the original dissenters, Justice White, remaining on the bench. To this day, however, the *Miranda* rule remains the law, albeit with some modifications.

In 1967 the Court extended the rule in holding that a defendant must have counsel present if he were required to participate in a police lineup for identification purposes (*United States* v. *Wade,* and *Gilbert* v. *California*), and that a probationer was entitled to a state-appointed lawyer at a combined probation revocation and sentencing hearing. Prior to any changes in its personnel the Court also held that a defendant who was questioned by an internal revenue agent while serving time in a state prison was entitled to *Miranda* warnings and to the presence of counsel (*Mathis* v. *United States,* 1968) and that a preliminary hearing to determine whether sufficient evidence existed to present the case to a grand jury was a critical part of the criminal process and required the appointment of counsel for the accused (*Coleman* v. *Alabama,* 1970).

When it was given the opportunity in 1972 to overrule *Miranda,* a new Supreme Court led by Nixon-appointed Chief Justice Warren Burger instead actually expanded the rule by unanimously extending it to include misdemeanors and petty offenses as well as felonies whenever a prison sentence was possible (*Argersinger* v. *Hamlin*). In numerous cases well into the 1980s the Court continued to give *Miranda's* core principles positive reinforcement while at the same time softening the rule by permitting certain qualifications and exceptions.

Cases Reinforcing Miranda

Brewer v. *Williams* (1977). Held that a new trial be provided for a man convicted of a brutal murder because the police had persuaded him, in the absence of counsel, to lead them to the victim's body.

Estelle v. *Smith* (1981). Held a death sentence void on the ground that the defendant should have been warned, prior to his giving consent to a psychiatric examination, that the results might be used against him and that he had the right to the assistance of counsel before consenting to the interview.

Edwards v. *Arizona* (1981). Held that the police may not continue to interrogate a suspect who has asked for an attorney.

Minnick v. *Mississippi* (1990). Held that once a suspect in custody asserts his right to a lawyer the police may not begin a new interrogation unless the lawyer is present.

Cases Qualifying Miranda

Harris v. *New York* (1971). Held that a statement made to police without *Miranda* warnings, while inadmissible at a defendant's trial, was usable to impeach his credibility should the defendant take the witness stand.

Kirby v. *Illinois* (1972). Held that counsel was not required in an identification lineup conducted before indictment.

United States v. *Ash* (1973). Held that counsel was not required after indictment when the prosecution permitted witnesses to the crime to examine photographs containing the defendant's picture to determine whether they could identify him.

United States v. *Mandujano* (1976). Held that the *Miranda* rule does not apply to witnesses before grand juries even though they may be suspects.

Oregon v. *Mathiason* (1977). Held that a suspect who voluntarily went to the police station was not under arrest and could, therefore, be questioned without being given the *Miranda* warnings.

California v. *Prysock* (1981). Held that police officers need not use the precise language of the *Miranda* warning so long as they clearly indicate that the suspect has the right to a lawyer.

Illinois v. *Perkins* (1990). Held that a law-enforcement officer can pose as a prison inmate and elicit a confession from an actual inmate without giving *Miranda* warnings. *Miranda* forbids coercion, not mere strategic deception, and does not protect suspects from boasting about their criminal activities in front of persons whom they believe to be their cellmates.

Pennsylvania v. *Muniz* (1990). Held that a videotape of a drunk driving suspect's booking made prior to his being advised of his *Miranda* rights is not inadmissible in court, except for his response to a question about the date of his sixth birthday, which was protected by the privilege against self-incrimination.

And what of Ernest Miranda, whose name has entered the annals of law enforcement as each day thousands of criminal suspects are routinely "Mirandized"—read their rights—by arresting officers? One year after his conviction was overturned by the Supreme Court, Miranda was retried by the state of Arizona. Barred from using Miranda's station house confession as evidence, prosecutors instead introduced testimony by Miranda's common-law wife that he had admitted his guilt to her during a jail house visit. Although this evidence too was challenged by the defense, the trial judge ruled that it was admissible and Miranda was again found guilty and again sentenced to 20 to 30 years in prison, with credit for time served. After his conviction was upheld by the Arizona Supreme Court, the United States Supreme Court rejected his petition for *certiorari*. Released on parole in 1972, Miranda returned to Phoenix where he sometimes earned pocket money by signing police "Miranda cards" and selling them for a dollar apiece. In 1975 Miranda spent several months in prison on a parole violation after being found in possession of drugs and a firearm. The following year he died of stab wounds sustained in a knife fight. A suspect was arrested but after being read his rights he chose to remain silent and was released. Although additional evidence against him was later found, the suspect was never apprehended.

San Antonio Independent School District v. Rodriguez

411 U.S. 1(1973)

Progress toward legal and social equality for United States citizens has not been accompanied by comparable gains in economic equality. Except for a brief flurry of activity during President Lyndon Johnson's "war on poverty" in the 1960s, the American political system has had minimal success in addressing the problems of persistent poverty in the midst of general affluence. The explanation is both cultural and institutional. The American political tradition emphasizes "equality of opportunity" rather than "equality of condition." The judiciary, which was the catalyst for eliminating legal barriers to racial equality, has been reluctant to use its power of judicial review to legitimize demands for economic equality that the other branches of government, and perhaps the economic system itself, may be unable to fulfill.

Texas, like most states in the late 1960s, relied heavily upon local property taxes to finance public education. This meant not only that education budgets could vary considerably from one city to another, according to the local tax base, but also that school districts within a given city might have substantially different sums of money

available for education. Such a disparity was dramatically evident in the city of San Antonio, where the predominantly Hispanic district of Edgewood, though it had the city's highest tax rate, had such low property values that it was able to raise only $26 per student through property taxes, while nearby Alamo Heights, an affluent district with a lower tax rate, raised $333 per student. State and federal funding reduced the interdistrict disparity somewhat, but when all sources were added together Alamo Heights was spending about twice as much on each student as Edgewood. Nor could Edgewood residents raise more money by setting an even higher tax rate because of a state-mandated property-tax ceiling.

Frustrated by this economic and legal squeeze, a group of Edgewood parents organized by Demetrio Rodriguez in the late 1960s arranged with a local civil rights attorney to file a class action suit in federal court. Their claim, simply put, was that Texas' school financing law prevented their children from receiving the same quality of education as students in wealthier districts, and thus denied them the equal protection of the laws in violation of the Fourteenth Amendment. Although similar arguments had been made successfully against discriminatory laws based on race and to a lesser extent sex, the Fourteenth Amendment had never been mobilized against wealth-based distinctions.

Texas succeeded in keeping the *Rodriguez* case out of court for 3 years while the state legislature considered a series of school-financing reforms. Finally, with no legislative progress made and none in sight, a three-judge federal court panel heard the case and ruled in favor of the plaintiffs on all counts. Texas appealed the ruling to the United States Supreme Court, which heard the case at the beginning of its 1972 term. Twenty-five states had filed *amicus curiae* briefs in support of Texas' position. Anticipating political chaos if property-based school funding was ruled invalid, the states' attorneys general asked the Court to exercise judicial restraint by allowing state legislatures to solve the school financing problem without judicial intervention. Politically, that was the conservative position as well, since it was likely to involve less government activity than a court might require. Among those supporting the Edgewood parents' argument that the Supreme Court should overturn the Texas school financing law—essentially a politically liberal, judicially activist position—were the National Association for the Advancement of Colored People, the American Civil Liberties Union, the National Education Association, and the state of Minnesota. Interestingly, the San Antonio Independent School District, the nominal defendant in the case, filed a brief with the Court asking it to uphold the lower court's ruling. The key issues before the Court were (1) whether the lower court had been correct in its finding that wealth was a "suspect classification" requiring "strict scrutiny" by the Court to protect against discrimination by state officials; and (2) whether education was indeed a "fundamental right" that state officials were required to provide on an equal basis to all citizens.

LEWIS POWELL

Lewis Powell was appointed to the Supreme Court in 1971 by President Richard Nixon after a distinguished legal career that had included a term as president of the American Bar Association. His only previous political experience had been at the local level, as president of the Richmond, Virginia, Board of Education during the school desegregation era. Respected as a thoughtful, careful legal craftsman, Powell exercised considerable influence over case outcomes because his moderate views often gave him a crucial "swing" vote on a Court evenly divided between liberals and conservatives.

Mr. Justice **Powell** delivered the opinion of the Court.

. . . We must decide, first, whether the Texas system for financing public education operates to the disadvantage of some suspect class or impinges upon a fundamental right explicitly or implicitly protected by the Constitution, thereby requiring strict judicial scrutiny. If so, the judgment of the District Court should be affirmed. If not, the Texas scheme must still be examined to determine whether it rationally furthers some legitimate, articulated state purpose and therefore does not constitute an invidious discrimination in violation of the Equal Protection Clause of the Fourteenth Amendment.

. . .

The District Court's opinion does not reflect the novelty and complexity of the constitutional questions posed by appellees' challenge to Texas' system of school finance. In concluding that strict judicial scrutiny was required, that court relied on decisions dealing with the rights of indigents to equal treatment in the criminal trial and appellate processes, and on cases disapproving wealth restrictions on the right to vote. Those cases, the District Court concluded, established wealth as a suspect classification. Finding that the local property tax system discriminated on the basis of wealth, it regarded those precedents as controlling. It then reasoned, based on decisions of this Court affirming the undeniable

importance of education, that there is a fundamental right to education and that, absent some compelling state justification, the Texas system could not stand.

We are unable to agree that this case, which in significant aspects is *sui generis,* may be so neatly fitted into the conventional mosaic of constitutional analysis under the Equal Protection Clause. Indeed, for the several reasons that follow, we find neither the suspect classification nor the fundamental interest analysis persuasive.

. . .

The case comes to us with no definitive description of the classifying facts or delineation of the disfavored class. Examination of the District Court's opinion and of appellees' complaint, briefs, and contentions at oral argument suggests, however, at least three ways in which the discrimination claimed here might be described. The Texas system of school finance might be regarded as discriminating (1) against "poor" persons whose incomes fall below some identifiable level of poverty or who might be characterized as functionally "indigent," or (2) against those who are relatively poorer than others, or (3) against all those who, irrespective of their personal incomes, happen to reside in relatively poorer school districts. Our task must be to ascertain whether, in fact, the Texas system has been shown to discriminate on any of these possible bases. . . .

. . .

Only appellees' first possible basis for describing the class disadvantaged by the Texas school finance system discrimination against a class of definably "poor" persons might arguably meet the criteria established in . . . prior cases. Even a cursory examination, however, demonstrates that neither of the two distinguishing characteristics of wealth classifications can be found here. First, in support of their charge that the system discriminates against the "poor," appellees have made no effort to demonstrate that it operates to the peculiar disadvantage of any class fairly definable as indigent, or as composed of persons whose incomes are beneath any designated poverty level. Indeed, there is reason to believe that the poorest families are not necessarily clustered in the poorest property districts. A recent and exhaustive study of school districts in Connecticut concluded that "[i]t is clearly incorrect . . . to contend that the 'poor' live in 'poor' districts". . . . [T]he Connecticut study found, not surprisingly, that the poor were clustered around commercial and industrial areas—those same areas that provide the most attractive sources of property tax income for school districts. Whether a similar pattern would be discovered in Texas is not known, but there is no basis on the record in this case for assuming that the poorest people—defined by reference to any level of absolute impecunity—are concentrated in the poorest districts.

Second, neither appellees nor the District Court addressed the fact that . . . lack of personal resources has not occasioned an absolute deprivation of the desired benefit. The argument here is not that the children in districts having relatively low assessable property values are receiving no public education; rather, it is that they are receiving a poorer quality education than that available to children in districts having more assessable wealth. Apart from the unsettled and disputed question whether the quality of education may be determined by the amount of money expended for it, a sufficient answer to appellees' argument is that at least where wealth is involved the Equal Protection Clause does not require absolute equality or precisely equal advantages. Nor indeed, in view of the infinite variables affecting the educational process, can any system assure equal quality of education except in the most relative sense. Texas asserts that the Minimum Foundation Program provides an "adequate" education for all children in the State. By providing 12 years of free public school education, and by assuring teachers, books, transportation and operating funds, the Texas Legislature has endeavored to "guarantee, for the welfare of the state as a whole, that all people shall have at least an adequate program of education. This is what is meant by 'A Minimum Foundation Program of Education.'" The State repeatedly asserted in its briefs in this Court that it has fulfilled this desire and that it now assures "every child in every school district an adequate education." No proof was offered at trial persuasively discrediting or refuting the State's assertion.

For these two reasons—the absence of any evidence that the financing system discriminates against any definable category of "poor" people or that it results in the absolute deprivation of education—the disadvantaged class is not susceptible to identification in traditional terms.

[A]ppellees and the District Court may have embraced a second or third approach, the second of which might be characterized as a theory of relative or comparative discrimination based on family income. Appellees sought to prove that a direct correlation exists between the wealth of families within each district and the expenditures therein for education. That is, along a continuum, the poorer the family the lower the dollar amount of education received by the family's children.

The principal evidence adduced in support of this comparative discrimination claim is an affidavit submitted by Professor Joele S. Berke of Syracuse University's Educational Finance Policy Institute. The District Court, relying in major part upon this affidavit and apparently accepting the substance of appellees' theory, noted, first, a positive correlation between the wealth of school districts, measured in terms of assessable property per pupil, and their levels of per-pupil expenditures. Second, the court found a similar correlation between district wealth and the personal wealth of its residents, measured in terms of median family income.

If, in fact, these correlations could be sustained, then it might be argued that expenditures on education—equated by appellees to the quality of education—are dependent on personal wealth. Appellees' comparative discrimination theory would still face serious unanswered questions, including whether a bare positive correlation or some higher degree of correlation is necessary to provide a basis for concluding that the financing system is designated to operate to the peculiar disadvantage of the comparatively poor, and whether a class of this size and diversity could ever claim the special protection accorded "suspect" classes. These questions need not be addressed in this case, however, since appellees' proof fails to support their allegations or the District Court's conclusions. . . .

This brings us, then, to the third way in which the classification scheme might be defined—*district* wealth discrimination. Since the only correlation indicated by the evidence is between district property wealth and expenditures, it may be argued that discrimination might be found without regard to the individual income characteristics of district residents. Assuming a perfect correlation between district property wealth and expenditures from top to bottom, the disadvantaged class might be viewed as encompassing every child in every district except the district that has the most assessable wealth and spends the most on education. Alternatively, as suggested in Mr. Justice Marshall's dissenting opinion, the class might be defined more restrictively to include children in districts with assessable property which falls below the statewide average, or median, or below some other artificially defined level.

However described, it is clear that appellees' suit asks this Court to extend its most exacting scrutiny to review a system that allegedly discriminates against a large, diverse, and amorphous class, unified only by the common factor of residence in districts that happen to have less taxable wealth than other districts. The system of alleged discrimination and the class it defines have none of the traditional indicia of suspectness: the class is not saddled with such disabilities, or subjected to such a history of purposeful unequal treatment, or relegated to such a position of political powerlessness as to command extraordinary protection from the majoritarian political process.

. . . We thus conclude that the Texas system does not operate to the peculiar disadvantage of any suspect class. But in recognition of the fact that this Court has never heretofore held that wealth discrimination alone provides an adequate basis for invoking strict scrutiny, appellees have not relied solely on this contention. They also assert that the State's system impermissibly interferes with the exercise of a "fundamental" right and that accordingly the prior decisions of this Court require the application of the strict standard of judicial review. It is this question—whether education is a fundamental right, in the sense that it is among the rights and liberties protected by the Constitution—which has so consumed the attention of courts and commentators in recent years.

. . .

The lesson of [our] cases in addressing the question now before the Court is plain. It is not the province of this Court to create substantive constitutional rights in the name of guaranteeing equal protection of the laws. Thus the key to discovering whether education is "fundamental" is not to be found in comparisons of the relative societal significance of education as opposed to subsistence in housing. Nor is it to be found by weighing whether education is as important as the right to travel. Rather, the answer lies in assessing whether there is a right to education explicitly or implicitly guaranteed by the Constitution.

. . .

Education, of course, is not among the rights afforded explicit protection under our Federal Constitution. Nor do we find any basis for saying it is implicitly so protected. As we have said, the undisputed importance of education will not alone cause this Court to depart from the usual standard for reviewing a State's social and economic legislation. It is appellees' contention, however, that education is distinguishable from other services and benefits provided by the State because it bears a peculiarly close relationship to other rights and liberties accorded protection under the Constitution. Specifically, they insist that education is itself a fundamental personal right because it is essential to the effective exercise of First Amendment freedoms and to intelligent utilization of the right to vote. In asserting a nexus between speech and education, appellees urge that the right to speak is meaningless unless the speaker is capable of articulating his thoughts intelligently and persuasively. The "marketplace of ideas" is an empty forum for those lacking basic communicative tools. Likewise, they argue that the corollary right to receive information becomes little more than a hollow privilege when the recipient has not been taught to read, assimilate, and utilize available knowledge.

A similar line of reasoning is pursued with respect to the right to vote. . . .

We need not dispute any of these propositions. The Court has long afforded zealous protection against unjustifiable governmental interference with the individual's rights to speak and to vote. Yet we have never presumed to possess either the ability or the authority to guarantee to the citizenry the most *effective* speech or the most *informed* electoral choice. That these may be desirable goals of a system of freedom of expression and a representative form of government is not to be doubted. These are indeed goals to be pursued by a people whose thoughts and beliefs are freed from governmental interference. But they are not values to be implemented by judicial intrusion into otherwise legitimate state activities.

. . .

We need not rest our decision, however, solely on the inappropriateness of the strict scrutiny test. A century of Supreme Court adjudication under the Equal Protection Clause affirmatively supports the application of the traditional standard of review, which requires only that the State's system be shown to bear some rational relationship to legitimate state purposes. This case represents far more than a challenge to the manner in which Texas provides for the education of its children. We have here nothing less than a direct attack on the way in which Texas has chosen to raise and disburse state and local tax revenues. We are asked to condemn the State's judgment in conferring on political subdivisions the power to tax local property to supply revenues for local interests. In so doing,

appellees would have the Court intrude in an area in which it has traditionally deferred to state legislatures. This Court has often admonished against such interferences with the State's fiscal policies under the Equal Protection Clause. . . .

Thus we stand on familiar grounds when we continue to acknowledge that the Justices of this Court lack both the experience and the familiarity with local problems so necessary to the making of wise decisions with respect to the raising and disposition of public revenues. . . . No scheme of taxation, whether the tax is imposed on property, income, or purchases of goods and services, has yet been devised which is free of all discriminatory impact. In such a complex arena in which no perfect alternatives exist, the Court does well not to impose too rigorous a standard of scrutiny lest all local fiscal schemes become subjects of criticism under the Equal Protection Clause.

In addition to matters of fiscal policy, this case also involves the most persistent and difficult questions of educational policy, another area in which this Court's lack of specialized knowledge and experience counsels against premature interference with the informed judgments made at the state and local levels. Education, perhaps even more than welfare assistance, presents a myriad of "intractable economic, social, and even philosophical problems." The very complexity of the problems of financing and managing a statewide public school system suggest that "there will be more than one constitutionally permissible method of solving them," and that, within the limits of rationality, "the legislature's efforts to tackle the problems" should be entitled to respect. . . . In such circumstances the judiciary is well advised to refrain from interposing on the States inflexible constitutional restraints that could circumscribe or handicap the continued research and experimentation so vital to finding even partial solutions to educational problems and to keeping abreast of ever changing conditions.

. . .

Appellees further urge that the Texas system is unconstitutionally arbitrary because it allows the availability of local taxable resources to turn on "happenstance." They see no justification for a system that allows, as they contend, the quality of education to fluctuate on the basis of the fortuitous positioning of the boundary lines of political subdivisions and the location of valuable commercial and industrial property. But any scheme of local taxation—indeed the very existence of identifiable local governmental units—requires the establishment of jurisdictional boundaries that are inevitably arbitrary. It is equally inevitable that some localities are going to be blessed with more taxable assets than others. Nor is local wealth a static quantity. Changes in the level of taxable wealth within any district may result from any number of events, some of which local residents can and do influence. For instance, commercial and industrial enterprises may be encouraged to locate within a district by various actions—public and private.

Moreover, if local taxation for local expenditure is an unconstitutional method of providing for education then it may be an equally impermissible means of providing other necessary services customarily financed largely from local property taxes, including local police and fire protection, public health and hospitals, and public utility facilities of various kinds. We perceive no justification for such a severe denigration of local property taxation and control as would follow from appellees' contentions. It has simply never been within the constitutional prerogative of this Court to nullify statewide measures for financing public services merely because the burdens or benefits thereof fall unevenly depending upon the relative wealth of the political subdivisions in which citizens live.

In sum, to the extent that the Texas system of school finance results in unequal expenditures between children who happen to reside in different districts, we cannot say that such disparities are the product of a system that is so irrational as to be invidiously discriminary. . . . We are unwilling to assume for ourselves a level of wisdom superior to that of legislators, scholars, and educational authorities in 49 States, especially where the alternatives proposed are only recently conceived and nowhere yet tested. The constitutional standard under the Equal Protection Clause is whether the challenged state action rationally furthers a legitimate state purpose or

interest. We hold that the Texas plan abundantly satisfied this standard. . . .

Reversed.

Mr. Justice **Marshall,** with whom Mr. Justice **Douglas** joins, dissenting:

The Court today decides, in effect, that a State may constitutionally vary the quality of education which it offers its children in accordance with the amount of taxable wealth located in the school districts within which they reside. The majority's decision represents an abrupt departure from the mainstream of recent state and federal court decisions concerning the unconstitutionality of state educational financing schemes dependent upon taxable local wealth. More unfortunately, though, the majority's holding can only be seen as a retreat from our historic commitment to equality of educational opportunity and as unsupportable acquiescence in a system which deprives children in their earliest years of the change to reach their full potential as citizens. The Court does this despite the absence of any substantial justification for a scheme which arbitrarily channels educational resources in accordance with the fortuity of the amount of taxable wealth within each district.

In my judgment, the right of every American to an equal start in life, so far as the provision of a state service as important as education is concerned, is far too vital to permit state discrimination on grounds as tenuous as those presented by this record. Nor can I accept the notion that it is sufficient to remit these appellees to the vagaries of the political process which, contrary to the majority's suggestion, has proven singularly unsuited to the task of providing a remedy for this discrimination. I, for one, am unsatisfied with the hope of an ultimate "political" solution sometime in the indefinite future while, in the meantime, countless children unjustifiably receive inferior educations that "may affect their hearts and minds in a way unlikely ever to be undone." I must therefore respectfully dissent.

. . .

I believe it is sufficient that the over-arching form of discrimination in this case is between the school children of Texas on the basis of the taxable property wealth of the districts in which they happen to live. To understand both the precise nature of this discrimination and the parameters of the disadvantaged class it is sufficient to consider the constitutional principle which appellees contend is controlling in the context of educational financing. In their complaint appellees asserted that the Constitution does not permit local district wealth to be determinative of educational opportunity. This is simply another way of saying, as the District Court concluded, that consistent with the guarantee of equal protection of the laws, "the quality of public education may not be a function of wealth, other than the wealth of the state as a whole." Under such a principle, the children of a district are excessively advantaged if that district has more taxable property per pupil than the average amount of taxable property per pupil considering the State as a whole. By contrast, the children of a district are disadvantaged if that district has less taxable property per pupil than the state average. The majority attempts to disparage such a definition of the disadvantaged class as the product of an "artificially defined level" of district wealth. But such is clearly not the case, for this is the definition unmistakably dictated by the constitutional principle for which appellees have argued throughout the course of this litigation. And I do not believe that a clearer definition of either the disadvantaged class of Texas school children or the allegedly unconstitutional discrimination suffered by the members of that class under the present Texas financing scheme could be asked for, much less needed. Whether this discrimination, against the school children of property poor districts, inherent in the Texas financing scheme is violative of the Equal Protection Clause is the question to which we must now turn.

. . .

To begin, I must once more voice my disagreement with the Court's rigidified approach to equal protection analysis. The Court apparently seeks to establish today that equal protection cases fall into one of two neat categories which dictate the appropriate standard of review—strict scrutiny or mere rationality. But this Court's decisions in the field of equal protection defy such easy categorization. A principled reading of what this Court has done reveals that it has applied a spectrum of standards in reviewing discrimination allegedly violative of the Equal Protection Clause. This spectrum clearly comprehends variations in the degree of care with which the Court will scrutinize particular classifications, depending, I believe, on the constitutional and societal importance of the interest adversely affected and the recognized invidiousness of the basis upon which the particular classification is drawn. I find in fact that many of the Court's recent decisions embody the very sort of reasoned approach to equal protection analysis for which I previously argued—that is, an approach in which "concentration [is] placed upon the character of the classification in question, the relative importance to the individuals in the class discriminated against of the governmental benefits that they do not receive, and the asserted state interests in support of the classification."

I therefore cannot accept the majority's labored efforts to demonstrate that fundamental interests, which call for strict scrutiny of the challenged classification, encompass only established rights which we are somehow bound to recognize from the text of the Constitution itself. To be sure, some interests which the Court has deemed to be fundamental for purposes of equal protection analysis are themselves constitutionally protected rights. . . . But it will not do to suggest that the "answer" to whether an interest is fundamental for purposes of equal protection analysis is *always* determined by whether that interest "is a right . . . explicitly or implicitly guaranteed by the Constitution."

. . .

Aftermath of San Antonio Independent School District *v.* Rodriguez

The Supreme Court's decision in *Rodriguez* was a victory for conservative restraint, and caused state officials to breath a collective sigh of relief. Although the case had focused a great deal of attention on the issue of school financing and generated considerable pressure for reform, the process could now proceed at a more measured pace than would have been possible had the Court declared wealth-based school financing laws unconstitutional. A handful of states moved with dispatch to develop new funding schemes that reduced the effects of local tax-base disparities on educational expenditures, but elsewhere the process soon bogged down. In the mid-1970s, with the help of the Ford Foundation and other school reform-minded organizations, parents' groups began a new round of litigation to spur state officials to action. This time, however, the cases were filed in state rather than federal courts. Most state constitutions have "equal protection" provisions much like the Fourteenth Amendment's, and a number of state constitutions explicitly define education as a right to which all citizens are equally entitled. Three years before *Rodriguez,* the California Supreme Court had struck down that state's school financing law citing the equal protection guarantees of both the United States and the California constitutions. In the following decade, a substantial number of state supreme courts followed suit. In 1989 the Texas Supreme Court, in a case whose plaintiffs included Demetrio Rodriguez, found that the state's school finance law violated the Texas constitution. Two years later a new law, passed after four special sessions of the state legislature, was also struck down by the state supreme court.

3   Structural Conflicts: Federalism and Separation of Powers

ince the initiation of judicial review in *Marbury* v. *Madison* in 1803, the Court has policed the boundaries of state and national authority (federalism), as well as the boundaries of executive, legislative, and judicial authority (the separation of powers). Our purpose in this chapter is to illustrate those conflicts by appropriate cases placed in historical context.

FEDERALISM

The federal system, like the written Constitution itself, was an American invention, a creative, novel approach by eighteenth-century statesmen to the art and science of government. The idea of having several local governmental units organized around a central authority was not without precedent. Such an arrangement, called a confederation or confederacy, could be found in several European states. Until the adoption of the U.S. Constitution, however, the local units in such confederations had always retained their full autonomy or sovereignty, with the central governing apparatus being simply a pivot around which a group of individual states organized themselves for the purpose of collective action in a few precisely defined areas. This central government had no power to coerce individual citizens, and any member state could remove itself from the confederation at will.

In the newly created American version the central government was granted specific powers, the local units (states) retained traditional governing powers, and both governments were prohibited from exercising certain powers altogether. Some of the framers wished to abolish the states entirely, a practical impossibility since the states in 1787 were already going concerns with deeply rooted political cultures. With some justification, the states considered themselves the guardians of popular government and individual rights, a role which they were loathe to surrender to an all-encompassing central government. Thus, American federalism was in one sense a political compromise. But it was also a structural formula with strong theoretical underpinnings, intended to limit power at all levels of government and to create barriers against arbitrariness and despotism. American federalism was a design for a constitutional system that was intended to be permanent and was arrived at after much deliberation and debate, but how it would work, or even *whether* it would work, could not be known by its architects in 1787. Time was to validate this bold, creative enterprise of the nation's founders, but there were moments when even the most optimistic of statesmen were uncertain that the federal union would remain intact. The Supreme Court, despite some egregious errors in judgment, has played a paramount role in settling the inevitable conflicts that arise in a federal system between the states and the central government, and thus has contributed markedly to the stability and permanence of the Constitution of the United States.

With respect to federalism there are two aspects of judicial power at issue. One involves the conflict between state and federal laws, the other between state laws and the mandates of the Constitution. Before beginning to function as an umpire in conflicts between the national and state governments, the Supreme Court had to establish its constitutional authority to play such a role. In *Marbury* v. *Madison*, the Court had announced its intention to act as a constitutional watchdog over acts of Congress, and in 1809, in its decision in *United States* v. *Judge Peters*, the Court first strongly asserted federal judicial power over state authority as well. The latter case had its origin in a dispute under the Articles of Confederation, when the old Court of Appeals had awarded Gideon Olmstead a prize claim which his home state of Pennsylvania then refused to honor. When some years later, pursuant to Supreme Court authorization, a federal district judge ordered that the prize money be paid to Olmstead, an obdurate Pennsylvania legislature still refused to comply. Olmstead then obtained a *mandamus* from the Supreme Court compelling the judge to enforce his decision. In awarding the *mandamus*, John Marshall declared that the ultimate right to determine the jurisdiction of the federal courts resided in the Supreme Court and not in the state legislatures. In Marshall's words:

> If the legislatures of the several states may, at will, annul the judgments of the courts of the United States, and destroy the rights acquired under those judgments, the constitution itself becomes a solemn mockery . . . the people of Pennsylvania, not less than the citizens of every other state, must feel a deep interest in resisting principles so destructive of the union and in averting consequences so fatal to themselves.

When the United States marshal attempted to serve process against the holders of the prize money, he was met by the state militia, an incident which came close to causing bloodshed. Ultimately the Pennsylvania legislature ungraciously acquiesced by issuing a resolution recognizing national supremacy, while maintaining that it would not tolerate an infringement of states' rights by an unconstitutional exercise of power in United States courts.

This serious controversy between the Supreme Court and Pennsylvania was the first in a series of battles between the states and the Court over the proper spheres of power in the new federal system. By 1820 the Court had invalidated laws in seven states and by 1825 in 10 states. Of special significance were the cases of *Cohens* v. *Virginia* and *Green* v. *Biddle*, which were handed down during the 1821 and 1823 terms. These cases pitted Virginia and Kentucky against the Supreme Court, but as in many such cases the issue was more that of national supremacy than of judicial sovereignty. What propelled the relatively insignificant *Cohens* case into one of crucial national importance was Chief Justice

Marshall's insistence—over Virginia's vehement protest—that the Supreme Court had jurisdiction in the case. The Cohen brothers, who had been fined for selling lottery tickets in violation of state law, maintained that an act of Congress authorizing a lottery in the District of Columbia protected their commercial activities in Virginia. Upholding the Cohens' conviction, Marshall observed that Congress had no intention of applying the ordinance beyond the confines of Washington. In this respect Virginia was vindicated. But in dealing with the more significant question of jurisdiction, Marshall used the case as an occasion to declare that nothing in the Constitution, including the Eleventh Amendment which prohibits nonconsenting suits between a state and a citizen of another state, precludes the appearance of a state as a defendant-in-error in the Supreme Court. Once a state initiates a suit against a citizen of another state, the outcome may involve an appeal to the Supreme Court in which the state becomes the defendant. Said Marshall in answer to the states' rights arguments:

> We think that in a government acknowledgedly supreme, with respect to objects of vital interest to the nation, there is nothing inconsistent with sound reason, nothing incompatible with the nature of government, in making all its departments supreme, so far as respects those objects, and so far as necessary to their attainment. The exercise of appellate power over those judgments of the state tribunals which may contravene the constitution or laws of the United States, is, we believe, essential to the attainment of those objects.

In *Green* v. *Biddle*, the ordinance creating the separate states of Virginia and Kentucky had specified that all private rights and interests in Kentucky lands derived from the laws of Virginia should be determined by the laws then in force in Virginia. Kentucky, however, in order to settle disputed land claims, enacted statutes providing somewhat different rules governing land occupancy and claimants' rights. Holding the Kentucky laws unconstitutional, the Supreme Court maintained that the agreement between Kentucky and Virginia was a contract, and as such, was entitled to protection under the Constitution. As in the *Cohens* case, the Court in *Green* simultaneously asserted the principle of national supremacy and reinforced its own role as arbiter of conflicts arising under the federal system.

These decisions set off a series of debates in Congress over the nature of the Union that continued until John Marshall's death in 1835. During this period many proposals were set forth which would have curbed the judiciary in its role as umpire of the federal system. The most serious of these were bills that would have removed appellate jurisdiction from the Supreme Court in cases involving the states. Other proposals introduced for consideration included subjecting federal judges to removal by votes of both houses of Congress, limiting judicial tenure, vesting final appellate authority in the Senate, and requiring a vote of at least five of the then seven justices to render a state law invalid. Although the states were exercised over the Supreme Court's construction of the Constitution, there was little agreement on what *method* should be used to curb the judiciary. As a result, none of the suggested proposals became law.

With a few notable exceptions such as *McCulloch* v. *Maryland* (excerpted in this chapter), the early cases during the Marshall years, as well as those heard by the Court while Roger B. Taney was chief justice (1836–1864), did not involve conflicts between state and federal laws. They involved instead the matching of state statutes against prohibitions in the Constitution itself, particularly the contract clause of Article I. Thus the Court's decisions in such cases did much to order the role of the states in the federal system in the first half of the nineteenth century. Later the slavery issue and the Court's failure to deal with it in the *Dred Scott* case brought unprecedented criticism upon the judicial branch and almost resulted in curtailment of its powers. Ironically, after the Civil War the Court as referee of the federal system emerged stronger than ever, primarily because the adoption of the Fourteenth Amendment placed at the Court's disposal a new weapon with which to contain state power.

From the 1870s until the turn of the century the Court tended to uphold state authority over business enterprises against challenges brought under the contract clause and under the new due process clause of the Fourteenth Amendment. State power was restricted only in a few instances where it was found to conflict with congressional authority under the commerce clause. In the twentieth century, however, the Fourteenth Amendment became the primary mechanism for judicially readjusting national and state spheres of authority as the Supreme Court began to place greater and greater curbs on state power by invalidating state laws, first in the economic sphere and then in all areas of due process and equal protection.

With respect to the other aspect of federalism, the conflict between state and federal laws, until 1937 the Court had intermittently decided cases on the basis of a doctrine called *dual federalism,* which held that the Tenth Amendment to the Constitution was an implied limit on national power. Such an interpretation of the federal system enabled the Court to annul federal laws validly enacted under a delegated power such as commerce or taxation on the ground that they had encroached upon state prerogatives. That is, the national and state governments were viewed as equal sovereigns operating within strictly defined spheres.

During the past half century the Court, however, has looked favorably upon national programs that involve state participation in federally controlled projects. Known as *cooperative federalism,* these programs have embraced matters as diverse as highway construction, welfare, and education. Once the states agreed to participate, they received federal money, but with the largesse has come control from Washington, control that has penetrated deeply into areas once assumed to be exclusively the domain of state authority. For example, the national government was able to coerce the states to enact lower speed limits on interstate highways with the threat of loss of federal funds, a policy upheld by the Supreme Court in *South Dakota* v. *Dole* (1987), bringing to mind the old adage that he who pays the piper calls the tune. In fact, in the view of many observers the states have become what some of the framers had hoped for and others had feared from the beginning: administrative units of a supreme national government. On the whole the Supreme Court has deferred to an expansive national power at the expense of the states. Even with the much-trumpeted efforts by President Reagan to diminish national power, and with the Court's returning some aspects of the abortion question to state control in the 1980s, the national government today remains very much the engine of policy-making in the United States.

Congress at any time could have limited the Court's power of judicial review over state laws but has never done so. Why not? Acting as a restraint on Congress in the early years was a Court constituency that respected a judicially formulated rule of law and stood to profit from a stable national government. Combined with this was the realization by the intellectual leadership of the country that only under a strong national government could the nation's destiny as envisioned by the framers be fulfilled. They had early taken to heart the wise words of Alexander Hamilton in *The Federalist* no. 80:

> What, for instance, would avail restrictions on the authority of the State legislatures without some constitutional mode of enforcing them? The States, by the plan of the convention, are prohibited from doing a variety of things, some of which are incompatible with the interests of the Union, and others with the principles of government. . . . No man of sense will believe that such prohibitions would be scrupulously regarded without some effectual power in the government to restrain or correct infractions of them. This power must either be a direct negative on the State laws or an authority in the federal courts to overrule such as might be in manifest contravention of the articles of Union. There is no third course that I can imagine. The latter appears to have been thought by the convention preferable to the former.

By the mid-twentieth century, despite the outcries of those who were aggrieved by individual decisions of the Court, a national consensus was so firmly in place that a majority could never be mustered to alter the Supreme Court's role. Even under extremely hostile pressures following rulings with multifarious social implications, such as desegregation, criminal procedure, legislative appointments, and abortion, all of which in a constitutional sense placed strong limits on state authority, the Court was not curbed. As Justice Robert Jackson concluded in 1941:

> It is now an accepted part of our constitutional doctrine that conflicts between state legislation and the federal Constitution are to be resolved by the Supreme Court, and had it not been, it is difficult to see how the Union could have survived.

Our cases demonstrate primarily the manner in which the Supreme Court viewed the federal system in the early stages of constitutional interpretation under John Marshall. In two of Marshall's greatest opinions, *McCulloch* v. *Maryland* and *Gibbons* v. *Ogden,* he established the principle that when both the state and federal governments are acting within their proper spheres, conflicts must be resolved in favor of the nation. In *Dartmouth College* v. *Woodward* he gave expansive meaning to the contract clause in order to restrain state power. In *Garcia* v. *San Antonio Metropolitan Transit Authority* one can see the disparate views of the current justices on the constitutional requirements of federalism in the contemporary context.

SEPARATION OF POWERS

In the minds of the framers of the Constitution the separation of powers was, like federalism, a structural defense against tyranny. Taken together, the vertical division of powers between states and nation and the horizontal separation of power among three branches—executive, legislative and judicial—created a formidable barrier to the concentration of power in a single part of a complex system. The framers were familiar with the French political philosopher Montesquieu's classic work, *The Spirit of the Laws,* in which the author warned that there can be no liberty when legislative and executive powers are united in the same person or in the same body of magistrates *and* when judicial power is not separated from both. It may be that Montesquieu simply confirmed what American political leaders of the late eighteenth century had already come to believe as a result of their troubled prerevolutionary experiences, since all of the state constitutions in force prior to the adoption of the national document reflected the principle of separation of powers.

Article I of the Constitution vests "all legislative power herein granted" in Congress; Article II vests "the executive power" in the President; Article III vests "the judicial power" in the federal courts. While all three articles describe the operational dominion of each of the government's branches, the text of Article I is the most expansive in that it grants specific powers to Congress, places limits in some instances on the manner in which a power is to be exercised (no suspension of the writ of habeas corpus except in cases of rebellion, invasion, or threat to the public safety) and prohibits Congress absolutely from enacting certain specified laws (bills of attainder, ex post facto laws, taxes on exports).

Certainly the most loosely constructed article is that governing presidential power since it sets no boundaries to executive prerogatives or to presidential discretion. In the words of the great constitutional scholar, Edward S. Corwin, executive power "is still indefinite as to *function* and retains, particularly when it is exercised by a single individual, much of its original plasticity as regards method." He suggests that to those who think a constitution ought to settle all public issues, Article II is a "nightmare," but for those who believe that a constitution should retain great flexibility, the executive article is a "vision realized."

In Article III the judicial branch is dealt with more briefly, although less vaguely, than the executive. In the article's first section, directing Congress to create a Supreme Court and, at its discretion, a system of federal courts, it authorizes the lifetime appointment of judges but says nothing about qualifications for office or the size of the Court. In the remaining two sections the article deals with jurisdiction, impeachment, and a definition of treason. Although nothing is said about the possibility of the Supreme Court's being the guarantor of the integrity of the separation of powers, it was an unconstitutional encroachment by Congress upon the judicial branch that was at issue in *Marbury* v. *Madison.* In this instance the Court was simply protecting its own sphere of authority, and it was always assumed by the framers, and even by Anti-Federalists like Jefferson, that each branch would always possess that self-protective ability. Only after many decades would the Supreme Court assume a referee function vis-à-vis Congress and the presidency.

In contrast to constitutional issues growing out of discord in the federal system, relatively few conflicts in which executive invasion of legislative prerogative or the reverse have reached the Court for resolution, but more usually have found solution in the political process. At the same time the Court has decided numerous cases arising in the context of the misuse of presidential and/or congressional power that allegedly resulted in harm to individual interests. Although some of the framers supported the separate, three-branch structure on grounds of efficiency, for most of the founding fathers, the system was a means of avoiding despotism. In 1927 Justice Louis Brandeis wrote in *Myers* v. *United States,* "The doctrine of the separation of powers was adopted by the Convention of 1787, not to promote efficiency but to preclude the exercise of arbitrary power. The purpose was, not to avoid friction, but, by means of the inevitable friction incident to the distribution of governmental powers among the three departments, to save the people from autocracy."

When deciding cases involving conflicts among the executive, legislative, and judicial branches, the Supreme Court is in a very different position politically than when it acts as umpire of the federal system. In the latter role it decides which of two conflicting authorities is paramount and, since the states are represented in Congress, the Court cannot expect support from the states' representatives when it diminishes state power. Indeed, we have seen that members of the House and Senate frequently have expressed loyalty and sympathy to the states that they represent rather than to a somewhat abstract national constituency. Theoretically, the Supreme Court does not represent either the nation or the states but is accountable to the Constitution and the laws made pursuant to it.

When rendering judgment on the proper scope of executive or legislative authority, the Court is in a somewhat different position since it frequently curbs the excesses of one branch on behalf of the constitutional prerogatives of the other. When acting with the support of one of its equal branches, the Court is in the advantageous position of being in the majority of two against one. When, however, the Court decides that the other two branches have *jointly* acted unconstitutionally, those "two" become an alliance of the President and Congress against the "one" judicial branch, putting the Court at an institutional disadvantage. Throughout its history the Court has tended to sidestep or finesse issues that would place its authority and prestige in jeopardy through confrontations with the executive and legislative branches acting cooperatively, as in times of war and other national emergencies.

Cases involving the separation of powers begin with *Myers* v. *United States,* which demonstrates the reluctance of the Supreme Court to interfere with the procedural aspects of presidential power. *Myers* was directly concerned with the scope of executive power left undefined by the Constitution, and the alliance in this instance was Court and President against Congress. *United States* v. *Belmont* similarly involved a broad construction of presidential authority—specifically in foreign affairs—with the President obviously in agreement with the Court. In *McGrain* v. *Daugherty* the Court approved a broad authority in a congressional procedure—legislative investigations—with Court and Congress now in alliance against the executive. In *Korematsu* v. *United States* we see the Court's deference to the executive in wartime, in this instance buttressed by overwhelming congressional support. In an uncharacteristic stance the Court in *Schechter Poultry Corporation* v. *United States* boldly challenged the executive-legislative New Deal coalition, but it retreated within 2 years to the more usual deferential posture in *National Labor Relations Board* v. *Jones and Laughlin Steel Corporation.* In *Youngstown Sheet and Tube Corporation* v. *Sawyer* the Court relied implicitly on congressional support for its ruling that President Harry Truman had overstepped his constitutional and statutory authority. This same pattern is discernible in *United States* v. *Nixon*—Congress being in agreement with the decision—when the Court ruled against the President, although the Court's deference to the principle of executive privilege transformed a defeat for a sitting President into a victory for the presidency. The *Nixon* case, incidentally, is a good illustration of the Court's institutional independence, given the fact that none of the three Nixon appointees who participated in the decision (Warren Burger, Lewis Powell, and Harry Blackmun) voted to support the President.

In the remaining cases, the Court was again politically in a more comfortable position in this two-against-one alliance as it curbed powers in one branch with the support of the other. In *Immigration and Naturalization Service* v. *Chadha* and *Bowsher* v. *Synar,* the Court espoused the cause of the executive branch as it invalidated a stronghold of congressional authority, the legislative veto, and declared unconstitutional a provision of the Gramm-Rudman Act which assigned the comptroller general, an agent of Congress, the duty of executing budget reductions (*Bowsher*). Supporting the position of Congress is the holding in *Morrison* v. *Olson,* which sustained a provision of the Ethics in Government Act permitting the judicial appointment of an "independent counsel" to investigate alleged criminal behavior in the executive department.

Bibliography

CHOPER, JESSE H. *Judicial Review and the National Political Process.* Chicago: University of Chicago Press, 1980.

CORWIN, EDWARD S. *The President: Office and Powers.* New York: New York University Press, 1948.

FISHER, LOUIS. *Constitutional Conflicts Between Congress and the President.* Princeton: Princeton University Press, 1985.

GOLDWIN, ROBERT A., and Schambra, WILLIAM A. *How Federal Is the Constitution?* Washington, D.C.: American Enterprise Institute, 1982.

GOLDWIN, ROBERT A., and KAUFMAN, ART. *Separation of Powers: Does It Still Work?* Washington, D.C.: American Enterprise Institute, 1986.

IRONS, PETER. *The Courage of Their Convictions.* New York: The Free Press, 1988.

MCDONALD, FORREST. *Novus Ordo Seclorum: The Intellectual Origins of the Constitution.* Lawrence, Kans.: University of Kansas Press, 1985.

POLSBY, NELSON W. *Congress and the Presidency,* 3d ed. Englewood Cliffs, N.J.: Prentice-Hall, 1976.

PRITCHETT, C. HERMAN. *Constitutional Law of the Federal System.* Englewood Cliffs, N.J.: Prentice-Hall, 1984.

McCulloch v. Maryland

4 WHEATON 316 (1819)

In the context of constitutional history *McCulloch* v. *Maryland,* like most landmark cases, arose out of political controversy and it is paramount among those decisions that reflect the bold genius of Chief Justice John Marshall.

As part of Alexander Hamilton's financial plan, a national bank was chartered in 1791 for a period of 20 years. Despite the important services it rendered, political pressures, in part from competing state banks, were sufficient to prevent renewal of the charter and the bank went out of business. A few years of financial troubles, however, convinced a majority of Congress and the President that a national banking institution was essential to the efficient functioning of the national government, and a second bank was chartered in 1816. Neither the original nor the new bank was wholly government-owned, the United States subscribing to only 20 percent of its stock and appointing one-fifth of its directors. In its operation, however, the bank had special fiscal relationships with the government which were profitable for both the bank and the United States.

Inevitably, the bank ran into conflicts with local financial institutions, in part by overlending and then calling on state banks to redeem their notes. State banks in turn pressed their debtors, and state legislatures, responding to demands of their constituents, enacted restrictive laws against the United States Bank. Some measures prohibited any bank chartered outside the state from doing business within its borders; others levied heavy taxes on branches of the United States Bank within the state. Maryland took the latter course. When McCulloch, a cashier of the Baltimore branch, failed to comply with requirements of the Maryland law, a suit was begun which eventually reached the Supreme Court.

Marshall, Ch. J., delivered the opinion of the court:

In the case now to be determined, the defendant, a sovereign state, denies the obligation of a law enacted by the legislature of the Union and the plaintiff, on his part, contests the validity of an act which has been passed by the legislature of that state. The constitution of our country, in its most interesting and vital parts, is to be considered; the conflicting powers of the government of the Union and of its members, as marked in that constitution, are to be discussed; and an opinion given, which may essentially influence the great operations of the government. No tribunal can approach such a question without a deep sense of its importance, and of the awful responsibility involved in its decision. But it must be decided peacefully, or remain a source of hostile legislation, perhaps of hostility of a still more serious nature; and if it is to be so decided, by this tribunal alone can the decision be made. On the Supreme Court of the United States has the constitution of our country devolved this important duty.

The first question made in the cause is, has Congress power to incorporate a bank?

It has been truly said that this can scarcely be considered as an open question, entirely unprejudiced by the former proceedings of the nation respecting it. The principle now contested was introduced at a very early period of our history, has been recognized by many successive legislatures, and has been acted upon by the judicial department, in cases of peculiar delicacy, as a law of undoubted obligation.

It will not be denied that a bold and daring usurpation might be resisted, after an acquiescence still longer and more complete than this. But it is conceived that a doubtful question, one on which human reason may pause, and the human judgment be suspended, in the decision of which the great principles of liberty are not concerned, but the respective powers of those who are equally the representatives of the people, are to be adjusted; if not put at rest by the practice of the government, ought to receive a considerable impression from that practice. An exposition of the constitution, deliberately established by the legislative acts, on the faith of which an immense property has been advanced, ought not to be lightly disregarded.

. . .

In discussing this question, the counsel for the state of Maryland have deemed it of some importance, in the construction of the constitution, to consider that instrument not as emanating from the people, but as the act of sovereign and independent states. The powers of the general government, it has been said, are delegated by the states, who alone are truly sovereign; and must be exercised in subordination to the states, who alone possess supreme dominion.

It would be difficult to sustain this proposition. The convention which framed the constitution was indeed elected by the state legislatures. But the instrument, when it came from their hands, was a mere proposal, without obligation, or pretensions to it. It was reported to the then existing Congress of the United States, with a request that it might "be submitted to a convention of delegates, chosen in each state by the people thereof, under the recommendation of its legislature, for their assent and ratification." This mode of proceeding was adopted; and by the convention, by Congress, and by the state legislatures, the instrument was submitted to the people. They acted upon it in the only manner in which they can act safely, effectively, and wisely, on such a subject, by assembling in convention. It is true, they assembled in their several states—and where else should they have assembled? No political dreamer was ever wild enough to think of breaking down the lines which separate the states, and of compounding the American people into one common mass. Of consequence, when they act, they act in their states. But the measures they adopt do not, on that account, cease to be the measures of the people themselves, or become the measures of the state governments.

From these conventions the constitution derives its whole authority. The government proceeds directly from the people; is "ordained and established" in the name of the people; and is declared to be ordained, "in order to form a more perfect union, establish justice, insure domestic tranquillity, and secure the blessings of liberty to themselves and to their posterity." The assent of the states, in their sovereign capacity, is implied in calling a convention, and thus submitting that instrument to the people. But the people were at perfect liberty to accept or reject it; and their act was final. It required not the affirmance, and could not be negatived, by the state governments. The constitution, when thus adopted, was of complete obligation, and bound the state sovereignties.

It has been said that the people had already surrendered all their powers to the state sovereignties, and had nothing more to give. But, surely, the question whether they may resume and modify the powers granted to government does not remain to be settled in this country. Much more might the legitimacy of the general government be doubted, had it been created by the states. The powers delegated to the state sovereignties were to be exercised by themselves, not by a distinct and independent sovereignty, created by themselves. To the formation of a league, such as was the confederation, the state sovereignties were certainly competent. But when, "in order to form a more perfect union," it was deemed necessary to change this alliance into an effective government, possessing great and sovereign powers, and acting directly on the people, the necessity of referring it to the people, and of deriving its powers directly from them, was felt and acknowledged by all.

The government of the Union, then (whatever may be the influence of this fact on the case), is, emphatically, and truly, a government of the people. In form and in substance it emanates from them. Its powers are granted by them, and are to be exercised directly on them, and for their benefit.

This government is acknowledged by all to be one of enumerated powers. The principle, that it can exercise only the powers granted to it, would seem too apparent to have required to be enforced by all those arguments which its enlightened friends, while it was depending before the people, found it necessary to urge. That principle is now universally admitted. But the question respecting the extent of the powers actually granted, is perpetually arising, and will probably continue to arise, as long as our system shall exist.

In discussing these questions, the conflicting powers of the general and state governments must be brought into view, and the supremacy of their respective laws, when they are in opposition, must be settled.

If any one proposition could command the universal assent of mankind, we might expect it would be this—that the government of the Union, though limited in its powers, is supreme within its sphere of action. This would seem to result necessarily from its nature. It is the government of all; its powers are delegated by all; it represents all, and acts for all. Though any one state may be willing to control its operations, no state is willing to allow others to control them. The nation, on those subjects on which it can act, must necessarily bind its component parts.

. . .

Among the enumerated powers, we do not find that of establishing a bank or creating a corporation. But there is no phrase in the instrument which, like the articles of confederation, excludes incidental or implied powers; and which requires that everything granted shall be expressly and minutely described.

. . .

A constitution, to contain an accurate detail of all the subdivisions of which its great powers will admit, and of all the means by which they may be carried into execution, would partake of a prolixity of a legal code, and could scarcely be embraced by the human mind. It would probably never be understood by the public. Its nature, therefore, requires, that only its great outlines should be marked, its important objects designated, and the minor ingredients which compose those objects be deduced from the nature of the objects themselves. That this idea was entertained by the framers of the American constitution, is not only to be inferred from the nature of the instrument, but from the language. Why else were some of the limitations, found in the ninth section of the 1st article, introduced? It is also, in some degree, warranted by their having omitted to use any restrictive term which might prevent its receiving a fair and just interpretation. In considering this question, then, we must never forget that it is a constitution we are expounding.

Although, among the enumerated powers of government, we do not find the word "bank" or "incorporation," we find the great powers to lay and collect taxes; to borrow money; to regulate commerce; to declare and conduct a war; and to raise and support armies and navies. The sword and the purse, all the external relations, and no inconsiderable portion of the industry of the nation, are entrusted to its government. It can never be pretended that these vast powers draw after them others of inferior importance, merely because they are inferior. Such an idea can never be advanced. But it may with great reason be contended, that a government, entrusted with such ample powers, on the due execution of which the happiness and prosperity of the nation so vitally depends, must also be entrusted with ample means for their execution.

. . .

But the constitution of the United States has not left the right of Congress to employ the necessary means for the execution of the powers conferred on the government to general reasoning. To its enumeration of powers is added that of making "all laws which shall be necessary and proper, for carrying into execution the foregoing powers, and all other powers vested by this constitution, in the government of the United States, or in any department thereof."

The counsel for the State of Maryland have urged various arguments, to prove that this clause, though in terms a grant of power, is not so in effect; but is really restrictive of the general right, which might otherwise be implied, of selecting means for executing the enumerated powers.

. . .

But the argument on which most reliance is placed, is drawn from the peculiar language of this clause. Congress is not empowered by it to make all laws, which may have relation to the powers conferred on the government, but such only as may be "necessary and proper" for carrying them into execution. The word "necessary" is considered as controlling the whole sentence, and as limiting the right to pass laws for the exe-

cution of the granted powers, to such as are indispensable, and without which the power would be nugatory. That it excludes the choice of means, and leaves to Congress, in each case, that only which is most direct and simple.

Is it true that this is the sense in which the word "necessary" is always used? Does it always import an absolute physical necessity, so strong that one thing, to which another may be termed necessary, cannot exist without that other? We think it does not. If reference be had to its use, in the common affairs of the world, or in approved authors, we find that it frequently imports no more than that one thing is convenient, or useful, or essential to another. To employ the means necessary to an end, is generally understood as employing any means calculated to produce the end, and not as being confined to those single means, without which the end would be entirely unattainable. Such is the character of human language, that no word conveys to the mind, in all situations, one single definite idea; and nothing is more common than to use words in a figurative sense. Almost all compositions contain words, which, taken in their rigorous sense, would convey a meaning different from that which is obviously intended. It is essential to just construction, that many words which import something excessive should be understood in a more mitigated sense—in that sense which common usage justifies. The word "necessary" is of this description. It has not a fixed character peculiar to itself. It admits of all degrees of comparison; and is often connected with other words, which increase or diminish the impression the mind receives of the urgency it imports. A thing may be necessary, very necessary, absolutely or indispensably necessary. To no mind would the same idea be conveyed by these several phrases. This comment on the word is well illustrated by the passage cited at the bar, from the 10th section of the 1st article of the constitution. It is, we think, impossible to compare the sentence which prohibits a state from laying "imposts or duties on imports or exports, except what may be absolutely necessary for executing its inspection laws," with that which authorizes Congress "to make all laws which shall be necessary and proper for carrying into execution" the powers of the general government, without feeling a conviction that the convention understood itself to change material-ly the meaning of the word "necessary," by prefixing the word "absolutely." This word, then, like others, is used in various senses; and, in its construction, the subject, the context, the inten-tion of the person using them, are all to be taken into view.

Let this be done in the case under considera-tion. The subject is the execution of those great powers on which the welfare of a nation essen-tially depends. It must have been the intention of those who gave these powers, to insure, as far as human prudence could insure, their bene-ficial execution. This could not be done by confiding the choice of means to such narrow limits as not to leave it in the power of Congress to adopt any which might be appropriate, and which were conducive to the end. This provision is made in a constitution intended to endure for ages to come, and, consequently, to be adapted to the various crises of human affairs. To have prescribed the means by which government should, in all future time, execute its powers, would have been to change, entirely, the charac-ter of the instrument, and give it the properties of a legal code. It would have been an unwise attempt to provide, by immutable rules, for exi-gencies which, if foreseen at all, must have been seen dimly, and which can be best provided for as they occur. To have declared that the best means shall not be used, but those alone without which the power given would be nugatory, would have been to deprive the legislature of the capacity to avail itself of experience, to exercise its reason, and to accommodate its legislation to circumstances.

. . .

Take, for example, the power "to establish post-offices and post-roads." This power is exe-cuted by the single act of making the establish-ment. But, from this has been inferred the power and duty of carrying the mail along the post-road, from one post-office to another. And, from this implied power, has again been inferred the right to punish those who steal let-ters from the post-office, or rob the mail. It may be said, with some plausibility, that the right to carry the mail, and to punish those who rob it, is

not indispensably necessary to the establishment of a post-office and post-road. This right is indeed essential to the beneficial exercise of the power, but not indispensably necessary to its existence. So, of the punishment of the crimes of stealing or falsifying a record or process of a court of the United States, or of perjury in such court. To punish these offenses is certainly con-ducive to the due administration of justice. But courts may exist, and may decide the causes brought before them, though such crimes escape punishment.

. . .

In ascertaining the sense in which the word "necessary" is used in this clause of the constitu-tion, we may derive some aid from that with which it is associated. Congress shall have power "to make all laws which shall be neces-sary and proper to carry into execution" the powers of the government. If the word "neces-sary" was used in that strict and rigorous sense for which the counsel for the state of Maryland contend, it would be an extraordinary departure from the usual course of the human mind, as exhibited in composition, to add a word, the only possible effect of which is to qualify that strict and rigorous meaning; to present to the mind the idea of some choice of means of legis-lation not straightened and compressed within the narrow limits for which gentlemen contend.

But the argument which most conclusively demonstrates the error of the construction con-tended for by the counsel for the state of Maryland, is founded on the intention of the convention, as manifested in the whole clause. To waste time and argument in proving that without it Congress might carry its powers into execution, would be not much less idle than to hold a lighted taper to the sun. As little can it be required to prove, that in the absence of this clause, Congress would have some choice of means. That it might employ those which, in its judgment, would most advantageously effect the object to be accomplished. That any means adapted to the end, any means which tended directly to the execution of the constitutional powers of the government, were in themselves constitutional. This clause, as construed by the state of Maryland, would abridge, and almost annihilate this useful and necessary right of the legislature to select its means. That this could not be intended, is, we should think, had it not been already controverted, too apparent for controversy. We think so for the following reasons:

1st. The clause is placed among the powers of Congress, not among the limitations on those powers.

2d. Its terms purport to enlarge, not to diminish the powers vested in the government. It purports to be an additional power, not a restriction on those already granted. No reason has been, or can be assigned for thus concealing an intention to narrow the discretion of the national legislature under words which purport to enlarge it. The framers of the constitution wished its adoption, and well knew that it would be endangered by its strength, not by its weakness. Had they been capable of using language which would convey to the eye one idea, and, after deep reflection, impress on the mind another, they would rather have disguised the grant of power than its limitation. If, then, their intention had been, by this clause, to restrain the free use of means which might otherwise have been implied, that intention would have been inserted in another place, and would have been expressed in terms resembling these. "In carrying into execution the foregoing powers, and all others," etc., "no laws shall be passed but such as are necessary and proper." Had the intention been to make this clause restrictive, it would unquestionably have been so in form as well as in effect.

. . .

But, were its necessity less apparent, none can deny its being an appropriate measure; and if it is, the degree of its necessity, as has been very justly observed, is to be discussed in another place. Should Congress, in the execution of its powers, adopt measures which are prohibited by the constitution; or should Congress, under the pretext of executing its powers, pass laws for the accomplishment of objects not entrusted to the government, it would become the painful duty of this tribunal, should a case requiring such a decision come before it, to say that such an act was not the law of the land. But where the law is not prohibited, and is really calculated to effect any of the objects entrusted to the government, to undertake here to inquire into the degree of its necessity, would be to pass the line which circumscribes the judicial department, and to tread on legislative ground. This court disclaims all pretensions to such a power.

. . .

After the most deliberate consideration, it is the unanimous and decided opinion of this court that the act to incorporate the bank of the United States is a law made in pursuance of the constitution, and is a part of the supreme law of the land.

. . .

It being the opinion of the court that the act incorporating the bank is constitutional, and that the power of establishing a branch in the state of Maryland might be properly exercised by the bank itself, we proceed to inquire:

Whether the state of Maryland may, without violating the constitution, tax that branch?

That the power of taxation is one of vital importance; that it is retained by the states; that it is not abridged by the grant of a similar power to the government of the Union; that it is to be concurrently exercised by the two governments: are truths which have never been denied. But, such is the paramount character of the constitution that its capacity to withdraw any subject from the action of even this power, is admitted.

. . .

This great principle is, that the constitution and the laws made in pursuance thereof are supreme; that they control the constitution and laws of the respective states, and cannot be controlled by them. From this, which may be almost termed an axiom, other propositions are deduced as corollaries, on the truth or error of which, and on their application to this case the cause has been supposed to depend. These are, 1st. that a power to create implies a power to preserve. 2d. That a power to destroy, if wielded by a different hand, is hostile to, and incompatible with these powers to create and to preserve. 3d. That where this repugnancy exists, that authority which is supreme must control, not yield to that over which it is supreme.

These propositions, as abstract truths, would perhaps, never be controverted. Their application to this case, however, has been denied; and both in maintaining the affirmative and the negative, a splendor of eloquence, and strength of argument seldom, if ever, surpassed, have been displayed.

. . .

The sovereignty of a state extends to everything which exists by its own authority, or is introduced by its permission; but does it extend to those means which are employed by Congress to carry into execution—powers conferred on that body by the people of the United States? We think it demonstrable that it does not. Those powers are not given by the people of a single state. They are given by the people of the United States, to a government whose laws, made in pursuance of the constitution, are declared to be supreme. Consequently, the people of a single state cannot confer a sovereignty which will extend over them.

If we measure the power of taxation residing in a state, by the extent of sovereignty which the people of a single state possess, and can confer on its government, we have an intelligible standard, applicable to every case to which the power may be applied. We have a principle which leaves the power of taxing the people and property of a state unimpaired; which leaves to a state the command of all its resources, and which places beyond its reach, all those powers which are conferred by the people of the United States on the government of the Union, and all those means which are given for the purpose of carrying those powers into execution. We have a principle which is safe for the states, and safe for the Union.

. . .

We find, then, on just theory, a total failure of this original right to tax the means employed by the government of the Union, for the execution of its powers. The right never existed, and the question whether it has been surrendered, cannot arise.

But, waiving this theory for the present, let us resume the inquiry, whether this power can be exercised by the respective states, consistently with a fair construction of the constitution.

That the power to tax involves the power to destroy; that the power to destroy may defeat and render useless the power to create; that there is a plain repugnance, in conferring on one government a power to control the constitutional measures of another, which other, with respect to those very measures, is declared to be supreme over that which exerts the control, are propositions not to be denied. But all inconsistencies are to be reconciled by the magic of the word confidence. Taxation, it is said, does not necessarily and unavoidably destroy. To carry it to the excess of destruction would be an abuse, to presume which, would banish that confidence which is essential to all government.

But is this a case of confidence? Would the people of any one state trust those of another with a power to control the most insignificant operations of their state government? We know they would not. Why, then, should we suppose that the people of any one state should be willing to trust those of another with a power to control the operations of a government to which they have confided the most important and most valuable interests? In the legislature of the Union alone, are all represented. The legislature of the Union alone, therefore, can be trusted by the people with the power of controlling measures which concern all, in the confidence that it will not be abused. This, then, is not a case of confidence, and we must consider it as it really is.

If we apply the principle for which the state of Maryland contends, to the constitution generally, we shall find it capable of changing totally the character of that instrument. We shall find it capable of arresting all the measures of the government, and of prostrating it at the foot of the states. The American people have declared their constitution, and the laws made in pursuance thereof, to be supreme; but this principle would transfer the supremacy, in fact, to the states.

If the states may tax one instrument, employed by the government in the execution of its powers, they may tax any and every other instrument. They may tax the mail; they may tax the mint; they may tax patent-rights; they may tax the papers of the custom-house; they may tax judicial process; they may tax all the means employed by the government, to an excess which would defeat all the ends of government. This was not intended by the American people. This did not design to make their government dependent on the states.

. . .

The question is, in truth, a question of supremacy; and if the right of the states to tax the means employed by the general government be conceded, the declaration that the constitution, and the laws made in pursuance thereof, shall be the supreme law of the land, is empty and unmeaning declamation.

. . .

It has also been insisted, that, as the power of taxation in the general and state governments is acknowledged to be concurrent, every argument which would sustain the right of the general government to tax banks chartered by the states, will equally sustain the right of the states to tax banks chartered by the general government.

But the two cases are not on the same reason. The people of all the states have created the general government, and have conferred upon it the general power of taxation. The people of all the states, and the states themselves, are represented in Congress, and, by their representatives, exercise this power. When they tax the chartered institutions of the states, they tax their constituents; and these taxes must be uniform. But, when a state taxes the operations of the government of the United States, it acts upon institutions created, not by their own constituents, but by people over whom they claim no control. It acts upon the measures of a government created by others as well as themselves, for the benefit of others in common with themselves. The difference is that which always exists, and always must exist, between the action of the whole on a part, and the action of a part on the whole—between the laws of a government declared to be supreme, and those of a government which, when in opposition to those laws, is not supreme.

But if the full application of this argument could be admitted, it might bring into question the right of Congress to tax the state banks, and could not prove the right of the states to tax the Bank of the United States.

The court has bestowed on this subject its most deliberate consideration. The result is a conviction that the states have no power, by taxation or otherwise, to retard, impede, burden, or in any manner control the operations of the constitutional laws enacted by Congress to carry into execution the powers vested in the general government. This is, we think, the unavoidable consequence of that supremacy which the constitution has declared.

We are unanimously of opinion that the law passed by the legislature of Maryland, imposing a tax on the Bank of the United States, is unconstitutional and void.

Aftermath of McCulloch v. Maryland

In his opinion John Marshall enunciated and ably defended two great constitutional doctrines—*implied powers* and *national supremacy*—but the immediate effect of the decision was to bring a torrent of criticism on the Court from the then powerful states. These were days of competitive federalism, and acquiescence in a doctrine which allowed the national government to expand its sphere of lawmaking at the expense of the states was grudging. Clearly, this decision opened the door to a tremendous expansion of federal power and a consequent weakening of the states within this dual structure.

With respect to the specific issues of limits on the power of a state to levy taxes, *McCulloch* settled the question that a state may not tax an instrumentality of the national government. Scores of cases have arisen over the years, however, involving such issues as state and local taxes that allegedly obstruct interstate commerce, the constitutionality of state income taxes on salaries of federal employees, and regulatory taxes that might be unfairly discriminatory. Unfortunately, there has been considerable vacillation on the part of the justices as they attempted to arrive at a formula which would protect the states' revenue-sharing potential without diminishing federal powers or unduly burdening commercial transactions. Written into the Constitution is only one prohibition on the states' taxing powers—no taxation of exports or imports—and there are no restrictions as to any other objects nor are there any limits on the amount of a tax. For the Supreme Court the task has been one of settling these inevitable disputes in a federal system with a maximum of accommodation and a minimum of friction.

Gibbons v. Ogden

9 WHEATON 1 (1824)

Second in this "Marshall trilogy" involving disputes growing out of state-national rivalry is *Gibbons* v. *Ogden*. Unlike *McCulloch*, the controversy in this instance was not one in which the congressional statute at issue had any great significance for national policy. It was rather a vehicle which the Court was able to use to define and strengthen the reach of national power when regulating commerce, and to a lesser extent to circumscribe the role of the states when dealing with the instruments of commerce that spill across state lines. In the constitutional sense the issue in *Gibbons* was the constitutional—and practical—meaning of the words "regulate," and "among the several states."

The case of *Gibbons* v. *Ogden* reached the Supreme Court after a long train of events following the invention and initial use of the steamboat. In 1808 the New York legislature granted to Robert Fulton and Robert Livingston a 30-year monopoly of steam navigation on New York's waterways and permitted others to engage in such navigation only after a license had been obtained from the grantees. When New Jersey citizens who engaged in commercial navigation were unable to enter New York waters without procuring the required license, New Jersey authorized the owner of any vessel seized under New York law to compensate for the loss by confiscating New York boats in Jersey waters. Connecticut prohibited outright the use of its rivers by New York vessels licensed by Fulton and Livingston. Now at hand was full-blown commercial warfare among the states, the very evil the Constitution was supposed to prevent.

Complicating matters even further was the existence of a federal law that granted licenses to persons to sail their ships along coastal areas. Aaron Ogden of New York and Thomas Gibbons of New Jersey had been partners in a venture which included a ferry service between New York and the Jersey shore, but after a falling-out, they became competitors in the ferry trade, with Ogden, licensed by Fulton and Livingston, and Gibbons, operating under a federal coasting license. A New York court enjoined Gibbons from trafficking in New York waters and he appealed to the United States Supreme Court. The immediate question was the constitutionality of the New York law, but Chief Justice Marshall took the opportunity to define and clarify the meaning of the commerce clause. Marshall painted his canvas with such a broad brush that the clause became the primary vehicle for the eventual reach of national regulatory power into such diverse areas as gambling, the purity of food and drugs, labor relations, and racial discrimination.

Mr. Chief Justice **Marshall** delivered the opinion of the Court, and after stating the case, proceeded as follows:

The appellant contends that this decree is erroneous, because the laws which purport to give the exclusive privilege it sustains, are repugnant to the constitution and laws of the United States.

They are said to be repugnant:

To that clause in the constitution which authorizes Congress to regulate commerce.

. . .

As preliminary to the very able discussions of the constitution, which we have heard from the bar, and as having some influence on its construction, reference has been made to the political situation of these states, anterior to its formation. It has been said that they were sovereign, were completely independent, and were connected with each other only by a league. This is true. But when these allied sovereigns converted their league into a government, when they converted their Congress of Ambassadors, deputed to deliberate on their common concerns, and to recommend measures of general utility, into a legislature, empowered to enact laws on the most interesting subjects, the whole character in which the states appear, underwent a change, the extent of which must be determined by a fair consideration of the instrument by which that change was effected.

This instrument contains an enumeration of powers expressly granted by the people to their government. It has been said that these powers ought to be construed strictly. But why ought they to be so construed? Is there one sentence in the constitution which gives countenance to this rule? In the last of the enumerated powers, that which grants, expressly, the means of carrying all others into execution, Congress is authorized "to make all laws which shall be necessary and proper" for the purpose. But this limitation on the means which may be used, is not extended to the powers which are conferred; nor is there one sentence in the constitution which has been pointed out by the gentlemen of the bar, or which we have been able to discern, that prescribes this rule. We do not, therefore, think ourselves justified in adopting it. What do gentlemen mean by a strict construction? If they contend only against that enlarged construction which would extend words beyond their natural and obvious import, we might question the application of the term, but should not controvert the principle. If they contend for that narrow construction which, in support of some theory not to be found in the constitution, would deny to the government those powers which the words of the grant, as usually understood, import, and which are consistent with the general views and objects of the instrument; for that narrow construction, which would cripple the government and render it unequal to the objects for which it is declared to be instituted, and to which the powers given, as fairly understood, render it competent; then we cannot perceive the propriety of this strict construction, nor adopt it as the rule by which the constitution is to be expounded. As men, whose intentions require no concealment, generally employ the words which most directly and aptly express the ideas they intend to convey, the enlightened patriots who framed our constitution, and the people who adopted it, must be understood to have employed words in their natural sense, and to have intended what they have said. If, from the imperfection of human language, there should be serious doubts respecting the extent of any given power, it is a well-settled rule that the objects for which it was given, especially when those objects are expressed in the instrument itself, should have great influence in the construction. We know of no reason for excluding this rule from the present case. The grant does not convey power which might be beneficial to the grantor, if retained by himself, or which can ensure solely to the benefit of the grantee, but is an investment of power for the general advantage, in the hands of agents selected for that purpose; which power can never be exercised by the people themselves, but must be placed in the hands of agents or lie dormant. We know of no rule for construing the extent of such powers, other than is given by the language of the instrument which confers them, taken in connection with the purposes for which they were conferred.

The words are: "Congress shall have power to regulate commerce with foreign nations, and among the several states, and with the Indian tribes."

The subject to be regulated is commerce; and our constitution being, as was aptly said at the bar, one of enumeration, and not of definition, to ascertain the extent of the power it becomes necessary to settle the meaning of the word. The counsel for the appellee would limit it to traffic, to buying and selling, or the interchange of commodities, and do not admit that it comprehends navigation. This would restrict a general term, applicable to many objects, to one of its significations. Commerce, undoubtedly, is traffic, but it is something more; it is intercourse. It describes the commercial intercourse between nations and parts of nations, in all its branches, and is regulated by prescribing rules for carrying on that intercourse. The mind can scarcely conceive a system for regulating commerce between nations, which shall exclude all laws concerning navigation, which shall be silent on the admission of the vessels of the one nation into the ports of the other, and be confined to prescribing rules for the conduct of individuals, in the actual employment of buying and selling, or of barter.

If commerce does not include navigation, the government of the Union has no direct power over that subject, and can make no law prescribing what shall constitute American vessels, or requiring that they shall be navigated by American seamen. Yet this power has been exercised from the commencement of the government, has been exercised with the consent of all, and has been understood by all to be a commercial regulation. All America understands, and has uniformly understood, the word "commerce" to comprehend navigation. It was so understood, and must have been so understood, when the constitution was framed. The power over commerce, including navigation, was one of the primary objects for which the people of America adopted their government, and must have been contemplated in forming it. The convention must have used the word in that sense; because all have understood it in that sense, and the attempt to restrict it comes too late.

If the opinion that "commerce" as the word is used in the constitution, comprehends navigation also, requires any additional confirmation, that additional confirmation is, we think, furnished by the words of the instrument itself.

. . .

The word used in the constitution, then, comprehends, and has been always understood to comprehend, navigation within its meaning; and a power to regulate navigation is as expressly granted as if that term had been added to the word "commerce."

To what commerce does this power extend? The constitution informs us, to commerce "with foreign nations, and among the several states, and with the Indian tribes."

It has, we believe, been universally admitted that these words comprehend every species of commercial intercourse between the United States and foreign nations. No sort of trade can be carried on between this country and any other, to which this power does not extend. It has been truly said, that commerce, as the word is used in the constitution, is a unit, every part of which is indicated by the term.

If this be the admitted meaning of the word, in its application to foreign nations, it must carry the same meaning throughout the sentence, and remain a unit, unless there be some plain intelligible cause which alters it.

The subject to which the power is next applied, is to commerce "among the several states." The word "among" means intermingled with. A thing which is among others, is intermingled with them. Commerce among the states cannot stop at the external boundary line of each state, but may be introduced into the interior.

It is not intended to say that these words comprehend that commerce which is completely internal, which is carried on between man and man in a state, or between different parts of the same state, and which does not extend to or affect other states. Such a power would be inconvenient, and is certainly unnecessary.

Comprehensive as the word "among" is, it may very properly be restricted to that commerce which concerns more states than one. The phrase is not one which would probably have been selected to indicate the completely interior traffic of a state, because it is not an apt phrase for that purpose; and the enumeration of the particular classes of commerce to which the power was to be extended, would not have been made had the intention been to extend the power to every description. The enumeration presupposes something not enumerated; and that something, if we regard the language or the subject of the sentence, must be the exclusively internal commerce of a state. The genius and character of the whole government seem to be, that its action is to be applied to all the external concerns of the nation, and to those internal concerns which affect the states generally; but not to those which are completely within a particular state, which do not affect other states, and with which it is not necessary to interfere, for the purpose of executing some of the general powers of the government. The completely internal commerce of a state, then, may be considered as reserved for the state itself.

But, in regulating commerce with foreign nations, the power of Congress does not stop at the jurisdictional lines of the several states. It would be a very useless power if it could not pass those lines. The commerce of the United States with foreign nations, is that of the whole United States. Every district has a right to participate in it. The deep streams which penetrate our country in every direction, pass through the interior of almost every state in the Union, and furnish the means of exercising this right. If Congress has the power to regulate it, that power must be exercised whenever the subject exists. If it exists within the states, if a foreign voyage may commence or terminate at a port within a state, then the power of Congress may be exercised within a state.

This principle is, if possible, still more clear, when applied to commerce "among the several states." They either join each other, in which case they are separated by a mathematical line, or they are remote from each other, in which case other states lie between them. What is commerce "among" them; and how is it to be conducted? Can a trading expedition between two adjoining states commence and terminate outside of each? And if the trading intercourse be between two states remote from each other, must it not commence in one, terminate in the other, and probably pass through a third? Commerce among the states must, of necessity, be commerce with the states.

. . .

We are now arrived at the inquiry, What is this power?

It is the power to regulate; that is, to prescribe the rule by which commerce is to be governed. This power, like all others vested in Congress, is complete in itself, may be exercised to its utmost extent, and acknowledges no limitations, other than are prescribed in the constitution. These are expressed in plain terms, and do not affect the questions which arise in this case, or which have been discussed at the bar. If, as has always been understood, the sovereignty of Congress, though limited to specified objects, is plenary as to those objects, the power over commerce with foreign nations, and among the several States, is vested in Congress as absolutely as it would be in a single government, having in its constitution the same restrictions on the exercise of the power as are found in the constitution of the United States. The wisdom and the discretion of Congress, their identity with the people, and the influence which their constituents possess at election, are, in this, as in many other instances, as that, for example, of declaring war, the sole restraints on which they have relied, to secure them from its abuse. They are the restraints on which the people must often rely solely, in all representative governments.

The power of Congress, then, comprehends navigation within the limits of every state in the Union; so far as that navigation may be, in any manner, connected with "commerce with foreign nations, or among the several states, or with the Indian tribes." It may, of consequence, pass the jurisdictional line of New York, and act upon the very waters to which the prohibition now under consideration applies.

But it has been urged with great earnestness, that although the power of Congress to regulate commerce with foreign nations, and among the several states, be co-extensive with the subject itself, and have no other limits than are prescribed in the constitution, yet the states may severally exercise the same power within their respective jurisdictions. In support of this argument, it is said that they possessed it as an inseparable attribute of sovereignty, before the formation of the constitution, and still retain it, except so far as they have surrendered it by that instrument; that this principle results from the nature of the government, and is secured by the tenth amendment; that an affirmative grant of power is not exclusive, unless in its own nature it be such that the continued exercise of it by the former possessor is inconsistent with the grant, and that this is not of that description.

The appellant, conceding these postulates, except the last, contends that full power to regulate a particular subject, implies the whole power, and leaves no residuum; that a grant of the whole is incompatible with the existence of a right in another to any part of it.

Both parties have appealed to the constitution, to legislative acts, and judicial decisions; and have drawn arguments from all these sources to support and illustrate the propositions they respectively maintain.

The grant of the power to lay and collect taxes is, like the power to regulate commerce, made in general terms, and has never been understood to interfere with the exercise of the same power by the states; and hence has been drawn an argument which has been applied to the question under consideration. But the two grants are not, it is conceived, similar in their terms or their nature. Although many of the powers formerly exercised by the states, are transferred to the government of the Union, yet the state governments remain, and constitute a most important part of our system. The power of taxation is indispensable to their existence, and is a power which, in its own nature, is capable of residing in, and being exercised by, different authorities at the same time. We are accustomed to see it placed, for different purposes, in different hands. Taxation is the simple operation of taking small portions from a perpetually accumulating mass, susceptible of almost infinite division; and a power in one to take what is necessary for certain purposes, is not, in its nature, incompatible with a power in another to take what is necessary for other purposes. Congress is authorized to lay and collect taxes, etc., to pay the debts, and provide for the common defense and general welfare of the United States. This does not interfere with the power of the states to tax for the support of their own governments; nor is the exercise of that power by the states an exercise of any portion of the power that is granted to the United States. In imposing taxes for state purposes, they are not doing what Congress is empowered to do. Congress is not empowered to tax for those purposes which are within the exclusive province of the states. When, then, each government exercises the power of taxation, neither is exercising the power of the other. But, when a state proceeds to regulate commerce with foreign nations, or among the several states, it is exercising the very power that is granted to Congress, and is doing the very thing which Congress is authorized to do. There is no analogy, then, between the power of taxation and the power of regulating commerce.

. . .

Powerful and ingenious minds, taking, as postulates, that the powers expressly granted to the government of the Union are to be contracted, by construction, into the narrowest possible compass, and that the original powers of the States are retained, if any possible construction will retain them, may, by a course of well digested, but refined and metaphysical reasoning, founded on these premises, explain away the constitution of our country; and leave it a magnificent structure indeed, to look at, but totally unfit for use. They may so entangle and perplex the understanding, as to obscure principles which were before thought quite plain, and induce doubts where, if the mind were to pursue its own course, none would be perceived. In such a case, it is peculiarly necessary to recur to safe and fundamental principles to sustain those principles, and, when sustained, to make them the tests of the arguments to be examined.

Aftermath of Gibbons *v.* Ogden

Broad as Marshall's opinion was in *Gibbons,* the nature of the controversy precluded, or at least did not require, answers to some nagging questions. Foremost among them was whether the power of Congress to regulate commerce was exclusive. In a practical sense if the power is exclusive, then that which Congress chooses not to regulate remains free of any statutory constraints. Such a rule was bound to lead and did lead to controversies in which the Court was asked to define what areas of commercial activity, if any, might permissibly be subject to state and local control. While the Supreme Court, wisely or unwisely, has never held that all interstate commerce falls within the exclusive jurisdiction of the federal government, the decisions following *Gibbons* indicate that the Court had strung a constitutional tightrope on which it would walk precariously as it sought to balance the spheres of national and state authority.

Just 5 years after the decision in *Gibbons,* John Marshall had the opportunity to press the claim of exclusive national control under the commerce power, but he declined to do so. In *Willson* v. *Blackbird Creek Marsh Company* (1829), he wrote the opinion of the Court upholding the state of Delaware when it authorized a company to erect a dam across a small, navigable creek. Sailing under a federal license, a boat had broken through the dam and its owners were sued for damages. Ruling for the state, the Court maintained that since Congress had not specifically prohibited state legislation governing small navigable streams, the state's action was valid. Said Marshall:

> We do not think that the act empowering the Blackbird Creek Marsh Company to place a dam across the creek, can, under all the circumstances of the case, be considered as repugnant to the power to regulate commerce in its dormant state, or as being in conflict with any law passed on the subject.

One should note the words "dormant state" in Marshall's opinion, since this indicates that the Constitution by itself does not automatically exclude the states from acting on those aspects of interstate commerce carried on within their borders.

Yet Justice Joseph Story, a close associate of Marshall who remained on the bench after the death of the chief justice, insisted that federal power over interstate commerce was exclusive and that Marshall had said as much! In *New York* v. *Milne* (1837), Story wrote a dissent in which he declared that from the time of *Gibbons* the question

> . . . has been considered (as far as I know) to be at rest. The power given to Congress to regulate commerce with foreign nations, and among the states, has been deemed exclusive, from the nature and objects of the power, and the necessary implications growing out of its exercise. . . .

At bottom the issue was that of national power as opposed to states' rights and it continued to divide the court as it groped its way through a series of decisions in an attempt to formulate a judicial rule. Such a rule was forthcoming in *Cooley* v. *Board of Port Wardens* (1852) and it still remains a viable, if complicated, doctrine today. At issue in the *Cooley* case was a Pennsylvania law of 1803 that required ships using the Port of Philadelphia to employ a local pilot, or pay an amount up to one-half the fee set by the Board of Port Wardens to a pension fund for the pilots. Although Congress had authorized state laws on pilotage, Aaron Cooley argued that the state fee amounted to an unconstitutional tax on commerce. In rejecting Cooley's claim the Court announced what became known as the "doctrine of selective exclusiveness," a formula that could be applied to future controversies. Essentially, the rule is this: When the commerce to be regulated requires a national uniform rule, only Congress may act, and any state laws on the subject matter are invalid; but when the commerce has a peculiarly local application, and Congress has not legislated on the subject matter, the state may validly regulate it. Experience has shown the *Cooley* doctrine to be more useful as a clear statement of the problem than as a solution, since application of the rule has been difficult in concrete cases. Nevertheless, it gave permanence to the principle that depending upon circumstances the states are not totally excluded from dealing with that part of interstate commerce within their borders (*intrastate* commerce) as it affects their local interests.

Dartmouth College v. Woodward
4 WHEATON 518 (1819)

Unlike *McCulloch* and *Gibbons*, both of which involved state statutes that were in collision with acts of Congress, *Dartmouth College* v. *Woodward* faced the more direct issue of a state law allegedly in contravention of a specific prohibition found in Article I, Section 10, of the Constitution. At issue was the contract clause which provides in simple, direct language that no state shall pass any "law impairing the obligation of contracts." While the framers assumed that common law precedents defined *contract* and *obligation*, nothing in the phraseology prevented U.S. courts from rounding out the meaning, and John Marshall did just that. In 1810 in the case of *Fletcher* v. *Peck* (excerpted in Chapter 2), the Supreme Court first had the opportunity to analyze the contract clause and it was the first case in which the Court declared a state law unconstitutional. There Marshall interpreted the clause broadly to include executed as well as executory agreements, and to apply not only to a contract made by private parties but to one made by the state itself.

Expanding the meaning of the contract clause to perhaps its outermost limits was the *Dartmouth College* decision in 1819. Chartered by the English Crown in 1769, Dartmouth College was empowered to make the usual academic decisions including appointing a president and a board of trustees. During the 1800s the college became embroiled in New Hampshire politics when the Federalist-oriented trustees removed the Republican president, John Wheelock. Later, when the Republicans gained control of the legislature, they altered the college's charter by giving the governor of the state the authority to appoint a majority of the trustees. Once in place the new trustees proceeded to reappoint Wheelock, a decision which the old trustees refused to accept as they brought suit against Wheelock, other officers of the college, and the new trustees, requesting that they turn over the college's official documents. In the Supreme Court the chief issue was the constitutional status of the college charter, that is, was it a contract in the constitutional sense?

The opinion of the Court was delivered by Chief Justice John **Marshall:**

. . .

The single question now to be considered is, do the acts to which the verdict refers violate the constitution of the United States?

. . .

It can require no argument to prove, that the circumstances of this case constitute a contract. An application is made to the crown for a charter to incorporate a religious and literary institution. In the application, it is stated, that large contributions have been made

for the object, which will be conferred on the corporation, as soon as it shall be created. The charter is granted, and on its faith the property is conveyed. Surely, in this transaction every ingredient of a complete and legitimate contract is to be found. The points for consideration are, 1. Is this contract protected by the constitution of the United States? 2. Is it impaired by the acts under which the defendant holds?

1. On the first point, it has been argued, that the word "contract," in its broadest sense, would comprehend the political relations between the government and its citizens, would extend to offices held within a state, for state purposes, and to many of those laws concerning civil insti-

tutions, which must change with circumstances, and be modified by ordinary legislation; which deeply concern the public, and which, to preserve good government, the public judgment must control. That even marriage is a contract, and its obligations are affected by the laws respecting divorces. That the clause in the constitution, if construed in its greatest latitude, would prohibit these laws. Taken in its broad, unlimited sense, the clause would be an unprofitable and vexatious interference with the internal concerns of a state, would unnecessarily and unwisely embarrass its legislation, and render immutable those civil institutions, which are established for purposes of internal government, and which, to subserve those purposes, ought to vary with varying circumstances. That as the framers of the constitution could never have intended to insert in that instrument, a provision so unnecessary, so mischievous, and so repugnant to its general spirit, the term "contract" must be understood in a more limited sense. That it must be understood as intended to guard against a power, of at least doubtful utility, the abuse of which had been extensively felt; and to restrain the legislature in future from violating the right to property. That, anterior to the formation of the constitution, a course of legislation had prevailed in many, if not in all, of the states, which weakened the confidence of man in man, and embarrassed all transactions between individuals, by dispensing with a faithful performance of engagements. To correct this mischief, by restraining the power which produced it, the state legislatures were forbidden "to pass any law impairing the obligation of contracts," that is, of contracts respecting property, under which some individual could claim a right to something beneficial to himself; and that, since the clause in the constitution must in construction receive some limitation, it may be confined, and ought to be confined, to cases of this description; to cases within the mischief it was intended to remedy.

The general correctness of these observations cannot be controverted. That the framers of the constitution did not intend to restrain the states in the regulation of their civil institutions, adopted for internal government, and that the instrument they have given us, is not to be so construed, may be admitted. The provision of the constitution never has been understood to embrace other contracts, than those which respect property, or some object of value, and confer rights which may be asserted in a court of justice. It never has been understood to restrict the general right of the legislature to legislate on the subject of divorces. Those acts enable some tribunals, not to impair a marriage contract, but to liberate one of the parties, because it has been broken by the other. When any state legislature shall pass an act annulling all marriage contracts, or allowing either party to annul it, without the consent of the other, it will be time enough to inquire, whether such an act be constitutional.

The parties in this case differ less on general principles, less on the true construction of the constitution in the abstract, than on the application of those principles to this case, and on the true construction of the charter of 1769. This is the point on which the cause essentially depends. If the act of incorporation be a grant of political power, if it create a civil institution, to be employed in the administration of the government, or if the funds of the college be public property, or if the state of New Hampshire, as a government, be alone interested in its transactions, the subject is one in which the legislature of the state may act according to its own judgment, unrestrained by any limitation of its power imposed by the constitution of the United States.

But if this be a private eleemosynary institution, endowed with a capacity to take property, for objects unconnected with government, whose funds are bestowed by individuals, on the faith of the charter; if the donors have stipulated for the future disposition and management of those funds, in the manner prescribed by themselves; there may be more difficulty in the case, although neither the persons who have made these stipulations, nor those for whose benefit they were made, should be parties to the cause. Those who are no longer interested in the property, may yet retain such an interest in the preservation of their own arrangements, as to have a right to insist, that those arrangements shall be held sacred. Or, if they have themselves disappeared, it becomes a subject of serious and anxious inquiry, whether those whom they have legally empowered to represent them for ever, may not assert all the rights which they possessed, while in being; whether, if they be without personal representatives, who may feel injured by a violation of the compact, the trustees be not so completely their representatives, in the eye of the law, as to stand in their place, not only as respects the government of the college, but also as respects the maintenance of the college charter. It becomes then the duty of the court, most seriously to examine this charter, and to ascertain its true character.

. . .

A corporation is an artificial being, invisible, intangible, and existing only in contemplation of law. Being the mere creature of law, it possesses only those properties which the charter of its creation confers upon it, either expressly, or as incidental to its very existence. These are such as are supposed best calculated to effect the object for which it was created. Among the most important are immortality, and, if the expression may be allowed, individuality; properties, by which a perpetual succession of many persons are considered as the same, and may act as a single individual. They enable a corporation to manage its own affairs, and to hold property, without the perplexing intricacies, the hazardous and endless necessity, of perpetual conveyances for the purpose of transmitting it from hand to hand. It is chiefly for the purpose of clothing bodies of men, in succession, with these qualities and capacities, that corporations were invented, and are in use. By these means, a perpetual succession of individuals are capable of acting for the promotion of the particular object, like one immortal being. But this being does not share in the civil government of the country, unless that be the purpose for which it was created. Its immortality no more confers on it political power, or a political character, than immortality would confer such power or character on a natural person. It is no more a state instrument, than a natural person exercising the same powers would be. If, then, a natural person, employed by individuals in the education of youth, or for the government of a seminary in which youth is educated, would not become a public officer, or be considered as a member of the civil government, how is it, that this artificial being,

created by law, for the purpose of being employed by the same individuals, for the same purposes, should become a part of the civil government of the country? Is it because its existence, its capacities, its powers, are given by law? Because the government has given it the power to take and to hold property, in a particular form, and for particular purposes, has the government a consequent right substantially to change that form, or to vary the purposes to which the property is to be applied? This principle has never been asserted or recognized, and is supported by no authority. Can it derive aid from reason?

The objects for which a corporation is created are universally such as the government wishes to promote. They are deemed beneficial to the country; and this benefit constitutes the consideration, and in most cases, the sole consideration of the grant. In most eleemosynary institutions, the object would be difficult, perhaps unattainable, without the aid of a charter of incorporation. Charitable or public-spirited individuals, desirous of making permanent appropriations for charitable or other useful purposes, find it impossible to effect their design securely and certainly, without an incorporating act. They apply to the government, state their beneficent object, and offer to advance the money necessary for its accomplishment, provided the government will confer on the instrument which is to execute their designs the capacity to execute them. The proposition is considered and approved. The benefit to the public is considered as an ample compensation for the faculty it confers, and the corporation is created. If the advantages to the public constitute a full compensation for the faculty it gives, there can be no reason for exacting a further compensation, by claiming a right to exercise over this artificial being, a power which changes its nature, and touches the fund, for the security and application for which it was created. There can be no reason for implying in a charter, given for a valuable consideration, a power which is not only not expressed, but is in direct contradiction to its express stipulations.

From the fact, then, that a charter of incorporation has been granted, nothing can be inferred, which changes the character of the institution, or transfers to the government any new power over it. The character of civil institutions does not grow out of their incorporation, but out of the manner in which they are formed, and the objects for which they are created. The right to change them is not founded on their being incorporated, but on their being the instruments of government, created for its purposes. The same institutions, created for the same objects, though not incorporated, would be public institutions, and, of course, be controllable by the legislature. The incorporating act neither gives nor prevents this control. Neither, in reason, can the incorporating act change the character of a private eleemosynary institution.

. . .

This is plainly a contract to which the donors, the trustees and the crown (to whose rights and obligations New Hampshire succeeds) were the original parties. It is a contract made on a valuable consideration. It is a contract for the security and disposition of property. It is a contract, on the faith of which, real and personal estate has been conveyed to the corporation. It is, then, a contract within the letter of the constitution, and within its spirit also, unless the fact, that the property is invested by the donors in trustees, for the promotion of religion and education, for the benefit of persons who are perpetually changing, though the objects remain the same, shall create a particular exception, taking this case out of the prohibition contained in the constitution.

It is more than possible, that the preservation of rights of this description was not particularly in the view of the framers of the constitution, when the clause under consideration was introduced into that instrument. It is probable, that interferences of more frequent occurrence, to which the temptation was stronger, and of which the mischief was more extensive, constituted the great motive for imposing this restriction on the state legislatures. But although a particular and a rare case may not, in itself, be of sufficient magnitude to induce a rule, yet it must be governed by the rule, when established, unless some plain and strong reason for excluding it can be given. It is not enough to say, that this particular case was not in the mind of the convention, when the article was framed, nor of the American people, when it was adopted. It is

necessary to go further, and to say that, had this particular case been suggested, the language would have been so varied, as to exclude it, or it would have been made a special exception. The case being within the words of the rule, must be within its operation likewise, unless there be something in the literal construction, so obviously absurd or mischievous, or repugnant to the general spirit of the instrument, as to justify those who expound the constitution in making it an exception.

On what safe and intelligible ground, can this exception stand? There is no expression in the constitution, no sentiment delivered by its contemporaneous expounders, which would justify us in making it. In the absence of all authority of this kind, is there, in the nature and reason of the case itself, that which would sustain a construction of the constitution, not warranted by its words? Are contracts of this description of a character to excite so little interest, that we must exclude them from the provisions of the constitution, as being unworthy of the attention of those who framed the instrument? Or does public policy so imperiously demand their remaining exposed to legislative alteration, as to compel us, or rather permit us, to say, that these words, which were introduced to give stability to contracts, and which in their plain import comprehend this contract, must yet be so construed as to exclude it?

[These questions were answered in the negative.]

. . .

The opinion of the court, after mature deliberation, is, that this is a contract, the obligation of which cannot be impaired, without violating the constitution of the United States. This opinion appears to us to be equally supported by reason, and by the former decisions of this court.

2. We next proceed to the inquiry, whether its obligation has been impaired by those acts of the legislature of New Hampshire, to which the special verdict refers?

. . .

On the effect of this law, two opinions cannot be entertained. Between acting directly, and acting through the agency of trustees and overseers, no essential difference is perceived. The whole power of governing the college is transferred from trustees, appointed according to the will of the founder, expressed in the charter, to the executive of New Hampshire. The management and application of the funds of this eleemosynary institution, which are placed by the donors in the hands of trustees named in the charter, and empowered to perpetuate themselves, are placed by this act under the control of the government of the state. The will of the state is substituted for the will of the donors, in every essential operation of the college. This is not an immaterial change. The founders of the college contracted, not merely for the perpetual application of the funds which they gave, to the objects for which those funds were given; they contracted also, to secure that application by the constitution of the corporation. They contracted for a system, which should, so far as human foresight can provide, retain for ever the government of the literary institution they had formed, in the hands of persons approved by themselves. This system is totally changed. The charter of 1769 exists no longer. It is re-organized; and re-organized in such a manner, as to convert a literary institution, moulded according to the will of its founders, and placed under the control of private literary men, into a machine entirely subservient to the will of government. This may be for the advantage of this college in particular, and may be for the advantage of literature in general; but it is not according to the will of the donors, and is subversive of that contract, on the faith of which their property was given.

In the view which has been taken of this interesting case, the court has confined itself to the rights possessed by the trustees, as the assignees and representatives of the donors and founders, for the benefit of religion and literature. Yet, it is not clear, that the trustees ought to be consid-

ered as destitute of such beneficial interest in themselves, as the law may respect. In addition to their being the legal owners of the property, and to their having a freehold right in the powers confided to them, the charter itself countenances the idea, that trustees may also be tutors, with salaries. The first president was one of the original trustees; and the charter provides, that in case of vacancy in that office, "the senior professor or tutor, being one of the trustees, shall exercise the office of president, until the trustees shall make choice of, and appoint a president." According to the tenor of the charter, then, the trustees might, without impropriety, appoint a president and other professors from their own body. This is a power not entirely unconnected with an interest. Even if the proposition of the counsel for the defendant were sustained; if it were admitted, that those contracts only are protected by the constitution, a beneficial interest in which is vested in the party, who appears in court to assert that interest; yet it is by no means clear, that the trustees of Dartmouth College have no beneficial interest in themselves.

But the court has deemed it unnecessary to investigate this particular point, being of opinion, on general principles, that in these private eleemosynary institutions, the body corporate, as possessing the whole legal and equitable interest, and completely representing the donors, for the purpose of executing the trust, has rights which are protected by the constitution.

It results from this opinion, that the acts of the legislature of New Hampshire, which are stated in the special verdict found in this cause, are repugnant to the constitution of the United States; and that the judgment on this special verdict ought to have been for the plaintiffs. The judgment of the state court must, therefore, be reversed.

Aftermath of Dartmouth College v. Woodward

As a result of the *Peck* and *Dartmouth College* decisions, state legislatures were severely limited in their ability to undo any damage perpetrated by a previous miscreant legislature since all agreements made between a state and a private party, including charters of incorporation, became ironclad, permanent contracts. In 1837, however, not long after John Marshall's death, a new Supreme Court under the leadership of Chief Justice Roger Brooke Taney decided the case of *Charles River Bridge* v. *Warren Bridge*, which, while not repudiating earlier doctrine, served notice that charters of incorporation—or public contracts of any nature—would be construed narrowly, that they contained no rights or privileges by implication, and that any ambiguities must be decided in the interest of the public. It was after the decision in *Stone* v. *Mississippi* in 1880, however, that the contract clause was relegated to a position of only minor constitutional protection for corporate rights when the Court held, in principle, that a state might repudiate the terms of a charter if circumstances required legislative action in behalf of public health, welfare, safety, or morals. That is, a state may not bargain away its police powers when it becomes party to a public contract. Thus, through changes in judicial thinking the contract clause lost much of its force as a barrier to state authority. But the Supreme Court now had a new constitutional shield that it might use to protect the public and the individual against arbitrary state power: the Fourteenth Amendment. Although technically in force since its adoption in 1868, until the turn of the century this post–Civil War alteration in the Constitution had been almost quiescent in its effects (see discussion in Chapter 4).

Garcia v. *San Antonio Metropolitan Transit Authority*

469 U.S. 528 (1985)

One of the most important pieces of legislation of the "second New Deal" was the Fair Labor Standards Act (FLSA) of 1938, which replaced the National Industrial Recovery Act declared unconstitutional 2 years earlier by the Supreme Court. The act set a minimum hourly wage and a 40-hour work week for most private employees and established national standards for child labor. In 1941, the FLSA was upheld unanimously in *United States* v. *Darby Lumber Company* as a proper use of congressional power under the commerce clause. The following year, in *Wickard* v. *Filburn*, the Court was again unanimous in upholding the Agricultural Adjustment Act on commerce clause grounds. After *Heart of Atlanta Motel* v. *United States* (excerpted in Chapter 2) in 1964, Congress's commerce power seemed virtually limitless.

Responding to considerable political pressure from public employee unions, Congress in 1974 voted to broaden the coverage of the FLSA's wage and hour provisions to include state and municipal employees who had previously been exempt from the law. Although Congress had been moving incrementally in this direction since the 1960s, most recently by bringing persons employed in state hospitals, institutions, and schools within the scope of the act, state and local officials viewed the 1974 amendments as particularly ominous because they would require significantly larger budgets for basic services such as police, fire protection, and sanitation, particularly in the area of overtime pay. Nineteen states, three cities, and one county joined the National League of Cities and the National Governors Conference in challenging the constitutionality of the 1974 amendments on the ground that they had interfered with the states' freedom to perform traditional governmental functions, and thus had exceeded congressional authority under the commerce clause. In a decision that surprised many observers, the Court accepted this argument in *National League of Cities* v. *Usery*(1976) and invalidated the FLSA amendments. This conservative-activist decision proved to be of limited significance, however. In 1981 the Court was unanimous in rejecting *Usery* as precedent in a case challenging a federal law covering surface mining on private lands because, unlike the 1974 FLSA amendments, the statute did not regulate the "states as states" (*Hodel* v. *Virginia Surface Mining and Reclamation Association*). Two years later, in *Equal Employment Opportunity Commission* v. *Wyoming,* the Court by a 5–4 vote (Justice Blackmun having reversed his *Usery* position) held that a federal law prohibiting age discrimination applied to state and local governments. In 1984 the Court heard an appeal in the case of *Garcia* v. *San Antonio Metropolitan Transit Authority.* The United States Department of Labor had ruled in 1979 that SAMTA, a public mass transit authority in San Antonio, Texas, was covered by the minimum wage and overtime requirements of the Fair Labor Standards Act. A federal appeals court, citing the Supreme Court's *National League of Cities* decision, held that operation of a mass transit system is a "traditional government function" and thus is immune from congressional authority.

Justice **Blackmun** delivered the opinion of the Court.

We revisit in these cases an issue raised in National League of Cities v Usery. In that litigation, this Court, by a sharply divided vote, ruled that the Commerce Clause does not empower Congress to enforce the minimum-wage and overtime provisions of the Fair Labor Standards Act (FLSA) against the States "in areas of traditional governmental functions." Although National League of Cities supplied some examples of "traditional governmental functions," it did not offer a general explanation of how a "traditional" function is to be distinguished from a "nontraditional" one. Since then, federal and state courts have struggled with the task, thus imposed, of identifying a traditional function for purposes of state immunity under the Commerce Clause.

In the present cases, a Federal District Court concluded that municipal ownership and operation of a mass-transit system is a traditional governmental function and thus, under National League of Cities, is exempt from the obligations imposed by the FLSA. Faced with the identical question, three Federal Courts of Appeals and one state appellate court have reached the opposite conclusion.

Our examination of this "function" standard applied in these and other cases over the last eight years now persuades us that the attempt to draw the boundaries of state regulatory immunity in terms of "traditional governmental function" is not only unworkable but is inconsistent with established principles of federalism and, indeed, with those very federalism principles on

which National League of Cities purported to rest. That case, accordingly, is overruled.

. . .

Appellees have not argued that SAMTA is immune from regulation under the FLSA on the ground that it is a local transit system engaged in intrastate commercial activity. In a practical sense, SAMTA's operations might well be characterized as "local." Nonetheless, it long has been settled that Congress' authority under the Commerce Clause extends to intrastate economic activities that affect interstate commerce. Were SAMTA a privately owned and operated enterprise, it could not credibly argue that Congress exceeded the bounds of its Commerce Clause powers in prescribing minimum wages and overtime rates for SAMTA's employees. Any constitutional exemption from the requirements of the FLSA therefore must rest on SAMTA's status as a governmental entity rather than on the "local" nature of its operations.

The prerequisites for governmental immunity under National League of Cities were summarized by this Court in Hodel. Under that summary, four conditions must be satisfied before a state activity may be deemed immune from a particular federal regulation under the Commerce Clause. First, it is said that the federal statute at issue must regulate "the 'States as States.'" Second, the statute must "address matters that are indisputably 'attribute[s] of state sovereignty.'" Third, state compliance with the federal obligation must "directly impair [the States'] ability 'to structure integral operations in areas of traditional governmental functions.'" Finally, the relation of state and federal interests must not be such that "the nature of the federal interest . . . justifies state submission."

The controversy in the present cases has focused on the third Hodel requirement—that the challenged federal statute trench on "traditional governmental functions." The District Court voiced a common concern: "Despite the abundance of adjectives, identifying which particular state functions are immune remains difficult."

. . .

The distinction the Court discarded as unworkable in the field of tax immunity has proved no more fruitful in the field of regulatory immunity under the Commerce Clause. Neither do any of the alternative standards that might be employed to distinguish between protected and unprotected governmental functions appear manageable. We rejected the possibility of making immunity turn on a purely historical standard of "tradition" in Long Island, and properly so. The most obvious defect of a historical approach to state immunity is that it prevents a court from accommodating changes in the historical functions of States, changes that have resulted in a number of once-private functions like education being assumed by the States and their subdivisions. At the same time, the only apparent virtue of a rigorous historical standard, namely, its promise of a reasonably objective measure for state immunity, is illusory. Reliance on history as an organizing principle results in linedrawing of the most arbitrary sort; the genesis of state governmental functions stretches over a historical continuum from before the Revolution to the present, and courts would have to decide by fiat precisely how longstanding a pattern of state involvement had to be for federal regulatory authority to be defeated.

A nonhistorical standard for selecting immune governmental functions is likely to be just as unworkable as is a historical standard. The goal of identifying "uniquely" governmental functions, for example, has been rejected by the Court in the field of government tort liability in part because the notion of a "uniquely" governmental function is unmanageable. Another possibility would be to confine immunity to "necessary" governmental services, that is, services that

would be provided inadequately or not at all unless the government provided them. The set of services that fits into this category, however, may well be negligible. The fact that an unregulated market produces less of some service than a State deems desirable does not mean that the State itself must provide the service; in most if not all cases, the State can "contract out" by hiring private firms to provide the service or simply by providing subsidies to existing suppliers. It also is open to question how well equipped courts are to make this kind of determination about the workings of economic markets.

We believe, however, that there is a more fundamental problem at work here, a problem that explains why the Court was never able to provide a basis for the governmental/proprietary distinction in the intergovernmental tax immunity cases and why an attempt to draw similar distinctions with respect to federal regulatory authority under National League of Cities is unlikely to succeed regardless of how the distinctions are phrased. The problem is that neither the governmental/proprietary distinction nor any other that purports to separate out important governmental functions can be faithful to the role of federalism in a democratic society. The essence of our federal system is that within the realm of authority left open to them under the Constitution, the States must be equally free to engage in any activity that their citizens choose for the common weal, no matter how unorthodox or unnecessary anyone else—including the judiciary—deems state involvement to be. Any rule of state immunity that looks to the "traditional," "integral," or "necessary" nature of governmental functions inevitably invites an unelected federal judiciary to make decisions about which state policies it favors and which ones it dislikes. "The science of government . . . is the science of experiment," and the States cannot serve as laboratories for social and economic experiment, if they must pay an added price when they meet the changing needs of their citizenry by taking up functions that an earlier day and a different society left in private hands. In the words of Justice Black:

"There is not, and there cannot be, any unchanging line of demarcation between essential and nonessential governmental functions. Many governmental functions of today have at some time in the past been non-governmental. The genius of our government provides that, within the sphere of constitutional action, the people—acting not through the courts but through their elected legislative representatives—have the power to determine as conditions demand, what services and functions the public welfare requires."

We therefore now reject, as unsound in principle and unworkable in practice, a rule of state immunity from federal regulation that turns on a judicial appraisal of whether a particular governmental function is "integral" or "traditional." Any such rule leads to inconsistent results at the same time that it disserves principles of democratic self-governance, and it breeds inconsistency precisely because it is divorced from those principles. If there are to be limits on the Federal Government's power to interfere with state functions—as undoubtedly there are—we must look elsewhere to find them. We accordingly return to the underlying issue that confronted this Court in National League of Cities—the manner in which the Constitution insulates States from the reach of Congress' power under the Commerce Clause.

The central theme of National League of Cities was that the States occupy a special position in our constitutional system and that the scope of Congress' authority under the Commerce Clause must reflect that position. Of course, the Commerce Clause by its specific language does not provide any special limitation on Congress' actions with respect to the States. It is equally true, however, that the text of the Constitution provides the beginning rather than the final answer to every inquiry into questions of federalism, for "[b]ehind the words of the constitutional provisions are postulates which limit and control." National League of Cities reflected the general conviction that the Constitution precludes "the National Government [from] devour[ing] the essentials of state sovereignty." In order to be faithful to the underlying federal premises of the Constitution, courts must look for the "postulates which limit and control."

. . .

We realize that changes in the structure of the Federal Government have taken place since 1789, not the least of which has been the substitution of popular election of Senators by the adoption of the Seventeenth Amendment in 1913, and that these changes may work to alter the influence of the States in the federal political process. Nonetheless, against this background, we are convinced that the fundamental limitation that the constitutional scheme imposes on the Commerce Clause to protect the "States as States" is one of process rather than one of result. Any substantive restraint on the exercise of Commerce Clause powers must find its justification in the procedural nature of this basic limitation, and it must be tailored to compensate for possible failings in the national political process rather than to dictate a "sacred province of state autonomy."

Insofar as the present cases are concerned, then, we need go no further than to state that we perceive nothing in the overtime and minimum-wage requirements of the FLSA, as applied to SAMTA, that is destructive of state sovereignty or violative of any constitutional provision. SAMTA faces nothing more than the same minimum-wage and overtime obligations that hundreds of thousands of other employers, public as well as private, have to meet.

In these cases, the status of public mass transit simply underscores the extent to which the structural protections of the Constitution insulate the States from federally imposed burdens. When Congress first subjected state mass-transit systems to FLSA obligations in 1966, and when it expanded those obligations in 1974, it simultaneously provided extensive funding for state and local mass transit through UMTA. In the two decades since its enactment, UMTA has provided over $22 billion in mass transit aid to States and localities. In 1983 alone, UMTA funding amounted to $3.7 billion. As noted above, SAMTA and its immediate predecessor have received a substantial amount of UMTA funding, including over $12 million during SAMTA's first two fiscal years alone. In short, Congress has not simply placed a financial burden on the shoulders of States and localities that operate mass-transit systems, but has provided substantial counter-vailing financial assistance as well, assistance that may leave individual mass transit systems better off than they would have been had Congress never intervened at all in the area. Congress' treatment of public mass transit rein-forces our conviction that the national political process systematically protects States from the risk of having their functions in that area handi-capped by Commerce Clause regulation.

This analysis makes clear that Congress' action in affording SAMTA employees the pro-tections of the wage and hour provisions of the FLSA contravened no affirmative limit on Congress' power under the Commerce Clause. The judgment of the District Court therefore must be reversed.

Of course, we continue to recognize that the States occupy a special and specific position in our constitutional system and that the scope of Congress' authority under the Commerce Clause must reflect that position. But the principal and basic limit on the federal commerce power is that inherent in all congressional action—the built-in restraints that our system provides through state participation in federal govern-mental action. The political process ensures that laws that unduly burden the States will not be promulgated. In the factual setting of these cases the internal safeguards of the political pro-cess have performed as intended.

These cases do not require us to identify or define what affirmative limits the constitutional structure might impose on federal action affect-ing the States under the Commerce Clause.

. . .

Though the separate concurrence providing the fifth vote in National League of Cities was "not untroubled by certain possible implica-tions" of the decision, the Court in that case attempted to articulate affirmative limits on the Commerce Clause power in terms of core gov-ernmental functions and fundamental attributes of state sovereignty. But the model of democrat-ic decisionmaking the Court there identified underestimated, in our view, the solicitude of the national political process for the continued vitality of the States. Attempts by other courts since then to draw guidance from this model

have proved it both impracticable and doctrinal-ly barren. In sum, in National League of Cities the Court tried to repair what did not need repair.

We do not lightly overrule recent precedent. We have not hesitated, however, when it has become apparent that a prior decision has departed from a proper understanding of con-gressional power under the Commerce Clause. Due respect for the reach of congressional power within the federal system mandates that we do so now.

National League of Cities v Usery is over-ruled. The judgment of the District Court is reversed, and these cases are remanded to that court for further proceedings consistent with this opinion.

It is so ordered.

Justice **Powell,** with whom The **Chief Justice,** Justice **Rehnquist,** and Justice **O'Connor** join, dissenting.

The Court today, in its 5–4 decision, overrules National League of Cities v Usery (1976), a case in which we held that Congress lacked authority to impose the requirements of the Fair Labor Standards Act on state and local governments. Because I believe this decision substantially alters the federal system embodied in the Constitution, I dissent.

There are, of course, numerous examples over the history of this Court in which prior decisions have been reconsidered and overruled. There have been few cases, however, in which the principle of stare decisis and the rationale of recent decisions were ignored as abruptly as we now witness. The reasoning of the Court in National League of Cities, and the principle applied there, have been reiterated consistently over the past eight years. . . .

. . .

Whatever effect the Court's decision may have in weakening the application of stare deci-sis, it is likely to be less important than what the Court has done to the Constitution itself. A unique feature of the United States is the *federal system* of government guaranteed by the Con-stitution and implicit in the very name of our country. Despite some genuflecting in Court's opinion to the concept of federalism, today's decision effectively reduces the Tenth Amendment to meaningless rhetoric when Congress acts pursuant to the Commerce Clause. . . .

. . .

In our federal system, the States have a major role that cannot be preempted by the national government. As contemporaneous writings and the debates at the ratifying conventions make clear, the States' ratification of the Constitution was predicated on this understanding of federalism. Indeed, the Tenth Amendment was adopted specifically to ensure that the important role promised the States by the proponents of the Constitution was realized.

Much of the initial opposition to the Constitution was rooted in the fear that the national government would be too powerful and eventually would eliminate the States as viable political entities. This concern was voiced repeatedly until proponents of the Constitution made assurances that a bill of rights, including a provision explicitly reserving powers in the States, would be among the first business of the new Congress. . . .

Antifederalists raised these concerns in almost every State ratifying convention. As a result, eight States voted for the Constitution only after proposing amendments to be adopted after ratification. All eight of these included among their recommendations some version of what later became the Tenth Amendment. So strong was the concern that the proposed Constitution was seriously defective without a specific bill of rights, including a provision reserving powers to the States, that in order to secure the votes for ratification, the Federalists eventually conceded that such provisions were necessary. It was thus generally agreed that consideration of a bill of rights would be among the first business of the new Congress. Accordingly, the 10 amendments that we know as the Bill of Rights were proposed and adopted early in the first session of the First Congress.

This history, which the Court simply ignores, documents the integral role of the Tenth Amendment in our constitutional theory. It exposes as well, I believe, the fundamental character of the Court's error today. Far from being "unsound in principle," judicial enforcement of the Tenth Amendment is essential to maintaining the federal system so carefully designed by the Framers and adopted in the Constitution.

. . .

The emasculation of the powers of the States that can result from the Court's decision is predicated on the Commerce Clause as a power "delegated to the United States" by the Constitution. The relevant language states: "Congress shall have power . . . to regulate commerce with foreign nations and among the several states and with the Indian tribes." Art I, § 8. Section eight identifies a score of powers, listing the authority to lay taxes, borrow money on the credit of the United States, pay its debts, and provide for the common defense and the general welfare *before* its brief reference to "Commerce." It is clear from the debates leading up to the adoption of the Constitution that the commerce to be regulated was that which the states themselves lacked the practical capability to regulate. Indeed, the language of the clause itself focuses on activities that only a national government could regulate: commerce with foreign nations and Indian tribes and *"among"* the several states.

To be sure, this Court has construed the Commerce Clause to accommodate unanticipated changes over the past two centuries. As these changes have occurred, the Court has had to decide whether the federal government has exceeded its authority by regulating activities beyond the capability of a single state to regulate or beyond legitimate federal interests that outweighed the authority and interests of the States. In so doing, however, the Court properly has been mindful of the essential role of the States in our federal system.

The opinion for the Court in National League of Cities was faithful to history in its understanding of federalism. The Court observed that "our federal system of government imposes definite limits upon the authority of Congress to regulate the activities of States as States by means of the commerce power." The Tenth Amendment was invoked to prevent Congress from exercising its "power in a fashion that impairs the States' integrity or their ability to function effectively in a federal system."

. . .

In contrast, the Court today propounds a view of federalism that pays only lip service to the role of the States. Although it says that the States "unquestionably do 'retai[n] a significant measure of sovereign authority,'" it fails to recognize the broad, yet specific areas of sovereignty that the Framers intended the States to retain. Indeed, the Court barely acknowledges that the Tenth Amendment exists. That Amendment states explicitly that "[t]he powers not delegated to the United States . . . are reserved to the States." The Court recasts this language to say that the States retain their sovereign powers "only to the extent that the Constitution has not divested them of their original powers and transferred those powers to the Federal Government." This rephrasing is not a distinction without a difference; rather, it reflects the Court's unprecedented view that Congress is free under the Commerce Clause to assume a State's traditional sovereign power, and to do so without judicial review of its action. Indeed, the Court's view of federalism appears to relegate the States to precisely the trivial role that opponents of the Constitution feared they would occupy.

In National League of Cities, we spoke of fire prevention, police protection, sanitation, and public health as "typical of [the services] performed by state and local governments in discharging their dual functions of administering the public law and furnishing public services." Not only are these activities remote from any normal concept of interstate commerce, they are also activities that epitomize the concerns of local, democratic self-government. In emphasizing the need to protect traditional governmental functions, we identified the kinds of activities engaged in by state and local governments that affect the everyday lives of citizens. These are services that people are in a position to understand and evaluate, and in a democracy, have the right to oversee. We recognized that "it is functions such as these which governments are created to provide . . . " and that the states and local governments are better able than the national government to perform them.

The Court maintains that the standard approved in National League of Cities "disserves principles of democratic self government." In reaching this conclusion, the Court looks myopically only to persons elected to positions in the federal government. It disregards entirely the far more effective role of democratic self-government at the state and local levels. One must compare realistically the operation of the state and local governments with that of the federal government. Federal legislation is drafted primarily by the staffs of the congressional committees. In view of the hundreds of bills introduced at each session of Congress and the complexity of many of them, it is virtually impossible for even the most conscientious legislators to be truly familiar with many of the statutes enacted. Federal departments and agencies customarily are authorized to write regulations. Often these are more important than the text of the statutes. As is true of the original legislation, these are drafted largely by staff personnel. The administration and enforcement of federal laws and regulations necessarily are largely in the hands of staff and civil service employees. These employees may have little or no knowledge of the States and localities that will be affected by the statutes and regulations for which they are responsible. In any case, they hardly are as accessible and responsive as those who occupy analogous positions in State and local governments.

In drawing this contrast, I imply no criticism of these federal employees or the officials who are ultimately in charge. The great majority are conscientious and faithful to their duties. My point is simply that members of the immense federal bureaucracy are not elected, know less about the services traditionally rendered by States and localities, and are inevitably less responsive to recipients of such services, than are state legislatures, city councils, boards of supervisors, and state and local commissions, boards, and agencies. It is at these state and local levels—not in Washington as the Court so mistakenly thinks—that "democratic self-government" is best exemplified.

. . .

Aftermath of Garcia *v.* San Antonio Metropolitan Transit Authority

One of the ironies of the *Garcia* case is that the decision gave the Labor Department enforcement power that it no longer wanted. President Reagan had long championed less regulation of states and communities by the federal government.

Although a majority of the Court clearly remains wary of restricting congressional authority under the commerce clause, it has been more deferential to state claims when the national government has not acted. For example, in 1989 the Court unanimously upheld a 5 percent tax imposed by the state of Illinois on interstate telephone calls, holding that the tax did not violate the interstate commerce clause because it was reasonably related to state services and benefits (*Goldberg* v. *Sweet*). Also unanimous was the decision in *Perpich* v. *Defense Department* (1990) which involved federal authority over National Guard military units that are controlled by the state governors under peacetime conditions. Congress may authorize National Guard training missions abroad, said the Court, despite the opposition of a state governor.

Myers v. *United States*
272 U.S. 52 (1926)

When one looks to the specific language of the Constitution, the only reference to any power of removal of any officer of the federal government from office is the power of impeachment. Does this mean that the framers had so circumscribed the executive that a President has no authority to fire one of his own appointees? Given the constitutional silence on the matter, the issue was bound to rise and did so in 1789 in the very first Congress. After a debate over the act to establish the Department of State (originally called the Department of Foreign Affairs) in which several viewpoints were expressed, a clause was incorporated in the measure which implied that the head of the new department might be removed at the President's discretion. In a strict sense this principle would apply only to officers such as cabinet-level appointees whose terms were not fixed. Constitutional scholars continued to debate the question, with dominant opinion contending that the power of removal was incident to the power of appointment and that those officers appointed by the President with the advice and consent of the Senate could not be removed without obtaining that same advice and consent. However, it was not until 1926, in *Myers* v. *United States*, that the Supreme Court made a decisive pronouncement on the rule governing presidential removal of executive officers.

Under orders from President Woodrow Wilson the postmaster general removed Frank Myers, a first-class postmaster in Portland, Oregon, from office, an act which appeared to be in direct conflict with a statute that had been in force since 1876. The law required that all first-, second-, and third-class postmasters should be appointed and removed by and with the consent of the Senate and should hold office for 4 years "unless sooner removed or suspended according to law." Myers lost his suit in the U.S. Court of Claims where he attempted to recover his salary. After his death an appeal was taken to the Supreme Court by Lois Myers, the administratrix of his estate.

In reading this opinion one should keep in mind that it was written by Chief Justice William Howard Taft, the only man to hold the chief justiceship and the presidency as well. It is ironic that Taft, who as President was known for his restrictive view of executive authority (in contrast to his predecessor, Theodore Roosevelt's expansive view), should have authored an opinion characterized as "the fountainhead of latitudinarian construction" of presidential power.

WILLIAM HOWARD TAFT

William Howard Taft is the only chief justice to have served as President of the United States. A conservative, property-oriented lawyer, Taft was appointed chief justice by President Warren Harding in 1922. Despite his laissez-faire views, Taft wrote several opinions upholding national regulation of business enterprise and dissented from his own Court when it resurrected economic due process to strike down state regulatory legislation. Reflecting his experience as chief executive, Taft wrote opinions giving broad scope to the pardoning power and to presidential authority to remove his appointees.

Mr. Chief Justice **Taft** delivered the opinion of the Court.

This case presents the question whether under the Constitution the President has the exclusive power of removing executive officers of the United States whom he has appointed by and with the advice and consent of the Senate.

. . .

The question where the power of removal of executive officers appointed by the President by and with the advice and consent of the Senate was vested, was presented early in the first session of the First Congress. There is no express provision respecting removals in the Constitution, except as section 4 of article 2 provides for removal from office by impeachment. The subject was not discussed in the Constitutional Convention. Under the Articles of Confederation, Congress was given the power of appointing certain executive officers of the Confederation, and during the Revolution and while the articles were given effect, Congress exercised the power of removal.

. . .

Made responsible under the Constitution for the effective enforcement of the law, the President needs as an indispensable aid to meet

it the disciplinary influence upon those who act under him of a reserve power of removal. But it is contended that executive officers appointed by the President with the consent of the Senate are bound by the statutory law, and are not his servants to do his will, and that his obligation to care for the faithful execution of the laws does not authorize him to treat them as such. The degree of guidance in the discharge of their duties that the President may exercise over executive officers varies with the character of their service as prescribed in the law under which they act. The highest and most important duties which his subordinates perform are those in which they act for him. In such cases they are exercising not their own but his discretion. This field is a very large one. It is sometimes described as political. Each head of a department is and must be the President's alter ego in the matters of that department where the President is required by law to exercise authority.

. . .

In all such cases, the discretion to be exercised is that of the President in determining the national public interest and in directing the action to be taken by his executive subordinates to protect it. In this field his cabinet officers must do his will. He must place in each member of his official family, and his chief executive subordinates, implicit faith. The moment that he loses confidence in the intelligence, ability, judgment, or loyalty of any one of them, he must have the power to remove him without delay. To require him to file charges and submit them to the consideration of the Senate might make impossible that unity and co-ordination in executive administration essential to effective action.

The duties of the heads of departments and bureaus in which the discretion of the President is exercised and which we have described are the most important in the whole field of executive action of the government. There is nothing in the Constitution which permits a distinction between the removal of the head of a department or a bureau, when he discharges a political duty of the President or exercises his discretion, and the removal of executive officers engaged in the discharge of their other normal duties. The imperative reasons requiring an unrestricted power to remove the most important of his subordinates in their most important duties must therefore control the interpretation of the Constitution as to all appointed by him.

But this is not to say that there are not strong reasons why the President should have a like power to remove his appointees charged with other duties than those above described. The ordinary duties of officers prescribed by statute come under the general administrative control of the President by virtue of the general grant to him of the executive power, and he may properly supervise and guide their construction of the statutes under which they act in order to secure that unitary and uniform execution of the laws which article 2 of the Constitution evidently contemplated in vesting general executive power in the President alone. Laws are often passed with specific provision for the adoption of regulations by a department or bureau head to make the law workable and effective. The ability and judgment manifested by the official thus empowered, as well as his energy and stimulation of his subordinates, are subjects which the President must consider and supervise in his administrative control. Finding such officers to be negligent and inefficient, the President should have the power to remove them. Of course there may be duties so peculiarly and specifically committed to the discretion of a particular officer as to raise a question whether the President may overrule or revise the officer's interpretation of his statutory duty in a particular instance. Then there may be duties of a quasi judicial character imposed on executive officers and members of executive tribunals whose decisions after hearing affect interests of individuals, the discharge of which the President cannot in a particular case properly influence or control. But even in such a case he may consider the decision after its rendition as a reason for removing the officer, on the ground that the discretion regularly entrusted to that officer by statute has not been on the whole intelligently or wisely exercised. Otherwise he does not discharge his own constitutional duty of seeing that the laws be faithfully executed.

We have devoted much space to this discussion and decision of the question of the presidential power of removal in the First Congress, not because a congressional conclusion on a constitutional issue is conclusive, but first because of our agreement with the reasons upon which it was avowedly based, second because this was the decision of the First Congress on a question of primary importance in the organization of the government made within two years after the Constitutional Convention and within a much shorter time after its ratification, and third because that Congress numbered among its leaders those who had been members of the convention. It must necessarily constitute a precedent upon which many future laws supplying the machinery of the new government would be based and, if erroneous, would be likely to evoke dissent and departure in future Congresses. It would come at once before the executive branch of the government for compliance and might well be brought before the judicial branch for a test of its validity. As we shall see, it was soon accepted as a final decision of the question by all branches of the government.

It was, of course, to be expected that the decision would be received by lawyers and jurists with something of the same division of opinion as that manifested in Congress, and doubts were often expressed as to its correctness. But the acquiescence which was promptly accorded it after a few years was universally recognized.

. . .

Summing up, then, the facts as to acquiescence by all branches of the government in the legislative decision of 1789 as to executive officers, whether superior or inferior, we find that from 1789 until 1863, a period of 74 years, there was no act of Congress, no executive act, and no decision of this court at variance with the declaration of the First Congress; but there was, as we have seen, clear affirmative recognition of it by each branch of the government.

Our conclusion on the merits, sustained by the arguments before stated, is that article 2 grants to the President the executive power of the government—i. e., the general administrative control of those executing the laws, including the power of appointment and removal of executive officers—a conclusion confirmed by his obligation to take care that the laws be faithfully executed; that article 2 excludes the exercise of legislative power by Congress to provide for appointments and removals, except only as granted therein to Congress in the matter of inferior offices; that Congress is only given power to provide for appointments and removals of inferior officers after it has vested, and on condition that it does vest, their appointment in other authority than the President with the Senate's consent; that the provisions of the second section of article 2, which blend action by the legislative branch, or by part of it, in the work of the executive, are limitations to be strictly construed, and not to be extended by implication; that the President's power of removal is further established as an incident to his specifically enumerated function of appointment by and with the advice of the Senate, but that such incident does not by implication extend to removals the Senate's power of checking appointments; and, finally, that to hold otherwise would make it impossible for the President, in case of political or other difference with the Senate or Congress, to take care that the laws be faithfully executed.

. . .

What, then, are the elements that enter into our decision of this case? We have, first, a construction of the Constitution made by a Congress which was to provide by legislation for the organization of the government in accord with the Constitution which had just then been adopted, and in which there were, as Representatives and Senators, a considerable number of those who had been members of the convention that framed the Constitution and presented it for ratification. It was the Congress that launched the government. It was the Congress that rounded out the Constitution itself by the proposing of the first 10 amendments, which had in effect been promised to the people as a consideration for the ratification. It was the Congress in which Mr. Madison, one of the first in the framing of the Constitution, led also in the organization of the government under it. It was a Congress whose constitutional decisions have always been regarded, as they should be regarded, as of the greatest weight in the interpretation of that fundamental instrument. This construction was followed by the legislative department and the executive department continuously for 73 years, and this, although the matter in the heat of political differences between the executive and the Senate in President Jackson's time, was the subject of bitter controversy, as we have seen. This court has repeatedly laid down the principle that a contemporaneous legislative exposition of the Constitution, when the founders of our government and framers of our Constitution were actively participating in public affairs, acquiesced in for a long term of years, fixes the construction to be given its provisions.

We are now asked to set aside this construction thus buttressed and adopt an adverse view, because the Congress of the United States did so during a heated political difference of opinion between the then President and the majority leaders of Congress over the reconstruction measures adopted as a means of restoring to their proper status the states which attempted to withdraw from the Union at the time of the Civil War. The extremes to which the majority in both Houses carried legislative measures in that matter are now recognized by all who calmly review the history of that episode in our government leading to articles of impeachment against President Johnson and his acquittal. Without animadverting on the character of the measures taken, we are certainly justified in saying that they should not be given the weight affecting proper constitutional construction to be accorded to that reached by the First Congress of the United States during a political calm and acquiesced in by the whole government for three-quarters of a century, especially when the new construction contended for has never been acquiesced in by either the executive or the judicial departments. While this court has studiously avoided deciding the issue until it was presented in such a way that it could not be avoided, in the references it has made to the history of the question, and in the presumptions it has indulged in favor of a statutory construction not inconsistent with the legislative decision of 1789, it has indicated a trend of view that we should not and cannot ignore. When on the merits we find our conclusion strongly favoring the view which prevailed in the First Congress, we have no hesitation in holding that conclusion to be correct; and it therefore follows that the Tenure of Office Act of 1867, in so far as it attempted to prevent the President from removing executive officers who had been appointed by him by and with the advice and consent of the Senate, was invalid, and that subsequent legislation of the same effect was equally so.

For the reasons given, we must therefore hold that the provision of the law of 1876 by which the unrestricted power of removal of first-class postmasters is denied to the President is in violation of the Constitution and invalid. This leads to an affirmance of the judgment of the Court of Claims.

. . .

The separate opinion of Mr. Justice **McReynolds.**

In any rational search for answer to the questions arising upon this record, it is important not to forget—

That this is a government of limited powers, definitely enumerated and granted by a written Constitution.

That the Constitution must be interpreted by attributing to its words the meaning which they bore at the time of its adoption, and in view of commonly-accepted canons of construction, its history, early and long-continued practices under it, and relevant opinions of this court.

That the Constitution endows Congress with plenary powers "to establish post offices and post roads."

That, exercising this power during the years from 1789 to 1836, Congress provided for postmasters and vested the power to appoint and remove all of them at pleasure in the Postmaster General.

That the Constitution contains no words which specifically grant to the President power to remove duly appointed officers. And it is definitely settled that he cannot remove those whom he has not appointed—certainly they can be removed only as Congress may permit.

That postmasters are inferior officers within the meaning of article 2, § 2, of the Constitution.

That from its first session to the last one Congress has often asserted its right to restrict the President's power to remove inferior officers, although appointed by him with consent of the Senate.

That many Presidents have approved statutes limiting the power of the executive to remove, and that from the beginning such limitations have been respected in practice.

That this court, as early as 1803, in an opinion never overruled and rendered in a case where it was necessary to decide the question, positively declared that the President had no power to remove at will an inferior officer appointed with consent of the Senate to serve for a definite term fixed by an act of Congress.

That the power of Congress to restrict removals by the President was recognized by this court as late as 1903, in Shurtleff v. United States.

That the proceedings in the Constitutional Convention of 1787, the political history of the times, contemporaneous opinion, common canons of construction, the action of Congress from the beginning and opinions of this court, all oppose the theory that by vesting "the executive power" in the President the Constitution gave him an illimitable right to remove inferior officers.

That this court has emphatically disapproved the same theory concerning "the judicial power" vested in the courts by words substantially the same as those which vest "the executive power" in the President. "The executive power shall be vested in a President of the United States of America." "The judicial power of the United States, shall be vested in one Supreme Court, and in such inferior courts as the Congress may from time to time ordain and establish."

That to declare the President vested with indefinite and illimitable executive powers would extend the field of his possible action far beyond the limits observed by his predecessors, and would enlarge the powers of Congress to a degree incapable of fair appraisement.

Considering all these things, it is impossible for me to accept the view that the President may dismiss, as caprice may suggest, any inferior officer whom he has appointed with consent of the Senate, notwithstanding a positive inhibition by Congress. In the last analysis, that view has no substantial support, unless it be the polemic opinions expressed by Mr. Madison (and eight others) during the debate of 1789, when he was discussing questions relating to a "superior officer" to be appointed for an indefinite term. Notwithstanding his justly exalted reputation as one of the creators and early expounder of the Constitution, sentiments expressed under such circumstances ought not now to outweigh the conclusion which Congress affirmed by deliberate action while he was leader in the House and has consistently maintained down to the present year, the opinion of this court solemnly announced through the great Chief Justice more than a century ago, and the canons of construction approved over and over again.

Judgment should go for the appellant.

Mr. Justice **Brandeis,** dissenting.

. . .

To imply a grant to the President of the uncontrollable power of removal from statutory inferior executive offices involves an unnecessary and indefensible limitation upon the constitutional power of Congress to fix the tenure of the inferior statutory offices. That such a limitation cannot be justified on the ground of necessity is demonstrated by the practice of our governments, state and national. In none of the original 13 states did the chief executive possess such power at the time of the adoption of the federal Constitution. In none of the 48 states has such power been conferred at any time since by a state Constitution, with a single possible exception. In a few states the Legislature has granted to the Governor, or other appointing power, the absolute power of removal. The legislative practice of most states reveals a decided tendency to limit, rather than to extend, the Governor's power of removal. The practice of the federal government will be set forth in detail.

Over removal from inferior civil offices, Congress has, from the foundation of our government, exercised continuously some measure of control by legislation. The instances of such laws are many. Some of the statutes were directory in character. Usually, they were mandatory. Some of them, comprehensive in scope, have endured for generations. During the first 40 years of our government, there was no occasion to curb removals.

. . .

The practice of Congress to control the exercise of the executive power of removal from inferior offices is evidenced by many statutes which restrict it in many ways besides the removal clause here in question. Each of these restrictive statutes became law with the approval of the President. Every President who has held office since 1861, except President Garfield, approved one or more of such statutes. Some of these statutes, prescribing a fixed term, provide that removal shall be made only for one of several specified causes. Some provide a fixed term, subject generally to removal for cause. Some provide for removal only after hearing. Some provide a fixed term, subject to removal for reasons to be communicated by the President to the Senate. Some impose the restriction in still other ways.

. . .

The assertion that the mere grant by the Constitution of executive power confers upon the President as a prerogative the unrestricted power of appointment and of removal from executive offices, except so far as otherwise expressly provided by the Constitution, is clearly inconsistent also with those statutes which restrict the exercise by the President of the power of nomination. There is not a word in the Constitution which in terms authorizes Congress to limit the President's freedom of choice in making nominations for executive offices. It is to appointment as distinguished from nomination that the Constitution imposes in terms the requirement of Senatorial consent. But a multitude of laws have been enacted which limit the President's power to make nominations, and which, through the restrictions imposed, may prevent the selection of the person deemed by him best fitted. Such restriction upon the power to nominate has been exercised by Congress continuously since the foundation of the government. Every President has approved one or more of such acts. Every President has consistently observed them. This is true of those offices to which he makes appointments without the advice and consent of the Senate as well as of those for which its consent is required.

. . .

The historical data submitted present a legislative practice, established by concurrent affirmative action of Congress and the President, to make consent of the Senate a condition of removal from statutory inferior, civil, executive offices to which the appointment is made for a fixed term by the President with such consent. They show that the practice has existed, without interruption, continuously for the last 58 years; that throughout this period, it has governed a great majority of all such offices; that the legislation applying the removal clause specifically to the office of postmaster was enacted more than half a century ago; and that recently the practice has, with the President's approval, been extended to several newly created offices. The data show further that the insertion of the removal clause in acts creating inferior civil offices with fixed tenures is part of the broader legislative practice, which has prevailed since the formation of our government, to restrict or regulate in many ways both removal from and nomination to such offices. A persistent legislative practice which involves a delimitation of the respective powers of Congress and the President, and which has been so established and maintained, should be deemed tantamount to judicial construction, in the absence of any decision by any court to the contrary.

The persuasive effect of this legislative practice is strengthened by the fact that no instance has been found, even in the earlier period of our history, of concurrent affirmative action of Congress and the President which is inconsistent with the legislative practice of the last 58 years to impose the removal clause. Nor has any instance been found of action by Congress which involves recognition in any other way of the alleged uncontrollable executive power to remove an inferior civil officer. The action taken by Congress in 1789 after the great debate does not present such an instance. The vote then taken did not involve a decision that the President had uncontrollable power. It did not involve a decision of the question whether Congress could confer upon the Senate the right, and impose upon it the duty, to participate in removals. It involved merely the decision that the Senate does not, in the absence of legislative grant thereof, have the right to share in the removal of an officer appointed with its consent, and that the President has, in the absence of restrictive legislation, the constitutional power of removal without such consent. Moreover, as Chief Justice Marshall recognized, the debate and the decision related to a high political office, not to inferior ones.

. . .

The separation of the powers of government did not make each branch completely autonomous. It left each in some measure, dependent upon the others, as it left to each power to exercise, in some respects, functions in their nature executive, legislative and judicial. Obviously the President cannot secure full execution of the laws, if Congress denies to him adequate means of doing so. Full execution may be defeated because Congress declines to create offices indispensable for that purpose; or because Congress, having created the office, declines to make the indispensable appropriation; or because Congress, having both created the office and made the appropriation, prevents, by restrictions which it imposes, the appointment of officials who in quality and character are indispensable to the efficient execution of the law. If, in any such way, adequate means are denied to the President, the fault will lie with Congress. The President performs his full constitutional duty, if, with the means and instruments provided by Congress and within the limitations prescribed by it; he uses his best endeavors to secure the faithful execution of the laws enacted.

Checks and balances were established in order that this should be "a government of laws and not of men." As White said in the House in 1789, an uncontrollable power of removal in the Chief Executive "is a doctrine not to be learned in American governments." Such power had been denied in colonial charters, and even under proprietary grants and royal commissions. It had been denied in the thirteen states before the framing of the federal Constitution. The doctrine of the separation of powers was adopted by the convention of 1787 not to promote efficiency but to preclude the exercise of arbitrary power. The purpose was not to avoid friction, but, by means of the inevitable friction incident to the distribution of the governmental powers among three departments, to save the people from autocracy. In order to prevent arbitrary executive action, the Constitution provided in terms that presidential appointments be made with the consent of the Senate, unless Congress should otherwise provide; and this clause was construed by Alexander Hamilton in The Federalist, No. 77, as requiring like consent to removals. Limiting further executive prerogatives customary in monarchies, the Constitution empowered Congress to vest the appointment of inferior officers, "as we think proper, in the President alone, in the Courts of Law, or in the Heads of Departments." Nothing in support of the claim of uncontrollable power can be inferred from the silence of the convention of 1787 on the subject of removal. For the outstanding fact remains that every specific proposal to confer such uncontrollable power upon the President was rejected. In America, as in England, the conviction prevailed then that the people must look to representative assemblies for the protection of their liberties. And protection of the individual, even if he be an official, from the arbitrary or capricious exercise of power was then believed to be an essential of free government.

Mr. Justice **Holmes,** dissenting.

My Brothers McReynolds and Brandeis have discussed the question before us with exhaustive research and I say a few words merely to emphasize my agreement with their conclusion.

The arguments drawn from the executive power of the President, and from his duty to appoint officers of the United States (when Congress does not vest the appointment elsewhere), to take care that the laws be faithfully executed, and to commission all officers of the United States, seem to me spiders' webs inadequate to control the dominant facts.

We have to deal with an office that owes its existence to Congress and that Congress may abolish to-morrow. Its duration and the pay attached to it while it lasts depend on Congress alone. Congress alone confers on the President the power to appoint to it and at any time may transfer the power to other hands. With such power over its own creation, I have no more trouble in believing that Congress has power to prescribe a term of life for it free from any interference than I have in accepting the undoubted power of Congress to decree its end. I have equally little trouble in accepting its power to prolong the tenure of an incumbent until Congress or the Senate shall have assented to his removal. The duty of the President to see that the laws be executed is a duty that does not go beyond the laws or require him to achieve more than Congress sees fit to leave within his power.

Aftermath of Myers v. United States

The Supreme Court's sweeping support of unlimited presidential removal power in *Myers* was later modified as the Court gave the term "executive officer" a very literal and somewhat circumscribed meaning. In 1935, in *Humphrey's Executor* v. *United States,* the Court, without overruling *Myers,* drew some boundaries around the original holding.

President Franklin Roosevelt had removed Humphrey from the Federal Trade Commission for reasons of policy disagreement and Humphrey brought suit for back salary, alleging that he was illegally removed. In a unanimous opinion the

Court, upholding Humphrey's claim, distinguished between strictly executive officers such as postmasters and those members of independent regulatory bodies such as the Federal Trade Commission whose duties were quasi-legislative and quasi-judicial as well as executive. Independent commissioners not only made rules (legislative in nature) but held hearings and then ordered that the rules be enforced (judicial in nature). Since these regulatory bodies are designed to carry out the legislative will, declared the Court, Congress may require them to act independently of executive control. Incident to that control is the power to fix the period they shall remain in office and to forbid their removal except for causes named in the statute, that is, incompetence, illness, and so forth.

Following the *Humphrey* decision the Court added another restriction, albeit not of major proportions, on the President's power of removal. In 1958 it decided the case of *Wiener* v. *United States,* which involved the unresolved question of whether the President, in the absence of an express limitation on his authority in a statute creating an agency endowed with quasi-judicial functions, might remove members of such agencies. At issue was the removal of Myron Wiener by President Dwight Eisenhower from the War Claims Commission, a body whose duties were wholly adjudicatory and whose determinations were not subject to review by any other agency. In a unanimous opinion the Court concluded that inasmuch as the President had no supervisory control over the commission, he lacked the power to remove a commissioner during his fixed term.

Despite some crimping of the presidential prerogative in the *Humphrey* and *Wiener* cases, the rule in *Myers* remains solidly in place, underscoring the Supreme Court's reluctance to curb the powers of its coordinate branches of government.

United States v. Belmont

301 U.S. 324 (1937)

Undoubtedly the area in which the Supreme Court is most reluctant to intrude on the powers of the coordinate branches is that of foreign affairs. Although the Senate with its consenting role on treaties and ambassadorial appointments, and the Congress with its control over appropriations and expenditures are an integral part of the foreign policy machinery, the President is dominant. *How* dominant has been made clear in several judicial decisions, a major one of which is *United States* v. *Belmont.* When a treaty with a foreign nation has been negotiated by the President and agreed to by two-thirds of the Senate, it has legal force, both as international and domestic law. In the latter sense it supersedes any previous acts of Congress on the subject and, under the doctrine of national supremacy, it takes precedence over any state laws in force. What, however, are the legal consequences if the President enters into an "executive agreement" with a foreign power, an agreement made only in his constitutional capacity as chief executive with no prior authorization or post concurrence by Congress? Does such an agreement have the binding force of a formal treaty? In short, are treaties and executive agreements legally interchangeable? Although executive initiatives had been taken by presidents historically, beginning with George Washington, such agreements neither required financial commitments from Congress nor conflicted with state policies.

It was not until 1937 in the *Belmont* case that the Supreme Court had to face squarely the constitutionality of "executive agreements." At issue was whether a district court of the United States might dismiss a suit, instituted by the national government in its capacity as assignee of the Soviet Union, to collect money which was once the property of a Russian corporation whose assets had been appropriated by the Soviet government. Prior to the Russian Revolution in 1917 the Petrograd Metal Works had deposited funds in the New York City bank of August Belmont & Company and when the Soviet government nationalized the company and appropriated assets, the Soviets held title to the money in the New York bank. In 1933, when President Roosevelt and representatives of the Soviet Union established diplomatic relations, they agreed that each government would act as an agent to prosecute the claims of the other. When the United States government requested the funds from Belmont— actually, his executors, since Belmont had died in the interim—they refused to comply and the United States brought suit to recover the assets. Both the U.S. District Court and the U.S. Circuit Court of Appeals refused to grant title to the government, arguing that the policy of New York State, which was opposed to the acquisition of property by confiscation, was controlling in any bank located within the state.

GEORGE SUTHERLAND

A conservative Republican senator from Utah, George Sutherland was appointed to the Supreme Court by President Warren G. Harding in 1922 and served until 1938. Sutherland saw great evils in the control of the individual by government and believed in the use of judicial power to keep government restraint to a minimum. He was a judge of great learning and became the intellectual leader of the Court's conservative wing in the 1930s. Sutherland will be remembered for his influential opinions in foreign affairs cases and his enlightened views on the administration of justice, as exemplified by his opinion in Powell v. Alabama.

Mr. Justice **Sutherland** delivered the opinion of the Court.

. . .

First. We do not pause to inquire whether in fact there was any policy of the State of New York to be infringed, since we are of opinion that no state policy can prevail against the international compact here involved.

This court has held that every sovereign state must recognize the independence of every other sovereign state; and that the courts of one will not sit in judgment upon the acts of the government of another, done within its own territory.

. . .

We take judicial notice of the fact that coincident with the assignment set forth in the complaint, the President recognized the Soviet Government, and normal diplomatic relations were established between that government and the Government of the United States, followed by an exchange of ambassadors. The effect of this was to validate, so far as this country is concerned, all acts of the Soviet Government here involved from the commencement of its existence. The recognition, establishment of diplomatic relations, the assignment, and agreements with respect thereto, were all parts of one transaction, resulting in an international compact between the two governments. That the negotiations, acceptance of the assignment and agreements and understandings in respect thereof were within the competence of the President may not be doubted. Governmental power over internal affairs is distributed between the national government and the several states. Governmental power over external affairs is not distributed, but is vested exclusively in the national government. And in respect of what was done here, the Executive had authority to speak as the sole organ of that government. The assignment and the agreements in connection therewith did not, as in the case of treaties, as that term is used in the treaty making clause of the Constitution (Art. II, § 2), require the advice and consent of the Senate.

A treaty signifies "a compact made between two or more independent nations with a view to the public welfare." But an international compact, as this was, is not always a treaty which requires the participation of the Senate. There are many such compacts, of which a protocol, a modus vivendi, a postal convention, and agreements like that now under consideration are illustrations.

. . .

Plainly, the external powers of the United States are to be exercised without regard to state laws or policies. The supremacy of a treaty in this respect has been recognized from the beginning. Mr. Madison, in the Virginia Convention, said that if a treaty does not supersede existing state laws, as far as they contravene its operation, the treaty would be ineffective. "To counteract it by the supremacy of the state laws, would bring on the Union the just charge of national perfidy, and involve us in war." And while this rule in respect of treaties is established by the express language of cl. 2, Art. VI, of the Constitution, the same rule would result in the case of all international compacts and agreements from the very fact that complete power over international affairs is in the national gov-

ernment and is not and cannot be subject to any curtailment or interference on the part of the several states. In respect of all international negotiations and compacts, and in respect of our foreign relations generally, state lines disappear. As to such purposes the State of New York does not exist. Within the field of its powers, whatever the United States rightfully undertakes, it necessarily has warrant to consummate. And when judicial authority is invoked in aid of such consummation, state constitutions, state laws, and state policies are irrelevant to the inquiry and decision. It is inconceivable that any of them can be interposed as an obstacle to the effective operation of a federal constitutional power.

Second. The public policy of the United States relied upon as a bar to the action is that declared by the Constitution, namely, that private property shall not be taken without just compensation. But the answer is that our Constitution, laws and policies have no extraterritorial operation, unless in respect of our own citizens. What another country has done in the way of taking over property of its nationals, and especially of its corporations, is not a matter for judicial consideration here. Such nationals must look to their own government for any redress to which they may be entitled. So far as the record shows, only the rights of the Russian corporation have been affected by what has been done; and it will be time enough to consider the rights of our nationals when, if ever, by proper judicial proceeding, it shall be made to appear that they are so affected as to entitle them to judicial relief. The substantive right to the moneys, as now disclosed, became vested in the Soviet Government as the successor to the corporation; and this right that government has passed to the United States. It does not appear that respondents have any interest in the matter beyond that of a custodian. Thus far no question under the Fifth Amendment is involved.

Aftermath of United States v. Belmont

Five years after the decision in *Belmont,* the Court adhered to its earlier position in unvarnished language when it decided the case of *United States* v. *Pink*(1942). Involved was the question of whether the government under the 1933 United States–Russia protocol might recover the assets of the New York branch of a Russian insurance company. It was the company's position that the decrees of Soviet confiscation could not constitutionally apply to property in New York, but the Court, speaking through Justice William O. Douglas, disagreed. Referring to the President again as the "sole organ of the Federal Government in the field of international relations," the opinion went on to say that since it was the judgment of the executive that to give full recognition required the settlement of outstanding problems, including the claims of nationals, the judiciary would be usurping the executive function if it were to hold that the decision was not fully binding on the nation's courts. Given this fact, Douglas contended that a state law that "is inconsistent with, or impairs the policy or provisions of, a treaty or an international compact or agreement" must yield, that no state "can rewrite foreign policy to conform to its own domestic policies."

This singularly broad reading of executive power would seem to fly in the face of the constitutional language that requires Senate approval of a treaty, particularly since the Court, for the purposes of domestic law at least, equated executive agreements with treaties. Nevertheless the rule remains in force and supports the proposition that, constitutional language aside, the Court exercises considerable restraint when asked to place limits on institutional procedures. A similar restraint was shown by Congress when some of its members proposed amending the Constitution to negate the Court's ruling in the *Belmont* and *Pink* decisions. Among the provisions of a proposed constitutional amendment introduced by Senator John W. Bricker of Ohio in 1954 was a section providing, "Congress shall have the power to regulate all executive and other agreements with any foreign power or international organization. All such agreements shall be subject to the limitations imposed on treaties by the article." In slightly different form the Bricker Amendment was defeated by a vote of 60–31, one vote short of the required two-thirds majority for passage. Similar amendments were introduced in subsequent Congresses but all died in committee. All of this indicates that the status of executive agreements and of their judicial underpinning remains, and probably will remain, unchanged.

McGrain v. *Daugherty*

273 U.S. 135 (1927)

This case is yet another example of how the principle of separate, independent executive and legislative bodies powerfully restrains the Supreme Court's exercise of judicial review. In those sections of Article I of the Constitution that expressly detail the procedures and powers of Congress, no mention is made of the power to conduct investigations or of any rules surrounding the calling and questioning of witnesses. Following the tradition of the British Parliament and of the American colonial legislatures, both of which engaged in investigations, the power was simply assumed when, in 1792, the House of Representatives appointed a committee to investigate the defeat of General St. Clair's army by the Native Americans in the northwest, and authorized it to call witnesses and subpoena records to aid in the inquiry. Other investigations followed and eventually these procedures and the constitutionality of their very existence were called into question before the Supreme Court. Prior to the *McGrain* case in 1927 several decisions were handed down, all supporting the power of Congress to engage in an investigatory function. Since the opinion in *McGrain*

gives a careful summary of those previous rulings, there is no need to outline them here.

Empowered to investigate charges that Attorney General Harry M. Daugherty had failed to prosecute oil company officers and government officials involved in the Teapot Dome scandals of the Harding Administration, a Senate committee entered a subpoena ordering Mally S. Daugherty, the brother-in-law of the attorney general, to appear before it as a witness. When Daugherty failed to answer the summons, the Senate directed John McGrain, deputy sergeant-at-arms, to execute a warrant to bring him into custody, whereupon Daugherty sought and obtained a writ of habeas corpus from the federal district court in Cincinnati. In a hearing in the lower federal court Daugherty obtained his release, the court's opinion declaring that he had been unlawfully detained because the Senate had acted unconstitutionally. The case was appealed to the Supreme Court.

WILLIS VAN DEVANTER

A successful railroad lawyer in Wyoming during the years of westward expansion, Willis Van Devanter became active in Republican politics and was rewarded with a seat on the Eighth Circuit Court of Appeals. In 1910 President William Howard Taft appointed him to the Supreme Court, where he proved to be a resolute conservative activist throughout his 27-year career. A meticulous legal technician, Van Devanter wrote relatively few opinions on the High Court. McGrain v. Daugherty *is by far his most important.*

Mr. Justice **Van Devanter** delivered the opinion of the court.

This is an appeal from the final order in a proceeding in *habeas corpus* discharging a recusant witness held in custody under process of attachment issued from the United States Senate in the course of an investigation which it was making of the administration of the Department of Justice.

. . .

The first of the principal questions—the one which the witness particularly presses on our attention—is, as before shown, whether the Senate—or the House of Representatives, both being on the same plane in this regard—has power, through its own process, to compel a private individual to appear before it or one of its committees and give testimony needed to enable it efficiently to exercise a legislative function belonging to it under the Constitution.

The Constitution provides for a Congress consisting of a Senate and House of Representatives and invests it with "all legislative powers" granted to the United States, and with power "to make all laws which shall be necessary and proper" for carrying into execution these powers and "all other powers" vested by the Constitution in the United States or in any department or officer thereof. Art. I, secs. 1, 8. Other provisions show that, while bills can become laws only after being considered and passed by both houses of Congress, each house is to be distinct from the other, to have its own officers and rules, and to exercise its legislative function independently. Art. I, secs. 2, 3, 5, 7. But there is no provision expressly investing either house with power to make investigations and exact testimony to the end that it may exercise its legislative function advisedly and effectively. So the question arises whether this power is so far incidental to the legislative function as to be implied.

In actual legislative practice power to secure needed information by such means has long been treated as an attribute of the power to legislate. It was so regarded in the British Parliament and in the Colonial legislatures before the American Revolution; and a like view has prevailed and been carried into effect in both houses of Congress and in most of the state legislatures.

This power was both asserted and exerted by the House of Representatives in 1792, when it appointed a select committee to inquire into the St. Clair expedition and authorized the committee to send for necessary persons, papers and records. Mr. Madison, who had taken an important part in framing the Constitution only five years before, and four of his associates in that work, were members of the House of Representatives at the time, and all voted for the inquiry. Other exertions of the power by the House of Representatives, as also by the Senate, are shown in the citations already made. Among those by the Senate, the inquiry ordered in 1859 respecting the raid by John Brown and his adherents on the armory and arsenal of the United States at Harper's Ferry is of special significance. The resolution directing the inquiry authorized the committee to send for persons and papers, to inquire into the facts pertaining to the raid and the means by which it was organized and supported, and to report what legislation, if any, was necessary to preserve the peace of the country and protect the public property. The resolution was briefly discussed and adopted without opposition. Later on the committee reported that Thaddeus Hyatt, although subpoenaed to appear as a witness, had refused to do so; whereupon the Senate ordered that he be attached and brought before it to answer for his refusal. When he was brought in he answered by challenging the power of the Senate to direct the inquiry and exact testimony to aid it in exercising its legislative function. The question of power thus presented was thoroughly discussed by several senators—Mr. Sumner of Massachusetts taking the lead in denying the power and Mr. Fessenden of Maine in supporting it. Sectional and party lines were put aside and the

question was debated and determined with special regard to principle and precedent. The vote was taken on a resolution pronouncing the witness's answer insufficient and directing that he be committed until he should signify that he was ready and willing to testify. The resolution was adopted—44 senators voting for it and 10 against.

. . .

The deliberate solution of the question on that occasion has been accepted and followed on other occasions by both houses of Congress, and never has been rejected or questioned by either.

The state courts quite generally have held that the power to legislate carries with it by necessary implication ample authority to obtain information needed in the rightful exercise of that power, and to employ compulsory process for the purpose.

. . .

We have referred to the practice of the two houses of Congress; and we now shall notice some significant congressional enactments. May 3, 1798, Congress provided that oaths or affirmations might be administered to witnesses by the President of the Senate, the Speaker of the House of Representatives, the chairman of a committee of the whole, or the chairman of a select committee, "in any case under their examination." February 8, 1817, it enlarged that provision so as to include the chairman of a standing committee. January 24, 1857, it passed "An Act more effectually to enforce the attendance of witnesses on the summons of either house of Congress, and to compel them to discover testimony." This act provided, first, that any person summoned as a witness to give testimony or produce papers in any matter under inquiry before either house of Congress, or any committee of either house, who should wilfully make default, or, if appearing, should refuse to answer any question pertinent to the inquiry, should, in addition to the pains and penalties then existing, be deemed guilty of a misdemeanor and be subject to indictment and punishment as there prescribed; and secondly, that no person should be excused from giving evidence in such an inquiry on the ground that it might tend to incriminate or disgrace him, nor be held to answer criminally, or be subjected to any penalty or forfeiture, for any fact or act as to which he was required to testify, excepting that he might be subjected to prosecution for perjury committed while so testifying. January 24, 1862, Congress modified the immunity provision in particulars not material here. These enactments are now embodied in §§ 101–104 and 859 of Revised Statutes. They show very plainly that Congress intended thereby (a) to recognize the power of either house to institute inquiries and exact evidence touching subjects within its jurisdiction and on which it was disposed to act; (b) to recognize that such inquiries may be conducted through committees; (c) to subject defaulting and contumacious witnesses to indictment and punishment in the courts, and thereby to enable either house to exert the power of inquiry "more effectually"; and (d) to open the way for obtaining evidence in such an inquiry, which otherwise could not be obtained, by exempting witnesses required to give evidence therein from criminal and penal prosecutions in respect of matters disclosed by their evidence.

Four decisions of this Court are cited and more or less relied on, and we now turn to them.

The first decision was in *Anderson* v. *Dunn* (1821). The question there was whether, under the Constitution, the House of Representatives has power to attach and punish a person other than a member for contempt of its authority—in fact, an attempt to bribe one of its members. The Court regarded the power as essential to the effective exertion of other powers expressly granted, and therefore as implied.

. . .

The next decision was in *Kilbourn* v. *Thompson* (1880). The question there was whether the House of Representatives had exceeded its power in directing one of its committees to make a particular investigation. The decision was that it had. The principles announced and applied in the case are—that neither house of Congress possesses a "general power of making inquiry into the private affairs of the citizen"; that the power actually possessed is limited to inquiries relating to matters of which the particular house "has jurisdiction"

and in respect of which it rightfully may take other action; that if the inquiry relates to "a matter wherein relief or redress could be had only by a judicial proceeding" it is not within the range of this power, but must be left to the courts, conformably to the constitutional separation of governmental powers; and that for the purpose of determining the essential character of the inquiry recourse may be had to the resolution or order under which it is made. The court examined the resolution which was the basis of the particular inquiry, and ascertained therefrom that the inquiry related to a private real-estate pool or partnership in the District of Columbia. Jay Cooke & Co. had had an interest in the pool, but had become bankrupts, and their estate was in course of administration in a federal bankruptcy court in Pennsylvania. The United States was one of their creditors. The trustee in the bankruptcy proceeding had effected a settlement of the bankrupts' interest in the pool, and of course his action was subject to examination and approval or disapproval by the bankruptcy court. Some of the creditors, including the United States, were dissatisfied with the settlement. In these circumstances, disclosed in the preamble, the resolution directed the committee "to inquire into the matter and history of said real-estate pool and the character of said settlement, with the amount of property involved in which Jay Cooke & Co. were interested, and the amount paid or to be paid in said settlement, with power to send for persons and papers and report to this House." The Court pointed out that the resolution contained no suggestion of contemplated legislation; that the matter was one in respect to which no valid legislation could be had; that the bankrupts' estate and the trustee's settlement were still pending in the bankruptcy court; and that the United States and other creditors were free to press their claims in that proceeding. And on these grounds the Court held that in undertaking the investigation "the House of Representatives not only exceeded the limit of its own authority, but assumed power which could only be properly exercised by another branch of the government, because it was in its nature clearly judicial."

The case has been cited at times, and is cited to us now, as strongly intimating, if not holding, that neither house of Congress has power to make inquiries and exact evidence in aid of contemplated legislation. There are expressions in the opinion which, separately considered, might bear such an interpretation; but that this was not intended is shown by the immediately succeeding statement that "This latter proposition is one which we do not propose to decide in the present case because we are able to decide the case without passing upon the existence or nonexistence of such a power in aid of the legislative function."

Next in order is *In re Chapman* (1897). The inquiry there in question was conducted under a resolution of the Senate and related to charges, published in the press, that senators were yielding to corrupt influences in considering a tariff bill then before the Senate and were speculating in stocks the value of which would be affected by pending amendments to the bill. Chapman appeared before the committee in response to a subpoena, but refused to answer questions pertinent to the inquiry, and was indicted and convicted under the act of 1857 for his refusal. The Court sustained the constitutional validity of the act of 1857, and, after referring to the constitutional provision empowering either house to punish its members for disorderly behavior and by a vote of two-thirds to expel a member, held that the inquiry related to the integrity and fidelity of senators in the discharge of their duties, and therefore to a matter "within the range of the constitutional powers of the Senate" and in respect of which it could compel witnesses to appear and testify. In overruling an objection that the inquiry was without any defined or admissible purpose, in that the preamble and resolution made no reference to any contemplated expulsion, censure, or other action by the Senate, the Court held that they adequately disclosed a subject-matter of which the Senate had jurisdiction, that it was not essential that the Senate declare in advance what it meditated doing, and that the assumption could not be indulged that the Senate was making the inquiry without a legitimate object.

The case is relied on here as fully sustaining the power of either house to conduct investigations and exact testimony from witnesses for legislative purposes. In the course of the opinion

it is said that disclosures by witnesses may be compelled constitutionally "'to enable the respective bodies to discharge their legitimate functions,' and that it was to effect this that the act of 1857 was passed"; and also "We grant that Congress could not divest itself, or either of its houses, of the essential and inherent power to punish for contempt, in cases to which the power of either house properly extended; but, because Congress, by the act of 1857, sought to aid each of the houses in the discharge of its constitutional functions, it does not follow that any delegation of the power in each to punish for contempt was involved." The terms "legitimate functions" and "constitutional functions" are broad and might well be regarded as including the legislative function, but as the case in hand did not call for any expression respecting that function, it hardly can be said that these terms were purposely used as including it.

The latest case is *Marshall* v. *Gordon* (1917). The question there was whether the House of Representatives exceeded its power in punishing, as for a contempt of its authority, a person—not a member—who had written, published and sent to the chairman of one of its committees an ill-tempered and irritating letter respecting the action and purposes of the committee. Power to make inquiries and obtain evidence by compulsory process was not involved. The Court recognized distinctly that the House of Representatives has implied power to punish a person not a member for contempt, as was ruled in *Anderson* v. *Dunn*, but held that its action in this instance was without constitutional justification. The decision was put on the ground that the letter, while offensive and vexatious, was not calculated or likely to affect the House in any of its proceedings or in the exercise of any of its functions—in short, that the act which was punished as a contempt was not of such a character as to bring it within the rule that an express power draws after it others which are necessary and appropriate to give effect to it.

While these cases are not decisive of the question we are considering, they definitely settle two propositions which we recognize as entirely sound and having a bearing on its solution: One, that the two houses of Congress, in their separate relations, possess not only such powers as are expressly granted to them by the Constitution, but such auxiliary powers as are necessary and appropriate to make the express powers effective; and, the other, that neither house is invested with "general" power to inquire into private affairs and compel disclosures, but only with such limited power of inquiry as is shown to exist when the rule of constitutional interpretation just stated is rightly applied.

With this review of the legislative practice, congressional enactments and court decisions, we proceed to a statement of our conclusions on the question.

We are of opinion that the power of inquiry—with process to enforce it—is an essential and appropriate auxiliary to the legislative function. It was so regarded and employed in American legislatures before the Constitution was framed and ratified. Both houses of Congress took this view of it early in their history—the House of Representatives with the approving votes of Mr. Madison and other members whose service in the convention which framed the Constitution gives special significance to their action—and both houses have employed the power accordingly up to the present time. The acts of 1798 and 1857, judged by their comprehensive terms, were intended to recognize the existence of this power in both houses and to enable them to employ it "more effectually" than before. So, when their practice in the matter is appraised according to the circumstances in which it was begun and to those in which it has been continued, it falls nothing short of a practical construction, long continued, of the constitutional provisions respecting their powers, and therefore should be taken as fixing the meaning of those provisions, if otherwise doubtful.

We are further of opinion that the provisions are not of doubtful meaning, but, as was held by this Court in the cases we have reviewed, are intended to be effectively exercised, and therefore to carry with them such auxiliary powers as are necessary and appropriate to that end. While the power to exact information in aid of the legislative function was not involved in those cases, the rule of interpretation applied there is applicable here. A legislative body cannot legislate wisely or effectively in the absence of information respecting the conditions which the legislation is intended to affect or change; and where the legislative body does not itself possess the requisite information—which not infrequently is true—recourse must be had to others who do possess it. Experience has taught that mere requests for such information often are unavailing, and also that information which is volunteered is not always accurate or complete; so some means of compulsion are essential to obtain what is needed. All this was true before and when the Constitution was framed and adopted. In that period the power of inquiry—with enforcing process—was regarded and employed as a necessary and appropriate attribute of the power to legislate—indeed, was treated as inhering in it. Thus there is ample warrant for thinking, as we do, that the constitutional provisions which commit the legislative function to the two houses are intended to include this attribute to the end that the function may be effectively exercised.

The contention is earnestly made on behalf of the witness that this power of inquiry, if sustained, may be abusively and oppressively exerted. If this be so, it affords no ground for denying the power. The same contention might be directed against the power to legislate, and of course would be unavailing. We must assume, for present purposes, that neither house will be disposed to exert the power beyond its proper bounds, or without due regard to the rights of witnesses. But if, contrary to this assumption, controlling limitations or restrictions are disregarded, the decisions in *Kilbourn* v. *Thompson* and *Marshall* v. *Gordon* point to admissible measures of relief. And it is a necessary deduction from the decisions in *Kilbourn* v. *Thompson* and *In re Chapman* that a witness rightfully may refuse to answer where the bounds of the power are exceeded or the questions are not pertinent to the matter under inquiry.

We come now to the question whether it sufficiently appears that the purpose for which the witness's testimony was sought was to obtain information in aid of the legislative function. The court below answered the question in the negative. . . .

. . .

We are of opinion that the Court's ruling on this question was wrong, and that it sufficiently appears, when the proceedings are rightly interpreted, that the object of the investigation and of the effort to secure the witness's testimony was to obtain information for legislative purposes.

It is quite true that the resolution directing the investigation does not in terms avow that it is intended to be in aid of legislation; but it does show that the subject to be investigated was the administration of the Department of Justice—whether its functions were being properly discharged or were being neglected or misdirected, and particularly whether the Attorney General and his assistants were performing or neglecting their duties in respect of the institution and prosecution of proceedings to punish crimes and enforce appropriate remedies against the wrongdoers—specific instances of alleged neglect being recited. Plainly the subject was one on which legislation could be had and would be materially aided by the information which the investigation was calculated to elicit. This becomes manifest when it is reflected that the functions of the Department of Justice, the powers and duties of the Attorney General and the duties of his assistants, are all subject to regulation by congressional legislation, and that the department is maintained and its activities are carried on under such appropriations as in the judgment of Congress are needed from year to year.

The only legitimate object the Senate could have in ordering the investigation was to aid it in legislating; and we think the subject-matter was such that the presumption should be indulged that this was the real object. An express avowal of the object would have been better; but in view of the particular subject-matter was not indispensable.

. . .

We conclude that the investigation was ordered for a legitimate object; that the witness wrongfully refused to appear and testify before the committee and was lawfully attached; that the Senate is entitled to have him give testimony pertinent to the inquiry, either at its bar or before the committee; and that the district court erred in discharging him from custody under the attachment.

. . .

What has been said requires that the final order in the district court discharging the witness from custody be reversed.

Final order reversed.

Aftermath of McGrain v. Daugherty

While upholding almost unlimited investigatory powers for congressional committees, including the power to issue subpoenas and to punish recalcitrant witnesses for contempt, the *McGrain* opinion said nothing about the rights of witnesses and contained only the vague constraint that an investigation must be in aid of a legislative function. It was not until the 1950s and 1960s that legislative investigations once again came under judicial scrutiny. Then the Supreme Court was afforded the opportunity to come to grips with some of *McGrain's* unanswered questions.

In a long and somewhat discursive opinion Chief Justice Earl Warren, in *Watkins* v. *United States*(1957), gave Congress a stern lecture on what its committees might and might not do when conducting investigations and, in this instance, overturned a contempt citation against a witness. Yet the decision was more in the nature of a judicial warning than a real curbing of power.

John Watkins, a labor leader, had testified before a subcommittee of the House Committee on Un-American Activities where he admitted that he had cooperated with the Communist party and volunteered information about people whom he believed were still active in Communist organizations. He refused, however, to answer questions concerning past activities of persons whom he believed were no longer participants in the Communist movement, contending that these questions were not relevant to the purpose of the investigation and that the subcommittee had no authority to expose a person's past associations.

In reversing a lower court's decision that Watkins was, indeed, guilty of contempt of Congress, the Supreme Court based its ruling on a very narrow point. Watkins, said the Court, was not clearly apprised of the pertinence to the investigation of the question that he was asked. Therefore he had been, because of the "vice of vagueness," denied due process of law. In the rest of the opinion, all *dicta,* the Court spoke eloquently of how witnesses before congressional committees were protected by the Bill of Rights, particularly the First Amendment, but in the final analysis Congress's powers had been curbed only slightly, if at all.

A more direct challenge to investigation committees allegedly denying First Amendment rights to witnesses came in 1959 in *Barenblatt* v. *United States.* Once again the Court, over the strong protests of four dissenters, refused to interfere with congressional committee procedures. Lloyd Barenblatt, pursuant to a subpoena and accompanied by an attorney, appeared as a witness before a subcommittee of the House Un-American Activities Committee where he refused to answer questions about his alleged Communist associations. Barenblatt contended that the subcommittee had no right to inquire into his political and religious or any other personal and private affairs or associational activities, since all were barred from government invasion under the First Amendment. He also argued that, as in *Watkins,* the committee had not adequately apprised him of the pertinence of the questions to the subject matter of the inquiry. Finally, he argued that the charter authorizing the compelling of testimony, particularly Rule XI, was unconstitutionally vague. Dismissing all contentions, Justice John Marshall Harlan II, speaking for the majority, wrote that so long as "Congress acts in pursuance of its constitutional power, the Judiciary lacks authority to intervene on the basis of motives which spurred the exercise of that power." He concluded that the balance between the individual and the governmental interests at stake must be struck in favor of the government and that the provisions of the First Amendment had not been offended. These cases, like those involving the use of presidential power, support the general thesis that "institutional restraints" bear heavily on the Court when it is faced with a lawsuit that challenges the modus operandi of either Congress or the presidency.

Korematsu v. United States

323 U.S. 214 (1944)

Following the destruction of much of the American naval fleet during the Japanese attack on Pearl Harbor, the United States government feared that an invasion of the west coast was imminent and had doubts about the loyalty of thousands of Japanese-Americans living in California, Washington, and Oregon. As a result, on February 19, 1942, President Franklin Roosevelt issued an order as Commander in Chief of the Army and Navy, empowering military commanders to designate areas from which persons could be removed and relocated. In March, Congress, in Public Law 503, ratified the President's decree and made it a misdemeanor, punishable by a fine of $5000, a year in jail, or both, to violate any order of the President, Secretary of War,

or a military commander. An initial military order required all persons of Japanese ancestry, alien or citizen, to remain in their homes from 8 p.m. to 6 a.m. A series of exclusion orders followed, requiring Japanese-Americans in specified "military" areas to report to assembly centers for evacuation to hastily constructed camps in the interior western states. Within 6 months after Pearl Harbor, some 112,000 persons of Japanese descent, 70 percent of whom were American citizens, were living in these primitive relocation centers.

One of the handful of persons who resisted the military orders was Gordon Hirabayashi, a 24-year-old student at the University of Washington. Hirabayashi, a devout Quaker, refused on religious grounds to register for evacuation. After his constitutional challenge to the evacuation order had been rejected by a judge who characterized the Japanese as "unbelievably treacherous and wholly ruthless" people, Hirabayashi was found guilty and sentenced to three months in jail on each of two criminal counts. Hirabayashi was represented by an American Civil Liberties Union attorney—a mixed blessing, as it turned out, since the ACLU's national board, anxious that the organization's patriotism not be questioned, had decided that the appeal should not directly challenge President Roosevelt's executive order but should confine itself instead to an attack on the military orders implementing the presidential directive. After the court of appeals took the unusual step of sending the case on to the Supreme Court without making a decision, the Court unanimously upheld the curfew order (which Hirabayashi had also acknowledged violating), leaving the evacuation issue undecided. Justice Frank Murphy had written a strong dissent comparing the "gigantic round-up" of Japanese-Americans to the Nazi persecution and extermination of Jews, but he was dissuaded from filing his opinion by Justice Frankfurter, who argued that a less than unanimous opinion would undermine the war effort.

The constitutionality of the evacuation itself came to the Supreme Court the following year in a case involving Fred Korematsu, a shipyard worker from Oakland, California. Korematsu, who had been rejected for military service on medical grounds, lost his job when his union expelled persons of Japanese descent. Wishing to move to the midwest with his fiancée, who was not of Japanese ancestry, Korematsu stayed behind when his parents were relocated and underwent crude plastic surgery on his nose and eyelids in hopes of concealing his racial identity. He was soon apprehended living under an assumed name. After a brief trial, Korematsu was convicted, given a 5-year probationary sentence, and sent to join his family at an internment camp.

Korematsu had set out to evade the evacuation order, not to challenge it, but while awaiting trial he decided to allow his case to become a test of the constitutionality of the government's authority to employ such sweeping measures against all members of a racial group. On appeal, Korematsu's lawyers, aware of the Court's traditional reluctance to challenge actions supported jointly by the President and Congress (which had been reinforced in its *Hirabayashi* decision), argued that Public Law 503 had authorized the military to evacuate but *not* to detain Japanese-Americans; thus the military was exceeding its legal authority by operating detention camps. Beyond the merits of their arguments, however, Korematsu's lawyers also rested their hopes on the fact that "war fever" was beginning to subside as the Allies gained the advantage both in Europe and in the South Pacific. Indeed, as the Supreme Court deliberated on the case, an official end to internment was under active consideration in the President's cabinet.

Mr. Justice **Black** delivered the opinion of the Court.

The petitioner, an American citizen of Japanese descent, was convicted in a federal district court for remaining in San Leandro, California, a "Military Area," contrary to Civilian Exclusion Order No. 34 of the Commanding General of the Western

Command, U.S. Army, which directed that after May 9, 1942, all persons of Japanese ancestry should be excluded from that area. No question was raised as to petitioner's loyalty to the United States. The Circuit Court of Appeals affirmed, and the importance of the constitutional question involved caused us to grant certiorari.

. . .

In the light of the principles we announced in the Hirabayashi case, we are unable to conclude that it was beyond the war power of Congress and the Executive to exclude those of Japanese ancestry from the West Coast war area at the time they did. True, exclusion from the area in which one's home is located is a far greater deprivation than constant confinement to the home from 8 p.m. to 6 a.m. Nothing short of apprehension by the proper military authorities of the gravest imminent danger to the public safety can constitutionally justify either. But exclusion from a threatened area, no less than curfew, has a definite and close relationship to the prevention of espionage and sabotage. The military authorities, charged with the primary responsibility of defending our shores, concluded that curfew provided inadequate protection and ordered exclusion. They did so, as pointed out in our Hirabayashi opinion, in accordance with Congressional authority to the military to say who should, and who should not, remain in the threatened areas.

In this case the petitioner challenges the assumptions upon which we rested our conclusions in the Hirabayashi case. He also urges that by May 1942, when Order No. 34 was promulgated, all danger of Japanese invasion of the West Coast had disappeared. After careful consideration of these contentions we are compelled to reject them.

Here, as in the Hirabayashi case, we cannot reject as unfounded the judgment of the military authorities and of Congress that there were disloyal members of that population, whose number and strength could not be precisely and quickly ascertained. We cannot say that the warmaking branches of the Government did not have ground for believing that in a critical hour such persons could not readily be isolated and

separately dealt with, and constituted a menace to the national defense and safety, which demanded that prompt and adequate measures be taken to guard against it.

Like curfew, exclusion of those of Japanese origin was deemed necessary because of the presence of an unascertained number of disloyal members of the group, most of whom we have no doubt were loyal to this country. It was because we could not reject the finding of the military authorities that it was impossible to bring about an immediate segregation of the disloyal from the loyal that we sustained the validity of the curfew order as applying to the whole group. In the instant case, temporary exclusion of the entire group was rested by the military on the same ground. The judgment that exclusion of the whole group was for the same reason a military operative answers the contention that the exclusion was in the nature of group punishment based on antagonism to those of Japanese origin. That there were members of the group who retained loyalties to Japan has been confirmed by investigations made subsequent to the exclusion. Approximately five thousand American citizens of Japanese ancestry refused to swear unqualified allegiance to the United States and to renounce allegiance to the Japanese Emperor, and several thousand evacuees requested repatriation to Japan.

We uphold the exclusion order as of the time it was made and when the petitioner violated it. In doing so, we are not unmindful of the hardships imposed by it upon a large group of American citizens. But hardships are part of war, and war is an aggregation of hardships. All citizens alike, both in and out of uniform, feel the impact of war in greater or lesser measure. Citizenship has its responsibilities as well as its privileges, and in time of war the burden is always heavier. Compulsory exclusion of large groups of citizens from their homes, except under circumstances of direst emergency and peril, is inconsistent with our basic governmental institutions. But when under conditions of modern warfare our shores are threatened by hostile forces, the power to protect must be commensurate with the threatened danger.

It is argued that on May 30, 1942, the date the petitioner was charged with remaining in the prohibited area, there were conflicting orders outstanding, forbidding him both to leave the area and to remain there. Of course, a person cannot be convicted for doing the very thing which it is a crime to fail to do. But the outstanding orders here contained no such contradictory commands.

There was an order issued March 27, 1942, which prohibited petitioner and others of Japanese ancestry from leaving the area, but its effect was specifically limited in time "until and to the extent that a future proclamation or order should so permit or direct." That "future order," the one for violation of which petitioner was convicted, was issued May 3, 1942, and it did "direct" exclusion from the area of all persons of Japanese ancestry, before 12 o'clock noon, May 9; furthermore it contained a warning that all such persons found in the prohibited area would be liable to punishment under the March 21, 1942 Act of Congress. Consequently, the only order in effect touching the petitioner's being in the area on May 30, 1942, the date specified in the information against him, was the May 3 order which prohibited his remaining there, and it was that same order, which he stipulated in his trial that he had violated, knowing of its existence. There is therefore no basis for the argument that on May 30, 1942, he was subject to punishment, under the March 27 and May 3rd orders, whether he remained in or left the area.

It does appear, however, that on May 9, the effective date of the exclusion order, the military authorities had already determined that the evacuation should be effected by assembling together and placing under guard all those of Japanese ancestry, at central points, designated as "assembly centers," in order "to insure the orderly evacuation and resettlement of Japanese voluntarily migrating from military area No. 1 to restrict and regulate such migration." And on May 19, 1942, eleven days before the time petitioner was charged with unlawfully remaining in the area, Civilian Restrictive Order No. 1 provided for detention of those of Japanese ancestry in assembly or relocation centers. It is now argued that the validity of the exclusion order cannot be considered apart from the orders requiring him, after departure from the area, to report and to remain in an assembly or relocation center. The

contention is that we must treat these separate orders as one and inseparable; that, for this reason, if detention in the assembly or relocation center would have illegally deprived the petitioner of his liberty, the exclusion order and his conviction under it cannot stand.

We are thus being asked to pass at this time upon the whole subsequent detention program in both assembly and relocation centers, although the only issues framed at the trial related to petitioner's remaining in the prohibited area in violation of the exclusion order. Had petitioner here left the prohibited area and gone to an assembly center we cannot say either as a matter of fact or law, that his presence in that center would have resulted in his detention in a relocation center. Some who did report to the assembly center were not sent to relocation centers, but were released upon condition that they remain outside the prohibited zone until the military orders were modified or lifted. This illustrates that they pose different problems and may be governed by different principles. The lawfulness of one does not necessarily determine the lawfulness of the others. This is made clear when we analyze the requirements of the separate provisions of the separate orders. These separate requirements were that those of Japanese ancestry (1) depart from the area; (2) report to and temporarily remain in an assembly center; (3) go under military control to a relocation center there to remain for an indeterminate period until released conditionally or unconditionally by the military authorities. Each of these requirements, it will be noted, imposed distinct duties in connection with the separate steps in a complete evacuation program. Had Congress directly incorporated into one Act the language of these separate orders, and provided sanctions for their violations, disobedience of any one would have constituted a separate offense. There is no reason why violations of these orders, insofar as they were promulgated pursuant to congressional enactment, should not be treated as separate offenses.

Since the petitioner has not been convicted of failing to report or to remain in an assembly or relocation center, we cannot in this case determine the validity of those separate provisions of the order. It is sufficient here for us to pass upon the order which petitioner violated. To do more would be to go beyond the issues raised, and to decide momentous questions not contained within the framework of the pleadings or the evidence in this case. It will be time enough to decide the serious constitutional issues which petitioner seeks to raise when an assembly or relocation order is applied or is certain to be applied to him, and we have its terms before us.

Some of the members of the Court are of the view that evacuation and detention in an Assembly Center were inseparable. After May 3, 1942, the date of Exclusion Order No. 34, Korematsu was under compulsion to leave the area not as he would choose but via an Assembly Center. The Assembly Center was conceived as a part of the machinery for group evacuation. The power to exclude includes the power to do it by force if necessary. And any forcible measure must necessarily entail some degree of detention or restraint whatever method of removal is selected. But whichever view is taken, it results in holding that the order under which petitioner was convicted was valid.

It is said that we are dealing here with the case of imprisonment of a citizen in a concentration camp solely because of his ancestry, without evidence or inquiry concerning his loyalty and good disposition towards the United States. Our task would be simple, our duty clear, were this a case involving the imprisonment of a loyal citizen in a concentration camp because of racial prejudice. Regardless of the true nature of the assembly and relocation centers—and we deem it unjustifiable to call them concentration camps with all the ugly connotations that term implies—we are dealing specifically with nothing but an exclusion order. To cast this case into outlines of racial prejudice, without reference to the real military dangers which were presented, merely confuses the issue. Korematsu was not excluded from the Military Area because of hostility to him or his race. He was excluded because we are at war with the Japanese Empire, because the properly constituted military authorities feared an invasion of our West Coast and felt constrained to take proper securi-

ty measures, because they decided that the military urgency of the situation demanded that all citizens of Japanese ancestry be segregated from the West Coast temporarily, and finally, because Congress, reposing its confidence in this time of war in our military leaders—as inevitably it must—determined that they should have the power to do just this. There was evidence of disloyalty on the part of some, the military authorities considered that the need for action was great, and time was short. We cannot—by availing ourselves of the calm perspective of hindsight—now say that at that time these actions were unjustified.

Affirmed.

Mr. Justice **Roberts,** dissenting.

I dissent, because I think the indisputable facts exhibit a clear violation of Constitutional rights.

This is not a case of keeping people off the streets at night as was Kiyoshi Hirabayashi v. United States, nor a case of temporary exclusion of a citizen from an area for his own safety or that of the community, nor a case of offering him an opportunity to go temporarily out of an area where his presence might cause danger to himself or to his fellows. On the contrary, it is the case of convicting a citizen as a punishment for not submitting to imprisonment in a concentration camp, based on his ancestry, and solely because of his ancestry, without evidence or inquiry concerning his loyalty and good disposition towards the United States. If this be a correct statement of the facts disclosed by this record, and facts of which we take judicial notice, I need hardly labor the conclusion that Constitutional rights have been violated.

. . .

Mr. Justice **Murphy,** dissenting.

This exclusion of "all persons of Japanese ancestry, both alien and non-alien," from the Pacific Coast area on a plea of military necessity in the absence of martial law ought not to be approved. Such exclusion goes over "the very brink of constitutional power" and falls into the ugly abyss of racism.

In dealing with matters relating to the prosecution and progress of a war, we must accord great respect and consideration to the judgments of the military authorities who are on the scene and who have full knowledge of the military facts. The scope of their discretion must, as a matter of necessity and common sense, be wide. And their judgments ought not to be overruled lightly by those whose training and duties ill-equip them to deal intelligently with matters so vital to the physical security of the nation.

At the same time, however, it is essential that there be definite limits to military discretion, especially where martial law has not been declared. Individuals must not be left impoverished of their constitutional rights on a plea of military necessity that has neither substance nor support. Thus, like other claims conflicting with the asserted constitutional rights of the individual, the military claim must subject itself to the judicial process of having its reasonableness determined and its conflicts with other interests reconciled. "What are the allowable limits of military discretion, and whether or not they have been overstepped in a particular case, are judicial questions."

The judicial test of whether the Government, on a plea of military necessity, can validly deprive an individual of any of his constitutional rights is whether the deprivation is reasonably related to a public danger that is so "immediate, imminent, and impending" as not to admit of delay and not to permit the intervention of ordinary constitutional processes to alleviate the danger. Civilian Exclusion Order No. 34, banishing from a prescribed area of the Pacific Coast "all persons of Japanese ancestry, both alien and non-alien," clearly does not meet that test. Being an obvious racial discrimination, the order deprives all those within its scope of the equal protection of the laws as guaranteed by the Fifth Amendment. It further deprives these individuals of their constitutional rights to live and work where they will, to establish a home where they choose and to move about freely. In excommunicating them without benefit of hearings, this order also deprives them of all their constitutional rights to procedural due process. Yet no reasonable relation to an "immediate, imminent, and impending" public danger is evident to support this racial restriction which is one of the most sweeping and complete deprivations of constitutional rights in the history of this nation in the absence of martial law. . . .

I dissent, therefore, from this legalization of racism. Racial discrimination in any form and in any degree has no justifiable part whatever in our democratic way of life. It is unattractive in any setting but it is utterly revolting among a free people who have embraced the principles set forth in the Constitution of the United States. All residents of this nation are kin in some way by blood or culture to a foreign land. Yet they are primarily and necessarily a part of the new and distinct civilization of the United States. They must accordingly be treated at all times as the heirs of the American experiment and as entitled to all the rights and freedoms guaranteed by the Constitution.

Mr. Justice **Jackson,** dissenting.

Korematsu was born on our soil, of parents born in Japan. The Constitution makes him a citizen of the United States by nativity and a citizen of California by residence. No claim is made that he is not loyal to this country. There is no suggestion that apart from the matter involved here he is not law-abiding and well disposed. Korematsu, however, has been convicted of an act not commonly a crime. It consists merely of being present in the state whereof he is a citizen, near the place where he was born, and where all his life he has lived.

Even more unusual is the series of military orders which made this conduct a crime. They forbid such a one to remain, and they also forbid him to leave. They were so drawn that the only way Korematsu could avoid violation was to give himself up to the military authority. This meant submission to custody, examination, and transportation out of the territory, to be followed by indeterminate confinement in detention camps.

A citizen's presence in the locality, however, was made a crime only if his parents were of Japanese birth. Had Korematsu been one of four—the others being, say, a German alien enemy, an Italian alien enemy, and a citizen of American-born ancestors, convicted of treason but out on parole—only Korematsu's presence would have violated the order. The difference between their innocence and his crime would result, not from anything he did, said, or thought, different than they, but only in that he was born of different racial stock.

Now, if any fundamental assumption underlies our system, it is that guilt is personal and not inheritable. Even if all of one's antecedents had been convicted of treason, the Constitution forbids its penalties to be visited upon him, for it provides that "no Attainder of Treason shall work Corruption of Blood, or Forfeiture except during the Life of the Person attained." Article 3, § 3, cl. 2. But here is an attempt to make an otherwise innocent act a crime merely because this prisoner is the son of parents as to whom he had no choice, and belongs to a race from which there is no way to resign. If Congress in peacetime legislation should enact such a criminal law, I should suppose this Court would refuse to enforce it.

But the "law" which this prisoner is convicted of disregarding is not found in an act of Congress, but in a military order. Neither the Act of Congress nor the Executive Order of the President, nor both together, would afford a basis for this conviction. It rests on the orders of General DeWitt. And it is said that if the military commander had reasonable military grounds for promulgating the orders, they are constitutional and become law, and the Court is required to enforce them. There are several reasons why I cannot subscribe to this doctrine.

It would be impracticable and dangerous idealism to expect or insist that each specific military command in an area of probable operations will conform to conventional tests of constitutionality. When an area is so beset that it must be put under military control at all, the paramount consideration is that its measures be successful, rather than legal. The armed services must protect a society, not merely its Constitution. The very essence of the military job is to marshal physical force, to remove every obstacle to its effectiveness, to give it every strategic advantage. Defense measures will not, and often should not, be held within the limits that bind civil authority in peace. No court can

require such a commander in such circumstances to act as a reasonable man; he may be unreasonably cautious and exacting. Perhaps, he should be. But a commander in temporarily focusing the life of a community on defense is carrying out a military program; he is not making law in the sense the courts know the term. He issues orders, and they may have a certain authority as military commands, although they may be very bad as constitutional law.

But if we cannot confine military expedients by the Constitution, neither would I distort the Constitution to approve all that the military may deem expedient. That is what the Court appears to be doing, whether consciously or not. I cannot say, from any evidence before me, that the orders of General DeWitt were not reasonably expedient military precautions, nor could I say that they were. But even if they were permissible military procedures, I deny that it follows that they are constitutional. If, as the Court holds, it does follow, then we may as well say that any military order will be constitutional and have done with it.

The limitation under which courts always will labor in examining the necessity for a military order are illustrated by this case. How does the Court know that these orders have a reasonable basis in necessity? No evidence whatever on that subject has been taken by this or any other court. There is sharp controversy as to the credibility of the DeWitt report. So the Court, having no real evidence before it, has no choice but to accept General DeWitt's own unsworn, self-serving statement, untested by any cross-examination, that what he did was reasonable. And thus it will always be when courts try to look into the reasonableness of a military order.

In the very nature of things military decisions are not susceptible of intelligent judicial appraisal. They do not pretend to rest on evidence, but are made on information that often would not be admissible and on assumptions that could not be proved. Information in support of an order could not be disclosed to courts without danger that it would reach the enemy. Neither can courts act on communications made in confidence. Hence courts can never have any real alternative to accepting the mere declaration of the authority that issued the order that it was reasonably necessary from a military viewpoint.

Much is said of the danger to liberty from the Army program for deporting and detaining these citizens of Japanese extraction. But a judicial construction of the due process clause that will sustain this order is a far more subtle blow to liberty than the promulgation of the order itself. A military order, however unconstitutional, is not apt to last longer than the military emergency. Even during that period a succeeding commander may revoke it all. But once a judicial opinion rationalizes such an order to show that it conforms to the Constitution, or rather rationalizes the Constitution to show that the Constitution sanctions such an order, the Court for all time has validated the principle of racial discrimination in criminal procedure and of transplanting American citizens. The principle then lies about like a loaded weapon ready for the hand of any authority that can bring forward a plausible claim of an urgent need. Every repetition imbeds that principle more deeply in our law and thinking and expands it to new purposes. All who observe the work of courts are familiar with what Judge Cardozo described as "the tendency of a principle to expand itself to the limit of its logic." A military commander may overstep the bounds of constitutionality, and it is an incident. But if we review and approve, that passing incident becomes the doctrine of the Constitution. There it has a generative power of its own, and all that it creates will be in its own image. Nothing better illustrates this danger than does the Court's opinion in this case.

It argues that we are bound to uphold the conviction of Korematsu because we upheld one in Kiyshi Hirabayashi v. United States, when we sustained these orders in so far as they applied a curfew requirement to a citizen of Japanese ancestry. I think we should learn something from that experience.

In that case we were urged to consider only the curfew feature, that being all that technically was involved, because it was the only count necessary to sustain Hirabayashi's conviction and sentence. We yielded, and the Chief Justice guarded the opinion as carefully as language will do. He said: "Our investigation here does not go beyond the inquiry whether, in the light of all the relevant circumstances preceding and attending their promulgation, the challenged orders and statute *afforded a reasonable basis for the action taken in imposing the curfew.*" "We decide only the issue as we have defined it—we decide only that the *curfew order* as applied, and at the time it was applied, was within the boundaries of the war power." And again: "It is unnecessary to consider whether or to what extent *such findings would support orders differing from the curfew order.*" (Italics supplied.) However, in spite of our limiting words we did validate a discrimination on the basis of ancestry for mild and temporary deprivation of liberty. Now the principle of racial discrimination is pushed from support of mild measures to very harsh ones, and from temporary deprivations to indeterminate ones. And the precedent which it is said requires us to do so is Hirabayashi. The Court is now saying that in Hirabayashi we did decide the very things we there said we were not deciding. Because we said that these citizens could be made to stay in their homes during the hours of dark, it is said we must require them to leave home entirely; and if that, we are told they may also be taken into custody for deportation; and if that, it is argued they may also be held for some undetermined time in detention camps. How far the principle of this case would be extended before plausible reasons would play out, I do not know.

I should hold that a civil court cannot be made to enforce an order which violates constitutional limitations even if it is a reasonable exercise of military authority. The courts can exercise only the judicial power, can apply only law, and must abide by the Constitution, or they cease to be civil courts and become instruments of military policy.

Of course, the existence of a military power resting on force, so vagrant, so centralized, so necessarily heedless of the individual, is an inherent threat to liberty. But I would not lead people to rely on this Court for a review that seems to me wholly delusive. The military reasonableness of these orders can only be determined by military superiors. If the people ever let command of the war power fall into irresponsible and unscrupulous hands, the courts wield no power equal to its restraint. The chief restraint upon those who command the physical forces of the country, in the future as in the past, must be their responsibility to the political judgments of their contemporaries and to the moral judgments of history.

My duties as a justice as I see them do not require me to make a military judgment as to whether General DeWitt's evacuation and detention program was a reasonable military necessity. I do not suggest that the courts should have attempted to interfere with the Army in carrying out its task. But I do not think they may be asked to execute a military expedient that has no place in law under the Constitution. I would reverse the judgment and discharge the prisoner.

Aftermath of Korematsu *v.* United States

On the same day the *Korematsu* decision was announced, the Court decided a third exclusion case, *Ex parte Endo.* Mitsuye Endo, an employee of the California Civil Service and an American citizen of demonstrated loyalty, had been evacuated to a relocation center near Tule Lake, California, and subsequently moved to a camp in Utah, where she filed a legal petition for her release in July 1942. Two years later the Court ruled that Endo was entitled to an unconditional release. In this case as in *Hirabayashi* and *Korematsu,* however, the Supreme Court refused to restrain the executive and the military or to face head-on the crucial constitutional questions. It would not substitute a judicial judgment for that of the President and the military even after the emergency had ended. In 1983 Fred Korematsu persuaded a federal district court to vacate his criminal conviction on the ground that the government had suppressed crucial evidence at his trial. Two years later Gordon Hirabayashi's conviction was vacated by a federal appeals court after it concluded that the curfew order had been "based on racism rather than military necessity."

In 1948 Congress authorized payment of compensation to Japanese-Americans for their documented property losses; about $37 million was eventually distributed, although the Federal Reserve Board had estimated Japanese-American property losses at more than 10 times that amount. In 1988 Congress enacted the Civil Liberties Act, providing payments of $20,000 to each of the 65,000 survivors of the relocation, beginning with the oldest living detainees. Five hundred million dollars was to be distributed in 1990, with a similar amount to be paid in 1991 and the remaining payments to be sent the following year. In October 1990 U.S. Attorney General Dick Thornburgh presented nine of the oldest Japanese-American internees checks for $20,000 and a letter of apology from President George Bush.

Not long after the end of World War II the concept of rounding up potential saboteurs in time of national emergency and incarcerating them in detention camps was written into Title II of the Internal Security Act of 1950 as the Emergency Detention Act. In sweeping language the statute authorized the President to proclaim an "internal security emergency" and to "apprehend and detain" any person as to whom there is reasonable ground to believe that such person will "probably engage in" or "probably will conspire to engage in, acts of espionage or sabotage." In 1971 Congress repealed the act including language declaring, "No citizen shall be imprisoned or otherwise detained by the United States except pursuant to an Act of Congress." While the repealing act prohibits the President from acting arbitrarily as Commander in Chief, it does not prevent Congress from empowering the President to act in future emergencies, the form, substance, and nature of which are unpredictable.

National Labor Relations Board v. Jones and Laughlin Steel Corporation

301 U.S. 1 (1937)

In the spring of 1937, during the debate over President Roosevelt's "Court-packing" plan, three major decisions were handed down, all of which positioned the Court in its more traditional role vis-à-vis Congress and the President during a time of national crisis. The first of the three, *Jones and Laughlin,* came on April 12 and the remaining two *(Helvering* v. *Davis* and *Steward Machine Company* v. *Davis)* on May 24. Less than 2 months after this trio of judicial reversals of the Court's earlier posture, FDR's Court-packing plan was given a public burial and interred in the grave holding all the Court-curbing measures of the past. Many close observers of this executive-judicial confrontation contended that the justices' altered view of the Constitution, as evidenced by their opinions in the *Jones and Laughlin, Helvering,* and *Steward Machine Company* cases, was brought about by the President's "threat" to restructure the Supreme Court. One justice in particular, Owen Roberts, was said to have reversed his earlier position and voted to uphold congressional commerce clause power in the *Jones and Laughlin* case to avert passage of Roosevelt's bill (a hypothesis immortalized as "the switch in time that saved nine"). As Robert H. Jackson—then attorney general and later an associate justice of the Supreme Court—phrased it: "In politics the black-robed reactionary justices won over the master liberal politicians of our day. In law the President defeated the recalcitrant justices in their own Court." Disagreeing with this assessment was Chief Justice Charles Evans Hughes, who was to write in retirement that the notion that any cases "were influenced in the slightest degree by the President's attitude, or his proposal to reorganize the Court is utterly baseless" and that the decision in *Jones and Laughlin* "would have been the same if the President's bill had never been proposed."

Passed by Congress in 1935 to replace the labor provisions of the NIRA which had been declared unconstitutional, the National Labor Relations Act protected the right of labor to organize into unions and prohibited certain unfair practices of employers engaged in interstate commerce. The National Labor Relations Board found the Jones and Laughlin Steel Company in violation of the law and petitioned the United States Circuit Court of Appeals to order the company to comply with its findings. The court of appeals declared the law unconstitutional and the NLRB appealed to the Supreme Court.

Mr. Chief Justice **Hughes** delivered the opinion of the Court.

. . .

The scheme of the National Labor Relations Act—which is too long to be quoted in full—may be briefly stated. The first section sets forth findings with respect to the injury to commerce resulting from the denial by employers of the right of employees to organize and from the refusal of employers to accept the procedure of collective bargaining. There follows a declaration that it is the policy of the United States to eliminate these causes of obstruction to the free flow of commerce. The act then defines the terms it uses, including the terms "commerce" and "affecting commerce." It creates the National Labor Relations Board and prescribes its organization. It sets forth the right of employees to self-organization and to bargain collectively through representatives of their own choosing. It defines "unfair labor practices." It lays down rules as to the representation of employees for the purpose of collective bargaining. The Board is empowered to prevent the described unfair labor practices affecting commerce and the act prescribes the procedure to that end. The Board is authorized to petition designated courts to secure the enforcement of its order. . . .

. . .

The facts as to the nature and scope of the business of the Jones & Laughlin Steel Corporation have been found by the Labor Board, and, so far as they are essential to the determination of this controversy, they are not in dispute. The Labor Board has found: The corporation is organized under the laws of Pennsylvania and has its principal office at Pittsburgh. It is engaged in the business of manufacturing iron and steel in plants situated in Pittsburgh and nearby Aliquippa, Pa. It manufactures and distributes a widely diversified line of steel and pig iron, being the fourth largest producer of steel in the United States. With its subsidiaries—nineteen in number—it is a completely integrated enterprise, owning and operating ore, coal and limestone properties, lake and river transportation facilities and terminal railroads located at its manufacturing plants. It owns or controls mines in Michigan and Minnesota. It operates four ore steamships on the Great Lakes, used in the transportation of ore to its factories. It owns coal mines in Pennsylvania. It operates towboats and steam barges used in carrying coal to its factories. It owns limestone properties in various places in Pennsylvania and West Virginia. It owns the Monongahela connecting railroad which connects the plants of the Pittsburgh works and forms an interconnection with the Pennsylvania, New York Central and Baltimore & Ohio Railroad systems. It owns the Aliquippa & Southern Railroad Company, which connects the Aliquippa works with the Pittsburgh & Lake Erie, part of the New York Central system. Much of its product is shipped to its warehouses in Chicago, Detroit, Cincinnati and Memphis—to the last two places by means of its own barges and transportation equipment. In Long Island City, New York, and in New Orleans it operates structural steel fabricating shops in connection with the warehousing of

semifinished materials sent from its works. Through one of its wholly-owned subsidiaries it owns, leases, and operates stores, warehouses, and yards for the distribution of equipment and supplies for drilling and operating oil and gas wells and for pipe lines, refineries and pumping stations. It has sales offices in twenty cities in the United States and a wholly-owned subsidiary which is devoted exclusively to distributing its product in Canada. Approximately 75 per cent, of its product is shipped out of Pennsylvania.

Summarizing these operations, the Labor Board concluded that the works in Pittsburgh and Aliquippa "might be likened to the heart of a self-contained, highly integrated body. They draw in the raw materials from Michigan, Minnesota, West Virginia, Pennsylvania in part through arteries and by means controlled by the respondent; they transform the materials and then pump them out to all parts of the nation through the vast mechanism which the respondent has elaborated."

To carry on the activities of the entire steel industry, 33,000 men mine ore, 44,000 men mine coal, 4,000 men quarry limestone, 16,000 men manufacture coke, 343,000 men manufacture steel, and 83,000 men transport its product. Respondent has about 10,000 employees in its Aliquippa plant, which is located in a community of about 30,000 persons.

Respondent points to evidence that the Aliquippa plant, in which the discharged men were employed, contains complete facilities for the production of finished and semifinished iron and steel products from raw materials; that its works consist primarily of a by-product coke plant for the production of coke; blast furnaces for the production of pig iron; open hearth furnaces and Bessemer converters for the production of steel; blooming mills for the reduction of steel ingots into smaller shapes; and a number of finishing mills such as structural mills, rod mills, wire mills, and the like. In addition, there are other buildings, structures and equipment, storage yards, docks and an intraplant storage system. Respondent's operations at these works are carried on in two distinct stages, the first being the conversion of raw materials into pig iron and the second being the manufacture of semifinished and finished iron and steel products; and in both cases the operations result in substantially changing the character, utility and value of the materials wrought upon, which is apparent from the nature and extent of the processes to which they are subjected and which respondent fully describes. Respondent also directs attention to the fact that the iron ore which is procured from mines in Minnesota and Michigan and transported to respondent's plant is stored in stock piles for future use, the amount of ore in storage varying with the season but usually being enough to maintain operations from nine to ten months; that the coal which is procured from the mines of a subsidiary located in Pennsylvania and taken to the plant at Aliquippa is there, like ore, stored for future use, approximately two to three months' supply of coal being always on hand; and that the limestone which is obtained in Pennsylvania and West Virginia is also stored in amounts usually adequate to run the blast furnaces for a few weeks. Various details of operation, transportation, and distribution are also mentioned which for the present purpose it is not necessary to detail.

Practically all the factual evidence in the case, except that which dealt with the nature of respondent's business, concerned its relations with the employees in the Aliquippa plant whose discharge was the subject of the complaint. These employees were active leaders in the labor union. Several were officers and others were leaders of particular groups. Two of the employees were motor inspectors; one was a tractor driver; three were crane operators; one was a washer in the coke plant; and three were laborers. Three other employees were mentioned in the complaint but it was withdrawn as to one of them and no evidence was heard on the action taken with respect to the other two.

While respondent criticizes the evidence and the attitude of the Board, which is described as being hostile toward employers and particularly toward those who insisted upon their constitutional rights, respondent did not take advantage of its opportunity to present evidence to refute that which was offered to show discrimination and coercion. In this situation, the record pre-

sents no ground for setting aside the order of the Board so far as the facts pertaining to the circumstances and purpose of the discharge of the employees are concerned. Upon that point it is sufficient to say that the evidence supports the findings of the Board that respondent discharged these men "because of their union activity and for the purpose of discouraging membership in the union." We turn to the questions of law which respondent urges in contesting the validity and application of the Act.

First. The Scope of the Act.—The act is challenged in its entirety as an attempt to regulate all industry, thus invading the reserved powers of the States over their local concerns.

. . .

. . . The authority of the federal government may not be pushed to such an extreme as to destroy the distinction, which the commerce clause itself establishes, between commerce "among the several States" and the internal concerns of a state. That distinction between what is national and what is local in the activities of commerce is vital to the maintenance of our federal system.

But we are not at liberty to deny effect to specific provisions, which Congress has constitutional power to enact, by superimposing upon them inferences from general legislative declarations of an ambiguous character, even if found in the same statute. The cardinal principle of statutory construction is to save and not to destroy. We have repeatedly held that as between two possible interpretations of a statute, by one of which it would be unconstitutional and by the other valid, our plain duty is to adopt that which will save the act. Even to avoid a serious doubt the rule is the same.

We think it clear that the National Labor Relations Act may be construed so as to operate within the sphere of constitutional authority. The jurisdiction conferred upon the Board, and invoked in this instance, is found in section 10(a): 29 U.S.C.A. § 160(a), which provides: "Sec. 10(a). The Board is empowered, as hereinafter provided, to prevent any person from engaging in any unfair labor practice (listed in section 8 [section 158]) affecting commerce."

The critical words of this provision, prescribing the limits of the Board's authority in dealing with the labor practices, are "affecting commerce." . . .

. . .

The act also defines the term "affecting commerce" section 2(7), 29 U.S.C.A. § 152(7):

"The term 'affecting commerce' means in commerce, or burdening or obstructing commerce or the free flow of commerce, or having led or tending to lead to a labor dispute burdening or obstructing commerce or the free flow of commerce."

This definition is one of exclusion as well as inclusion. The grant of authority to the Board does not purport to extend to the relationship between all industrial employees and employers. Its terms do not impose collective bargaining upon all industry regardless of effects upon interstate or foreign commerce. It purports to reach only what may be deemed to burden or obstruct that commerce and, thus qualified, it must be construed as contemplating the exercise of control within constitutional bounds. It is a familiar principle that acts which directly burden or obstruct interstate or foreign commerce, or its free flow, are within the reach of the congressional power. Acts having that effect are not rendered immune because they grow out of labor disputes. . . .

Second. The Unfair Labor Practices in Question.— . . .

. . .

. . . [I]n its present application, the statute goes no further than to safeguard the right of employees to self-organization and to select representatives of their own choosing for collective bargaining or other mutual protection without restraint or coercion by their employer.

That is a fundamental right. Employees have as clear a right to organize and select their representatives for lawful purposes as the respondent has to organize its business and select its own officers and agents. Discrimination and coercion to prevent the free exercise of the right of employees to self-organization and represen-

tation is a proper subject for condemnation by competent legislative authority. . . .

. . .

Third. The Application of the Act to Employees Engaged in Production.—The Principle Involved.—Respondent says that, whatever may be said of employees engaged in interstate commerce, the industrial relations and activities in the manufacturing department of respondent's enterprise are not subject to federal regulation. The argument rests upon the proposition that manufacturing in itself is not commerce.

The government distinguishes these cases. The various parts of respondent's enterprise are described as interdependent and as thus involving "a great movement of iron ore, coal and limestone along well-defined paths to the steel mills, thence through them, and thence in the form of steel products into the consuming centers of the country—a definite and well-understood course of business." It is urged that these activities constitute a "stream" or "flow" of commerce, of which the Aliquippa manufacturing plant is the focal point, and that industrial strife at that point would cripple the entire movement. Reference is made to our decision sustaining the Packers and Stockyards Act. The Court found that the stockyards were but a "throat" through which the current of commerce flowed and the transactions which there occurred could not be separated from that movement. Hence the sales at the stockyards were not regarded as merely local transactions, for, while they created "a local change of title," they did not "stop the flow," but merely changed the private interests in the subject of the current. . . .

. . .

Respondent contends that the instant case presents material distinctions. Respondent says that the Aliquippa plant is extensive in size and represents a large investment in buildings, machinery and equipment. The raw materials which are brought to the plant are delayed for long periods and, after being subjected to manufacturing processes "are changed substantially as to character, utility and value." The finished products which emerge "are to a large extent manufactured without reference to pre-existing orders and contracts and are entirely different from the raw materials which enter at the other end." Hence respondent argues that, "If importation and exportation in interstate commerce do not singly transfer purely local activities into the field of congressional regulation, it should follow that their combination would not alter the local situation."

We do not find it necessary to determine whether these features of defendant's business dispose of the asserted analogy to the "stream of commerce" cases. The instances in which that metaphor has been used are but particular, and not exclusive, illustrations of the protective power which the government invokes in support of the present act. The congressional authority to protect interstate commerce from burdens and obstructions is not limited to transactions which can be deemed to be an essential part of a "flow" of interstate or foreign commerce. Burdens and obstructions may be due to injurious action springing from other sources. The fundamental principle is that the power to regulate commerce is the power to enact "all appropriate legislation" for its "protection or advancement"; to adopt measures "to promote its growth and insure its safety"; "to foster, protect, control, and restrain." That power is plenary and

may be exerted to protect interstate commerce "no matter what the source of the dangers which threaten it." Although activities may be intrastate in character when separately considered, if they have such a close and substantial relation to interstate commerce that their control is essential or appropriate to protect that commerce from burdens and obstructions, Congress cannot be denied the power to exercise that control. Undoubtedly the scope of this power must be considered in the light of our dual system of government and may not be extended so as to embrace effects upon interstate commerce so indirect and remote that to embrace them, in view of our complex society, would effectually obliterate the distinction between what is national and what is local and create a completely centralized government. The question is necessarily one of degree. . . .

. . .

Our conclusion is that the order of the Board was within its competency and that the act is valid as here applied. The judgment of the Circuit Court of Appeals is reversed and the cause is remanded for further proceedings in conformity with this opinion. It is so ordered.

Reversed and remanded.

Aftermath of NLRB v. Jones and Laughlin Steel Corporation

As a result of the Roosevelt assault the high bench had received a severe shock. No act of Congress was invalidated for the next 6 years, and only two minor statutes were declared unconstitutional in the 18 years between 1937 and 1955. Closely following *Jones & Laughlin* were cases contesting the ever-widening incursions of Congress into what were once considered local matters, with the Court now granting its approval to measures that in earlier times would never have passed muster. In *United States* v. *Darby* (1941), the Court upheld the Fair Labor Standards Act of 1938 which provided for minimum wages and maximum hours and effectively terminated child labor by prohibiting the shipment in interstate commerce of all goods not meeting standards fixed by federal law. Overruling a 23-year-old precedent, *Hammer* v. *Dagenhart* (1918), the Court abandoned the old distinction between "production" and "transportation" in holding that Congress may prohibit the shipment of goods manufactured under substandard labor conditions from entering the channels of interstate commerce. Among other reversals were *Wickard* v. *Filburn* (1942) which upheld the wheat marketing provisions of the Agricultural Adjustment Act of 1938 and discarded another old doctrine, that of dual federalism which held that the Tenth Amendment was a limit on the enumerated powers of Congress; and *United States* v. *Southeastern Underwriters Association* (1944) which overturned a long-standing precedent by holding that the insurance business was a part of interstate commerce and subject to the Sherman Antitrust Act. These and other decisions set the stage for congressional movement into the area of race relations in the 1960s based on the Supreme Court's broad, post-1937 reading of the interstate commerce clause.

Youngstown Sheet and Tube Company v. *Sawyer*

343 U.S. 579 (1952)

In 1952 the United States, while constitutionally not in a state of war since none had been declared by Congress, was in fact engaged in what was termed a "limited war" or "police action" in Korea. Technically in pursuit of a "treaty obligation" to the United Nations, President Truman had sent hundreds of thousands of American troops to South Korea to aid in repelling an invasion by North Korea, backed by the Soviet Union and later joined in battle by the forces of Communist China. In the latter part of 1951, a domestic dispute between management and labor in the steel industry arose over the terms of a new collective bargaining agreement. When the United Steelworkers of America announced on December 18 that they would strike when existing bargaining agreements expired on December 31, the Federal Mediation and Conciliation Service and the Federal War Stabilization Board intervened but were unsuccessful in effecting an agreement. When the union gave notice of a nationwide strike on April 4, 1952, the President issued an executive order directing Secretary of Commerce Charles Sawyer to take possession of and to operate most of the steel mills throughout the nation. President Truman based his order not on any specific statutory authority, but simply upon his powers as President, as Commander in Chief of the armed forces and "under the Constitution and laws of the United States." The order contained a finding that the seizure was necessary to avoid a national catastrophe since the work stoppage would imperil the national defense at a time when American troops were fighting in Korea.

Obeying the order under protest, the steel companies brought proceedings against the Secretary of Commerce in which they charged that the seizure was not authorized either by Congress or by the Constitution. Issuing a preliminary injunction, the district court rejected the government's contention that the President had "inherent power"—power supported by the Constitution, by historical precedent and court decision—to do what he had done. Following a stay of the injunction in the District of Columbia Court of Appeals, the case landed in the lap of the Supreme Court.

This case was a manifestation of the ever-present potential power conflict between Congress and the President which, when it reaches a flash point, requires settlement by a third party, traditionally the Supreme Court. In this instance two acts of Congress, the Selective Service Act of 1948 and the Defense Production Act of 1950, had both authorized seizure of industrial plants which failed to give priority to defense orders, but neither measure said anything about seizing plants to resolve labor disputes. Furthermore, when debating the Taft-Hartley Act of 1947 prior to its passage, Congress had considered and rejected authorizing executive seizure of an industry. One of the act's provisions, however, permitted the President to obtain an injunction postponing for 80 days any strike which threatened the national welfare. It was President Truman's position that since the strike had already been delayed more than 80 days, there was no point in invoking the procedure. He chose instead

to rely on the general executive prerogative which was not without precedent in times of crisis, notably during the Civil War and World Wars I and II.

Mr. Justice **Black** delivered the opinion of the Court.

We are asked to decide whether the President was acting within his constitutional power when he issued an order directing the Secretary of Commerce to take possession of and operate most of the Nation's steel mills. The mill owners argue that the President's order amounts to law-making, a legislative function which the Constitution has expressly confided to the Congress and not to the President. The Government's position is that the order was made on findings of the President that his action was necessary to avert a national catastrophe which would inevitably result from a stoppage of steel production, and that in meeting this grave emergency the President was acting within the aggregate of his constitutional powers as the Nation's Chief Executive and the Commander in Chief of the Armed Forces of the United States.

. . .

The President's power, if any, to issue the order must stem either from an act of Congress or from the Constitution itself. There is no statute that expressly authorizes the President to take possession of property as he did here. Nor is there any act of Congress to which our attention has been directed from which such a power can fairly be implied. Indeed, we do not understand the Government to rely on statutory authorization for this seizure. There are two statutes which do authorize the President to take both personal and real property under certain conditions. However, the Government admits that these conditions were not met and that the President's order was not rooted in either of the statutes. The Government refers to the seizure provisions of one of these statutes (§ 201 (b) of the Defense Production Act) as "much too cumbersome, involved, and time-consuming for the crisis which was at hand."

Moreover, the use of the seizure technique to solve labor disputes in order to prevent work stoppages was not only unauthorized by any congressional enactment; prior to this controversy, Congress had refused to adopt that method of settling labor disputes. When the Taft-Hartley Act was under consideration in 1947, Congress rejected an amendment which would have authorized such governmental seizures in cases of emergency. Apparently it was thought that the technique of seizure, like that of compulsory arbitration, would interfere with the process of collective bargaining. Consequently, the plan Congress adopted in that Act did not provide for seizure under any circumstances. Instead, the plan sought to bring about settlements by use of the customary devices of mediation, conciliation, investigation by boards of inquiry, and public reports. In some instances temporary injunctions were authorized to provide cooling-off periods. All this failing, unions were left free to strike after a secret vote by employees as to whether they wished to accept their employers' final settlement offer.

It is clear that if the President had authority to issue the order he did, it must be found in some provision of the Constitution. And it is not claimed that express constitutional language grants this power to the President. The contention is that presidential power should be implied from the aggregate of his powers under the Constitution. Particular reliance is placed on provisions in Article II which say that "The executive Power shall be vested in a President . . ."; that "he shall take Care that the Laws be faithfully executed"; and that he "shall be Commander in Chief of the Army and Navy of the United States."

The order cannot properly be sustained as an exercise of the President's military power as Commander in Chief of the Armed Forces. The Government attempts to do so by citing a number of cases upholding broad powers in military commanders engaged in day-to-day fighting in a theater of war. Such cases need not concern us here. Even though "theater of war" be an expanding concept, we cannot with faithfulness to our constitutional system hold that the Commander in Chief of the Armed Forces has the ultimate power as such to take possession of private property in order to keep labor disputes from stopping production. This is a job for the Nation's lawmakers, not for its military authorities.

Nor can the seizure order be sustained because of the several constitutional provisions that grant executive power to the President. In the framework of our Constitution, the President's power to see that the laws are faithfully executed refutes the idea that he is to be a lawmaker. The Constitution limits his functions in the lawmaking process to the recommending of laws he thinks wise and the vetoing of laws he thinks bad. And the Constitution is neither silent nor equivocal about who shall make laws which the President is to execute. The first section of the first article says that "All legislative Powers herein granted shall be vested in a Congress of the United States. . . ." After granting many powers to the Congress, Article I goes on to provide that Congress may "make all Laws which shall be necessary and proper for carrying into Execution the foregoing Powers, and all other Powers vested by this Constitution in the Government of the United States, or in any Department or Officer thereof."

The President's order does not direct that a congressional policy be executed in a manner prescribed by Congress—it directs that a presidential policy be executed in a manner prescribed by the President. The preamble of the order itself, like that of many statutes, sets out reasons why the President believes certain policies should be adopted, proclaims these policies as rules of conduct to be followed, and again, like a statute, authorizes a government official to promulgate additional rules and regulations consistent with the policy proclaimed and needed to carry that policy into execution. The power of Congress to adopt such public policies as those proclaimed by the order is beyond question. It can authorize the taking of private property for public use. It can make laws regulating the relationships between employers and employees, prescribing rules designed to settle labor disputes, and fixing wages and working conditions in certain fields of our economy. The Constitution does not subject this lawmaking power of Congress to presidential or military supervision or control.

It is said that other Presidents without congressional authority have taken possession of private business enterprises in order to settle labor disputes. But even if this be true, Congress has not thereby lost its exclusive constitutional authority to make laws necessary and proper to carry out the powers vested by the Constitution "in the Government of the United States, or any Department or Officer thereof."

The Founders of this Nation entrusted the lawmaking power to the Congress alone in both good and bad times. It would do no good to recall the historical events, the fears of power and the hopes for freedom that lay behind their choice. Such a review would but confirm our holding that this seizure order cannot stand.

The judgment of the District Court is

Affirmed.

. . .

Mr. Justice **Jackson,** concurring in the judgment and opinion of the Court.

That comprehensive and undefined presidential powers hold both practical advantages and grave dangers for the country will impress anyone who has served as legal adviser to a President in time of transition and public anxiety. While an interval of detached reflection may temper teachings of that experience, they probably are a more realistic influence on my views than the conventional materials of judicial decision which seem unduly to accentuate doctrine and legal fiction. But as we approach the question of presidential power, we half overcome mental hazards by recognizing them. The opinions of judges, no less than executives and publicists, often suffer the infirmity of confusing the issue of a power's validity with the cause it is invoked to promote, of confounding the permanent executive office with its temporary occupant. The tendency is strong to emphasize transient results upon policies—such as wages or stabilization—and lose sight of enduring consequences upon the balanced power structure of our Republic.

A judge, like an executive adviser, may be surprised at the poverty of really useful and unambiguous authority applicable to concrete problems of executive power as they actually present themselves. Just what our forefathers did envision, or would have envisioned had they foreseen modern conditions, must be divined from materials almost as enigmatic as the dreams Joseph was called upon to interpret for Pharaoh. A century and a half of partisan debate and scholarly speculation yields no net result but only supplies more or less apt quotations from respected sources on each side of any question. They largely cancel each other. And court decisions are indecisive because of the judicial practice of dealing with the largest questions in the most narrow way.

The actual art of governing under our Constitution does not and cannot conform to judicial definitions of the power of any of its branches based on isolated clauses or even single Articles torn from context. While the Constitution diffuses power the better to secure liberty, it also contemplates that practice will integrate the dispersed powers into a workable government. It enjoins upon its branches separateness but interdependence, autonomy but reciprocity. Presidential powers are not fixed but fluctuate, depending upon their disjunction or conjunction with those of Congress. We may well begin by a somewhat over-simplified grouping of practical situations in which a President may doubt, or others may challenge, his powers, and by distinguishing roughly the legal consequences of this factor of relativity.

1. When the President acts pursuant to an express or implied authorization of Congress, his authority is at its maximum, for it includes all that he possesses in his own right plus all that Congress can delegate. In these circumstances, and in these only, may he be said (for what it may be worth) to personify the federal sovereignty. If his act is held unconstitutional under these circumstances, it usually means that the Federal Government as an undivided whole lacks power. A seizure executed by the President pursuant to an Act of Congress would be supported by the strongest of presumptions and the widest latitude of judicial interpretation, and the burden of persuasion would rest heavily upon any who might attack it.

2. When the President acts in absence of

either a congressional grant or denial of authority, he can only rely upon his own independent powers, but there is a zone of twilight in which he and Congress may have concurrent authority, or in which its distribution is uncertain. Therefore, congressional inertia, indifference or quiescence may sometimes, at least as a practical matter, enable, if not invite, measures on independent presidential responsibility. In this area, any actual test of power is likely to depend on the imperatives of events and contemporary imponderables rather than on abstract theories of law.

3. When the President takes measures incompatible with the expressed or implied will of Congress, his power is at its lowest ebb, for then he can rely only upon his own constitutional powers minus any constitutional powers of Congress over the matter. Courts can sustain exclusive presidential control in such a case only by disabling the Congress from acting upon the subject. Presidential claim to a power at once so conclusive and preclusive must be scrutinized with caution, for what is at stake is the equilibrium established by our constitutional system.

Into which of these classifications does this executive seizure of the steel industry fit? It is eliminated from the first by admission, for it is conceded that no congressional authorization exists for this seizure. That takes away also the support of the many precedents and declarations which were made in relation, and must be confined, to this category.

Can it then be defended under flexible tests available to the second category? It seems clearly eliminated from that class because Congress has not left seizure of private property an open field but has covered it by three statutory policies inconsistent with this seizure. In cases where the purpose is to supply needs of the Government itself, two courses are provided: one, seizure of a plant which fails to comply with obligatory orders placed by the Government; another, condemnation of facilities, including temporary use under the power of eminent domain. The third is applicable where it is the general economy of the country that is to be protected rather than exclusive governmental interests. None of these were invoked. In choosing a different and inconsistent way of his own, the President cannot claim that it is necessitated or invited by failure of Congress to legislate upon the occasions, grounds and methods for seizure of industrial properties.

This leaves the current seizure to be justified only by the severe tests under the third grouping, where it can be supported only by any remainder of executive power after subtraction of such powers as Congress may have over the subject. In short, we can sustain the President only by holding that seizure of such strike-bound industries is within his domain and beyond control by Congress. Thus, this Court's first review of such seizures occurs under circumstances which leave presidential power most vulnerable to attack and in the least favorable of possible constitutional postures.

. . .

We should not use this occasion to circumscribe, much less to contract, the lawful role of the President as Commander in Chief. I should indulge the widest latitude of interpretation to sustain his exclusive function to command the instruments of national force, at least when turned against the outside world for the security of our society. But, when it is turned inward, not because of rebellion but because of a lawful economic struggle between industry and labor, it should have no such indulgence. His command power is not such an absolute as might be implied from that office in a militaristic system but is subject to limitations consistent with a constitutional Republic whose law and policy-making branch is a representative Congress. The purpose of lodging dual titles in one man was to insure that the civilian would control the military, not to enable the military to subordinate the presidential office. No penance would ever expiate the sin against free government of holding that a President can escape control of executive powers by law through assuming his military role. What the power of command may include I do not try to envision, but I think it is not a military prerogative, without support of law, to seize persons or property because they are important or even essential for the military and naval establishment.

. . .

Loose and irresponsible use of adjectives colors all nonlegal and much legal discussion of presidential powers. "Inherent" powers, "implied" powers, "incidental" powers, "plenary" powers, "war" powers and "emergency" powers are used, often interchangeably and without fixed or ascertainable meanings.

The vagueness and generality of the clauses that set forth presidential powers afford a plausible basis for pressures within and without an administration for presidential action beyond that supported by those whose responsibility it is to defend his actions in court. The claim of inherent and unrestricted presidential powers has long been a persuasive dialectical weapon in political controversy. While it is not surprising that counsel should grasp support from such unadjudicated claims of power, a judge cannot accept self-serving press statements of the attorney for one of the interested parties as authority in answering a constitutional question, even if the advocate was himself. But prudence has counseled that actual reliance on such nebulous claims stop short of provoking a judicial test.

. . .

The appeal, however, that we declare the existence of inherent powers *ex necessitate* to meet an emergency asks us to do what many think would be wise, although it is something the forefathers omitted. They knew what emergencies were, knew the pressures they engender for authoritative action, knew, too, how they afford a ready pretext for usurpation. We may also suspect that they suspected that emergency powers would tend to kindle emergencies. Aside from suspension of the privilege of the writ of habeas corpus in time of rebellion or invasion, when the public safety may require it, they made no express provision for exercise of extraordinary authority because of a crisis. I do not think we rightfully may so amend their work, and, if we could, I am not convinced it would be wise to do so, although many modern nations have forthrightly recognized that war and economic crises may upset the normal balance between liberty and authority. Their experience with emergency powers may not be irrelevant to the argument here that we should say that the Executive, of his own volition, can invest himself with undefined emergency powers.

. . .

In the practical working of our Government we already have evolved a technique within the framework of the Constitution by which normal executive powers may be considerably expanded to meet an emergency. Congress may and has granted extraordinary authorities which lie dormant in normal times but may be called into play by the Executive in war or upon proclamation of a national emergency. In 1939, upon congressional request, the Attorney General listed ninety-nine such separate statutory grants by Congress of emergency or wartime executive powers. They were invoked from time to time as need appeared. Under this procedure we retain Government by law—special, temporary law, perhaps, but law nonetheless. The public may know the extent and limitations of the powers that can be asserted, and persons affected may be informed from the statute of their rights and duties.

In view of the ease, expedition and safety with which Congress can grant and has granted large emergency powers, certainly ample to embrace this crisis, I am quite unimpressed with the argument that we should affirm possession of them without statute. Such power either has no beginning or it has no end. If it exists, it need submit to no legal restraint. I am not alarmed that it would plunge us straightway into dictatorship, but it is at least a step in that wrong direction.

. . .

Executive power has the advantage of concentration in a single head in whose choice the whole Nation has a part, making him the focus of public hopes and expectations. In drama, magnitude and finality his decisions so far overshadow any others that almost alone he fills the public eye and ear. No other personality in public life can begin to compete with him in access to the public mind through modern methods of communications. By his prestige as head of state and his influence upon public opinion he exerts a leverage upon those who are supposed to check and balance his power which often cancels their effectiveness.

. . .

But I have no illusion that any decision by this Court can keep power in the hands of Congress if it is not wise and timely in meeting its problems. A crisis that challenges the President equally, or perhaps primarily, challenges Congress. If not good law, there was worldly wisdom in the maxim attributed to Napoleon that "The tools belong to the man who can use them." We may say that power to legislate for emergencies belongs in the hands of Congress, but only Congress itself can prevent power from slipping through its fingers.

The essence of our free Government is "leave to live by no man's leave, underneath the law"— to be governed by those impersonal forces which we call law. Our Government is fashioned to fulfill this concept so far as humanly possible. The Executive, except for recommendation and veto, has no legislative power. The executive action we have here originates in the individual will of the President and represents an exercise of authority without law. No one, perhaps not even the President, knows the limits of the power he may seek to exert in this instance and the parties affected cannot learn the limit of their rights. We do not know today what powers over labor or property would be claimed to flow from Government possession if we should legalize it, what rights to compensation would be claimed or recognized, or on what contingency it would end. With all its defects, delays and inconveniences, men have discovered no technique for long preserving free government except that the Executive be under the law, and that the law be made by parliamentary deliberations.

Such institutions may be destined to pass away. But it is the duty of the Court to be last, not first, to give them up.

Mr. Chief Justice **Vinson,** with whom Mr. Justice **Reed** and Mr. Justice **Minton** join, dissenting.

In passing upon the question of Presidential powers in this case, we must first consider the context in which those powers were exercised.

Those who suggest that this is a case involving extraordinary powers should be mindful that these are extraordinary times. A world not yet recovered from the devastation of World War II has been forced to face the threat of another and more terrifying global conflict.

Accepting in full measure its responsibility in the world community, the United States was instrumental in securing adoption of the United Nations Charter, approved by the Senate by a vote of 89 to 2. The first purpose of the United Nations is to "maintain international peace and security, and to that end: to take effective collective measures for the prevention and removal of threats to the peace, and for the suppression of acts of aggression or other breaches of the peace. . . ." In 1950, when the United Nations called upon member nations "to render every assistance" to repel aggression in Korea, the United States furnished its vigorous support. For almost two full years, our armed forces have been fighting in Korea, suffering casualties of over 108,000 men. Hostilities have not abated. The "determination of the United Nations to continue its action in Korea to meet the aggression" has been reaffirmed. Congressional support of the action in Korea has been manifested by provisions for increased military manpower and equipment and for economic stabilization, as hereinafter described.

Further efforts to protect the free world from aggression are found in the congressional enactments of the Truman Plan for assistance to Greece and Turkey and the Marshall Plan for economic aid needed to build up the strength of our friends in Western Europe. In 1949, the Senate approved the North Atlantic Treaty under which each member nation agrees that an armed attack against one is an armed attack against all. Congress immediately implemented the North Atlantic Treaty by authorizing military assistance to nations dedicated to the principles of mutual security under the United Nations Charter. The concept of mutual security recently has been extended by treaty to friends in the Pacific.

Our treaties represent not merely legal obligations but show congressional recognition that mutual security for the free world is the best security against the threat of aggression on a global scale. The need for mutual security is shown by the very size of the armed forces outside the free world. Defendant's brief informs us that the Soviet Union maintains the largest air force in the world and maintains ground forces much larger than those presently available to the United States and the countries joined with us in mutual security arrangements. Constant international tensions are cited to demonstrate how precarious is the peace.

Even this brief review of our responsibilities in the world community discloses the enormity of our undertaking. Success of these measures may, as has often been observed, dramatically influence the lives of many generations of the world's peoples yet unborn. Alert to our responsibilities, which coincide with our own self-preservation through mutual security, Congress has enacted a large body of implementing legislation. As an illustration of the magnitude of the over-all program, Congress has appropriated $130 billion for our own defense and for military assistance to our allies since the June, 1950, attack in Korea.

In the Mutual Security Act of 1951, Congress authorized "military, economic, and technical assistance to friendly countries to strengthen the mutual security and individual and collective defenses of the free world. . . ." Over $5½ billion were appropriated for military assistance for fiscal year 1952, the bulk of that amount to be devoted to purchase of military equipment. A request for over $7 billion for the same purpose for fiscal year 1953 is currently pending in Congress. In addition to direct shipment of military equipment to nations of the free world, defense production in those countries relies upon shipment of machine tools and allocation of steel tonnage from the United States.

Congress also directed the President to build up our own defenses. Congress, recognizing the "grim fact . . . that the United States is now engaged in a struggle for survival" and that "it is imperative that we now take those necessary steps to make our strength equal to the peril of the hour," granted authority to draft men into the armed forces. As a result, we now have over 3,500,000 men in our armed forces.

Appropriations for the Department of Defense, which had averaged less than $13 billion per year for the three years before attack in Korea, were increased by Congress to $48 billion for fiscal year 1951 and to $60 billion for fiscal year 1952. A request for $51 billion for the Department of Defense for fiscal year 1953 is currently pending in Congress. The bulk of the increase is for military equipment and supplies—guns, tanks, ships, planes and ammunition—all of which require steel. Other defense programs requiring great quantities of steel include the large scale expansion of facilities for the Atomic Energy Commission and the expansion of the Nation's productive capacity affirmatively encouraged by Congress.

Congress recognized the impact of these defense programs upon the economy. Following the attack in Korea, the President asked for authority to requisition property and to allocate and fix priorities for scarce goods. In the Defense Production Act of 1950, Congress granted the powers requested and, *in addition,* granted power to stabilize prices and wages and to provide for settlement of labor disputes arising in the defense program. The Defense Production Act was extended in 1951, a Senate Committee noting that in the dislocation caused by the programs for purchase of military equipment "lies the seed of an economic disaster that might well destroy the military might we are straining to build." Significantly, the Committee examined the problem "in terms of just one commodity, steel," and found "a graphic picture of the overall inflationary danger growing out of reduced civilian supplies and rising incomes." Even before Korea, steel production at levels above theoretical 100% capacity was not capable of supplying civilian needs alone. Since Korea, the tremendous military demand for steel has far exceeded the increases in productive capacity. This Committee emphasized that the shortage of steel, even with the mills operating at full capacity, coupled with increased civilian purchasing power, presented grave danger of disastrous inflation.

The President has the duty to execute the foregoing legislative programs. Their successful execution depends upon continued production of steel and stabilized prices for steel. Accordingly, when the collective bargaining agreements between the Nation's steel producers and their

employees, represented by the United Steel Workers, were due to expire on December 31, 1951, and a strike shutting down the entire basic steel industry was threatened, the President acted to avert a complete shutdown of steel production. On December 22, 1951, he certified the dispute to the Wage Stabilization Board, requesting that the Board investigate the dispute and promptly report its recommendation as to fair and equitable terms of settlement. The Union complied with the President's request and delayed its threatened strike while the dispute was before the Board. After a special Board panel had conducted hearings and submitted a report, the full Wage Stabilization Board submitted its report and recommendations to the President on March 20, 1952.

The Board's report was acceptable to the Union but was rejected by plaintiffs. The Union gave notice of its intention to strike as of 12:01 a.m., April 9, 1952, but bargaining between the parties continued with hope of settlement until the evening of April 8, 1952. After bargaining had failed to avert the threatened shutdown of steel production, the President issued the following Executive Order:

. . .

"WHEREAS in order to assure the continued availability of steel and steel products during the existing emergency, it is necessary that the United States take possession of and operate the plants, facilities, and other property of the said companies as hereinafter provided:

"NOW, THEREFORE, by virtue of the authority vested in me by the Constitution and laws of the United States, and as President of the United States and Commander in Chief of the armed forces of the United States, it is hereby ordered as follows:

"1. The Secretary of Commerce is hereby authorized and directed to take possession of all or such of the plants, facilities, and other property of the companies named in the list attached hereto, or any part thereof, as he may deem necessary in the interests of national defense; and to operate or to arrange for the operation thereof and to do all things necessary for, or incidental to, such operation. . . ."

. . .

Focusing now on the situation confronting the President on the night of April 8, 1952, we cannot but conclude that the President was performing his duty under the Constitution to "take Care that the Laws be faithfully executed"—a duty described by President Benjamin Harrison as "the central idea of the office."

The President reported to Congress the morning after the seizure that he acted because a work stoppage in steel production would immediately imperil the safety of the Nation by preventing execution of the legislative programs for procurement of military equipment. And, while a shutdown could be averted by granting the price concessions requested by plaintiffs, granting such concessions would disrupt the price stabilization program also enacted by Congress. Rather than fail to execute either legislative program, the President acted to execute both.

Much of the argument in this case has been directed at straw men. We do not now have before us the case of a President acting solely on the basis of his own notions of the public welfare. Nor is there any question of unlimited executive power in this case. The President himself closed the door to any such claim when he sent his Message to Congress stating his purpose to abide by any action of Congress, whether approving or disapproving his seizure action. Here, the President immediately made sure that Congress was fully informed of the temporary action he had taken only to preserve the legislative programs from destruction until Congress could act.

The absence of a specific statute authorizing seizure of the steel mills as a mode of executing the laws—both the military procurement program and the anti-inflation program—has not until today been thought to prevent the President from executing the laws. Unlike an administrative commission confined to the enforcement of the statute under which it was created, or the head of a department when administering a particular statute, the President is a constitutional officer charged with taking care that a "mass of legislation" be executed. Flexibility as to mode of execution to meet critical situations is a matter of practical necessity.

This practical construction of the "Take Care" clause, advocated by John Marshall, was adopted by this Court in *In re Neagle, In re Debs.* . . . Although more restrictive views of executive power, advocated in dissenting opinions of Justices Holmes, McReynolds and Brandeis, were emphatically rejected by this Court in *Myers* v. *United States,* members of today's majority treat these dissenting views as authoritative.

There is no statute prohibiting seizure as a method of enforcing legislative programs. Congress has in no wise indicated that its legislation is not to be executed by the taking of private property (subject of course to the payment of just compensation) if its legislation cannot otherwise be executed. Indeed, the Universal Military Training and Service Act authorizes the seizure of *any* plant that fails to fill a Government contract or the properties of *any* steel producer that fails to allocate steel as directed for defense production. And the Defense Production Act authorizes the President to requisition equipment and condemn real property needed without delay in the defense effort. Where Congress authorizes seizure in instances not necessarily crucial to the defense program, it can hardly be said to have disclosed an intention to prohibit seizures where essential to the execution of that legislative program.

Whatever the extent of Presidential power on more tranquil occasions, and whatever the right of the President to execute legislative programs as he sees fit without reporting the mode of execution to Congress, the single Presidential purpose disclosed on this record is to faithfully execute the laws by acting in an emergency to maintain the status quo, thereby preventing collapse of the legislative programs until Congress could act. The President's action served the same purposes as a judicial stay entered to maintain the status quo in order to preserve the jurisdiction of a court. In his Message to Congress immediately following the seizure, the President explained the necessity of his action in executing the military procurement and anti-inflation legislative programs and expressed his desire to cooperate with any legislative proposals approving, regulating or rejecting the seizure of the steel mills. Consequently, there is no evidence whatever of any Presidential purpose to defy Congress or act in any way inconsistent with the legislative will.

. . .

The diversity of views expressed in the six opinions of the majority, the lack of reference to authoritative precedent, the repeated reliance upon prior dissenting opinions, the complete disregard of the uncontroverted facts showing the gravity of the emergency and the temporary nature of the taking all serve to demonstrate how far afield one must go to affirm the order of the District Court.

The broad executive power granted by Article II to an officer on duty 365 days a year cannot, it is said, be invoked to avert disaster. Instead, the President must confine himself to sending a message to Congress recommending action. Under this messenger-boy concept of the Office, the President cannot even act to preserve legislative programs from destruction so that Congress will have something left to act upon. There is no judicial finding that the executive action was unwarranted because there was in fact no basis for the President's finding of the existence of an emergency for, under this view, the gravity of the emergency and the immediacy of the threatened disaster are considered irrelevant as a matter of law.

Seizure of plaintiffs' property is not a pleasant undertaking. Similarly unpleasant to a free country are the draft which disrupts the home and military procurement which causes economic dislocation and compels adoption of price controls, wage stabilization and allocation of materials. The President informed Congress that even a temporary Government operation of plaintiffs' properties was "thoroughly distasteful" to him, but was necessary to prevent immediate paralysis of the mobilization program. Presidents have been in the past, and any man worthy of the Office should be in the future, free to take at least interim action necessary to execute legislative programs essential to survival of the Nation. A sturdy judiciary should not be swayed by the unpleasantness or unpopularity of necessary executive action, but must independently determine for itself whether the President was acting, as required by the Constitution, to "take Care that the Laws be faithfully executed."

As the District Judge stated, this is no time for "timorous" judicial action. But neither is this a time for timorous executive action. Faced with the duty of executing the defense programs which Congress had enacted and the disastrous effects that any stoppage in steel production would have on those programs, the President acted to preserve those programs by seizing the steel mills. There is no question that the possession was other than temporary in character and subject to congressional direction—either approving, disapproving or regulating the manner in which the mills were to be administered and returned to the owners. The President immediately informed Congress of his action and clearly stated his intention to abide by the legislative will. No basis for claims of arbitrary action, unlimited powers or dictatorial usurpation of congressional power appears from the facts of this case. On the contrary, judicial, legislative and executive precedents throughout our history demonstrate that in this case the President acted in full conformity with his duties under the Constitution. Accordingly, we would reverse the order of the District Court.

Aftermath of Youngstown Sheet and Tube Company v. Sawyer

In the *Youngstown* case we observe the Supreme Court curbing the power of one of the branches of government (the executive) while being firmly supported by another (the legislature). At the same time, however, we can see the Court's unwillingness, perhaps incapacity, to resolve clearly and definitely a conflict involving the limits of executive power under the Constitution. The fact that all of the justices in the majority wrote separate opinions indicates an inability to agree on a rationale for the decision and illustrates anew the tenuous nature of constitutional limits on the presidency during a national emergency. Those justices in the majority could agree only that the President can act constitutionally under powers prescribed in the document itself or in pursuance of a congressional statute. The executive has no "inherent" powers whatsoever in domestic affairs and only a possible residue that allows for elasticity in foreign affairs. However, even in this case repudiating the excessive use of the presidential prerogative, only Justices Hugo Black and William O. Douglas would have held the President strictly to constitutional and/or statutory language. In addition to the three dissenters, four of the majority hinted or assumed that the President might exercise extraordinary powers in an extreme emergency. All six in the majority agreed on one crucial point: the President had usurped legislative power because Congress had specifically refused to grant authority for executive seizures in emergencies when it enacted the Taft-Hartley law.

Issues of this type have continued to plague the nation, particularly as a result of modern technology which tends to move events swiftly to a crisis stage which, in turn, requires immediate action by the government to avoid catastrophe. Only the President is capable of such quick reaction, and more often than not, his efforts, though frequently constitutionally borderline, are not litigable in court; that is, there may be no definable individual injury that would give a person or a corporate entity standing to sue. For example, during the Vietnam War, also carried on through executive action without a formal congressional declaration, the Court rejected all attempts on the part of litigants to obtain a ruling on the war's constitutionality. In this instance, as in the Korean conflict, the President was not without legislative support since Congress in 1964 had passed the Gulf of Tonkin Resolution supporting the President's use of armed force in Southeast Asia. At the war's end, however, Congress enacted the War Powers Resolution(1973) which requires the President when using the armed forces in a combat situation to report the fact to the Congress within 48 hours and to terminate such action within 60 days unless Congress gives its approval. Congressional moves of this nature have automatically driven the body into a confrontational mode with the executive, as Presidents have interpreted the act narrowly. President Reagan sent Marines to Lebanon, bombed Libya, invaded the island of Grenada, and used the Navy to escort tankers in the Persian Gulf, always skirting the War Powers Act and avoiding a direct confrontation with Congress or with any court order.

The separation of powers helps to prevent tyranny, especially when a cautious legislature curtails an adventurous executive. It also may prevent the executive from taking forcible action ostensibly to preclude greater troubles for the nation down the road. Unfortunately, it is seldom clear at the time which policies would best ensure the nation's future security, and the Supreme Court has wisely decided that unless there is a clear constitutional mandate, it will not intervene in legislative-executive squabbles over foreign policy matters. Illustrative of this point is the 1979 case of *Goldwater* v. *Carter,* which arose after President Jimmy Carter, acting on his own initiative, terminated a mutual defense treaty between the United States and Taiwan. Eight senators, a former senator, and 16 congressmen brought suit in the district court of the District of Columbia, alleging that the President had acted unconstitutionally in that he had not obtained some form of legislative concurrence. The district court ruled against the President but was reversed by the circuit court of appeals. Acting in accord with tradition and precedent, the Supreme Court ordered the district court to dismiss the case, thus leaving the final solution up to the "political branches" of the government.

United States v. *Nixon*

418 U.S. 683 (1974)

Not since 1867, when the Supreme Court decided the case of *Mississippi* v. *Johnson*, had there been a case in which the Supreme Court was asked to issue a direct order to the President. In the case of *United States* v. *Nixon* for the first time ever the Court issued such an order. The *Nixon* case differed markedly from controversies of the past in that it did not involve a policy conflict with Congress, but was grounded upon allegations of corruption and wrongdoing in the executive department. Ultimately the constitutional issue turned on the question of executive privilege, that is, the extent to which a President might withhold information from Congress, the courts and the public.

This complex case had its origin in what at the time seemed a rather minor event. On June 17, 1972, a private security guard in Washington's Watergate apartment hotel noticed a door with its lock taped open and called the police, who caught and arrested five men who were burglarizing the headquarters of the Democratic National Committee. Eventually it became known that the burglary was part of a much larger operation set in motion by Attorney General John Mitchell and his staff to help ensure the reelection of President Richard Nixon, all of which was subsequently denied by Mitchell and other members of the Nixon White House staff. As a result of a massive "coverup" and a major congressional investigation, a federal grand jury sitting in the District of Columbia returned indictments against then-resigned Attorney General Mitchell and six others, alleging conspiracy to defraud the United States and obstruction of justice. Also named by the grand jury as a co-conspirator was President Nixon. Following the indictments, District Judge John Sirica issued a *subpoena duces tecum* directing the President to produce tape recordings of conversations with his aides and advisors that might be relevant to the upcoming trials of those indicted. Releasing transcripts to the public of 43 conversations, the President declined to release additional material on the ground, among others, that it was protected by the principle of executive privilege.

WARREN E. BURGER

*Warren Earl Burger, who served as chief justice from 1969 to 1986, was appointed by President Richard Nixon with the expectation that he would help move the Supreme Court away from the liberal activism of the Earl Warren era. Under Burger the Court became somewhat more middle-of-the-road politically, but the years of his leadership saw no radical transformation of judicial doctrine. As a judge Burger produced no coherent jurisprudence but he wrote opinions stabilizing the rules on obscenity (*Miller v. California*) and formulating principles covering state aid to religious schools (*Lemon v. Kurtzman*). Burger devoted much attention as chief justice to promoting greater efficiency in the federal judicial system.*

Mr. Chief Justice **Burger** delivered the opinion of the Court.

This litigation presents for review the denial of a motion, filed in the District Court on behalf of the President of the United States, in the case of United States v Mitchell to quash a third-party subpoena duces tecum issued by the United States District Court for the District of Columbia, pursuant to Fed Rul Crim Proc 17(c). The subpoena directed the President to produce certain tape recordings and documents relating to his conversations with aides and advisers. The court rejected the President's claims of absolute executive privilege, of lack of jurisdiction, and of failure to satisfy the requirements of Rule 17(c). The President appealed to the Court of Appeals. We granted both the United States' petition for certiorari before judgment and also the President's cross-petition for certiorari before judgment because of the public importance of the issues presented and the need for their prompt resolution.

On March 1, 1974, a grand jury of the United States District Court for the District of Columbia returned an indictment charging seven named individuals with various offenses, including conspiracy to defraud the United States and to obstruct justice. Although he was not designated as such in the indictment, the grand jury named the President, among others, as an unindicted coconspirator. On April 18, 1974, upon motion of the Special Prosecutor, a subpoena duces tecum was issued pursuant to Rule 17(c) to the President by the United States District Court and made returnable on May 2, 1974. This subpoena required the production, in advance of the September 9 trial date, of certain tapes, memoranda, papers, transcripts, or other writings relating to certain precisely identified meetings between the President and others. The Special Prosecutor was able to fix the time, place, and persons present at these discussions because the White House daily logs and appointment records had been delivered to him. On April 30, the President publicly released edited transcripts of 43 conversations; portions of 20 conversations subject to subpoena in the present case were included. On May 1, 1974, the President's counsel filed a "special appearance" and a motion to quash the subpoena under Rule 17(c). This motion was accompanied by a formal claim of privilege. At a subsequent hearing, further motions to expunge the grand jury's action naming the President as an unindicted coconspirator and for protective orders against the disclosure of that information were filed or raised orally by counsel for the President.

. . .

THE CLAIM OF PRIVILEGE

A

. . . [W]e turn to the claim that the subpoena should be quashed because it demands "confidential conversations between a President and his close advisers that it would be inconsistent with the public interest to produce." The first contention is a broad claim that the separation of powers doctrine precludes judicial review of a President's claim of privilege. The second contention is that if he does not prevail on the claim of absolute privilege, the court should hold as a matter of constitutional law that the privilege prevails over the subpoena duces tecum.

In the performance of assigned constitutional duties each branch of the Government must initially interpret the Constitution, and the interpretation of its powers by any branch is due great respect from the others. The President's counsel, as we have noted, reads the Constitution as providing an absolute privilege of confidentiality for all Presidential communications. Many decisions of this Court, however, have unequivocally reaffirmed the holding of Marbury v Madison, that "[i]t is emphatically the province and duty of the judicial department to say what the law is."

No holding of the Court has defined the scope of judicial power specifically relating to the enforcement of a subpoena for confidential Presidential communications for use in a criminal prosecution, but other exercises of power by the Executive Branch and the Legislative Branch have been found invalid as in conflict with the Constitution. In a series of cases, the Court interpreted the explicit immunity conferred by express provisions of the Constitution on Members of the House and Senate by the Speech or Debate Clause, US Const Art I, § 6. Since this Court has consistently exercised the power to construe and delineate claims arising under express powers, it must follow that the Court has authority to interpret claims with respect to powers alleged to derive from enumerated powers.

Our system of government "requires that federal courts on occasion interpret the Constitution in a manner at variance with the construction given the document by another branch."

. . .

Notwithstanding the deference each branch must accord the others, the "judicial Power of the United States" vested in the federal courts by Art III, § 1, of the Constitution can no more be shared with the Executive Branch than the Chief Executive, for example, can share with the Judiciary the veto power, or the Congress share with the Judiciary the power to override a Presidential veto. Any other conclusion would be contrary to the basic concept of separation of powers and the checks and balances that flow from the scheme of a tripartite government. We therefore reaffirm that it is the province and duty of this Court "to say what the law is" with respect to the claim of privilege presented in this case.

B

In support of his claim of absolute privilege, the President's counsel urges two grounds, one of which is common to all governments and one of which is peculiar to our system of separation of powers. The first ground is the valid need for protection of communications between high Government officials and those who advise and assist them in the performance of their manifold duties; the importance of this confidentiality is too plain to require further discussion. Human experience teaches that those who expect public dissemination of their remarks may well temper candor with a concern for appearances and for their own interests to the detriment of the decisionmaking process. Whatever the nature of the privilege of confidentiality of Presidential communications in the exercise of Art II powers, the

privilege can be said to derive from the supremacy of each branch within its own assigned area of constitutional duties. Certain powers and privileges flow from the nature of enumerated powers; the protection of the confidentiality of Presidential communications has similar constitutional underpinnings.

The second ground asserted by the President's counsel in support of the claim of absolute privilege rests on the doctrine of separation of powers. Here it is argued that the independence of the Executive Branch within its own sphere, insulates a President from a judicial subpoena in an ongoing criminal prosecution, and thereby protects confidential Presidential communications.

However, neither the doctrine of separation of powers, nor the need for confidentiality of high-level communications, without more, can sustain an absolute, unqualified Presidential privilege of immunity from judicial process under all circumstances. The President's need for complete candor and objectivity from advisers calls for great deference from the courts. However, when the privilege depends solely on the broad, undifferentiated claim of public interest in the confidentiality of such conversations, a confrontation with other values arises. Absent a claim of need to protect military, diplomatic, or sensitive national security secrets, we find it difficult to accept the argument that even the very important interest in confidentiality of Presidential communications is significantly diminished by production of such material for in camera inspection with all the protection that a district court will be obliged to provide.

The impediment that an absolute, unqualified privilege would place in the way of the primary constitutional duty of the Judicial Branch to do justice in criminal prosecutions would plainly conflict with the function of the courts under Art III. In designing the structure of our Government and dividing and allocating the sovereign power among three co-equal branches, the Framers of the Constitution sought to provide a comprehensive system, but the separate powers were not intended to operate with absolute independence.

To read the Art II powers of the President as providing an absolute privilege as against a subpoena essential to enforcement of criminal statutes on no more than a generalized claim of the public interest in confidentiality of nonmilitary and nondiplomatic discussions would upset the constitutional balance of "a workable government" and gravely impair the role of the courts under Art III.

C

Since we conclude that the legitimate needs of the judicial process may outweigh Presidential privilege, it is necessary to resolve those competing interests in a manner that preserves the essential functions of each branch. The right and indeed the duty to resolve that question does not free the judiciary from according high respect to the representations made on behalf of the President. The expectation of a President to the confidentiality of his conversations and correspondence, like the claim of confidentiality of judicial deliberations, for example, has all the values to which we accord deference for the privacy of all citizens and added to those values the necessity for protection of the public interest in candid, objective, and even blunt or harsh opinions in Presidential decision making. A President and those who assist him must be free to explore alternatives in the process of shaping policies and making decisions and to do so in a way many would be unwilling to express except privately. These are the considerations justifying a presumptive privilege for Presidential communications. The privilege is fundamental to the operation of government and inextricably rooted in the separation of powers under the Constitution. In Nixon v Sirica, the Court of Appeals held that such Presidential communications are "presumptively privileged," and this position is accepted by both parties in the present litigation. We agree with Mr. Chief Justice Marshall's observation, therefore, that "[i]n no case of this kind would a court be required to proceed against the President as against an ordinary individual."

But this presumptive privilege must be considered in light of our historic commitment to the rule of law. This is nowhere more profoundly manifest than in our view that "the twofold aim [of criminal justice] is that guilt shall not escape or innocence suffer." We have elected to employ an adversary system of criminal justice in which the parties contest all issues before a court of law. The need to develop all relevant facts in the adversary system is both fundamental and comprehensive. The ends of criminal justice would be defeated if judgments were to be founded on a partial or speculative presentation of the facts. The very integrity of the judicial system and public confidence in the system depend on full disclosure of all the facts, within the framework of the rules of evidence. To ensure that justice is done, it is imperative to the function of courts that compulsory process be available for the production of evidence needed either by the prosecution or by the defense.

. . .

The privileges referred to by the Court are designed to protect weighty and legitimate competing interests. Thus, the Fifth Amendment to the Constitution provides that no man "shall be compelled in any criminal case to be a witness against himself." And, generally, an attorney or a priest may not be required to disclose what has been revealed in professional confidence. These and other interests are recognized in law by privileges against forced disclosure, established in the Constitution, by statute, or at common law. Whatever their origins, these exceptions to the demand for every man's evidence are not lightly created nor expansively construed, for they are in derogation of the search for truth.

In this case the President challenges a subpoena served on him as a third party requiring the production of materials for use in a criminal prosecution; he does so on the claim that he has a privilege against disclosure of confidential communications. He does not place his claim of privilege on the ground they are military or diplomatic secrets. As to these areas of Art II duties the courts have traditionally shown the utmost deference to Presidential responsibilities.

. . .

No case of the Court, however, has extended this high degree of deference to a President's generalized interest in confidentiality. Nowhere in the Constitution, as we have noted earlier, is there any explicit reference to a privilege of confidentiality, yet to the extent this interest relates to the effective discharge of a President's powers, it is constitutionally based.

The right to the production of all evidence at a criminal trial similarly has constitutional dimensions. The Sixth Amendment explicitly confers upon every defendant in a criminal trial the right "to be confronted with the witnesses against him" and "to have compulsory process for obtaining witnesses in his favor." Moreover, the Fifth Amendment also guarantees that no person shall be deprived of liberty without due process of law. It is the manifest duty of the courts to vindicate those guarantees, and to accomplish that it is essential that all relevant and admissible evidence be produced.

In this case we must weigh the importance of the general privilege of confidentiality of Presidential communications in performance of his responsibilities against the inroads of such a privilege on the fair administration of criminal justice. The interest in preserving confidentiality is weighty indeed and entitled to great respect. However, we cannot conclude that advisers will be moved to temper the candor of their remarks by the infrequent occasions of disclosure because of the possibility that such conversations will be called for in the context of a criminal prosecution.

On the other hand, the allowance of the privilege to withhold evidence that is demonstrably relevant in a criminal trial would cut deeply into the guarantee of due process of law and gravely impair the basic function of the courts. A President's acknowledged need for confidentiality in the communications of his office is general in nature, whereas the constitutional need for production of relevant evidence in a criminal proceeding is specific and central to the fair adjudication of a particular criminal case in the administration of justice. Without access to specific facts a criminal prosecution may be totally frustrated. The President's broad interest in confidentiality of communications will not be vitiated by disclosure of a limited number of conversations preliminarily shown to have some bearing on the pending criminal cases.

We conclude that when the ground for asserting privilege as to subpoenaed materials sought for use in a criminal trial is based only on the generalized interest in confidentiality, it cannot prevail over the fundamental demands of due process of law in the fair administration of criminal justice. The generalized assertion of privilege must yield to the demonstrated, specific need for evidence in a pending criminal trial.

D

We have earlier determined that the District Court did not err in authorizing the issuance of the subpoena. If a President concludes that compliance with a subpoena would be injurious to the public interest he may properly, as was done here, invoke a claim of privilege on the return of the subpoena. Upon receiving a claim of privilege from the Chief Executive, it became the further duty of the District Court to treat the subpoenaed material as presumptively privileged and to require the Special Prosecutor to demonstrate that the Presidential material was "essential to the justice of the [pending criminal] case." Here the District Court treated the material as presumptively privileged, proceeded to find that the Special Prosecutor had made a sufficient showing to rebut the presumption, and ordered an in camera examination of the subpoenaed material. On the basis of our examination of the record we are unable to conclude that the District Court erred in ordering the inspection. Accordingly we affirm the order of the District Court that subpoenaed materials be transmitted to that court. We now turn to the important question of the District Court's responsibilities in conducting the in camera examination of Presidential materials or communications delivered under the compulsion of the subpoena duces tecum.

E

Enforcement of the subpoena duces tecum was stayed pending this Court's resolution of the issues raised by the petitions for certiorari. Those issues now having been disposed of, the matter of implementation will rest with the District Court. "[T]he guard, furnished to [the President] to protect him from being harassed by vexatious and unnecessary subpoenas, is to be looked for in the conduct of a [district] court after those subpoenas have issued; not in any circumstance which is to precede their being issued." Statements that meet the test of admissibility and relevance must be isolated; all other material must be excised. At this stage the District Court is not limited to representations of the Special Prosecutor as to the evidence sought by the subpoena; the material will be available to the District Court. It is elementary that in camera inspection of evidence is always a procedure calling for scrupulous protection against any release or publication of material not found by the court, at that stage, probably admissible in evidence and relevant to the issues of the trial for which it is sought. That being true of an ordinary situation, it is obvious that the District Court has a very heavy responsibility to see to it that Presidential conversations, which are either not relevant or not admissible, are accorded that high degree of respect due the President of the United States. Mr. Chief Justice Marshall, sitting as a trial judge in the Burr case, was extraordinarily careful to point out that "[i]n no case of this kind would a court be required to proceed against the president as an ordinary individual." Marshall's statement cannot be read to mean in any sense that a President is above the law, but relates to the singularly unique role under Art II of a President's communications and activities, related to the performance of duties under that Article. Moreover, a President's communications and activities encompass a vastly wider range of sensitive material than would be true of any "ordinary individual." It is therefore necessary in the public interest to afford Presidential confidentiality the greatest protection consistent with the fair administration of justice. The need for confidentiality even as to idle conversations with associates in which casual reference might be made concerning political leaders within the country or foreign statesmen is too obvious to call for further treatment. We have no doubt that the District Judge will at all times accord to Presidential records that high degree of deference suggested in United States v Burr, and will discharge his responsibility to see to it that until released to the Special Prosecutor no in camera material is revealed to anyone. This burden applies with even greater force to excised material; once the decision is made to excise, the material is restored to its privileged status and should be returned under seal to its lawful custodian.

Since this matter came before the Court during the pendency of a criminal prosecution, and on representations that time is of the essence, the mandate shall issue forthwith.

Affirmed.

Mr. Justice **Rehnquist** took no part in the consideration or decision of these cases.

Aftermath of United States *v.* Nixon

Although Chief Justice Warren Burger in the majority opinion ruled against the President, he nevertheless gave broad constitutional sanction to the principle of executive privilege, a precept that the Chief admitted was not specifically stated in the Constitution. Burger took great pains to give the broadest possible scope to what he called "this presumptive privilege," and his opinion appeared to authorize the President to withhold any information from a court if he decides it is in the interest of national security.

On August 9, 1975, just 2 weeks after the Court's decision, an embattled Richard Nixon resigned from office, the first President to do so in the two-century history of the republic. As the record unfolded, it became clear that the President was the man behind the web of Watergate, that he had taken the irreversible step on June 23, 1972, 6 days after the break-in, of ordering his aides to ensure that the FBI not learn about the network of wrongdoing—wiretapping, burglaries, coverups, laundering of money, secret funds, forgeries, Internal Revenue Service audits—authorized by the White House. When Gerald Ford succeeded to the presidency upon Nixon's resignation, he pardoned the former President of all possible criminal activity, but many of those people who had served in the Nixon White House ended up in jail.

On the matter of executive privilege a footnote was written in 1977 when the Court handed down the opinion in *Nixon* v. *Administrator of General Services.* Following his resignation Richard Nixon entered into an agreement with the General Services Administration for the storage and conditions of access to the millions of documents and several hundred tape recordings accumulated during his tenure as President. Subsequently, Congress passed the Presidential Recordings and Materials Preservation Act which directed the Administrator of the GSA to screen the materials and return personal papers to the former President, but to preserve all documents of historic value and maintain the availability of any materials for use in judicial proceedings conditioned upon "any rights, defenses, or privileges which the Federal Government or any person may invoke." On the day the Act took effect Mr. Nixon initiated a suit in a federal district court, alleging that the law violated the Constitution in several respects, particularly in its contravention of the separation of powers and executive privilege. On appeal the Supreme Court rejected all of the former President's claims, holding that no infringements of the separation of powers existed since the screening and control of the materials remained within the executive branch, and that the law contained clear guidelines regulating access to the materials and protection against indiscriminate disclosures. With respect to executive privilege, the Court concluded that "the screening process contemplated by the Act will not constitute a more severe intrusion into Presidential confidentiality than the *in camera* inspection by the District Court approved in *United States* v. *Nixon.*"

Another component of the presidential prerogative was addressed in 1982 in *Nixon* v. *Fitzgerald,* when the Supreme Court held that a former President of the United States is entitled to absolute immunity from damages liability predicated on his official acts.

Immigration and Naturalization Service v. *Chadha*

462 U.S. 919 (1983)

Adopted as a means of dealing expeditiously with the problems inherent in a complex, administrative bureaucracy, the legislative veto was first used in the Reorganization Act of 1932. Under the Act the President might, in the interests of efficiency, reorganize the administrative structure of the government on his own initiative, the new organization to take effect unless disapproved by Congress within a specified period of time. This seemingly sensible concept caught on immediately and was used in some 200 laws over the next half century, albeit in many different forms. Generally it was to be exercised by both houses of Congress, although in some instances the measure provided for a veto by one house or even by a permanent committee of either house.

The concept went unchallenged until the early 1980s when Jagdish Rai Chadha, an alien who had been lawfully admitted to the United States but had remained in the country after the expiration of his visa, was ordered by the Immigration and Naturalization Service (INS) to show cause why he should not be deported. Chadha, an East Indian born in Kenya and holding a British passport, was admitted to the United States in 1966 on a nonimmigrant student visa which had expired in 1972. At his deportation hearing the immigration judge found that Chadha had met the requirements of the law, namely, that he had resided continually in the United States for over 7 years, was of good moral character, and would suffer extreme hardship if deported. In pursuance of the act, the attorney general recommended to Congress that Chadha's deportation be suspended. By resolution, however, the House of Representatives "vetoed" the actions of the immigration judge and the attorney general, thus closing the avenue of permanent alien residence to Chadha and upholding his deportation. Chadha filed a petition for review of the deportation order in the U.S. Court of Appeals, arguing that the law authorizing the procedures was unconstitutional. Agreeing with him, the court of appeals held, in essence, that Section 244(c)(2) of the act violated the doctrine of separation of powers. The Supreme Court granted *certiorari*.

Chief Justice **Burger** delivered the opinion of the Court.

. . .

A

We turn . . . to the question whether action of one House of Congress under § 244(c)(2) violates strictures of the Constitution. We begin, of course, with the presumption that the challenged statute is valid. Its wisdom is not the concern of the courts; if a challenged action does not violate the Constitution, it must be sustained:

"Once the meaning of an enactment is discerned and its constitutionality determined, the judicial process comes to an end. We do not sit as a committee of review, nor are we vested with the power of veto." Tennessee Valley Authority v Hill (1978).

By the same token, the fact that a given law or procedure is efficient, convenient, and useful in facilitating functions of government, standing alone, will not save it if it is contrary to the Constitution. Convenience and efficiency are not the primary objectives—or the hallmarks—of democratic government and our inquiry is sharpened rather than blunted by the fact that Congressional veto provisions are appearing with increasing frequency in statutes which delegate authority to executive and independent agencies:

"Since 1932, when the first veto provision was enacted into law, 295 congressional veto-type procedures have been inserted in 196 different statutes as follows: from 1932 to 1939, five statutes were affected; from 1940–49, nineteen statutes; between 1950–59, thirty-four statutes; and from 1960–69, forty-nine. From the year 1970 through 1975, at least one hundred sixty-three such provisions were included in eighty-nine laws."

Justice White undertakes to make a case for the proposition that the one-House veto is a useful "political invention," and we need not challenge that assertion. We can even concede this utilitarian argument although the long range political wisdom of this "invention" is arguable. It has been vigorously debated and it is instructive to compare the views of the protagonists. But policy arguments supporting even useful "political inventions" are subject to the demands of the Constitution which defines powers and, with respect to this subject, sets out just how those powers are to be exercised.

Explicit and unambiguous provisions of the Constitution prescribe and define the respective functions of the Congress and of the Executive in the legislative process. Since the precise terms of those familiar provisions are critical to the resolution of this case, we set them out verbatim. Art I provides:

"All legislative Powers herein granted shall be vested in a Congress of the United States, which shall consist of a Senate *and* a House of Representatives." Art I, §1. (Emphasis added).

"Every Bill which shall have passed the House of Representatives *and* the Senate, *shall,* before it becomes a Law, be presented to the President of the United States; . . ." Art I, § 7, cl 2. (Emphasis added).

"*Every* Order, Resolution, or Vote to which the Concurrence of the Senate and House of Representatives may be necessary (except on a question of Adjournment) *shall be* presented to the President of the United States; and before the Same shall take Effect, *shall* be approved by him, or being disapproved by him, *shall be* repassed by two thirds of the Senate and House of Representatives, according to the Rules and Limitations prescribed in the Case of a Bill." Art I, § 7, cl 3. (Emphasis added.)

These provisions of Art I are integral parts of the constitutional design for the separation of powers. We have recently noted that "[t]he principle of separation of powers was not simply an abstract generalization in the minds of the Framers: it was woven into the documents that they drafted in Philadelphia in the summer of 1787." Buckley v Valeo (1976). Just as we relied on the textual provision of Art II, § 2, cl 2, to vindicate the principle of separation of powers in Buckley, we find that the purposes underlying the Presentment Clauses, Art I, § 7, cls 2, 3, and the bicameral requirement of Art I, § 1 and § 7, cl 2, guide our resolution of the important question presented in this case. The very structure of the articles delegating and separating powers under Arts I, II, and III exemplify the concept of separation of powers and we now turn to Art I.

B

The Presentment Clauses

The records of the Constitutional Convention reveal that the requirement that all legislation be presented to the President before becoming law was uniformly accepted by the Framers. Presentment to the President and the Presidential veto were considered so imperative that the draftsmen took special pains to assure that these requirements could not be circumvented. During the final debate on Art I, § 7, cl 2, James Madison expressed concern that it might easily be evaded by the simple expedient of calling a proposed law a "resolution" or "vote" rather than a "bill." As a consequence, Art I, § 7, cl 3 was added.

The decision to provide the President with a limited and qualified power to nullify proposed legislation by veto was based on the profound conviction of the Framers that the powers conferred on Congress were the powers to be most carefully circumscribed. It is beyond doubt that lawmaking was a power to be shared by both

Houses and the President. In The Federalist No. 73, Hamilton focused on the President's role in making laws:

"If even no propensity had ever discovered itself in the legislative body to invade the rights of the Executive, the rules of just reasoning and theoretic propriety would of themselves teach us that the one ought not to be left to the mercy of the other, but ought to possess a constitutional and effectual power of self-defense."

. . .

The President's role in the lawmaking process also reflects the Framers' careful efforts to check whatever propensity a particular Congress might have to enact oppressive, improvident, or ill-considered measures. The President's veto role in the legislative process was described later during public debate on ratification:

"It establishes a salutary check upon the legislative body, calculated to guard the community against the effects of faction, precipitancy, or of any impulse unfriendly to the public good which may happen to influence a majority of that body. . . . The primary inducement to conferring the power in question upon the Executive is to enable him to defend himself; the secondary one is to increase the chances in favor of the community against the passing of bad laws through haste, inadvertence, or design." The Court also has observed that the Presentment Clauses serve the important purpose of assuring that a "national" perspective is grafted on the legislative process:

"The President is a representative of the people just as the members of the Senate and of the House are, and it may be, at some times, on some subjects, that the President elected by all the people is rather more representative of them all than are the members of either body of the Legislature whose constituencies are local and not countrywide. . . ." Myers v United States (1926).

C

Bicameralism

The bicameral requirement of Art I, §§ 1, 7 was of scarcely less concern to the Framers than was the Presidential veto and indeed the two concepts are interdependent. By providing that no law could take effect without the concurrence of the prescribed majority of the Members of both Houses, the Framers reemphasized their belief, already remarked upon in connection with the Presentment Clauses, that legislation should not be enacted unless it has been carefully and fully considered by the Nation's elected officials. In the Constitutional Convention debates on the need for a bicameral legislature, James Wilson, later to become a Justice of this Court, commented:

"Despotism comes on mankind in different shapes. Sometimes in an Executive, sometimes in a military, one. Is there danger of a Legislative despotism? Theory & practice both proclaim it. If the Legislative authority be not restrained, there can be neither liberty nor stability; and it can only be restrained by dividing it within itself, into distinct and independent branches. In a single house there is no check, but the inadequate one, of the virtue & good sense of those who compose it."

Hamilton argued that a Congress comprised of a single House was antithetical to the very purposes of the Constitution. Were the Nation to adopt a Constitution providing for only one legislative organ, he warned:

"we shall finally accumulate, in a single body, all the most important prerogatives of sovereignty, and thus entail upon our posterity one of the most execrable forms of government that human infatuation ever contrived. Thus we should create in reality that very tyranny which the adversaries of the new Constitution either are, or affect to be, solicitous to avert."

This view was rooted in a general skepticism regarding the fallibility of human nature later commented on by Joseph Story:

"Public bodies, like private persons, are occasionally under the dominion of strong passions and excitements; impatient, irritable, and impetuous. . . . If [a legislature] feels no check but its own will, it rarely has the firmness to insist upon holding a question long enough under its own view, to see and mark it in all its bearings and relations to society."

These observations are consistent with what many of the Framers expressed, none more cogently than Hamilton in pointing up the need to divide and disperse power in order to protect liberty:

"In republican government, the legislative authority necessarily predominates. The remedy for this inconveniency is to divide the legislature into different branches; and to render them, by different modes of election and different principles of action, as little connected with each other as the nature of their common functions and their common dependence on the society will admit."

. . .

We see therefore that the Framers were acutely conscious that the bicameral requirement and the Presentment Clauses would serve essential constitutional functions. The President's participation in the legislative process was to protect the Executive Branch from Congress and to protect the whole people from improvident laws. The division of the Congress into two distinctive bodies assures that the legislative power would be exercised only after opportunity for full study and debate in separate settings. The President's unilateral veto power, in turn, was limited by the power of two thirds of both Houses of Congress to overrule a veto thereby precluding final arbitrary action of one person. It emerges clearly that the prescription for legislative action in Art I, §§ 1, 7 represents the Framers' decision that the legislative power of the Federal government be exercised in accord with a single, finely wrought and exhaustively considered, procedure.

The Constitution sought to divide the delegated powers of the new Federal government into three defined categories, legislative, executive and judicial, to assure, as nearly as possible, that each Branch of government would confine itself to its assigned responsibility. The hydraulic pressure inherent within each of the separate Branches to exceed the outer limits of its power, even to accomplish desirable objectives, must be resisted.

Although not "hermetically" sealed from one another, the powers delegated to the three Branches are functionally identifiable. When any

Branch acts, it is presumptively exercising the power the Constitution has delegated to it. When the Executive acts, it presumptively acts in an executive or administrative capacity as defined in Art II. And when, as here, one House of Congress purports to act, it is presumptively acting within its assigned sphere.

Beginning with this presumption, we must nevertheless establish that the challenged action under § 244(c)(2) is of the kind to which the procedural requirements of Art I, § 7 apply. Not every action taken by either House is subject to the bicameralism and presentment requirements of Art I. Whether actions taken by either House are, in law and fact, an exercise of legislative power depends not on their form but upon "whether they contain matter which is properly to be regarded as legislative in its character and effect."

Examination of the action taken here by one House pursuant to § 244(c)(2) reveals that it was essentially legislative in purpose and effect. In purporting to exercise power defined in Art I, § 8, cl 4 to "establish an uniform Rule of Naturalization," the House took action that had the purpose and effect of altering the legal rights, duties and relations of persons, including the Attorney General, Executive Branch officials and Chadha, all outside the legislative branch. Section 244(c)(2) purports to authorize one House of Congress to require the Attorney General to deport an individual alien whose deportation otherwise would be cancelled under § 244. The one-House veto operated in this case to overrule the Attorney General and mandate Chadha's deportation; absent the House action, Chadha would remain in the United States. Congress has *acted* and its action has altered Chadha's status.

The legislative character of the one-House veto in this case is confirmed by the character of the Congressional action it supplants. Neither the House of Representatives nor the Senate contends that, absent the veto provision in § 244(c)(2), either of them, or both of them acting together, could effectively require the Attorney General to deport an alien once the Attorney General, in the exercise of legislatively delegated authority, had determined the alien should remain in the United States. Without the chal-

lenged provision in § 244(c)(2), this could have been achieved, if at all, only by legislation requiring deportation. Similarly, a veto by one House of Congress under § 244(c)(2) cannot be justified as an attempt at amending the standards set out in § 244(a)(1), or as a repeal of § 244 as applied to Chadha. Amendment and repeal of statutes, no less than enactment, must conform with Art I.

The nature of the decision implemented by the one-House veto in this case further manifests its legislative character. After long experience with the clumsy, time consuming private bill procedure, Congress made a deliberate choice to delegate to the Executive Branch, and specifically to the Attorney General, the authority to allow deportable aliens to remain in this country in certain specified circumstances. It is not disputed that this choice to delegate authority is precisely the kind of decision that can be implemented only in accordance with the procedures set out in Art I. Disagreement with the Attorney General's decision on Chadha's deportation—that is, Congress' decision to deport Chadha—no less than Congress' original choice to delegate to the Attorney General the authority to make that decision, involves determinations of policy that Congress can implement in only one way; bicameral passage followed by presentment to the President. Congress must abide by its delegation of authority until that delegation is legislatively altered or revoked.

Finally, we see that when the Framers intended to authorize either House of Congress to act alone and outside of its prescribed bicameral legislative role, they narrowly and precisely defined the procedure for such action. There are but four provisions in the Constitution, explicit and unambiguous, by which one House may act alone with the unreviewable force of law, not subject to the President's veto:

(a)　The House of Representatives alone was given the power to initiate impeachments. Art I, § 2, cl 6;

(b)　The Senate alone was given the power to conduct trials following impeachment on charges initiated by the House and to convict following trial. Art I, § 3, cl 5;

(c)　The Senate alone was given final unreviewable power to approve or to disapprove presidential appointments. Art II, § 2, cl 2;

(d) The Senate alone was given unreviewable power to ratify treaties negotiated by the President. Art II, § 2, cl 2.

Clearly, when the Draftsmen sought to confer special powers on one House, independent of the other House, or of the President, they did so in explicit, unambiguous terms. These carefully defined exceptions from presentment and bicameralism underscore the difference between the legislative functions of Congress and other unilateral but important and binding one-House acts provided for in the Constitution. These exceptions are narrow, explicit, and separately justified; none of them authorizes the action challenged here. On the contrary, they provide further support for the conclusion that Congressional authority is not to be implied and for the conclusion that the veto provided for in § 244(c)(2) is not authorized by the constitutional design of the powers of the Legislative Branch.

Since it is clear that the action by the House under § 244(c)(2) was not within any of the express constitutional exceptions authorizing one House to act alone, and equally clear that it was an exercise of legislative power, that action was subject to the standards prescribed in Article I. The bicameral requirement, the Presentment Clauses, the President's veto, and Congress' power to override a veto were intended to erect enduring checks on each Branch and to protect the people from the improvident exercise of power by mandating certain prescribed steps. To preserve those checks, and maintain the separation of powers, the carefully defined limits on the power of each Branch must not be eroded. To accomplish what has been attempted by one House of Congress in this case requires action in conformity with the express procedures of the Constitution's prescription for legislative action: passage by a majority of both Houses and presentment to the President.

The veto authorized by § 244(c)(2) doubtless has been in many respects a convenient shortcut; the "sharing" with the Executive by Congress of its authority over aliens in this manner is, on its face, an appealing compromise. In purely practical terms, it is obviously easier for action to be taken by one House without submission to the President; but it is crystal clear from the records of the Convention, contemporaneous writings and debates, that the Framers ranked other values higher than efficiency. The records of the Convention and debates in the States preceding ratification underscore the common desire to define and limit the exercise of the newly created federal powers affecting the states and the people. There is unmistakable expression of a determination that legislation by the national Congress be a step-by-step, deliberate and deliberative process.

The choices we discern as having been made in the Constitutional Convention impose burdens on governmental processes that often seem clumsy, inefficient, even unworkable, but those hard choices were consciously made by men who had lived under a form of government that permitted arbitrary governmental acts to go unchecked. There is no support in the Constitution or decisions of this Court for the proposition that the cumbersomeness and delays often encountered in complying with explicit Constitutional standards may be avoided, either by the Congress or by the President. With all the obvious flaws of delay, untidiness, and potential for abuse, we have not yet found a better way to preserve freedom than by making the exercise of power subject to the carefully crafted restraints spelled out in the Constitution.

. . .

We hold that the Congressional veto provision in § 244(c)(2) is severable from the Act and that it is unconstitutional. Accordingly, the judgment of the Court of Appeals is affirmed.

Justice **White,** dissenting.

Today the Court not only invalidates § 244(c)(2) of the Immigration and Nationality Act, but also sounds the death knell for nearly 200 other statutory provisions in which Congress has reserved a "legislative veto." For this reason, the Court's decision is of surpassing importance. And it is for this reason that the Court would have been well-advised to decide the case, if possible, on the narrower grounds of separation of powers, leaving for full consideration the constitutionality of other congressional review statutes operating on such varied matters as war powers and agency rulemaking, some of which concern the independent regulatory agencies.

The prominence of the legislative veto mechanism in our contemporary political system and its importance to Congress can hardly be overstated. It has become a central means by which Congress secures the accountability of executive and independent agencies. Without the legislative veto, Congress is faced with a Hobson's choice: either to refrain from delegating the necessary authority, leaving itself with a hopeless task of writing laws with the requisite specificity to cover endless special circumstances across the entire policy landscape, or in the alternative, to abdicate its lawmaking function to the executive branch and independent agencies. To choose the former leaves major national problems unresolved; to opt for the latter risks unaccountable policymaking by those not elected to fill that role. Accordingly, over the past five decades, the legislative veto has been placed in nearly 200 statutes. The device is known in every field of governmental concern: reorganization, budgets, foreign affairs, war powers, and regulation of trade, safety, energy, the environment and the economy.

. . .

The legislative veto developed initially in response to the problems of reorganizing the sprawling government structure created in response to the Depression. The Reorganization Acts established the chief model for the legislative veto. When President Hoover requested authority to reorganize the government in 1929, he coupled his request that the "Congress be willing to delegate its authority over the problem (subject to defined principles) to the Executive" with a proposal for legislative review. He proposed that the Executive "should act upon approval of a joint committee of Congress or with the reservation of power of revision by Congress within some limited period adequate for its consideration." Congress followed President Hoover's suggestion and authorized reorganization subject to legislative review. Although the reorganization authority reenacted in 1933 did not contain a legislative veto provision, the provision returned during the

Roosevelt Administration and has since been renewed numerous times. Over the years, the provision was used extensively. Presidents submitted 115 reorganization plans to Congress of which 23 were disapproved by Congress pursuant to legislative veto provisions.

Shortly after adoption of the Reorganization Act of 1939, Congress and the President applied the legislative veto procedure to resolve the delegation problem for national security and foreign affairs. World War II occasioned the need to transfer greater authority to the President in these areas. The legislative veto offered the means by which Congress could confer additional authority while preserving its own constitutional role. During World War II, Congress enacted over thirty statutes conferring powers on the Executive with legislative veto provisions. President Roosevelt accepted the veto as the necessary price for obtaining exceptional authority.

Over the quarter century following World War II, Presidents continued to accept legislative vetoes by one or both Houses as constitutional, while regularly denouncing provisions by which Congressional committees reviewed Executive activity. The legislative veto balanced delegations of statutory authority in new areas of governmental involvement: the space program, international agreements on nuclear energy, tariff arrangements, and adjustment of federal pay rates.

During the 1970s the legislative veto was important in resolving a series of major constitutional disputes between the President and Congress over claims of the President to broad impoundment, war, and national emergency powers. The key provision of the War Powers Resolution authorizes the termination by concurrent resolution of the use of armed forces in hostilities. A similar measure resolved the problem posed by Presidential claims of inherent power to impound appropriations. Congressional Budget and Impoundment Control Act of 1974. In conference, a compromise was achieved under which permanent impoundments, termed "rescissions," would require approval through enactment of legislation. In contrast, temporary impoundments, or "deferrals," would become effective unless disapproved by one House. This compromise provided the President with flexibility, while preserving ultimate Congressional control over the budget. Although the War Powers Resolution was enacted over President Nixon's veto, the Impoundment Control Act was enacted with the President's approval. These statutes were followed by others resolving similar problems: the National Emergencies Act, resolving the longstanding problems with unchecked Executive emergency power; the Arms Export Control Act, resolving the problem of foreign arms sales; and the Nuclear Non-Proliferation Act of 1978, resolving the problem of exports of nuclear technology.

. . .

If the legislative veto were as plainly unconstitutional as the Court strives to suggest, its broad ruling today would be more comprehensible. But, the constitutionality of the legislative veto is anything but clearcut. The issue divides scholars, courts, attorneys general, and the two other branches of the National Government. If the veto devices so flagrantly disregarded the requirements of Article I as the Court today suggests, I find it incomprehensible that Congress, whose members are bound by oath to uphold the Constitution, would have placed these mechanisms in nearly 200 separate laws over a period of 50 years.

The reality of the situation is that the constitutional question posed today is one of immense difficulty over which the executive and legislative branches—as well as scholars and judges—have understandably disagreed. That disagreement stems from the silence of the Constitution on the precise question: The Constitution does not directly authorize or prohibit the legislative veto. Thus, our task should be to determine whether the legislative veto is consistent with the purposes of Art I and the principles of Separation of Powers which are reflected in that Article and throughout the Constitution. We should not find the lack of a specific constitutional authorization for the legislative veto surprising, and I would not infer disapproval of the mechanism from its absence. From the summer of 1787 to the present the government of the United States has become an endeavor far beyond the contemplation of the Framers. Only within the last half century has the complexity and size of the Federal Government's responsi-

bilities grown so greatly that the Congress must rely on the legislative veto as the most effective if not the only means to insure their role as the nation's lawmakers. But the wisdom of the Framers was to anticipate that the nation would grow and new problems of governance would require different solutions. Accordingly, our Federal Government was intentionally chartered with the flexibility to respond to contemporary needs without losing sight of fundamental democratic principles.

. . .

The Court holds that the disapproval of a suspension of deportation by the resolution of one House of Congress is an exercise of legislative power without compliance with the prerequisites for lawmaking set forth in Art I of the Constitution. Specifically, the Court maintains that the provisions of § 244(c)(2) are inconsistent with the requirement of bicameral approval, implicit in Art I, § 1, and the requirement that all bills and resolutions that require the concurrence of both Houses be presented to the President, Art I, § 7, cl 2 and 3.

I do not dispute the Court's truismatic exposition of these clauses. There is no question that a bill does not become a law until it is approved by both the House and the Senate, and presented to the President. Similarly, I would not hesitate to strike an action of Congress in the form of a concurrent resolution which constituted an exercise of original lawmaking authority. I agree with the Court that the President's qualified veto power is a critical element in the distribution of powers under the Constitution, widely endorsed among the Framers, and intended to serve the President as a defense against legislative encroachment and to check the "passing of bad laws through haste, inadvertence, or design." The records of the Convention reveal that it is the first purpose which figured most prominently but I acknowledge the vitality of the second. I also agree that the bicameral approval required by Art I, §§ 1, 7 "was of scarcely less concern to the Framers than was the Presidential veto," and that the need to divide and disperse legislative power figures significantly in our scheme of Government. All of this, the Third Part of the Court's opinion, is entirely unexceptionable.

It does not, however, answer the constitutional question before us. The power to exercise a legislative veto is not the power to write new law without bicameral approval or presidential consideration. The veto must be authorized by statute and may only negative what an Executive department or independent agency has proposed. On its face, the legislative veto no more allows one House of Congress to make law than does the presidential veto confer such power upon the President.

. . .

The central concern of the presentation and bicameralism requirements of Article I is that when a departure from the legal status quo is undertaken, it is done with the approval of the President and both Houses of Congress—or, in the event of a presidential veto, a two-thirds majority in both Houses. This interest is fully satisfied by the operation of § 244(c)(2). The President's approval is found in the Attorney General's action in recommending to Congress that the deportation order for a given alien be suspended. The House and the Senate indicate their approval of the Executive's action by not passing a resolution of disapproval within the statutory period. Thus, a change in the legal status quo—the deportability of the alien—is consummated only with the approval of each of the three relevant actors. The disagreement of any one of the three maintains the alien's pre-existing status: the Executive may choose not to recommend suspension; the House and Senate may each veto the recommendation. The effect on the rights and obligations of the affected individuals and upon the legislative system is precisely the same as if a private bill were introduced but failed to receive the necessary approval.

. . .

Thus understood, § 244(c)(2) fully effectuates the purposes of the bicameralism and presentation requirements. I now briefly consider possible objections to the analysis.

First, it may be asserted that Chadha's status before legislative disapproval is one of nondeportation and that the exercise of the veto, unlike the failure of a private bill, works a change in the status quo. This position plainly ignores the statutory language. At no place in § 244 has Congress delegated to the Attorney General any final power to determine which aliens shall be allowed to remain in the United States. Congress has retained the ultimate power to pass on such changes in deportable status.

. . .

Second, it may be said that this approach leads to the incongruity that the two-House veto is more suspect than its one-House brother. Although the idea may be initially counter-intuitive, on close analysis, it is not at all unusual that the one-House veto is of more certain constitutionality than the two-House version. If the Attorney General's action is a proposal for legislation, then the disapproval of but a single House is all that is required to prevent its passage. Because approval is indicated by the failure to veto, the one-House veto satisfies the requirement of bicameral approval.

. . .

Third, it may be objected that Congress cannot indicate its approval of legislative change by inaction. In the Court of Appeals' view, inaction by Congress "could equally imply endorsement, acquiescence, passivity, indecision or indifference." . . . the Court appears to echo this concern. This objection appears more properly directed at the wisdom of the legislative veto than its constitutionality. The Constitution does not and cannot guarantee that legislators will carefully scrutinize legislation and deliberate before acting. In a democracy it is the electorate that holds the legislators accountable for the wisdom of their choices.

. . .

The Court of Appeals struck § 244(c)(2) as violative of the constitutional principle of separation of powers. It is true that the purpose of separating the authority of government is to prevent unnecessary and dangerous concentration of power in one branch. For that reason, the Framers saw fit to divide and balance the powers of government so that each branch would be checked by the others. Virtually every part of our constitutional system bears the mark of this judgment.

But the history of the separation of powers doctrine is also a history of accommodation and practicality. Apprehensions of an overly powerful branch have not led to undue prophylactic measures that handicap the effective working of the national government as a whole. . . .

Section 244(c)(2) survives this test. The legislative veto provision does not "prevent the Executive Branch from accomplishing its constitutionally assigned functions." First, it is clear that the Executive Branch has no "constitutionally assigned" function of suspending the deportation of aliens. "'Over no conceivable subject is the legislative power of Congress more complete than it is over' the admission of aliens."

. . .

Moreover, the Court believes that the legislative veto we consider today is best characterized as an exercise of legislative or quasi-legislative authority. Under this characterization, the practice does not, even on the surface, constitute an infringement of executive or judicial prerogative. The Attorney General's suspension of deportation is equivalent to a proposal for legislation. The nature of the Attorney General's role as recommendatory is not altered because § 244 provides for congressional action through disapproval rather than by ratification. In comparison to private bills, which must be initiated in the Congress and which allow a Presidential veto to be overriden by a two-thirds majority in both Houses of Congress, § 244 augments rather than reduces the executive branch's authority. So

understood, congressional review does not undermine, as the Court of Appeals thought, the "weight and dignity" that attends the decisions of the Executive Branch.

. . .

I do not suggest that all legislative vetoes are necessarily consistent with separation of powers principles. A legislative check on an inherently executive function, for example that of initiating prosecutions, poses an entirely different question. But the legislative veto device here—and in many other settings—is far from an instance of legislative tyranny over the Executive. It is a necessary check on the unavoidably expanding power of the agencies, both executive and independent, as they engage in exercising authority delegated by Congress.

I regret that I am in disagreement with my colleagues on the fundamental questions that this case presents. But even more I regret the destructive scope of the Court's holding. It reflects a profoundly different conception of the Constitution than that held by the Courts which sanctioned the modern administrative state. Today's decision strikes down in one fell swoop provisions in more laws enacted by Congress than the Court has cumulatively invalidated in its history. I fear it will now be more difficult "to insure that the fundamental policy decisions in our society will be made not by an appointed official but by the body immediately responsible to the people," *Arizona v California* (1963). I must dissent.

Aftermath of Immigration and Naturalization Service *v.* Chadha

In the *Chadha* case the Court was dealing with a "one-House veto," but the broad standard promulgated in Chief Justice Burger's opinion extends the ban to "two-House vetoes" as well as to those of any House or Senate committees. It has been suggested that the Court's willingness to decide *Chadha*—which it could easily have avoided—was in part a matter of its own role in the constitutional system. Given the nature of the legislative veto involved in *Chadha,* a matter of administrative rule making and an accommodation between the executive and legislative branches, the judiciary was removed from the decision-making loop.

What has been the effect of this case? As a practical matter the effect on legislative-executive relations has been relatively minimal as Congress has continued to rely on the legislative veto. At the time of the *Chadha* decision there were 120 laws on the books permitting the veto and theoretically all would be unconstitutional. Yet, invalidation of these measures would require a specific challenge to each, and such challenges have not been forthcoming. In fact, since the Court's ruling, more than 100 new laws have been written with a legislative veto provision, most involving spending bills that require the administration to obtain written approval of the House and Senate appropriations committees on matters ranging from military authorizations to foreign aid, to housing and urban development. Moreover, there have been presidential/congressional accords—informal agreements—as exemplified by that reached early in 1989 between President George Bush and both houses of Congress, under which only limited aid may be sent to the Nicaraguan insurgents (Contras) housed in Honduras. Under its terms President Bush agreed to send money to the Contras only upon obtaining letters of approval from four congressional committees. This is not a law but rather an informal understanding, a "deal" in political jargon. It is not enforceable in the courts nor is there anything in the Constitution that prevents it. Louis Fisher of the Congressional Research Service of the Library of Congress who has written extensively on the legislative veto calls it "a classic quid pro quo," an attempt to reconcile the interests of both branches: the desire of administrative agencies to retain discretionary authority on the one hand and the need of Congress to maintain ultimate control, short of passing another law. Thus the *Chadha* case illustrates the judicial restraintist's worst nightmare, in which the Court moves into an area where its decision is so at odds with historic and current practice that the other branches are bound to find ways to evade and circumvent its rulings.

Bowsher v. *Synar*

478 U.S. 714 (1986)

In an attempt to cope with spiralling federal budget deficits, Congress enacted the Balanced Budget and Emergency Deficit Control Act of 1985, popularly known as the Gramm-Rudman-Hollings Act, named after its bipartisan sponsors, Senators Philip Gramm of Texas, Warren Rudman of New Hampshire, both Republicans, and Ernest Hollings of South Carolina, a Democrat. Under its terms a deficit target for federal spending for each of fiscal years 1986–1991 was fixed, and if in any fiscal year the budget deficit were to exceed the maximum deficit amount by more than a specified sum, cuts were to be made across the board in order to reach the targeted deficit level. These "automatic" reductions were to be accomplished through provisions under which the comptroller general of the United States would prepare and submit to the President a report containing detailed estimates of projected federal revenues and expenditures and specify what reductions, if any, were needed to meet the target for a given fiscal year. The President was then to issue an order mandating the spending reductions specified by the comptroller general. Contemplating the possibility of judicial invalidation of the procedure, the act contained a "fallback" provision under which deficit reduction proposals would be submitted to the President in a joint resolution of both houses of Congress rather than in a report by the comptroller general.

After the act was signed into law, 12 members of Congress challenged its constitutionality in the federal district court for the District of Columbia. This action was consolidated with a similar suit filed by the National Treasury Employees Union which alleged that its members were injured by the act's automatic spending reduction provisions in that scheduled cost-of-living benefits would be suspended. Invalidating the reporting provisions, the district court declared that the role of the

comptroller general, an officer who was subservient to the Congress, was a violation of the separation of powers. The case then went to the Supreme Court.

Chief Justice **Burger** delivered the opinion of the Court.

The question presented by these appeals is whether the assignment by Congress to the Comptroller General of the United States of certain functions under the Balanced Budget and Emergency Deficit Control Act of 1985 violates the doctrine of separation of powers.

. . .

We noted recently that "[t]he Constitution sought to divide the delegated powers of the new Federal Government into three defined categories, Legislative, Executive, and Judicial." INS v Chadha (1983). The declared purpose of separating and dividing the powers of government, of course, was to "diffus[e] power the better to secure liberty." Youngstown Sheet & Tube Co. v Sawyer (1952). Justice Jackson's words echo the famous warning of Montesquieu, quoted by James Madison in The Federalist No. 47, that "'there can be no liberty where the legislative and executive powers are united in the same person, or body of magistrates.' . . ."

Even a cursory examination of the Constitution reveals the influence of Montesquieu's thesis that checks and balances were the foundation of a structure of government that would protect liberty. The Framers provided a vigorous legislative branch and a separate and wholly independent executive branch, with each branch responsible ultimately to the people. The Framers also provided for a judicial branch equally independent with "[t]he judicial Power . . . extend[ing] to all Cases, in Law and Equity, arising under this Constitution, and the Laws of the United States." Art III, § 2.

Other, more subtle, examples of separated powers are evident as well. Unlike parliamentary systems such as that of Great Britain, no person who is an officer of the United States may serve as a Member of the Congress. Art I, § 6. Moreover, unlike parliamentary systems, the President, under Article II, is responsible not to the Congress but to the people, subject only to impeachment proceedings which are exercised by the two Houses as representatives of the people.

Art II, § 4. And even in the impeachment of a President the presiding officer of the ultimate tribunal is not a member of the legislative branch, but the Chief Justice of the United States, Art I, § 3.

That this system of division and separation of powers produces conflicts, confusion, and discordance at times is inherent, but it was deliberately so structured to assure full, vigorous and open debate on the great issues affecting the people and to provide avenues for the operation of checks on the exercise of governmental power.

The Constitution does not contemplate an active role for Congress in the supervision of officers charged with the execution of the laws it enacts. The President appoints "Officers of the United States" with the "Advice and Consent of the Senate . . ." Article II, § 2. Once the appointment has been made and confirmed, however, the Constitution explicitly provides for removal of Officers of the United States by Congress only upon impeachment by the House of Representatives and conviction by the Senate. An impeachment by the House and trial by the Senate can rest only on "Treason, Bribery or other high Crimes and Misdemeanors." Article II, § 4. A direct congressional role in the removal of officers charged with the execution of the laws beyond this limited one is inconsistent with separation of powers.

This was made clear in debate in the First Congress in 1789. When Congress considered an amendment to a bill establishing the Department of Foreign Affairs, the debate centered around whether the Congress "should recognize and declare the power of the President under the Constitution to remove the Secretary of Foreign Affairs without the advice and consent of the Senate." James Madison urged rejection of a congressional role in the removal of Executive Branch officers, other than by impeachment, saying in debate:

"Perhaps there was no argument urged with more success, or more plausibly grounded against the Constitution, under which we are now deliberating, than that founded on the mingling of the Executive and Legislative branches of the Government in one body. It has been objected, that the Senate have too much of the Executive power even, by having a control over the President in the appointment to office. Now, shall we extend this connexion between the Legislative and Executive departments, which will strengthen the objection, and diminish the responsibility we have in the head of the Executive?"

Madison's position ultimately prevailed, and a congressional role in the removal process was rejected. This "Decision of 1789" provides "contemporaneous and weighty evidence" of the Constitution's meaning since many of the Members of the first Congress "had taken part in framing that instrument."

. . .

In light of . . . precedents, we conclude that Congress cannot reserve for itself the power of removal of an officer charged with the execution of the laws except by impeachment. To permit the execution of the laws to be vested in an officer answerable only to Congress would, in practical terms, reserve in Congress control over the execution of the laws. As the District Court observed, "Once an officer is appointed, it is only the authority that can remove him, and not the authority that appointed him, that he must fear and, in the performance of his functions, obey." The structure of the Constitution does not permit Congress to execute the laws; it follows that Congress cannot grant to an officer under its control what it does not possess.

Our decision in INS v Chadha supports this conclusion. In Chadha, we struck down a one house "legislative veto" provision by which each House of Congress retained the power to reverse a decision Congress had expressly authorized the Attorney General to make. . . .

. . .

To permit an officer controlled by Congress to execute the laws would be, in essence, to permit a congressional veto. Congress could simply remove, or threaten to remove, an officer for executing the laws in any fashion found to be unsatisfactory to Congress. This kind of congres-

sional control over the execution of the laws, Chadha makes clear, is constitutionally impermissible.

. . .

Appellants urge that the Comptroller General performs his duties independently and is not subservient to Congress. We agree with the District Court that this contention does not bear close scrutiny.

The critical factor lies in the provisions of the statute defining the Comptroller General's office relating to removability. Although the Comptroller General is nominated by the President from a list of three individuals recommended by the Speaker of the House of Representatives and the President pro tempore of the Senate, and confirmed by the Senate, he is removable only at the initiative of Congress. He may be removed not only by impeachment but also by Joint Resolution of Congress "at any time" resting on any one of the following bases:

"(i)   permanent disability;
"(ii) inefficiency;
"(iii) neglect of duty;
"(iv) malfeasance; or
"(v)   a felony or conduct involving moral turpitude."

This provision was included, as one Congressman explained in urging passage of the Act, because Congress "felt that [the Comptroller General] should be brought under the sole control of Congress, so that Congress at the moment when it found he was inefficient and was not carrying on the duties of his office as he should and as the Congress expected, could remove him without the long, tedious process of a trial by impeachment."

The removal provision was an important part of the legislative scheme, as a number of Congressmen recognized. Representative Hawley commented: "[H]e is our officer, in a measure, getting information for us. . . . If he does not do his work properly, we, as practically his employers, ought to be able to discharge him from office." Representative Sisson observed that the removal provisions would give "[t]he Congress of the United States . . . absolute control of the man's destiny in office." The ultimate design was to "give the legislative branch of the Government control of the audit, not through the power of appointment, but through the power of removal."

Justice White contends that "[t]he statute does not permit anyone to remove the Comptroller at will; removal is permitted only for specified cause, with the existence of cause to be determined by Congress following a hearing. Any removal under the statute would presumably be subject to post-termination judicial review to ensure that a hearing had in fact been held and the finding of cause for removal was not arbitrary." That observation by the dissenter rests on at least two arguable premises: (a) that the enumeration of certain specified causes of removal excludes the possibility of removal for other causes, cf. Shurtleff v United States; and (b) that any removal would be subject to judicial review, a position that appellants were unwilling to endorse.

Glossing over these difficulties, the dissent's assessment of the statute fails to recognize the breadth of the grounds for removal. The statute permits removal for "inefficiency," "neglect of duty," or "malfeasance." These terms are very broad and, as interpreted by Congress, could sustain removal of a Comptroller General for any number of actual or perceived transgressions of the legislative will. The Constitutional Convention chose to permit impeachment of executive officers only for "Treason, Bribery, or other high Crimes and Misdemeanors." It rejected language that would have permitted impeachment for "maladministration," with Madison arguing that "[s]o vague a term will be equivalent to a tenure during pleasure of the Senate."

We need not decide whether that "inefficiency" or "malfeasance" are terms as broad as "maladministration" in order to reject the dissent's position that removing the Comptroller General requires "a feat of bipartisanship more difficult than that required to impeach and convict." Surely no one would seriously suggest that judicial independence would be strengthened by allowing removal of federal judges only by a joint resolution finding "inefficiency," "neglect of duty," or "malfeasance."

Justice White, however, assures us that "[r]ealistic consideration" of the "practical result of the removal provision," reveals that the Comptroller General is unlikely to be removed by Congress. The separated powers of our government can not be permitted to turn on judicial assessment of whether an officer exercising executive power is on good terms with Congress. The Framers recognized that, in the long term, structural protections against abuse of power were critical to preserving liberty. In constitutional terms, the removal powers over the Comptroller General's office dictate that he will be subservient to Congress.

This much said, we must also add that the dissent is simply in error to suggest that the political realities reveal that the Comptroller General is free from influence by Congress. The Comptroller General heads the General Accounting Office, "an instrumentality of the United States Government independent of the executive departments," which was created by Congress in 1921 as part of the Budget and Accounting Act of 1921, 42 Stat 23. Congress created the office because it believed that it "needed an officer, responsible to it alone, to check upon the application of public funds in accordance with appropriations."

It is clear that Congress has consistently viewed the Comptroller General as an officer of the Legislative Branch. The Reorganization Acts of 1945 and 1949, for example, both stated that the Comptroller General and the GAO are "a part of the legislative branch of the Government." Similarly, in the Accounting and Auditing Act of 1950, Congress required the Comptroller General to conduct audits "as an agent of the Congress."

Over the years, the Comptrollers General have also viewed themselves as part of the Legislative Branch. In one of the early Annual Reports of Comptroller General, the official seal of his office was described as reflecting:

"the independence of judgment to be exercised by the General Accounting Office, subject to the control of the legislative branch. . . . The combination represents an agency of the Congress independent of other authority auditing and checking the expenditures of the Government as required by law and subjecting any questions arising in that connection to quasi-judicial determination."

Later, Comptroller General Warren, who had been a member of Congress for 15 years before being appointed Comptroller General, testified that: "During most of my public life, . . . I have been a member of the legislative branch. Even now, although heading a great agency, it is an agency of the Congress, and *I am an agent of the Congress*" (emphasis added). And, in one conflict during Comptroller General McCarl's tenure he asserted his independence of the Executive Branch, stating:

> "Congress . . . is . . . the only authority to which there lies an appeal from the decision of this office. . . .
>
> ". . . I may not accept the opinion of any official, inclusive of the Attorney General, as controlling my duty under the law."

Against this background, we see no escape from the conclusion that, because Congress had retained removal authority over the Comptroller General, he may not be entrusted with executive powers. The remaining question is whether the Comptroller General has been assigned such powers in the Balanced Budget and Emergency Deficit Control Act of 1985.

. . .

The primary responsibility of the Comptroller General under the instant Act is the preparation of a "report." This report must contain detailed estimates of projected federal revenues and expenditures. The report must also specify the reductions, if any, necessary to reduce the deficit to the target for the appropriate fiscal year. The reductions must be set forth on a program-by-program basis.

In preparing the report, the Comptroller General is to have "due regard" for the estimates and reductions set forth in a joint report submitted to him by the Director of CBO and the Director of OMB, the President's fiscal and budgetary advisor. However, the Act plainly contemplates that the Comptroller General will exercise his independent judgment and evaluation with respect to those estimates. The Act also provides that the Comptroller General's report "shall explain fully any differences between the contents of such reports and the report of the Directors."

Appellants suggest that the duties assigned to the Comptroller General in the Act are essentially ministerial and mechanical so that their performance does not constitute "execution of the law" in a meaningful sense. On the contrary, we view these functions as plainly entailing execution of the law in constitutional terms. Interpreting a law enacted by Congress to implement the legislative mandate is the very essence of "execution" of the law. Under § 251, the Comptroller General must exercise judgment concerning facts that affect the application of the Act. He must also interpret the provisions of the Act to determine precisely what budgetary calculations are required. Decisions of that kind are typically made by officers charged with executing a statute.

The executive nature of the Comptroller General's functions under the Act is revealed in § 252(a)(3) which gives the Comptroller General the ultimate authority to determine the budget cuts to be made. Indeed, the Comptroller General commands the President himself to carry out, without the slightest variation (with exceptions not relevant to the constitutional issues presented), the directive of the Comptroller General as to the budget reductions:

> "The [Presidential] order *must provide* for reductions in the manner specified in section 251(a)(3), must incorporate the provisions of the [Comptroller General's] report submitted under section 251(b), and *must be consistent with such report in all respects*. The President *may not modify or recalculate any of the estimates, determinations, specifications, bases, amounts, or percentages* set forth in the report submitted under section 251(b) in determining the reductions to be specified in the order with respect to programs, projects, and activities, or with respect to budget activities, within an account. . . ." (emphasis added).

Congress of course initially determined the content of the Balanced Budget and Emergency Deficit Control Act; and undoubtedly the content of the Act determines the nature of the executive duty. However, as Chadha makes clear, once Congress makes its choice in enacting legislation, its participation ends. Congress can thereafter control the execution of its enactment only indirectly—by passing new legislation. By placing the responsibility for execution of the Balanced Budget and Emergency Deficit Control Act in the hands of an officer who is subject to removal only by itself, Congress in effect has retained control over the execution of the Act and has intruded into the executive function. The Constitution does not permit such intrusion.

. . .

No one can doubt that Congress and the President are confronted with fiscal and economic problems of unprecedented magnitude, but "the fact that a given law or procedure is efficient, convenient, and useful in facilitating functions of government, standing alone, will not save it if it is contrary to the Constitution. Convenience and efficiency are not the primary objectives—or the hallmarks—of democratic government. . . ."

We conclude the District Court correctly held that the powers vested in the Comptroller General under § 251 violate the command of the Constitution that the Congress play no direct role in the execution of the laws. Accordingly, the judgment and order of the District Court are affirmed.

Our judgment is stayed for a period not to exceed 60 days to permit Congress to implement the fallback provisions.

. . .

Justice **White,** dissenting.

The Court, acting in the name of separation of powers, takes upon itself to strike down the Gramm-Rudman-Hollings Act, one of the most novel and far-reaching legislative responses to a national crisis since the New Deal. The basis of the Court's action is a solitary provision of another statute that was passed over sixty years ago and has lain dormant since that time. I cannot concur in the Court's action. Like the Court, I will not purport to speak to the wisdom of the policies incorporated in the legislation the Court invalidates; that is a matter for the Congress and the Executive, *both* of which expressed their assent to the statute barely half a year ago. I

will, however, address the wisdom of the Court's willingness to interpose its distressingly formalistic view of separation of powers as a bar to the attainment of governmental objectives through the means chosen by the Congress and the President in the legislative process established by the Constitution. Twice in the past four years I have expressed my view that the Court's recent efforts to police the separation of powers have rested on untenable constitutional propositions leading to regrettable results. Today's result is even more misguided. As I will explain, the Court's decision rests on a feature of the legislative scheme that is of minimal practical significance and that presents no substantial threat to the basic scheme of separation of powers. In attaching dispositive significance to what should be regarded as a triviality, the Court neglects what has in the past been recognized as a fundamental principle governing consideration of disputes over separation of powers:

"The actual art of governing under our Constitution does not and cannot conform to judicial definitions of the power of any of its branches based on isolated clauses or even single Articles torn from context. While the Constitution diffuses power the better to secure liberty, it also contemplates that practice will integrate the dispersed powers into a workable government."

. . .

The Court's recognition of the legitimacy of legislation vesting "executive" authority in officers independent of the President does not imply derogation of the President's own constitutional authority—indeed, duty—to "take Care that the Laws be faithfully executed," Art II, § 3, for any such duty is necessarily limited to a great extent by the content of the laws enacted by the Congress. As Justice Holmes put it, "The duty of the President to see that the laws be executed is a duty that does not go beyond the laws or require him to achieve more than Congress sees fit to leave within his power." Myers v United States. Justice Holmes perhaps overstated his case, for there are undoubtedly executive functions that, regardless of the enactments of Congress, must be performed by officers subject to removal at will by the President. Whether a particular function falls within this class or within the far larger class that may be relegated to independent officers "will depend upon the character of the office." Humphrey's Executor. In determining whether a limitation on the President's power to remove an officer performing executive functions constitutes a violation of the constitutional scheme of separation of powers, a court must "focu[s] on the extent to which [such a limitation] prevents the Executive Branch from accomplishing its constitutionally assigned functions." Nixon v Administrator of General Services. "Only where the potential for disruption is present must we then determine whether that impact is satisfied by an overriding need to promote objectives within the constitutional authority of Congress." Ibid. This inquiry is, to be sure, not one that will beget easy answers; it provides nothing approaching a bright-line rule or set of rules. Such an inquiry, however, is necessitated by the recognition that "formalistic and unbending rules" in the area of separation of powers may "unduly constrict Congress' ability to take needed and innovative action pursuant to its Article I powers." Commodity Futures Trading Commission v Schor.

It is evident (and nothing in the Court's opinion is to the contrary) that the powers exercised by the Comptroller General under the Gramm-Rudman Act are not such that vesting them in an officer not subject to removal at will by the President would in itself improperly interfere with Presidential powers. Determining the level of spending by the Federal Government is not by nature a function central either to the exercise of the President's enumerated powers or to his general duty to ensure execution of the laws; rather, appropriating funds is a peculiarly legislative function, and one expressly committed to Congress by Art I, § 9, which provides that "[n]o Money shall be drawn from the Treasury, but in Consequence of Appropriations made by Law." In enacting Gramm-Rudman, Congress has chosen to exercise this legislative power to establish the level of federal spending by providing a detailed set of criteria for reducing expenditures below the level of appropriations in the event that certain conditions are met. Delegating the execution of this legislation—that is, the power to apply the Act's criteria and make the required

calculations—to an officer independent of the President's will does not deprive the President of any power that he would otherwise have or that is essential to the performance of the duties of his office. Rather, the result of such a delegation, from the standpoint of the President, is no different from the result of more traditional forms of appropriation: under either system, the level of funds available to the Executive branch to carry out its duties is not within the President's discretionary control. To be sure, if the budget-cutting mechanism required the responsible officer to exercise a great deal of policymaking discretion, one might argue that having created such broad discretion Congress had some obligation based upon Art II to vest it in the Chief Executive or his agents. In Gramm-Rudman, however, Congress has done no such thing; instead, it has created a precise and articulated set of criteria designed to minimize the degree of policy choice exercised by the officer executing the statute and to ensure that the relative spending priorities established by Congress in the appropriations it passes into law remain unaltered. Given that the exercise of policy choice by the officer executing the statute would be inimical to Congress' goal in enacting "automatic" budget-cutting measures, it is eminently reasonable and proper for Congress to vest the budget-cutting authority in an officer who is to the greatest degree possible nonpartisan and independent of the President and his political agenda and who therefore may be relied upon not to allow his calculations to be colored by political considerations. Such a delegation deprives the President of no authority that is rightfully his.

If, as the Court seems to agree, the assignment of "executive" powers under Gramm-Rudman to an officer not removable at will by the President would not in itself represent a violation of the constitutional scheme of separated powers, the question remains whether, as the Court concludes, the fact that the officer to whom Congress has delegated the authority to implement the Act is removable by a joint resolution of Congress should require invalidation of the Act. The Court's decision, as I have stated above, is based on a syllogism: the Act vests the

Comptroller with "executive power"; such power may not be exercised by Congress or its agents; the Comptroller is an agent of Congress because he is removable by Congress; therefore the Act is invalid. I have no quarrel with the proposition that the powers exercised by the Comptroller under the Act may be characterized as "executive" in that they involve the interpretation and carrying out of the Act's mandate. I can also accept the general proposition that although Congress has considerable authority in designating the officers who are to execute legislation, the constitutional scheme of separated powers does prevent Congress from reserving an executive role for itself or for its "agents." Buckley v Valeo. I cannot accept, however, that the exercise of authority by an officer removable for cause by a joint resolution of Congress is analogous to the impermissible execution of the law by Congress itself, nor would I hold that the congressional role in the removal process renders the Comptroller an "agent" of the Congress, incapable of receiving "executive" power.

· · ·

The deficiencies in the Court's reasoning are apparent. First, the Court baldly mischaracterizes the removal provision when it suggests that it allows Congress to remove the Comptroller for "executing the laws in any fashion found to be unsatisfactory"; in fact, Congress may remove the Comptroller only for one or more of five specified reasons, which "although not so narrow as to deny Congress any leeway, circumscribe Congress' power to some extent by providing a basis for judicial review of congressional removal." Ameron, Inc. v United States Army Corps of Engineers, Second, and more to the point, the Court overlooks or deliberately ignores the decisive difference between the congressional removal provision and the legislative veto struck down in Chadha; under the Budget and Accounting Act, Congress may remove the Comptroller only through a joint resolution, which by definition must be passed by both Houses and signed by the President. In other words, a removal of the Comptroller under the statute *satisfies the requirements of bicameralism and presentment laid down in Chadha.* The majority's citation of Chadha for the proposition

that Congress may only control the acts of officers of the United States "by passing new legislation," in no sense casts doubt on the legitimacy of the removal provision, for that provision allows Congress to effect removal only through action that constitutes legislation as defined in Chadha.

To the extent that it has any bearing on the problem now before us, Chadha would seem to suggest the legitimacy of the statutory provision making the Comptroller removable through joint resolution, for the Court's opinion in Chadha reflects the view that the bicameralism and presentment requirements of Art I represent the principal assurances that Congress will remain within its legislative role in the constitutionally prescribed scheme of separated powers. Action taken in accordance with the "single, finely wrought, and exhaustively considered, procedure" established by Art I, should be presumptively viewed as a legitimate exercise of legislative power. That such action may represent a more or less successful attempt by Congress to "control" the actions of an officer of the United States surely does not in itself indicate that it is unconstitutional, for no one would dispute that Congress has the power to "control" administration through legislation imposing duties or substantive restraints on executive officers, through legislation increasing or decreasing the funds made available to such officers, or through legislation actually abolishing a particular office. Indeed, Chadha expressly recognizes that while congressional meddling with administration of the laws outside of the legislative process is impermissible, congressional control over executive officers exercised through the legislative process is valid. Thus, if the existence of a statute permitting removal of the Comptroller through joint resolution (that is, through the legislative process) renders his exercise of executive powers unconstitutional, it is for reasons having virtually nothing to do with Chadha.

That a joint resolution removing the Comptroller General would satisfy the requirements for legitimate legislative action laid down in Chadha does not fully answer the separation of powers argument, for it is apparent that even the results of the constitutional legislative process may be unconstitutional if those results are in fact destructive of the scheme of separation of powers. Nixon v Administrator of General Services. The question to be answered is whether the threat of removal of the Comptroller General for cause through joint resolution as authorized by the Budget and Accounting Act renders the Comptroller sufficiently subservient to Congress that investing him with "executive" power can be realistically equated with the unlawful retention of such power by Congress itself; more generally, the question is whether there is a genuine threat of "encroachment or aggrandizement of one branch at the expense of the other," Buckley v Valeo. Common sense indicates that the existence of the removal provision poses no such threat to the principle of separation of powers.

The statute does not permit anyone to remove the Comptroller at will; removal is permitted only for specified cause, with the existence of cause to be determined by Congress following a hearing. Any removal under the statute would presumably be subject to post-termination judicial review to ensure that a hearing had in fact been held and that the finding of cause for removal was not arbitrary. These procedural and substantive limitations on the removal power militate strongly against the characterization of the Comptroller as a mere agent of Congress by virtue of the removal authority. Indeed, similarly qualified grants of removal power are generally deemed to protect the officers to whom they apply and to establish their independence from the domination of the possessor of the removal power. Removal authority limited in such a manner is more properly viewed as motivating adherence to a substantive standard established by law than as inducing subservience to the particular institution that enforces that standard. That the agent enforcing the standard is Congress may be of some significance to the Comptroller, but Congress' substantively limited removal power will undoubtedly be less of a spur to subservience than Congress' unquestionable and unqualified power to enact legislation reducing the Comptroller's salary, cutting the funds available to his department, reducing his personnel, limiting or expanding his duties, or even abolishing his position altogether.

More importantly, the substantial role played by the President in the process of removal through joint resolution reduces to utter insignificance the possibility that the threat of removal will induce subservience to the Congress. As I have pointed out above, a joint resolution must be presented to the President and is ineffective if it is vetoed by him, unless the veto is overridden by the constitutionally prescribed two-thirds majority of both Houses of Congress. The requirement of presidential approval obviates the possibility that the Comptroller will perceive himself as so completely at the mercy of Congress that he will function as its tool. If the Comptroller's conduct in office is not so unsatisfactory to the President as to convince the latter that removal is required under the statutory standard, Congress will have no independent power to coerce the Comptroller unless it can muster a two-thirds majority in both Houses—a feat of bipartisanship more difficult than that required to impeach and convict. The incremental in terrorem effect of the possibility of congressional removal in the face of a presidential veto is therefore exceedingly unlikely to have any discernible impact on the extent of congressional influence over the Comptroller.

The practical result of the removal provision is not to render the Comptroller unduly dependent upon or subservient to Congress, but to render him one of the most independent officers in the entire federal establishment. Those who have studied the office agree that the procedural and substantive limits on the power of Congress and the President to remove the Comptroller make dislodging him against his will practically impossible. As one scholar put it nearly fifty years ago, "Under the statute the Comptroller General, once confirmed, is safe so long as he avoids a public exhibition of personal immorality, dishonesty, or failing mentality." The passage of time has done little to cast doubt on this view; of the six Comptrollers who have served since 1921, none has been threatened with, much less subjected to, removal. Recent students of the office concur that "[b]arring resignation, death, physical or mental incapacity, or extremely bad behavior, the Comptroller General is assured his tenure if he wants it, and not a day more." The threat of "here-and-now subservience" is obviously remote indeed.

Realistic consideration of the nature of the Comptroller General's relation to Congress thus reveals that the threat to separation of powers conjured up by the majority is wholly chimerical. The power over removal retained by the Congress is not a power that is exercised outside the legislative process as established by the Constitution, nor does it appear likely that it is a power that adds significantly to the influence Congress may exert over executive officers through other, undoubtedly constitutional exercises of legislative power and through the constitutionally guaranteed impeachment power. Indeed, the removal power is so constrained by its own substantive limits and by the requirement of presidential approval "that, as a practical matter, Congress has not exercised, and probably will never exercise, such control over the Comptroller General that his non-legislative powers will threaten the goal of dispersion of power, and hence the goal of individual liberty, that separation of powers serves." Ameron, Inc. v United States Army Corps of Engineers.

The majority's contrary conclusion rests on the rigid dogma that, outside of the impeachment process, any "direct congressional role in the removal of officers charged with the execution of the laws . . . is inconsistent with separation of powers." Reliance on such an unyielding principle to strike down a statute posing no real danger of aggrandizement of congressional power is extremely misguided and insensitive to our constitutional role. The wisdom of vesting "executive" powers in an officer removable by joint resolution may indeed be debatable—as may be the wisdom of the entire scheme of permitting an unelected official to revise the budget enacted by Congress—but such matters are for the most part to be worked out between the Congress and the President through the legislative process, which affords each branch ample opportunity to defend its interests. The Act vesting budget-cutting authority in the Comptroller General represents Congress' judgment that the delegation of such authority to counteract ever-mounting deficits is "necessary and proper" to the exercise of the powers granted the Federal Government by the Constitution; and the President's approval of the statute signifies his unwillingness to reject the choice made by Congress. Under such circumstances, the role of this Court should be limited to determining whether the Act so alters the balance of authority among the branches of government as to pose a genuine threat to the basic division between the lawmaking power and the power to execute the law. Because I see no such threat, I cannot join the Court in striking down the Act.

I dissent.

Aftermath of Bowsher *v.* Synar

In this somewhat cautiously crafted opinion, not only were the "fallback" provisions left intact, but the Court also suspended its holding for up to 60 days in order to allow Congress time to reaffirm a first round of budget reductions for fiscal year 1986 that had taken effect automatically in March prior to the handing down of this decision in July. Congress also faced the task of applying the "fallback" provisions to implement a second round of budget reductions for the new fiscal year beginning October 1.

Initially the House and Senate disagreed on precisely what direction the budget process should take, although both were unhappy with the "fallback" under which the Congress jointly would submit deficit reduction proposals to the President. They clearly preferred the executive to be involved in the "cutting" process so that the President would bear some responsibility along with the legislature. In September both houses concurred in a new bill which established a mechanism that triggered across the board cuts by the Office of Management and Budget, an arm of the executive, unless Congress and the President agreed on specific reductions. On September 29, 1986, just prior to the October 1 deadline for the start of the new fiscal year, President Reagan signed "Gramm-Rudman-Hollings II" into law.

Morrison v. Olson

487 U.S. 654 (1988)

After the decisions in the *Chadha* and *Bowsher* cases, both of which adhered to a formalistic construction of the abstract and somewhat elusive concept of the separation of powers, the Court in *Morrison* v. *Olson*—decided 5 years after *Chadha* and 2 years after *Bowsher*—executed an abrupt about-face and accepted a more pragmatic view of the doctrine. Inspired by the wrongdoing in the executive branch exposed in the Watergate scandal, Congress enacted a "special prosecutor" (later changed to "independent counsel") provision of the Ethics in Government Act of 1978, which was reenacted with minor amendments in 1982. Under its terms, when allegations are made that high-ranking executive officials may have engaged in criminal activity, the Attorney General must conduct a preliminary investigation. He then requests that a special three-judge federal appellate court in the District of Columbia appoint an independent counsel to complete the investigation and conduct any prosecutions unless the allegations prove to be without merit. In order to insulate the independent counsel from any undue pressure, the law provides further that the Attorney General may remove a special prosecutor from office "only for good cause" and subject to judicial review.

This case faced the issue of the constitutionality of the independent counsel provisions of the Ethics of Government Act and arose when the House Judiciary Committee began an investigation into the Justice Department's role in a controversy between the House of Representatives and the Environmental Protection Agency (EPA). In a report of the House Judiciary Committee it was suggested that an official of the Attorney General's office, Theodore Olson, had given false testimony during an earlier EPA investigation and that two other members of the Attorney General's staff, Edward Schmultz and Carol Dinkins, had obstructed the investigation by wrongfully withholding documents. Pursuant to the act the House committee requested the Attorney General to appoint an independent counsel to investigate the allegations. Ultimately, Alexia Morrison, who was appointed counsel to check into the matter and to prosecute any violations of federal law, convinced a grand jury to issue subpoenas to Olson, Schmultz, and Dinkins. They in turn moved to quash the subpoenas in federal district court, claiming that the independent counsel provisions of the act were unconstitutional because they authorized a nonexecutive branch employee to exercise a purely executive function, namely criminal prosecution. However, the lower court upheld the law, denied all motions, and ordered that Olson and the others be held in contempt for refusing to comply with the subpoenas. The court of appeals reversed, holding that the act violated the appointments clause of Article II of the Constitution as well as the principle of the separation of powers.

WILLIAM REHNQUIST

William Rehnquist was named an associate justice by President Richard Nixon in 1971, and elevated to the chief justiceship by President Ronald Reagan in 1986 upon the retirement of Warren Burger. The 38 Senate votes cast against his nomination as chief justice—the largest negative vote ever recorded against a successful nominee— attest to his reputation as an articulate spokesperson for conservative principles. Early in his Court career Rehnquist was often a lone dissenter from liberal activist rulings. As changes in personnel have moved the Court to the right, and particularly since he became chief justice, Rehnquist has become the intellectual leader of an increasingly solid conservative majority in due process and equal protection cases.

Chief Justice **Rehnquist** delivered the opinion of the Court.

This case presents us with a challenge to the independent counsel provisions of the Ethics in Government Act of 1978. We hold today that these provisions of the Act do not violate the Appointments Clause of the Constitution, Art II, § 2, cl 2, or the limitations of Article III, nor do they impermissibly interfere with the President's authority under Article II in violation of the constitutional principle of separation of powers.

. . .

The Appointments Clause of Article II reads as follows:

"[The President] shall nominate, and by and with the Advice and Consent of the Senate, shall appoint Ambassadors, other public Ministers and Consuls, Judges of the supreme Court, and all other Officers of the United States, whose Appointments are not herein otherwise provided for, and which shall be established by Law: but the Congress may by Law vest the Appointment of such inferior Officers, as they think proper, in the President alone, in the Courts of Law, or in the Heads of Departments."

The parties do not dispute that "[t]he Constitution for purposes of appointment . . . divides all its officers into two classes." As we

stated in Buckley v Valeo, "[p]rincipal officers are selected by the President with the advice and consent of the Senate. Inferior officers Congress may allow to be appointed by the President alone, by the heads of departments, or by the Judiciary." The initial question is, accordingly, whether appellant is an "inferior" or a "principal" officer. If she is the latter, as the Court of Appeals concluded, then the Act is in violation of the Appointments Clause.

The line between "inferior" and "principal" officers is one that is far from clear, and the Framers provided little guidance into where it should be drawn. We need not attempt here to decide exactly where the line falls between the two types of officers, because in our view appellant clearly falls on the "inferior officer" side of that line. Several factors lead to this conclusion.

First, appellant is subject to removal by a higher Executive Branch official. Although appellant may not be "subordinate" to the Attorney General (and the President) insofar as she possesses a degree of independent discretion to exercise the powers delegated to her under the Act, the fact that she can be removed by the Attorney General indicates that she is to some degree "inferior" in rank and authority. Second, appellant is empowered by the Act to perform only certain, limited duties. An independent counsel's role is restricted primarily to investigation and, if appropriate, prosecution for certain federal crimes. Admittedly, the Act delegates to appellant "full power and independent authority to exercise all investigative and prosecutorial functions and powers of the Department of Justice," § 594(a), but this grant of authority does not include any authority to formulate policy for the Government or the Executive Branch, nor does it give appellant any administrative duties outside of those necessary to operate her office. The Act specifically provides that in policy matters appellant is to comply to the extent possible with the policies of the Department § 594(f).

Third, appellant's office is limited in jurisdiction. Not only is the Act itself restricted in applicability to certain federal officials suspected of certain serious federal crimes, but an independent counsel can only act within the scope of the jurisdiction that has been granted by the Special Division pursuant to a request by the Attorney General. Finally, appellant's office is limited in tenure. There is concededly no time limit on the appointment of a particular counsel. Nevertheless, the office of independent counsel is "temporary" in the sense that an independent counsel is appointed essentially to accomplish a single task, and when that task is over the office is terminated, either by the counsel herself or by action of the Special Division. Unlike other prosecutors, appellant has no ongoing responsibilities that extend beyond the accomplishment of the mission that she was appointed for and authorized by the Special Division to undertake. In our view, these factors relating to the "ideas of tenure, duration . . . and duties" of the independent counsel, are sufficient to establish that appellant is an "inferior" officer in the constitutional sense.

This conclusion is consistent with our few previous decisions that considered the question of whether a particular government official is a "principal" or an "inferior" officer. In United States v Eaton, for example, we approved Department of State regulations that allowed executive officials to appoint a "vice-consul" during the temporary absence of the consul, terming the "vice-consul" a "subordinate officer" notwithstanding the Appointment Clause's specific reference to "Consuls" as principal officers. As we stated, "Because the subordinate officer is charged with the performance of the duty of the superior for a limited time and under special and temporary conditions he is not thereby transformed into the superior and permanent official." In Ex parte Siebold, the Court found that federal "supervisor[s] of elections," who were charged with various duties involving oversight of local congressional elections, were inferior officers for purposes of the Clause. In Go-Bart Importing Co. v United States, we held that "United States commissioners are inferior officers." These commissioners had various judicial and prosecutorial powers, including the power to arrest and imprison for trial, to issue warrants, and to institute prosecutions under "laws relating to the elective franchise and civil rights." All of this consistent with our reference in United States v Nixon, to the office of Watergate Special Prosecutor—whose authority was similar to that of appellant, a "subordinate officer."

This does not, however, end our inquiry under the Appointments Clause. Appellees argue that even if appellant is an "inferior" officer, the Clause does not empower Congress to place the power to appoint such an officer outside the Executive Branch. They contend that the Clause does not contemplate congressional authorization of "interbranch appointments," in which an officer of one branch is appointed by officers of another branch. The relevant language of the Appointments Clause is worth repeating. It reads: ". . . but the Congress may by Law vest the Appointment of such inferior Officers, as they think proper, in the President alone, in the courts of Law, or in the Heads of Departments." On its face, the language of this "excepting clause" admits of no limitation on interbranch appointments. Indeed, the inclusion of "as they think proper" seems clearly to give Congress significant discretion to determine whether it is "proper" to vest the appointment of, for example, executive officials in the "courts of Law." We recognized as much in one of our few decisions in this area, Ex parte Siebold, where we stated:

"It is no doubt usual and proper to vest the appointment of inferior officers in that department of the government, executive or judicial, or in that particular executive department to which the duties of such officers appertain. But there is no absolute requirement to this effect in the Constitution; and, if there were, it would be difficult in many cases to determine to which department an office properly belonged. . .

"But as the Constitution stands, the selection of the appointing power, as between the functionaries named, is a matter resting in the discretion of Congress. And, looking at the subject in a practical light, it is perhaps better that it should rest there, than that the country should be harassed by the endless controversies to which a more specific direction on this subject might have given rise."

. . .

We also note that the history of the clause provides no support for appellees' position. Throughout most of the process of drafting the Constitution, the Convention concentrated on the problem of who should have the authority to appoint judges. At the suggestion of James Madison, the Convention adopted a proposal that the Senate should have this authority, and several attempts to transfer the appointment power to the president were rejected. The August 6, 1787, draft of the Constitution reported by the Committee of Detail retained Senate appointment of Supreme Court Judges, provided also for Senate appointment of ambassadors, and vested in the president the authority to "appoint officers in all cases not otherwise provided for by this Constitution." This scheme was maintained until September 4, when the Committee of Eleven reported its suggestions to the Convention. This Committee suggested that the Constitution be amended to state that the president "shall nominate and by and with the advice and consent of the Senate shall appoint ambassadors, and other public Ministers, Judges of the Supreme Court, and all other Officers of the [United States], whose appointments are not otherwise herein provided for." After the addition of "Consuls" to the list, the Committee's proposal was adopted, and was subsequently reported to the Convention by the Committee of Style. It was at this point, on September 15, that Gouverneur Morris moved to add the Excepting Clause to Art II, §2. The one comment made on this motion was by Madison, who felt that the Clause did not go far enough in that it did not allow Congress to vest appointment powers in "Superior Officers below Heads of Departments." The first vote on Morris's motion ended in tie. It was then put forward a second time, with the urging that "some such provision [was] too necessary, to be omitted." This time the proposal was adopted. As this discussion shows, there was little or no debate on the question of whether the Clause empowers Congress to provide for interbranch appointments, and there is nothing to suggest that the Framers intended to prevent Congress from having that power.

We do not mean to say that Congress' power to provide for interbranch appointments of "inferior officers" is unlimited. In addition to separation of powers concerns, which would arise if such provisions for appointment had the potential to impair the constitutional functions assigned to one of the branches, Siebold itself suggested that Congress' decision to vest the appointment power in the courts would be improper if there was some "incongruity" beween the functions normally performed by the courts and the performance of their duty to appoint. In this case, however, we do not think it impermissible for Congress to vest the power to appoint independent counsels in a specially created federal court. We thus disagree with the Court of Appeals' conclusion that there is an inherent incongruity about a court having the power to appoint prosecutorial officers.

. . .

We now turn to consider whether the Act is invalid under the constitutional principle of separation of powers. Two related issues must be addressed: The first is whether the provision of the Act restricting the Attorney General's power to remove the independent counsel to only those instances in which he can show "good cause," taken by itself, impermissibly interferes with the President's exercise of his constitutionally appointed functions. The second is whether, taken as a whole, the Act violates the separation of powers by reducing the President's ability to control the prosecutorial powers wielded by the independent counsel.

Two Terms ago we had occasion to consider whether it was consistent with the separation of powers for Congress to pass a statute that authorized a government official who is removable only by Congress to participate in what we found to be "executive powers." We held in Bowsher that "Congress cannot reserve for itself the power of removal of an officer charged with the execution of the laws except by impeachment." A primary antecedent for this ruling was our 1926 decision in Myers v United States. Myers had considered the propriety of a federal statute by which certain postmasters of the United States could be removed by the President only "by and with the advice and consent of the Senate." There too, Congress' attempt to involve itself in the removal of an executive official was found to be sufficient grounds to render the statute invalid. As we observed in Bowsher, the essence of the decision in Myers was the judgment that the Constitution prevents Congress from "draw[ing] to itself . . . the power to remove or the right to participate in the exercise of that power. To do this would be to go beyond the words and implications of the [Appointments Clause] and to infringe the constitutional principle of the separation of governmental powers."

Unlike both Bowsher and Myers, this case does not involve an attempt by Congress itself to gain a role in the removal of executive officials other than its established powers of impeachment and conviction. The Act instead puts the removal power squarely in the hands of the Executive Branch; an independent counsel may be removed from office, "only by the personal action of the Attorney General, and only for good cause." There is no requirement of congressional approval of the Attorney General's removal decision, though the decision is subject to judicial review. In our view, the removal provisions of the Act make this case more analogous to Humphrey's Executor v United States, and Wiener v United States, than to Myers or Bowsher.

. . .

We undoubtedly did rely on the terms "quasi-legislative" and "quasi-judicial" to distinguish the officials involved in Humphrey's Executor and Wiener from those in Myers, but our present considered view is that the determination of whether the Constitution allows Congress to impose a "good cause" type restriction on the President's power to remove an official cannot be made to turn on whether or not that official is classified as "purely executive." The analysis contained in our removal cases is designed not to define rigid categories of those officials who may or may not be removed at will by the President, but to ensure that Congress does not interfere with the President's exercise of the "executive power" and his constitutionally appointed duty to "take care that the laws be faithfully executed" under Article II. Myers was undoubtedly correct in its holding, and in its broader suggestion that there are some "purely executive" officials who must be removable by the President at will if he is to be able to accomplish his constitutional role.

. . .

Considering for the moment the "good cause" removal provision in isolation from the other parts of the Act at issue in this case, we cannot say that the imposition of a "good cause" standard for removal by itself unduly trammels on executive authority. There is no real dispute that the functions performed by the independent counsel are "executive" in the sense that they are law enforcement functions that typically have been undertaken by officials within the Executive Branch. As we noted above, however, the independent counsel is an inferior officer under the Appointments Clause, with limited jurisdiction and tenure and lacking policymaking or significant administrative authority. Although the counsel exercises no small amount of discretion and judgment in deciding how to carry out her duties under the Act, we simply do not see how the President's need to control the exercise of that discretion is so central to the functioning of the Executive Branch as to require as a matter of constitutional law that the counsel be terminable at will by the President.

Nor do we think that the "good cause" removal provision at issue here impermissibly burdens the President's power to control or supervise the independent counsel, as an executive official, in the execution of her duties under the Act. This is not a case in which the power to remove an executive official has been completely stripped from the President, thus providing no means for the President to ensure the "faithful execution" of the laws. Rather, because the independent counsel may be terminated for "good cause," the Executive, through the Attorney General, retains ample authority to assure that the counsel is competently performing her statutory responsibilities in a manner that comports with the provisions of the Act. Although we need not decide in this case exactly what is encompassed within the term "good cause" under the Act, the legislative history of the removal provision also makes clear that the Attorney General may remove an independent counsel for "misconduct." Here, as with the provision of the Act conferring the appointment authority of the independent counsel on the special court, the congressional determination to limit the removal power of the Attorney General was essential, in the view of Congress, to establish the necessary independence of the office. We do not think that this limitation as it presently stands sufficiently deprives the President of control over the independent counsel to interfere impermissibly with his constitutional obligation to ensure the faithful execution of the laws.

The final question to be addressed is whether the Act, taken as a whole, violates the principle of separation of powers by unduly interfering with the role of the Executive Branch. Time and again we have reaffirmed the importance in our constitutional scheme of the separation of governmental powers into the three coordinate branches.

. . .

We observe first that this case does not involve an attempt by Congress to increase its own powers at the expense of the Executive Branch. Unlike some of our previous cases, most recently Bowsher v Synar, this case simply does not pose a "dange[r] of congressional usurpation of Executive Branch functions." Indeed, with the exception of the power of impeachment—which applies to all officers of the United States—Congress retained for itself no powers of control or supervision over an independent counsel. The

Act does empower certain members of Congress to request the Attorney General to apply for the appointment of an independent counsel, but the Attorney General has no duty to comply with the request, although he must respond within a certain time limit. Other than that, Congress' role under the Act is limited to receiving reports or other information and oversight of the independent counsel's activities, functions that we have recognized generally as being incidental to the legislative function of Congress.

Similarly, we do not think that the Act works any *judicial* usurpation of properly executive functions. As should be apparent from our discussion of the Appointments Clause above, the power to appoint inferior officers such as independent counsels is not in itself an "executive" function in the constitutional sense, at least when Congress has exercised its power to vest the appointment of an inferior office in the "courts of Law." We note nonetheless that under the Act the Special Division has no power to appoint an independent counsel sua sponte; it may only do so upon the specific request of the Attorney General, and the courts are specifically prevented from reviewing the Attorney General's decision not to seek appointment. In addition, once the court has appointed a counsel and defined her jurisdiction, it has no power to supervise or control the activities of the counsel. As we pointed out in our discussion of the Special Division in relation to Article III, the various powers delegated by the statute to the Division are not supervisory or administrative, nor are they functions that the Constitution requires be performed by officials within the Executive Branch. The Act does give a federal court the power to review the Attorney General's decision to remove an independent counsel, but in our view this is a function that is well within the traditional power of the judiciary.

Finally, we do not think that the Act "impermissibly undermine[s]" the powers of the Executive Branch, or "disrupts the proper balance between the coordinate branches [by] prevent[ing] the Executive Branch from accomplishing its constitutionally assigned functions," Nixon v Administrator of General Services. . . . It is undeniable that the Act reduces the amount of control or supervision that the Attorney

General and, through him, the President exercises over the investigation and prosecution of a certain class of alleged criminal activity. The Attorney General is not allowed to appoint the individual of his choice; he does not determine the counsel's jurisdiction; and his power to remove a counsel is limited. Nonetheless, the Act does give the Attorney General several means of supervising or controlling the prosecutorial powers that may be wielded by an independent counsel. Most importantly, the Attorney General retains the power to remove the counsel for "good cause," a power that we have already concluded provides the Executive with substantial ability to ensure that the laws are "faithfully executed" by an independent counsel. No independent counsel may be appointed without a specific request by the Attorney General and the Attorney General's decision not to request appointment if he finds "no reasonable grounds to believe that further investigation is warranted" is committed to his unreviewable discretion. The Act thus gives the Executive a degree of control over the power to initiate an investigation by the independent counsel. In addition, the jurisdiction of the independent counsel is defined with reference to the facts submitted by the Attorney General, and once a counsel is appointed, the Act requires that the counsel abide by Justice Department policy unless it is not "possible" to do so. Notwithstanding the fact that the counsel is to some degree "independent" and free from Executive supervision to a greater extent than other federal prosecutors, in our view these features of the Act give the Executive Branch sufficient control over the independent counsel to ensure that the President is able to perform his constitutionally assigned duties.

In sum, we conclude today that it does not violate the Appointments Clause for Congress to vest the appointment of independent counsels in the Special Division; that the powers exercised by the Special Division under the Act do not violate Article III; and that the Act does not violate the separation of powers principle by impermissibly interfering with the functions of the Executive Branch. The decision of the Court of Appeals is therefore reversed.

Justice **Scalia,** dissenting.

It is the proud boast of our democracy that we have "a government of laws and not of men." Many Americans are familiar with that phrase; not many know its derivation. It comes from Part the First, Article XXX of the Massachusetts Constitution of 1780, which reads in full as follows:

"In the government of this commonwealth, the legislative department shall never exercise the executive and judicial powers, or either of them; the executive shall never exercise the legislative and judicial powers, or either of them; the judicial shall never exercise the legislative and executive powers, or either of them; to the end it may be a government of laws, and not of men."

The framers of the Federal Constitution similarly viewed the principle of separation of powers as the absolutely central guarantee of a just government. In No. 47 of The Federalist, Madison wrote that "[n]o political truth is certainly of greater intrinsic value, or is stamped with the authority of more enlightened patrons of liberty." Without a secure structure of separated powers, our Bill of Rights would be worthless, as are the bills of rights of many nations of the world that have adopted, or even improved upon, the mere words of ours.

The principle of separation of powers is expressed in our Constitution in the first section of each of the first three Articles. Article I, § 1 provides that "[a]ll legislative Powers herein granted shall be vested in a Congress of the United States, which shall consist of a Senate and House of Representatives." Article III, § 1 provides that "[t]he judicial Power of the United States, shall be vested in one supreme Court, and in such inferior Courts as the Congress may from time to time ordain and establish." And the provision at issue here, Art II, § 1, cl 1 provides that "[t]he executive Power shall be vested in a President of the United States of America."

But just as the mere words of a Bill of Rights are not self-effectuating, the framers recognized "[t]he insufficiency of a mere parchment delineation of the boundaries" to achieve the separation of powers. "[T]he great security," wrote

Madison, "against a gradual concentration of the several powers in the same department consists in giving to those who administer each department the necessary constitutional means and personal motives to resist encroachments of the others. The provision for defense must in this, as in all other cases, be made commensurate to the danger of attack." Madison continued:

"But it is not possible to give to each department an equal power of self-defense. In republican government, the legislative authority necessarily predominates. The remedy for this inconveniency is to divide the legislature into different branches; and to render them, by different modes of election and different principles of action, as little connected with each other as the nature of their common functions and their common dependence on the society will admit. . . . As the weight of the legislative authority requires that it should be thus divided, the weakness of the executive may require, on the other hand, that it should be fortified."

The major "fortification" provided, of course, was the veto power. But in addition to providing fortification, the founders conspicuously and very consciously declined to sap the executive's strength in the same way they had weakened the legislature: by dividing the executive power. Proposals to have multiple executives, or a council of advisors with separate authority were rejected. Thus, while "[a]ll legislative Powers herein granted shall be vested in a Congress of the United States, which shall consist of a Senate *and* House of Representatives," US Const. Art I, § 1 (emphasis added), "[t]he executive Power shall be vested in *a President of the United States*" (emphasis added).

That is what this suit is about. Power. The allocation of power among Congress, the President and the courts in such fashion as to preserve the equilibrium the Constitution sought to establish—so that "a gradual concentration of the several powers in the same department," can effectively be resisted. Frequently an issue of this sort will come before the Court clad, so to speak, in sheep's clothing: the potential of the asserted principle to effect important change in the equilibrium of power is not immediately evi-

dent, and must be discerned by a careful and perceptive analysis. But this wolf comes as a wolf.

. . .

Thus, by the application of this statute in the present case, Congress has effectively compelled a criminal investigation of a high-level appointee of the President in connection with his actions arising out of a bitter power dispute between the President and the Legislative Branch. Mr. Olson may or may not be guilty of a crime; we do not know. But we do know that the investigation of him has been commenced, not necessarily because the President or his authorized subordinates believe it is in the interest of the United States, in the sense that it warrants the diversion of resources from other efforts, and is worth the cost in money and in possible damage to other governmental interests and not even, leaving aside those normally considered factors, because the President or his authorized subordinates necessarily believe that an investigation is likely to unearth a violation worth prosecuting; but only because the Attorney General cannot affirm, as Congress demands, that there are *no reasonable grounds to believe* that further investigation is warranted. The decisions regarding the scope of that further investigation, its duration, and, finally, whether or not prosecution should ensue, are likewise beyond the control of the President and his subordinates.

. . .

If to describe this case is not to decide it, the concept of a government of separate and coordinate powers no longer has meaning. The Court devotes most of its attention to such relatively technical details as the Appointments Clause and the removal power, addressing briefly and only at the end of its opinion the separation of powers. As my prologue suggests, I think that has it backwards. Our opinions are full of the recognition that it is the principle of separation of powers, and the inseparable corollary that each department's "defense must . . . be made commensurate to the danger of attack," which gives comprehensible content to the appointments clause, and determines the appropriate scope of the removal power. Thus, while I will subsequently discuss why our appointments and removal jurisprudence does not support today's holding, I begin with a consideration of the fountainhead of that jurisprudence, the separation and equilibration of powers.

. . .

To repeat, Art III, § 1, cl 1 of the Constitution provides:

"The executive Power shall be vested in a President of the United States."

As I described at the outset of this opinion, this does not mean *some* of the executive power, but *all* of the executive power. It seems to me, therefore, that the decision of the Court of Appeals invalidating the present statute must be upheld on fundamental separation-of-powers principles if the following two questions are answered affirmatively: (1) Is the conduct of a criminal prosecution (and of an investigation to decide whether to prosecute) the exercise of purely executive power? (2) Does the statute deprive the President of the United States of exclusive control over the exercise of that power? Surprising to say, the Court appears to concede an affirmative answer to both questions, but seeks to avoid the inevitable conclusion that since the statute vests some purely executive power in a person who is not the President of the United States it is void.

. . .

As for the second question, whether the statute before us deprives the President of exclusive control over the quintessentially executive activity: The Court does not, and could not possibly, assert that it does not. That is indeed the whole object of the statute. Instead, the Court points out that the President, through his Attorney General, has at least some control. That concession is alone enough to invalidate the statute, but I cannot refrain from pointing out that the Court greatly exaggerates the extent of that "some" presidential control. "Most importan[t]" among these controls, the Court asserts, is the Attorney General's "power to remove the counsel for `good cause.'" This is somewhat like referring to shackles as an effec-

tive means of locomotion. As we recognized in Humphrey's Executor v United States—indeed, what Humphrey's Executor was all about—limiting removal power to "good cause" is an impediment to, not an effective grant of, presidential control. We said that limitation was necessary with respect to members of the Federal Trade Commission, which we found to be "an agency of the legislative and judicial departments," and "wholly disconnected from the executive department," because "it is quite evident that one who holds his office only during the pleasure of another, cannot be depended upon to maintain an attitude of independence against the latter's will." What we in Humphrey's Executor found to be a means of eliminating presidential control, the Court today considers the "most importan[t]" means of assuring presidential control. Congress, of course, operated under no such illusion when it enacted this statute, describing the "good cause" limitation as "protecting the independent counsel's ability to act independently of the President's direct control" since it permits removal only for "misconduct."

. . .

The utter incompatibility of the Court's approach with our constitutional traditions can be made more clear, perhaps, by applying it to the powers of the other two Branches. Is it conceivable that if Congress passed a statute depriving itself of less than full and entire control over some insignificant area of legislation, we would inquire whether the matter was *"so central* to the functioning of the Legislative Branch," as really to require complete control, or whether the statute gives Congress *"sufficient* control over the surrogate legislator to ensure that Congress is able to perform its constitutionally assigned duties"? Of course we would have none of that. Once we determined that a purely legislative power was at issue we would require it to be exercised, wholly and entirely, by Congress. Or to bring the point closer to home, consider a statute giving to non-Article III judges just a tiny bit of purely judicial power in a relatively insignificant field, with substantial control, though not total control, in the courts—perhaps "clear error" review, which would be a fair judicial equivalent of the Attorney General's "for cause" removal power here. Is there any doubt that we would not pause to inquire whether the matter was *"so central* to the functioning of the Judicial Branch" as really to require complete control, or whether we retained *"sufficient* control over the matters to be decided that we are able to perform our constitutionally assigned duties"? We would say that our "constitutionally assigned duties" include *complete* control over all exercises of the judicial power—or, as the plurality opinion said in Northern Pipeline Construction Co. v Marathon Pipe Line Co. that "[t]he inexorable command of [Article III] is clear and definite: The judicial power of the United States must be exercised by courts having the attributes prescribed in Art III." We should say here that the President's constitutionally assigned duties include *complete* control over investigation and prosecution of violations of the law, and that the inexorable command of Article II is clear and definite: the executive power must be vested in the President of the United States.

. . .

The purpose of the separation and equilibration of powers in general, and of the unitary Executive in particular, was not merely to assure effective government but to preserve individual freedom. Those who hold or have held offices covered by the Ethics in Government Act are entitled to that protection as much as the rest of us, and I conclude my discussion by considering the effect of the Act upon the fairness of the process they receive.

Only someone who has worked in the field of law enforcement can fully appreciate the vast power and the immense discretion that are placed in the hands of a prosecutor with respect to the objects of his investigation. Justice Robert Jackson, when he was Attorney General under President Franklin Roosevelt, described it in a memorable speech to United States Attorneys, as follows:

"There is a most important reason why the prosecutor should have, as nearly as possible, a detached and impartial view of all groups in his community. Law enforcement is not automatic. It isn't blind. One of the greatest difficulties of the position of prosecutor is that he must pick his cases, because no prosecutor can even investigate all of the cases in which he receives complaints. If the Department of Justice were to make even a pretense of reaching every probable violation of federal law, ten times its present staff will be inadequate. We know that no local police force can strictly enforce the traffic laws, or it would arrest half the driving population on any given morning. What every prosecutor is practically required to do is to select the cases for prosecution and to select those in which the offense is the most flagrant, the public harm the greatest, and the proof the most certain.

"If the prosecutor is obliged to choose his case, it follows that he can choose his defendants. Therein is the most dangerous power of the prosecutor: that he will pick people that he thinks he should get, rather than cases that need to be prosecuted. With the law books filled with a great assortment of crimes, a prosecutor stands a fair chance of finding at least a technical violation of some act on the part of almost anyone. In such a case, it is not a question of discovering the commission of a crime and then looking for the man who has committed it, it is a question of picking the man and then searching the law books, or putting investigators to work, to pin some offense on him. It is in this realm—in which the prosecutor picks some person whom he dislikes or desires to embarrass, or selects some group of unpopular persons and then looks for an offense, that the greatest danger of abuse of prosecuting power lies. It is here that law enforcement becomes personal, and the real crime becomes that of being unpopular with the predominant or governing group, being attached to the wrong political views, or being personally obnoxious to or in the way of the prosecutor himself."

Under our system of government, the primary check against prosecutorial abuse is a political one. The prosecutors who exercise this awesome discretion are selected and can be removed by a President, whom the people have trusted enough to elect. Moreover, when crimes are not investigated and prosecuted fairly, nonselectively, with a reasonable sense of proportion, the President pays the cost in political damage to his administration. If federal prosecutors "pick people that

[they] thin[k] [they] should get, rather than cases that need to be prosecuted," if they amass many more resources against a particular prominent individual, or against a particular class of political protesters, or against members of a particular political party, than the gravity of the alleged offenses or the record of successful prosecutions seems to warrant, the unfairness will come home to roost in the Oval Office. I leave it to the reader to recall the examples of this in recent years. That result, of course, was precisely what the Founders had in mind when they provided that all executive powers would be exercised by a *single* Chief Executive. As Hamilton put it, "[t]he ingredients which constitute safety in the republican sense are a due dependence on the people, and a due responsibility." The President is directly dependent on the people, and since there is only *one* President, *he* is responsible. The people know whom to blame, whereas "one of the weightiest objections to a plurality in the executive . . . is that it tends to conceal faults and destroy responsibility."

That is the system of justice the rest of us are entitled to, but what of that select class consisting of present or former high-level executive-branch officials? If an allegation is made against them of any violation of any federal criminal law (except Class B or C misdemeanors or infractions) the Attorney General must give it his attention. That in itself is not objectionable. But if, after a 90-day investigation without the benefit of normal investigatory tools, the Attorney General is unable to say that there are "no reasonable grounds to believe" that further investigation is warranted, a process is set in motion that is *not* in the full control of persons "dependent on the people," and whose flaws cannot be blamed on the President. An independent counsel is selected, and the scope of her authority prescribed, by a panel of judges. What if they are politically partisan, as judges have been known to be, and select a prosecutor antagonistic to the administration, or even to the particular individual who has been selected for this special treatment? There is no remedy for that, not even a political one. Judges, after all, have life tenure, and appointing a sure-fire enthusiastic prosecutor could hardly be considered an impeachable offense. So if there is anything

wrong with the selection, there is effectively no one to blame. The independent counsel thus selected proceeds to assemble a staff. As I observed earlier, in the nature of things this has to be done by finding lawyers who are willing to lay aside their current careers for an indeterminate amount of time, to take on a job that has no prospect of permanence and little prospect for promotion. One thing is certain, however: it involves investigating and perhaps prosecuting a particular individual. Can one imagine a less equitable manner of fulfilling the Executive responsibility to investigate and prosecute? What would be the reaction if, in an area not covered by this statute, the Justice Department posted a public notice inviting applicants to assist in an investigation and possible prosecution of a certain prominent person? Does this not invite what Justice Jackson described as "picking the man and then searching the law books, or putting investigators to work, to pin some offense on him"? To be sure, the investigation must relate to the area of criminal offense specified by the life-tenured judges. But that has often been (and nothing prevents it from being) very broad—and should the independent counsel or her staff come up with something beyond that scope, nothing prevents her from asking the judges to expand her authority or, if that does not work, referring it to the Attorney General, whereupon the whole process would recommence and, if there was "reasonable basis to believe" that further investigation was warranted, that new offense would be referred to the Special Tribunal, which would in all likelihood assign it to the same independent counsel. It seems to me not conducive to fairness. But even if it were entirely evident that unfairness was in fact the result—the judges hostile to the administration, the independent counsel an old foe of the President, the staff refugees from the recently defeated administration—*there would be no one accountable to the public to whom the blame could be assigned.*

I do not mean to suggest that anything of this sort (other than the inevitable self-selection of the prosecutory staff) occurred in the present case. I know and have the highest regard for the judges on the Special Division, and the independent counsel herself is a woman of accomplishment, impartiality and integrity. But the fairness of a process must be adjudged on the basis of what it permits to happen, not what it produced in a particular case. It is true, of course, that a similar list of horribles could be attributed to an ordinary Justice Department prosecution—a vindictive prosecutor, an antagonistic staff, etc. But the difference is the difference that the Founders envisioned when they established a single Chief Executive accountable to the people: the blame can be assigned to someone who can be punished.

The above described possibilities of irresponsible conduct must, as I say, be considered in judging the constitutional acceptability of this process. But they will rarely occur, and in the average case the threat to fairness is quite different. As described in the brief filed on behalf of three ex-Attorneys General from each of the last three administrations:

"The problem is less spectacular but much more worrisome. It is that the institutional environment of the Independent Counsel—specifically, her isolation from the Executive Branch and the internal checks and balances it supplies—is designed to heighten, not to check, all of the occupational hazards of the dedicated prosecutor; the danger of too narrow a focus, of the loss of perspective, of preoccupation with the pursuit of one alleged suspect to the exclusion of other interests."

It is, in other words, an additional advantage of the unitary Executive that it can achieve a more uniform application of the law. Perhaps that is not always achieved, but the mechanism to achieve it is there. The mini-Executive that is the independent counsel, however, operating in an area where so little is law and so much is discretion, is intentionally cut off from the unifying influence of the Justice Department, and from the perspective that multiple responsibilities provide. What would normally be regarded as a technical violation (there are no rules defining such things), may in her small world assume the proportions of an indictable offense. What would normally be regarded as an investigation that has reached the level of pursuing such picayune matters that it should be concluded, may to her be an investigation that ought to go

on for another year. How frightening it must be to have your own independent counsel and staff appointed, with nothing else to do but to investigate you until investigation is no longer worthwhile—with whether it is worthwhile not depending upon what such judgments usually hinge on, competing responsibilities. And to have that counsel and staff decide, with no basis for comparison, whether what you have done is bad enough, willful enough, and provable enough, to warrant an indictment. How admirable the constitutional system that provides the means to avoid such a distortion. And how unfortunate the judicial decision that has permitted it.

The notion that every violation of law should be prosecuted, including—indeed, *especially*—every violation by those in high places, is an attractive one, and it would be risky to argue in an election campaign that that is not an absolutely overriding value. Fiat justitia, ruat coelum. Let justice be done, though the heavens may fall. The reality is, however, that it is not an absolutely overriding value, and it was with the hope that we would be able to acknowledge and apply such realities that the Constitution spared us, by life tenure, the necessity of election campaigns. I cannot imagine that there are not many thoughtful men and women in Congress who realize that the benefits of this legislation are far outweighed by its harmful effect upon our system of government, and even upon the nature of justice received by those men and women who agree to serve in the Executive Branch. But it is difficult to vote not to enact, and even more difficult to vote to repeal, a statute called, appropriately enough, the Ethics in Government Act. If Congress is controlled by the party other than the one to which the President belongs, it has little incentive to repeal it; if it is controlled by the same party, it dare not. By its short-sighted action today, I fear the Court has permanently encumbered the Republic with an institution that will do it great harm.

Worse than what it has done, however, is the manner in which it has done it. A government of laws means a government of rules. Today's decision on the basic issue of fragmentation of executive power is ungoverned by rule, and hence ungoverned by law. It extends into the very heart of our most significant constitutional function the "totality of the circumstances" mode of analysis that this Court has in recent years become fond of. Taking all things into account, we conclude that the power taken away from the President here is not really *too* much. The next time executive power is assigned to someone other than the President we may conclude, taking all things into account, that it *is* too much. That opinion, like this one, will not be confined by any rule. We will describe, as we have today (though I hope more accurately) the effects of the provision in question, and will authoritatively announce: "The President's need to control the exercise of the [subject officer's] discretion *is* so central to the functioning of the Executive Branch as to require complete control." This is not analysis; it is ad hoc judgment. And it fails to explain why it is not true that—as the text of the Constitution seems to require, as the Founders seemed to expect, and as our past cases have uniformly assumed—all purely executive power must be under the control of the President.

The ad hoc approach to constitutional adjudication has real attraction, even apart from its work-saving potential. It is guaranteed to produce a result, in every case, that will make a majority of the Court happy with the law. The law is, by definition, precisely what the majority thinks, taking all things into account, it *ought* to be. I prefer to rely upon the judgment of the wise men who constructed our system, and of the people who approved it, and of two centuries of history that have shown it to be sound. Like it or not, that judgment says, quite plainly, that "[t]he executive Power shall be vested in a President of the United States."

Aftermath of Morrison v. Olson

In a political sense this decision was a major defeat for the administration of President Ronald Reagan whose solicitor general had entered the case against Morrison arguing that the special prosecutor statute threatened the existence of a vigorous, independent executive, responsible directly to the people and essential to the functioning of the American system. In response, Chief Justice William Rehnquist maintained that the law did not impermissibly undermine the powers of the executive branch since the law contained enough safeguards to ensure that "the President is able to perform his constitutionally assigned duties." The law, argued Rehnquist, did not amount to congressional usurpation of executive branch functions since it gave Congress no voice in the appointment of special prosecutors and no control over their actions. Only the most recently appointed Reagan justices, Anthony Kennedy and Antonin Scalia, did not join the majority of seven. Kennedy had disqualified himself in the case without giving reasons but Scalia wrote a blistering 38-page dissent in which he accused the Court of subverting the separation of powers and diluting executive authority.

Long-term significance aside, the immediate effect of the decision was to remove all impediments to the independent counsel, Lawrence E. Walsh, who had recently obtained indictments of Oliver North, John Poindexter, and three others, all of whom were to go to trial as a result of alleged illegal actions growing out of the Iran-Contra affair. Moreover, the decision now made it impossible for two of President Reagan's closest advisers, Michael Deaver and Lyn Nofziger, both convicted on criminal indictments obtained by independent counsel, to raise constitutional objections on appeal based on the Ethics in Government Act.

In 1989, a year after the *Morrison* decision, the Court continued to adhere to the *Morrison* rationale when it decided *Mistretta* v. *United States*. For almost a century federal judges exercised broad discretion over offenders in criminal cases. Under the usual arrangement of indeterminate sentencing it was the judge's prerogative to decide whether and for how long the defendant should be imprisoned, whether there should be a fine and/or probation. Eventually those caught in the web of criminal justice began to charge unfairness in a system that resulted in a serious disparity among sentences imposed by federal judges upon similarly situated offenders. Responding to growing criticism, Congress passed the Sentencing Reform Act of 1984, creating the United States Sentencing Commission as an independent body located in the judicial branch of the government. The commission was to consist of seven members appointed by the President and approved by the Senate, with a provision that no more than four may be members of the same political party. In addition at least three members were to be federal judges selected from a list of six recommended by the Judicial Conference of the United States. Using the independent regulatory commission concept as a model, the law provided that members would be appointed to six-year terms with service limited to two terms and that they might be removed only for neglect of duty, malfeasance in office, or other shown causes. It was the commission's duty to promulgate sentence guidelines by establishing a range of determinate sentences for all categories of federal offenses and defendants. The new guidelines provided judges with a range of sentences to follow on a mathematical grid with such variables as the amount of money involved in fraud, whether a weapon was used in violent crime, and whether a criminal was a repeat offender. Judges might depart from the guidelines but must give written reasons for doing so, and any departure would be subject to review in the appellate courts. In addition to reducing disparity in sentencing for like crimes, the system was designed to increase the likelihood of imprisonment for crimes involving drugs and for white-collar offenses such as insider trading, price fixing, and tax evasion.

After pleading guilty to a charge of conspiring to distribute cocaine, John Mistretta, pursuant to the commission's guidelines, was fined $1,000 and sentenced to 18 months' imprisonment, to be followed by a term of 3 years' supervised release. Mistretta's counsel contended that the conviction should be overturned on the ground that the commission was constituted in violation of the separation of powers (nonjudicial duties exercised by a judicial institution) and that Congress had delegated excessive authority to the commission by giving it discretion in formulating sentencing guidelines. Speaking for the Supreme Court majority, Justice Blackmun wrote an opinion upholding the Sentencing Reform Act and rejecting all of Mistretta's contentions. Blackmun concluded that "Congress neither delegated excessive legislative power nor upset the constitutionally mandated balance of powers among the coordinate Branches."

Indicative of the cleavage among federal judges over sentencing procedures was the fact that prior to *Mistretta*, 158 federal judges had ruled the guidelines set by the commission unconstitutional and had sentenced convicted criminals under prior existing rules, while 116 judges had used the new system. After the commission's guidelines took effect on November 1, 1987, 1,200 persons who committed crimes after the effective date were sentenced under the old system and, as a result of *Mistretta*, some may require resentencing.

After the Supreme Court's ruling Attorney General Dick Thornburgh said that the guidelines "make the punishment for crime not only fairer but more certain." But at the same time it is likely that the new guidelines may increase the burden on the already overcrowded federal courts, since sentences will generally be stiffer and less likely to be altered on appeal. It is possible that more offenders will opt for trial rather than enter a guilty plea, increasing the load of the trial judges, and that more appeals will be taken in which defendants contend that judges improperly applied the guidelines. Moreover, a greater certainty of prison sentences might lead to an overload on the federal prisons.

To return to our main point, the separation of powers debate continues. Justice Harry Blackmun's *Mistretta* opinion highlighted the proposition that past Supreme Court rulings on the separation of powers focused on the efforts of one branch of government to aggrandize power for itself, but that such was not the case with the sentencing commission. At the same time Justice Scalia's argument that this case is about the creation of a new branch of government—"a sort of junior-varsity Congress"—cannot be dismissed out of hand. The structure of the Constitution does matter, and while not as glamorous as the right to free speech or the right to due process of law, there is a constitutional right in the United States to a particular kind of government structure. Among the Constitution's framers there was an acute awareness that tyrannical governments concentrate power in a single residuum—a party, a group, a person—and they designed a Constitution in which governmental power was dispersed. That is what the separation of powers is all about, and any intermingling of powers should always be viewed with some suspicion.

4   Due Process of Law

At the heart of the Anglo-American legal tradition stands the principle that citizens should be treated fairly by their government. Such treatment is called *due process of law*, a venerable term which made its first appearance in an act of Parliament in 1354. The idea that a government's authority over its citizens should be subject to specific limitations can be traced back even further, at least to the signing of the Magna Carta in 1215, when a group of English nobles forced King John to accept a set of written prohibitions on the royal power which had previously been accepted as absolute.

Over the next several centuries, due process in England consisted of a gradually expanding set of common law protections for the criminally accused which eventually included the right to indictment by grand jury and trial by jury; the privilege against self-incrimination, protection against double jeopardy, and the right to counsel. While the definition of due process was periodically updated and codified by judges and legal scholars, most notably by Chief Justice Edward Coke in the seventeenth century, the phrase was generally understood to have an open-ended rather than a fixed meaning. Like another term with which it was used interchangeably—"the law of the land"—due process of law was intended to incorporate changing ideas about the proper scope and nature of state powers.

The due process principle appears twice in the U.S. Constitution, first in the Fifth Amendment where it qualifies the authority of the national government to deprive its citizens of "life, liberty, or property," and again in the Fourteenth Amendment where it imposes a similar restriction on the states. When the Bill of Rights was being debated in Congress, a number of the states already had similar (though generally less extensive) lists of checks written into their own constitutions. Nevertheless, the main author of the Bill of Rights, James Madison of Virginia, proposed in his original draft that at least some of its prohibitions be explicitly applied to the states. His suggestion was summarily rejected by the Senate, and thus the words with which the First Amendment begins, "Congress shall make no law . . . ," establish the interpretive context for the entire Bill of

Rights. In *Barron* v. *Baltimore*, decided in 1833, the Supreme Court confirmed that the Bill of Rights limits national, not state, power.

This situation began to change after the Civil War, with the adoption of three constitutional amendments, each intended by its sponsors to address part of the problem faced by newly freed slaves living in the former confederate states. These amendments reflected a conviction (widely held in the north, though not in the south) that the Constitution could properly be used to protect citizens against the actions of state governments. The Thirteenth Amendment, ratified in 1865, was a formal renunciation of the institution of slavery, a step thought at least symbolically necessary since the Constitution had originally legitimized slavery through its "three-fifths" rule for determining the voting strength of slave states in the House of Representatives. The Fifteenth Amendment, which became effective in 1870, was similarly straightforward, guaranteeing former slaves the right to vote.

The Fourteenth Amendment, ratified in 1868, was the most ambitious—and ambiguous—of the Civil War amendments. After stating that "all persons born or naturalized in the United States" were United States citizens (thereby nullifying the *Dred Scott* decision), as well as citizens of their state of residence, the amendment went on to erect a "triple barrier" against state-sponsored discrimination: through the privileges and immunities clause, the due process clause, and the equal protection clause. It also granted Congress the power to enforce the amendment's prohibitions.

In theory, then, citizens could now look to the Constitution, and to the national government, for protection from abuse of their rights by state and local officials. But exactly what personal rights did the Fourteenth Amendment protect? Given its power of judicial review, it was inevitable that the Supreme Court would be called on to provide answers to this question. As we shall later see, the Court dealt so summarily with the privileges and immunities clause that it became a constitutional dead letter. The much more complex story of equal protection will be taken up in Chapter 7. The rest of this chapter will be devoted to the equally entangled history of the Supreme Court's interpretation of the due process clause.

At the core of all due process clause cases are two closely related questions: Exactly what kind of liberty does due process protect? How broadly does it protect it? To answer these questions the Supreme Court has also had to decide what relationship, if any, exists between the Fourteenth Amendment and the Bill of Rights. Specifically, are the restrictions imposed on the states through the due process clause the same as those already applied against the national government in the Bill of Rights? Over the years a variety of responses to this question have issued from the Supreme Court, out of which three distinct positions have emerged. We will now examine each of these positions in turn.

DUE PROCESS AS FUNDAMENTAL FAIRNESS

The oldest, best-known, and most widely accepted interpretation of the due process clause is known as the fundamental fairness position. Its most prominent advocates on the Supreme Court have been Justices Benjamin Cardozo, Felix Frankfurter, and John Marshall Harlan II. Supporters of this approach argue that the due process clause of the Fourteenth Amendment was intended by its authors to protect those personal rights which are, as Cardozo put it, of the "essence of a scheme of ordered liberty." Some of those freedoms happen to be included in the

Bill of Rights, while others are not. Speaking for the Court in *Rochin* v. *California* in 1952, for example, Frankfurter held that police had deprived a criminal suspect of due process when they pumped his stomach for evidence, even though no specific provision of the Bill of Rights had been violated. To Frankfurter, it was enough to find that such "conduct . . . shocks the conscience," and "offend(s) the community's sense of fair play and decency," for it to be unconstitutional under the due process clause of the Fourteenth Amendment. Even when a fundamental right happens to be provided for in the Bill of Rights, it is the nature of the liberty rather than its inclusion in the Bill of Rights that qualifies it for Fourteenth Amendment protection. As Harlan put it in his concurrence in *Griswold* v. *Connecticut* (excerpted in this chapter), the due process clause "stands . . . on its own bottom."

Under the fundamental fairness doctrine not all of the guarantees in the Bill of Rights are considered crucial to the concept of due process. In three of its earliest due process decisions, for example, the Court held that grand jury indictment, the 12-person criminal jury, and self-incrimination protection—although required in federal cases under provisions of the Bill of Rights—were not essential to due process in state proceedings. Later, in *Palko* v. *Connecticut* (1937) (excerpted in this chapter), the Court ruled that the Fifth Amendment protection against double jeopardy was not a due process requirement for the states either, although it noted in passing that the First Amendment freedoms of speech and press, among others, had already been incorporated.

There is no necessary relationship in the fundamental fairness theory between the Fourteenth Amendment and the specific guarantees of the Bill of Rights. Supreme Court justices who subscribe to this view thus have the burden of deciding on a case-by-case basis whether a given form of treatment is consistent with due process. In making this judgment they must look primarily to history and traditions, searching through common law, statutes, and past practices to locate the procedures that have played an essential role in ensuring just treatment of individuals by government. Although advocates of fundamental fairness are heavily influenced by history, they would deny being bound by it. On the contrary, in their view the concept of due process is still evolving; judges can and must recognize that practices acceptable to previous generations may violate contemporary standards of fairness.

DUE PROCESS AS TOTAL INCORPORATION

A second interpretation of the due process clause is most commonly, indeed almost exclusively, associated with Justice Hugo Black, whose reading of the congressional debates surrounding the adoption of the Fourteenth Amendment persuaded him that the purpose of the due process clause was to *incorporate* each of the specific guarantees found in the Bill of Rights, where they originally applied to the national government, making them applicable to the states. According to Black, after the ratification of the Fourteenth Amendment the national and state governments were subject to identical limitations on their power to deprive citizens of life, liberty, or property. Unlike the fundamental rights interpretation, the total incorporation position looks to the text of the Bill of Rights as the alpha and omega of due process. All of its provisions are protected against state action by the Fourteenth Amendment, but any rights excluded from the Bill of Rights cannot claim such protection. Black, for example, concurred in the "stomach pump" decision (*Rochin* v. *California*) not on Frankfurter's ground that the practice violated fundamental fairness, but rather because such an involuntary extraction of evidence was in his view prohibited by the Fifth Amendment's command, "No person . . . shall be compelled in any criminal case to be a witness against himself."

Throughout much of his career Black was a vigorous champion of personal freedoms that he believed to be protected by the Bill of Rights against government abuse. He was particularly prominent in the development of the right to counsel, and in protecting speech and press freedom through his *absolutist* interpretation of the First Amendment (see Chapter 5 for more extended discussion of Black's position). Toward the end of his life, however, Black's total incorporation position, which had greatly endeared him to civil libertarians, sometimes caused him to part company with those who wished to stretch the concept of due process farther than his reading of the Bill of Rights would allow it to go. This split was most noticeable with regard to privacy rights, which Black claimed to value "as well as the next one," but nonetheless did not find among the specific guarantees of the Bill of Rights. For this reason Black dissented from the majority opinion in *Griswold* v. *Connecticut*, overturning on privacy grounds a state law prohibiting the sale or use of contraceptives.

DUE PROCESS AS TOTAL INCORPORATION PLUS FUNDAMENTAL FAIRNESS

A third position on the relationship between the Fourteenth Amendment and the Bill of Rights is essentially a hybrid of the two previous positions and thus might be called total incorporation plus fundamental rights. Such justices as Wiley Rutledge, Frank Murphy, and, most prominently, William O. Douglas, subscribed to Black's total incorporation theory, but were unwilling to stop there for fear of neglecting other unspecified rights such as personal privacy. Like fundamental fairness, this position is open-ended in its conception of due process. Unlike fundamental fairness, however, it embraces the entire Bill of Rights within the meaning of due process. Both Frankfurter and Black found Douglas's position exasperating because it seemed to ignore the theoretical underpinnings of their interpretations, which they regarded as mutually exclusive. As he did in so many areas, however, Douglas charted his own course on due process without much concern for his colleagues' intellectual sensibilities.

Out of this amalgam of views has come a collective Supreme Court position on due process that might be called selective incorporation plus fundamental rights. As the following table shows, the Supreme Court either explicitly or implicitly has incorporated every specific provision of the First, Fourth, Fifth, Sixth, and Eighth Amendments, with only two exceptions: the Fifth Amendment's grand jury requirement, and the Eighth Amendment's ban on excessive bail and fines. (The Second and Seventh Amendments, which do not involve criminal procedure or individual rights, have not been adjudicated in the context of due process, and the Third Amendment has never reached the Supreme Court at all.) The requirement that state criminal defendants be indicted by a grand jury (as opposed to the procedure used in some western states where a judge determines whether an indictment should be issued after being presented with "information" by the prosecution) was explicitly excluded from due process over a century ago in *Hurtado* v. *California*, and the Court has shown no inclination to reexamine that.

Bill of Rights Provisions Made Applicable to the States through the Fourteenth Amendment

Amendment	Clause	Case	Year
First	Establishment of religion	*Everson* v. *Board of Education*	1947
	Free exercise of religion	*Cantwell* v. *Connecticut*	1940
	Freedom of speech	*Gitlow* v. *New York*	1925
	Freedom of press	*Gitlow* v. *New York*	1925
	Right of assembly	*DeJonge* v. *Oregon*	1937
	Right to petition	*DeJonge* v. *Oregon*	1937
Fourth	Search and seizure	*Wolf* v. *Colorado*	1949
Fifth	Double jeopardy	*Benton* v. *Maryland*	1969
	Self-incrimination	*Malloy* v. *Hogan*	1964
	Just compensation	*Chicago, Burlington & Quincy RR Co.* v. *Chicago*	1897
Sixth	Speedy trial	*Klopfer* v. *North Carolina*	1967
	Public trial	*In re Oliver*	1948
	Jury trial	*Duncan* v. *Louisiana*	1968
	Impartial jury	*Irvin* v. *Dowd*	1961
	Nature of accusation	*In re Oliver*	1948
	Confrontation of witnesses	*Pointer* v. *Texas*	1965
	Compulsory process for witnesses	*Washington* v. *Texas*	1967
	Assistance of counsel	*Gideon* v. *Wainwright*	1963
Eighth	Cruel and unusual punishment	*Robinson* v. *California*	1962

judgment. The Eighth Amendment matter is more complicated; while the Court has never explicitly incorporated the prohibition against excessive bail and fines, it has sometimes spoken as if the issue were settled, as in a 1989 case holding that state laws permitting unrestricted civil damage awards did not violate the provision.

It would appear that Justice Black has come very close to winning the Fourteenth Amendment interpretive war, not through wholesale incorporation of the Bill of Rights as he would have liked, but rather through a piecemeal, incremental process which has taken nearly 50 years to complete. Black might consider this something of a hollow victory, however, because along the way the Court has also accepted the quite different logic of fundamental fairness by defining due process to include rights that are not grounded in specific provisions of the Bill of Rights, the most notable of these being privacy. Although it is unlikely that Justice Frankfurter, given his deference to state authority, would have joined the Court majority in *Roe* v. *Wade*, there is no doubt that it was his definition of due process as fundamental fairness, especially its emphasis on evolving standards of justice, that provided the theoretical foundation for that decision.

Clearly, then, the concept of liberty has been "nationalized" by the Supreme Court—that is, made nearly uniform as a limitation on national and state governments. This means that American citizens enjoy virtually the same set of constitutional protections whether they be in Maine, Mississippi, or Washington, D.C. To understand more completely what this liberty consists of, we will now look at two different versions of the concept of due process—procedural and substantive—that have evolved over the last century. In general, procedural due process relates to the *enforcement* of government decisions, prohibiting government from acting arbitrarily as it carries out its policies. Substantive due process, on the other hand, demands that the *content* of those policies be fair, that any statutory restrictions on personal freedom be reasonably related to legitimate government functions. Obviously these two dimensions of due process are closely related conceptually; both seek to ensure that citizens are treated fairly in their encounters with government. Functionally, however, they are separate and distinct. For example, many perfectly acceptable laws run into constitutional difficulties because their implementation does not meet procedural due process requirements. At the same time, procedurally correct enforcement cannot save a statute whose substance violates basic principles of fairness. While substantive due process generally involves *legislative* actions, procedural due process is usually associated with *judicial, executive,* or *administrative* actions.

PROCEDURAL DUE PROCESS

To Englishmen of the seventeenth and eighteenth centuries, the term *procedural due process* would have seemed redundant. Due process of law was then understood to be concerned entirely with procedures, and almost exclusively with *criminal* procedures. While most of the procedural protections delineated in the Bill of Rights are criminal in nature, the list does contain a few noncriminal procedural rights as well. Examples include the Fifth Amendment's prohibition against government's taking private property without just compensation and the Seventh Amendment's command that civil suits involving claims of more than 20 dollars be tried before a jury. It is clear that both the Fifth and Fourteenth Amendments contemplate noncriminal applications of due process by requiring that the concept be employed whenever a citizen's "life, liberty, or property" is at stake.

It is ironic, considering the principle's deep roots in Anglo-American legal practice, that the first half of the nineteenth century was almost devoid of Supreme Court litigation involving procedural due process. This is partly because at that time the United States government played only a small role in criminal matters, and also because the Bill of Rights was not then understood to limit state authority. Thus for many years the Supreme Court had little opportunity to review either federal or state criminal procedures. As we will see in the section on substantive due process, for many years after the Fourteenth Amendment was adopted, the Supreme Court's primary interest in due process was as a bulwark against state interference with economic liberty and corporate property. Not until the twentieth century did the Court began to pay much attention to developing procedural due process as a constitutional doctrine. Once that process began, however, it proceeded apace, and between the 1930s and the 1960s the Court presided over a virtual "due process revolution" which effected comprehensive, top-down reform of criminal procedures at both the national and state levels. The incorporation table in the previous section gives some indication of the scope and nature of that reform, but of course those cases are only the tip of the constitutional iceberg. For each landmark incorporation case there are scores of others which apply that particular Bill of Rights provision to the myriad procedural circumstances that arise in the American criminal justice system. Some of the most important of these cases are excerpted in this chapter, and others are discussed in the accompanying commentaries. Here we will limit ourselves to a brief sketch of the major procedural due process developments at three crucial states of criminal proceedings—the pretrial stage, which includes criminal investigation and arrest; the trial itself; and the posttrial phase, including punishment—specifying what the Supreme Court has said about due process requirements at each of these stages.

DUE PROCESS BEFORE TRIAL

The Fourth Amendment's prohibition against "unreasonable searches and seizures" has been interpreted by the Supreme Court as placing some restrictions on the activities of law enforcement officers in search of either evidence or suspects in criminal cases. Since *Mapp* v. *Ohio* in 1961, state and local police have had to operate under the same due process standards as federal agents. Since few fact situations are identical, no area of procedural due process has so many minutely detailed rules as the law of search and seizure. In general, a "reasonable" search is one that has been authorized by a magistrate who is satisfied that there is "probable cause" to believe that a search of a particular place will yield evidence relating to a particular crime. A warrant is required to search any area where a suspect has a "reasonable expectation of privacy." This clearly includes one's place of residence and probably one's automobile, but does not generally include public places. Wiretaps and other forms of electronic surveillance are considered searches and must meet the warrant requirements of the Fourth Amendment.

An arrest is considered a seizure of a person and therefore falls within the scope of the Fourth Amendment. A suspect may be arrested in a public place without a warrant, but except in emergency situations warrantless home arrests cannot be made. A police officer making a lawful arrest with or without a warrant may search the person and the immediate area for weapons or contraband that might be destroyed. In the case of an automobile, this means the entire passenger compartment, including the glove compartment, but not the trunk.

Under the "exclusionary rule," evidence obtained through a search or seizure that falls short of due process standards cannot be used in a subsequent prosecution. This rule, which has been in effect in federal cases since 1914 and in state cases since 1961, has had many vigorous critics, including former Chief Justice Warren Burger, who objected to having criminal convictions lost because of harmless "technicalities" or even occasional police misconduct. For a time it appeared that a majority of the Court might throw out the exclusionary rule altogether, but in 1984 the Court limited itself to carving out an exception to the rule for police officers who rely in good faith on a defective search warrant.

Once the police have arrested a suspect and charged him or her with a particular crime, an array of Fifth and Sixth Amendment procedural safeguards come into play. In general, a suspect is protected by the right against self-incrimination and the right to counsel. This area of procedural due process is treated at length in Chapter 1 in the commentary accompanying *Gideon* v. *Wainwright* and that discussion need not be reiterated here. Suffice it to say that the Court has recognized that station-house detention is inherently coercive and that failure to observe due process at this stage may taint all subsequent phases of the criminal proceedings.

Under most state constitutions or statutes a defendant is entitled to be released on appropriate bail prior to the trial unless charged with a capital crime or (in noncapital punishment states) its equivalent. There is no such guarantee in the United States Constitution (though "excessive bail" is prohibited) and the Supreme Court has upheld against a Fifth Amendment challenge the Bail Reform Act of 1984 which permits pretrial "preventive detention" of federal defendants deemed to pose a danger to the community.

DUE PROCESS AT TRIAL

Since the 1960s the Supreme Court has made every aspect of the Bill of Rights relating to trial procedures applicable to the states through the Fourteenth Amendment. Under the Sixth Amendment criminal defendants are entitled to "a speedy and public trial" before an impartial jury. In 1967 the Court ruled that it was a violation of the speedy trial rule for the prosecution to suspend charges "without prejudice," a procedure which permitted their reinstatement at any time. It has also held that, notwithstanding the Sixth Amendment requirement that a criminal trial be held in the district where the crime took place, a trial must be moved to another jurisdiction if pretrial publicity has made it unlikely that an unbiased jury can be found. The Court has held that a criminal jury may consist of no fewer than six members, who must be drawn from a pool that is representative of the community. Although the jury itself need not be a cross section of the community, due process requires that no distinct and numerically significant groups be underrepresented in the jury pool. The public may not be excluded from a criminal trial, including pretrial hearings, without a finding that such exclusion is necessary to guarantee a fair trial.

The Sixth Amendment also requires that criminal defendants "have the assistance of counsel." As we noted in Chapter 1, in the discussion of *Gideon* v. *Wainwright*, about half of the states had made this right available by the time the Supreme Court incorporated it into the due process clause in 1963. In *Gideon* the right to counsel was made applicable in felony cases, those involving a possible jail term of 6 months or more. Later the Court extended the rule to all crimes carrying possible jail terms of any length.

Another aspect of procedural due process which is relevant at the trial stage is the Fifth Amendment privilege against self-incrimination. In the early twentieth century the Supreme Court refused to extend this protection to state proceedings, ruling that a state trial judge's comment on the fact that defendants had not testified on their own behalf did not violate due process. In 1961 the Court incorporated the self-incrimination privilege (*Malloy* v. *Hogan*), and has since ruled that due process requires that a trial judge must, on the defendant's request, instruct the jury not to draw a negative inference from the defendant's failure to testify at trial. Moreover, under the Fifth and Fourteenth Amendments a prosecutor is prohibited from commenting on a defendant's failure to testify on his or her own behalf. On the other hand, the Court has held that the Fifth Amendment protects testimonial rather than physical evidence, and hence does not forbid a state from requiring a defendant from providing voice, blood, or handwriting samples even if such evidence may be used against him or her.

DUE PROCESS AFTER TRIAL

The Eighth Amendment prohibition against "cruel and unusual punishment," which was made applicable to the states in 1962, has been used since then to restrict state criminal punishments in a variety of ways. The most spectacular of these was the Court's decision in 1972 holding all state capital punishment statutes then in effect unconstitutional (see *Furman* v. *Georgia*, excerpted and discussed in Chapter 1). With respect to noncapital punishments, the Court has held that a penalty which is disproportionate to the crime for which it is inflicted is cruel and unusual. It has also employed the Eighth Amendment to strike down statutes that punish so-called status offenses such as "being a common drunkard," while emphasizing that related *activities* such as appearing in public while intoxicated may still be made illegal.

DUE PROCESS IN NONCRIMINAL SETTINGS

It should be clear from the foregoing discussion that in the last several decades the Supreme Court has played an extraordinarily active role in setting constitutional standards of procedural due process. Indeed, it might be argued that the application of due process to state criminal procedures has been the Court's most impressive sustained policy-making achievement in this century. But the Court's leadership of the due process revolution has not been confined to the criminal area. Following the vast expansion of government benefits and services under President Franklin Roosevelt's New Deal, later supplemented and extended by President Lyndon Johnson's Great Society, the Court began to recognize that what government gives it may also try to take away. In the 1960s, therefore, the Court moved its revolution to a second stage by extending procedural due process to noncriminal encounters with government in which citizens' liberty and property interests were at risk. This led to a series of decisions in which the Supreme Court interpreted the Fifth and Fourteenth Amendments' due process clauses as prohibiting federal and state agencies from withholding or withdrawing statutory entitlements without observing fair procedures.

For example, the Court has held that due process applies whenever the government seeks to deprive persons of parental rights, welfare benefits, certain kinds of government jobs, or national citizenship. Similarly, procedural due process must be observed before a public utility can terminate gas or electric service for nonpayment of a disputed bill, before an individual can be involuntarily hospitalized or medicated, before a person's wages can be garnished without a court order, and before a student can be suspended or expelled from a public school. Under certain emergency situations the Court has permitted the due process hearing to take place *after* the deprivation has occurred, as in the case of a state law requiring immediate suspension of a driver's license when a person arrested for drunk driving refuses to take a breathalyzer test.

What does procedural due process involve in such cases? At a minimum, the Supreme Court has said, an individual must be given an opportunity to speak to a proposed action before an impartial decision maker. Due process may also require, or at least permit, the calling of witnesses, confrontation of one's accusers, if any, and the assistance of legal counsel in making one's case. The Supreme Court has resisted imposing a uniform, across-the-board standard of procedural due process and generally has allowed less rigorous procedures when liberty or property interests that it deems less important are involved. For example, the hearing requirements for short disciplinary suspensions from public school are considerably less stringent than those that must precede a longer suspension or expulsion (see *Goss* v. *Lopez,* excerpted in this chapter). Similarly, a lesser standard of proof is required to withdraw medical disability payments than to take away welfare benefits.

Most of the liberty and property interests protected by procedural due process are not themselves required by the Constitution. For example, a state is under no constitutional obligation to grant its citizens licenses to practice a particular trade or profession. However, the Supreme Court has ruled that once a state has made the policy choice to license a profession, enforcement of that policy in particular cases—specifically, the decision to grant and to withdraw licenses—is subject under the Constitution to procedural due process. Thus, while prisoners have no constitutional right to a parole hearing, if a state law confers such a right, due process requires a fair system for determining whether a prisoner should be released on parole.

The high water mark of noncriminal procedural due process occurred in the mid-1970s, when the Supreme Court defined liberty and property interests expansively enough to include entitlements derived not only from specific statutes but even from the general expectations fostered by past governmental practices. Since then, however, a more politically conservative Court has insisted that rights be grounded more explicitly in state or federal laws, and has tolerated less formality in the procedures that it has required.

SUBSTANTIVE DUE PROCESS

We turn now to the second version of due process, which traces its constitutional roots to the late nineteenth century, a time of rapid economic and social change in the United States. The Civil War spurred the rise of the railroads, which in turn created new markets, encouraged westward expansion, and generally stimulated the emergence of an industrial sector based largely on the cheap labor supplied by new European immigrants. Eventually state legislatures began to respond to worker and consumer demands by passing legislation regulating wages, prices, hours, and working conditions. Outgunned in the legislatures, the railroads and other corporate interests counterattacked in the federal courts, thus becoming the first of many interest groups to look to the judiciary for their political salvation. The legal profession as a whole was not yet the economic and social elite that it would later become; until well into the twentieth century there were few law schools, and most lawyers entered the profession by "reading law" in the office of an established practitioner and then sitting for a perfunctory examination. However, the federal courts of the day were heavily staffed by judges who had achieved their high status through previous service as corporation lawyers, and who could be counted on to give their former employers a respectful hearing. The corporations' task was to fashion a plausible constitutional case for reversing the considerable body of nineteenth-century precedent supporting government regulation of economic activities. To persuade the courts that the constitutional environment had changed, the corporations seized upon the Fourteenth Amendment, whose open-ended phraseology seemed to offer several hooks on which to hang a constitutional case against state regulation.

Of the three key limits on state action in the Fourteenth Amendment—the privileges and immunities clause, the due process clause, and the equal protection clause—privileges and immunities seemed at first to offer the greatest potential for advancing the corporations' cause. If the courts could be persuaded that the right to do business was one of the privileges and immunities of United States citizenship which under the amendment could not be abridged by state action, then virtually any law that regulated a business enterprise would be unconstitutional. This argument was made before the Supreme Court in *The Slaughterhouse Cases* in 1873, but the Court responded with such a restrictive reading of the privileges and immunities of United States citizenship (see the case excerpt and discussion in this chapter) that the clause virtually disappeared from the Constitution.

Bloody but unbowed, the corporations then turned to their second line of defense, the Fourteenth Amendment's due process clause. Soon they unveiled an ingenious two-part argument, asserting first that businesses were "persons" within the meaning of the due process clause, and second that the "liberty and property" protected under the clause included private economic rights. Thus, under the Fourteenth Amendment, states were severely limited in the extent to which they could regulate businesses.

The Supreme Court responded skeptically at first. In *Munn* v. *Illinois* in 1877, Chief Justice Morrison Waite held that an Illinois law setting storage rates for grain-elevator operators did not violate due process because grain elevators were a "business affected with a public interest," and thus subject to traditional state police powers exercised for the public good. Waite's reasoning held out the possibility that the Court might someday find that a state had violated due process by regulating a business that was ostensibly private and not sufficiently connected to a valid public interest. *Munn* has been described as a "promissory note" on which the corporations were determined to collect. For the next decade the Supreme Court continued to uphold state regulatory laws, while issuing increasingly urgent reminders that there were limits to their police powers.

Finally in 1890, in *Chicago, Milwaukee & St. Paul Railway Co.* v. *Minnesota,* the Supreme Court for the first time declared a state regulatory act unconstitutional on due process grounds because it contained no provision for judicial review of the rates established by a railroad commission. Although the decision was made on traditional procedural grounds, it opened the door for an altogether different standard of due process to be employed. Henceforth the Court would have the last word on the reasonableness of state economic legislation, and in each case would be reviewing the substance of the law to make that determination. If a majority of the Court concluded that the law constituted an unnecessary or arbitrary interference with the plaintiff's economic liberty, it would be struck down as a violation of due process. Thus was born the doctrine of substantive due process, which later became a vehicle for protecting noneconomic rights, such as privacy, from abridgment by the states.

Between 1890 and 1937, a Supreme Court dominated by strong supporters of laissez-faire economics found several hundred state laws to be unreasonable and therefore unconstitutional. During this sustained period of conservative activism the Court was not without its critics. One of the most eloquent was Justice Oliver

Wendell Holmes, Jr., who dissented from most of the Court's substantive due process decisions (see his dissent in *Lochner* v. *New York*, excerpted in this chapter). As a political conservative, Holmes had little sympathy with workers' interests and even less confidence that regulatory schemes could work in their behalf, but as a judicial restraintist he believed that the political marketplace ought to be allowed to function without interference from the judiciary. Later Holmes was joined in frequent dissent by Associate Justice Louis Brandeis, a leading figure in the progressive movement who had inspired much of the legislation that the Court found constitutionally invalid.

The Court maintained its role as a "super-legislature" in economic regulation cases until 1937. Then, in the wake of the political crisis provoked by President Roosevelt's Court-packing plan, it finally lowered the flag on substantive due process in the case of *West Coast Hotel* v. *Parrish*. Claiming that new economic conditions required "fresh consideration" of the Court's earlier position on the reasonableness of state economic regulations, Chief Justice Charles Evans Hughes spoke for a 5–4 majority upholding a minimum wage law as a reasonable exercise of state power. The public interest, he said, was not served by having workers exploited by employers. Despite the outraged dissents of conservative justices, the new majority held firm, and the economic version of substantive due process was laid to rest. Justice William O. Douglas provided a belated epitaph for the doctrine in a 1955 case in which the Supreme Court rejected a due process challenge to an Oklahoma law prohibiting opticians from fitting new frames without a prescription by an optometrist or an opthalmologist. "The day is done," Douglas wrote, "when this Court uses the Due Process Clause of the Fourteenth Amendment to strike down state laws, regulatory of business and industrial conditions, because they may be unwise, improvident, or out of harmony with a particular school of thought" (*Williamson* v. *Lee Optical Co.*).

Substantive due process, however, remains alive and well in relation to other personal freedoms. In 1925, when the Court began the long process of selectively incorporating Bill of Rights guarantees through the Fourteenth Amendment, the first liberties it chose to so recognize were the free speech and press guarantees of the First Amendment (*Gitlow* v. *New York*). By declaring these to be among the liberties protected by the First Amendment, the Court was giving states the same message as in the economic regulation area, namely that only the most compelling state interest would justify interference with such a fundamental right. Later this would come to be called the *strict scrutiny* test, and would be applied in equal protection cases as well (see Chapter 7 for a more extended discussion of strict scrutiny). The Court has subsequently brought the other provisions of the First Amendment under the same standard (see Chapters 5 and 6 for consideration of these areas of constitutional law).

Other fundamental rights that the Court has held to be covered by substantive due process include privacy, voting, and interstate travel. The right of privacy encompasses a woman's freedom to obtain an abortion without state interference (except in the last trimester of pregnancy), the right to buy contraceptives, the right to marry and to raise and educate children, and the freedom to read obscene material in one's home. It does not, however, include the right to engage in acts of sodomy. Both the right to vote and the right to travel from state to state are protected by the equal protection clause as well as by the due process clause.

CONCLUSION

Few areas of constitutional law have been as controversial, both inside and outside the Supreme Court, as that of due process. In interpreting the requirements of the Fifth and the Fourteenth Amendments' due process clauses, the Court has found itself dealing with each of the three most divisive issues in America's political history: the relationship between the nation and the states, the relationship between government and industry, and the relationship between government and its citizens. In the latter area, of course, the issue of due process is particularly compelling, and the Court has played a major role not only in seeing that government obeys the constitutional command that it treat its citizens fairly, but also in determining just what that treatment must entail.

Bibliography

ABRAHAM, HENRY J. *Freedom and the Court.* New York: Oxford University Press, 1972.

JAMES, JOSEPH B. *The Framing of the Fourteenth Amendment.* Urbana: University of Illinois Press, 1956.

LEVY, LEONARD. *Origins of the Fifth Amendment.* New York: Oxford University Press, 1968.

McCLOSKEY, ROBERT. *The Modern Supreme Court.* Cambridge: Harvard University Press, 1972.

STEAMER, ROBERT J. *The Supreme Court in Crisis.* Amherst: University of Massachusetts Press, 1971.

The Slaughterhouse Cases

16 WALLACE 36 (1873)

The Civil War resolved the political question of how the states and the national government would relate to one another, but constitutionally, despite the passage of the Thirteenth, Fourteenth, and Fifteenth Amendments, the old principle that the states and the national government each retained sovereign, independent powers, and that each had a sovereign realm not to be subverted by the other, was to be a long time dying. Well into the twentieth century the term *states' rights* continued to be a part of constitutional discourse with the Supreme Court frequently raising the Tenth Amendment as a bar to federal intrusion into state matters. In *The Slaughterhouse Cases* the Court, in its first interpretation of the Fourteenth Amendment, refused to see any but minimal constitutional limits on state power and thus little alteration in the dynamics of the federal system.

In 1869 the Louisiana legislature enacted a law "to protect the health of the city of New Orleans" by incorporating a single slaughterhouse company and empowering it to do the exclusive slaughtering of animals in the city. All remaining butchers in the city were required to use and pay for that company's facilities. The state courts sustained the law and on appeal to the Supreme Court it was alleged by those challenging the law's constitutionality that it violated the Thirteenth Amendment as well as the three main clauses of the Fourteenth: privileges and immunities, equal protection, and due process of law.

SAMUEL F. MILLER

Appointed to the Supreme Court by President Abraham Lincoln in 1862, Samuel Miller, who had never held public office of any kind, became one of the Court's towering figures during his 28 years on the bench. A moderate on a Court generally dedicated to laissez-faire economics and Social Darwinism, Miller became the intellectual leader of the liberal wing that would cautiously permit some government regulation of the mushrooming corporate enterprises. With the exception of his restrictive interpretation of the privileges and immunities clause, however, Miller's opinions in Fourteenth Amendment cases were to be reversed while he remained on the Court.

Mr. Justice **Miller** delivered the opinion of the court.

[The Court discusses the state "police powers" upon which the Louisiana legislature relied in incorporating a single slaughterhouse for New Orleans and its environs, concluding that such powers are well grounded in the Constitution.]

. . .

It may, therefore, be considered as established, that the authority of the legislature of Louisiana to pass the present statute is ample, unless some restraint in the exercise of that power be found in the constitution of that State or in the amendments to the Constitution of the United States, adopted since the date of the decisions we have already cited.

If any such restraint is supposed to exist in the constitution of the State, the Supreme Court of Louisiana having necessarily passed on that question, it would not be open to review in this court.

The plaintiffs in error accepting this issue, allege that the statute is a violation of the Constitution of the United States in these several particulars:

That it creates an involuntary servitude forbidden by the thirteenth article of amendment;

That it abridges the privileges and immunities of citizens of the United States;

That it denies to the plaintiffs the equal protection of the laws; and,

That it deprives them of their property without due process of law; contrary to the provisions of the first section of the fourteenth article of amendment.

This court is thus called upon for the first time to give construction to these articles.

. . .

Twelve articles of amendment were added to the Federal Constitution soon after the original organization of the government under it in 1789. Of these all but the last were adopted so soon afterwards as to justify the statement that they were practically contemporaneous with the adoption of the original; and the twelfth, adopted in eighteen hundred and three, was so nearly so as to have become, like all the others, historical and of another age. But within the last eight years three other articles of amendment of vast importance have been added by the voice of the people to that now venerable instrument.

The most cursory glance at these articles discloses a unity of purpose, when taken in connection with the history of the times, which cannot fail to have an important bearing on any question of doubt concerning their true meaning. Nor can such doubts, when any reasonably exist, be safely and rationally solved without a reference to that history; for in it is found the occasion and the necessity for recurring again to the great source of power in this country, the people of the States, for additional guarantees of human rights; additional powers to the Federal government; additional restraints upon those of the States. Fortunately that history is fresh within the memory of us all, and its leading features, as they bear upon the matter before us, free from doubt.

The institution of African slavery, as it existed in about half the States of the Union, and the contests pervading the public mind for many years, between those who desired its curtailment and ultimate extinction and those who desired additional safeguards for its security and perpetuation, culminated in the effort, on the part of most of the States in which slavery existed, to separate from the Federal government, and to resist its authority. This constituted the war of the rebellion, and whatever auxiliary causes may have contributed to bring about this war, undoubtedly the overshadowing and efficient cause was African slavery.

In that struggle slavery, as a legalized social relation, perished. It perished as a necessity of the bitterness and force of the conflict. When the armies of freedom found themselves upon the soil of slavery they could do nothing less than free the poor victims whose enforced servitude was the foundation of the quarrel. And when hard pressed in the contest these men (for they proved themselves men in that terrible crisis) offered their services and were accepted by thousands to aid in suppressing the unlawful rebellion, slavery was at an end wherever the Federal government succeeded in that purpose. The proclamation of President Lincoln expressed an accomplished fact as to a large portion of the insurrectionary districts, when he declared slavery abolished in them all. But the war being over, those who had succeeded in re-establishing the authority of the Federal government were not content to permit this great act of emancipation to rest on the actual results of the contest or the proclamation of the Executive, both of which might have been questioned in after times, and they determined to place this main and most valuable result in the Constitution of the restored Union as one of its fundamental articles. Hence the thirteenth article of amendment of that instrument.

. . .

. . . Among the first acts of legislation adopted by several of the States in the legislative bodies which claimed to be in their normal relations with the Federal government, were laws which imposed upon the colored race onerous disabilities and burdens, and curtailed their rights in the pursuit of life, liberty, and property to such an extent that their freedom was of little value, while they had lost the protection which they had received from their former owners from motives both of interest and humanity.

. . .

These circumstances, whatever of falsehood or misconception may have been mingled with their presentation, forced upon the statesmen who had conducted the Federal government in safety through the crisis of the rebellion, and who supposed that by the thirteenth article of amendment they had secured the result of their labors, the conviction that something more was necessary in the way of constitutional protection to the unfortunate race who had suffered so much. They accordingly passed through Congress the proposition for the fourteenth amendment, and they declined to treat as restored to their full participation in the government of the Union the States which had been in insurrection, until they ratified that article by a formal vote of their legislative bodies.

Before we proceed to examine more critically the provisions of this amendment, on which the plaintiffs in error rely, let us complete and dismiss the history of the recent amendments, as that history relates to the general purpose which pervades them all. A few years' experience satisfied the thoughtful men who had been the authors of the other two amendments that, notwithstanding the restraints of those articles on the States, and the laws passed under the additional powers granted to Congress, these were inadequate for the protection of life, liberty, and property, without which freedom to the slave was no boon. They were in all those States denied the right of suffrage. The laws were administered by the white man alone. It was urged that a race of men distinctively marked as was the negro, living in the midst of another and dominant race, could never be fully secured in their person and their property without the right of suffrage.

Hence the fifteenth amendment, which declares that "the right of a citizen of the United States to vote shall not be denied or abridged by any State on account of race, color, or previous condition of servitude." The negro having, by the fourteenth amendment, been declared to be a citizen of the United States, is thus made a voter in every State of the Union.

. . .

We do not say that no one else but the negro can share in this protection. Both the language and spirit of these articles are to have their fair and just weight in any question of construction. Undoubtedly while negro slavery alone was in the mind of the Congress which proposed the thirteenth article, it forbids any other kind of slavery, now or hereafter. If Mexican peonage or the Chinese coolie labor system shall develop slavery of the Mexican or Chinese race within our territory, this amendment may safely be trusted to make it void. And so if other rights are assailed by the States which properly and necessarily fall within the protection of these articles, that protection will apply, though the party interested may not be of African descent. But what we do say, and what we wish to be understood is, that in any fair and just construction of any section or phrase of these amendments, it is necessary to look to the purpose which we have said was the pervading spirit of them all, the evil which they were designed to remedy, and the process of continued addition to the Constitution, until that purpose was supposed to be accomplished, as far as constitutional law can accomplish it.

The first section of the fourteenth article, to which our attention is more specially invited, opens with a definition of citizenship—not only citizenship of the United States, but citizenship of the States. No such definition was previously found in the Constitution, nor had any attempt been made to define it by act of Congress. It had been the occasion of much discussion in the courts, by the executive departments, and in the public journals. It had been said by eminent judges that no man was a citizen of the United States, except as he was a citizen of one of the States composing the Union. Those, therefore, who had been born and resided always in the District of Columbia or in the Territories, though within the United States, were not citi-

zens. Whether this proposition was sound or not had never been judicially decided. But it had been held by this court, in the celebrated Dred Scott case, only a few years before the outbreak of the civil war, that a man of African descent, whether a slave or not, was not and could not be a citizen of a State or of the United States. This decision, while it met the condemnation of some of the ablest statesmen and constitutional lawyers of the country, had never been overruled; and if it was to be accepted as a constitutional limitation of the right of citizenship, then all the negro race who had recently been made freemen, were still, not only not citizens, but were incapable of becoming so by anything short of an amendment to the Constitution.

To remove this difficulty primarily, and to establish a clear and comprehensive definition of citizenship which should declare what should constitute citizenship of the United States, and also citizenship of a State, the first clause of the first section was framed.

"All persons born or naturalized in the United States, and subject to the jurisdiction thereof, are citizens of the United States and of the State wherein they reside."

The first observation we have to make on this clause is, that it puts at rest both the questions which we stated to have been the subject of differences of opinion. It declares that persons may be citizens of the United States without regard to their citizenship of a particular State, and it overturns the Dred Scott decision by making *all persons* born within the United States and subject to its jurisdiction citizens of the United States. That its main purpose was to establish the citizenship of the negro can admit of no doubt. . . .

The next observation is more important in view of the arguments of counsel in the present case. It is, that the distinction between citizenship of the United States and citizenship of a State is clearly recognized and established. Not only may a man be a citizen of the United States without being a citizen of a State, but an important element is necessary to convert the former into the latter. He must reside within the State to make him a citizen of it, but it is only necessary that he should be born or naturalized in the United States to be a citizen of the Union.

It is quite clear, then, that there is a citizenship of the United States, and a citizenship of a State, which are distinct from each other, and which depend upon different characteristics or circumstances in the individual.

We think this distinction and its explicit recognition in this amendment of great weight in this argument, because the next paragraph of this same section, which is the one mainly relied on by the plaintiffs in error, speaks only of privileges and immunities of citizens of the United States, and does not speak of those of citizens of the several States. The argument, however, in favor of the plaintiffs rests wholly on the assumption that the citizenship is the same, and the privileges and immunities guaranteed by the clause are the same.

The language is, "No State shall make or enforce any law which shall abridge the privileges or immunities of citizens of *the United States.*" It is a little remarkable, if this clause was intended as a protection to the citizen of a State against the legislative power of his own State, that the word citizen of the State should be left out when it is so carefully used, and used in contradistinction to citizens of the United States, in the very sentence which precedes it. It is too clear for argument that the change in phraseology was adopted understandingly and with a purpose.

Of the privileges and immunities of the citizen of the United States, and of the privileges and immunities of the citizen of the State, and what they respectively are, we will presently consider; but we wish to state here that it is only the former which are placed by this clause under the protection of the Federal Constitution, and that the latter, whatever they may be, are not intended to have any additional protection by this paragraph of the amendment.

. . .

Having shown that the privileges and immunities relied on in the argument are those which belong to citizens of the States as such, and that they are left to the State governments for security and protection, and not by this article placed under the special care of the Federal government, we may hold ourselves excused from defining the privileges and immunities of citizens

of the United States which no State can abridge, until some case involving those privileges may make it necessary to do so.

But lest it should be said that no such privileges and immunities are to be found if those we have been considering are excluded, we venture to suggest some which owe their existence to the Federal government, its National character, its Constitution, or its laws.

One of these is well described in the case of *Crandall* v. *Nevada.* It is said to be the right of the citizen of this great country, protected by implied guarantees of its Constitution, "to come to the seat of government to assert any claim he may have upon that government, to transact any business he may have with it, to seek its protection, to share its offices, to engage in administering its functions. He has the right of free access to its seaports, through which all operations of foreign commerce are conducted, to the subtreasuries, land offices, and courts of justice in the several States." . . .

Another privilege of a citizen of the United States is to demand the care and protection of the Federal government over his life, liberty, and property when on the high seas or within the jurisdiction of a foreign government. Of this there can be no doubt, nor that the right depends upon his character as a citizen of the United States. The right to peaceably assemble and petition for redress of grievances, the privilege of the writ of *habeas corpus*, are rights of the citizen guaranteed by the Federal Constitution. The right to use the navigable waters of the United States, however they may penetrate the territory of the several States, all rights secured to our citizens by treaties with foreign nations, are dependent upon citizenship of the United States, and not citizenship of a State. One of these privileges is conferred by the very article under consideration. It is that a citizen of the United States can, of his own volition, become a citizen of any State of the Union by a *bonâ fide* residence therein, with the same rights as other citizens of that State. To these may be added the rights secured by the thirteenth and fifteenth articles of amendment, and by the other clause of the fourteenth, next to be considered.

But it is useless to pursue this branch of the inquiry, since we are of opinion that the rights claimed by these plaintiffs in error, if they have any existence, are not privileges and immunities of citizens of the United States within the meaning of the clause of the fourteenth amendment under consideration.

"All persons born or naturalized in the United States, and subject to the jurisdiction thereof, are citizens of the United States and of the State wherein they reside. No State shall make or enforce any law which shall abridge the privileges or immunities of citizens of the United States; nor shall any State deprive any person of life, liberty, or property without due process of law, nor deny to any person within its jurisdiction the equal protection of its laws."

The argument has not been much pressed in these cases that the defendant's charter deprives the plaintiffs of their property without due process of law, or that it denies to them the equal protection of the law. The first of these paragraphs has been in the Constitution since the adoption of the fifth amendment, as a restraint upon the Federal power. It is also to be found in some form of expression in the constitutions of nearly all the States, as a restraint upon the power of the States. This law then, has practically been the same as it now is during the existence of the government, except so far as the present amendment may place the restraining power over the States in this matter in the hands of the Federal government.

We are not without judicial interpretation, therefore, both State and National, of the meaning of this clause. And it is sufficient to say that under no construction of that provision that we have ever seen, or any that we deem admissible, can the restraint imposed by the State of Louisiana upon the exercise of their trade by the butchers of New Orleans be held to be a deprivation of property within the meaning of that provision.

"Nor shall any State deny to any person within its jurisdiction the equal protection of the laws."

In the light of the history of these amendments, and the pervading purpose of them, which we have already discussed, it is not difficult to give a meaning to this clause. The existence of laws in the States where the newly emancipated negroes resided, which discrimi-

nated with gross injustice and hardship against them as a class, was the evil to be remedied by this clause, and by it such laws are forbidden.

. . .

Mr. Justice **Field,** with whom the Chief Justice Mr. Justice **Swayne,** and Mr. Justice **Bradley** concurred, dissenting.

. . .

In the law in question there are only two provisions which can properly be called police regulations—the one which requires the landing and slaughtering of animals below the city of New Orleans, and the other which requires the inspection of the animals before they are slaughtered. When these requirements are complied with, the sanitary purposes of the act are accomplished. In all other particulars the act is a mere grant to a corporation created by it of special and exclusive privileges by which the health of the city is in no way promoted. It is plain that if the corporation can, without endangering the health of the public, carry on the business of landing, keeping, and slaughtering cattle within a district below the city embracing an area of over a thousand square miles, it would not endanger the public health if other persons were also permitted to carry on the same business within the same district under similar conditions as to the inspection of the animals. The health of the city might require the removal from its limits and suburbs of all buildings for keeping and slaughtering cattle, but no such object could possibly justify legislation removing such buildings from a large part of the State for the benefit of a single corporation. The pretence of sanitary regulations for the grant of the exclusive privileges is a shallow one, which merits only this passing notice.

. . .

The act of Louisiana presents the naked case, unaccompanied by any public considerations, where a right to pursue a lawful and necessary calling, previously enjoyed by every citizen, and in connection with which a thousand persons were daily employed, is taken away and vested exclusively for twenty-five years, for an extensive district and a large population, in a single corporation, or its exercise is for that period restricted to the establishments of the corporation, and there allowed only upon onerous conditions.

. . .

The question presented is, therefore, one of the gravest importance, not merely to the parties here, but to the whole country. It is nothing less than the question whether the recent amendments to the Federal Constitution protect the citizens of the United States against the deprivation of their common rights by State legislation. In my judgment the fourteenth amendment does afford such protection, and was so intended by the Congress which framed and the States which adopted it.

. . .

. . . The provisions of the fourteenth amendment, which is properly a supplement to the thirteenth, cover, in my judgment, the case before us, and inhibit any legislation which confers special and exclusive privileges like these under consideration. The amendment was adopted to obviate objections which had been raised and pressed with great force to the validity of the Civil Rights Act, and to place the common rights of American citizens under the protection of the National government. . . .

. . .

The first clause of the fourteenth amendment . . . recognizes in express terms, if it does not create, citizens of the United States, and it makes their citizenship dependent upon the place of their birth, or the fact of their adoption, and not upon the constitution or laws of any State or the condition of their ancestry. A citizen of a State is now only a citizen of the United States residing in that State. The fundamental rights, privileges, and immunities which belong to him as a free man and a free citizen, now belong to him as a citizen of the United States, and are not dependent upon his citizenship of any State. The exercise of these rights and privileges, and the degree of enjoyment received from such exercise, are always more or less affected by the condition and the local institutions of the State, or city, or town where he resides. They are thus affected in a State by the wisdom of its laws, the ability of its officers, the efficiency of its magistrates, the education and morals of its people, and by many other considerations. This is a result which follows from the constitution of society, and can never be avoided, but in no other way can they be affected by the action of the State, or by the residence of the citizen therein. They do not derive their existence from its legislation, and cannot be destroyed by its power.

The amendment does not attempt to confer any new privileges or immunities upon citizens, or to enumerate or define those already existing. It assumes that there are such privileges and immunities which belong of right to citizens as such, and ordains that they shall not be abridged by State legislation. If this inhibition has no reference to privileges and immunities of this character, but only refers, as held by the majority of the court in their opinion, to such privileges and immunities as were before its adoption specially designated in the Constitution or necessarily implied as belonging to citizens of the United States, it was a vain and idle enactment, which accomplished nothing, and most unnecessarily excited Congress and the people on its passage. With privileges and immunities thus designated or implied no State could ever have interfered by its laws, and no new constitutional provision was required to inhibit such interference. The supremacy of the Constitution and the laws of the United States always controlled any State legislation of that character. But if the amendment refers to the natural and inalienable rights which belong to all citizens, the inhibition has a profound significance and consequence.

What, then, are the privileges and immunities which are secured against abridgment by State legislation?

. . .

. . . The privileges and immunities designated are those *which of right belong to the citizens of all free governments.* Clearly among these must be placed the right to pursue a lawful employment in a lawful manner, without other restraint than such as equally affects all persons.

. . .

. . . The privileges and immunities of citizens of the United States, of every one of them, is secured against abridgment in any form by any State. The fourteenth amendment places them under the guardianship of the National authority. All monopolies in any known trade or manufacture are an invasion of these privileges, for they encroach upon the liberty of citizens to acquire property and pursue happiness. . . .

. . .

This equality of right, with exemption from all disparaging and partial enactments, in the lawful pursuits of life throughout the whole country, is the distinguishing privilege of citizens of the United States. To them, everywhere, all pursuits, all professions, all avocations are open without other restrictions than such as are imposed equally upon all others of the same age, sex, and condition. The State may prescribe such regulations for every pursuit and calling of life as will promote the public health, secure the good order and advance the general prosperity of society, but when once prescribed, the pursuit or calling must be free to be followed by every citizen who is within the conditions designated, and will conform to the regulations. This is the fundamental idea upon which our institutions rest, and unless adhered to in the legislation of the country our government will be a republic only in name. The fourteenth amendment, in my judgment, makes it essential to the validity of the legislation of every State that this equality of right should be respected. How widely this equality has been departed from, how entirely rejected and trampled upon by the act of Louisiana, I have already shown. And it is to me a matter of profound regret that its validity is recognized by a majority of this court, for by it the right of free labor, one of the most sacred and imprescriptible rights of man, is violated.

Aftermath of The Slaughterhouse Cases

Permanence was not the hallmark of *The Slaughterhouse Cases;* only the majority's interpretation of the privileges and immunities clause was to remain the law. Justice Stephen Field's dissenting opinion eventually prevailed with respect to judicial interpretation of due process and equal protection. It was some time, however, before the justices were to embrace a new federalism in which the balance of power lay overwhelmingly with the national government. In two cases decided soon after the *Slaughterhouse* decision the Court again faced challenges under the privileges and immunities clause and continued to construe it narrowly, holding in *Minor* v. *Happersett* (1875) that voting was not a privilege of national citizenship and that the clause did not prohibit a state from excluding women from the franchise. Similarly in *Walker* v. *Sauvinet* (1876) it was held that the privileges and immunities clause did not require the states to grant jury trials in common law cases. Although the clause has been used on occasion in oral and written briefs by lawyers arguing against the validity of various state laws, the Supreme Court has never amended the narrow construction given to the privileges and immunities clause by Justice Samuel Miller.

Palko v. *Connecticut*

302 U.S. 319 (1937)

By the 1930s the Supreme Court had made it clear that the Fourteenth Amendment did not make the entire Bill of Rights automatically binding on the states, but it had

also begun the process of selectively incorporating specific Bill of Rights provisions through the due process clause. A number of guarantees—just compensation, freedom of speech, press, and assembly, and the right to counsel in capital cases—had been incorporated, while several others, including jury trials, grand jury indictments, and the privilege against self-incrimination had been specifically excluded.

In the state of Connecticut a prosecutor was permitted by law to seek a retrial after a criminal defendant was either acquitted or convicted of a lesser offense, if it could be shown that the jury's verdict was based upon a mistaken interpretation of the law. Palko, on trial for first degree murder, was convicted of second degree murder instead, and sentenced to life imprisonment. The state entered an appeal on the ground that evidence of the defendant's confession and testimony impeaching his credibility had been incorrectly excluded at the trial, and further because the trial judge had failed to properly instruct the jury as to the difference between first and second degree murder. The state supreme court then ordered a retrial, at which Palko was convicted of first degree murder and given a death sentence. On appeal, Palko argued that the retrial violated the double jeopardy clause of the Fifth Amendment which was applicable to the states through the Fourteenth Amendment. Since Palko's brief also made the claim that the due process clause incorporated *all* of the provisions of the Bill of Rights, the Court's opinion became the occasion for its most comprehensive consideration to date of the scope of the Fourteenth Amendment.

BENJAMIN CARDOZO

In 18 years on the New York Court of Appeals, Benjamin Cardozo became one of the most respected jurists and legal scholars in America. When Oliver Wendell Holmes retired from the Court in 1932, there was an unprecedented public demand for President Herbert Hoover to name Cardozo to succeed him. Hoover made the appointment despite the fact that there were already two other New Yorkers on the Court at the time. In his brief (6-year) Court career Cardozo carried on Holmes's commitment to judicial restraint. Although too intellectually detached to be a political liberal in the Brandeis mold, Cardozo usually supported expansive readings of government power under the commerce clause.

Mr. Justice **Cardozo** delivered the opinion of the Court.

. . .

The argument for appellant is that whatever is forbidden by the Fifth Amendment is forbidden by the Fourteenth also. The Fifth Amendment, which is not directed to the states, but solely to the federal government, creates immunity from double jeopardy. No person shall be "subject for the same offense to be twice put in jeopardy of life or limb." The Fourteenth Amendment ordains, "nor shall any State deprive any person of life, liberty, or property, without due process of law." To retry a defendant, though under one indictment and only one, subjects him, it is said, to double jeopardy in violation of the Fifth Amendment, if the prosecution is one on behalf of the United States. From this the consequence is said to follow that there is a denial of life or liberty without due process of law, if the prosecution is one on behalf of the People of a State. Thirty-five years ago a like argument was made to this court in *Dreyer* v. *Illinois*, and was passed without consideration of its merits as unnecessary to a decision. The question is now here.

. . .

We have said that in appellant's view the Fourteenth Amendment is to be taken as embodying the prohibitions of the Fifth. His thesis is even broader. Whatever would be a violation of the original bill of rights (Amendments I to VIII) if done by the federal government is now equally unlawful by force of the Fourteenth Amendment if done by a state. There is no such general rule.

The Fifth Amendment provides, among other things, that no person shall be held to answer for a capital or otherwise infamous crime unless on presentment or indictment of a grand jury. This court has held that, in prosecutions by a state, presentment or indictment by a grand jury may give way to informations at the instance of a public officer. *Hurtado* v. *California*. The Fifth Amendment provides also that no person shall be compelled in any criminal case to be a witness against himself. This court has said that, in prosecutions by a state, the exemption will fail if the state elects to end it. *Twining* v. *New Jersey*. The Sixth Amendment calls for a jury trial in criminal cases and the Seventh for a jury trial in civil cases at common law where the value in controversy shall exceed twenty dollars. This court has ruled that consistently with those amendments trial by jury may be modified by a state or abolished altogether. As to the Fourth Amendment, one should refer to *Weeks* v. *United States*, and as to other provisions of the Sixth, to *West* v. *Louisiana*.

On the other hand, the due process clause of the Fourteenth Amendment may make it unlawful for a state to abridge by its statutes the freedom of speech which the First Amendment safeguards against encroachment by the Congress,

De Jonge v. *Oregon;* or the like freedom of the press, *Grosjean* v. *American Press Co.;* or the free exercise of religion, *Hamilton* v. *Regents;* or the right of peaceable assembly, without which speech would be unduly trammeled, *De Jonge* v. *Oregon;* or the right of one accused of crime to the benefit of counsel, *Powell* v. *Alabama*. In these and other situations immunities that are valid as against the federal government by force of the specific pledges of particular amendments have been found to be implicit in the concept of ordered liberty, and thus, through the Fourteenth Amendment, become valid as against the states.

The line of division may seem to be wavering and broken if there is a hasty catalogue of the cases on the one side and the other. Reflection and analysis will induce a different view. There emerges the perception of a rationalizing principle which gives to discrete instances a proper order and coherence. The right to trial by jury and the immunity from prosecution except as the result of an indictment may have value and importance. Even so, they are not of the very essence of a scheme of ordered liberty. To abolish them is not to violate a "principle of justice so rooted in the traditions and conscience of our people as to be ranked as fundamental." *Snyder* v. *Massachusetts*. Few would be so narrow or provincial as to maintain that a fair and enlightened system of justice would be impossible without them. What is true of jury trials and indictments is true also, as the cases show, of the immunity from compulsory self-incrimination. This too might be lost, and justice still be done. Indeed, today as in the past there are students of our penal system who look upon the immunity as a mischief rather than a benefit, and who would limit its scope, or destroy it altogether. No doubt there would remain the need to give protection against torture, physical or mental. Justice, however, would not perish if the accused were subject to a duty to respond to orderly inquiry. The exclusion of these immunities and privileges from the privileges and immunities protected against the action of the states has not been arbitrary or casual. It has been dictated by a study and appreciation of the meaning, the essential implications, of liberty itself.

We reach a different plane of social and moral values when we pass to the privileges and immunities that have been taken over from the earlier articles of the federal bill of rights and brought within the Fourteenth Amendment by a process of absorption. These in their origin were effective against the federal government alone. If the Fourteenth Amendment has absorbed them, the process of absorption has had its source in the belief that neither liberty nor justice would exist if they were sacrificed. This is true, for illustration, of freedom of thought, and speech. Of that freedom one may say that it is the matrix, the indispensable condition, of nearly every other form of freedom. With rare aberrations a pervasive recognition of that truth can be traced in our history, political and legal. So it has come about that the domain of liberty, withdrawn by the Fourteenth Amendment from encroachment by the states, has been enlarged by latter-day judgments to include liberty of the mind as well as liberty of action. The extension became, indeed, a logical imperative when once it was recognized, as long ago it was, that liberty is something more than exemption from physical restraint, and that even in the field of substantive rights and duties the legislative judgment, if oppressive and arbitrary, may be overridden by the courts. Fundamental too in the concept of due process, and so in that of liberty, is the thought that condemnation shall be rendered only after trial. The hearing, moreover, must be a real one, not a sham or a pretense. For that reason, ignorant defendants in a capital case were held to have been condemned unlawfully when in truth, though not in form, they were refused the aid of counsel. The decision did not turn upon the fact that the benefit of counsel would have been guaranteed to the defendants by the provisions of the Sixth Amendment if they had been prosecuted in a federal court. The decision turned upon the fact that in the particular situation laid before us in the evidence the benefit of counsel was essential to the substance of a hearing.

Our survey of the cases serves, we think, to justify the statement that the dividing line between them, if not unfaltering throughout its course, has been true for the most part to a unifying principle. On which side of the line the case made out by the appellant has appropriate location must be the next inquiry and the final one. Is that kind of double jeopardy to which the statute has subjected him a hardship so acute and shocking that our polity will not endure it? Does it violate those "fundamental principles of liberty and justice which lie at the base of all our civil and political institutions"? *Hebert* v. *Louisiana*. The answer surely must be "no." What the answer would have to be if the state were permitted after a trial free from error to try the accused over again or to bring another case against him, we have no occasion to consider. We deal with the statute before us and no other. The state is not attempting to wear the accused out by a multitude of cases with accumulated trials. It asks no more than this, that the case against him shall go on until there shall be a trial free from the corrosion of substantial legal error. This is not cruelty at all, nor even vexation in any immoderate degree. If the trial had been infected with error adverse to the accused, there might have been review at his instance, and as often as necessary to purge the vicious taint. A reciprocal privilege, subject at all times to the discretion of the presiding judge, has now been granted to the state. There is here no seismic innovation. The edifice of justice stands, its symmetry, to many, greater than before.

. . .

The judgment is affirmed.

Aftermath of Palko v. Connecticut

The *Palko* decision stood until 1969, when the Court ruled in *Benton* v. *Maryland* that the double jeopardy guarantee was such a "fundamental ideal in our constitutional heritage . . . that it should apply to the States through the Fourteenth Amendment." In the three decades between *Palko* and *Benton*, the Court, using *Palko's* conceptual framework, but applying it much more expansively, had selectively incorporated virtually the entire Bill of Rights into the due process clause. In the 1960s alone the Court had already incorporated eight provisions of the Bill of Rights (see Incorporation Table, p. 239). After Benton, however, incorporation came to an abrupt halt. In the last two decades the Court has refused to consider the few remaining provisions of the Bill of Rights as fundamental to a concept of fairness.

Mapp v. *Ohio*
367 U.S. 643 (1961)

As the previous discussion of incorporation shows, for many years the Supreme Court was reluctant to dictate constitutional requirements for the states in the field of criminal justice. Even when the Court held that a particular provision of the Bill of Rights applied to the states, it did not always insist that state criminal procedures conform exactly to the standards previously set for the national government. A particularly interesting example of this dualism arises in connection with the admissibility of evidence obtained in violation of constitutional standards.

In a 1914 case, *Weeks* v. *United States*, the Supreme Court held that evidence seized without a valid search warrant could not be used in a federal criminal case. This prohibition, known as the exclusionary rule, was controversial from the start. To some, the possible loss of a criminal conviction was an unnecessarily harsh penalty for society to pay for the mistakes of the police, while others believed that it was unjust for society to benefit from illegal acts committed in its name. When the Court ruled in 1949, in *Wolf* v. *Colorado*, that the Fourth Amendment's prohibition against unreasonable searches and seizures was applicable to the states, a majority of the justices pointedly refused to require the states to observe the exclusionary rule as well. They reasoned that there were other remedies, both civil and criminal, available for punishing police officers who conducted improper searches. In subsequent years a number of states adopted their own versions of the exclusionary rule.

On the afternoon of May 23, 1957, three plainclothes police officers arrived without a search warrant at the Cleveland home of Dollree Mapp to investigate a report that a bombing suspect might be hiding there. Mapp, who lived in a second-floor apartment with her 15-year-old daughter, refused to admit them. After watching the house for several hours (while the suspect's car was parked outside), the plainclothes police, now accompanied by a number of uniformed officers, entered the house by breaking a pane of glass and unlatching the door. Mapp met them on the stairway leading to her apartment and demanded to see a search warrant. One of the officers waved a sheet of paper (which it later turned out was not a warrant but an affidavit requesting a warrant) which Mapp grabbed from him and stuffed into her sweater. The police retrieved the paper, handcuffed Mapp, and proceeded to search her apartment, where they found some sexually explicit pamphlets and pictures. In the basement they located a box filled with gambling equipment. Dollree Mapp was arrested on a misdemeanor charge of possessing betting paraphernalia and a felony charge of possession of obscene material. At her jury trial on the obscenity count (after she had been acquitted on the gambling charge) Mapp's lawyer sought to have the evidence excluded because it had not been identified in a proper search warrant. The trial judge rejected the motion—Ohio did not have an exclusionary rule—and Mapp was found guilty and sentenced to 1 to 7 years in prison. On appeal, the Ohio

Supreme Court voted 4–3 to find the state's obscenity law unconstitutional. However, since the state constitution required that such a decision have the support of at least all but one of the judges, Dollree Mapp's conviction remained in effect. The United States Supreme Court then granted *certiorari*. It also took the unprecedented step of inviting the Ohio affiliate of the American Civil Liberties Union to participate in the oral arguments. Mapp's attorney based his appeal on the narrow point that the Cleveland police had violated an Ohio statute by conducting a warrantless search. The civil liberties lawyer argued much more broadly that the time had come for the Supreme Court to overturn *Wolf* v. *Colorado* and require the states to observe the exclusionary rule.

Mr. Justice **Clark** delivered the opinion of the Court.

. . .

In 1949, 35 years after *Weeks* was announced, this Court, in *Wolf* v. *Colorado*, . . . discussed the effect of the Fourth Amendment upon the States through the operation of the Due Process Clause of the Fourteenth Amendment. It said:

"[W]e have no hesitation in saying that were a State affirmatively to sanction such police incursion into privacy it would run counter to the guaranty of the Fourteenth Amendment."

Nevertheless, after declaring that the "security of one's privacy against arbitrary intrusion by the police" is "implicit in 'the concept of ordered liberty' and as such enforceable against the States through the Due Process Clause," *Palko* v. *Connecticut*, (1937), and announcing that it "stoutly adhere[d]" to the *Weeks* decision, the Court decided that the *Weeks* exclusionary rule would not then be imposed upon the States as "an essential ingredient of the right." The Court's reasons for not considering essential to the right to privacy, as a curb imposed upon the States by the Due Process Clause, that which decades before had been posited as part and parcel of the Fourth Amendment's limitation upon federal encroachment of individual privacy, were bottomed on factual considerations.

While they are not basically relevant to a decision that the exclusionary rule is an essential ingredient of the Fourth Amendment as the right it embodies is vouchsafed against the States by the Due Process Clause, we will consider the current validity of the factual grounds upon which *Wolf* was based.

The Court in *Wolf* first stated that "[t]he contrariety of views of the States" on the adoption of the exclusionary rule of *Weeks* was "particularly impressive"; and, in this connection, that it could not "brush aside the experience of States which deem the incidence of such conduct by the police too slight to call for a deterrent remedy . . . by overriding the [States'] relevant rules of evidence." While in 1949, prior to the *Wolf* case, almost two-thirds of the States were opposed to the use of the exclusionary rule, now, despite the *Wolf* case, more than half of those since passing upon it, by their own legislative or judicial decision, have wholly or partly adopted or adhered to the *Weeks* rule. Significantly, among those now following the rule is California, which, according to its highest court, was "compelled to reach that conclusion because other remedies have completely failed to secure compliance with the constitutional provisions. . . ." *People* v. *Cahan* (1955). In connection with this California case, we note that the second basis elaborated in *Wolf* in support of its failure to enforce the exclusionary doctrine against the States was that "other means of protection" have been afforded "the right to privacy." The experience of California that such other remedies have been worthless and futile is buttressed by the experience of other States. The obvious futility of relegating the Fourth Amendment to the protection of other remedies has, moreover, been recognized by this Court since *Wolf*.

. . . It, therefore, plainly appears that the factual considerations supporting the failure of the *Wolf* Court to include the *Weeks* exclusionary rule when it recognized the enforceability of the right to privacy against the States in 1949, while not basically relevant to the constitutional consideration, could not, in any analysis, now be deemed controlling. . . . Today we once again examine *Wolf's* constitutional documentation of the right to privacy free from unreasonable state intrusion, and, after its dozen years on our books, are led by it to close the only courtroom door remaining open to evidence secured by official lawlessness in flagrant abuse of that basic right, reserved to all persons as a specific guarantee against that very same unlawful conduct. We hold that all evidence obtained by searches and seizures in violation of the Constitution is, by that same authority, inadmissible in a state court.

Since the Fourth Amendment's right of privacy has been declared enforceable against the States through the Due Process Clause of the Fourteenth, it is enforceable against them by the same sanction of exclusion as is used against the Federal Government. Were it otherwise, then just as without the *Weeks* rule the assurance against unreasonable federal searches and seizures would be "a form of words," valueless and undeserving of mention in a perpetual charter of inestimable human liberties, so too, without that rule the freedom from state invasions of privacy would be so ephemeral and so neatly severed from its conceptual nexus with the freedom from all brutish means of coercing evidence as not to merit this Court's high regard as a freedom "implicit in the concept of ordered liberty." At the time that the Court held in *Wolf* that the Amendment was applicable to the States through the Due Process Clause, the cases of this Court, as we have seen, had steadfastly held that as to federal officers the Fourth Amendment included the exclusion of the evidence seized in violation of its provisions. Even *Wolf* "stoutly adhered" to that proposition. The right to privacy, when conceded operatively enforceable against the States, was not susceptible of destruction by avulsion of the sanction upon which its protection and enjoyment had always been deemed dependent under the *Boyd*, *Weeks* and *Silverthorne* cases. Therefore, in extending the substantive protections of due process to all constitutionally unreasonable searches—state or federal—it was logically and constitutionally necessary that the exclusion doctrine—an essential part of the right to privacy—be also insisted upon as an essential ingredient of the right newly recognized by the *Wolf* case. In short, the admission of the new constitutional right by *Wolf* could not consistently tolerate denial of its most important constitutional privilege, namely, the exclusion of the evidence which an accused had been forced to give by reason of the unlawful seizure. To hold otherwise is to grant the right but in reality to withhold its privilege and enjoyment.

. . .

Moreover, our holding that the exclusionary rule is an essential part of both the Fourth and Fourteenth Amendments is not only the logical dictate of prior cases, but it also makes very good sense. There is no war between the Constitution and common sense. Presently, a federal prosecutor may make no use of evidence illegally seized, but a States's attorney across the street may, although he supposedly is operating under the enforceable prohibitions of the same Amendment. Thus the State, by admitting evidence unlawfully seized, serves to encourage disobedience to the Federal Constitution which it is bound to uphold.

. . .

There are those who say, as did Justice (then Judge) Cardozo, that under our constitutional exclusionary doctrine "[t]he criminal is to go free because the constable has blundered." *People* v. *Defore*. In some cases this will undoubtedly be the result. But, as was said in *Elkins*, "there is another consideration—the imperative of judicial integrity." The criminal goes free, if he must, but it is the law that sets him free. Nothing can destroy a government more quickly than its failure to observe its own laws, or worse, its disregard of the charter of its own existence. As Mr. Justice Brandeis, dissenting, said in *Olmstead* v. *United States* (1928): "Our Government is the potent, the omnipresent teacher. For good or for ill, it teaches the whole people by its example. . . . If the Government becomes a lawbreaker, it breeds contempt for law; it invites every man to become a law unto himself; it invites anarchy." Nor can it lightly be assumed that, as a practical matter, adoption of the exclusionary rule fetters law enforcement.

Only last year this Court expressly considered that contention and found that "pragmatic evidence of a sort" to the contrary was not wanting. *Elkins* v. *United States*. The Court noted that

"The federal courts themselves have operated under the exclusionary rule of *Weeks* for almost half a century; yet it has not been suggested either that the Federal Bureau of Investigation has thereby been rendered ineffective, or that the administration of criminal justice in the federal courts has thereby been disrupted. Moreover, the experience of the states is impressive. . . . The movement towards the rule of exclusion has been halting but seemingly inexorable."

The ignoble shortcut to conviction left open to the State tends to destroy the entire system of constitutional restraints on which the liberties of the people rest. Having once recognized that the right to privacy embodied in the Fourth Amendment is enforceable against the States, and that the right to be secure against rude invasions of privacy by state officers is, therefore, constitutional in origin, we can no longer permit that right to remain an empty promise. Because it is enforceable in the same manner and to like effect as other basic rights secured by the Due Process Clause, we can no longer permit it to be revocable at the whim of any police officer who, in the name of law enforcement itself, chooses to suspend its enjoyment. Our decision, founded on reason and truth, gives to the individual no more than that which the Constitution guarantees him, to the police officer no less than that to which honest law enforcement is entitled, and, to the courts, that judicial integrity so necessary in the true administration of justice.

The judgment of the Supreme Court of Ohio is reversed and the cause remanded for further proceedings not inconsistent with this opinion.

Mr. Justice **Black,** concurring.

. . .

I am still not persuaded that the Fourth Amendment, standing alone, would be enough to bar the introduction into evidence against an accused of papers and effects seized from him in violation of its commands. For the Fourth Amendment does not itself contain any provision expressly precluding the use of such evidence, and I am extremely doubtful that such a provision could properly be inferred from nothing more than the basic command against unreasonable searches and seizures. Reflection on the problem, however, in the light of cases coming before the Court since *Wolf,* has led me to conclude that when the Fourth Amendment's ban against unreasonable searches and seizures is considered together with the Fifth Amendment's ban against compelled self-incrimination, a constitutional basis emerges which not only justifies but actually requires the exclusionary rule.

The close interrelationship between the Fourth and Fifth Amendments, as they apply to this problem, has long been recognized and, indeed, was expressly made the ground for this Court's holding in *Boyd* v. *United States.* There the Court fully discussed this relationship and declared itself "unable to perceive that the seizure of a man's private books and papers to be used in evidence against him is substantially different from compelling him to be a witness against himself." It was upon this ground that Mr. Justice Rutledge largely relied in his dissenting opinion in the *Wolf* case. And, although I rejected the argument at that time, its force has, for me at least, become compelling with the more thorough understanding of the problem brought on by recent cases. In the final analysis, it seems to me that the *Boyd* doctrine, though perhaps not required by the express language of the Constitution strictly construed, is amply justified from an historical standpoint, soundly based in reason, and entirely consistent with what I regard to be the proper approach to interpretation of our Bill of Rights—an approach well set out by Mr. Justice Bradley in the *Boyd* case:

"[C]onstitutional provisions for the security of person and property should be liberally construed. A close and literal construction deprives them of half their efficacy, and leads to gradual depreciation of the right, as if it consisted more in sound than in substance. It is the duty of the courts to be watchful for the constitutional rights of the citizen, and against any stealthy encroachments thereon."

The case of *Rochin* v. *California*, which we decided three years after the *Wolf* case, authenticated, I think, the soundness of Mr. Justice Bradley's and Mr. Justice Rutledge's reliance upon the interrelationship between the Fourth and Fifth Amendments as requiring the exclusion of unconstitutionally seized evidence. In the *Rochin* case, three police officers, acting with neither a judicial warrant nor probable cause, entered Rochin's home for the purpose of conducting a search and broke down the door to a bedroom occupied by Rochin and his wife. Upon their entry into the room, the officers saw Rochin pick up and swallow two small capsules. They immediately seized him and took him in handcuffs to a hospital where the capsules were recovered by use of a stomach pump. Investigation showed that the capsules contained morphine and evidence of that fact was made the basis of his conviction of a crime in a state court.

When the question of the validity of that conviction was brought here, we were presented with an almost perfect example of the interrelationship between the Fourth and Fifth Amendments. Indeed, every member of this Court who participated in the decision of that case recognized this interrelationship and relied on it, to some extent at least, as justifying reversal of Rochin's conviction. The majority, though careful not to mention the Fifth Amendment's provision that "[n]o person . . . shall be compelled in any criminal case to be a witness against himself," showed at least that it was not unaware that such a provision exists, stating: "Coerced confessions offend the community's sense of fair play and decency. . . . It would be a stultification of the responsibility which the course of constitutional history has cast upon this Court to hold that in order to convict a man the police cannot extract by force what is in his mind but can extract what is in his stomach." The methods used by the police thus were, according to the majority, "too close to the rack and the screw to permit of constitutional differentiation," and the case was reversed on the ground that these methods had violated the Due Process Clause of the Fourteenth Amendment in that the treatment accorded Rochin was of a kind that "shocks the conscience," "offend[s] 'a sense of justice'" and fails to "respect certain decencies of civilized conduct."

I concurred in the reversal of the *Rochin* case, but on the ground that the Fourteenth Amendment made the Fifth Amendment's provision against self-incrimination applicable to the States and that, given a broad rather than a narrow construction, that provision barred the introduction of this "capsule" evidence just as much as it would have forbidden the use of words Rochin might have been coerced to speak. In reaching this conclusion I cited and relied on the *Boyd* case, the constitutional doctrine of which was, of course, necessary to my disposition of the case. At that time, however, these views were very definitely in the minority for only Mr. Justice Douglas and I rejected the flexible and uncertain standards of the "shock-the-conscience test" used in the majority opinion.

Two years after *Rochin*, in *Irvine* v. *California*, we were again called upon to consider the validity of a conviction based on evidence which had been obtained in a manner clearly unconstitutional and arguably shocking to the conscience. The five opinions written by this Court in that case demonstrate the utter confusion and uncertainty that had been brought about by the *Wolf* and *Rochin* decisions. In concurring, Mr. Justice Clark emphasized the unsatisfactory nature of the Court's "shock-the-conscience test," saying that this "test" "makes for such uncertainty and unpredictability that it would be impossible to foretell—other than by guesswork—just how brazen the invasion of the intimate privacies of one's home must be in order to shock itself into the protective arms of the Constitution. In truth, the practical result of this *ad hoc* approach is simply that when five Justices are sufficiently revolted by local police action, a conviction is overturned and a guilty man may go free."

Only one thing emerged with complete clarity from the *Irvine* case—that is that seven Justices rejected the "shock-the-conscience" constitutional standard enunciated in the *Wolf* and *Rochin* cases. But even this did not lessen the confusion in this area of the law because the continued existence of mutually inconsistent precedents together with the Court's inability to settle upon a majority opinion in the *Irvine* case left the situation at least as uncertain as it had been before. Finally, today, we clear up that uncertainty. As I understand the Court's opinion in this case, we again reject the confusing "shock-the-conscience" standard of the *Wolf* and *Rochin* cases and, instead, set aside this state conviction in reliance upon the precise, intelligible and more predictable constitutional doctrine enunciated in the *Boyd* case. I fully agree with Mr. Justice Bradley's opinion that the two Amendments upon which the *Boyd* doctrine rests are of vital importance in our constitutional scheme of liberty and that both are entitled to a liberal rather than a niggardly interpretation. The courts of the country are entitled to know with as much certainty as possible what scope they cover. The Court's opinion, in my judgment, dissipates the doubt and uncertainty in this field of constitutional law and I am persuaded, for this and other reasons stated, to depart from my prior views, to accept the *Boyd* doctrine as controlling in this state case and to join the Court's judgment and opinion which are in accordance with that constitutional doctrine.

Mr. Justice **Harlan,** whom Mr. Justice **Frankfurter** and Mr. Justice **Whittaker** join, dissenting.

In overruling the *Wolf* case the Court, in my opinion, has forgotten the sense of judicial restraint which, with due regard for *stare decisis,* is one element that should enter into deciding whether a past decision of this Court should be overruled. Apart from that I also believe that the *Wolf* rule represents sounder Constitutional doctrine than the new rule which now replaces it.

. . .

The action of the Court finds no support in the rule that decision of Constitutional issues should be avoided wherever possible. For in overruling *Wolf* the Court, instead of passing upon the validity of Ohio's § 2905.34, has simply chosen between two Constitutional questions. Moreover, I submit that it has chosen the more difficult and less appropriate of the two questions. The Ohio statute which, as construed by the State Supreme Court, punishes knowing possession or control of obscene material, irrespective of the purposes of such possession or control (with exceptions not here applicable) and irrespective of whether the accused had any reasonable opportunity to rid himself of the material after discovering that it was obscene, surely presents a Constitutional question which is both simpler and less far-reaching than the question which the Court decides today. It seems to me that justice might well have been done in this case without overturning a decision on which the administration of criminal law in many of the States has long justifiably relied.

. . .

At the heart of the majority's opinion in this case is the following syllogism: (1) the rule excluding in federal criminal trials evidence which is the product of an illegal search and seizure is "part and parcel" of the Fourth Amendment; (2) *Wolf* held that the "privacy" assured against federal action by the Fourth Amendment is also protected against state action by the Fourteenth Amendment; and (3) it is therefore "logically and constitutionally necessary" that the *Weeks* exclusionary rule should also be enforced against the States.

This reasoning ultimately rests on the unsound premise that because *Wolf* carried into the States, as part of "the concept of ordered liberty" embodied in the Fourteenth Amendment, the principle of "privacy" underlying the Fourth Amendment, it must follow that whatever configurations of the Fourth Amendment have been developed in the particularizing federal precedents are likewise to be deemed a part of "ordered liberty," and as such are enforceable against the States. For me, this does not follow at all.

It cannot be too much emphasized that what was recognized in *Wolf* was not that the Fourth Amendment *as such* is enforceable against the States as a facet of due process, a view of the Fourteenth Amendment which, as *Wolf* itself pointed out, has long since been discredited, but the principle of privacy "which is at the core of the Fourth Amendment." It would not be proper to expect or impose any precise equivalence, either as regards the scope of the right or the means of its implementation, between the requirements of the Fourth and Fourteenth Amendments. For the Fourth, unlike what was said in *Wolf* of the Fourteenth, does not state a general principle only; it is a particular command, having its setting in a pre-existing legal context on which both interpreting decisions and enabling statutes must at least build.

. . .

I would not impose upon the States this federal exclusionary remedy. The reasons given by the majority for now suddenly turning its back on *Wolf* seem to me notably unconvincing.

First, it is said that "the factual grounds upon which *Wolf* was based" have since changed, in that more States now follow the *Weeks* exclusionary rule than was so at the time *Wolf* was decided. While that is true, a recent survey indicates that at present one-half of the States still adhere to the common-law non-exclusionary rule, and one, Maryland, retains the rule as to felonies. But in any case surely all this is beside the point, as the majority itself indeed seems to recognize. Our concern here, as it was in *Wolf*, is not with the desirability of that rule but only with the question whether the States are Constitutionally free to follow it or not as they may themselves determine, and the relevance of the disparity of views among the States on this point lies simply in the fact that the judgment involved is a debatable one. Moreover, the very fact on which the majority relies, instead of lending support to what is now being done, points away from the need of replacing voluntary state action with federal compulsion.

The preservation of a proper balance between state and federal responsibility in the administration of criminal justice demands patience on the part of those who might like to see things move faster among the States in this respect. Problems of criminal law enforcement vary widely from State to State. One State, in considering the totality of its legal picture, may conclude that the need for embracing the *Weeks* rule is pressing because other remedies are unavailable or inadequate to secure compliance with the substantive Constitutional principle involved. Another, though equally solicitous of Constitutional rights, may choose to pursue one purpose at a time, allowing all evidence relevant to guilt to be brought into a criminal trial, and dealing with Constitutional infractions by other means. Still another may consider the exclusionary rule too rough-and-ready a remedy, in that it reaches only unconstitutional intrusions which eventuate in criminal prosecution of the victims. Further, a State after experimenting with the *Weeks* rule for a time may, because of unsatisfactory experience with it, decide to revert to a non-exclusionary rule. And so on. From the standpoint of Constitutional permissibility in pointing a State in one direction or another, I do not see at all why "time has set its face against" the considerations which led Mr. Justice Cardozo, then chief judge of the New York Court of Appeals, to reject for New York in *People* v. *Defore*, the *Weeks* exclusionary rule. For us the question remains, as it has always been, one of state power, not one of passing judgment on the wisdom of one state course or another. In my view this Court should continue to forbear from fettering the States with an adamant rule which may embarrass them in coping with their own peculiar problems in criminal law enforcement.

. . .

I regret that I find so unwise in principle and so inexpedient in policy a decision motivated by the high purpose of increasing respect for Constitutional rights. But in the last analysis I think this Court can increase respect for the Constitution only if it rigidly respects the limitations which the Constitution places upon it, and respects as well the principles inherent in its own processes. In the present case I think we exceed both, and that our voice becomes only a voice of power, not of reason.

Aftermath of Mapp *v.* Ohio

Dollree Mapp later moved to New York City, where in 1973 she was convicted of drug possession and, under the state's draconian "Rockefeller laws," sentenced to 20 years to life in prison. She served 9 years of her sentence.

In cases decided subsequent to *Mapp* v. *Ohio*, the Court gradually softened its position that the exclusionary rule was part of the procedural due process required by the Constitution, suggesting instead that it was merely a judge-made rule of evidence intended to deter police misconduct. As such, it could be qualified or even eliminated without altering the basic *Wolf* holding that the Fourth Amendment itself was applicable to the states. In 1984, in *United States* v. *Leon,* the Court explicitly defined a "good faith" exception to the exclusionary rule. Beginning with the premise that the purpose of the rule was deterrence, the majority reasoned that it made little sense to apply the rule in situations where police had reason to believe that they were acting on a proper search warrant— even if the warrant later turned out to be invalid. In dissent, Justices William Brennan and Thurgood Marshall objected that the decision would "put a premium on police ignorance of the law" and send a "message to magistrates that their decisions to issue warrants are now insulated from subsequent judicial review."

Goss v. *Lopez*
419 U.S. 565 (1975)

Throughout much of its history the Supreme Court has been notably reluctant to interfere with the operation of the nation's public schools, which traditionally have been among the strongest bastions of "local control" in American society. As the twentieth century progressed, however, public education came to be viewed both as a resource of fundamental importance to individuals and to society-at-large and as an institution with potentially great coercive power over a huge captive audience. Responding to the proddings of civil rights and civil liberties activists, the Supreme Court gradually began to fashion a number of constitutional protections for public school students and teachers. Notable among these were the equal protection clause of the Fourteenth Amendment (see Chapter 7) and the religion and speech clauses of the First Amendment (see Chapters 5 and 6). With the onset of the "due process revolution" in the 1960s, it was inevitable that the Court would be asked to determine whether the Fourteenth Amendment applied to disciplinary matters in public schools.

During a period of considerable student unrest in the 1970s, nine students at two high schools and one junior high school in Columbus, Ohio, were summarily suspended from school for 10-day periods. Under Ohio law, school principals were permitted to order such suspensions without first holding a hearing. A three-judge federal court, citing recent Supreme Court precedents establishing procedural due process rights outside the criminal setting, held that suspensions without prior hearings violated the Fourteenth Amendment. The Supreme Court took the case and announced its decision in 1975.

BYRON WHITE

Before his nomination to the Supreme Court by President John F. Kennedy in 1962, Byron White had been a Rhodes Scholar, a professional football player, and an attorney in private practice in Denver. His previous political experience consisted of helping manage Kennedy's presidential campaign in 1960 and then a brief stint in the Justice Department under Attorney General Robert Kennedy. At the time of his appointment White was generally expected to help strengthen the liberal bloc which then held sway on the Court, but with the exception of equal protection cases, his voting record throughout his career has been decidedly conservative.

Mr. Justice **White** delivered the opinion of the Court.

. . .

At the outset, appellants contend that because there is no constitutional right to an education at public expense, the Due Process Clause does not protect against expulsions from the public school system. This position misconceives the nature of the issue and is refuted by prior decisions. The Fourteenth Amendment forbids the State to deprive any person of life, liberty or property without due process of law. Protected interests in property are normally "not created by the Constitution. Rather, they are created and their dimensions are defined" by an independent source such as state statutes or rules entitling the citizen to certain benefits.

Accordingly, a state employee who under state law, or rules promulgated by state officials, has a legitimate claim of entitlement to continued employment absent sufficient cause for discharge may demand the procedural protections of due process. So may welfare recipients who have statutory rights to welfare as long as they maintain the specified qualifications. Morrissey v Brewer(1972) applied the limitations of the Due Process Clause to governmental decisions to revoke parole, although a parolee has no constitutional right to that status. In like vein was Wolff v McDonnell(1974), where the procedural protections of the Due Process Clause were triggered by official cancellation of a prisoner's

good-time credits accumulated under state law, although those benefits were not mandated by the Constitution.

Here, on the basis of state law, appellees plainly had legitimate claims of entitlement to a public education. Ohio Rev Code §§ 3313.48 and 3313.64 direct local authorities to provide a free education to all residents between six and 21 years of age, and a compulsory attendance law requires attendance for a school year of not less than 32 weeks. Ohio Rev Code § 3321.04. It is true that § 3313.66 of the Code permits school principals to suspend students for up to two weeks; but suspensions may not be imposed without any grounds whatsoever. All of the schools had their own rules specifying the grounds for expulsion or suspension. Having chosen to extend the right to an education to people of appellees' class generally, Ohio may not withdraw that right on grounds of misconduct absent fundamentally fair procedures to determine whether the misconduct has occurred.

Although Ohio may not be constitutionally obligated to establish and maintain a public school system, it has nevertheless done so and has required its children to attend. Those young people do not "shed their constitutional rights" at the schoolhouse door. "The Fourteenth Amendment, as now applied to the States, protects the citizen against the State itself and all of its creatures . . . Boards of Education not excepted." The authority possessed by the State to prescribe and enforce standards of conduct in its schools, although concededly very broad, must be exercised consistently with constitutional safeguards. Among other things, the State is constrained to recognize a student's legitimate entitlement to a public education as a property interest which is protected by the Due Process Clause and which may not be taken away for misconduct without adherence to the minimum procedures required by that Clause.

The Due Process Clause also forbids arbitrary deprivations of liberty. "Where a person's good name, reputation, honor, or integrity is at stake because of what the government is doing to him," the minimal requirements of the clause must be satisfied. School authorities here suspended appellees from school for periods of up to 10 days based on charges of misconduct. If sustained and recorded, those charges could seriously damage the students' standing with their fellow pupils and their teachers as well as interfere with later opportunities for higher education and employment. It is apparent that the claimed right of the State to determine unilaterally and without process whether that misconduct has occurred immediately collides with the requirements of the Constitution.

Appellants proceed to argue that even if there is a right to a public education protected by the Due Process Clause generally, the clause comes into play only when the State subjects a student to a "severe detriment or grievous loss." The loss of 10 days, it is said, is neither severe nor grievous and the Due Process Clause is therefore of no relevance. Appellee's argument is again refuted by our prior decisions; for in determining "whether due process requirements apply in the first place, we must look not to the 'weight' but to the *nature* of the interest at stake." Appellees were excluded from school only temporarily, it is true, but the length and consequent severity of a deprivation, while another factor to weigh in determining the appropriate form of hearing, "is not decisive of the basic right" to a hearing of some kind. The Court's view has been that as long as a property deprivation is not de minimis, its gravity is irrelevant to the question whether account must be taken of the Due Process Clause. A 10-day suspension from school is not de minimis in our view and may not be imposed in complete disregard of the Due Process Clause. . . .

"Once it is determined that due process applies, the question remains what process is due." We turn to that question, fully realizing as our cases regularly do that the interpretation and application of the Due Process Clause are intensely practical matters. . . .

There are certain bench marks to guide us, however. . . . At the very minimum . . . students facing suspension and the consequent interference with a protected property interest must be given some kind of notice and afforded some kind of hearing. . . .

It also appears from our cases that the timing and content of the notice and the nature of the hearing will depend on appropriate accommodation of the competing interests involved. The student's interest is to avoid unfair or mistaken exclusion from the educational process, with all of its unfortunate consequences. The Due Process Clause will not shield him from suspensions properly imposed, but it disserves both his interest and the interest of the State if his suspension is in fact unwarranted. The concern would be mostly academic if the disciplinary process were a totally accurate, unerring process, never mistaken and never unfair. Unfortunately, that is not the case, and no one suggests that it is. Disciplinarians, although proceeding in utmost good faith, frequently act on the reports and advice of others; and the controlling facts and the nature of the conduct under challenge are often disputed. The risk of error is not at all trivial, and it should be guarded against if that may be done without prohibitive cost or interference with the educational process.

The difficulty is that our schools are vast and complex. Some modicum of discipline and order is essential if the educational function is to be performed. Events calling for discipline are frequent occurrences and sometimes require immediate, effective action. Suspension is considered not only to be a necessary tool to maintain order but a valuable educational device. The prospect of imposing elaborate hearing requirements in every suspension case is viewed with great concern, and many school authorities may well prefer the untrammeled power to act unilaterally, unhampered by rules about notice and hearing. But it would be a strange disciplinary system in an educational institution if no communication was sought by the disciplinarian with the student in an effort to inform him of his defalcation and to let him tell his side of the story in order to make sure that an injustice is not done. . . .

We do not believe that school authorities must be totally free from notice and hearing requirements if their schools are to operate with acceptable efficiency. Students facing temporary suspension have interests qualifying for protection of the Due Process Clause, and due process requires, in connection with a suspension of 10 days or less, that the student be given oral or written notice of the charges against him and, if he denies them, an explanation of the evidence the authorities have and an opportunity to present his side of the story. The clause requires at least these rudimentary precautions against unfair or mistaken findings of misconduct and arbitrary exclusion from school.

There need be no delay between the time "notice" is given and the time of the hearing. In the great majority of cases the disciplinarian may informally discuss the alleged misconduct with the student minutes after it has occurred. We hold only that, in being given an opportunity to explain his version of the facts at this discussion, the student first be told what he is accused of doing and what the basis of the accusation is. . . .

In holding as we do, we do not believe that we have imposed procedures on school disciplinarians which are inappropriate in a classroom setting. Instead we have imposed requirements which are, if anything, less than a fair-minded school principal would impose upon himself in order to avoid unfair suspensions. Indeed, according to the testimony of the principal of Marion-Franklin High School, that school had an informal procedure, remarkably similar to that which we now require, applicable to suspensions generally but which was not followed in this case. Similarly, according to the most recent memorandum applicable to the entire CPSS, school principals in the CPSS are now required by local rule to provide at least as much as the constitutional minimum which we have described.

We stop short of construing the Due Process Clause to require, countrywide, that hearings in connection with short suspensions must afford the student the opportunity to secure counsel, to confront and cross-examine witnesses supporting the charge or to call his own witnesses to verify his version of the incident. Brief disciplinary suspensions are almost countless. To impose in each such case even truncated trial type procedures might well overwhelm administrative facilities in many places and, by diverting resources, cost more than it would save in educational effectiveness. Moreover, further formalizing the suspension process and escalating its formality and adversary nature may not only make it too costly as a regular disciplinary tool but also destroy its effectiveness as part of the teaching process.

On the other hand, requiring effective notice and informal hearing permitting the student to give his version of the events will provide a meaningful hedge against erroneous action. At least the disciplinarian will be alerted to the existence of disputes about facts and arguments about cause and effect. He may then determine himself to summon the accuser, permit cross-examination and allow the student to present his own witnesses. In more difficult cases, he may permit counsel. In any event, his discretion will be more informed and we think the risk of error substantially reduced. . . .

Mr. Justice **Powell,** with whom The **Chief Justice,** Mr. Justice **Blackmun,** and Mr. Justice **Rehnquist** join, dissenting.

The Court today invalidates an Ohio statute that permits student suspensions from school without a hearing "for not more than ten days." The decision unnecessarily opens avenues for judicial intervention in the operation of our public schools that may affect adversely the quality of education. The Court holds for the first time that the federal courts, rather than educational officials and state legislatures, have the authority to determine the rules applicable to routine classroom discipline of children and teenagers in the public schools. It justifies this unprecedented intrusion into the process of elementary and secondary education by identifying a new constitutional right: the right of a student not to be suspended for as much as a single day without notice and a due process hearing either before or promptly following the suspension.

The Court's decision rests on the premise that, under Ohio law, education is a property interest protected by the Fourteenth Amendment's Due Process Clause and therefore that any suspension requires notice and a hearing. In my view, a student's interest in education is not infringed by a suspension within the limited period prescribed by Ohio law. Moreover, to the extent that there may be some arguable infringement, it is too speculative, transitory and insubstantial to justify imposition of a *constitutional* rule.

. . .

The Ohio suspension statute allows no serious or significant infringement of education. It authorizes only a maximum suspension of eight school days, less than 5% of the normal 180-day school year. Absences of such limited duration will rarely affect a pupil's opportunity to learn or his scholastic performance. Indeed, the record in this case reflects no educational injury to appellees. Each completed the semester in which the suspension occurred and performed at least as well as he or she had in previous years. Despite the Court's unsupported speculation that a suspended student could be "seriously damaged," there is no factual showing of any such damage to appellees.

The Court also relies on a perceived deprivation of "liberty" resulting from any suspension, arguing—again without factual support in the record pertaining to these appellees—that a suspension harms a student's reputation. In view of the Court's decision in Board of Regents v Roth, I would have thought that this argument was plainly untenable. Underscoring the need for "serious damage" to reputation, the Roth Court held that a nontenured teacher who is not rehired by a public university could not claim to suffer sufficient reputational injury to require constitutional protections. Surely a brief suspension is of less serious consequence to the reputation of a teenage student.

In prior decisions, this Court has explicitly recognized that school authorities must have broad discretionary authority in the daily operation of public schools. This includes wide latitude with respect to maintaining discipline and good order. . . . Unlike the divergent and even

sharp conflict of interests usually present where due process rights are asserted, the interests here implicated—of the State through its schools and of the pupils—are essentially congruent.

The State's interest, broadly put, is in the proper functioning of its public school system for the benefit of *all* pupils and the public generally. Few rulings would interfere more extensively in the daily functioning of schools than subjecting routine discipline to the formalities and judicial oversight of due process. Suspensions are one of the traditional means—ranging from keeping a student after class to permanent expulsion—used to maintain discipline in the schools. It is common knowledge that maintaining order and reasonable decorum in school buildings and classrooms is a major educational problem, and one which has increased significantly in magnitude in recent years. Often the teacher, in protecting the rights of other children to an education (if not his or their safety), is compelled to rely on the power to suspend. . . .

The State's generalized interest in maintaining an orderly school system is not incompatible with the individual interest of the student. Education in any meaningful sense includes the inculcation of an understanding in each pupil of the necessity of rules and obedience thereto. This understanding is no less important than learning to read and write. One who does not comprehend the meaning and necessity of discipline is handicapped not merely in his education but throughout his subsequent life. In an age when the home and church play a diminishing role in shaping the character and value judgments of the young, a heavier responsibility falls upon the schools. When an immature student merits censure for his conduct, he is rendered a disservice if appropriate sanctions are not applied or if procedures for their application are so formalized as to invite a challenge to the teacher's authority—an invitation which rebellious or even merely spirited teenagers are likely to accept. . . .

One of the more disturbing aspects of today's decision is its discriminate reliance upon the judiciary, and the adversary process, as the means of resolving many of the most routine problems arising in the classroom. In mandating due process procedures the Court misapprehends the reality of the normal teacher-pupil relationship. There is an ongoing relationship, one in which the teacher must occupy many roles—educator, adviser, friend and, at times, parent-substitute. It is rarely adversary in nature except with respect to the chronically disruptive or insubordinate pupil whom the teacher must be free to discipline without frustrating formalities.

. . .

No one can foresee the ultimate frontiers of the new "thicket" the Court now enters. Today's ruling appears to sweep within the protected interest in education a multitude of discretionary decisions in the educational process. Teachers and other school authorities are required to make many decisions that may have serious consequences for the pupil. They must decide, for example, how to grade the student's work, whether a student passes or fails a course, whether he is to be promoted, whether he is required to take certain subjects, whether he may be excluded from interscholastic athletics or other extracurricular activities, whether he may be removed from one school and sent to another, whether he may be bused long distances when available schools are nearby, and whether he should be placed in a "general," "vocational," or "college-preparatory" track.

In these and many similar situations claims of impairment of one's educational entitlement identical in principle to those before the Court today can be asserted with equal or greater justification. Likewise, in many of these situations, the pupil can advance the same types of speculative and subjective injury given critical weight in this case. The District Court, relying upon gener-

alized opinion evidence, concluded that a suspended student may suffer psychological injury in one or more of the ways set forth in the margin below.

It hardly need be said that if a student, as a result of a day's suspension, suffers "a blow" to his "self esteem," "feels powerless," views "teachers with resentment," or feels "stigmatized by his teachers," identical psychological harms will flow from many other routine and necessary school decisions. The student who is given a failing grade, who is not promoted, who is excluded from certain extracurricular activities, who is assigned to a school reserved for children of less than average ability, or who is placed in the "vocational" rather than the "college preparatory" track, is unlikely to suffer any less psychological injury than if he were suspended for a day for a relatively minor infraction.

If, as seems apparent, the Court will now require due process procedures whenever such routine school decisions are challenged, the impact upon public education will be serious indeed. The discretion and judgment of federal courts across the land often will be substituted for that of the 50-state legislatures, the 14,000 school boards and the 2,000,000 teachers who heretofore have been responsible for the administration of the American public school system. If the Court perceives a rational and analytically sound distinction between the discretionary decision by school authorities to suspend a pupil for a brief period, and the types of discretionary school decisions described above, it would be prudent to articulate it in today's opinion. Otherwise, the federal courts should prepare themselves for a vast new role in society.

Aftermath of Goss v. Lopez

In its public education cases, the Supreme Court has continued to seek a balance between students' constitutional rights and the order necessary for a school to accomplish its educational mission. Although the Court has not qualified its *Goss* holding, in 1978 it did remove some of the incentive to pursue legal redress for constitutional violations by ruling that students suspended from school without a hearing could not receive compensatory damages without a showing of actual injury (*Carey* v. *Piphus*). In several recent cases the Court has also given school authorities more latitude in restricting students' First Amendment rights. In 1986 in *Bethel School District No. 403* v. *Fraser*, the Court upheld a 3-day suspension of a student who made a sexually suggestive speech at a school assembly. Although the speech was vulgar rather than obscene, the Court held that such speech was not constitutionally protected because public schools are uniquely responsible for inculcating fundamental values, including habits of civility. Two years later the Court held in *Hazelwood School District* v. *Kuhlmeier* that a high school principal could delete articles from a school-sponsored student newspaper, so long as the action was "reasonably related to legitimate pedagogical concerns." In both cases the Court stressed that any limitations on student speech must be politically neutral. Several states have reacted to *Hazelwood* by passing laws that restrict administrative censorship of student publications to stories that may be libelous, threaten privacy, or incite unlawful acts.

Lochner v. *New York*

198 U.S. 45 (1905)

In 1890, in *Chicago, Milwaukee, and St. Paul Railway Co.* v. *Minnesota,* the Supreme Court assumed ultimate responsibility for determining the reasonableness, and hence the constitutionality, of virtually all state economic regulation. Three years earlier, in *Mugler* v. *Kansas,* the Court had already served notice that regulations limiting economic freedom would be considered invalid unless the state could show that they were necessary to protect the health, safety, and morals of its citizens. Otherwise, individual or corporate liberty and property rights would prevail. In an 1897 case, *Allgeyer* v. *Louisiana,* the Court explicitly applied the doctrine of substantive due process for the first time in determining that a law regulating out-of-state marine insurance companies lacked sufficient justification under the state's police powers. However, the following year, in *Holden* v. *Hardy,* the Court found that a Utah law limiting underground miners to an 8-hour day was justified because of the health hazard involved in such work.

In 1897 the state of New York passed a statute called the Labor Law, one section of which limited bakery and confectionery workers to a 10-hour day and a 60-hour week. A Utica, New York, bakery owner named Joseph Lochner was charged with violating the law, found guilty, and fined $50. The New York Court of Appeals (the state's supreme court) upheld the conviction, and Lochner appealed the decision to the Supreme Court. In his brief, Lochner's attorney fired a fusillade of questions designed to place the state on the defensive:

> Does a danger exist which the enactment is designed to meet? Is it of sufficient magnitude? Does it concern the public? Does the proposed measure tend to remove it? Is the restraint or requirement in proportion to the danger? Is it possible to secure the objects sought without impairing essential rights and principles? Does the choice of a particular measure show that some other interest than safety or health was the actual motive of legislation?

As the following excerpt from *Lochner* shows, a majority of the justices were not impressed with the state's answers to these questions.

RUFUS W. PECKHAM

Rufus W. Peckham was appointed to the Supreme Court by President Grover Cleveland in 1895 after serving as a New York state judge for 10 years. A conservative Democrat, his opinions involving government regulation of the economy reflected his strong Social Darwinist views. Considered an able judge, Peckham wrote with a clear, straightforward style.

Mr. Justice **Peckham** delivered the opinion of the court.

. . .

The statute necessarily interferes with the right of contract between the employer and employés, concerning the number of hours in which the latter may labor in the bakery of the employer. The general right to make a contract in relation to his business is part of the liberty of the individual protected by the Fourteenth Amendment of the Federal Constitution. Under that provision no State can deprive any person of life, liberty or property without due process of law. The right to purchase or to sell labor is part of the liberty protected by this amendment, unless there are circumstances which exclude the right. There are, however, certain powers, existing in the sovereignty of each State in the Union, somewhat vaguely termed police powers, the exact description and limitation of which have not been attempted by the courts. Those powers, broadly stated and without, at present, any attempt at a more specific limitation, relate to the safety, health, morals and general welfare of the public. Both property and liberty are held on such reasonable conditions as may be imposed by the governing power of the State in the exercise of those powers, and with such conditions the Fourteenth Amendment was not designed to interfere.

The State, therefore, has power to prevent the individual from making certain kinds of con-

tracts, and in regard to them the Federal Constitution offers no protection. If the contract be one which the State, in the legitimate exercise of its police power, has the right to prohibit, it is not prevented from prohibiting it by the Fourteenth Amendment. Contracts in violation of a statute, either of the Federal or state government, or a contract to let one's property for immoral purposes, or to do any other unlawful act, could obtain no protection from the Federal Constitution, as coming under the liberty of person or of free contract. Therefore, when the State, by its legislature, in the assumed exercise of its police powers, has passed an act which seriously limits the right to labor or the right of contract in regard to their means of livelihood between persons who are *sui juris* (both employer and employé), it becomes of great importance to determine which shall prevail—the right of the individual to labor for such time as he may choose, or the right of the State to prevent the individual from laboring or from entering into any contract to labor, beyond a certain time prescribed by the State.

This court has recognized the existence and upheld the exercise of the police powers of the States in many cases which might fairly be considered as border ones, and it has, in the course of its determination of questions regarding the asserted invalidity of such statutes, on the ground of their violation of the rights secured by the Federal Constitution, been guided by rules of a very liberal nature, the application of which has resulted, in numerous instances, in upholding the validity of state statutes thus assailed. Among the later cases where the state law has been upheld by this court is that of *Holden* v. *Hardy.* . . .

. . .

It must, of course, be conceded that there is a limit to the valid exercise of the police power by the State. There is no dispute concerning this general proposition. Otherwise the Fourteenth Amendment would have no efficacy and the legislatures of the States would have unbounded power, and it would be enough to say that any piece of legislation was enacted to conserve the morals, the health or the safety of the people; such legislation would be valid, no matter how absolutely without foundation the claim might be. The claim of the police power would be a mere pretext—become another and delusive name for the supreme sovereignty of the State to be exercised free from constitutional restraint. This is not contended for. In every case that comes before this court, therefore, where legislation of this character is concerned and where the protection of the Federal Constitution is sought, the question necessarily arises: Is this a fair, reasonable and appropriate exercise of the police power of the State, or is it an unreasonable, unnecessary and arbitrary interference with the right of the individual to his personal liberty or to enter into those contracts in relation to labor which may seem to him appropriate or necessary for the support of himself and his family? Of course the liberty of contract relating to labor includes both parties to it. The one has as much right to purchase as the other to sell labor.

This is not a question of substituting the judgment of the court for that of the legislature. If the act be within the power of the State it is valid, although the judgment of the court might be totally opposed to the enactment of such a law. But the question would still remain: Is it within the police power of the State? and that question must be answered by the court.

. . .

We think the limit of the police power has been reached and passed in this case. There is,

in our judgment, no reasonable foundation for holding this to be necessary or appropriate as a health law to safeguard the public health or the health of the individuals who are following the trade of a baker. If this statute be valid, and if, therefore, a proper case is made out in which to deny the right of an individual, *sui juris*, as employer or employé, to make contracts for the labor of the latter under the protection of the provisions of the Federal Constitution, there would seem to be no length to which legislation of this nature might not go. The case differs widely, as we have already stated, from the expressions of this court in regard to laws of this nature, as stated in *Holden* v. *Hardy.* . . .

We think that there can be no fair doubt that the trade of a baker, in and of itself, is not an unhealthy one to that degree which would authorize the legislature to interfere with the right to labor, and with the right of free contract on the part of the individual, either as employer or employé. In looking through statistics regarding all trades and occupations, it may be true that the trade of a baker does not appear to be as healthy as some other trades, and is also vastly more healthy than still others. To the common understanding the trade of a baker has never been regarded as an unhealthy one. Very likely physicians would not recommend the exercise of that or of any other trade as a remedy for ill health. Some occupations are more healthy than others, but we think there are none which might not come under the power of the legislature to supervise and control the hours of working therein, if the mere fact that the occupation is not absolutely and perfectly healthy is to confer that right upon the legislative department of the Government. It might be safely affirmed that almost all occupations more or less affect the health. There must be more than the mere fact of the possible existence of some small amount of unhealthiness to warrant legislative interference with liberty. It is unfortunately true that labor, even in any department, may possibly carry with it the seeds of unhealthiness. But are we all, on that account, at the mercy of legislative majorities? A printer, a tinsmith, a locksmith, a carpenter, a cabinetmaker, a dry goods clerk, a bank's, a lawyer's or a physician's clerk, or a clerk in almost any kind of business, would all come under the power of the legislature, on this assumption. No trade, no occupation, no mode of earning one's living, could escape this all-pervading power, and the acts of the legislature in limiting the hours of labor in all employments would be valid, although such limitation might seriously cripple the ability of the laborer to support himself and his family. In our large cities there are many buildings into which the sun penetrates for but a short time in each day, and these buildings are occupied by people carrying on the business of bankers, brokers, lawyers, real estate, and many other kinds of business, aided by many clerks, messengers, and other employés. Upon the assumption of the validity of this act under review, it is not possible to say that an act, prohibiting lawyers' or bank clerks, or others, from contracting to labor for their employers more than eight hours a day, would be invalid. It might be said that it is unhealthy to work more than that number of hours in an apartment lighted by artificial light during the working hours of the day; that the occupation of the bank clerk, the lawyer's clerk, the real estate clerk, or the broker's clerk in such offices is therefore unhealthy, and the legislature in its paternal wisdom must, therefore, have the right to legislate on the subject of and to limit the hours for such labor, and if it exercises that power and its validity be questioned, it is sufficient to say, it has reference to the public health; it has reference to the health of the employés condemned to labor day after day in buildings where the sun never shines; it is a health law, and therefore it is valid, and cannot be questioned by the courts.

It is also urged, pursuing the same line of argument, that it is to the interest of the State that its population should be strong and robust, and therefore any legislation which may be said to tend to make people healthy must be valid as health laws, enacted under the police power. If this be a valid argument and a justification for this kind of legislation, it follows that the protection of the Federal Constitution from undue interference with liberty of person and freedom of contract is visionary, wherever the law is sought to be justified as a valid exercise of the police power. Scarcely any law but might find shelter under such assumptions, and conduct,

properly so called, as well as contract, would come under the restrictive sway of the legislature. Not only the hours of employés, but the hours of employers, could be regulated, and doctors, lawyers, scientists, all professional men, as well as athletes and artisans, could be forbidden to fatigue their brains and bodies by prolonged hours of exercise, lest the fighting strength of the State be impaired. We mention these extreme cases because the contention is extreme. We do not believe in the soundness of the views which uphold this law. On the contrary, we think that such a law as this, although passed in the assumed exercise of the police power, and as relating to the public health, or the health of the employés named, is not within that power, and is invalid. The act is not, within any fair meaning of the term, a health law, but is an illegal interference with the rights of individuals, both employers and employés, to make contracts regarding labor upon such terms as they may think best, or which they may agree upon with the other parties to such contracts. Statutes of the nature of that under review, limiting the hours in which grown and intelligent men may labor to earn their living, are mere meddlesome interferences with the rights of the individual, and they are not saved from condemnation by the claim that they are passed in the exercise of the police power and upon the subject of the health of the individual whose rights are interfered with, unless there be some fair ground, reasonable in and of itself, to say that there is material danger to the public health or to the health of the employés, if the hours of labor are not curtailed.

. . .

It is manifest to us that the limitation of the hours of labor as provided for in this section of the statute under which the indictment was found, and the plaintiff in error convicted, has no such direct relation to and no such substantial effect upon the health of the employé, as to justify us in regarding the section as really a health law. It seems to us that the real object and purpose were simply to regulate the hours of labor between the master and his employés (all being men, *sui juris*), in a private business, not dangerous in any degree to morals or in any real and substantial degree, to the health of the employés. Under such circumstances the freedom of master and employé to contract with each other in relation to their employment, and in defining the same, cannot be prohibited or interfered with, without violating the Federal Constitution.

The judgment of the Court of Appeals of New York as well as that of the Supreme Court and of the County Court of Oneida County must be reversed and the case remanded to the County Court for further proceedings not inconsistent with this opinion.

Mr. Justice **Harlan,** with whom Mr. Justice **White** and Mr. Justice **Day** concurred, dissenting.

. . .

Granting . . . that there is a liberty of contract which cannot be violated even under the sanction of direct legislative enactment, but assuming, as according to settled law we may assume, that such liberty of contract is subject to such regulations as the State may reasonably prescribe for the common good and the well-being of society, what are the conditions under which the judiciary may declare such regulations to be in excess of legislative authority and void? Upon this point there is no room for dispute; for, the rule is universal that a legislative enactment, Federal or state, is never to be disregarded or held invalid unless it be, beyond question, plainly and palpably in excess of legislative power. In *Jacobson* v. *Massachusetts,* we said that the power of the courts to review legislative action in respect of a matter affecting the general welfare exists *only* "when that which the legislature has done comes within the rule that if a statute purporting to have been enacted to protect the public health, the public morals or the public safety, has no real or substantial relation to those objects, or is, beyond all question, a plain, palpable invasion of rights secured by the fundamental law." . . . If there be doubt as to the validity of the statute, that doubt must therefore be resolved in favor of its validity, and the courts must keep their hands off, leaving the legislature to meet the responsibility for unwise legislation. If the end which the legislature seeks

to accomplish be one to which its power extends, and if the means employed to that end, although not the wisest or best, are yet not plainly and palpably unauthorized by law, then the court cannot interfere. In other words, when the validity of a statute is questioned, the burden of proof, so to speak, is upon those who assert it to be unconstitutional. *McCulloch* v. *Maryland.*

Let these principles be applied to the present case. By the statute in question it is provided that, "No employé shall be required or permitted to work in a biscuit, bread or cake bakery or confectionery establishment more than sixty hours in any one week, or more than ten hours in any one day, unless for the purpose of making a shorter work day on the last day of the week; nor more hours in any one week than will make an average of ten hours per day for the number of days during such week in which such employé shall work."

It is plain that this statute was enacted in order to protect the physical well-being of those who work in bakery and confectionery establishments. It may be that the statute had its origin, in part, in the belief that employers and employés in such establishments were not upon an equal footing, and that the necessities of the latter often compelled them to submit to such exactions as unduly taxed their strength. Be this as it may, the statute must be taken as expressing the belief of the people of New York that, as a general rule, and in the case of the average man, labor in excess of sixty hours during a week in such establishments may endanger the health of those who thus labor. Whether or not this be wise legislation it is not the province of the court to inquire. Under our systems of government the courts are not concerned with the wisdom or policy of legislation. So that in determining the question of power to interfere with liberty of contract, the court may inquire whether the means devised by the State are germane to an end which may be lawfully accomplished and have a real or substantial relation to the protection of health, as involved in the daily work of the persons, male and female, engaged in bakery and confectionery establishments. But when this inquiry is entered upon I find it impossible, in view of common experience, to say that there is here no real or substantial relation between the means employed by the State and the end sought to be accomplished by its legislation. Nor can I say that the statute has no appropriate or direct connection with that protection to health which each State owes to her citizens; or that it is not promotive of the health of the employés in question; or that the regulation prescribed by the State is utterly unreasonable and extravagant or wholly arbitrary. Still less can I say that the statute is, beyond question, a plain, palpable invasion of rights secured by the fundamental law. Therefore I submit that this court will transcend its functions if it assumes to annul the statute of New York. It must be remembered that this statute does not apply to all kinds of business. It applies only to work in bakery and confectionery establishments, in which, as all know, the air constantly breathed by workmen is not as pure and healthful as that to be found in some other establishments or out of doors.

Professor Hirt in his treatise on the "Diseases of the Workers" has said: "The labor of the bakers is among the hardest and most laborious imaginable, because it has to be performed under conditions injurious to the health of those engaged in it. It is hard, very hard work, not only because it requires a great deal of physical exertion in an overheated workshop and during unreasonably long hours, but more so because of the erratic demands of the public, compelling the baker to perform the greater part of his work at night, thus depriving him of an opportunity to enjoy the necessary rest and sleep, a fact which is highly injurious to his health." Another writer says: "The constant inhaling of flour dust causes inflammation of the lungs and of the bronchial tubes. The eyes also suffer through this dust, which is responsible for the many cases of running eyes among the bakers. The long hours of toil to which all bakers are subjected produce rheumatism, cramps and swollen legs. The intense heat in the workshops induces the workers to resort to cooling drinks, which together with their habit of exposing the greater part of their bodies to the change in the atmosphere, is another source of a number of diseases of various organs. Nearly all bakers are pale-faced and of more delicate health than the workers of other crafts, which is chiefly due to their hard

work and their irregular and unnatural mode of living, whereby the power of resistance against disease is greatly diminished. The average age of a baker is below that of other workmen; they seldom live over their fiftieth year, most of them dying between the ages of forty and fifty. During periods of epidemic diseases the bakers are generally the first to succumb to the disease, and the number swept away during such periods far exceeds the number of other crafts in comparison to the men employed in the respective industries. When, in 1720, the plague visited the city of Marseilles, France, every baker in the city succumbed to the epidemic, which caused considerable excitement in the neighboring cities and resulted in measures for the sanitary protection of the bakers."

. . .

We also judicially know that the number of hours that should constitute a day's labor in particular occupations involving the physical strength and safety of workmen has been the subject of enactments by Congress and by nearly all of the States. Many, if not most, of those enactments fix eight hours as the proper basis of a day's labor.

I do not stop to consider whether any particular view of this economic question presents the sounder theory. What the precise facts are it may be difficult to say. It is enough for the determination of this case, and it is enough for this court to know, that the question is one about which there is room for debate and for an honest difference of opinion. There are many reasons of a weighty, substantial character, based upon the experience of mankind, in support of the theory that, all things considered, more than ten hours' steady work each day, from week to week, in a bakery or confectionery establishment, may endanger the health, and shorten the lives of the workmen, thereby diminishing their physical and mental capacity to serve the State, and to provide for those dependent upon them.

If such reasons exist that ought to be the end of this case, for the State is not amenable to the judiciary, in respect of its legislative enactments, unless such enactments are plainly, palpably, beyond all question, inconsistent with the Constitution of the United States. We are not to presume that the State of New York has acted in bad faith. Nor can we assume that its legislature acted without due deliberation, or that it did not determine this question upon the fullest attainable information, and for the common good. We cannot say that the State has acted without reason nor ought we to proceed upon the theory that its action is a mere sham. Our duty, I submit, is to sustain the statute as not being in conflict with the Federal Constitution, for the reason—and such is an all-sufficient reason—it is not shown to be plainly and palpably inconsistent with that instrument. Let the State alone in the management of its purely domestic affairs, so long as it does not appear beyond all question that it has violated the Federal Constitution. This view necessarily results from the principle that the health and safety of the people of a State are primarily for the State to guard and protect.

I take leave to say that the New York statute, in the particulars here involved, cannot be held to be in conflict with the Fourteenth Amendment, without enlarging the scope of the Amendment far beyond its original purpose and without bringing under the supervision of this court matters which have been supposed to belong exclusively to the legislative departments of the several States when exerting their conceded power to guard the health and safety of their citizens by such regulations as they in their wisdom deem best. . . .

Mr. Justice **Holmes** dissenting.

I regret sincerely that I am unable to agree with the judgment in this case, and that I think it my duty to express my dissent.

This case is decided upon an economic theory which a large part of the country does not entertain. If it were a question whether I agreed with that theory, I should desire to study it further and long before making up my mind. But I do not conceive that to be my duty, because I strongly believe that my agreement or disagreement has nothing to do with the right of a majority to embody their opinions in law. It is settled by various decisions of this court that state constitutions and state laws may regulate life in many ways which we as legislators might think as injudicious or if you like as tyrannical as this, and which equally with this interfere with the liberty to contract. Sunday laws and usury laws are ancient examples. A more modern one is the prohibition of lotteries. The liberty of the citizen to do as he likes so long as he does not interfere with the liberty of others to do the same, which has been a shibboleth for some well-known writers, is interfered with by school laws, by the Post Office, by every state or municipal institution which takes his money for purposes thought desirable, whether he likes it or not. The Fourteenth Amendment does not enact Mr. Herbert Spencer's Social Statics. The other day we sustained the Massachusetts vaccination law. *Jacobson* v. *Massachusetts*. United States and state statutes and decisions cutting down the liberty to contract by way of combination are familiar to this court. *Northern Securities Co.* v. *United States*. Two years ago we upheld the prohibition of sales of stock on margins or for future delivery in the constitution of California. *Otis* v. *Parker*. The decision sustaining an eight hour law for miners is still recent. *Holden* v. *Hardy*. Some of these laws embody convictions or prejudices which judges are likely to share. Some may not. But a constitution is not intended to embody a particular economic theory, whether of paternalism and the organic relation of the citizen to the State or of *laissez faire*. It is made for people of fundamentally differing views, and the accident of our finding certain opinions natural and familiar or novel and even shocking ought not to conclude our judgment upon the question whether statutes embodying them conflict with the Constitution of the United States.

General propositions do not decide concrete cases. The decision will depend on a judgment or intuition more subtle than any articulate major premise. But I think that the proposition just stated, if it is accepted, will carry us far toward the end. Every opinion tends to become a law. I think that the word liberty in the Fourteenth Amendment is perverted when it is held to prevent the natural outcome of a dominant opinion, unless it can be said that a rational and fair man necessarily would admit that the statute proposed would infringe fundamental principles as they have been understood by the traditions of our people and our law. It does not need research to show that no such sweeping condemnation can be passed upon the statute before us. A reasonable man might think it a proper measure on the score of health. Men whom I certainly could not pronounce unreasonable would uphold it as a first installment of a general regulation of the hours of work. Whether in the latter aspect it would be open to the charge of inequality I think it unnecessary to discuss.

Aftermath of Lochner v. New York

Lochner is remembered today more for the stinging dissent by Justice Holmes accusing his brethren of acting on the basis of economic rather than constitutional theory, than for its majority opinion by Justice Peckham. Yet, with a few notable exceptions, it was Peckham's enshrinement of liberty of contract in the Fourteenth Amendment that would prevail on the Court over the next several decades. In 1908, for example, a Boston lawyer named Louis Brandeis was retained by the National Consumers League to defend an Oregon Law mandating a 10-hour day for women against a challenge in the Supreme Court. Brandeis in effect picked up the gauntlet thrown down by Lochner's lawyer three years earlier by submitting a 116-page brief consisting of three pages of constitutional arguments and 113 pages of scientific data demonstrating the negative effects of excessive working hours on women. The famous "Brandeis Brief" persuaded the Court that the law addressed a public interest which in this instance outweighed the sanctity of contract. Ten years later the Court upheld on similar grounds another Oregon law providing a 10-hour day for all industrial workers, and on the same day upheld Oregon's minimum wage law. Significantly, in both cases the Court shifted the burden of proof from the defenders to the challengers of the law.

In the 1920s, however, the Supreme Court returned to its *Lochner* position with a vengeance by striking down minimum wage laws in two states and the District of Columbia, and in 1936 it invalidated a New York law mandating minimum wages for women and children. (*Morehead* v. *New York ex rel Tipaldo.*) Between 1900 and 1936 the vast majority of the public welfare, worker protection, and consumer protection statutes brought before the Supreme Court were overturned on substantive due process grounds. It was not until President Roosevelt, reelected overwhelmingly in 1936, unveiled his plan for reorganizing the Supreme Court that a bare majority of the justices finally backed away from the doctrine of substantive due process restriction on state police powers in the economic area. In *West Coast Hotel* v. *Parrish*(1937) the Court upheld a state minimum wage law almost identical to one it had overturned the previous year.

Griswold v. *Connecticut*

381 U.S. 479 (1965)

Substantive due process ceased to serve as a vehicle for laissez-faire economics after 1937, but it did not disappear from constitutional discourse. Over the next several decades the doctrine became increasingly important as a source of limitations on the capacity of local, state, and national officials to interfere with personal freedoms.

While many of the Court's substantive due process decisions have involved liberties specifically located in the Bill of Rights, as in the speech, press, and religious clauses of the First Amendment, from time to time the Court has included as well liberties not specifically named under the rubric of due process. Probably the most notable of these is the right of privacy, an important dimension of which is sexual privacy.

In 1879 Connecticut became the only state to prohibit not only the distribution but also the use of contraceptives. Although rarely enforced, the law remained on the books despite persistent efforts by groups like Margaret Sanger's Planned Parenthood Federation to have it repealed. Opponents of the law emphasized its unfairness because as a practical matter the law could be applied only against birth control clinics, not private doctors. Middle-class women had access to birth control but poor women did not. In the 1930s the Connecticut Birth Control League set up a network of clinics around the state to provide services for married women with one or more children, an action that led to a criminal prosecution and in 1940, to a state supreme court decision upholding the anti-birth control law.

Birth control advocates renewed their attack on the law in the 1950s, initiating a constitutional challenge involving plaintiffs whose health problems were such that their lives would be endangered by future pregnancies. However, when the case *Poe v. Ullman* reached the Supreme Court in 1961, the Court refused to decide it on its merits, citing the absence of a real controversy because in practice the law was being enforced only against clinics and not against individual married women like the plaintiffs.

Determined to bring a case that the Court could not deflect or ignore, Connecticut Planned Parenthood immediately announced plans to open a birth control clinic in New Haven. City officials were reluctant to move against the clinic, but after prodding by a local anti-birth control activist the clinic was "raided" and its director, Estelle Griswold, and its medical director were arrested—with their full and enthusiastic cooperation. Following a perfunctory trial the codefendants were found guilty and fined $100 apiece. After the convictions were upheld by the state supreme court, the case reached the United States Supreme Court in 1965. In its appeal, Planned Parenthood argued that the First, Third, Fourth, and Ninth Amendments, taken together, created a right of privacy which was protected against state interference by the due process clause of the Fourteenth Amendment. Connecticut defended the law as a legitimate exercise of its police power, a measure justified by the need to protect the "health, safety, and morals" of the citizenry.

WILLIAM O. DOUGLAS

Named to the Supreme Court by President Franklin Roosevelt in 1939 at the age of 41, William O. Douglas was the youngest Court appointee since Joseph Story in 1811. His 36-year tenure is the longest in the Court's history. Although Douglas had made his legal reputation as an expert in financial law, as a Supreme Court justice his greatest concern was for individual liberty, which he saw as the preeminent value protected by the U.S. Constitution. In his 1300 opinions (about half of them dissents) and his nearly 30 books, Douglas promoted a philosophy of uncompromising individualism. He was also an ardent conservationist and naturalist.

Mr. Justice **Douglas** delivered the opinion of the Court.

. . .

Coming to the merits, we are met with a wide range of questions that implicate the Due Process Clause of the Fourteenth Amendment. Overtones of some arguments suggest that Lochner v New York should be our guide. But we decline that invitation. . . .

We do not sit as a super-legislature to determine the wisdom, need, and propriety of laws that touch economic problems, business affairs, or social conditions. This law, however, operates directly on an intimate relation of husband and wife and their physician's role in one aspect of that relation.

The association of people is not mentioned in the Constitution nor in the Bill of Rights. The right to educate a child in a school of the parents' choice—whether public or private or parochial—is also not mentioned. Nor is the right to study any particular subject or any foreign language. Yet the First Amendment has been construed to include certain of those rights.

By Pierce v Society of Sisters, the right to educate one's children as one chooses is made applicable to the States by the force of the First and Fourteenth Amendments. By Meyer v Nebraska, the same dignity is given the right to study the German language in a private school. In other words, the State may not, consistently with the spirit of the First Amendment, contract the spectrum of available knowledge. The right of freedom of speech and press includes not only the right to utter or to print, but the right to distribute, the right to receive, the right to read and freedom of inquiry, freedom of thought, and freedom to teach—indeed the freedom of the entire university community. Without those peripheral rights the specific rights would be less secure. And so we reaffirm the principle of the Pierce and the Meyer cases.

In NAACP v Alabama, we protected the "freedom to associate and privacy in one's association," noting that freedom of association was a peripheral First Amendment right. Disclosure of membership lists of a constitutionally valid association, we held, was invalid "as entailing the

likelihood of a substantial restraint upon the exercise by petitioner's members of their right to freedom of association." In other words, the First Amendment has a penumbra where privacy is protected from governmental intrusion. In like context, we have protected forms of "association" that are not political in the customary sense but pertain to the social, legal, and economic benefit of the members. In Schware v Board of Bar Examiners, we held it not permissible to bar a lawyer from practice, because he had once been a member of the Communist Party. The man's "association with that Party" was not shown to be "anything more than a political faith in a political party" and not action of a kind proving bad moral character.

Those cases involved more than the "right of assembly"—a right that extends to all irrespective of their race or ideology. The right of "association," like the right of belief, is more than the right to attend a meeting; it includes the right to express one's attitudes or philosophies by membership in a group or by affiliation with it or by other lawful means. Association in that context is a form of expression of opinion; and while it is not expressly included in the First Amendment its existence is necessary in making the express guarantees fully meaningful.

The foregoing cases suggest that specific guarantees in the Bill of Rights have penumbras, formed by emanations from those guarantees that help give them life and substance. Various guarantees create zones of privacy. The right of association contained in the penumbra of the First Amendment is one, as we have seen. The Third Amendment in its prohibition against the quartering of soldiers "in any house" in time of peace without the consent of the owner is another facet of that privacy. The Fourth Amendment explicitly affirms the "right of the people to be secure in their persons, houses, papers, and effects against unreasonable searches and seizures." The Fifth Amendment in its Self-Incrimination Clause enables the citizen to create a zone of privacy which government may not force him to surrender to his detriment. The Ninth Amendment provides: "The enumeration in the Constitution, of certain rights, shall not be construed to deny or disparage others retained by the people."

The Fourth and Fifth Amendments were described in Boyd v United States, as protection against all governmental invasions "of the sanctity of a man's home and the privacies of life. We recently referred in Mapp v Ohio, to the Fourth Amendment as creating a "right of privacy, no less important than any other right carefully and particularly reserved to the people." . . .

The present case, then, concerns a relationship lying within the zone of privacy created by several fundamental constitutional guarantees. And it concerns a law which, in forbidding the *use* of contraceptives rather than regulating their manufacture or sale, seeks to achieve its goals by means having a maximum destructive impact upon that relationship. Such a law cannot stand in light of the familiar principle, so often applied by this Court, that a "governmental purpose to control or prevent activities constitutionally subject to state regulation may not be achieved by means which sweep unnecessarily broadly and thereby invade the area of protected freedom." NAACP v Alabama. Would we allow the police to search the sacred precincts of marital bedrooms for telltale signs of the use of contraceptives? The very idea is repulsive to the notions of privacy surrounding the marriage relationship.

We deal with a right of privacy older than the Bill of Rights—older than our political parties, older than our school system. Marriage is a coming together for better or for worse, hopefully enduring, and intimate to the degree of being sacred. It is an association that promotes a way of life, not causes; a harmony in living, not political faiths; a bilateral loyalty, not commercial or social projects. Yet it is an association for as noble a purpose as any involved in our prior decisions.

Reversed.

Mr. Justice **Goldberg,** whom The **Chief Justice** and Mr. Justice **Brennan** join, concurring.

I agree with the Court that Connecticut's birth control law unconstitutionally intrudes upon the right of marital privacy, and I join in its opinion and judgment. Although I have not accepted the view that "'due process' as used in the Fourteenth Amendment incorporates all of the first eight Amendments," I do agree that the concept of liberty protects those personal rights that are fundamental, and is not confined to the specific terms of the Bill of Rights. My conclusion that the concept of liberty is not so restricted and that it embraces the right of marital privacy though that right is not mentioned explicitly in the Constitution is supported both by numerous decisions of this Court, referred to in the Court's opinion, and by the language and history of the Ninth Amendment. In reaching the conclusion that the right of marital privacy is protected, as being within the protected penumbra of specific guarantees of the Bill of Rights, the Court refers to the Ninth Amendment, ante, at 515. I add these words to emphasize the relevance of that Amendment to the Court's holding.

The Court stated many years ago that the Due Process Clause protects those liberties that are "so rooted in the traditions and conscience of our people as to be ranked as fundamental." . . .

This Court, in a series of decisions, has held that the Fourteenth Amendment absorbs and applies to the States those specifics of the first eight amendments which express fundamental personal rights. The language and history of the Ninth Amendment reveal that the Framers of the Constitution believed that there are additional fundamental rights, protected from governmental infringement, which exist alongside those fundamental rights specifically mentioned in the first eight constitutional amendments.

The Ninth Amendment reads, "The enumeration in the Constitution, of certain rights, shall not be construed to deny or disparage others retained by the people." The Amendment is almost entirely the work of James Madison. It was introduced in Congress by him and passed the House and Senate with little or no debate and virtually no change in language. It was proffered to quiet expressed fears that a bill of specifically enumerated rights could not be sufficiently broad to cover all essential rights and that the specific mention of certain rights would be interpreted as a denial that others were protected.

While this Court has had little occasion to interpret the Ninth Amendment, "[i]t cannot be presumed that any clause in the constitution is intended to be without effect." Marbury v Madison. In interpreting the Constitution, "real effect should be given to all the words it uses." Myers v United States. The Ninth Amendment to the Constitution may be regarded by some as a recent discovery and may be forgotten by others, but since 1791 it has been a basic part of the Constitution which we are sworn to uphold. To hold that a right so basic and fundamental and so deep-rooted in our society as the right of privacy in marriage may be infringed because that right is not guaranteed in so many words by the first eight amendments to the Constitution is to ignore the Ninth Amendment and to give it no effect whatsoever. Moreover, a judicial construction that this fundamental right is not protected by the Constitution because it is not mentioned in explicit terms by one of the first eight amendments or elsewhere in the Constitution would violate the Ninth Amendment, which specifically states that "[t]he enumeration in the Constitution, of certain rights, shall not be *construed* to deny or disparage others retained by the people." (Emphasis added.)

. . .

The entire fabric of the Constitution and the purposes that clearly underlie its specific guarantees demonstrate that the rights to marital privacy and to marry and raise a family are of similar order and magnitude as the fundamental rights specifically protected.

Although the Constitution does not speak in so many words of the right of privacy in marriage, I cannot believe that it offers these fundamental rights no protection. The fact that no particular provision of the Constitution explicitly forbids the State from disrupting the traditional relation of the family—a relation as old and as fundamental as our entire civilization—surely does not show that the Government was meant to have the power to do so. Rather, as the Ninth Amendment expressly recognizes, there are fundamental personal rights such as this one, which are protected from abridgment by the Government though not specifically mentioned in the Constitution. . . .

Although the Connecticut birth-control law obviously encroaches upon a fundamental personal liberty, the State does not show that the law serves any "subordinating state interest which is compelling" or that it is "necessary . . . to the accomplishment of a permissible state policy." The State, at most, argues that there is some rational relation between this statute and what is admittedly a legitimate subject of state concern—the discouraging of extra-marital relations. It says that preventing the use of birth control devices by married persons helps prevent the indulgence by some in such extra-marital relations. The rationality of this justification is dubious, particularly in light of the admitted widespread availability to all persons in the State of Connecticut, unmarried as well as married, of birth control devices for the prevention of disease, as distinguished from the prevention of conception. But, in any event, it is clear that the State interest in safeguarding marital fidelity can be served by a more discriminately tailored statute, which does not, like the present one, sweep unnecessarily broadly, reaching far beyond the evil sought to be dealt with and intruding upon the privacy of all married couples. . . .

In sum, I believe that the right of privacy in the marital relation is fundamental and basic—a personal right "retained by the people" within the meaning of the Ninth Amendment. Connecticut cannot constitutionally abridge this fundamental right, which is protected by the Fourteenth Amendment from infringement by the States. I agree with the Court that petitioners' convictions must therefore be reversed.

Mr. Justice **Harlan,** concurring in the judgment.

I fully agree with the judgment of reversal, but find myself unable to join the Court's opinion. The reason is that it seems to me to evince an approach to this case very much like that taken by my Brothers Black and Stewart in dissent, namely: the Due Process Clause of the Fourteenth Amendment does not touch this Connecticut statute unless the enactment is found to violate some right assured by the letter or penumbra of the Bill of Rights.

In other words, what I find implicit in the Court's opinion is that the "incorporation" doctrine may be used to *restrict* the reach of Fourteenth Amendment Due Process. For me this is just as unacceptable constitutional doctrine as is the use of the "incorporation" approach to *impose* upon the States all the requirements of the Bill of Rights as found in the provisions of the first eight amendments and in the decisions of this Court interpreting them.

In my view, the proper constitutional inquiry in this case is whether this Connecticut statute infringes the Due Process Clause of the Fourteenth Amendment because the enactment violates basic values "implicit in the concept of ordered liberty," Palko v Connecticut. For reasons stated at length in my dissenting opinion in Poe v Ullman, I believe that it does. While the relevant inquiry may be aided by resort to one or more of the provisions of the Bill of Rights, it is not dependent on them or any of their radiations. The Due Process Clause of the Fourteenth Amendment stands, in my opinion, on its own bottom.

A further observation seems in order respecting the justification of my Brothers Black and Stewart for their "incorporation" approach to this case. Their approach does not rest on historical reasons, which are of course wholly lacking, but on the thesis that by limiting the content of the Due Process Clause of the Fourteenth Amendment to the protection of rights which can be found elsewhere in the Constitution, in this instance in the Bill of Rights, judges will thus be confined to "interpretation" of specific constitutional provisions, and will thereby be restrained from introducing their own notions of constitutional right and wrong into the "vague contours of the Due Process Clause." Rochin v California.

While I could not more heartily agree that judicial "self restraint" is an indispensable ingredient of sound constitutional adjudication, I do submit that the formula suggested for achieving it is more hollow than real. "Specific" provisions of the Constitution, no less than "due process," lend themselves as readily to "personal" interpretations by judges whose constitutional outlook is simply to keep the Constitution in supposed "tune with the times." Need one go further than to call up last Term's reapportionment cases, Wesberry v Sanders, and Reynolds v Sims, where a majority of the Court "interpreted" "by the People" (Art I, § 2) and "equal protection" (Amd 14) to command "one person, one vote," an interpretation that was made in the face of irrefutable and still unanswered history to the contrary?

Judicial self-restraint will not, I suggest, be brought about in the "due process" area by the historically unfounded incorporation formula long advanced by my Brother Black, and now in part espoused by my Brother Stewart. It will be achieved in this area, as in other constitutional areas, only by continual insistence upon respect for the teachings of history, solid recognition of the basic values that underlie our society, and wise appreciation of the great roles that the doctrines of federalism and separation of powers have played in establishing and preserving American freedoms. Adherence to these principles will not, of course, obviate all constitutional differences of opinion among judges, nor should it. Their continued recognition will, however, go farther toward keeping most judges from roaming at large in the constitutional field than will the interpolation into the Constitution of an artificial and largely illusory restriction on the content of the Due Process Clause.

Mr. Justice **Black,** with whom Mr. Justice **Stewart** joins, dissenting.

I agree with my Brother Stewart's dissenting opinion. And like him I do not to any extent whatever base my view that this Connecticut law is constitutional on a belief that the law is wise or that its policy is a good one. In order that there may be no room at all to doubt why I vote as I do, I feel constrained to add that the law is every bit as offensive to me as it is to my Brethren of the majority and my Brothers Harlan, White and Goldberg who, reciting reasons why it is offensive to them, hold it unconstitutional. There is no single one of the graphic and eloquent strictures and criticisms fired at the policy of this Connecticut law either by the Court's opinion or by those of my concurring Brethren to which I cannot subscribe—except their conclusion that the evil qualities they see in the law make it unconstitutional.

Had the doctor defendant here, or even the

nondoctor defendant, been convicted for doing nothing more than expressing opinions to persons coming to the clinic that certain contraceptive devices, medicines or practices would do them good and would be desirable, or for telling people how devices could be used, I can think of no reasons at this time why their expressions of views would not be protected by the First and Fourteenth Amendments, which guarantee freedom of speech. But speech is one thing; conduct and physical activities are quite another.

The two defendants here were active participants in an organization which gave physical examinations to women, advised them what kind of contraceptive devices or medicines would most likely be satisfactory for them, and then supplied the devices themselves, all for a graduated scale of fees, based on the family income. Thus these defendants admittedly engaged with others in a planned course of conduct to help people violate the Connecticut law. Merely because some speech was used in carrying on that conduct—just as in ordinary life some speech accompanies most kinds of conduct—we are not in my view any more justified in holding that the First Amendment forbids the State to punish their conduct. Strongly as I desire to protect all First Amendment freedoms, I am unable to stretch the Amendment so as to afford protection to the conduct of these defendants in violating the Connecticut law. What would be the constitutional fate of the law if hereafter applied to punish nothing but speech is, as I have said, quite another matter.

The Court talks about a constitutional "right of privacy" as though there is some constitutional provision or provisions forbidding any law ever to be passed which might abridge the "privacy" of individuals. But there is not. There are, of course, guarantees in certain specific constitutional provisions which are designed in part to protect privacy at certain times and places with respect to certain activities. Such, for example, is the Fourth Amendment's guarantee against "unreasonable searches and seizures." But I think it belittles that Amendment to talk about it as though it protects nothing but "privacy." To treat it that way is to give it a niggardly interpretation, not the kind of liberal reading I think any Bill of Rights provision should be given. The

average man would very likely not have his feelings soothed any more by having his property seized openly than by having it seized privately and by stealth. He simply wants his property left alone. And a person can be just as much, if not more, irritated, annoyed and injured by an unceremonious public arrest by a policeman as he is by a seizure in the privacy of his office or home.

One of the most effective ways of diluting or expanding a constitutionally guaranteed right is to substitute for the crucial word or words of a constitutional guarantee another word, more or less flexible and more or less restricted in its meaning. This fact is well illustrated by the use of the term "right of privacy" as a comprehensive substitute for the Fourth Amendment's guarantee against "unreasonable searches and seizures." "Privacy" is a broad, abstract and ambiguous concept which can easily be shrunken in meaning but which can also, on the other hand, easily be interpreted as a constitutional ban against many things other than searches and seizures. I have expressed the view many times that First Amendment freedoms, for example, have suffered from a failure of the courts to stick to the simple language of the First Amendment in construing it, instead of invoking multitudes of words substituted for those the Framers used. For these reasons I get nowhere in this case by talk about a constitutional "right of privacy" as an emanation from one or more constitutional provisions. I like my privacy as well as the next one, but I am nevertheless compelled to admit that government has a right to invade it unless prohibited by some specific constitutional provision. For these reasons I cannot agree with the Court's judgment and the reasons it gives for holding this Connecticut law unconstitutional.

This brings me to the arguments made by my Brothers Harlan, White and Goldberg for invalidating the Connecticut law. Brothers Harlan and White would invalidate it by reliance on the Due Process Clause of the Fourteenth Amendment, but Brother Goldberg, while agreeing with Brother Harlan, relies also on the Ninth Amendment. I have no doubt that the Connecticut law could be applied in such a way as to abridge freedom of speech and press and therefore violate the First and Fourteenth Amendments. My disagreement with the Court's opinion holding that there is such a violation here is a narrow one, relating to the application of the First Amendment to the facts and circumstances of this particular case. But my disagreement with Brothers Harlan, White and Goldberg is more basic. I think that if properly construed neither the Due Process Clause nor the Ninth Amendment, nor both together, could under any circumstances be a proper basis for invalidating the Connecticut law. I discuss the due process and Ninth Amendment arguments together because on analysis they turn out to be the same thing—merely using different words to claim for this Court and the federal judiciary power to invalidate any legislative act which the judges find irrational, unreasonable or offensive.

The due process argument which my Brothers Harlan and White adopt here is based, as their opinions indicate, on the premise that this Court is vested with power to invalidate all state laws that it considers to be arbitrary, capricious, unreasonable, or oppressive, or because of this Court's belief that a particular state law under scrutiny has no "rational or justifying purpose," or is offensive to a "sense of fairness and justice." If these formulas based on "natural justice," or others which mean the same thing, are to prevail, they require judges to determine what is or is not constitutional on the basis of their own appraisal of what laws are unwise or unnecessary. The power to make such decisions is of course that of a legislative body. Surely it has to be admitted that no provision of the Constitution specifically gives such blanket power to courts to exercise such a supervisory veto over the wisdom and value of legislative policies and to hold unconstitutional those laws which they believe unwise or dangerous. I readily admit that no legislative body, state or national, should pass laws that can justly be given any of the invidious labels invoked as constitutional excuses to strike down state laws. But perhaps it is not too much to say that no legislative body ever does pass laws without believing that they will accomplish a sane, rational, wise and justifiable purpose. While I completely subscribe to the holding of Marbury v Madison, and subsequent cases, that our Court has constitutional power to strike down statutes, state or federal, that violate commands of the Federal Constitution, I do not believe that we are granted power by the Due Process Clause or any other constitutional provision or provisions to measure constitutionality by our belief that legislation is arbitrary, capricious or unreasonable, or accomplishes no justifiable purpose, or is offensive to our own notions of "civilized standards of conduct." Such an appraisal of the wisdom of legislation is an attribute of the power to make laws, not of the power to interpret them. The use by federal courts of such a formula or doctrine or whatnot to veto federal or state laws simply takes away from Congress and States the power to make laws based on their own judgment of fairness and wisdom and transfers that power to this Court for ultimate determination—a power which was specifically denied to federal courts by the convention that framed the Constitution. . . .

Aftermath of Griswold *v.* Connecticut

Although the *Griswold* case marked the first appearance of a potentially expansive constitutional freedom, the right of privacy, the Court was careful to limit its application to the decision of a married couple to have or not to have children. Seven years later, in *Eisenstadt* v. *Baird* (1972), the Supreme Court broadened this privacy right to apply to all persons, married or not, and the following year, in *Roe* v. *Wade* (excerpted in Chapter 1), it was further extended to include a woman's decision to terminate her pregnancy.

Bowers v. *Hardwick*

478 U.S. 186 (1986)

After the Supreme Court's decisions in *Griswold* v. *Connecticut* and *Roe* v. *Wade* had established a substantive due process protection for some forms of sexual privacy, many felt that it was only a matter of time before the Court declared state laws prohibiting homosexual activities unconstitutional. The Court had never ruled directly on the issue, although in 1976 it had let stand without formal review a three-judge federal court decision upholding Virginia's sodomy law.

Sodomy (technically, oral and anal sex acts, whether committed by persons of the same sex or different sexes) was considered a criminal offense in all of the original 13 states. As late as 1961 it was illegal in all 50 states, although in many jurisdictions, private, consensual homosexual contact between adults was prosecuted infrequently, and heterosexual sodomy never at all (in some states only homosexual sodomy is forbidden by law). In the late 1950s the American Law Institute, a prestigious legal reform organization, issued a Model Penal Code recommending that all such conduct be decriminalized, and in 1961 Illinois became the first state to do so. At the end of the 1960s the newly formed "gay rights movement" was making its political presence felt through a well-organized legislative-litigative strategy which by 1975 had led to the repeal of sodomy laws in more than half of the states. Much public prejudice and a considerable amount of discrimination against homosexuals remained, however.

Michael Hardwick, a 28-year-old Atlanta, Georgia, bartender, was arrested by a police officer in 1982 for engaging in oral sex with another adult male in the bedroom of his home. The officer, who had come to Hardwick's house with a warrant for a previous unrelated violation, was admitted and directed to the bedroom by another guest. It later developed that the arrest warrant had expired 3 weeks earlier. Because of this, and because of his policy against prosecuting private homosexual acts, the county attorney refused to take the matter before the grand jury. By this time, although he was in no immediate danger of prosecution, Hardwick had decided to challenge the Georgia sodomy statute. With the help of a volunteer attorney provided by the American Civil Liberties Union, he brought suit in federal court asserting that the law violated his constitutional rights of privacy, due process, and freedom of expression and association. The district court rejected Hardwick's claim, but that decision was overturned by the federal appeals court, which ruled that on the basis of Supreme Court precedents providing constitutional protections for all kinds of "intimate association," whether related to marriage or not, homosexual activity should be considered part of the "liberty" protected by the Fourteenth Amendment against government interference. The Supreme Court granted *certiorari* and heard the case in 1986.

Justice **White** delivered the opinion of the Court.

. . .

Because other Courts of Appeals have arrived at judgments contrary to that of the Eleventh Circuit in this case, we granted the State's petition for certiorari questioning the holding that its sodomy statute violates the fundamental rights of homosexuals. We agree with the State that the Court of Appeals erred, and hence reverse its judgment.

This case does not require a judgment on whether laws against sodomy between consenting adults in general, or between homosexuals in particular, are wise or desirable. It raises no question about the right or propriety of state legislative decisions to repeal their laws that criminalize homosexual sodomy, or of state court decisions invalidating those laws on state constitutional grounds. The issue presented is whether the Federal Constitution confers a fundamental right upon homosexuals to engage in sodomy and hence invalidates the laws of the many States that still make such conduct illegal and have done so for a very long time. The case also calls for some judgment about the limits of the Court's role in carrying out its constitutional mandate.

We first register our disagreement with the Court of Appeals and with respondent that the Court's prior cases have construed the Constitution to confer a right of privacy that extends to homosexual sodomy and for all intents and purposes have decided this case. . . .

[Here follows a list of previous Court decisions dealing with childrearing and education, family relationships, procreation, marriage, contraception, and abortion.]

Accepting the decisions in these cases and the above description of them, we think it evident that none of the rights announced in those cases bears any resemblance to the claimed constitutional right of homosexuals to engage in acts of sodomy that is asserted in this case. No connection between family, marriage, or procreation on the one hand and homosexual activity on the other has been demonstrated, either by the Court of Appeals or by respondent. Moreover, any claim that these cases nevertheless stand for the proposition that any kind of private sexual conduct between consenting adults is constitutionally insulated from state proscription is unsupportable. . . .

Precedent aside, however, respondent would have us announce, as the Court of Appeals did, a fundamental right to engage in homosexual sodomy. This we are quite unwilling to do. It is true that despite the language of the Due Process Clauses of the Fifth and Fourteenth Amendments, which appears to focus only on the processes by which life, liberty, or property is taken, the cases are legion in which those Clauses have been interpreted to have substantive content, subsuming rights that to a great extent are immune from federal or state regulation or pro-

scription. Among such cases are those recognizing rights that have little or no textual support in the constitutional language. . . .

Striving to assure itself and the public that announcing rights not readily identifiable in the Constitution's text involves much more than the imposition of the Justices' own choice of values on the States and the Federal Government, the Court has sought to identify the nature of the rights qualifying for heightened judicial protection. In Palko v Connecticut, it was said that this category includes those fundamental liberties that are "implicit in the concept of ordered liberty," such that "neither liberty nor justice would exist if [they] were sacrificed." A different description of fundamental liberties appeared in Moore v East Cleveland(1977) (opinion of Powell, J.), where they are characterized as those liberties that are "deeply rooted in this Nation's history and tradition." . . .

It is obvious to us that neither of these formulations would extend a fundamental right to homosexuals to engage in acts of consensual sodomy. Proscriptions against that conduct have ancient roots. . . . Sodomy was a criminal offense at common law and was forbidden by the laws of the original thirteen States when they ratified the Bill of Rights. In 1868, when the Fourteenth Amendment was ratified, all but 5 of the 37 States in the Union had criminal sodomy laws. In fact, until 1961, all 50 States outlawed sodomy, and today, 24 States and the District of Columbia continue to provide criminal penalties for sodomy performed in private and between consenting adults. . . . Against this background, to claim that a right to engage in such conduct is "deeply rooted in this Nation's history and tradition" or "implicit in the concept of ordered liberty" is, at best, facetious.

Nor are we inclined to take a more expansive view of our authority to discover new fundamental rights imbedded in the Due Process Clause. The Court is most vulnerable and comes nearest to illegitimacy when it deals with judge-made constitutional law having little or no cognizable roots in the language or design of the Constitution. That this is so was painfully demonstrated by the face-off between the Executive and the Court in the 1930's, which resulted in the repudiation of much of the substantive gloss that the

Court had placed on the Due Process Clause of the Fifth and Fourteenth Amendments. There should be, therefore, great resistance to expand the substantive reach of those Clauses, particularly if it requires redefining the category of rights deemed to be fundamental. Otherwise, the Judiciary necessarily takes to itself further authority to govern the country without express constitutional authority. The claimed right pressed on us today falls far short of overcoming this resistance.

Respondent, however, asserts that the result should be different where the homosexual conduct occurs in the privacy of the home. He relies on Stanley v Georgia, where the Court held that the First Amendment prevents conviction for possessing and reading obscene material in the privacy of his home: "If the First Amendment means anything, it means that a State has no business telling a man, sitting alone in his house, what books he may read or what films he may watch."

Stanley did protect conduct that would not have been protected outside the home, and it partially prevented the enforcement of state obscenity laws; but the decision was firmly grounded in the First Amendment. The right pressed upon us here has no similar support in the text of the Constitution, and it does not qualify for recognition under the prevailing principles for construing the Fourteenth Amendment. Its limits are also difficult to discern. Plainly enough, otherwise illegal conduct is not always immunized whenever it occurs in the home. Victimless crimes, such as the possession and use of illegal drugs do not escape the law where they are committed at home. Stanley itself recognized that its holding offered no protection for the possession in the home of drugs, firearms, or stolen goods. And if respondent's submission is limited to the voluntary sexual conduct between consenting adults, it would be difficult, except by fiat, to limit the claimed right to homosexual conduct while leaving exposed to prosecution adultery, incest, and other sexual crimes even though they are committed in the home. We are unwilling to start down that road.

Even if the conduct at issue here is not a fundamental right, respondent asserts that there must be a rational basis for the law and that

there is none in this case other than the presumed belief of a majority of the electorate in Georgia that homosexual sodomy is immoral and unacceptable. This is said to be an inadequate rationale to support the law. The law, however, is constantly based on notions of morality, and if all laws representing essentially moral choices are to be invalidated under the Due Process Clause, the courts will be very busy indeed. Even respondent makes no such claim, but insists that majority sentiments about the morality of homosexuality should be declared inadequate. We do not agree, and are unpersuaded that the sodomy laws of some 25 States should be invalidated on this basis.

Accordingly, the judgment of the Court of Appeals is reversed.

Chief Justice **Burger,** concurring.

I join the Court's opinion, but I write separately to underscore my view that in constitutional terms there is no such thing as a fundamental right to commit homosexual sodomy.

As the Court notes, the proscriptions against sodomy have very "ancient roots." Decisions of individuals relating to homosexual conduct have been subject to state intervention throughout the history of Western Civilization. Condemnation of those practices is firmly rooted in Judeo-Christian moral and ethical standards. Homosexual sodomy was a capital crime under Roman law. During the English Reformation when powers of the ecclesiastical courts were transferred to the King's Courts, the first English statute criminalizing sodomy was passed. Blackstone described "the infamous crime against nature" as an offense of "deeper malignity" than rape, an heinous act "the very mention of which is a disgrace to human nature," and "a crime not fit to be named." The common law of England, including its prohibition of sodomy, became the received law of Georgia and the other Colonies. In 1816 the Georgia Legislature passed the statute at issue here, and that statute has been continuously in force in one form or another since that time. To hold that the act of homosexual sodomy is somehow protected as a fundamental right would be to cast aside millennia of moral teaching.

This is essentially not a question of personal "preferences" but rather that of the legislative authority of the State. I find nothing in the Constitution depriving a State of the power to enact the statute challenged here.

Justice **Powell,** concurring.

I join the opinion of the Court. I agree with the Court that there is no fundamental right— i.e., no substantive right under the Due Process Clause—such as that claimed by respondent, and found to exist by the Court of Appeals. This is not to suggest, however, that respondent may not be protected by the Eighth Amendment of the Constitution. The Georgia statute at issue in this case, Ga Code Ann § 16-6-2, authorizes a court to imprison a person for up to 20 years for a single private, consensual act of sodomy. In my view, a prison sentence for such conduct— certainly a sentence of long duration—would create a serious Eighth Amendment issue. Under the Georgia statute a single act of sodomy, even in the private setting of a home, is a felony comparable in terms of the possible sentence imposed to serious felonies such as aggravated battery, § 16-5-24, first degree arson, § 16-7-60 and robbery, § 16-8-40.

In this case, however, respondent has not been tried, much less convicted and sentenced. Moreover, respondent has not raised the Eighth Amendment issue below. For these reasons this constitutional argument is not before us.

Justice **Blackmun,** with whom Justice **Brennan,** Justice **Marshall,** and Justice **Stevens** join, dissenting.

This case is no more about "a fundamental right to engage in homosexual sodomy," as the Court purports to declare, than Stanley v Georgia was about a fundamental right to watch obscene movies, or Katz v United States was about a fundamental right to place interstate bets from a telephone booth. Rather, this case is about "the most comprehensive of rights and the right most valued by civilized men," namely, "the right to be let alone."

The statute at issue, Ga Code Ann § 16-6-2, denies individuals the right to decide for themselves whether to engage in particular forms of private, consensual sexual activity. The Court concludes that § 16-6-2 is valid essentially because "the laws of . . . many States . . . still make such conduct illegal and have done so for a very long time." But the fact that the moral judgments expressed by statutes like § 16-6-2 may be "natural and familiar . . . ought not to conclude our judgment upon the question whether statutes embodying them conflict with the Constitution of the United States." Like Justice Holmes, I believe that "[i]t is revolting to have no better reason for a rule of law than that so it was laid down in the time of Henry IV. It is still more revolting if the grounds upon which it was laid down have vanished long since, and the rule simply persists from blind imitation of the past." I believe we must analyze respondent's claim in the light of the values that underlie the constitutional right to privacy. If that right means anything, it means that, before Georgia can prosecute its citizens for making choices about the most intimate aspects of their lives, it must do more than assert that the choice they have made is an "'abominable crime not fit to be named among Christians.'"

. . .

"Our cases long have recognized that the Constitution embodies a promise that a certain private sphere of individual liberty will be kept largely beyond the reach of government." In construing the right to privacy, the Court has proceeded along two somewhat distinct, albeit complementary, lines. First, it has recognized a privacy interest with reference to certain decisions that are properly for the individual to make. Second, it has recognized a privacy interest with reference to certain *places* without regard for the particular activities in which the individuals who occupy them are engaged. The case before us implicates both the decisional and the spatial aspects of the right to privacy.

. . .

The Court concludes today that none of our prior cases dealing with various decisions that individuals are entitled to make free of governmental interference "bears any resemblance to the claimed constitutional right of homosexuals to engage in acts of sodomy that is asserted in this case." While it is true that these cases may be characterized by their connection to protection of the family, the Court's conclusion that they extend no further than this boundary ignores the warning in Moore v East Cleveland (plurality opinion), against "clos[ing] our eyes to the basic reasons why certain rights associated with the family have been accorded shelter under the Fourteenth Amendment's Due Process Clause." We protect those rights not because they contribute, in some direct and material way, to the general public welfare, but because they form so central a part of an individual's life.

. . .

Only the most willful blindness could obscure the fact that sexual intimacy is "a sensitive, key relationship of human existence, central to family life, community welfare, and the development of human personality," Paris Adult Theatre I v Slayton. The fact that individuals define themselves in a significant way through their intimate sexual relationships with others suggests, in a Nation as diverse as ours, that there may be many "right" ways of conducting those relationships, and that much of the richness of a relationship will come from the freedom an individual has to *choose* the form and nature of these intensely personal bonds.

In a variety of circumstances we have recognized that a necessary corollary of giving individuals freedom to choose how to conduct their lives is acceptance of the fact that different individuals will make different choices. . . . The Court claims that its decision today merely refuses to recognize a fundamental right to engage in homosexual sodomy; what the Court really has refused to recognize is the fundamental interest all individuals have in controlling the nature of their intimate associations with others.

. . .

The behavior for which Hardwick faces prosecution occurred in his own home, a place to which the Fourth Amendment attaches special significance. The Court's treatment of this aspect of the case is symptomatic of its overall refusal to consider the broad principles that have informed our treatment of privacy in specific cases. Just as the right to privacy is more than the mere aggregation of a number of entitle-

ments to engage in specific behavior, so too, protecting the physical integrity of the home is more than merely a means of protecting specific activities that often take place there. Even when our understanding of the contours of the right to privacy depends on "reference to a 'place,' . . . the essence of a Fourth Amendment violation is 'not the breaking of [a person's] doors, and the rummaging of his drawers,' but rather is 'the invasion of his indefeasible right of personal security, personal liberty and private property.'"

The Court's interpretation of the pivotal case of Stanley v Georgia is entirely unconvincing. Stanley held that Georgia's undoubted power to punish the public distribution of constitutionally unprotected, obscene material did not permit the State to punish the private possession of such material. According to the majority here, Stanley relied entirely on the First Amendment, and thus, it is claimed, sheds no light on cases not involving printed materials. But that is not what Stanley said. Rather, the Stanley Court anchored its holding in the Fourth Amendment's special protection for the individual in his home.

. . .

The Court's failure to comprehend the magnitude of the liberty interests at stake in this case leads it to slight the question whether petitioner, on behalf of the State, has justified Georgia's infringement on these interests. I believe that neither of the two general justifications for § 16-6-2 that petitioner has advanced warrants dismissing respondent's challenge for failure to state a claim.

First, petitioner asserts that the acts made criminal by the statute may have serious adverse consequences for "the general public health and welfare," such as spreading communicable diseases or fostering other criminal activity. Brief for Petitioner 37. Inasmuch as this case was dismissed by the District Court on the pleadings, it is not surprising that the record before us is barren of any evidence to support petitioner's claim. In light of the state of the record, I see no justification for the Court's attempt to equate the private, consensual sexual activity at issue here with the "possession in the home of drugs, firearms, or stolen goods," to which Stanley refused to extend its protection. None of the behavior so mentioned in Stanley can properly be viewed as "[v]ictimless": drugs and weapons are inherently dangerous, and for property to be "stolen," someone must have been wrongfully deprived of it. Nothing in the record before the Court provides any justification for finding the activity forbidden by § 16-6-2 to be physically dangerous, either to the persons engaged in it or to others.

The core of petitioner's defense of § 16-6-2, however, is that respondent and others who engage in the conduct prohibited by § 16-6-2 interfere with Georgia's exercise of the "'right of the Nation and of the States to maintain a decent society.'" Essentially, petitioner argues, and the Court agrees, that the fact that the acts described in § 16-6-2 "for hundreds of years, if not thousands, have been uniformly condemned as immoral" is a sufficient reason to permit a State to ban them today.

I cannot agree that either the length of time a majority has held its convictions or the passions with which it defends them can withdraw legislation from this Court's scrutiny. . . .

The assertion that "traditional Judeo-Christian values proscribe" the conduct involved cannot provide an adequate justification for § 16-6-2. That certain, but by no means all, religious groups condemn the behavior at issue gives the State no license to impose their judgments on the entire citizenry. The legitimacy of secular legislation depends instead on whether the State can advance some justification for its law beyond its conformity to religious doctrine. Thus, far from buttressing his case, petitioner's invocation of Leviticus, Romans, St. Thomas Aquinas, and sodomy's heretical status during the Middle Ages undermines his suggestion that § 16-6-2 represents a legitimate use of secular coercive power. A State can no more punish private behavior because of religious intolerance than it can punish such behavior because of racial animus. . . . No matter how uncomfortable a certain group may make the majority of

this Court, we have held that "[m]ere public intolerance or animosity cannot constitutionally justify the deprivation of a person's physical liberty."

Nor can § 16-6-2 be justified as a "morally neutral" exercise of Georgia's power to "protect the public environment." . . . Petitioner and the Court fail to see the difference between laws that protect public sensibilities and those that enforce private morality. Statutes banning public sexual activity are entirely consistent with protecting the individual's liberty interest in decisions concerning sexual relations: the same recognition that those decisions are intensely private which justifies protecting them from governmental interference can justify protecting individuals from unwilling exposure to the sexual activities of others. But the mere fact that intimate behavior may be punished when it takes place in public cannot dictate how States can regulate intimate behavior that occurs in intimate places. . . .

This case involves no real interference with the rights of others, for the mere knowledge that other individuals do not adhere to one's value system cannot be a legally cognizable interest, let alone an interest that can justify invading the houses, hearts, and minds of citizens who choose to live their lives differently.

It took but three years for the Court to see the error in its analysis in Minersville School District v Gobitis, and to recognize that the threat to national cohesion posed by a refusal to salute the flag was vastly outweighed by the threat to those same values posed by compelling such a salute. I can only hope that here, too, the Court soon will reconsider its analysis and conclude that depriving individuals of the right to choose for themselves how to conduct their intimate relationships poses a far greater threat to the values most deeply rooted in our Nation's history than tolerance of nonconformity could ever do. Because I think the Court today betrays those values, I dissent.

Aftermath of Bowers v. Hardwick

The Washington Post reported in July 1986 that according to unidentified "informed sources" Justice Lewis Powell had originally voted to overturn the Georgia law in Bowers v. Hardwick, but changed his mind shortly before the decision was announced and wrote a concurring opinion instead. If that is true, we can assume that Justice Harry Blackmun's impassioned dissent was first written as the majority opinion, which may explain both its length and its tone of outrage.

The reaction among homosexual activists and civil libertarians to the *Bowers* decision was swift and predictable. In addition to deploring the outcome, many expressed concern that the Court's dismissive, even hostile, attitude toward Hardwick's arguments might encourage increased harassment against homosexuals, stepped-up enforcement of antihomosexual statutes, and perhaps even undermine governmental efforts to respond to AIDS, a fatal disease prevalent primarily among homosexual men. One leading homosexual rights activist called the decision "our *Dred Scott* case." However, a *Newsweek* poll published shortly after *Bowers* was announced showed that 57 percent of those surveyed disapproved of the ruling, and some observers predicted that the Court's decision would galvanize homosexual rights activists in their efforts to repeal the remaining state sodomy laws and to achieve other objectives such as child custody rights for homosexuals. By 1990 judges in Texas, Kentucky, and Michigan had struck down state sodomy laws as violations of the states' constitutions.

One closely watched federal court case involved a United States Army sergeant, Perry J. Watkins, who was discharged after 14 years of service, although he had reported his homosexuality at the time of his enlistment and had been allowed repeatedly to re-enlist. In 1989 the Ninth Circuit Court of Appeals ordered the Army to reinstate Mr. Watkins, and the following year the Supreme Court let that ruling stand without comment. The Army then agreed to give Mr. Watkins retroactive pay of about $135,000, an honorable discharge, and full retirement benefits. The case was decided on narrow grounds and none of the constitutional issues in *Bowers* was revisited. The policy of all the military services prohibiting homosexuality remains unchanged, and more than 1,000 people a year are discharged from the military for homosexuality.

Another statutory issue before the federal courts is whether Section 504 of the Rehabilitation Act of 1973, which prohibits any institution that receives federal financing from discriminating on the basis of physical handicaps, prevents an employer from dismissing a person with AIDS. Ignoring a Justice Department opinion that the statute does not cover AIDS victims, the Department of Health and Human Services filed a complaint against a North Carolina hospital for dismissing a registered nurse who had been diagnosed as having AIDS.

Michael Hardwick, who had avoided all contact with the media while his case was in the courts, became much more visible after it was over, traveling and appearing on television on behalf of gay rights. In 1987 he was awarded an honorary degree by the City University of New York Law School.

Cruzan v. Director, Missouri Department of Health

497 U.S.——(1990)

In 1983, 25-year-old Nancy Beth Cruzan was involved in an automobile accident which left her in an anoxic state for 12 to 14 minutes resulting in permanent brain

damage. After being comatose for several weeks, Ms. Cruzan progressed to an unconscious state in which she received nutrition and hydration through an implanted gastronomy tube. When it became clear that Ms. Cruzan was in a "persistent vegetative state" with no chance of recovery or even of further rehabilitation, her parents, who had been appointed her legal guardians, asked that her artificial feeding and hydration be terminated, but officials at the state hospital where Ms. Cruzan resided refused to honor the request without court approval. The Cruzans then sought such an order from a state probate court. The court heard testimony that Nancy Cruzan had once told a friend that she would not wish to be kept alive if she were extremely ill or severely injured, though she had not prepared a formal document (commonly called a "living will") giving instructions to that effect. Concluding that under the state and federal constitutions she had a fundamental due process right to refuse or direct the termination of "death prolonging procedures," the court directed hospital employees to carry out the Cruzans' request. By a 4–3 vote, the Missouri Supreme Court reversed the trial court's decision, holding that that state's strong policy favoring the preservation of life outweighed Ms. Cruzan's right to refuse treatment. Evidence of that state policy, said the Missouri court, could be found in the antiabortion law adopted by the legislature in 1986 which declared that life began at conception (a law upheld in most respects by the United States Supreme Court in its 1989 decision, *Webster* v. *Reproductive Services*), as well as in the state's "living will" statute which requires specific instructions from the patient. Missouri also happens to be the only state in which the absence of a living will does not automatically place the decision to continue or to terminate life support for a comatose patient in the hands of family members. The United States Supreme Court, which had previously refused to hear four "right to die" cases, accepted the *Cruzan* case for review on the last day of its 1988–1989 term. The central questions before the Court were (1) whether a patient has a right under the due process clause of the Fourteenth Amendment to refuse life-sustaining treatment; and (2) if such a right exists, whether Missouri's refusal to accept the Cruzans' decision on their daughter's behalf constituted a denial of that right.

Chief Justice **Rehnquist** delivered the opinion of the Court.

. . .

We granted certiorari to consider the question of whether Cruzan has a right under the United States Constitution which would require the hospital to withdraw life-sustaining treatment from her under these circumstances.

At common law, even the touching of one person by another without consent and without legal justification was a battery. Before the turn of the century, this Court observed that "[n]o right is held more sacred, or is more carefully guarded, by the common law, than the right of every individual to the possession and control of his own person, free from all restraint or interference of others, unless by clear and unquestionable authority of law." Union Pacific R. Co. v Botsford (1891). This notion of bodily integrity has been embodied in the requirement that informed consent is generally required for medi-

cal treatment. . . . The informed consent doctrine has become firmly entrenched in American tort law.

The logical corollary of the doctrine of informed consent is that the patient generally possesses the right not to consent, that is, to refuse treatment. Until about 15 years ago and the seminal decision in In re Quinlan, the number of right-to-refuse-treatment decisions were relatively few. Most of the earlier cases involved patients who refused medical treatment forbidden by their religious beliefs, thus implicating First Amendment rights as well as common law rights of self-determination. More recently, however, with the advance of medical technology capable of sustaining life well past the point where natural forces would have brought certain death in earlier times, cases involving the right to refuse life-sustaining treatment have burgeoned.

. . .

As these cases demonstrate, the common-law doctrine of informed consent is viewed as generally encompassing the right of a competent individual to refuse medical treatment. Beyond that, these decisions demonstrate both similarity and diversity in their approach to decision of what all agree is a perplexing question with unusually strong moral and ethical overtones. State courts have available to them for decision a number of sources—state constitutions, statutes, and common law—which are not available to us. In this Court, the question is simply and starkly whether the United States Constitution prohibits Missouri from choosing the rule of decision which it did. This is the first case in which we have been squarely presented with the issue of whether the United States Constitution grants what is in common parlance referred to as a "right to die." We follow the judicious counsel of our decision in Twin City Bank v Nebeker (1897), where we said that in deciding "a question of such magnitude and importance . . . it is the [better] part of wisdom not to attempt, by any general statement, to cover every possible phase of the subject."

The Fourteenth Amendment provides that no State shall "deprive any person of life, liberty, or property, without due process of law." The principle that a competent person has a constitutionally protected liberty interest in refusing unwanted medical treatment may be inferred from our prior decisions. In Jacobson v Massachusetts (1905), for instance, the Court balanced an individual's liberty interest in declining an unwanted smallpox vaccine against the State's interest in preventing disease. Decisions prior to the incorporation of the Fourth Amendment into the Fourteenth Amendment analyzed searches and seizures involving the body under the Due Process Clause and were thought to implicate substantial liberty interests. . . .

Just this Term, in the course of holding that a State's procedures for administering antipsychotic medication to prisoners were sufficient to satisfy due process concerns, we recognized that prisoners possess "a significant liberty interest in avoiding the unwanted administration of antipsychotic drugs under the Due Process Clause of the Fourteenth Amendment." Washington v Harper (1990). Still other cases support the recognition of a general liberty interest in refusing medical treatment.

But determining that a person has a "liberty interest" under the Due Process Clause does not end the inquiry, "whether respondent's constitutional rights have been violated must be determined by balancing his liberty interests against the relevant state interests." Youngberg v Romeo (1982).

Petitioners insist that under the general holdings of our cases, the forced administration of life-sustaining medical treatment, and even of artificially-delivered food and water essential to life, would implicate a competent person's liberty interest. Although we think the logic of the cases discussed above would embrace such a liberty interest, the dramatic consequences involved in refusal of such treatment would inform the inquiry as to whether the deprivation of that interest is constitutionally permissible. But for purposes of this case, we assume that the United States Constitution would grant a competent person a constitutionally protected right to refuse lifesaving hydration and nutrition.

Petitioners go on to assert that an incompetent person should possess the same right in this respect as is possessed by a competent person.

. . .

The difficulty with petitioners' claim is that in a sense it begs the question: an incompetent person is not able to make an informed and voluntary choice to exercise a hypothetical right to refuse treatment or any other right. Such a "right" must be exercised for her, if at all, by some sort of surrogate. Here, Missouri has in effect recognized that under certain circumstances a surrogate may act for the patient in electing to have hydration and nutrition withdrawn in such a way as to cause death, but it has established a procedural safeguard to assure that the action of the surrogate conforms as best it may to the wishes expressed by the patient while competent. Missouri requires that evidence of the incompetent's wishes as to the withdrawal of treatment be proved by clear and convincing evidence. The question, then, is whether the United States Constitution forbids the establishment of this procedural requirement by the State. We hold that it does not.

Whether or not Missouri's clear and convincing evidence requirement comports with the United States Constitution depends in part on what interests the State may properly seek to protect in this situation. Missouri relies on its interest in the protection and preservation of human life, and there can be no gainsaying this interest. As a general matter, the States—indeed, all civilized nations—demonstrate their commitment to life by treating homicide as serious crime. Moreover, the majority of States in this country have laws imposing criminal penalties on one who assists another to commit suicide. We do not think a State is required to remain neutral in the face of an informed and voluntary decision by a physically-able adult to starve to death.

But in the context presented here, a State has more particular interests at stake. The choice between life and death is a deeply personal decision of obvious and overwhelming finality. We believe Missouri may legitimately seek to safeguard the personal element of this choice through the imposition of heightened evidentiary requirements. It cannot be disputed that the Due Process Clause protects an interest in life as well as an interest in refusing life-sustaining medical treatment. Not all incompetent patients will have loved ones available to serve as surrogate decisionmakers. And even where family members are present, "[t]here will, of course, be some unfortunate situations in which family members will not act to protect a patient." In re Jobes (1987). A State is entitled to guard against potential abuses in such situations. Similarly, a State is entitled to consider that a judicial proceeding to make a determination regarding an incompetent's wishes may very well not be an adversarial one, with the added guarantee of accurate factfinding that the adversary process brings with it. Finally, we think a State may properly decline to make judgments about the "quality" of life that a particular individual may enjoy, and simply assert an unqualified interest in the preservation of human life to be weighed against the constitutionally protected interests of the individual.

In our view, Missouri has permissibly sought to advance these interests through the adoption of a "clear and convincing" standard of proof to govern such proceedings.

. . .

We think it self-evident that the interests at stake in the instant proceedings are more substantial, both on an individual and societal level, than those involved in a run-of-the-mine civil dispute. But not only does the standard of proof reflect the importance of a particular adjudication, it also serves as "a societal judgment about how the risk of error should be distributed between the litigants." The more stringent the burden of proof a party must bear, the more that party bears the risk of an erroneous decision. We believe that Missouri may permissibly place an increased risk of an erroneous decision on those seeking to terminate an incompetent individual's life-sustaining treatment. An erroneous decision not to terminate results in a maintenance of the status quo; the possibility of subsequent developments such as advancements in medical science, the discovery of new evidence regarding the patient's intent, changes in the law, or simply the unexpected death of the patient despite the administration of life-sustaining treatment, at least create the potential that a wrong decision will eventually be corrected or its impact mitigated. An erroneous decision to withdraw life-sustaining treatment, however, is not susceptible of correction.

. . .

In sum, we conclude that a State may apply a clear and convincing evidence standard in proceedings where a guardian seeks to discontinue nutrition and hydration of a person diagnosed to be in a persistent vegetative state. We note that many courts which have adopted some sort of substituted judgment procedure in situations like this, whether they limit consideration of evidence to the prior expressed wishes of the incompetent individual, or whether they allow more general proof of what the individual's decision would have been, require a clear and convincing standard of proof for such evidence.

The Supreme Court of Missouri held that in this case the testimony adduced at trial did not amount to clear and convincing proof of the patient's desire to have hydration and nutrition withdrawn. In so doing, it reversed a decision of the Missouri trial court which had found that the evidence "suggest[ed]" Nancy Cruzan would not have desired to continue such measures, but which had not adopted the standard of "clear and convincing evidence" enunciated by the Supreme Court. The testimony adduced at trial consisted primarily of Nancy Cruzan's statements made to a housemate about a year before her accident that she would not want to live should she face life as a "vegetable," and other observations to the same effect. The observations did not deal in terms with withdrawal of medical treatment or of hydration and nutrition. We cannot say that the Supreme Court of Missouri committed constitutional error in reaching the conclusion that it did.

Petitioners alternatively contend that Missouri must accept the "substituted judgment" of close family members even in the absence of substantial proof that their views reflect the views of the patient. They rely primarily upon our decisions in Michael H. v. Gerald D. (1979). But we do not think these cases support their claim. In Michael H., we *upheld* the constitutionality of California's favored treatment of traditional family relationships; such a holding may not be turned around into a constitutional requirement that a State must recognize the primacy of those relationships in a situation like this. And in Parham, where the patient was a minor, we also *upheld* the constitutionality of a state scheme in which parents made certain decisions for mentally ill minors. Here again petitioners would seek to turn a decision which allowed a State to rely on family decisionmaking into a constitutional requirement that the State recognize such decisionmaking. But constitutional law does not work that way.

No doubt is engendered by anything in this record but that Nancy Cruzan's mother and father are loving and caring parents. If the State were required by the United States Constitution to repose a right of "substituted judgment" with anyone, the Cruzans would certainly qualify. But we do not think the Due Process Clause requires the State to repose judgment on these matters with anyone but the patient herself. Close family members may have a strong feeling—a feeling not at all ignoble or unworthy, but not entirely disinterested, either—that they do not wish to witness the continuation of the life of a loved one which they regard as hopeless, meaningless, and even degrading. But there is no automatic assurance that the view of close family members will necessarily be the same as the patient's would have been had she been confronted with the prospect of her situation while competent. All of the reasons previously discussed for allowing Missouri to require clear and convincing evidence of the patient's wishes lead us to conclude that the State may choose to defer only to those wishes, rather than confide the decision to close family members.

The judgment of the Supreme Court of Missouri is affirmed.

Justice **O'Connor,** concurring.

I agree that a protected liberty interest in refusing unwanted medical treatment may be inferred from our prior decisions, and that the refusal of artificially delivered food and water is encompassed within that liberty interest. I write separately to clarify why I believe this to be so.

As the Court notes, the liberty interest in refusing medical treatment flows from decisions involving the State's invasions into the body. Because our notions of liberty are inextricably entwined with our idea of physical freedom and self-determination, the Court has often deemed state incursions into the body repugnant to the interests protected by the Due Process Clause. . . .

The State's artificial provision of nutrition and hydration implicates identical concerns. Artificial feeding cannot readily be distinguished from other forms of medical treatment. Whether or not the techniques used to pass food and water into the patient's alimentary tract are termed "medical treatment," it is clear they all involve some degree of intrusion and restraint. Feeding a patient by means of a nasogastric tube requires a physician to pass a long flexible tube through the patient's nose, throat and esophagus and into the stomach. Because of the discomfort such a tube causes, "[m]any patients need to be restrained forcibly and their hands put into large mittens to prevent them from removing the tube." A gastrostomy tube (as was used to provide food and water to Nancy Cruzan) or jejunostomy tube must be surgically implanted into the stomach or small intestine. Requiring a competent adult to endure such procedures against her will burdens the patient's liberty, dignity, and freedom to determine the course of her own treatment. Accordingly, the liberty guaranteed by the Due Process Clause must protect, if it protects anything, an individual's deeply personal decision to reject medical treatment, including the artificial delivery of food and water.

I also write separately to emphasize that the Court does not today decide the issue whether a State must also give effect to the decisions of a surrogate decisionmaker. In my view, such a duty may well be constitutionally required to protect the patient's liberty interest in refusing medical treatment. Few individuals provide explicit oral or written instructions regarding their intent to refuse medical treatment should they become incompetent. States which decline to consider any evidence other than such instructions may frequently fail to honor a patient's intent. Such failures might be avoided if the State considered an equally probative source of evidence: the patient's appointment of a proxy to make health care decisions on her behalf. Delegating the authority to make medical decisions to a family member or friend is becoming a common method of planning for the future. Several States have recognized the practical wisdom of such a procedure by enacting durable power of attorney statutes that specifically authorize an individual to appoint a surrogate to make medical treatment decisions. Some state courts have suggested that an agent appointed pursuant to a general durable power of attorney statute would also be empowered to make health care decisions on behalf of the patient.

Other States allow an individual to designate a proxy to carry out the intent of a living will. These procedures for surrogate decisionmaking, which appear to be rapidly gaining in acceptance, may be a valuable additional safeguard of the patient's interest in directing his medical care. Moreover, as patients are likely to select a family member as a surrogate, giving effect to a proxy's decisions may also protect the "freedom of personal choice in matters of . . . family life."

Today's decisions, holding only that the Constitution permits a State to require clear and convincing evidence of Nancy Cruzan's desire to have artificial hydration and nutrition withdrawn, does not preclude a future determination that the Constitution requires the States to implement the decisions of a patient's duly appointed surrogate. Nor does it prevent States from developing other approaches for protecting an incompetent individual's liberty interest in refusing medical treatment. As is evident from the Court's survey of state court decisions, no national consensus has yet emerged on the best solution for this difficult and sensitive problem. Today we decide only that one State's practice does not violate the Constitution; the more challenging task of crafting appropriate procedures for safeguarding incompetents' liberty interests is entrusted to the "laboratory" of the States in the first instance.

Justice **Scalia,** concurring.

The various opinions in this case portray quite clearly the difficult, indeed agonizing, questions that are presented by the constantly increasing power of science to keep the human body alive for longer than any reasonable person would want to inhabit it. The States have begun to grapple with these problems through legislation. I am concerned, from the tenor of today's opinions, that we are poised to confuse that enterprise as successfully as we have confused the enterprise of legislating concerning abortion—requiring it to be conducted against a background of federal constitutional imperatives that are unknown because they are being newly crafted from Term to Term. That would be a great misfortune.

While I agree with the Court's analysis today, and therefore join in its opinion, I would have preferred that we announce, clearly and promptly, that the federal courts have no business in this field; that American law has always accorded the State the power to prevent, by force if necessary, suicide—including suicide by refusing to take appropriate measures necessary to preserve one's life; that the point at which life becomes "worthless," and the point at which the means necessary to preserve it become "extraordinary" or "inappropriate," are neither set forth in the Constitution nor known to the nine Justices of this Court any better than they are known to nine people picked at random from the Kansas City telephone directory; and hence, that even when it *is* demonstrated by clear and convincing evidence that a patient no longer wishes certain measures to be taken to preserve her life, it is up to the citizens of Missouri to decide, though their elected representatives, whether that wish will be honored. It is quite impossible (because the Constitution says nothing about the matter) that those citizens will decide upon a line less lawful than the one we would choose; and it is unlikely (because we know no more about "life-and-death" than they do) that they will decide upon a line less reasonable.

The text of the Due Process Clause does not protect individuals against deprivations of liberty simpliciter. It protects them against deprivations of liberty "without due process of law." To determine that such a deprivation would not occur if Nancy Cruzan were forced to take nourishment against her will, it is unnecessary to reopen the historically recurrent debate over whether "due process" includes substantive restrictions. It is at least true that no "substantive due process" claim can be maintained unless the claimant demonstrates that the State has deprived him of a right historically and traditionally protected against State interference. That cannot possibly be established here.

At common law in England, a suicide— defined as one who "deliberately puts an end to his own existence, or commits any unlawful malicious act, the consequence of which is his own death," was criminally liable. Although the States abolished the penalties imposed by the common law (i.e., forfeiture and ignominious burial), they did so to spare the innocent family, and not to legitimize the act. Case law at the time of the Fourteenth Amendment generally held that assisting suicide was a criminal offense. The System of Penal Law presented to the House of Representatives by Representative Livingston in 1828 would have criminalized assisted suicide. The Field Penal Code, adopted by the Dakota Territory in 1877, proscribed attempted suicide and assisted suicide. And most States that that did not explicitly prohibit assisted suicide in 1868 recognized, when the issue arose in the 50 years following the Fourteenth Amendment's ratification, that assisted and (in some cases) attempted suicide were unlawful. Thus, "there is no significant support for the claim that a right to suicide is so rooted in our tradition that it may be deemed 'fundamental' or 'implicit in the concept of ordered liberty.'"

Petitioners rely on three distinctions to separate Nancy Cruzan's case from ordinary suicide: (1) that she is permanently incapacitated and in pain; (2) that she would bring on her death not by any affirmative act but by merely declining treatment that provides nourishment; and (3) that preventing her from effectuating her presumed wish to die requires violation of her bodily integrity. None of these suffices. Suicide was not excused even when committed "to avoid those ills which [persons] had not the fortitude to endure." . . .

The second asserted distinction—suggested by the recent cases canvassed by the Court concerning the right to refuse treatment—relies on the dichotomy between action and inaction. Suicide, it is said, consists of an affirmative act to end one's life; refusing treatment is not an affirmative act "causing" death, but merely a passive acceptance of the natural process of dying. I readily acknowledge that the distinction between action and inaction has some bearing upon the legislative judgment of what ought to be prevented as suicide—though even there it would seem to me unreasonable to draw the line precisely between action and inaction, rather than between various forms of inaction. It would not make much sense to say that one may not kill oneself by walking into the sea, but may sit on the beach until submerged by the incoming tide; or that one may not intentionally lock oneself into a cold storage locker, but may refrain from coming indoors when the temperature drops below freezing. Even as a legislative matter, in other words, the intelligent line does not fall between action and inaction but between those forms of inaction that consist of abstaining from "ordinary" care and those that consist of abstaining from "excessive" or "heroic" measures. Unlike action *vs* inaction, that is not a line to be discerned by logic or legal analysis, and we should not pretend that it is.

But to return to the principal point for present purposes: the irrelevance of the action-inaction distinction. Starving oneself to death is no different from putting a gun to one's temple as far as the common-law definition of suicide is concerned; the cause of death in both cases is the suicide's conscious decision to "pu[t] an end to his own existence."

. . .

The third asserted basis of distinction—that frustrating Nancy Cruzan's wish to die in the present case requires interference with her bodily integrity—is likewise inadequate, because such interference is impermissible only if one begs the question whether her refusal to undergo the treatment on her own is suicide. It has always been lawful not only for the State, but even for private citizens, to interfere with bodily integrity to prevent a felony. That general rule has of course been applied to suicide. At common law, even a private person's use of force to prevent suicide was privileged. It is not even reasonable, much less required by the Constitution, to maintain that although the State has the right to prevent a person from slashing his wrists it does not have the power to apply physical force to prevent him from doing so, nor the power, should he succeed, to apply, coercively if necessary, medical measures to stop the flow of blood. The state-run hospital, I am certain, is not liable under 42 USC § 1983 for violation of constitutional rights, nor the private hospital liable under general tort law, if, in a State where suicide is unlawful, it pumps out the stomach of a person who has intentionally taken an overdose of barbiturates, despite that person's wishes to the contrary.

The dissents of Justices Brennan and Stevens make a plausible case for our intervention here only by embracing—the latter explicitly and the former by implication—a political principle that the States are free to adopt, but that is demonstrably not imposed by the Constitution. "The State," says Justice Brennan, "has no legitimate general interest in someone's life, completely abstracted from the interest of the person living that life, that could outweigh the person's choice to avoid medical treatment" (emphasis added). The italicized phrase sounds moderate enough, and is all that is needed to cover the present case—but the proposition cannot logically be so limited. One who accepts it must also accept, I think, that the State has no such legitimate interest that could outweigh "the person's choice to put an end to her life." Similarly, if one agrees with Justice Brennan that "the State's general interest in life must accede to Nancy Cruzan's particularized and intense interest in self-determination in her choice of medical treatment" (emphasis added), he must also believe that the State must accede to her "particularized and intense interest in self-determination in her choice whether to continue living or to die." For insofar as balancing the relative interests of the State and the individual is concerned, there is nothing distinctive about accepting death through the refusal of "medical treatment," as opposed to accepting it through the refusal of food or through the failure to shut off the engine and get out of the car after parking in one's garage after work. Suppose that Nancy Cruzan were in precisely the condition she is in today, except that she could be fed and digest food and water without artificial assistance. How is the State's "interest" in keeping her alive thereby increased, or her interest in deciding whether she wants to continue living reduced? It seems to me, in other words, that Justice Brennan's position ultimately rests upon the proposition that it is none of the State's business if a person wants to commit suicide. Justice Stevens is explicit on the point: "Choices about death touch the core of liberty. . . . [N]ot much may be said with confidence about death unless it is said from faith, and that alone is reason enough to protect the freedom to conform choices about death to individual conscience." This is a view that some societies have held, and that our States are free to adopt if they wish. But it is not a view imposed by our constitutional traditions, in which the power of the State to prohibit suicide is unquestionable.

What I have said above is not meant to suggest that I would think it desirable, if we were sure that Nancy Cruzan wanted to die, to keep her alive by means at issue here. I assert only that the Constitution has nothing to say about the subject. To raise up a constitutional right here we would have to create out of nothing (for it exists neither in text nor tradition) some constitutional principle whereby, although the State may insist that an individual come in out of the cold and eat food, it may not insist that he take medicine; and although it may pump his stomach empty of poison he has ingested, it may not fill his stomach with food he has failed to ingest. Are there, then, no reasonable and humane limits that ought not to be exceeded in requiring an individual to preserve his own life? There obviously are, but they are not set forth in the Due Process Clause. What assures us that those limits will not be exceeded is the same constitutional guarantee that is the source of most of our protection—what protects us, for example, from being assessed a tax of 100% of our income above the subsistence level, from being forbidden to drive cars, or from being required to send our children to school for 10 hours a day, none of which horribles is categorically prohibited by the Constitution. Our salvation is the Equal Protection Clause, which requires the democratic majority to accept for themselves and their loved ones what they impose on you and me. This Court need not, and has no authority to, inject itself into every field of human activity where irrationality and oppression may theoretically occur, and if it tries to do so it will destroy itself.

Justice **Brennan,** with whom Justice **Marshall** and Justice **Blackmun** join, dissenting.

. . .

Today the Court, while tentatively accepting that there is some degree of constitutionally protected liberty interest in avoiding unwanted medical treatment, including life-sustaining medical treatment such as artificial nutrition and hydration, affirms the decision of the Missouri Supreme Court. The majority opinion, as I read it, would affirm that decision on the ground that a State may require "clear and convincing" evidence of Nancy Cruzan's prior decision to forego life-sustaining treatment under circumstances such as hers in order to ensure that her actual wishes are honored. Because I believe that

Nancy Cruzan has a fundamental right to be free of unwanted artificial nutrition and hydration, which right is not outweighed by any interests of the state, and because I find that the improperly biased procedural obstacles imposed by the Missouri Supreme Court impermissibly burden that right, I respectfully dissent. Nancy Cruzan is entitled to choose to die with dignity.

. . .

The starting point for our legal analysis must be whether a competent person has a constitutional right to avoid unwanted medical care. Earlier this Term, this Court held that the Due Process Clause of the Fourteenth Amendment confers a significant liberty interest in avoiding unwanted medical treatment. Today, the Court concedes that our prior decisions "support the recognition of a general liberty interest in refusing medical treatment." The Court, however, avoids discussing either the measure of that liberty interest or its application by assuming, for purposes of this case only, that a competent person has a constitutionally protected liberty interest in being free of unwanted artificial nutrition and hydration. Justice O'Connor's opinion is less parsimonious. She openly affirms that "the Court has often deemed state incursions into the body repugnant to the interests protected by the Due Process Clause," that there is a liberty interest in avoiding unwanted medical treatment and that it encompasses the right to be free of "artificially delivered food and water."

But if a competent person has a liberty interest to be free of unwanted medical treatment, as both the majority and Justice O'Connor concede, it must be fundamental. "We are dealing here with [a decision] which involves one of the basic civil rights of man." Skinner v Oklahoma ex rel. Williamson, (1942) (invalidating a statute authorizing sterilization of certain felons). Whatever other liberties protected by the Due Process Clause are fundamental, "those liberties that are 'deeply rooted in this Nation's history and tradition'" are among them.

The right to be free from medical attention without consent, to determine what shall be done with one's own body, *is* deeply rooted in this Nation's traditions, as the majority acknowledges. This right has long been "firmly entrenched in American tort law" and is securely grounded in the earliest common law.

. . .

The right to be free from unwanted medical attention is a right to evaluate the potential benefit of treatment and its possible consequences according to one's own values and to make a personal decision whether to subject oneself to the intrusion. For a patient like Nancy Cruzan, the sole benefit of medical treatment is being kept metabolically alive. Neither artificial nutrition nor any other form of medical treatment available today can cure or in any way ameliorate her condition. Irreversibly vegetative patients are devoid of thought, emotion and sensation; they are permanently and completely unconscious. . . .

There are also affirmative reasons why someone like Nancy might choose to forego artificial nutrition and hydration under these circumstances. Dying is personal. And it is profound. For many, the thought of an ignoble end, steeped in decay, is abhorrent. A quiet, proud death, bodily integrity intact, is a matter of extreme consequence.

. . .

Although the right to be free of unwanted medical intervention, like other constitutionally protected interests, may not be absolute, no State interest could outweigh the rights of an individual in Nancy Cruzan's position. Whatever a State's possible interests in mandating life-support treatment under other circumstances, there is no good to be obtained here by Missouri's insistence that Nancy Cruzan remain on life-support systems if it is indeed her wish not to do so. Missouri does not claim, nor could it, that society as a whole will be benefited by Nancy's receiving medical treatment. No third party's situation will be improved and no harm to others will be averted.

The only state interest asserted here is a general interest in the preservation of life. But the State has no legitimate general interest in someone's life, completely abstracted from the interest of the person living that life, that could outweigh the person's choice to avoid medical treatment. Thus, the State's general interest in

life must accede to Nancy Cruzan's particularized and intense interest in self-determination in her choice of medical treatment. There is simply nothing legitimately within the State's purview to be gained by superseding her decision.

Moreover, there may be considerable danger that Missouri's rule of decision would impair rather than serve any interest the State does have in sustaining life. Current medical practice recommends use of heroic measures if there is a scintilla of a chance that the patient will recover, on the assumption that the measures will be discontinued should the patient improve. When the President's Commission in 1982 approved the withdrawal of life support equipment from irreversibly vegetative patients, it explained that "[a]n even more troubling wrong occurs when a treatment that might save life or improve health is not started because the health care personnel are afraid that they will find it very difficult to stop the treatment if, as is fairly likely, it proves to be of little benefit and greatly burdens the patient." A New Jersey court recognized that families as well as doctors might be discouraged by an inability to stop life-support measures from "even attempting certain types of care [which] could thereby force them into hasty and premature decisions to allow a patient to die." In re Conroy (1985).

This is not to say that the State has no legitimate interests to assert here. As the majority recognizes, Missouri has a parens patriae interest in providing Nancy Cruzan, now incompetent, with as accurate as possible a determination of how she would exercise her rights under these circumstances. Second, if and when it is determined that Nancy Cruzan would want to continue treatment, the State may legitimately assert an interest in providing that treatment. But *until* Nancy's wishes have been determined, the only state interest that may be asserted is an interest in safeguarding the accuracy of that determination.

Accuracy, therefore, must be our touchstone. Missouri may constitutionally impose only those procedural requirements that serve to enhance the accuracy of a determination of Nancy Cruzan's wishes or are at least consistent with an accurate determination. The Missouri "safeguard" that the Court upholds today does not meet that standard. The determination needed in this context is whether the incompetent person would choose to live in a persistent vegetative state on life-support or to avoid this medical treatment. Missouri's rule of decision imposes a markedly asymmetrical evidentiary burden. Only evidence of specific statements of treatment choice made by the patient when competent is admissible to support a finding that the patient, now in a persistent vegetative state, would wish to avoid further medical treatment. Moreover, this evidence must be clear and convincing. No proof is required to support a finding that the incompetent person would wish to continue treatment.

. . .

The Missouri court's disdain for Nancy's statements in serious conversations not long before her accident, for the opinions of Nancy's family and friends as to her values, beliefs and certain choice, and even for the opinion of an outside objective factfinder appointed by the State evinces a disdain for Nancy Cruzan's own right to choose. The rules by which an incompetent person's wishes are determined must represent every effort to determine those wishes. The rule that the Missouri court adopted and that this Court upholds, however, skews the result away from a determination that as accurately as possible reflects the individual's own preferences and beliefs. It is a rule that transforms human beings into passive subjects of medical technology.

. . .

I do not suggest that States must sit by helplessly if the choices of incompetent patients are in danger of being ignored. Even if the Court had ruled that Missouri's rule of decision is unconstitutional, as I believe it should have, States would nevertheless remain free to fashion procedural protections to safeguard the interests of incompetents under these circumstances. The Constitution provides merely a framework here: protections must be genuinely aimed at ensuring decisions commensurate with the will of the patient, and must be reliable as instruments to that end. Of the many States which have insti-

tuted such protections, Missouri is virtually the only one to have fashioned a rule that lessens the likelihood of accurate determinations. In contrast, nothing in the Constitution prevents States from reviewing the advisability of a family decision, by requiring a court proceeding or by appointing an impartial guardian ad litem.

There are various approaches to determining an incompetent patient's treatment choice in use by the several States today and there may be advantages and disadvantages to each and other approaches not yet envisioned. The choice, in largest part, is and should be left to the States, so long as each State is seeking, in a reliable manner, to discover what the patient would want. But with such momentous interests in the balance, States must avoid procedures that will prejudice the decision. "To err either way—to keep a person alive under circumstances under which he would rather have been allowed to die, or to allow that person to die when he would have chosen to cling to life—would be deeply unfortunate." In re Conroy.

. . .

Finally, I cannot agree with the majority that where it is not possible to determine what choice an incompetent patient would make, a State's role as parens patriae permits the State automatically to make that choice itself. Under fair rules of evidence, it is improbable that a court could not determine what the patient's choice would be. Under the rule of decision adopted by Missouri and upheld today by this Court, such occasions might be numerous. But in neither case does it follow that it is constitutionally acceptable for the State invariably to assume the role of deciding for the patient. A State's legitimate interest in safeguarding a patient's choice cannot be furthered by simply appropriating it.

The majority justifies its position by arguing that, while close family members may have a strong feeling about the question, "there is no automatic assurance that the view of close family members will necessarily be the same as the patient's would have been had she been confronted with the prospect of her situation while competent." I cannot quarrel with this observation. But it leads only to another question: Is there any reason to suppose that a State is *more* likely to make the choice that the patient would have made than someone who knew the patient intimately? To ask this is to answer it. As the New Jersey Supreme Court observed: "Family members are best qualified to make substituted judgments for incompetent patients not only because of their peculiar grasp of the patient's approach to life, but also because of their special bonds with him or her. . . . It is . . . they who treat the patient as a person, rather than a symbol of a cause." In re Jobes (1987). The State, in contrast, is a stranger to the patient.

A State's inability to discern an incompetent patient's choice still need not mean that a State is rendered powerless to protect that choice. But I would find that the Due Process Clause prohibits a State from doing more than that. A State may ensure that the person who makes the decision on the patient's behalf is the one whom the patient himself would have selected to make that choice for him. And a State may exclude from consideration anyone having improper motives. But a State generally must either repose the choice with the person whom the patient himself would most likely have chosen as proxy or leave the decision to the patient's family.

As many as 10,000 patients are being maintained in persistent vegetative states in the United States, and the number is expected to increase significantly in the near future. Medical technology, developed over the past 20 or so years, is often capable of resuscitating people after they have stopped breathing or their hearts have stopped beating. Some of those people are brought fully back to life. Two decades ago, those who were not and could not swallow and digest food, died. Intravenous solutions could not provide sufficient calories to maintain people for more than a short time. Today, various forms of artificial feeding have been developed that are able to keep people metabolically alive for years, even decades. In addition, in this century, chronic or degenerative ailments have replaced communicable diseases as the primary causes of death. The 80% of Americans who die in hospitals are "likely to meet their end . . . 'in a sedated or comatose state; betubed nasally, abdominally and intravenously; and far more like manipulated objects than like moral subjects.'" A fifth of all adults surviving to age 80 will suffer a progressive dementing disorder prior to death.

"[L]aw, equity and justice must not themselves quail and be helpless in the face of modern technological marvels presenting questions hitherto unthought of." In re Quinlan (1976). The new medical technology can reclaim those who would have been irretrievably lost a few decades ago and restore them to active lives. For Nancy Cruzan, it failed, and for others with wasting incurable diseases it may be doomed to failure. In these unfortunate situations, the bodies and preferences and memories of the victims do not escheat to the State; nor does our Constitution permit the State or any other government to commandeer them. No singularity of feeling exists upon which such a government might confidently rely as parens patriae. Yet Missouri and this Court have displaced Nancy's own assessment of the processes associated with dying. They have discarded evidence of her will, ignored her values, and deprived her of the right to a decision as closely approximating her own choice as humanly possible. They have done so disingenuously in her name, and openly in Missouri's own. That Missouri and this Court may truly be motivated only by concern for incompetent patients makes no matter. As one of our most prominent jurists warned us decades ago: "Experience should teach us to be most on our guard to protect liberty when the government's purposes are beneficent. . . . The greatest dangers to liberty lurk in insidious encroachment by men of zeal, well meaning but without understanding." Olmstead v United States (1928) (Brandeis, J., dissenting).

I respectfully dissent.

Aftermath of Cruzan *v.* Director, Missouri Department of Health

In November 1990, five months after the Supreme Court had decided the *Cruzan* case, the parents of Nancy Cruzan appeared again in state court to request that their daughter's feeding tube be disconnected. Missouri's Attorney General, declaring that his previous intervention had been intended to clarify the state law rather than to object specifically to the removal of Ms. Cruzan's feeding tube, announced that the state would not oppose the request. The same judge who had heard the case nearly three years earlier listened to new testimony from three of Nancy Cruzan's friends citing specific conversations in which she had expressed her wish never to live "like a vegetable" on life support machines. Ms. Cruzan's physician, who in the earlier proceeding had opposed the Cruzans' petition, this time supported it, describing his patient's life as "a living hell."

In December 1990, having found "clear and convincing" evidence that the Cruzans were acting as their daughter would have wished, the judge authorized the termination of Nancy Cruzan's feeding. This was done on December 14. Over the next 10 days a number of religious groups filed petitions in federal and state courts attempting to force resumption of Ms. Cruzan's intravenous feeding. All were summarily denied. On December 18, 19 demonstrators were arrested after trying unsuccessfully to get into Ms. Cruzan's hospital room to reconnect her feeding tube. Nancy Cruzan died on December 26, 1990.

In the fall of 1990 Congress passed the Patient Self-Determination Act, which requires that all health care facilities receiving federal funds inform patients of their rights to accept or refuse medical treatment and to use living wills to make their wishes known in advance. A majority of the states now have health-care proxy laws of one kind or another. Many states with living wills permit the removal of breathing equipment but prohibit the termination of food and water even at the patient's written request. While the Supreme Court did not distinguish in *Cruzan* between these two forms of life support, many medical and legal experts predict that in the future the Court will have to decide whether the "liberty" interest to discontinue life support embraces both procedures.

5 Freedom of Speech, Press, and Assembly

A lthough twentieth-century Americans take for granted the broad area of free expression guaranteed by those simple clauses in the First Amendment, "Congress shall make no law . . . abridging the freedom of speech, or of the press; or the right of the people peaceably to assemble . . . ," they need to be reminded from time to time that the freedom they exercise so cavalierly was unknown anywhere in the world prior to the nineteenth century and is still a luxury enjoyed by a small minority of the earth's teeming population. There are antecedents for the American model of "freedom of expression," the expanded term now used by judges and scholars to describe First Amendment guarantees, but prior to constitutional development in eighteenth-century England, the only parallels to modern practice are found in the brief, transient democracies of Athens and Rome. Neither of those ancient societies, however, countenanced the open, robust give-and-take we know today, and even England initially exercised firm control over the press and over speech critical of lawful governmental processes (sedition).

Evolving over some three centuries in England and Europe was a set of principles that formed the underpinning of the First Amendment as it was written into the Bill of Rights in 1791. These principles assert that free and open discussion (1) is essential to a society dedicated to political decision making by its citizens, (2) is the only way of ascertaining truth, and (3) provides enlightenment and self-fulfillment to the individual. Unquestionably, free, democratic government cannot function without open and unencumbered discussion among its citizens, but there is another side of the coin, namely, that a point may be reached whereby the exercise of free expression by an individual or a group becomes so harmful to others or to the public that some limits must be tolerated in order to maintain a fair and stable society. Thus, a dilemma: How can speech be free and limited at the same time? There is no perfect solution, but modern democracies have accepted the fact that freedom of speech, press, and association is not absolute, that reasonable restrictions are necessary to assure the continuity of the constitutional order and to prevent harm to innocent parties. Mechanisms for striking a balance between liberty and order vary from nation to nation, but the United

States, with its written constitutional guarantees, has relied on the judiciary to resolve conflicts between the claims of the individual and those of society at large. Primarily, although not exclusively, the Supreme Court, in deciding cases involving freedom of speech, press, and assembly, has formulated a complex system of rules within which those freedoms may be exercised.

Permissible limits on individual expression fall roughly into five categories: (1) sedition (advocacy of unlawful action and violence as a means of political change), (2) breach of the peace (the street-corner speech or demonstration), (3) obscenity (lascivious and pornographic material), (4) libel (defamation of character or injury to reputation), and (5) contempt of court (disruptive speech in a courtroom). Although the language of the First Amendment is explicit in its proscription that Congress shall make *no* law abridging freedom of speech or press, the Supreme Court has always maintained that there is flexibility in explicating the meaning of "abridging," "freedom," and even "speech" and "press," all of which are susceptible to differing interpretations. That is, not all speech is protected from government invasion, only that which can be categorized as "free," and not all laws regulating expression are necessarily an abridgment. Therefore, the guarantee in the First Amendment's language is not absolute, but subject to reasonable qualification.

There have been dissenters from this conventional construction, notably Justice Hugo Black who insisted that "no law" means *no* law and that all speech is protected from government intrusion. Justice Black in his liberalism, however, gave less protection to expression in general than did his more traditional colleagues who would not permit restrictions on "symbolic" speech such as students wearing black armbands in the classroom as a means of protest against the Vietnam war. To Black, the Constitution protects speech and press absolutely, but the wearing of a black armband is neither speech nor writing and thus falls outside the First Amendment mandate. These issues will be dealt with in greater depth in the commentary and cases to follow, but suffice to say, in spite of the overwhelming judicial and public consensus that some restrictions on speech and press are not only permissible but desirable, there is no nation, past or present, that has a better—albeit imperfect—record of protecting dissent, even when intemperate, insulting, disorderly, or vulgar.

It has only been since 1919 when the Court decided *Schenck* v. *United States* that press and speech issues have been subject to judicial examination, the reason being that with the exception of the short-lived Alien and Sedition Acts of 1798, the federal government had made little effort to regulate speech of any kind. It was not until the advent of World War I that Congress believed it prudent to punish seditious activity, including advocacy of unlawful action. At the state level there had always been either common law rules or legislation restricting speech in the five areas enumerated above, but any litigation that arose was limited to the state courts since the Bill of Rights, under the rubric of *Barron* v. *Baltimore* (discussed in Chapter 4), did not circumscribe the states in any way whatsoever. It was only after 1925 in *Gitlow* v. *New York* the Court decided that the Fourteenth Amendment's due process clause incorporated freedom of speech and press and made them federally guaranteed rights at the state level that the Supreme Court subsequently began to docket cases involving allegations of a denial of free speech by state legislatures and administrative officials. Thus, the judicial rules surrounding the exercise of free speech have, since 1925, been identical whether being applied to national or state legislative regulations, the former directly under the First Amendment, the latter indirectly under the word "liberty" of the due process clause of the Fourteenth Amendment's freedoms.

It should be noted that although Americans speak of constitutionally guaranteed rights, the Bill of Rights is essentially a negative restraint on the government. It tells the government that in legislating or in administering legislative acts, it cannot enter a constitutionally restricted area. Justice Robert Jackson explained the concept of rights and liberties with an apt sword/shield metaphor. He contended that the Bill of Rights is a *shield* that protects the citizen from government interference in specified areas, thus preserving a vast realm of *civil liberty*. At the same time the government may use positive intervention, a *sword*, to guarantee certain *civil rights* such as the right of a person to be free from racial discrimination in education, housing, or public accommodations. The *sword* is used to protect minorities from both public and private oppression, whereas the *shield* in its all-encompassing restraint applies only to government and protects all persons, citizen and alien alike. One can be punished by fine or imprisonment for violating a person's civil rights, but the individual citizen is under no legal restraint by the Bill of Rights or the Fourteenth Amendment which, respectively, restricts Congress and the state legislatures.

JUDICIAL DOCTRINES AND FREEDOM OF SPEECH

In the introductory essay preceding each case in this chapter, judicial tests used in the case will be elucidated, but since the justices in their opinions often allude elliptically to judicial doctrine, some familiarity with the development of the various principles is crucial to an understanding of the case law.

Bad Tendency, Clear and Present Danger, and Balancing of Interest

Although no longer used by the Supreme Court to determine the constitutionality of speech advocating unlawful action, the "bad tendency" test was in vogue on and off for many years. Under this doctrine, speech or writing was punishable if a legislature had determined that it had a tendency to produce a substantive evil, such as interfering with lawful governmental processes. In 1925 in *Gitlow* v. *New York* the doctrine was enunciated clearly when the Court declared that a state might punish persons who abuse free speech if their words were deemed "inimical to the public welfare, tending to corrupt public morals, incite to crime, or disturb the public peace. . . . " Although in principle this view of free speech was severely restrictive, technically it was not censorship since it did not outlaw specified words, but only permitted punishment if the utterance "tended" to produce specified evils. Nevertheless, speech was only minimally protected.

A test allegedly more protective of speech was articulated in 1919 by Justice Oliver Wendell Holmes, Jr., in *Schenck* v. *United States*. Known as the "clear and present danger" rule, it permits punishment for speaking or writing, but requires a much more stringent test for criminal liability. In Holmes's words: "The question in every case is whether the words used are used in such circumstances and are of such a nature as to create a clear and present danger that they will bring about the substantive evils that Congress has the right to prevent." Theoretically, in order for a person to be fined or sent to jail for advocacy through writing or speaking, the clear and present danger rule requires that the words used will produce the danger—usually violence or obstruction of the wheels of government—

clearly and immediately and not merely have a "tendency" to do so. Unfortunately, as with "bad tendency," "clear and present danger" is inherently vague and gives the speaker or writer as well as the police and prosecuting attorneys little guidance as to what is and what is not permissible. In our case discussions below, it will be seen how the Supreme Court has struggled over the years to arrive at a balance between protection of the individual's right to express ideas, no matter how radical or nonconformist, and the right of the public to be protected against abuse and violence. During the 1950s and 1960s a majority of the justices appeared to agree with Justice Felix Frankfurter's view that no matter what a test was named, each case called for a "balancing of interests" which in itself became a judicial test, albeit just as vague as those of the past. In 1969, however, a judicial consensus was reached in *Brandenburg* v. *Ohio* (see excerpted case in this chapter), the rule of which protects speech to the broadest extent possible in an orderly society.

Presumption of Constitutionality, Preferred Position, Void-for-Vagueness, Overbreadth

Despite the confusing history with respect to finding a judicial test that would satisfactorily balance the liberty-authority equation in free speech cases, the Supreme Court has created several devices that have enabled it to uphold various forms of individual expression. As a general rule the Court has maintained that when litigants allege that a statute or administrative action is unconstitutional, it is incumbent upon them to prove the allegation. That is, the Court assumes that the government has acted properly, that there exists at the outset of the case a "presumption of constitutionality," and the Court will declare a law invalid only as a last resort. Beginning in the 1930s, however, the Court took the position that laws abridging First Amendment rights are presumptively unconstitutional and the burden of proof of constitutionality rests with the government. This doctrine has not been applied consistently in all free speech cases, but it has generally helped to vindicate the rights of the speaker or writer.

Closely related to the reverse presumption rule is the "preferred position" doctrine, first enunciated by Chief Justice Harlan Fiske Stone and either overtly or tacitly accepted by the justices over the years. In 1943 in a dissenting opinion in *Jones* v. *Opelika*, Stone wrote:

> The First Amendment is not confined to safeguarding freedom of speech and freedom of religion against discriminatory attempts to wipe them out. On the contrary, the Constitution by virtue of the First and Fourteenth Amendments, has put those freedoms in a *preferred position*.

The idea that the First Amendment had an elevated status in the Bill of Rights, that the Court should take special cognizance of laws interfering with freedom of speech, press, assembly, or religion, had been alluded to prior to Stone's promulgation of that idealistic phrase and has since then often been reiterated. In 1937 Justice Benjamin Cardozo, for example, called free speech "the matrix, the indispensable condition of nearly every form of freedom," and Justice Hugo Black wrote in 1951 that "the First Amendment is the keystone of our Government." Although the phrase, "preferred position," has not been used in recent years, the justices continue to treat freedom of speech as a constitutional liberty deserving of a special status and respect whenever cases involving alleged government abridgment are before the Court.

Although the "void-for-vagueness" doctrine applies to any statute under review by the Court, it has special relevance for free speech cases. It is a judicial requirement to write a law with enough precision so that a normal person can know whether certain acts are illegal. That is, a statute must have an ascertainable standard of guilt on which persons of common intelligence can agree. For example, in 1971 the Court refused to accept as clear a city ordinance of Cincinnati (*Coates v. Cincinnati*) that forbade three or more persons from meeting on sidewalks and acting "in a manner annoying to persons passing by." The word, "annoying," was so vague as to embrace anything from outrageous conduct to protected speech, and gave police officers such broad discretion that the law might be applied unfairly.

Closely related to the vagueness principle is the doctrine of "overbreadth," described by the Court in *Thornhill* v. *Alabama* in 1940 as a law that "does not aim specifically at evils within the allowable area of state control [but] sweeps within its ambit other activities that in ordinary circumstances constitute an exercise of freedom of speech or of the press." A good example of the use of the overbreadth principle is seen in the case of *Erznoznik* v. *Jacksonville* (1975) in which the Court struck down an ordinance of Jacksonville, Florida, prohibiting the showing of films containing nudity at drive-in theaters with screens visible from public highways. Although properly concerned with the safety and privacy interests of passing motorists, the ordinance nevertheless was a restraint on the content of communication and therefore a violation of the First Amendment. A ban on all nudity, said the Court, was overbroad in that it "would bar a film containing a picture of a baby's buttocks, the nude body of a war victim, or scenes from a culture in which nudity is indigenous." Clearly, concluded the opinion, "all nudity cannot be deemed obscene even as to minors."

Such judicially imposed rules as presumption of unconstitutionality, preferred position, void-for-vagueness, and overbreadth, though not rigid in their application, have a positive effect in preserving a broad area of free expression. The doctrines put lawmakers on notice that in crafting legislation care must be taken to be precise and clear in their use of language and that any restriction on speech must be shown to have a compelling governmental interest in order to pass constitutional muster.

SYMBOLIC SPEECH AND "SPEECH PLUS"

Complicating the free speech picture are those situations in which a person is expressing a viewpoint, not by speaking or writing, but by performing a symbolic act such as destroying the American flag, burning one's draft card, carrying a sign, or simply wearing clothing bearing a special message. To what extent are these actions considered speech and to what constitutional protection are they entitled? Several cases have arisen since 1931 when the Court first extended protection to symbolic speech in *Stromberg v. California.* Involved in the case was a state statute that made it a felony to display a red flag as "an emblem of opposition to organized government." Overturning the conviction of Yetta Stromberg, a director of a children's summer camp who raised a red flag every morning as a salute to Communism, the Court said that the statute's vagueness permitted punishment for the fair use of "opportunity for free political discussion" and was therefore unconstitutional. By extending "speech" to include symbolism the Court opened the door to various modes of expression which, in turn, necessitated the drawing of lines when symbolic protest surfaced, such as defacing government documents by pouring blood on them, and when nude dancers argued that laws outlawing their gyrations were in violation of constitutionally protected "artistic expression."

Symbolism as a means of communication concerns action rather than "pure" speech and is akin but not identical to yet another form of speech protected by the First Amendment, namely, "speech plus" which involves expression combined with action. Here the problem is that of protecting speech made in conjunction with unlawful acts. Cases of this type have generally arisen as a result of street demonstrations, picketing, or marching used to convey an idea, either in support of a public issue or, more often, in protest against official policy or its enforcement. Taking to the streets to dramatize an issue and give it broad exposure is, as we know, a fact of modern life in all governmental systems, including those that tolerate it only within narrow limits. In democracies this access to a public forum is a significant means of expressing ideas and it has had judicial protection since the 1930s. As Justice Owen Roberts declared in *Hague* v. *CIO* in 1939: "Wherever the title of street and parks may rest, they have immemorially been held in trust for the use of the public and time out of mind have been used for the purpose of assembly, communicating thoughts between citizens and discussing public questions."

It must be emphasized, however, that public areas such as streets, sidewalks, and parks are dedicated to a primary use that has no relation to free speech. Thus, a city has an obligation to the public to facilitate the movement of traffic and to protect the casual user of recreational facilities from the harassment of a political rally. In practice, therefore, the Supreme Court has established rules that accommodate the primary purpose of communal areas with the public forum principle. In general, municipalities may require permits for the use of public facilities so long as there is no attempt to censor any ideas by denying permission to a particular group, no matter how extreme a position it may espouse. This principle has been applied to such extremist organizations as the Ku Klux Klan and the American Nazi party in spite of adamant resistance by much of the local citizenry to permitting such hate groups to march in the city's streets. Always with public demonstrations, particularly when they involve large numbers, there is the incipient danger of violence. At the point when violence erupts or even prior to its occurrence—if it is imminent, "clear and present"—the police may order demonstrators to desist under threat of arrest, fine, or imprisonment. The timing of police intervention is crucial. If an official restraint to a peaceful protest is made too early, First Amendment guarantees are violated, and if made too late, someone may be hurt or even killed. No perfect solution exists to this ever-present dilemma. What is clear is that the various doctrinal rules governing the practical application of the constitutional guarantee of freedom of speech load the dice in favor of open, robust debate.

FIGHTING WORDS, OBSCENITY, LIBEL

In our discussion so far we have been concerned primarily with speech used in certain contexts, whether "pure" or "symbolic," that might, in Justice Holmes's phrase, produce "the substantive evils that Congress has a right to prevent." There is nothing intrinsically bad about the words; it is the circumstance under which they are used—the time, place, and manner—that brings government strictures into play. However, there are a few carefully defined spheres in which the words, either spoken or written, are inherently suspect and fall outside constitutional protection. Although the circumstances surrounding the use of such words may have a bearing on the outcome of a case, persons using the proscribed language are subject to official restraint without proof that the words might result in harm to society.

"Fighting words," first used by the Supreme Court in 1942 in the case of *Chaplinsky* v. *New Hampshire,* fall into a judicially created category of unprotected speech. A unanimous Court upheld the conviction of a Jehovah's Witness who, in the midst of an argument, called a city marshal a "damned Fascist" and a "God-damned racketeer." Disagreeing with Chaplinsky's contention that his arrest and conviction violated his guarantee of free speech, the Court declared:

> There are certain well-defined and narrowly limited classes of speech, the prevention and punishment of which have never been thought to raise any Constitutional problem. These include . . . insulting or "fighting" words—those which by their very utterance inflict injury or tend to incite an immediate breach of the peace. It has been well observed that such utterances are no essential part of any exposition of ideas and are of such slight social value as a step to truth that any benefit that may be derived from them is clearly outweighed by the social interest in order and morality.

Despite the fact that the Supreme Court has retained the doctrine of "fighting words" in the lexicon of proscribed speech, it has not used it frequently nor given it any expanded meaning. The Court has in fact interpreted the rule narrowly, insisting that in order to be classed as "fighting" the words must be more than annoying or offensive and must be addressed to a specific individual. For example, in *Lewis* v. *New Orleans* in 1974, in overturning the conviction of a woman who had called an officer "you god damn m.f. police," the Court declared that words may or may not be "fighting words" depending upon the circumstances of their utterance. It is unlikely, continued the opinion, "that the words said to have been used here would have precipitated a physical confrontation between the middle-aged woman who made them and the police officer in whose presence they were uttered." Thus, even profanity addressed to a specific police officer was held to be protected speech, given the age and sex of the speaker.

Obscenity has always been held to be outside the protection of the First Amendment, but it has had a confusing history as the Supreme Court has struggled in case after case to arrive at an agreement on a legal meaning and to give firm guidance to the lower courts and the government-enforcement agencies. Facing yet another constitutional dilemma, the Court attempted to maintain the broadest possible freedom of artistic expression on the one hand while protecting the public from offensive language and the degradation of national culture on the other. As we shall see later, after deciding more than a score of cases over a 15-year period, the justices finally arrived at a consensus in 1973 in *Miller* v. *California.* Obscenity still remains, however, the most difficult of all the free speech issues to define with precision and has rightly been deemed "a constitutional disaster area."

A third category of unprotected speech is that of libel or defamation of character. While not quite as slippery as obscenity, libel is similarly not susceptible of simple characterization. A defamatory statement is one that tends to bring a person into disrepute in such a way as to lower his or her standing in the community and/or to deter others from associating with him or her. If written, the offensive language is libel; if spoken, slander. Prior to the case of *New York Times* v. *Sullivan* in 1964 the law of libel was applied within a complex arrangement of common law rules supplemented by state statutes, the entire system existing in the 50 states without guidance from the Supreme Court. All of that changed after 1964 when in the *New York Times* case and others following, the Court formulated rules that would accord First Amendment protection to the press while preserving the integrity of an individual's reputation. Libel, like obscenity, forces the Court to deal with insoluble problems; all it can do is settle the competing claims in a way that satisfies neither side fully but provides an acceptable balance for society in that it gives wide latitude to the press as political and social critic while insulating the individual from false and unfair accusations that might damage his or her reputation.

CONTEMPT OF COURT

Somewhat different and usually less controversial than the areas discussed above is contempt of court. Although again, one right is pitted against another—the right of free speech and the right of a person to a trial conducted in a spirit of fairness and proper decorum—it becomes a matter of striking an appropriate balance. A judge has total control over the courtroom, and the entire proceeding including the determination of who may speak and under what circumstances, within the confines of traditional judicial rules, is subject to the judge's discretion. If anyone in the courtroom—attorney, defendant, witness, member of the press, spectator—speaks in a manner that the judge believes is impairing the progress of a fair trial, that person may be punished for contempt. Such punishment may be summary—removal from the courtroom or fine on the spot—or the offender may be ordered to trial on the contempt citation before another judge and jury, subject to more stringent penalties including imprisonment.

Although speech is not very free in a courtroom, neither is the speaker totally at the mercy of a capricious judge, nor is his or her speech devoid of some constitutional safeguards. The Supreme Court has taken the position that a person cannot be held in contempt for merely talking unless it can be shown that the language used constitutes an imminent threat to the administration of justice. A good example is seen in the case of *Eaton* v. *City of Tulsa* (1974) in which the Court reversed a conviction for contempt based on the alleged use of an expletive during the course of a trial. During cross-examination the defendant, Terry Eaton, in answering the prosecutor's question about his defense posture during a physical assault on him, replied: "I think that would be a place where you would be able to get your feet to stand square so you would be half ready for some chicken shit that had jumped you from behind." At that point the judge said: "I'm not going to put up with that kind of language in this Court" and fined Eaton $50 plus costs. In reversing Eaton's conviction, the Supreme Court declared that a "single isolated usage of street vernacular, not directed at the judge or any officer of the court, cannot constitutionally support the conviction of criminal contempt." In a further observation the opinion suggested that it would have been a different matter if Eaton had acted boisterously or attempted to prevent any court official from carrying out his duties.

More controversial than punishment for contempt committed in the presence of a judge are citations for contempt by the news media allegedly for having prejudiced a trial through statements made in the press, on radio, or on television. In litigation of this nature the Court has tended to uphold the press. In the companion cases of *Bridges* v. *California* and *Times-Mirror Company* v. *Superior Court of California* (1941) the Court dealt with the issue for the first time and, while ruling against the judge's contempt citation, did so in a split 5–4 decision. While a motion was pending for a new trial in a dispute between the American Federation of Labor and the Congress of Industrial Organization, Harry Bridges, a left-wing labor leader, sent a telegram to the Secretary of Labor in which he called the judge's decision outrageous and threatened to paralyze the entire west coast with a union strike. In the *Times-Mirror* case the newspaper had been cited for contempt for suggesting in an editorial prior to sentencing, that the judge would be making a serious mistake if he granted probation to two union leaders who had been adjudged guilty of assaulting nonunion truck drivers.

In the majority opinion by Justice Hugo Black the Court first declared that there was no "clear and present danger" to the operation of justice. Further, said the Court, to suggest that a judge might be influenced by such publications would be to impute to judges "a lack of firmness, wisdom or honor." Justice Felix Frankfurter, in dissent, voiced a contrary view that would allow judges to punish the press for abusive criticism of a trial. "A trial," said Frankfurter, "is not a 'free trade in ideas,' nor is the best test of truth in a courtroom 'the power of the thought to get itself accepted in the competition of the market.' . . . A court is a forum with strictly defined limits for discussion. . . . To assure the impartial accomplishment of justice is not an abridgment of speech or freedom of the press. . . ." Despite Justice Frankfurter's plea, it has been the tendency of the Court to come down on the side of the media and freedom of speech in contempt citations for harshly critical statements made outside the courtroom.

COMMERCIAL SPEECH

For many years the Supreme Court treated commercial communications such as advertising as a purely business matter unprotected by the First Amendment. Beginning in 1914 when Congress established the Federal Trade Commission, various aspects of commercial speech, especially false or deceptive advertising, became subject to national regulation. In addition to the FTC, regulatory agencies such as the Food and Drug Administration, the Federal Communications Commission, the Securities and Exchange Commission, along with the United States Postal Service, have been charged by Congress with duties that involve some controls over commercial advertising. Traditionally the Supreme Court found no constitutional obstacles to such matters as the policing of product labeling and advertising, the banning of cigarette commercials on radio and television, the insistence on accurate advertising for the sale of securities, or the criminal punishment of persons who use the mails to perpetuate a fraudulent business.

It was not until 1942, however, that the Court officially declared that commercial speech was not covered by the protective blanket of the First Amendment. In *Valentine* v. *Chrestensen* the Court upheld a New York City ordinance that forbade the distribution of commercial handbills while permitting those of a political nature. F. J. Chrestensen, who owned an old Navy submarine, had docked it on the East River in New York and charged admission to those who wished to tour the vessel. When Chrestensen began to advertise by distributing handbills, the city authorities, acting under the New York ordinance, ordered him to desist. Chrestensen then had a new flyer printed with his ad on one side and a message protesting the city's action on the other. The city once again ordered him to cease distribution whereupon he obtained an injunction from the federal district court against enforcement of the ordinance. Lewis J. Valentine, New York police commissioner, took appeals all the way to the Supreme Court which in a 9–0 opinion reversed the lower courts and dissolved the injunction. It was the Court's view that a person could not be prevented from using the city streets for disseminating information or ideas, but the Constitution granted no such right for commercial advertising. Expansion of First Amendment protection to commercial speech was not to come for some 30 years.

In 1975 the Court made an exception to the Chrestensen rule when it decided *Bigelow* v. *Virginia.* Jeffrey C. Bigelow, managing editor of a Charlottesville, Virginia, newspaper, the *Virginia Weekly,* was convicted for violating a state law that made it illegal to advertise abortion services information. In 1971 the newspaper had run an advertisement of the Women's Pavilion of New York City which had listed an address and telephone numbers from which information could be obtained with respect to the availability of legal, low-cost abortions in accredited hospitals and clinics in New York.

In an opinion by Justice Blackmun the Supreme Court reversed Bigelow's conviction, noting that the advertisement contained material of clear public interest and that parts of the message involved the freedom to communicate information and disseminate opinion. Although the *Bigelow* decision did not involve comprehensive inclusion of all commercial speech under the First Amendment, it altered the old rules to the extent that truthful advertising conveying information of a public interest became protected speech. One year later in *Virginia State Board of Pharmacy* v. *Virginia Citizens Consumer Council* (1976) the Court, in declaring a Virginia law unconstitutional that made the advertising of prescription drug prices a matter of "unprofessional conduct," extended First Amendment coverage to commercial speech that disseminates "truthful information about entirely lawful activity." Inevitably further cases arose in which the Court had to refine and, to a certain degree, qualify the guarantees surrounding commercial speech.

In *Bates* v. *State Bar of Arizona* (1977) the Court held that constitutional protection for commercial advertising applied to lawyers subject to reasonable restrictions such as prohibitions on false, deceptive, or misleading material. In 1980 Justice Lewis Powell formulated a standard for commercial speech cases that was concurred in by all of the justices except Rehnquist. In *Central Hudson Gas & Electric Corporation* v. *Public Service Commission of New York* Powell argued that in commercial speech cases the Court must ask the following questions in order to determine constitutionality: (1) Is the activity lawful and not misleading? (2) Is the governmental interest substantial? (3) If the above are answered affirmatively, the Court must then determine (a) whether the regulation directly advances the asserted governmental interest and (b) whether it is not more extensive than is necessary to assert that interest. Justice Rehnquist in dissent suggested that the test devitalizes the First Amendment by elevating commercial speech "to a level that is virtually indistinguishable from that of noncommercial speech." Whether the Powell formula will hold up now that the Court's personnel has undergone considerable change is not yet clear.

Corruption of the Political Process: Party Patronage and Campaign Financing

Crucial to the integrity of a constitutional democracy is the guarantee of the right to vote, the right to organize political parties and to participate in the electoral process without fear of official reprisals for one's views or actions. Although not contemplated by the framers of the Constitution, very soon after the Constitution went into effect political parties became the vehicle for carrying on the democratic process. They perform essential functions such as nominating candidates, setting forth views on public policy, managing the government if successful in the election and, if unsuccessful, standing by as critic and as an available alternative. As the American system became more democratic in the twentieth century with the advent of universal suffrage through the addition of blacks and women to the voting rolls, problems arose that required governmental attention. Political parties are private organizations, not governmental agencies. Yet they are public or at least quasi-public in the sense that they are so inextricably bound up with the success of the entire governmental enterprise that some regulatory measures are essential in order to minimize the corruption that seems inevitable in any collective human endeavor. Although the Supreme Court has rendered many decisions over the years with respect to the political process, two areas, party patronage and campaign financing, have special relevance to First Amendment issues.

Handing out jobs to loyal party members goes back to the very early years of the republic and appears to have acquired respectability among practicing politicians with the acceptance of the "spoils system"—"to the victor belongs the spoils"—during the incumbency of President Andrew Jackson. Party leaders have defended patronage in principle as well as in practice on the ground that the winning candidates can better carry out the election mandate by placing their supporters in office. In recent years with the expansion of a merit system in the civil service, patronage positions are considerably fewer than in earlier times, and, in a series of decisions beginning with *Elrod* v. *Burns* in 1976, the Supreme Court has added insult to injury by ordering the diminishing of patronage almost to the vanishing point. In the *Elrod* case a majority of five, speaking through Justice Brennan, agreed with John Burns, a Republican who was fired solely on the basis of his party affiliation by newly elected Democratic sheriff, John Elrod, Jr., that his First Amendment rights had been violated. Brennan maintained that patronage dismissals "severely restricted political belief and association" since a member of the out-party maintains affiliation with his own party at the risk of losing his job or alternatively compromises his true beliefs. In 1990 the Court in *Rutan* v. *Republican Party of Illinois* extended the *Elrod* ruling to hold that the principle therein announced encompassed promotions, transfer, recall, or hiring decisions involving public employment for which party affiliation is not an appropriate requirement.

Congress has attempted to mitigate the undue influence of money on the outcome of elections by enacting regulations limiting both campaign spending and giving as well as requiring public disclosure of the sources and uses of funds. In 1907 Congress prohibited any national bank or corporation chartered by the government from contributing money to elections. A more comprehensive measure was enacted in 1910, the Federal Corrupt Practices Act, that required political committees to report their contributions to Congress and limited the amount of money that a candidate for election to Congress could spend on his or her own campaign. Initially the Supreme Court held in *Newberry* v. *United States* (1921) that the legislation could not constitutionally be applied to primary elections, the party not being an arm of the state, but later reversed its position in *United States v. Classic* (1941) since in some states, particularly in the south, the primary election, in theory only a nominating procedure, was in fact the only real choice the voters had. Given the overwhelming dominance of the Democratic party, victory in the primary was tantamount to election.

In the 1940s Congress extended the prohibition on campaign contributions by corporations and national banks to labor unions. The unions, however, reacted with a new device, the Political Action Committee (PAC) which used voluntary funds, segregated from union dues, to contribute to campaigns. This principle was upheld by the Court in *Pipefitters* v. *United States* (1972) and PAC money has now become the primary source of funding for candidates from corporations and myriad interest groups as well as labor unions.

In an attempt to tighten the rules over campaign finances Congress enacted the Federal Election Campaign Act in 1971 and a subsequent amending statute in 1974 which not only limited campaign expenditures and contributions but created a Federal Elections Commission to enforce the law. In 1976 a coalition of both conservative and liberal organizations and individuals challenged the law, alleging that the limits on campaign contributions and expenditures violated the First Amendment rights of both contributors and candidates. In *Buckley* v. *Valeo* (1976), while upholding limits on contributions by both PACs and individuals, the Court declared that limits on a candidate's use of personal funds were unconstitutional restraints on freedom of expression. "The First Amendment's protection against governmental abridgment of free expression," said the Court, "cannot properly be made to depend on a person's financial ability to engage in public discussion.

Following the rule of *Buckley* v. *Valeo* the Supreme Court struck down a Massachusetts law that prohibited business corporations from contributing funds to influence a referendum on the ground that it violated freedom of speech (*First National Bank of Boston* v. *Bellotti,* 1978). It should be noted that in this instance the speech being protected was not that of individuals but of a corporate entity. In another significant case, *Federal Elections Commission* v. *Massachusetts Citizens for Life, Inc.* (1986), the Court declared unconstitutional a ruling by the FEC prohibiting expenditures by nonprofit organizations to influence public issues such as abortion or gun control. Expending money for television or newspaper advertising in support of or in opposition to such issues is protected by the First Amendment.

In 1990 the Court upheld the Michigan Campaign Act of 1979 which, while permitting corporations to solicit contributions for a political fund from an enumerated list of persons associated with the corporation, prohibited any corporation from expending its official treasury monies to support or oppose any candidate running for office. The law, wrote Justice Thurgood Marshall, may impose a burden on First Amendment rights but is justified by a "compelling state interest" in reducing the threat of corporate political expenditures that might undermine the integrity of the political process (*Austin* v. *Michigan Chamber of Commerce*).

It has not been our purpose to canvass exhaustively the law of speech, press, and assembly, but only to introduce the student to some of the key issues that perennially require judicial intervention and to highlight the doctrinal response of the Supreme Court, past and present. It should be clear that the justices, in carrying out their obligations as trustees of the Constitution, are forced to make excruciatingly difficult choices between maintaining a broad area for free expression and protecting society at large or deciding between two or more equally valid claims of constitutional guarantees. We turn now to the language of the judges themselves.

Bibliography

BERNS, WALTER. *The First Amendment and the Future of American Democracy.* New York: Basic Books, 1976.

CHAFEE, ZECHARIAH. *Free Speech in the United States.* Cambridge: Harvard University Press, 1941.

CLOR, HARRY M. *Obscenity and Public Morality: Censorship in a Liberal Society.* Chicago: University of Chicago Press, 1969.

DUCAT, CRAIG R. *Modes of Constitutional Interpretation.* St. Paul: West Publishing Company, 1978.

EMERSON, THOMAS I. *The System of Freedom of Expression.* New York: Random House, 1970.

FRIENDLY, FRED W. *Minnesota Rag.* New York: Vintage Books, 1982.

HENTOFF, NAT. *The First Freedom: The Tumultuous History of Free Speech in America.* New York: Delacorte Press, 1980.

KALVEN, HARRY, JR., and JAMIE KALVEN. *A Worthy Tradition: Freedom of Speech in America.* New York: Harper & Row, 1988.

MEIKLEJOHN, ALEXANDER. *Political Freedom: The Constitutional Power of the People.* New York: Oxford University Press, 1965.

PRITCHETT, C. HERMAN. *Constitutional Civil Liberties.* Englewood Cliffs: Prentice-Hall, 1984.

TEDFORD, THOMAS L. *Freedom of Speech in the United States.* New York: Random House, 1985.

Schenck v. United States

249 U.S. 47 (1919)

Legal and historical scholarship has confirmed the proposition that all of the principals involved in placing the First Amendment in the Constitution—the men who wrote it, the senators and congressmen who proposed its adoption, and the state legislators who voted to ratify it—were sharply divided over its meaning. A general consensus did exist that the amendment outlawed advance prohibitions on speaking or writing, but did not constrain punishment after publication or vocal advocacy. At the state level, persons were prosecuted at common law and occasionally under statutes for seditious, defamatory speech and, in the early years, blasphemy. In 1798 Congress enacted four statutes, collectively known as the Alien and Sedition Acts, two of which expired within 3 years. A third was repealed in 1802 and the remaining one, the Alien Enemies Act, remains in force as a part of the President's wartime emergency power. When Thomas Jefferson became President, he pardoned everyone who had been convicted under the acts, and thus ended the initial federal interference with speech. Until 1917 the national government had no legislation on the books that could be used to prosecute persons who expressed ideas that were outside the mainstream of the American political tradition.

After the United States entered the war against Germany, Congress passed the Espionage Act, its primary purpose being to prevent sabotage. However, the statute contained a section that punished speech used with the intent to interfere with the military, the draft, or to cause insubordination, disloyalty, or mutiny in the armed forces. Charles T. Schenck, the general secretary of the Socialist party, was strongly opposed to the war and expressed his opposition by circulating leaflets urging young

men not to report for the draft. He was indicted under the Espionage Act for conspiring to obstruct the draft and for using the mails to send his messages. After being convicted by a jury and sentenced to prison, Schenck appealed to the Supreme Court on the ground that he had been deprived of his freedom of speech guaranteed by the First Amendment.

OLIVER WENDELL HOLMES, JR.

Oliver Wendell Holmes, Jr., the son of a well-known Boston physician and poet, was named to the Supreme Court by President Theodore Roosevelt in 1902 after nearly two decades of service as an associate and then chief justice of the Supreme Judicial Court of Massachusetts. He is without a doubt the greatest legal scholar to sit on the Court, having written a ground-breaking study of the common law. Although strongly conservative politically, Holmes was firmly committed to a philosophy of judicial restraint, which put him at odds with his conservative brethren who wished to use the power of the Court to prevent the government from regulating the economy. Holmes and his frequent partner in dissent, Louis Brandeis, formed one of the most intellectually formidable alliances in the Court's history.

Mr. Justice **Holmes** delivered the opinion of the court.

. . .

It is argued that the evidence, if admissible, was not sufficient to prove that the defendant Schenck was concerned in sending the documents. According to the testimony Schenck said he was general secretary of the Socialist party and had charge of the Socialist headquarters from which the documents were sent. He identified a book found there as the minutes of the Executive Committee of the party. The book showed a resolution of August 13, 1917, that 15,000 leaflets should be printed on the other side of one of them in use, to be mailed to men who had passed exemption boards, and for distribution. Schenck personally attended to the printing. On August 20 the general secretary's report said "Obtained new leaflets from printer and started work addressing envelopes" &c.; and there was a resolve that Comrade Schenck be allowed $125 for sending leaflets through the mail. He said that he had about fifteen or sixteen

thousand printed. There were files of the circular in question in the inner office which he said were printed on the other side of the one sided circular and were there for distribution. Other copies were proved to have been sent through the mails to drafted men. Without going into confirmatory details that were proved, no reasonable man could doubt that the defendant Schenck was largely instrumental in sending the circulars about.

. . .

The document in question upon its first printed side recited the first section of the Thirteenth Amendment, said that the idea embodied in it was violated by the Conscription Act and that a conscript is little better than a convict. In impassioned language it intimated that conscription was despotism in its worst form and a monstrous wrong against humanity in the interest of Wall Street's chosen few. It said "Do not submit to intimidation," but in form at least confined itself to peaceful measures such as a petition for the repeal of the act. The other and later printed side of the sheet was headed "Assert Your Rights." It stated reasons for alleging that any one violated the Constitution when he refused to recognize "your right to assert your opposition to the draft," and went on "If you do not assert and support your rights, you are helping to deny or disparage rights which it is the solemn duty of all citizens and residents of the United States to retain." It described the arguments on the other side as coming from cunning politicians and a mercenary capitalist press, and even silent consent to the conscription law as helping to support an infamous conspiracy. It denied the power to send our citizens away to foreign shores to shoot up the people of other lands, and added that words could not express the condemnation such cold-blooded ruthlessness deserves, &c., &c., winding up, "You must do your share to maintain, support and uphold the rights of the people of this country." Of course the document would not have been sent unless it had been intended to have some effect, and we do not see what effect it could be expected to have upon persons subject to the draft except to influence them to obstruct the carrying of it out. The defendants do not deny that the jury might find against them on this point.

But it is said, suppose that that was the tendency of this circular, it is protected by the First Amendment to the Constitution. Two of the strongest expressions are said to be quoted respectively from well-known public men. It well may be that the prohibition of laws abridging the freedom of speech is not confined to previous restraints, although to prevent them may have been the main purpose, as intimated in Patterson v. Colorado. We admit that in many places and in ordinary times the defendants in saying all that was said in the circular would have been within their constitutional rights. But the character of every act depends upon the circumstances in which it is done. The most stringent protection of free speech would not protect a man in falsely shouting fire in a theatre and causing a panic. It does not even protect a man from an injunction against uttering words that may have all the effect of force. The question in every case is whether the words used are used in such circumstances and are of such a nature as to create a clear and present danger that they will bring about the substantive evils that Congress has a right to prevent. It is a question of proximity and degree. When a nation is at war many things that might be said in time of peace are such a hindrance to its effort that their utterance will not be endured so long as men fight and that no Court could regard them as protected by any constitutional right. It seems to be admitted that if an actual obstruction of the recruiting service were proved, liability for words that produced that effect might be enforced. The statute of 1917 in § 4 punishes conspiracies to obstruct as well as actual obstruction. If the act, (speaking, or circulating a paper), its tendency and the intent with which it is done are the same, we perceive no ground for saying that success alone warrants making the act a crime. Indeed that case might be said to dispose of the present contention if the precedent covers all *media concludendi*. But as the right to free speech was not referred to specially, we have thought fit to add a few words.

It was not argued that a conspiracy to obstruct the draft was not within the words of the Act of 1917. The words are "obstruct the recruiting or enlistment service," and it might be suggested that they refer only to making it hard to get volunteers. Recruiting heretofore usually having been accomplished by getting volunteers the word is apt to call up that method only in our minds. But recruiting is gaining fresh supplies for the forces, as well by draft as otherwise. It is put as an alternative to enlistment or voluntary enrollment in this act. The fact that the Act of 1917 was enlarged by the amending Act of May 16, of course, does not affect the present indictment and would not, even if the former act had been repealed.

Judgments affirmed.

Aftermath of Schenck *v.* United States

For 10 years after Justice Holmes enunciated the "clear and present danger" rule, its effect appeared to be the opposite of Holmes's intention. What Holmes had tried to do was to draw the line between a speech that is made within the democratic process—one that is attempting to become accepted through debate—and one that is an incitement to activity that might result in injury to persons or impede the legitimate administration of public policy. Schenck, like someone who shouts fire in a crowded theater, was not inviting debate but was inciting persons to act. Thus, he met the test and went to jail for 10 years.

Within a week of the decision in *Schenck* a unanimous Court, again speaking through Justice Holmes, sent two more dissenters from the war to jail by upholding their convictions. Jacob Frohwerk, publisher of a pro-German newspaper, had been convicted of conspiracy to violate the Espionage Act by printing articles intended to cause disloyalty and mutiny in the armed forces (*Frohwerk* v. *United States,* 1919). Socialist leader Eugene v. Debs had appealed his conviction for delivering an antiwar speech which tended to obstruct conscription of men for the military (*Debs* v. *United States,* 1919). Like Schenck, Debs and Frohwerk were sentenced to 10 years in prison.

Eight months after the rendering of these decisions the Court decided *Abrams* v. *United States* (1919) in which Justices Holmes and Brandeis parted with their brethren, arguing for a more liberal (speech-protecting) interpretation of clear and present danger. Jacob Abrams and four associates, all aliens of Russian descent, were convicted under a 1918 amendment to the Espionage Act of conspiracy to write, print, and distribute seditious material and of advocating curtailment of production essential to the war effort. Abrams and his fellow defendants had distributed leaflets in and around New York City that were critical of President Wilson's policy of sending troops to Russia in support of anti-Communist forces, and urged workers to take part in a general strike in sympathy for the Russian Revolution.

Dissenting from the majority opinion which upheld Abrams's conviction, Holmes emphasized that the "surreptious publishing of a silly leaflet, by an unknown man" posed no immediate danger or hindrance to the success of the government's policy. Unfortunately, he did not prevail, and Jacob Abrams and his friends went to jail for 20 years.

For some two decades after its enunciation by Holmes, the clear and present danger doctrine was of little use in protecting speech, but it was kept alive by Holmes and Brandeis in concurrences and dissents. Eventually it became a safeguard for a full discussion of ideas, a test the Court would use to prevent official suppression of advocacy of ideas with which the general public may disagree or even passionately hate.

Dennis v. *United States*

341 U.S. 494 (1951)

In 1940 Congress passed the Alien Registration Act, more popularly known as the Smith Act because of its authorship by Representative Howard W. Smith of Virginia. This law was characterized by Professor Zechariah Chafee, Jr., as containing "the most drastic restrictions on freedom of speech ever enacted by the United States during peace." It was the first federal peacetime sedition law to appear since the

Alien and Sedition Acts were passed in 1798. Under the act's provisions it was a criminal offense to (1) advocate the necessity, desirability, or propriety of overthrowing the government by force; (2) organize any group to teach the overthrow of the government; and (3) conspire with others to violate the act. Anyone convicted of violating the statute was subject to maximum penalties of a $20,000 fine and imprisonment for 20 years.

Although this was the first federal prohibition on political speech in a century and a half, such was not the case in the states. New York, in passing the Criminal Anarchy Act of 1902, opened a veritable spillway for a flood of state statutes aimed at "subversion." State legislatures around the country soon followed New York in enacting laws encompassing everything from treason and criminal anarchy (defined as advocating the violent overthrow of organized government) to teacher loyalty oaths. The Smith Act, incidentally, was patterned almost word for word on the New York statute.

The Supreme Court decided some 50 First Amendment cases between *Schenck* in 1919 and *Dennis* in 1950, most originating in the states and with free speech claims being upheld more often than not. The one with the greatest doctrinal impact on First Amendment law was *Gitlow* v. *New York* in 1925. Two important rules resulted from *Gitlow*, one restrictive of political speech, the second, in its long-range implication, strongly protective. Benjamin Gitlow, a leader of the left-wing section of the Socialist party was convicted in New York of violating the state's criminal anarchy statute for, according to the indictment, distributing materials advocating the overthrow of organized government by force, violence, and unlawful means. The aspect of the *Gitlow* decision that was protective of speech was the rule that henceforth freedom of speech of the First Amendment would be incorporated into the Fourteenth Amendment as a limit on state power. In deciding the *Gitlow* case, however, the Court simply reiterated the old common law concept of "remote and indirect tendency," that is, if speech had a "tendency" to produce an evil it might be constitutionally restricted. As the majority contended: "The state cannot reasonably be required to measure the danger from every . . . utterance in the nice balance of a jeweler's scale. A single revolutionary spark *may* kindle a fire that, smouldering for a time, may burst into a sweeping and destructive conflagration." Justice Holmes, joined by Justice Brandeis, dissented, maintaining that there was no "present danger of an attempt to overthrow the government by force" on the part of Gitlow. Notwithstanding Holmes's protest, the judicial test for determining limits on political speech was that of "bad tendency" and not "clear and present danger."

In 1948 Eugene Dennis, secretary general of the American Communist party, and 10 of the top Communist party leaders in the nation were convicted in a federal district court in New York of violating the Smith Act in that they had advocated the overthrow of the government by force and violence, had organized a group to teach such advocacy, and had conspired to violate the law's prohibitions. This case arose during the early years of the cold war between the Soviet Union and the United States, and in the midst of a hot war with Communist forces in Korea. These events magnified the threat of internal Communist subversion—real or imagined—as an ever-present, highly charged topic in the nation's political discourse. As one can see in reading the various concurring and dissenting opinions, the justices were struggling to reach a consensus on a formula, old or new, that would give maximum protection to speech while not impeding the governmental efforts to protect its citizens from subversion and possible violence.

FRED M. VINSON

Before his nomination as chief justice by President Harry S. Truman in 1946, Fred M. Vinson had had a successful political career as a U.S. representative from Kentucky and then in several top administration posts, including that of Secretary of the Treasury. He was selected to head the Supreme Court partly because of his talent as a mediator since the Court at the time was rancorous and divided, but when he died 7 years later, the Court's divisiveness remained. Although conservative on free speech issues, Vinson wrote several significant opinions advancing equality for black Americans.

Mr. Chief Justice **Vinson** announced the judgment of the Court and an opinion in which Mr. Justice **Reed,** Mr. Justice **Burton** and Mr. Justice **Minton** join.

. . .

I

It will be helpful in clarifying the issues to treat next the contention that the trial judge improperly interpreted the statute by charging that the statute required an unlawful intent before the jury could convict. More specifically, he charged that the jury could not find the petitioners guilty under the indictment unless they found that petitioners had the intent "to overthrow . . . the Government of the United States by force and violence as speedily as circumstances would permit."

Section 2(a)(1) makes it unlawful "to knowingly or willfully advocate, . . . or teach the duty, necessity, desirability, or propriety of overthrowing or destroying any government in the United States by force or violence. . . ."; Section 2(a)(3), "to organize or help to organize any society, group, or assembly of persons who teach, advocate or encourage the overthrow. . . ." Because of the fact that § 2(a)(2) expressly requires a specific intent to overthrow the Government, and because of the absence of precise language in the foregoing subsections, it is claimed that Congress deliberately omitted any such requirement. We do not agree. It would require a far greater indication of congressional desire that intent not be made an element of the crime than the use of the disjunctive "knowingly *or* willfully" in § 2(a)(1), or the omission of exact language in § 2(a)(3). The structure and purpose of the statute demand the inclusion of intent as an element of the crime. Congress was concerned with those who advocate and organize for the overthrow of the Government. Certainly those who recruit and combine for the purpose of advocating overthrow intend to bring about that overthrow. We hold that the statute requires as an essential element of the crime proof of the intent of those who are charged with its violation to overthrow the Government by force and violence.

. . .

II

The obvious purpose of the statute is to protect existing Government, not from change by peaceable, lawful and constitutional means, but from change by violence, revolution and terrorism. That it is within the *power* of the Congress to protect the Government of the United States from armed rebellion is a proposition which requires little discussion. Whatever theoretical merit there may be to the argument that there is a "right" to rebellion against dictatorial governments is without force where the existing structure of the government provides for peaceful and orderly change. We reject any principle of governmental helplessness in the face of preparation for revolution, which principle, carried to its logical conclusion, must lead to anarchy. No one could conceive that it is not within the power of Congress to prohibit acts intended to overthrow the Government by force and violence. The question with which we are concerned here is not whether Congress has such *power*, but whether the *means* which it has employed conflict with the First and Fifth Amendments to the Constitution.

One of the bases for the contention that the means which Congress has employed are invalid takes the form of an attack on the face of the statute on the grounds that by its terms it prohibits academic discussion of the merits of Marxism-Leninism, that it stifles ideas and is contrary to all concepts of a free speech and a free press. Although we do not agree that the language itself has that significance, we must bear in mind that it is the duty of the federal courts to interpret federal legislation in a manner not inconsistent with the demands of the Constitution.

. . .

The very language of the Smith Act negates the interpretation which petitioners would have us impose on that Act. It is directed at advocacy, not discussion. Thus, the trial judge properly charged the jury that they could not convict if they found that petitioners did "no more than pursue peaceful studies and discussions or teaching and advocacy in the realm of ideas." He further charged that it was not unlawful "to conduct in an American college and university a course explaining the philosophical theories set forth in the books which have been placed in evidence." Such a charge is in strict accord with the statutory language, and illustrates the mean-

ing to be placed on those words. Congress did not intend to eradicate the free discussion of political theories, to destroy the traditional rights of Americans to discuss and evaluate ideas without fear of governmental sanction. Rather Congress was concerned with the very kind of activity in which the evidence showed these petitioners engaged.

III

But although the statute is not directed at the hypothetical cases which petitioners have conjured, its application in this case has resulted in convictions for the teaching and advocacy of the overthrow of the Government by force and violence, which, even though coupled with the intent to accomplish that overthrow, contains an element of speech. For this reason, we must pay special heed to the demands of the First Amendment marking out the boundaries of speech.

. . .

No important case involving free speech was decided by this Court prior to Schenck v. United States. Indeed, the summary treatment accorded an argument based upon an individual's claim that the First Amendment protected certain utterances indicates that the Court at earlier dates placed no unique emphasis upon that right. It was not until the classic dictum of Justice Holmes in the Schenck case that speech *per se* received that emphasis in a majority opinion.

. . .

The rule we deduce from these cases is that where an offense is specified by a statute in non-speech or nonpress terms, a conviction relying upon speech or press as evidence of violation may be sustained only when the speech or publication created a "clear and present danger" of attempting or accomplishing the prohibited crime, *e. g.,* interference with enlistment. The dissents, we repeat, in emphasizing the value of speech, were addressed to the argument of the sufficiency of the evidence.

. . .

In discussing the proper measure of evaluation of this kind of legislation, we suggested that the Holmes-Brandeis philosophy insisted that where there was a direct restriction upon speech, a "clear and present danger" that the substantive evil would be caused was necessary before the statute in question could be constitutionally applied. And we stated, "[The First] Amendment requires that one be permitted to believe what he will. It requires that one be permitted to advocate what he will unless there is a clear and present danger that substantial public evil will result therefrom." But we further suggested that neither Justice Holmes nor Justice Brandeis ever envisioned that a shorthand phrase should be crystallized into a rigid rule to be applied inflexibly without regard to the circumstances of each case. Speech is not an absolute, above and beyond control by the legislature when its judgment, subject to review here, is that certain kinds of speech are so undesirable as to warrant criminal sanction. Nothing is more certain in modern society than the principle that there are no absolutes, that a name, a phrase, a standard has meaning only when associated with the considerations which gave birth to the nomenclature. To those who would paralyze our Government in the face of impending threat by encasing it in a semantic straitjacket we must reply that all concepts are relative.

In this case we are squarely presented with the application of the "clear and present danger" test, and must decide what that phrase imports. We first note that many of the cases in which this Court has reversed convictions by use of this or similar tests have been based on the fact that the interest which the State was attempting to protect was itself too insubstantial to warrant restriction of speech.

Overthrow of the Government by force and violence is certainly a substantial enough interest for the Government to limit speech. Indeed, this is the ultimate value of any society, for if a society cannot protect its very structure from armed internal attack, it must follow that no subordinate value can be protected. If, then, this interest may be protected, the literal problem which is presented is what has been meant by the use of the phrase "clear and present danger" of the utterances bringing about the evil within the power of Congress to punish.

Obviously, the words cannot mean that before the Government may act, it must wait until the *putsch* is about to be executed, the plans have been laid and the signal is awaited. If Government is aware that a group aiming at its overthrow is attempting to indoctrinate its members and to commit them to a course whereby they will strike when the leaders feel the circumstances permit, action by the Government is required. The argument that there is no need for Government to concern itself, for Government is strong, it possesses ample powers to put down a rebellion, it may defeat the revolution with ease needs no answer. For that is not the question. Certainly an attempt to overthrow the Government by force, even though doomed from the outset because of inadequate numbers or power of the revolutionists, is a sufficient evil for Congress to prevent. The damage which such attempts create both physically and politically to a nation makes it impossible to measure the validity in terms of the probability of success, or the immediacy of a successful attempt. In the instant case the trial judge charged the jury that they could not convict unless they found that petitioners intended to overthrow the Government "as speedily as circumstances would permit." This does not mean, and could not properly mean, that they would not strike until there was certainty of success. What was meant was that the revolutionists would strike when they thought the time was ripe. We must therefore reject the contention that success or probability of success is the criterion.

The situation with which Justices Holmes and Brandeis were concerned in Gitlow was a comparatively isolated event, bearing little relation in their minds to any substantial threat to the safety of the community. They were not confronted with any situation comparable to the instant one—the development of an apparatus designed and dedicated to the overthrow of the Government, in the context of world crisis after crisis.

Chief Judge Learned Hand, writing for the majority below, interpreted the phrase as follows: "In each case [courts] must ask whether the gravity of the 'evil,' discounted by its improbability, justifies such invasion of free speech as is necessary to avoid the danger." We adopt this statement of the rule. As articulated by Chief Judge Hand, it is as succinct and inclusive as any other we might devise at this time. It takes into consideration those factors which we deem relevant, and relates their significances. More we cannot expect from words.

Likewise, we are in accord with the court below, which affirmed the trial court's finding that the requisite danger existed. The mere fact that from the period 1945 to 1948 petitioners' activities did not result in an attempt to overthrow the Government by force and violence is of course no answer to the fact that there was a group that was ready to make the attempt. The formation by petitioners of such a highly organized conspiracy, with rigidly disciplined members subject to call when the leaders, these petitioners, felt that the time had come for action, coupled with the inflammable nature of world conditions, similar uprisings in other countries, and the touch-and-go nature of our relations with countries with whom petitioners were in the very least ideologically attuned, convince us that their convictions were justified on this score. And this analysis disposes of the contention that a conspiracy to advocate, as distinguished from the advocacy itself, cannot be constitutionally restrained, because it comprises only the preparation. It is the existence of the conspiracy which creates the danger. If the ingredients of the reaction are present, we cannot bind the Government to wait until the catalyst is added.

IV

Although we have concluded that the finding that there was a sufficient danger to warrant the application of the statute was justified on the merits, there remains the problem of whether the trial judge's treatment of the issue was correct.

. . .

It is . . . clear that he reserved the question of the existence of the danger for his own determination, and the question becomes whether the issue is of such a nature that it should have been submitted to the jury.

The first paragraph of the quoted instructions calls for the jury to find the facts essential to establish the substantive crime, violation of §§ 2(a)(1) and 2(a)(3) of the Smith Act, involved in the conspiracy charge. There can be no doubt that if the jury found those facts against the petitioners violation of the Act would be established. The argument that the action of the trial court is erroneous, in declaring as a matter of law that such violation shows sufficient danger to justify the punishment despite the First Amendment, rests on the theory that a jury must decide a question of the application of the First Amendment. We do not agree.

When facts are found that establish the violation of a statute, the protection against conviction afforded by the First Amendment is a matter of law. The doctrine that there must be a clear and present danger of a substantive evil that Congress has a right to prevent is a judicial rule to be applied as a matter of law by the courts. The guilt is established by proof of facts. Whether the First Amendment protects the activity which constitutes the violation of the statute must depend upon a judicial determination of the scope of the First Amendment applied to the circumstances of the case.

. . .

The question in this case is whether the statute which the legislature has enacted may be constitutionally applied. In other words, the Court must examine judicially the application of the statute to the particular situation, to ascertain if the Constitution prohibits the conviction. We hold that the statute may be applied where there is a "clear and present danger" of the substantive evil which the legislature had the right to prevent. Bearing, as it does, the marks of a "question of law," the issue is properly one for the judge to decide.

V

There remains to be discussed the question of vagueness—whether the statute as we have interpreted it is too vague, not sufficiently advising those who would speak of the limitations upon their activity. It is urged that such vagueness contravenes the First and Fifth Amendments. This argument is particularly nonpersuasive when presented by petitioners, who, the jury found, intended to overthrow the Government as speedily as circumstances would permit.

We agree that the standard as defined is not a neat, mathematical formulary. Like all verbalizations it is subject to criticism on the score of indefiniteness. But petitioners themselves contend that the verbalization, "clear and present danger" is the proper standard. We see no difference, from the standpoint of vagueness, whether the standard of "clear and present danger" is one contained in *hac verba* within the statute, or whether it is the judicial measure of constitutional applicability. We have shown the indeterminate standard the phrase necessarily connotes. We do not think we have rendered that standard any more indefinite by our attempt to sum up the factors which are included within its scope. We think it well serves to indicate to those who would advocate constitutionally prohibited conduct that there is a line beyond which they may not go—a line which they, in full knowledge of what they intend and the circumstances in which their activity takes place, will well appreciate and understand.

. . .

We hold that §§ 2(a) (1), 2(a) (3) and 3 of the Smith Act, do not inherently, or as construed or applied in the instant case, violate the First Amendment and other provisions of the Bill of Rights, or the First and Fifth Amendments because of indefiniteness. Petitioners intended to overthrow the Government of the United States as speedily as the circumstances would permit. Their conspiracy to organize the Communist Party and to teach and advocate the overthrow of the Government of the United States by force and violence created a "clear and present danger" of an attempt to overthrow the Government by force and violence. They were properly and constitutionally convicted for violation of the Smith Act. The judgments of conviction are affirmed.

Affirmed.

Mr. Justice **Frankfurter,** concurring in affirmance of the judgment.

. . .

The language of the First Amendment is to be read not as barren words found in a dictionary but as symbols of historic experience illumined by the presuppositions of those who employed them. Not what words did Madison and Hamilton use, but what was it in their minds which they conveyed? Free speech is subject to prohibition of those abuses of expression which a civilized society may forbid. As in the case of every other provision of the Constitution that is not crystallized by the nature of its technical concepts, the fact that the First Amendment is not self-defining and self-enforcing neither impairs its usefulness nor compels its paralysis as a living instrument.

"The law is perfectly well settled," this Court said over fifty years ago, "that the first 10 amendments to the Constitution, commonly known as the 'Bill of Rights,' were not intended to lay down any novel principles of government, but simply to embody certain guaranties and immunities which we had inherited from our English ancestors, and which had from time immemorial, been subject to certain well-recognized exceptions, arising from the necessities of the case. In incorporating these principles into the fundamental law, there was no intention of disregarding the exceptions, which continued to be recognized as if they had been formally expressed." That this represents the authentic view of the Bill of Rights and the spirit in which it must be construed has been recognized again and again in cases that have come here within the last fifty years. Absolute rules would inevitably lead to absolute exceptions, and such exceptions would eventually corrode the rules. The demands of free speech in a democratic society as well as the interest in national security are better served by candid and informed weighing of the competing interests, within the confines of the judicial process, than by announcing dogmas too inflexible for the non-Euclidian problems to be solved.

But how are competing interests to be assessed? Since they are not subject to quantitative ascertainment, the issue necessarily resolves itself into asking, who is to make the adjustment?—who is to balance the relevant factors and ascertain which interest is in the circumstances to prevail? Full responsibility for the choice cannot be given to the courts. Courts are not representative bodies. They are not designed to be a good reflex of a democratic society. Their judgment is best informed, and therefore most dependable, within narrow limits. Their essential quality is detachment, founded on independence. History teaches that the independence of the judiciary is jeopardized when courts become embroiled in the passions of the day and assume primary responsibility in choosing between competing political, economic and social pressures.

Primary responsibility for adjusting the interests which compete in the situation before us of necessity belongs to the Congress. The nature of the power to be exercised by this Court has been delineated in decisions not charged with the emotional appeal of situations such as that now before us. We are to set aside the judgment of those whose duty it is to legislate only if there is no reasonable basis for it.

. . .

—A survey of the relevant decisions indicates that the results which we have reached are on the whole those that would ensue from careful weighing of conflicting interests. The complex issues presented by regulation of speech in public places, by picketing, and by legislation prohibiting advocacy of crime have been resolved by scrutiny of many factors besides the imminence and gravity of the evil threatened.

. . .

—Not every type of speech occupies the same position on the scale of values. There is no substantial public interest in permitting certain kinds of utterances: "the lewd and obscene, the profane, the libelous, and the insulting or 'fighting' words—those which by their very utterance inflict injury or tend to incite an immediate breach of the peace."

We have frequently indicated that the interest in protecting speech depends on the circumstances of the occasion. It is pertinent to the decision before us to consider where on the scale of values we have in the past placed the type of speech now claiming constitutional immunity.

The defendants have been convicted of conspiring to organize a party of persons who advocate the overthrow of the Government by force and violence. The jury has found that the object of the conspiracy is advocacy as "a rule or principle of action," "by language reasonably and ordinarily calculated to incite persons to such action," and with the intent to cause the overthrow "as speedily as circumstances would permit."

On any scale of values which we have hitherto recognized, speech of this sort ranks low.

. . .

It is true that there is no divining rod by which we may locate "advocacy." Exposition of ideas readily merges into advocacy. The same Justice who gave currency to application of the incitement doctrine in this field dissented four times from what he thought was its misapplication. As he said in the Gitlow dissent, "Every idea is an incitement." Even though advocacy of overthrow deserves little protection, we should hesitate to prohibit it if we thereby inhibit the interchange of rational ideas so essential to representative government and free society.

But there is underlying validity in the distinction between advocacy and the interchange of ideas, and we do not discard a useful tool because it may be misused. That such a distinction could be used unreasonably by those in power against hostile or unorthodox views does not negate the fact that it may be used reasonably against an organization wielding the power of the centrally controlled international Communist movement. The object of the conspiracy before us is so clear that the chance of error in saying that the defendants conspired to advocate rather than to express ideas is slight. Mr. Justice DOUGLAS quite properly points out that the conspiracy before us is not a conspiracy to overthrow the Government. But it would be equally wrong to treat it as a seminar in political theory.

. . .

These general considerations underlie decision of the case before us.

On the one hand is the interest in security. The Communist Party was not designed by these defendants as an ordinary political party. For the circumstances of its organization, its aims and methods, and the relation of the defendants to its organization and aims we are concluded by the jury's verdict. The jury found that the Party rejects the basic premise of our political system—that change is to be brought about by nonviolent constitutional process. The jury found that the Party advocates the theory that there is a duty and necessity to overthrow the Government by force and violence. It found that the Party entertains and promotes this view, not as a prophetic insight or as a bit of unworldly speculation, but as a program for winning adherents and as a policy to be translated into action.

In finding that the defendants violated the statute, we may not treat as established fact that the Communist Party in this country is of significant size, well-organized, well-disciplined, conditioned to embark on unlawful activity when given the command. But in determining whether application of the statute to the defendants is within the constitutional powers of Congress, we are not limited to the facts found by the jury. We must view such a question in the light of whatever is relevant to a legislative judgment. We may take judicial notice that the Communist doctrines which these defendants have conspired to advocate are in the ascendency in powerful nations who cannot be acquitted of unfriendliness to the institutions of this country. We may take account of evidence brought forward at this trial and elsewhere, much of which has long been common knowledge. In sum, it would amply justify a legislature in concluding that recruitment of additional members for the Party would create a substantial danger to national security.

. . .

On the other hand is the interest in free speech. The right to exert all governmental powers in aid of maintaining our institutions and resisting their physical overthrow does not include intolerance of opinions and speech that cannot do harm although opposed and perhaps alien to dominant, traditional opinion. The treatment of its minorities, especially their legal position, is among the most searching tests of the level of civilization attained by a society. It is better for those who have almost unlimited power of government in their hands to err on the side of freedom. We have enjoyed so much freedom for so long that we are perhaps in danger of forgetting how much blood it cost to establish the Bill of Rights.

. . .

It is not for us to decide how we would adjust the clash of interests which this case presents were the primary responsibility for reconciling it ours. Congress has determined that the danger created by advocacy of overthrow justifies the ensuing restriction on freedom of speech. The determination was made after due deliberation, and the seriousness of the congressional purpose is attested by the volume of legislation passed to effectuate the same ends.

. . .

In the light of their experience, the Framers of the Constitution chose to keep the judiciary dissociated from direct participation in the legislative process. In asserting the power to pass on the constitutionality of legislation, Marshall and his Court expressed the purposes of the Founders. But the extent to which the exercise of this power would interpenetrate matters of policy could hardly have been foreseen by the most prescient. The distinction which the Founders drew between the Court's duty to pass on the power of Congress and its complementary duty not to enter directly the domain of policy is fundamental. But in its actual operation it is rather subtle, certainly to the common understanding. Our duty to abstain from confounding policy with constitutionality demands perceptive humility as well as self-restraint in not declaring unconstitutional what in a judge's private judgment is deemed unwise and even dangerous.

Even when moving strictly within the limits of constitutional adjudication, judges are concerned with issues that may be said to involve vital finalities. The too easy transition from disapproval of what is undesirable to condemnation as unconstitutional, has led some of the wisest judges to question the wisdom of our scheme in lodging such authority in courts. But it is relevant to remind that in sustaining the power of Congress in a case like this nothing irrevocable is done. The democratic process at all events is not impaired or restricted. Power and responsibility remain with the people and immediately with their representation. All the Court says is that Congress was not forbidden by the Constitution to pass this enactment and that a prosecution under it may be brought against a conspiracy such as the one before us.

. . .

The wisdom of the assumptions underlying the legislation and prosecution is another matter. In finding that Congress has acted within its power, a judge does not remotely imply that he favors the implications that lie beneath the legal issues. Considerations there enter which go beyond the criteria that are binding upon judges within the narrow confines of their legitimate authority. The legislation we are here considering is but a truncated aspect of a deeper issue. For me it has been most illuminatingly expressed by one in whom responsibility and experience have fructified native insight, the Director-General of the British Broadcasting Corporation:

"We have to face up to the fact that there are powerful forces in the world today misusing the privileges of liberty in order to destroy her. The question must be asked, however, whether suppression of information or opinion is the true defense. We may have come a long way from Mill's famous dictum that: 'If all mankind minus one were of one opinion, and only one person were of the contrary opinion, mankind would be no more justified in silencing that one person, than he, if he had the power, would be justified in silencing mankind,' but Mill's reminders from history as to what has happened when suppression was most virulently exercised ought to warn us that no debate is ever permanently won by shutting one's ears or by even the most Draconian policy of silencing opponents. The *debate* must be won. And it must be won with full information. Where there are lies, they must be shown for what they are. Where there are errors, they must be refuted. It would be a major defeat if the enemies of democracy forced us to abandon our faith in the power of informed discussion and so brought us down to their own level.

Mankind is so constituted, moreover, that if, where expression and discussion are concerned, the enemies of liberty are met with a denial of liberty, many men of goodwill will come to suspect there is something in the proscribed doctrine after all. Erroneous doctrines thrive on being expunged. They die if exposed."

. . .

Civil liberties draw at best only limited strength from legal guaranties. Preoccupation by our people with the constitutionality, instead of with the wisdom, of legislation or of executive action is preoccupation with a false value. Even those who would most freely use the judicial brake on the democratic process by invalidating legislation that goes deeply against their grain, acknowledge, at least by paying lip service, that constitutionality does not exact a sense of proportion or the sanity of humor or an absence of fear. Focusing attention on constitutionality tends to make constitutionality synonymous with wisdom. When legislation touches freedom of thought and freedom of speech, such a tendency is a formidable enemy of the free spirit. Much that should be rejected as illiberal, because repressive and envenoming, may well be not unconstitutional. The ultimate reliance for the deepest needs of civilization must be found outside their vindication in courts of law; apart from all else, judges, howsoever they may conscientiously seek to discipline themselves against it, unconsciously are too apt to be moved by the deep undercurrents of public feeling. A persistent, positive translation of the liberating faith into the feelings and thoughts and actions of men and women is the real protection against attempts to strait-jacket the human mind. Such temptations will have their way, if fear and hatred are not exercised. The mark of a truly civilized man is confidence in the strength and security derived from the inquiring mind. We may be grateful for such honest comforts as it supports, but we must be unafraid of its incertitudes. Without open minds there can be no open society. And if society be not open the spirit of man is mutilated and becomes enslaved.

Mr. Justice **Jackson,** concurring.

This prosecution is the latest of neverending, because never successful, quests for some legal formula that will secure an existing order against revolutionary radicalism. It requires us to reappraise, in the light of our own times and conditions, constitutional doctrines devised under other circumstances to strike a balance between authority and liberty.

Activity here charged to be criminal is conspiracy—that defendants conspired to teach and advocate, and to organize the Communist Party to teach and advocate, overthrow and destruction of the Government by force and violence. There is no charge of actual violence or attempt at overthrow.

The principal reliance of the defense in this Court is that the conviction cannot stand under the Constitution because the conspiracy of these defendants presents no "clear and present danger" of imminent or foreseeable overthrow.

. . .

The "clear and present danger" test was an innovation by Mr. Justice Holmes in the Schenck case, reiterated and refined by him and Mr. Justice Brandeis in later cases, all arising before the era of World War II revealed the subtlety and efficacy of modernized revolutionary techniques used by totalitarian parties. In those cases, they were faced with convictions under so-called criminal syndicalism statutes aimed at anarchists but which, loosely construed, had been applied to punish socialism, pacifism, and left-wing ideologies, the charges often resting on far-fetched inferences which, if true, would establish only technical or trivial violations. They proposed "clear and present danger" as a test for the sufficiency of evidence in particular cases.

I would save it, unmodified, for application as a "rule of reason" in the kind of case for which it was devised. When the issue is criminality of a hot-headed speech on a street corner, or circulating of a few incendiary pamphlets, or parading by some zealots behind a red flag, or refusal of a handful of school children to salute our flag, it is not beyond the capacity of the judicial process to gather, comprehend, and weigh the necessary materials for decision whether it is a clear and present danger of substantive evil or a harmless letting off of steam. It

is not a prophecy, for the danger in such cases has matured by the time of trial or it was never present. The test applies and has meaning where a conviction is sought to be based on a speech or writing which does not directly or explicitly advocate a crime but to which such tendency is sought to be attributed by construction or by implication from external circumstances. The formula in such cases favors freedoms that are vital to our society, and, even if sometimes applied too generously, the consequences cannot be grave. But its recent expansion has extended, in particular to Communists, unprecedented immunities. Unless we are to hold our Government captive in a judge-made verbal trap, we must approach the problem of a well-organized, nation-wide conspiracy, such as I have described, as realistically as our predecessors faced the trivialities that were being prosecuted until they were checked with a rule of reason.

I think reason is lacking for applying that test to this case.

If we must decide that this Act and its application are constitutional only if we are convinced that petitioner's conduct creates a "clear and present danger" of violent overthrow, we must appraise imponderables, including international and national phenomena which baffle the best informed foreign offices and our most experienced politicians. We would have to foresee and predict the effectiveness of Communist propaganda, opportunities for infiltration, whether, and when, a time will come that they consider propitious for action, and whether and how fast our existing government will deteriorate. And we would have to speculate as to whether an approaching Communist *coup* would not be anticipated by a nationalistic fascist movement. No doctrine can be sound whose application requires us to make a prophecy of that sort in the guise of a legal decision. The judicial process simply is not adequate to a trial of such far-flung issues. The answers given would reflect our own political predilections and nothing more.

The authors of the clear and present danger test never applied it to a case like this, nor would I. If applied as it is proposed here, it means that the Communist plotting is protected during its period of incubation its preliminary stages of organization and preparation are immune from the law; the Government can move only after imminent action is manifest, when it would, of course, be too late.

. . .

The highest degree of constitutional protection is due to the individual acting without conspiracy. But even an individual cannot claim that the Constitution protects him in advocating or teaching overthrow of government by force or violence. I should suppose no one would doubt that Congress has power to make such attempted overthrow a crime. But the contention is that one has the constitutional right to work up a public desire and will to do what it is a crime to attempt. I think direct incitement by speech or writing can be made a crime, and I think there can be a conviction without also proving that the odds favored its success by 99 to 1, or some other extremely high ratio.

. . .

What really is under review here is a conviction of conspiracy, after a trial for conspiracy, on an indictment charging conspiracy, brought under a statute outlawing conspiracy. With due respect to my colleagues, they seem to me to discuss anything under the sun except the law of conspiracy.

. . .

When our constitutional provisions were written, the chief forces recognized as antagonists in the struggle between authority and liberty were the Government on the one hand and the individual citizen on the other. It was thought that if the state could be kept in its place the individual could take care of himself.

In more recent times these problems have been complicated by the intervention between the state and the citizen of permanently organized, well-financed, semisecret and highly disciplined political organizations. Totalitarian groups here and abroad perfected the technique of creating private paramilitary organizations to coerce both the public government and its citizens. These organizations assert as against our Government all of the constitutional rights and immunities of individuals and at the same time

exercise over their followers much of the authority which they deny to the Government. The Communist Party realistically is a state within a state, an authoritarian dictatorship within a republic. It demands these freedoms, not for its members, but for the organized party. It denies to its own members at the same time the freedom to dissent, to debate, to deviate from the party line, and enforces its authoritarian rule by crude purges, if nothing more violent.

The law of conspiracy has been the chief means at the Government's disposal to deal with the growing problems created by such organizations. I happen to think it is an awkward and inept remedy, but I find no constitutional authority for taking this weapon from the Government. There is no constitutional right to "gang up" on the Government.

While I think there was power in Congress to enact this statute and that, as applied in this case, it cannot be held unconstitutional, I add that I have little faith in the long-range effectiveness of this conviction to stop the rise of the Communist movement. Communism will not go to jail with these Communists. No decision by this Court can forestall revolution whenever the existing government fails to command the respect and loyalty of the people and sufficient distress and discontent is allowed to grow up among the masses. Many failures by fallen governments attest that no government can long prevent revolution by outlawry. Corruption, ineptitude, inflation, oppressive taxation, militarization, injustice, and loss of leadership capable of intellectual initiative in domestic or foreign affairs are allies on which the Communists count to bring opportunity knocking to their door. Sometimes I think they may be mistaken. But the Communists are not building just for today—the rest of us might profit by their example.

Mr. Justice **Black,** dissenting.

. . .

At the outset I want to emphasize what the crime involved in this case is, and what it is not. These petitioners were not charged with an attempt to overthrow the Government. They were not charged with overt acts of any kind designed to overthrow the Government. They were not even charged with saying anything or writing anything designed to overthrow the Government. The charge was that they agreed to assemble and to talk and publish certain ideas at a later date: The indictment is that they conspired to organize the Communist Party and to use speech or newspapers and other publications in the future to teach and advocate the forcible overthrow of the Government. No matter how it is worded, this is a virulent form of prior censorship of speech and press, which I believe the First Amendment forbids. I would hold § 3 of the Smith Act authorizing this prior restraint unconstitutional on its face and as applied.

. . . The opinions for affirmance indicate that the chief reason for jettisoning the rule is the expressed fear that advocacy of Communist doctrine endangers the safety of the Republic. Undoubtedly, a governmental policy of unfettered communication of ideas does entail dangers. To the Founders of this Nation, however, the benefits derived from free expression were worth the risk. They embodied this philosophy in the First Amendment's command that "Congress shall make no law . . . abridging the freedom of speech, or of the press. . . ." I have always believed that the First Amendment is the keystone of our Government, that the freedoms it guarantees provide the best insurance against destruction of all freedom. At least as to speech in the realm of public matters, I believe that the "clear and present danger" test does not "mark the furthermost constitutional boundaries of protected expression" but does "no more than recognize a minimum compulsion of the Bill of Rights."

So long as this Court exercises the power of judicial review of legislation, I cannot agree that the First Amendment permits us to sustain laws suppressing freedom of speech and press on the basis of Congress' or our own notions of mere "reasonableness." Such a doctrine waters down the First Amendment so that it amounts to little more than an admonition to Congress. The Amendment as so construed is not likely to protect any but those "safe" or orthodox views which rarely need its protection. I must also express my objection to the holding because, as Mr. Justice Douglas' dissent shows, it sanctions the determination of a crucial issue of fact by the judge rather than by the jury. Nor can I let this opportunity pass without expressing my objection to the severely limited grant of certiorari in this case which precluded consideration here of at least two other reasons for reversing these convictions: (1) the record shows a discriminatory selection of the jury panel which prevented trial before a representative cross-section of the community; (2) the record shows that one member of the trial jury was violently hostile to petitioners before and during the trial.

Public opinion being what it now is, few will protest the conviction of these Communist petitioners. There is hope, however, that in calmer times, when present pressures, passions and fears subside, this or some later Court will restore the First Amendment liberties to the high preferred place where they belong in a free society.

Mr. Justice **Douglas,** dissenting.

If this were a case where those who claimed protection under the First Amendment were teaching the techniques of sabotage, the assassination of the President, the filching of documents from public files, the planting of bombs, the art of street warfare, and the like, I would have no doubts. The freedom to speak is not absolute; the teaching methods of terror and other seditious conduct should be beyond the pale along with obscenity and immorality. This case was argued as if those were the facts. The argument imported much seditious conduct into the record. That is easy and it has popular appeal, for the activities of Communists in plotting and scheming against the free world are common knowledge. But the fact is that no such evidence was introduced at the trial. There is a statute which makes a seditious conspiracy unlawful. Petitioners, however, were not charged with a "conspiracy to overthrow" the Government. They were charged with a conspiracy to form a party and groups and assemblies of people who teach and advocate the overthrow of our Government by force or violence and with a conspiracy to advocate and teach its overthrow by force and violence. It may well be that indoctrination in the techniques of terror to destroy the Government would be indictable under either statute. But the teaching which is condemned here is of a different character.

. . .

The First Amendment provides that "Congress shall make no law . . . abridging the freedom of speech." The Constitution provides no exception. This does not mean, however, that the Nation need hold its hand until it is in such weakened condition that there is no time to protect itself from incitement to revolution. Seditious conduct can always be punished. But the command of the First Amendment is so clear that we should not allow Congress to call a halt to free speech except in the extreme case of peril from the speech itself. The First Amendment makes confidence in the common sense of our people and in their maturity of judgment the great postulate of our democracy. Its philosophy is that violence is rarely, if ever, stopped by denying civil liberties to those advocating resort to force. The First Amendment reflects the philosophy of Jefferson "that it is time enough for the rightful purposes of civil government, for its officers to interfere when principles break out into overt acts against peace and good order." The political censor has no place in our public debates. Unless and until extreme and necessitous circumstances are shown our aim should be to keep speech unfettered and to allow the processes of law to be invoked only when the provocateurs among us move from speech to action.

Vishinsky wrote in 1938 in The Law of the Soviet State, "In our state, naturally, there is and can be no place for freedom of speech, press, and so on for the foes of socialism."

Our concern should be that we accept no such standard for the United States. Our faith should be that our people will never give support to these advocates of revolution, so long as we remain loyal to the purposes for which our Nation was founded.

Aftermath of Dennis *v.* United States

Eugene Dennis and his associates went to jail for 5 years, but as Justice Robert Jackson observed prophetically in his concurrence, "Communism will not go to jail with these Communists" and "no government can prevent revolution by outlawry." Yet, although he believed the Smith Act to be "an awkward and inept remedy," Jackson could "find no constitutional authority for taking this weapon away from the Government." Chief Justice Fred Vinson, in writing for the majority of six, recast the language of the clear and present danger test as reformulated by Judge Learned Hand who had upheld the conviction of the Communist leaders in the Circuit Court of Appeals. This Hand-Vinson formula, "Whether the gravity of the 'evil,' discounted by its improbability, justified such invasion of free speech as is necessary to avoid the danger," so watered down "clear and present danger" as to make it indistinguishable from "bad tendency." Justice Frankfurter would have none of those judicial gymnastics and reasserted his view that it is all a matter of "balancing interests" and in this instance he would "balance" in favor of the government.

It was the dissenters, Justices Black and Douglas, who captured the future. In his concluding paragraph Black spoke of hope that in "calmer times" the Court would "restore the First Amendment liberties to the high preferred place where they belong in a free society." It was 18 years later while Justice Black still sat on the Court that his "hope" became a reality in *Brandenburg* v. *Ohio* (see following case). Meanwhile some 141 persons were indicted under the Smith Act, of whom 29 served time in prison, including those convicted in *Dennis*.

Just 6 years after the ruling in the *Dennis* case, the Court, with a changed personnel including a new Chief Justice, Earl Warren, virtually neutralized the Smith Act as a weapon for prosecuting members of the Communist party. In *Yates* v. *United States,* 14 members of the California Communist party had appealed from a conviction for conspiracy to violate the Smith Act. Fashioning a new rule of evidence, namely, that in order to be adjudged guilty under the act there must be clear proof that a person was advocating and exhorting people to action and not simply teaching abstract doctrine, the Court remanded the case to the district court with orders to acquit some of the defendants and to retry the others. Since the government prosecutors could not meet the new standard, all the charges were dismissed, and all other prosecutions under way—with one exception—were dropped. That exception was Junius Scales, the only person ever convicted for violating the membership clause of the Smith Act (being a member of a group that advocated seditious conduct) and he was released from prison after serving 6 months, on commutation orders by President John F. Kennedy. The *Yates* decision brought an end to government prosecutions of Communists in the United States.

Brandenburg v. *Ohio*

395 U.S. 444 (1969)

It was not a federal but a state case that elevated the free speech clause of the First Amendment to its highest level in American constitutional history, and the case involved dissent not from the left but from the right.

Clarence Brandenburg, a leader of the Ku Klux Klan, spoke at a rally in rural Ohio to which he had invited coverage by a television crew. It was on the basis of the television tapes that Brandenburg was convicted of violating Ohio's Criminal Syndicalism law. The Ohio statute made it a crime to advocate "the duty, necessity, or propriety of crime, sabotage, violence or unlawful methods of terrorism as a means of accomplishing industrial or political reform," and to assemble with any "groups . . . to teach or advocate the doctrines of criminal syndicalism." The rally included 12 hooded men, some carrying guns, standing before a burning cross. Brandenburg was shown on tape making a speech in which he threatened to take "revenge" if the President, Congress and the Supreme Court continued to "suppress the white, Caucasian race." In further remarks he said: "Personally, I believe the nigger should be returned to Africa, the Jew returned to Israel." On appeal, Brandenburg contended that the Ohio law was unconstitutional under the First and Fourteenth Amendments.

PER CURIAM.

The Ohio Criminal Syndicalism Statute was enacted in 1919. From 1917 to 1920, identical or quite similar laws were adopted by 20 States and two territories. In 1927, this Court sustained the constitutionality of California's Criminal Syndicalism Act, the text of which is quite similar to that of the laws of Ohio. *Whitney* v. *California,* (1927). The Court upheld the statute on the ground that, without more, "advocating" violent means to effect political and economic change involves such danger to the security of the State that the State may outlaw it. But *Whitney* has

been thoroughly discredited by later decisions. These later decisions have fashioned the principle that the constitutional guarantees of free speech and free press do not permit a State to forbid or proscribe advocacy of the use of force or of law violation except where such advocacy is directed to inciting or producing imminent lawless action and is likely to incite or produce such action. As we said in *Noto* v. *United States,* "the mere abstract teaching . . . of the moral propriety or even moral necessity for a resort to force and violence, is not the same as preparing a group for violent action and steeling it to such action." A statute which fails to draw this distinction impermissibly intrudes upon the freedoms guaranteed by the First and Fourteenth Amendments. It sweeps within its condemnation speech which our Constitution has immunized from governmental control.

Measured by this test, Ohio's Criminal Syndicalism Act cannot be sustained. The Act punishes persons who "advocate or teach the duty, necessity, or propriety" of violence "as a means of accomplishing industrial or political reform"; or who publish or circulate or display any book or paper containing such advocacy; or who "justify" the commission of violent acts "with intent to exemplify, spread or advocate the propriety of the doctrines of criminal syndicalism"; or who "voluntarily assemble" with a group formed "to teach or advocate the doctrines of criminal syndicalism." Neither the indictment nor the trial judge's instructions to the jury in any way refined the statute's bald definition of the crime in terms of mere advocacy not distinguished from incitement to imminent lawless action.

Accordingly, we are here confronted with a statute which, by its own words and as applied, purports to punish mere advocacy and to forbid, on pain of criminal punishment, assembly with others merely to advocate the described type of action. Such a statute falls within the condemnation of the First and Fourteenth Amendments. The contrary teaching of *Whitney* v. *California,* cannot be supported, and that decision is therefore overruled.

. . . .

Mr. Justice **Douglas,** concurring.

While I can join the opinion of the Court, I desire to enter a *caveat.*

. . .

The Court quite properly overrules *Whitney* v. *California,* which involved advocacy of ideas which the majority of the Court deemed unsound and dangerous.

Mr. Justice Holmes, though never formally abandoning the "clear and present danger" test, moved closer to the First Amendment ideal when he said in dissent in *Gitlow* v. *New York,*

"Every idea is an incitement. It offers itself for belief and if believed it is acted on unless some other belief outweighs it or some failure of energy stifles the movement at its birth. The only difference between the expression of an opinion and an incitement in the narrower sense is the speaker's enthusiasm for the result. Eloquence may set fire to reason. But whatever may be thought of the redundant discourse before us it had no chance of starting a present conflagration. If in the long run the beliefs expressed in proletarian dictatorship are destined to be accepted by the dominant forces of the community, the only meaning of free speech is that they should be given their chance and have their way."

We have never been faithful to the philosophy of that dissent.

. . .

Out of the "clear and present danger" test came other offspring. Advocacy and teaching of forcible overthrow of government as an abstract principle is immune from prosecution. *Yates* v. *United States.* But an "active" member, who has a guilty knowledge and intent of the aim to overthrow the Government by violence may be prosecuted. *Scales* v. *United States.* And the power to investigate, backed by the powerful sanction of contempt, includes the power to determine which of the two categories fits the particular witness. *Barenblatt* v. *United States.* And so the investigator roams at will through all of the beliefs of the witness, ransacking his conscience and his innermost thoughts.

Judge Learned Hand, who wrote for the Court of Appeals in affirming the judgment in *Dennis,* coined the "not improbable" test, which this Court adopted and which Judge Hand preferred over the "clear and present danger" test. Indeed, in his book, The Bill of Rights (1958), in referring to Holmes' creation of the "clear and present danger" test, he said, "I cannot help thinking that for once Homer nodded."

My own view is quite different. I see no place in the regime of the First Amendment for any "clear and present danger" test, whether strict and tight as some would make it, or free-wheeling as the Court in *Dennis* rephrased it.

When one reads the opinions closely and sees when and how the "clear and present danger" test has been applied, great misgivings are aroused. First, the threats were often loud but always puny and made serious only by judges so wedded to the *status quo* that critical analysis made them nervous. Second, the test was so twisted and perverted in *Dennis* as to make the trial of those teachers of Marxism an all-out political trial which was part and parcel of the cold war that has eroded substantial parts of the First Amendment.

Action is often a method of expression and within the protection of the First Amendment.

Suppose one tears up his own copy of the Constitution in eloquent protest to a decision of this Court. May he be indicted?

Suppose one rips his own Bible to shreds to celebrate his departure from one "faith" and his embrace of atheism. May he be indicted?

. . .

One's beliefs have long been thought to be sanctuaries which government could not invade. *Barenblatt* is one example of the ease with which that sanctuary can be violated. The lines drawn by the Court between the criminal act of being an "active" Communist and the innocent act of being a nominal or inactive Communist mark the difference only between deep and abiding belief and casual or uncertain belief. But I think that all matters of belief are beyond the reach of sub-

poenas or the probings of investigators. That is why the invasions of privacy made by investigating committees were notoriously unconstitutional. That is the deep-seated fault in the infamous loyalty-security hearings which, since 1947 when President Truman launched them, have processed 20,000,000 men and women. Those hearings were primarily concerned with one's thoughts, ideas, beliefs, and convictions. They were the most blatant violations of the First Amendment we have ever known.

The line between what is permissible and not subject to control and what may be made impermissible and subject to regulation is the line between ideas and overt acts.

The example usually given by those who would punish speech is the case of one who falsely shouts fire in a crowded theatre.

This is, however, a classic case where speech is brigaded with action. They are indeed inseparable and a prosecution can be launched for the overt acts actually caused. Apart from rare instances of that kind, speech is, I think, immune from prosecution. Certainly there is no constitutional line between advocacy of abstract ideas as in *Yates* and advocacy of political action as in *Scales*. The quality of advocacy turns on the depth of the conviction; and government has no power to invade that sanctuary of belief and conscience.

Aftermath of Brandenburg *v.* Ohio

It is interesting that such a brief *per curiam* opinion should elevate protection of freedom of speech to its highest level ever, and it is significant that all nine of the justices were in substantial agreement. Although the Court did not use the phrase "clear and present danger," it appeared to reinstate it with a special gloss. It is not permissible for the government to forbid "advocacy of the use of force or of law violation except where such advocacy is directed to inciting or producing imminent lawless action. . . ." In the 22 years since the decision in *Brandenburg*, the Court has never backed away from this test of "incitement to unlawful action."

In two cases in the 1970s, *Hess* v. *Indiana* (1973) and *Communist Party of Indiana* v. *Whitcomb* (1974), the Court cited *Brandenburg* in ruling for the defendants. Gregory Hess was ordered released after an appeal from a conviction for disorderly conduct at a street demonstration during the Vietnam war, and in *Whitcomb* it was held that the candidates of the Communist party in Indiana need not sign a loyalty oath pledging not to advocate the overthrow of the government by force or violence. In 1982 the Court again invoked *Brandenburg* to overturn judgments of liability in a complex case involving a boycott of white merchants by blacks (*NAACP* v. *Claiborne Hardware Co.*). While acknowledging that the boycott "included elements of criminality and elements of majesty," Justice

John Paul Stevens declared that "it clearly involved constitutionally protected activity" since it was through "speech, assembly and petition—rather than through riot or revolution—[that] petitioners sought to change a social order that had consistently treated them as second-class citizens."

Near v. *Minnesota*

283 U.S. 697 (1931)

All governments in the modern day, democratic as well as authoritarian, control abuses of free speech with postspeech penalties. As seen in our discussion above, the Supreme Court has fashioned various devices that give maximum protection to the speaker and permit fines or jail sentences for speaking or writing only under exceptional circumstances. Advance prohibitions—known as *prior restraints*—on speech and press, although anathema to free governments, have existed in the United States in the past and continue to exist today, though under severely restrictive judicial rules. Such restraints appear in four forms: (1) the injunction by which a court orders a person or group not to implement plans for a speech or demonstration, or prohibits a newspaper from publishing specified material, the violation of which may result in punishment for contempt; (2) the permit system whereby local authorities may refuse to issue a permit to use the city streets, parks, or other facilities; (3) a licensing system for modern communications such as radio and television; and (4) an official censoring agency which may disallow the showing of a movie or the distribution of a book, usually on the grounds of obscenity. Official movie censorship went out of business in 1981 when the last board in the United States ceased to exist. This was 29 years after the Court brought films within the protection of the First Amendment in *Burstyn* v. *Wilson*. The remaining devices—injunctions, permits, and licenses—may be valid modes of regulation so long as they are used neither to suppress ideas nor to prevent official information from reaching the public. (See *New York Times* v. *United States* in Chapter 1.) And beginning with the *Near* case in 1931 the Supreme Court has consistently ruled against any official attempts at censorship of the press.

Jay M. Near was the publisher of a sensationalized newspaper called *The Saturday Press*. In several issues he charged that a "Jewish gangster" was in control of gambling, bootlegging, and racketeering in Minneapolis. He also asserted that the chief of police was guilty of gross neglect of duty and was in league with gangsters and a participant in graft. Finally, Near accused the county attorney and the mayor of being aware of corruption and failing to take adequate measures to control it. Bringing action pursuant to a Minnesota law prohibiting the publication of "malicious, scandalous and defamatory" material, the county attorney was successful in the state's district court which adjudged *The Saturday Press* to be a public nuisance and enjoined it from further publication. The American Civil Liberties Union initially provided Near with legal support in his unsuccessful appeal to the Minnesota Supreme Court. Colonel Robert McCormick, the wealthy and powerful publisher of *The Chicago Tribune*, then financed an appeal to the United States Supreme Court.

Mr. Chief Justice **Hughes** delivered the opinion of the Court.

. . .

Without attempting to summarize the contents of the voluminous exhibits attached to the complaint, we deem it sufficient to say that the articles charged, in substance, that a Jewish gangster was in control of gambling, bootlegging, and racketeering in Minneapolis, and that law enforcing officers and agencies were not energetically performing their duties. Most of the charges were directed against the chief of police; he was charged with gross neglect of duty, illicit relations with gangsters, and with participation in graft. The county attorney was charged with knowing the existing conditions and with failure to take adequate measures to remedy them. The mayor was accused of inefficiency and dereliction. One member of the grand jury was stated to be in sympathy with the gangsters. A special grand jury and a special prosecutor were demanded to deal with the situation in general, and, in particular, to investigate an attempt to assassinate one Guilford, one of the original defendants, who, it appears from the articles, was shot by gangsters after the first issue of the periodical had been published. There is no question but that the articles made serious accusations against the public officers named and others in connection with the prevalence of crimes and the failure to expose and punish them.

. . .

The district court made findings of fact, which followed the allegations of the complaint and found in general terms that the editions in question were "chiefly devoted to malicious, scandalous and defamatory articles" concerning the individuals named. The court further found that the defendants through these publications "did engage in the business of regularly and customarily producing, publishing and circulating a malicious, scandalous and defamatory newspaper," and that "the said publication" "under said name of The Saturday Press, or any other name, constitutes a public nuisance under the laws of the State." Judgment was thereupon entered adjudging that "the newspaper, magazine and periodical known as The Saturday Press," as a public nuisance, "be and is hereby abated." The judgment perpetually enjoined the defendants "from producing, editing, publishing, circulating, having in their possession, selling or giving away any publication whatsoever which is a malicious, scandalous or defamatory newspaper, as defined by law," and also "from

further conducting said nuisance under the name and title of said The Saturday Press or any other name or title."

. . .

This statute, for the suppression as a public nuisance of a newspaper or periodical, is unusual, if not unique, and raises questions of grave importance transcending the local interests involved in the particular action. It is no longer open to doubt that the liberty of the press and of speech is within the liberty safeguarded by the due process clause of the Fourteenth Amendment from invasion by state action. It was found impossible to conclude that this essential personal liberty of the citizen was left unprotected by the general guaranty of fundamental rights of person and property.

. . .

First. The statute is not aimed at the redress of individual or private wrongs. Remedies for libel remain available and unaffected. The statute, said the state court "is not directed at threatened libel but at an existing business which, generally speaking, involves more than libel." It is aimed at the distribution of scandalous matter as "detrimental to public morals and to the general welfare," tending "to disturb the peace of the community" and "to provoke assaults and the commission of crime." In order to obtain an injunction to suppress the future publication of the newspaper or periodical, it is not necessary to prove the falsity of the charges that have been made in the publication condemned. In the present action there was no allegation that the matter published was not true. It is alleged, and the statute requires the allegation that the publication was "malicious." But, as in prosecutions for libel, there is no requirement of proof by the state of malice in fact as distinguished from malice inferred from the mere publication of the defamatory matter. The judgment in this case proceeded upon the mere proof of publication. The statute permits the defense, not of the truth alone, but only that the truth was published with good motives and for justifiable ends. It is apparent that under the statute the publication is to be regarded as defamatory if it injures reputation, and that it is scandalous if it circulates charges of reprehensible conduct, whether criminal or otherwise, and the publication is thus deemed to invite public reprobation and to constitute a public scandal.

. . .

Second. The statute is directed not simply at the circulation of scandalous and defamatory statements with regard to private citizens, but at the continued publication by newspapers and periodicals of charges against public officers of corruption, malfeasance in office, or serious neglect of duty. Such charges by their very nature create a public scandal. They are scandalous and defamatory within the meaning of the statute, which has its normal operation in relation to publications dealing prominently and chiefly with the alleged derelictions of public officers.

Third. The object of the statute is not punishment, in the ordinary sense, but suppression of the offending newspaper or periodical. The reason for the enactment, as the state court has said, is that prosecutions to enforce penal statutes for libel do not result in "efficient repression or suppression of the evils of scandal." Describing the business of publication as a public nuisance does not obscure the substance of the proceeding which the statute authorizes. It is the continued publication of scandalous and defamatory matter that constitutes the business and the declared nuisance. In the case of public officers, it is the reiteration of charges of official misconduct, and the fact that the newspaper or periodical is principally devoted to that purpose, that exposes it to suppression. In the present instance, the proof was that nine editions of the newspaper or periodical in question were published on successive dates, and that they were chiefly devoted to charges against public officers and in relation to the prevalence and protection of crime. In such a case, these officers are not left to their ordinary remedy in a suit for libel, or the authorities to a prosecution for criminal libel. Under this statute, a publisher of a newspaper or periodical, undertaking to conduct a campaign to expose and to censure official derelictions, and devoting his publication principally to that purpose, must face not simply the possibility of a verdict against him in a suit or prosecution for libel, but a determination that his newspaper or periodical is a public nuisance to be abated, and that this abatement and suppression will follow unless he is prepared with legal evidence to prove the truth of the charges and also to satisfy the court that, in addition to being true, the matter was published with good motives and for justifiable ends.

This suppression is accomplished by enjoining publication, and that restraint is the object and effect of the statute.

Fourth. The statute not only operates to suppress the offending newspaper or periodical, but to put the publisher under an effective censorship. When a newspaper or periodical is found to be "malicious, scandalous and defamatory," and is suppressed as such, resumption of publication is punishable as a contempt of court by fine or imprisonment. Thus where a newspaper or periodical has been suppressed because of the circulation of charges against public officers of official misconduct, it would seem to be clear that the renewal of the publication of such charges would constitute a contempt, and that the judgment would lay a permanent restraint upon the publisher, to escape which he must satisfy the court as to the character of a new publication. Whether he would be permitted again to publish matter deemed to be derogatory to the same or other public officers would depend upon the court's ruling. In the present instance the judgment restrained the defendants from "publishing, circulating, having in their possession, selling or giving away any publication whatsoever which is a malicious, scandalous or defamatory newspaper, as defined by law."

. . .

If we cut through mere details of procedure, the operation and effect of the statute in substance is that public authorities may bring the owner or publisher of a newspaper or periodical before a judge upon a charge of conducting a business of publishing scandalous and defamatory matter—in particular that the matter consists of charges against public officers of official dereliction—and, unless the owner or publisher is able and disposed to bring competent evidence to satisfy the judge that the charges are true and are published with good motives and for justifiable ends, his newspaper or periodical is suppressed and further publication is made punishable as a contempt. This is of the essence of censorship.

The question is whether a statute authorizing such proceedings in restraint of publication is consistent with the conception of the liberty of the press as historically conceived and guaranteed. In determining the extent of the constitutional protection, it has been generally, if not universally, considered that it is the chief purpose of the guaranty to prevent previous restraints upon publication. The struggle in England, directed against the legislative power of the licenser, resulted in renunciation of the censorship of the press. The liberty deemed to be established was thus described by Blackstone: "The liberty of the press is indeed essential to the nature of a free state; but this consists in laying no *previous* restraints upon publications, and not in freedom from censure for criminal matter when published. Every freeman has an undoubted right to lay what sentiments he pleases before the public; to forbid this, is to destroy the freedom of the press; but if he publishes what is improper, mischievous or illegal, he must take the consequence of his own temerity." The distinction was early pointed out between the extent of the freedom with respect to censorship under our constitutional system and that enjoyed in England. Here, as Madison said, "the great and essential rights of the people are secured against legislative as well as against executive ambition. They are secured, not by laws paramount to prerogative, but by constitutions paramount to laws. This security of the freedom of the press requires that it should be exempt not only from previous restraint by the Executive, as in Great Britain, but from legislative restraint also." This Court said, in Patterson v. Colorado, "In the first place, the main purpose of such constitutional provisions is 'to prevent all such previous restraints upon publications as had been practiced by other governments,' and they do not prevent the subsequent punishment of such as may be deemed contrary to the public welfare. The preliminary freedom extends as well to the false as to the true; the subsequent

punishment may extend as well to the true as to the false. This was the law of criminal libel apart from statute in most cases, if not in all.

. . .

In the present case, we have no occasion to inquire as to the permissible scope of subsequent punishment. For whatever wrong the appellant has committed or may commit, by his publications, the state appropriately affords both public and private redress by its libel laws. As has been noted, the statute in question does not deal with punishments; it provides for no punishment, except in case of contempt for violation of the court's order, but for suppression and injunction—that is, for restraint upon publication.

The objection has also been made that the principle as to immunity from previous restraint is stated too broadly, if every such restraint is deemed to be prohibited. That is undoubtedly true; the protection even as to previous restraint is not absolutely unlimited. But the limitation has been recognized only in exceptional cases. "When a nation is at war many things that might be said in time of peace are such a hindrance to its effort that their utterance will not be endured so long as men fight and that no Court could regard them as protected by any constitutional right." No one would question but that a government might prevent actual obstruction to its recruiting service or the publication of the sailing dates of transports or the number and location of troops. On similar grounds, the primary requirements of decency may be enforced against obscene publications. The security of the community life may be protected against incitements to acts of violence and the overthrow by force of orderly government. The constitutional guaranty of free speech does not "protect a man from an injunction against uttering words that may have all the effect of force." These limitations are not applicable here. Nor are we now concerned with questions as to the extent of authority to prevent publications in order to protect private rights according to the principles governing the exercise of the jurisdiction of courts of equity.

The exceptional nature of its limitations

places in a strong light the general conception that liberty of the press, historically considered and taken up by the Federal Constitution, has meant, principally although not exclusively, immunity from previous restraints or censorship.

. . .

The fact that for approximately one hundred and fifty years there has been almost an entire absence of attempts to impose previous restraints upon publications relating to the malfeasance of public officers is significant of the deep-seated conviction that such restraints would violate constitutional right. Public officers, whose character and conduct remain open to debate and free discussion in the press, find their remedies for false accusations in actions under libel laws providing for redress and punishment, and not in proceedings to restrain the publication of newspapers and periodicals. The general principle that the constitutional guaranty of the liberty of the press gives immunity from previous restraints has been approved in many decisions under the provisions of state constitutions.

The importance of this immunity has not lessened. While reckless assaults upon public men, and efforts to bring obloquy upon those who are endeavoring faithfully to discharge official duties, exert a baleful influence and deserve the severest condemnation in public opinion, it cannot be said that this abuse is greater, and it is believed to be less, than that which characterized the period in which our institutions took shape. Meanwhile, the administration of government has become more complex, the opportunities for malfeasance and corruption have multiplied, crime has grown to most serious proportions, and the danger of its protection by unfaithful officials and of the impairment of the fundamental security of life and property by criminal alliances and official neglect, emphasizes the primary need of a vigilant and courageous press, especially in great cities. The fact that the liberty of the press may be abused by miscreant purveyors of scandal does not make any the less necessary the immunity of the press from previous restraint in dealing with official misconduct. Subsequent pun-ishment for such abuses as may exist is the appropriate remedy, consistent with constitutional privilege.

. . .

Equally unavailing is the insistence that the statute is designed to prevent the circulation of scandal which tends to disturb the public peace and to provoke assaults and the commission of crime. Charges of reprehensible conduct, and in particular of official malfeasance, unquestionably create a public scandal, but the theory of the constitutional guaranty is that even a more serious public evil would be caused by authority to prevent publication. "To prohibit the intent to excite those unfavorable sentiments against those who administer the Government, is equivalent to a prohibition of the actual excitement of them; and to prohibit the actual excitement of them is equivalent to a prohibition of discussions having that tendency and effect; which, again, is equivalent to a protection of those who administer the Government, if they should at any time deserve the contempt or hatred of the people, against being exposed to it by free animadversions on their characters and conduct." There is nothing new in the fact that charges of reprehensible conduct may create resentment and the disposition to resort to violent means of redress, but this well-understood tendency did not alter the determination to protect the press against censorship and restraint upon publication.

. . .

For these reasons we hold the statute, so far as it authorized the proceedings in this action under clause (b) of section 1, to be an infringement of the liberty of the press guaranteed by the Fourteenth Amendment. We should add that this decision rests upon the operation and effect of the statute, without regard to the question of the truth of the charges contained in the particular periodical. The fact that the public officers named in this case, and those associated with the charges of official dereliction, may be deemed to be impeccable, does not affect the conclusion that the statute imposes an unconstitutional restraint upon publication.

Judgment reversed.

Aftermath of Near *v.* Minnesota

In 1932 *The Saturday Press* resumed publication, calling itself "The Paper That Refused to Stay Gagged." Editor Near, as combative and vitriolic as ever, managed to keep the paper going for another couple of years before it folded for lack of funds. Near had tried but failed to persuade Colonel McCormick to invest in his enterprise.

In dissolving the injunction and invalidating the Minnesota "gag" law under which it was issued, Chief Justice Charles Evans Hughes set a major precedent and a standard to which the Supreme Court has adhered ever since. It should be emphasized that Hughes, while condemning in this instance the suppression of charges of official corruption, outlined the conditions under which prior restraint might be permissible: the prevention of the publication of military information in time of war, the protection of public decency against obscenity, and the preservation of community life against incitement to violence. None of these exceptions to "prior restraint" was present in the *Near* case. Nor were they present in a score or more of cases decided by the Court over the half century following Hughes' memorable opinion in 1931.

It should be noted that for the most part prior restraint cases arise not because state or local authorities set out to censor ideas but rather as a result of ordinances enacted to preserve public order. For example, in 1939 the Court struck down several city ordinances as prior restraint on speech and press that forbade the distribution of handbills and leaflets on the public streets, the purpose of the measures being to prevent litter. These cases followed the decision in *Lovell* v. *Griffin* in 1938 that struck down a municipal ordinance requiring the written permission of the city manager before a person could distribute "circulars, handbills, advertising, or literature of any kind" within the city limits. Despite the city's good intentions of keeping its citizens free from the annoyances by hawkers, proselytizers and advertisers, the law was deemed "censorship" and overbroad since it encompassed all literature and all methods and places of distribution. In 1971 the Court affirmed this earlier stand when it overturned an Illinois court order that enjoined an organization from "passing out pamphlets, leaflets or literature of any kind, and from picketing, anywhere in the City of Westchester, Illinois." The injunction had been issued against a neighborhood group that had distributed leaflets protesting the business practices of a local realtor, and in dissolving the injunction, the Court chose free speech over the alleged invasion of an individual's privacy (*Organization for a Better Austin* v. *Keefe*). In the interest of preserving fair and orderly elections the state of Alabama prohibited all election day editorials since there would be no time for rebuttal prior to the election. Overturning the conviction of James F. Mills, editor of a Birmingham newspaper, who had deliberately violated the statute, the Court declared the law to be a "flagrant abridgement of . . . freedom of the press" (*Mills* v. *Alabama*, 1966).

In 1988 the Court decided the case of *Hazelwood School District* v. *Kuhlmeier*. For the first time since *Near*, the Court upheld what might be considered censorship of a newspaper. Complicating the issue, however, were the special circumstances under which the case arose. A high school newspaper, *Spectrum*, was written and edited by a journalism class as part of the school's curriculum. Pursuant to the school's practice the teacher in charge of the paper submitted page proofs to the principal. In one of the issues the principal deleted two pages that included articles describing students' experiences with pregnancy and a discussion of the impact of divorce on students of the school. He reasoned that students, while not named, might be identified by the text. Moreover, the principal maintained that references to sexual activity and birth control were inappropriate for younger students. Student members of the newspaper staff filed suit in federal district court, alleging a violation of First Amendment rights.

Upholding the school authorities, the Court referred to the *Tinker* case, indicating that students in public schools, while enjoying First Amendment guarantees, are subject to restriction by the school administration if their activities involve interference with school discipline or the rights of others. In this instance, declared the Court, the school authorities did not offend the First Amendment by exercising editorial control over the content of speech in a school-sponsored activity.

Implicit in the decision was the assumption that had this type of editorial censorship been taken outside a public school setting, it would have been condemned under the *Near* standard.

Edwards v. *South Carolina*

372 U.S. 229 (1963)

Street demonstrations involving marches, parades, and picketing have been used as means of protest ever since, and perhaps before, the Boston Tea Party and, while always posing a possible threat to peace and order, they represent a legitimate means of expression. Constitutionally, however, they present a special problem since as a mode of speech they are protected, but as conduct they are subject to reasonable regulation by the state. Such regulation may take the form of a permit or an injunction, both of which are frequently characterized as "prior restraint." However, unlike in *Near* v. *Minnesota* and the other prior restraint cases cited in the previous section, the Court is dealing with a constitutional hybrid known as "speech plus."

The Supreme Court first supported protection for "speech plus" in the area of labor disputes when in *Thornhill* v. *Alabama* (1941) it held that peaceful picketing came under the First Amendment's guarantees. For the Court, Justice Frank Murphy wrote that "the dissemination of information concerning the facts of a labor dispute must be regarded as within that area of free discussion that is guaranteed by the Constitution." In that same year, however, the Court unanimously upheld the conviction of a group of Jehovah's Witnesses who had marched on a downtown city street carrying signs to advertise a meeting without obtaining the required license from the state. (*Cox* v. *New Hampshire*, 1941). The opinion made it clear that the license requirement was a reasonable measure for traffic regulation and that a different issue would have been raised had the Witnesses been denied a permit because of the views they represented. Such was the case 10 years later when the Court reversed the conviction of members of the same religious group who had been denied a permit to use a public park. (*Niemotko* v. *Maryland*, 1951). Frequently the problem with a permit system is the discretion it places in an official who may ostensibly deny the use of the streets for reasons of safety or traffic control, but in fact is censoring the ideas of the persons involved. For example, in *Kunz* v. *New York* (1951) the Court invalidated a New York City ordinance that required a permit from the police commissioner to hold public meetings on the city streets. Since a single official had the discretionary power to determine in advance who might speak on the streets without appropriate standards to guide his decision, the measure was fatally flawed.

First Amendment litigation mushroomed in the 1960s and 1970s as more and more groups took to the streets. Such tactics were used in profusion by civil rights groups, Vietnam war protesters, and by peace and antinuclear activists. As the numbers in the various protests became larger, the stage was set for reaction in the form of governmental suppression. Such a response was evident in the *Edwards* case when the police intervened in what appeared to be a peaceful demonstration. Edwards and 186 associates were convicted in magistrate's court in Columbia, South Carolina, of the common law crime of breach of the peace. The convictions were affirmed by the South Carolina Supreme Court. Unlike the earlier cases described above, here there was no prior restraint either by a permit denial or a court injunction. The pertinent facts are stated in the Court's opinion.

POTTER STEWART

Potter Stewart became President Dwight Eisenhower's final Supreme Court nominee in 1958 when he was elevated from the Sixth Circuit Court of Appeals. A politically moderate justice with a strong commitment to continuity in the law, he dissented from many of the Warren Court's liberal activist opinions, but later resisted attempts by the Burger Court's conservatives to overturn them. Stewart was known for his ability to summarize complex issues with pithy phrases. Expressing impatience with the Court's effort to define obscenity, he said, "I know it when I see it." Stewart retired from the Court in 1981, at the relatively early age of 66, and died in 1985.

Mr. Justice **Stewart** delivered the opinion of the Court.

. . .

Late in the morning of March 2, 1961, the petitioners, high school and college students of the Negro race, met at the Zion Baptist Church in Columbia. From there, at about noon, they walked in separate groups of about 15 to the South Carolina State House grounds, an area of two city blocks open to the general public. Their purpose was "to submit a protest to the citizens of South Carolina, along with the Legislative Bodies of South Carolina, our feelings and our dissatisfaction with the present condition of discriminatory actions against Negroes, in general, and to let them know that we were dissatisfied and that we would like for the laws which prohibited Negro privileges in this State to be removed."

Already on the State House grounds when the petitioners arrived were 30 or more law enforcement officers, who had advance knowledge that the petitioners were coming. Each group of petitioners entered the grounds through a driveway and parking area known in the record as the "horseshoe." As they entered, they were told by the law enforcement officials that "they had a right, as a citizen, to go through the State House grounds, as any other citizen has, as long as they were peaceful." During the next half hour or 45 minutes, the petitioners, in the same small groups, walked single file or two abreast in an orderly way through the grounds, each group carrying placards bearing such messages as "I am proud to be a Negro" and "Down with segregation."

During this time a crowd of some 200 to 300 onlookers had collected in the horseshoe area and on the adjacent sidewalks. There was no evidence to suggest that these onlookers were anything but curious, and no evidence at all of any threatening remarks, hostile gestures, or offensive language on the part of any member of the crowd. The City Manager testified that he recognized some of the onlookers, whom he did not identify, as "possible trouble makers," but his subsequent testimony made clear that nobody among the crowd actually caused or threatened any trouble. There was no obstruction of pedestrian or vehicular traffic within the State House grounds. No vehicle was prevented from entering or leaving the horseshoe area. Although vehicular traffic at a nearby street intersection was slowed down somewhat, an officer was dispatched to keep traffic moving. There were a number of bystanders on the public sidewalks adjacent to the State House grounds, but they all moved on when asked to do so, and there was no impediment of pedestrian traffic. Police protection at the scene was at all times sufficient to meet any foreseeable possibility of disorder.

In the situation and under the circumstances thus described, the police authorities advised the petitioners that they would be arrested if they did not disperse within 15 minutes. Instead of dispersing, the petitioners engaged in what the City Manager described as "boisterous," "loud," and "flamboyant" conduct, which, as his later testimony made clear, consisted of listening to a "religious harangue" by one of their leaders, and loudly singing "The Star Spangled Banner" and other patriotic and religious songs, while stamping their feet and clapping their hands. After 15 minutes had passed, the police arrested the petitioners and marched them off to jail.

Upon this evidence the state trial court convicted the petitioners of breach of the peace, and imposed sentences ranging from a $10 fine or five days in jail, to a $100 fine or 30 days in jail. In affirming the judgments, the Supreme Court of South Carolina said that under the law of that State the offense of breach of the peace "is not susceptible of exact definition," but that the "general definition of the offense" is as follows:

"In general terms, a breach of the peace is a violation of public order, a disturbance of the public tranquility, by any act or conduct inciting to violence . . . , it includes any violation of any law enacted to preserve peace and good order. It may consist of an act of violence or an act likely to produce violence. It is not necessary that the peace be actually broken to lay the foundation for a prosecution for this offense. If what is done is unjustifiable and unlawful, tending with sufficient directness to break the peace, no more is required. Nor is actual personal violence an essential element in the offense. . . .

"By 'peace,' as used in the law in this connection, is meant the tranquility enjoyed by citizens of a municipality or community where good order reigns among its members, which is the natural right of all persons in political society."

The petitioners contend that there was a complete absence of any evidence of the commission of this offense, and that they were thus denied one of the most basic elements of due process of law. Whatever the merits of this contention, we need not pass upon it in the present case. The state courts have held that the petitioners' conduct constituted breach of the peace under state law, and we may accept their decision as binding upon us to that extent. But it nevertheless remains our duty in a case such as this to make an independent examination of the whole record. And it is clear to us that in arresting, convicting, and punishing the petitioners under the circumstances disclosed by this record, South Carolina infringed the petitioners' constitutionally protected rights of free speech, free assembly, and freedom to petition for redress of their grievances.

It has long been established that these First Amendment freedoms are protected by the Fourteenth Amendment from invasion by the States. The circumstances in this case reflect an exercise of these basic constitutional rights in their most pristine and classic form. The petitioners felt aggrieved by laws of South Carolina which allegedly "prohibited Negro privileges in this State." They peaceably assembled at the site of the State Government and there peaceably expressed their grievances "to the citizens of South Carolina, along with the Legislative Bodies of South Carolina." Not until they were told by police officials that they must disperse on pain of arrest did they do more. Even then, they but sang patriotic and religious songs after one of their leaders had delivered a "religious harangue." There was no violence or threat of violence on their part, or on the part of any member of the crowd watching them. Police protection was "ample."

This, therefore, was a far cry from the situation in *Feiner* v. *New York* where two policemen were faced with a crowd which was "pushing, shoving and milling around," where at least one member of the crowd "threatened violence if the police did not act," where "the crowd was pressing closer around petitioner and the officer," and where "the speaker passes the bounds of argument or persuasion and undertakes incitement to riot." And the record is barren of any evidence of "fighting words."

We do not review in this case criminal convictions resulting from the evenhanded application of a precise and narrowly drawn regulatory statute evincing a legislative judgment that certain specific conduct be limited or proscribed. If, for example, the petitioners had been convicted upon evidence that they had violated a law regulating traffic, or had disobeyed a law reasonably limiting the periods during which the State House grounds were open to the public, this would be a different case. These petitioners were convicted of an offense so generalized as to be, in the words of the South Carolina Supreme Court, "not susceptible of exact definition." And they were convicted upon evidence which showed no more than that the opinions which they were peaceably expressing were sufficiently opposed to the views of the majority of the community to attract a crowd and necessitate police protection.

The Fourteenth Amendment does not permit a State to make criminal the peaceful expression of unpopular views. "[A] function of free speech under our system of government is to invite dispute. It may indeed best serve its high purpose when it induces a condition of unrest, creates dissatisfaction with conditions as they are, or even stirs people to anger. Speech is often provocative and challenging. It may strike at prejudices and preconceptions and have profound unsettling effects as it presses for acceptance of an idea. That is why freedom of speech . . . is . . . protected against censorship or punishment, unless shown likely to produce a clear and present danger of a serious substan-

tive evil that rises far above public inconvenience, annoyance, or unrest. . . . There is no room under our Constitution for a more restrictive view. For the alternative would lead to standardization of ideas either by legislatures, courts, or dominant political or community groups." As in the *Terminiello* case, the courts of South Carolina have defined a criminal offense so as to permit conviction of the petitioners if their speech "stirred people to anger, invited public dispute, or brought about a condition of unrest. A conviction resting on any of those grounds may not stand."

As Chief Justice Hughes wrote in *Stromberg* v. *California*, "The maintenance of the opportunity for free political discussion to the end that government may be responsive to the will of the people and that changes may be obtained by lawful means, an opportunity essential to the security of the Republic, is a fundamental principle of our constitutional system. A statute which upon its face, and as authoritatively construed, is so vague and indefinite as to permit the punishment of the fair use of this opportunity is repugnant to the guaranty of liberty contained in the Fourteenth Amendment. . . ."

For these reasons we conclude that these criminal convictions cannot stand.

Reversed.

Mr. Justice **Clark,** dissenting.

The convictions of the petitioners, Negro high school and college students, for breach of the peace under South Carolina law are accepted by the Court "as binding upon us to that extent" but are held violative of "petitioners' constitutionally protected rights of free speech, free assembly, and freedom to petition for redress of their grievances." Petitioners, of course, had a right to peaceable assembly, to espouse their cause and to petition, but in my view the manner in which they exercised those rights was by no means the passive demonstration which this Court relates; rather, as the City Manager of Columbia testified, "a dangerous situation was really building up" which South Carolina's courts expressly found had created "an actual interference with traffic and an imminently threatened disturbance of the peace of the community."

Since the Court does not attack the state courts' findings and accepts the convictions as "binding" to the extent that the petitioners' conduct constituted a breach of the peace, it is difficult for me to understand its understatement of the facts and reversal of the convictions.

. . .

Ultimately, the petitioners were arrested, as they apparently planned from the beginning, and convicted on evidence the sufficiency of which the Court does not challenge. The question thus seems to me whether a State is constitutionally prohibited from enforcing laws to prevent breach of the peace in a situation where city officials in good faith believe, and the record shows, that disorder and violence are imminent, merely because the activities constituting that breach contain claimed elements of constitutionally protected speech and assembly. To me the answer under our cases is clearly in the negative.

. . .

The gravity of the danger here surely needs no further explication. The imminence of that danger has been emphasized at every stage of this proceeding, from the complaints charging that the demonstrations "tended directly to immediate violence" to the State Supreme Court's affirmance on the authority of *Feiner*. This record, then, shows no steps backward from a standard of "clear and present danger." But to say that the police may not intervene until the riot has occurred is like keeping out the doctor until the patient dies. I cannot subscribe to such a doctrine.

Aftermath of Edwards *v.* South Carolina

Implicit in the *Edwards* holding was the proposition that so long as protesters or marchers are not engaged in unlawful conduct, the government must show strong justification for intervention. Given the Court's clear approval, the peaceful demonstration became and remains a common occurrence in American life, but the problems it spawns will not go away. Another test of a permit system by civil rights marchers came in 1969 in *Shuttlesworth* v. *Birmingham,* when a group headed by civil rights leader Fred Shuttlesworth was arrested for parading without the permit required by Alabama law. Once again the Court reversed the conviction, citing lack of "narrow, objective and definite standards to guide the licensing authority." As with the New York ordinance at issue in *Kunz,* the Alabama law gave the city commission authority to deny a permit if "in its judgment the public welfare, peace, safety, health, decency, good order, morals or convenience required that it be refused." Unlike cases arising under a breach ordinance in which convictions are reversed because the law is invalidly applied but is not per se unconstitutional, the ordinance in *Shuttlesworth* was declared unconstitutional "on its face" for its lack of precise standards.

Two cases of more recent vintage, both complicated by special circumstances, illustrate how extremely difficult it is for the Court to maintain the appropriate equilibrium between free speech and community sensitivity when the possibility of violence hangs in the balance. In one, a demonstration was planned by the National Socialist party of America for Skokie, Illinois, in which some 50 demonstrators were to march in front of the village hall wearing Nazi uniforms with swastikas prominently displayed on armbands and banners. Not only was Skokie's population predominantly Jewish, but several thousand of its residents were survivors of Nazi concentration camps. Responding to outraged Skokie citizens, the Cook County Circuit Court issued an injunction forbidding anyone from marching or parading in a Nazi uniform, displaying the swastika in any manner, or distributing materials which incite or promote hatred of Jews or persons of any faith, ancestry, race, or religion. Frank Collin, the leader of the American Nazi party, first appealed to the Supreme Court of Illinois for a stay of the injunction, was turned down, and then moved to the United States Supreme Court. The Court reversed the Illinois ruling, holding that Skokie could not permanently bar a protest march of this nature and sending the question back to the lower court for reconsideration (*National Socialist Party* v. *Skokie*, 1977). Taking up the matter once again, the Illinois Appellate Court retained a modified injunction in force, deleting the sections forbidding the wearing of Nazi uniforms and the distribution of inflammatory literature. Not to be outdone, the city enacted several restrictive ordinances including a requirement that in order to obtain a parade permit, an organization must post a disproportionately large bond as insurance against possible property damage, in this instance, $350,000. Collin, denied a permit for inability to raise the bond, again appealed to the judiciary, this time to the federal district court. In striking down the insurance scheme, the court contended that it was "a drastic restriction of the right of freedom of speech and assembly." It was the city's turn to appeal as it requested reinstatement of the ordinance, but the appeal was rejected when the Supreme Court denied *certiorari* (*Smith* v. *Collin*, 1978). Now nothing stood in the way of Collin's provocative march. However, after pulling out all the legal stops to win, he canceled the Skokie march only to hold it later in Chicago where it came off without incident.

In the second case, *Frisby* v. *Schultz* (1988), the Court again dealt with a town ordinance, the purpose of which was the protection of individual privacy. Members of an antiabortion group in Brookfield, Wisconsin, were arrested for picketing a doctor's home on several occasions as a protest against his having performed abortions at clinics in neighboring towns. They were convicted of violating a town ordinance that made it "unlawful for any person to engage in picketing before or about the residence or dwelling of any individual in the Town of Brookfield." Upholding the ordinance as solely prohibiting picketing before a particular residence, the Court concluded that it did not restrict "marching through residential neighborhoods, or even walking a route in front of an entire block of houses." This is a classic example of the Court's leaving an ordinance on the books as constitutionally valid but reserving the right to reverse convictions if the measure is unconstitutionally applied.

Qualifications to First Amendment protections of the protest march do exist, but they apply almost exclusively in restricted physical areas. In *Adderley* v. *Florida* (1966) the Court held that demonstrations may be banned on the grounds of a county jail where security is essential. Access to shopping centers for picketing or distributing leaflets does not come under the free speech guarantee, nor does access to the Supreme Court building itself, although protests may be mounted on sidewalks on the building's perimeter (*United States* v. *Grace*, 1988). Recently the Court invalidated a section of the District of Columbia code making it unlawful to display within 500 feet of a foreign embassy any sign tending to bring a foreign government into "public disrepute." According to Justice Sandra Day O'Connor, this was clearly a restriction on the content of free speech. At the same time the Court upheld a second part of the ordinance which outlawed congregating and refusing to obey a police dispersal order outside a foreign embassy (*Boos* v. *Barry*, 1988).

Texas v. Johnson

491 U.S. 397 (1989)

As indicated in the introduction to this chapter, the first case in which the Supreme Court extended First Amendment protection to symbolic speech was that of *Stromberg* v. *California* in 1931. It is always a problem in cases such as *Stromberg* to separate conduct from speech, government regulation being permissible for the former but not for the latter. Since symbolic speech *is* conduct, what must be determined in these cases is whether the agent intended to communicate an idea through a symbolic act.

Although the Court dealt with scattered instances of symbolic protest after 1931, its use by dissidents proliferated during the Vietnam war and continues today in connection with such emotional issues as abortion, nuclear energy, and disarmament. During the Vietnam war in 1966, Paul David O'Brien burned his draft card on the steps of the courthouse in South Boston seeking to influence others, as he later told a jury, to adopt antiwar beliefs. He was convicted of destroying his Selective Service Registration Certificate in violation of federal law. Upholding his conviction in 1968 in *United States* v. *O'Brien*, Chief Justice Earl Warren, speaking for the Court majority, rejected the proposition that "an apparently limitless variety of conduct can be labeled 'speech' whenever the person engaging in the conduct intends thereby to express an idea." When "speech" and "nonspeech" elements are combined in the same conduct, Warren wrote, "a sufficiently important governmental interest in regulating the non-speech element can justify incidental limitations on First Amendment freedoms." However, the following year in *Tinker* v. *Des Moines School District* (1968) the Court saw no "sufficiently important governmental interest" when it held that 13-year-old Mary Tinker and her 15-year-old brother John were legitimately exercising their rights of free speech when they wore black armbands to school as a symbolic protest against the Vietnam war. Since the silent, passive expression of opinion was unaccompanied by any disorder or disturbance, the school authorities had acted unconstitutionally by suspending the students. In 1977 in *Wooley* v. *Maynard* the Court again found an insufficient state interest to support the conviction of the Maynard family who had covered the motto on New Hampshire's automobile license plates reading "Live Free or Die." It was the Maynards' First Amendment right, said the Court, not to become a courier for disseminating an ideology.

Desecrating the American flag as a means of protest has been especially controversial since it provokes angry responses from many Americans who view the flag as the preeminent symbol of unity and nationhood. Prior to the *Johnson* case in 1989 the Court dealt with the issue only peripherally. In *Street* v. *New York* (1969), a young black man, after learning of the attempted assassination of civil rights leader James Meredith in Mississippi, set fire to his flag and when approached by a policeman, said: "If they did that to Meredith, we don't need an American flag." Convicted of violating a New York statute making it a misdemeanor "to publicly mutilate, defile, or cast contempt upon an American flag" either by word or act, Street argued that his free speech had been constrained. The Court agreed, holding that Street had a constitutional right to express his opinion about the flag and that it was not clear whether he had been convicted for his deed or for what he said. Burning a flag as an exclusive issue was thus not addressed.

Two cases decided in 1974, *Smith* v. *Goguen* and *Spence* v. *Washington*, again left the issue of the constitutionality of statutes prohibiting desecration of the American flag undecided. In the first case the Court overturned the conviction of a man who wore a 4 by 4-inch flag sewn on the seat of his pants in violation of a Massachusetts law that prohibited contemptuous treatment of the United States flag. This statute, said the Court, was void for vagueness since it failed to draw "reasonably clear lines between the kinds of non-ceremonial treatment that are criminal and those that are not." In *Spence* the defendant had displayed the flag upside down from his window, with peace symbols attached to both front and back. Reversing his conviction, the Court declared that since the flag was privately owned and displayed on private property and had not been permanently disfigured or destroyed, it was legitimately used to convey an idea.

Not until 1989 did the Court deal head-on with flag destruction as symbolic speech. During a demonstration while the 1984 Republican National Convention was in progress in Dallas, Gregory Johnson unfurled the American flag in front of the city hall, doused it with kerosene and set it on fire. While the flag burned, Johnson and other protesters chanted "America, the red, white, and blue, we spit on you." Though he was convicted for desecrating a venerated object in violation of the Texas Penal Code, fined $2000 and sentenced to 1 year in prison, the Texas Court of Criminal Appeals reversed his conviction.

WILLIAM BRENNAN

William Brennan was a member of the New Jersey Supreme Court when he was selected by President Dwight Eisenhower in 1956 to fill the vacancy on the United States Supreme Court created by Justice Sherman Minton's retirement. Brennan, a Democrat, quickly became a leader in the Court's liberal-activist bloc and continued in that role until his retirement in 1990. Over the more than three decades of his tenure Brennan became one of the most vigorous and prolific exponents of libertarian values in the Court's history, though with the passage of time his voice was heard increasingly in dissent.

Justice **Brennan** delivered the opinion of the Court.

After publicly burning an American flag as a means of political protest, Gregory Lee Johnson was convicted of desecrating a flag in violation of Texas law. This case presents the question whether his conviction is consistent with the First Amendment. We hold that it is not.

. . .

Johnson was convicted of flag desecration for burning the flag rather than for uttering insulting words. This fact somewhat complicates our consideration of his conviction under the First

Amendment. We must first determine whether Johnson's burning of the flag constituted expressive conduct, permitting him to invoke the First Amendment in challenging his conviction. If his conduct was expressive, we next decide whether the State's regulation is related to the suppression of free expression. If the State's regulation is not related to expression, then the less stringent standard we announced in United States v O'Brien for regulations of noncommunicative conduct controls. If it is, then we are outside of O'Brien's test, and we must ask whether this interest justifies Johnson's conviction under a more demanding standard. A third possibility is that the State's asserted interest is simply not implicated on these facts, and in that event the interest drops out of the picture.

The First Amendment literally forbids the abridgement only of "speech," but we have long recognized that its protection does not end at the spoken or written word. While we have rejected "the view that an apparently limitless variety of conduct can be labeled 'speech' whenever the person engaging in the conduct intends thereby to express an idea," we have acknowledged that conduct may be "sufficiently imbued with elements of communication to fall within the scope of the First and Fourteenth Amendments."

In deciding whether particular conduct possesses sufficient communicative elements to bring the First Amendment into play, we have asked whether "[a]n intent to convey a particularized message was present, and [whether] the likelihood was great that the message would be understood by those who viewed it."

. . .

. . . Pregnant with expressive content, the flag as readily signifies this Nation as does the combination of letters found in "America."

We have not automatically concluded, however, that any action taken with respect to our flag is expressive. Instead, in characterizing such action for First Amendment purposes, we have considered the context in which it occurred.

. . .

The Government generally has a freer hand in restricting expressive conduct than it has in restricting the written or spoken word. It may not, however, proscribe particular conduct *because* it has expressive elements. "[W]hat might be termed the more generalized guarantee of freedom of expression makes the communicative nature of conduct an inadequate *basis* for singling out that conduct for proscription. A law *directed at* the communicative nature of conduct must, like a law directed at speech itself, be justified by the substantial showing of need that the First Amendment requires." . . .

Thus, although we have recognized that where "'speech' and 'nonspeech' elements are combined in the same course of conduct, a sufficiently important governmental interest in regulating the nonspeech element can justify

incidental limitations on First Amendment freedoms," we have limited the applicability of O'Brien's relatively lenient standard to those cases in which "the governmental interest is unrelated to the suppression of free expression." In stating, moreover, that O'Brien's test "in the last analysis is little, if any, different from the standard applied to time, place, or manner restrictions," we have highlighted the requirement that the governmental interest in question be unconnected to expression in order to come under O'Brien's less demanding rule.

In order to decide whether O'Brien's test applies here, therefore, we must decide whether Texas has asserted an interest in support of Johnson's conviction that is unrelated to the suppression of expression. If we find that an interest asserted by the State is simply not implicated on the facts before us, we need not ask whether O'Brien's test applies. The State offers two separate interests to justify this conviction: preventing breaches of the peace, and preserving the flag as a symbol of nationhood and national unity. We hold that the first interest is not implicated on this record and that the second is related to the suppression of expression.

. . .

Texas claims that its interest in preventing breaches of the peace justifies Johnson's conviction for flag desecration. However, no disturbance of the peace actually occurred or threatened to occur because of Johnson's burning of the flag. Although the State stresses the disruptive behavior of the protestors during their march toward City Hall, it admits that "no actual breach of the peace occurred at the time of the flagburning or in response to the flagburning." The State's emphasis on the protestors' disorderly actions prior to arriving at City Hall is not only somewhat surprising given that no charges were brought on the basis of this conduct, but it also fails to show that a disturbance of the peace was a likely reaction to *Johnson's* conduct. The only evidence offered by the State at trial to show the reaction to Johnson's actions was the testimony of several persons who had been seriously offended by the flagburning.

The State's position, therefore, amounts to a claim that an audience that takes serious offense at particular expression is necessarily likely to disturb the peace and that the expression may be prohibited on this basis. Our precedents do not countenance such a presumption. On the contrary, they recognize that a principal "function of free speech under our system of government is to invite dispute. It may indeed best serve its high purpose when it induces a condition of unrest, creates dissatisfaction with conditions as they are, or even stir . . . people to anger."

Nor does Johnson's expressive conduct fall within that small class of "fighting words" that are "likely to provoke the average person to retaliation, and thereby cause a breach of the peace." No reasonable onlooker would have regarded Johnson's generalized expression of dissatisfaction with the policies of the Federal Government as a direct personal insult or an invitation to exchange fisticuffs.

We thus conclude that the State's interest in maintaining order is not implicated on these facts. The State need not worry that our holding will disable it from preserving the peace.

. . .

The State also asserts an interest in preserving the flag as a symbol of nationhood and national unity. In Spence, we acknowledged that the Government's interest in preserving the flag's special symbolic value "is directly related to expression in the context of activity" such as affixing a peace symbol to a flag. We are equally persuaded that this interest is related to expression in the case of Johnson's burning of the flag. The State, apparently, is concerned that such conduct will lead people to believe either that the flag does not stand for nationhood and national unity, but instead reflects other, less positive concepts, or that the concepts reflected in the flag do not in fact exist, that is, we do not enjoy unity as a Nation. These concerns blossom only when a person's treatment of the flag communicates some message, and thus are related "to the suppression of free expression" within the meaning of O'Brien. We are thus outside of O'Brien's test altogether.

. . .

It remains to consider whether the State's interest in preserving the flag as a symbol of nationhood and national unity justifies Johnson's conviction.

. . .

The State's argument is not that it has an interest simply in maintaining the flag as a symbol of *something*, no matter what it symbolizes; indeed, if that were the State's position, it would be difficult to see how that interest is endangered by highly symbolic conduct such as Johnson's. Rather, the State's claim is that it has an interest in preserving the flag as a symbol of *nationhood* and *national unity*, a symbol with a determinate range of meanings. According to Texas, if one physically treats the flag in a way that would tend to cast doubt on either the idea that nationhood and national unity are the flag's referents or that national unity actually exists, the message conveyed thereby is a harmful one and therefore may be prohibited.

If there is a bedrock principle underlying the First Amendment, it is that the Government may not prohibit the expression of an idea simply because society finds the idea itself offensive or disagreeable.

. . .

In short, nothing in our precedents suggests that a State may foster its own view of the flag by prohibiting expressive conduct relating to it. To bring its argument outside our precedents, Texas attempts to convince us that even if its interest in preserving the flag's symbolic role does not allow it to prohibit words or some expressive conduct critical of the flag, it does permit it to forbid the outright destruction of the flag. The State's argument cannot depend here on the distinction between written or spoken words and nonverbal conduct. That distinction, we have shown, is of no moment where the nonverbal conduct is expressive, as it is here, and where the regulation of that conduct is related to expression, as it is here. . . .

Texas' focus on the precise nature of Johnson's expression, moreover, misses the point of our prior decisions: their enduring lesson, that the Government may not prohibit expression simply because it disagrees with its message, is not dependent on the particular mode in which one chooses to express an idea. If we were to hold that a State may forbid flagburning wherever it is likely to endanger the flag's symbolic role, but allow it wherever burning a flag promotes that role—as where, for example, a person ceremoniously burns a dirty flag—we would be saying that when it comes to impairing the flag's physical integrity, the flag itself may be used as a symbol—as a substitute for the written or spoken word or a "short cut from mind to mind"—only in one direction. We would be permitting a State to "prescribe what shall be orthodox" by saying that one may burn the flag to convey one's attitude toward it and its referents only if one does not endanger the flag's representation of nationhood and national unity.

. . .

There is, moreover, no indication—either in the text of the Constitution or in our cases interpreting it—that a separate juridical category exists for the American flag alone. Indeed, we would not be surprised to learn that the persons who framed our Constitution and wrote the Amendment that we now construe were not known for their reverence for the Union Jack. The First Amendment does not guarantee that other concepts virtually sacred to our Nation as a whole—such as the principle that discrimination on the basis of race is odious and destructive—will go unquestioned in the marketplace of ideas. We decline, therefore, to create for the flag an exception to the joust of principles protected by the First Amendment.

It is not the State's ends, but its means, to which we object. It cannot be gainsaid that there is a special place reserved for the flag in this Nation, and thus we do not doubt that the Government has a legitimate interest in making efforts to "preserv[e] the national flag as an unalloyed symbol of our country." We reject the suggestion, urged at oral argument by counsel for Johnson, that the Government lacks "any state interest whatsoever" in regulating the manner in which the flag may be displayed. Congress has, for example, enacted precatory regulations describing the proper treatment of the flag, and we cast no doubt on the legitimacy of its interest in making such recommendations. To say that the Government has an interest in encouraging proper treatment of the flag, however, is not to say that it may criminally punish a person for burning a flag as a means of political protest. "National unity as an end which officials may foster by persuasion and example is not in question. The problem is whether under our Constitution compulsion as here employed is a permissible means for its achievement."

We are fortified in today's conclusion by our conviction that forbidding criminal punishment for conduct such as Johnson's will not endanger the special role played by our flag or the feelings it inspires. To paraphrase Justice Holmes, we submit that nobody can suppose that this one gesture of an unknown man will change our Nation's attitude towards its flag.

. . .

We are tempted to say, in fact, that the flag's deservedly cherished place in our community will be strengthened, not weakened, by our holding today. Our decision is a reaffirmation of the principles of freedom and inclusiveness that the flag best reflects, and of the conviction that our toleration of criticism such as Johnson's is a sign and source of our strength. Indeed, one of the proudest images of our flag, the one immortalized in our own national anthem, is of the bombardment it survived at Fort McHenry. It is the Nation's resilience, not its rigidity, that Texas sees reflected in the flag—and it is that resilience that we reassert today.

The way to preserve the flag's special role is not to punish those who feel differently about these matters. It is to persuade them that they are wrong. "To courageous, self-reliant men, with confidence in the power of free and fearless reasoning applied through the processes of popular government, no danger flowing from speech can be deemed clear and present, unless the incidence of the evil apprehended is so imminent that it may befall before there is opportunity for full discussion. If there be time to expose through discussion the falsehood and fallacies, to avert the evil by the processes of education, the remedy to be applied is more speech, not enforced silence." And, precisely because it is our flag that is involved, one's response to the flag-burner may exploit the uniquely persuasive power of the flag itself. We can imagine no more appropriate response to burning a flag than waving one's own, no better way to counter a flag-burner's message than by saluting the flag that burns, no surer means of preserving the dignity even of the flag that burned than by—as one witness here did—according its remains a respectful burial. We do not consecrate the flag by punishing its desecration, for in doing so we dilute the freedom that this cherished emblem represents.

. . .

Johnson was convicted for engaging in expressive conduct. The State's interest in preventing breaches of the peace does not support his conviction because Johnson's conduct did not threaten to disturb the peace. Nor does the State's interest in preserving the flag as a symbol of nationhood and national unity justify his criminal conviction for engaging in political expression. The judgment of the Texas Court of Criminal Appeals is therefore affirmed.

. . .

Chief Justice **Rehnquist,** with whom Justice **White** and Justice **O'Connor** join, dissenting.

In holding this Texas statute unconstitutional, the Court ignores Justice Holmes' familiar aphorism that "a page of history is worth a volume of logic." For more than 200 years, the American flag has occupied a unique position as the symbol of our Nation, a uniqueness that justifies a governmental prohibition against flag burning in the way respondent Johnson did here.

. . .

The American flag . . . throughout more than 200 years of our history, has come to be the visible symbol embodying our Nation. It does not represent the views of any particular political party, and it does not represent any particular political philosophy. The flag is not simply another "idea" or "point of view" competing for recognition in the marketplace of ideas. Millions and millions of Americans regard it with an almost mystical reverence regardless of what sort of social, political, or philosophi-

cal beliefs they may have. I cannot agree that the First Amendment invalidates the Act of Congress, and the laws of 48 of the 50 States, which make criminal the public burning of the flag.

. . .

The Court upheld Chaplinsky's conviction under a state statute that made it unlawful to "address any offensive, derisive or annoying word to any person who is lawfully in any street or other public place." Chaplinsky had told a local Marshal, "You are a God damned racketeer" and a "damned Fascist and the whole government of Rochester are Fascists or agents of Fascists."

Here it may equally well be said that the public burning of the American flag by Johnson was no essential part of any exposition of ideas, and at the same time it had a tendency to incite a breach of the peace. Johnson was free to make any verbal denunciation of the flag that he wished; indeed, he was free to burn the flag in private. He could publicly burn other symbols of the Government or effigies of political leaders. He did lead a march through the streets of Dallas, and conducted a rally in front of the Dallas City Hall. He engaged in a "die-in" to protest nuclear weapons. He shouted out various slogans during the march, including: "Reagan, Mondale which will it be? Either one means World War III"; "Ronald Reagan, killer of the hour, Perfect example of US power"; and "red, white and blue, we spit on you, you stand for plunder, you will go under." For none of these acts was he arrested or prosecuted; it was only when he proceeded to burn publicly an American flag stolen from its rightful owner that he violated the Texas statute.

The Court could not, and did not, say that Chaplinsky's utterances were not expressive phrases—they clearly and succinctly conveyed an extremely low opinion of the addressee. The same may be said of Johnson's public burning of the flag in this case; it obviously did convey Johnson's bitter dislike of his country. But his act, like Chaplinsky's provocative words, conveyed nothing that could not have been conveyed and was not conveyed just as forcefully in a dozen different ways. As with "fighting words," so with flag burning, for purposes of the First

Amendment: It is "no essential part of any exposition of ideas, and [is] of such slight social value as a step to truth that any benefit that may be derived from [it] is clearly outweighed" by the public interest in avoiding a probable breach of the peace. The highest courts of several States have upheld state statutes prohibiting the public burning of the flag on the grounds that it is so inherently inflammatory that it may cause a breach of public order.

The result of the Texas statute is obviously to deny one in Johnson's frame of mind one of many means of "symbolic speech." Far from being a case of "one picture being worth a thousand words," flagburning is the equivalent of an inarticulate grunt or roar that, it seems fair to say, is most likely to be indulged in not to express any particular idea, but to antagonize others. Only five years ago we said in Los Angeles City Council v Taxpayers for Vincent, that "the First Amendment does not guarantee the right to employ every conceivable method of communication at all times and in all places." The Texas statute deprived Johnson of only one rather inarticulate symbolic form of protest—a form of protest that was profoundly offensive to many—and left him with a full panoply of other symbols and every conceivable form of verbal expression to express his deep disapproval of national policy. Thus, in no way can it be said that Texas is punishing him because his hearers—or any other group of people—were profoundly opposed to the message that he sought to convey. Such opposition is no proper basis for restricting speech or expression under the First Amendment. It was Johnson's use of this particular symbol, and not the idea that he sought to convey by it or by his many other expressions, for which he was punished.

. . .

The Court concludes its opinion with a regrettably patronizing civics lecture, presumably addressed to the Members of both Houses of Congress, the members of the 48 state legislatures that enacted prohibitions against flag burning, and the troops fighting under that flag in Vietnam who objected to its being burned: "The way to preserve the flag's special role is not to punish those who feel differently about these matters. It is to persuade them that they are wrong." The Court's role as the final expositor of the Constitution is well established, but its role as a platonic guardian admonishing those responsible to public opinion as if they were truant school children has no similar place in our system of government. The cry of "no taxation without representation" animated those who revolted against the English Crown to found our Nation—the idea that those who submitted to government should have some say as to what kind of laws would be passed. Surely one of the high purposes of a democratic society is to legislate against conduct that is regarded as evil and profoundly offensive to the majority of people—whether it be murder, embezzlement, pollution, or flag burning.

Our Constitution wisely places limits on powers of legislative majorities to act, but the declaration of such limits by this Court "is, at all times, a question of much delicacy, which ought seldom, if ever, to be decided in the affirmative, in a doubtful case." Uncritical extension of constitutional protection to the burning of the flag risks the frustration of the very purpose for which organized governments are instituted. The Court decides that the American flag is just another symbol, about which not only must opinions pro and con be tolerated, but for which the most minimal public respect may not be enjoined. The government may conscript men into the Armed Forces where they must fight and perhaps die for the flag, but the government may not prohibit the public burning of the banner under which they fight. I would uphold the Texas statute as applied in this case.

Aftermath of Texas v. Johnson

Responding to the public outcry that followed the Court's decision in *Johnson*, President George Bush supported a constitutional amendment that would protect the American flag from desecration, a move that would overrule the Supreme Court and make an explicit exception to the First Amendment. Many members of Congress preferred the less-sweeping approach of enacting a statute that would protect the flag from public insult and yet remain within the framework of the Supreme Court's language in *Johnson*. It was felt that a statute focusing on the *act* of flag burning, rather than the political message of the flag burners, might satisfy the Court's First Amendment concerns. A bill was soon drafted punishing anyone who knowingly mutilates, defaces, burns or tramples on an American flag. A few months after the Court's decision, the proposed constitutional amendment failed in the Senate on a vote of 51 to 48 (with 67 votes needed for passage). Soon thereafter, Congress passed the Flag Protection Act of 1989 which went into effect without the President's signature.

The relevant section of the new statute provided that: "Whoever knowingly mutilates, defaces, physically defiles, burns, maintains on the floor or ground, or tramples upon any flag of the United States shall be fined . . . or imprisoned for not more than one year, or both." It was not long before arrests were made of several persons who had burned flags in violation of the law. In June of 1990 the Supreme Court consolidated two appeals from the United States government, one originating in the District of Columbia (*United States* v. *Eichman*) and one in the state of Washington (*United States* v. *Haggerty*), in which the defendants had persuaded the lower courts to dismiss the flag-burning charge on the ground that the law violated the First Amendment.

In a 5–4 decision the Supreme Court, adhering to the recent precedent of *Texas* v. *Johnson*, agreed with the lower courts that the new law was, indeed, a violation of the First Amendment. Writing for the Court, Justice Brennan declared that "the mere destruction or disfigurement of a particular physical manifestation of the symbol, without more, does not diminish or otherwise affect the symbol itself in any way." While noting that the act of Congress was cast in broader terms than the Texas law at issue in the *Johnson* case, Brennan nevertheless maintained that "the Act still suffers from the same fundamental flaw: it suppresses expression out of concern for its likely communicative impact." Even assuming that a national consensus exists favoring a prohibition on flag burning, continued Justice Brennan, "any suggestion that the Government's interest in suppressing speech becomes more weighty as popular opposition to that speech grows is foreign to the First Amendment." Justice John Paul Stevens, adhering to his position in *Texas* v. *Johnson*, argued that the government may, and should, "protect the symbolic value of the flag without regard to the specific content of the flag burner's speech."

Reaction to the decision was swift as both houses of Congress debated and voted upon a constitutional amendment to outlaw flag burning. Neither the House nor the Senate could muster the necessary two-thirds vote required to propose an amendment to the Constitution, and the issue appears to have been resolved permanently.

New York Times v. *Sullivan*

376 U.S. 254 (1964)

Legal protection for persons claiming defamation of character has its roots in Greek and Roman civilizations and in the ecclesiastical courts of the Middle Ages. It came

to fruition in the English common law of defamation, the general principles of which were transplanted to the American colonies and eventually provided the basis for the law of libel in the states. In the United States there are no federal laws pertaining to defamation, or libel as it has come to be known, and thus the evolving law on the subject embodies a complex arrangement of common law rules modified by diverse statutes in the 50 states. Prior to the *New York Times* case the Supreme Court had assumed that libelous actions were matters for state resolution and were outside First Amendment protection.

Although the law of libel differs from state to state, there are significant similarities. In all jurisdictions a suit for damages becomes actionable only after a specific person or publication (newspaper, pamphlet, etc.) has been identified as having communicated a harmful, insulting or derogatory message to a third person. In the case of a publication the message is assumed to have been read by its recipients. Initially, libel referred to written defamation and slander to the spoken word, but with modern electronic communications and the fact that radio and television project a message to a broad audience, the distinction has become blurred and the mass media—whatever their form—are subject to libel actions. Traditionally, the subject of a lawsuit has had three plausible defenses: (1) that the message was true; (2) that the allegedly libelled person's reputation was of dubious integrity prior to the message; (3) that the communication was privileged, either absolutely as in the case of a legislator's remarks in a floor debate and certain judicial relationships, or qualifiedly as for the case of reviewers of artistic work or journalistic reports of public proceedings.

If a person proves to the satisfaction of a jury that he or she has been defamed, the jurors in awarding damages face a perplexing scheme of arcane legalisms. Damages are *presumed* if the statements are automatically destructive of a person's reputation, that is, if they accuse one of criminality, carrying a contagious disease, or professional or business wrongdoing or of sexual immorality. If the statement is not defamatory on its face but is tied to particular circumstances, injury to reputation must be specifically proved. Once the jury agrees that damages should be awarded, whether presumed or as the result of proof of defamation, they must then translate the decision into monetary terms. This is done through a calculus based upon three assessments: *special* damages which compensate a person for precise loss of salary or business income as a result of the libel; *general* damages which include "presumed" and are simply a jury's judgment of the seriousness of the harm inflicted; and *punitive* damages which permit the jury to add money to the award as punishment. If the trial judge or an appeals court believes the jury's award to be excessive, either may reduce the money damages accordingly. Most libel actions are *civil* suits for damages, but the government may also initiate a prosecution for *criminal* libel, subjecting the defendant to fine and/or imprisonment.

When libel suits are between private parties, they seemingly have little implication for constitutional rights, but the First Amendment comes into play when the suit is against a public official or when the media are party to the suit. This was the situation when the Supreme Court dealt with the issues in the following case and altered the common law of defamation with its announcement of the "actual malice" rule.

On March 29, 1960 *The New York Times* published a full-page advertisement which urged support for the civil rights movement in the south. Purporting to dramatize events in Montgomery, Alabama, the ad contained several references which turned out to be inaccurate. L. B. Sullivan, a former commissioner of public affairs in Montgomery, whose duties included supervision of the police department, claimed that although he was not personally named, the errors of fact in the ad had defamed his reputation. An Alabama jury awarded Sullivan $500,000 in damages and the verdict was subsequently affirmed by the Alabama Supreme Court.

Mr. Justice **Brennan** delivered the opinion of the Court.

We are required in this case to determine for the first time the extent to which the constitutional protections for speech and press limit a State's power to award damages in a libel action brought by a public official against critics of his official conduct.

. . .

Under Alabama law as applied in this case, a publication is "libelous per se" if the words "tend to injure a person . . . in his reputation" or to "bring [him] into public contempt"; the trial court stated that the standard was met if the words are such as to "injure him in his public office, or impute misconduct to him in his office, or want of official integrity, or want of fidelity to a public trust. . . ." The jury must find that the words were published "of and concerning" the plaintiff, but where the plaintiff is a public official his place in the governmental hierarchy is sufficient evidence to support a finding that his reputation has been affected by statements that reflect upon the agency of which he is in charge. Once "libel per se" has been established, the defendant has no defense as to stated facts unless he can persuade the jury that they were true in all their particulars. His privilege of "fair comment" for expressions of opinion depends on the truth of the facts upon which the comment is based. Unless he can discharge the burden of proving the truth, general damages are presumed, and may be awarded without proof of pecuniary injury. A showing of actual malice is apparently a prerequisite to recovery of punitive damages, and the defendant may in any event forestall a primitive award by a retraction meeting the statutory requirements. Good motives and belief in truth do not negate an inference of malice, but are relevant only in mitigation of punitive damages if the jury chooses to accord them weight.

The question before us is whether this rule of liability, as applied to an action brought by a public official against critics of his official conduct, abridges the freedom of speech and of the press that is guaranteed by the First and Fourteenth Amendments.

Respondent relies heavily, as did the Alabama courts, on statements of this Court to the effect that the Constitution does not protect libelous publications. Those statements do not foreclose our inquiry here. None of the cases sustained the use of libel laws to impose sanctions upon expression critical of the official conduct of public officials.

. . .

Thus we consider this case against the background of a profound national commitment to the principle that debate on public issues should be uninhibited, robust, and wide-open, and that it may well include vehement, caustic, and sometimes unpleasantly sharp attacks on government and public officials. The present advertisement, as an expression of grievance and protest on one of the major public issues of our time, would seem clearly to qualify for the constitutional protection. The question is whether it forfeits that protection by the falsity of some of its factual statements and by its alleged defamation of respondent.

Authoritative interpretations of the First Amendment guarantees have consistently refused to recognize an exception for any test of truth—whether administered by judges, juries, or administrative officials—and especially one that puts the burden of proving truth on the speaker. The constitutional protection does not turn upon "the truth, popularity, or social utility of the ideas and beliefs which are offered."

. . .

Injury to official reputation affords no more warrant for repressing speech that would otherwise be free than does factual error. Where judicial officers are involved, this Court has held that concern for the dignity and reputation of the courts does not justify the punishment as criminal contempt of criticism of the judge or his decision. This is true even though the utterance contains "half-truths" and "misinformation." Such repression can be justified, if at all, only by a clear and present danger of the obstruction of justice. If judges are to be treated as "men of fortitude, able to thrive in a hardy climate," surely the same must be true of other government officials, such as elected city commissioners. Criticism of their official conduct does not lose its constitutional protection merely because it is effective criticism and hence diminishes their official reputations.

If neither factual error nor defamatory content suffices to remove the constitutional shield from criticism of official conduct, the combination of the two elements is no less inadequate.

. . .

A rule compelling the critic of official conduct to guarantee the truth of all his factual assertions—and to do so on pain of libel judgments virtually unlimited in amount—leads to a comparable "self-censorship." Allowance of the defense of truth, with the burden of proving it on the defendant, does not mean that only false speech will be deterred. Even courts accepting this defense as an adequate safeguard have recognized the difficulties of adducing legal proofs that the alleged libel was true in all its factual particulars. Under such a rule, would-be critics of official conduct may be deterred from voicing their criticism, even though it is believed to be true and even though it is in fact true, because of doubt whether it can be proved in court or fear of the expense of having to do so. They tend to make only statements which "steer far wider of the unlawful zone." The rule thus dampens the vigor and limits the variety of public debate. It is inconsistent with the First and Fourteenth Amendments.

The constitutional guarantees require, we think, a federal rule that prohibits a public official from recovering damages for a defamatory falsehood relating to his official conduct unless he proves that the statement was made with "actual malice"—that is, with knowledge that it was false or with reckless disregard of whether it was false or not.

. . .

We conclude that such a privilege is required by the First and Fourteenth Amendments. . . .

We hold today that the Constitution delimits a State's power to award damages for libel in actions brought by public officials against critics of their official conduct. Since this is such an action, the rule requiring proof of actual malice is applicable. While Alabama law apparently

requires proof of actual malice for an award of punitive damages, where general damages are concerned malice is "presumed." Such a presumption is inconsistent with the federal rule. "The power to create presumptions is not a means of escape from constitutional restrictions, the showing of malice required for the forfeiture of the privilege is not presumed but is a matter for proof by the plaintiff. . . ." Since the trial judge did not instruct the jury to differentiate between general and punitive damages, it may be that the verdict was wholly an award of one or the other. But it is impossible to know, in view of the general verdict returned. Because of this uncertainty, the judgment must be reversed and the case remanded.

Since respondent may seek a new trial, we deem that considerations of effective judicial administration require us to review the evidence in the present record to determine whether it could constitutionally support a judgment for respondent.

. . .

Applying these standards, we consider that the proof presented to show actual malice lacks the convincing clarity which the constitutional standard demands, and hence that it would not constitutionally sustain the judgment for respondent under the proper rule of law. The case of the individual petitioners requires little discussion. Even assuming that they could constitutionally be found to have authorized the use of their names on the advertisement, there was no evidence whatever that they were aware of any erroneous statements or were in any way reckless in that regard. The judgment against them is thus without constitutional support.

As to the Times, we similarly conclude that the facts do not support a finding of actual malice. The statement by the Times' Secretary that, apart from the padlocking allegation, he thought the advertisement was "substantially correct," affords no constitutional warrant for the Alabama Supreme Court's conclusion that it was a "cavalier ignoring of the falsity of the advertisement [from which] the jury could not have but been impressed with the bad faith of The Times, and its maliciousness inferable therefrom." The statement does not indicate malice at the time of the publication; even if the advertisement was not "substantially correct"—although respondent's own proofs tend to show that it was—that opinion was at least a reasonable one, and there was no evidence to impeach the witness' good faith in holding it. The Times' failure to retract upon respondent's demand, although it later retracted upon the demand of Governor Patterson, is likewise not adequate evidence of malice for constitutional purposes. Whether or not a failure to retract may ever constitute such evidence, there are two reasons why it does not here. *First*, the letter written by the Times reflected a reasonable doubt on its part as to whether the advertisement could reasonably be taken to refer to respondent at all. *Second*, it was not a final refusal, since it asked for an explanation on this point—a request that respondent chose to ignore. Nor does the retraction upon the demand of the Governor supply the necessary proof. It may be doubted that a failure to retract which is not itself evidence of malice can retroactively become such by virtue of a retraction subsequently made to another party. But in any event that did not happen here, since the explanation given by the Times' Secretary for the distinction drawn between respondent and the Governor was a reasonable one, the good faith of which was not impeached.

Finally, there is evidence that the Times published the advertisement without checking its accuracy against the news stories in the Times'

own files. The mere presence of the stories in the files does not, of course, establish that the Times "knew" the advertisement was false, since the state of mind required for actual malice would have to be brought home to the persons in the Times' organization having responsibility for the publication of the advertisement. With respect to the failure of those persons to make the check, the record shows that they relied upon their knowledge of the good reputation of many of those whose names were listed as sponsors of the advertisement, and upon the letter from A. Philip Randolph, known to them as a responsible individual, certifying that the use of the names was authorized. There was testimony that the persons handling the advertisement saw nothing in it that would render it unacceptable under the Times' policy of rejecting advertisements containing "attacks of a personal character"; their failure to reject it on this ground was not unreasonable. We think the evidence against the Times supports at most a finding of negligence in failing to discover the misstatements, and is constitutionally insufficient to show the recklessness that is required for a finding of actual malice.

. . .

The judgment of the Supreme Court of Alabama is reversed and the case is remanded to that court for further proceedings not inconsistent with this opinion.

Reversed and remanded.

Aftermath of New York Times *v.* Sullivan

In the *Sullivan* case the Supreme Court significantly altered the old common law and statutory rules governing the law of libel. First, it thereafter became extremely difficult for a public official to collect damages under the principle that "actual malice" had to be proved; second, the subject of a libel suit now had a new element available—the First Amendment—along with the traditional three (truth, known bad reputation of the plaintiff, and privileged communication) that could be used as a defense. Extensive litigation generally follows an abrupt judicial alteration in the law and the *Times-Sullivan* case was no exception. Eventually the "public official" category was expanded to encompass not only officials serving in all public posts from judge to police officer to school board member, but to candidates for office as well (*Monitor Patriot* v. *Roy*, 1971).

Three additional questions reached the Court for resolution very quickly: Does the *Times-Sullivan* rule apply to criminal libel as well as to civil? Do the rules that apply to "public officials" also fit persons who are "public figures" such as actors, television personalities, professional athletes, etc.? Do "non-public" persons who become involved in a libel suit become "public" figures when the litigation receives extensive coverage by the media? Within a year after the decision in *Sullivan* the Court answered the first question in the affirmative in *Garrison* v. *Louisiana* (1964). Unanimously reversing the conviction of the New Orleans district attorney, Jim Garrison, who had been convicted under a Louisiana criminal libel law for accusing certain state judges of laziness and inefficiency, the Court applied the *Times-Sullivan* rule in declaring the Louisiana statute unconstitutional.

In 1967 the Court expanded the term *public official* to include *public persons* when it decided *Curtis Publishing Co.* v. *Butts.* Wally Butts, the University of Georgia football coach, had been the subject of a story in the *Saturday Evening Post* which stated that Butts had revealed significant information about Georgia's football strategy to Bear Bryant, the coach at the University of Alabama, just prior to a meeting of the two teams. Butts sued the magazine and won a jury verdict of $3 million, later reduced to $460,000 by the trial judge. In affirming the decision of the state courts, the Supreme Court held that the *Times-Sullivan* standard was applicable to public figures as well as to public officials. Precise definition of the terms, however, was not easy to ascertain. At one point a frustrated federal judge characterized attempts at defining *public figures* as comparable to "trying to nail a jellyfish to a wall."

In *Gertz* v. *Welsh* in 1974 the Court promulgated a rough formula for determining who had the status of public figure. Justice Lewis Powell in his opinion declared that some persons occupy positions of such pervasive power that they may be deemed public figures for all purposes. Others, Powell maintained, attain notoriety as a result of being thrust to the forefront of a public controversy, but they do not thereby become public figures in the constitutional sense. Elmer Gertz, a Chicago attorney, had been awarded damages of $50,000 by a jury; an appellate court vacated the verdict and denied the damages. On appeal the Supreme Court reversed the proceedings of the lower courts and sent the case back for another trial with instructions that were to alter the old common law rules. In handing down new guidelines, Justice Powell contended that "private individuals are not only more vulnerable to injury than public figures; they are also more deserving of recovery." Thus they need not meet the tough "actual malice" standard even if the suit has attained public notoriety. Nevertheless, in order to protect the First Amendment rights of the media, the Court abolished the concept of "strict liability" (liability without fault, meaning that a party is liable for damages even with the best of motives) in suits between private persons and the press and substituted a standard of fault that is no less than "negligence" (to act or not to act in accordance with a normal standard of human prudence and reasonableness). Furthermore, the Court outlawed the use of punitive or presumed damages, permitting only damages for actual injury, such as financial loss or diminution of reputation.

Following *Gertz* the Court faced the question in several cases whether a normally private person becomes a public figure as a result of media attention, and answered in the negative. In *Time Inc.* v. *Firestone* (1976) a Florida jury brought in a verdict against *Time* magazine and awarded the plaintiff, Mrs. Harvey Firestone, $100,000. A story in *Time*, discussing the sordid details of a highly publicized divorce proceeding, referred to Mrs. Firestone as an "adulteress" although the divorce decree had not found her guilty of adultery. The Court sent the case back to the Florida courts, indicating that Mrs. Firestone was not a *public figure* as a result of the publicity given the controversy, but that the case might be retried for a finding of negligence. Similarly, the nephew of an admitted Russian spy who had been held in contempt for refusal to answer a subpoena, was later erroneously named in a book as a Russian agent. His contempt conviction did not make him a public figure, said the Court, and he therefore needed only to prove negligence and not actual malice against the publisher (*Walston* v. *Reader's Digest Association,* 1979). Also held not to be public figures were corporations that advertise for the public's business (*American Broadcasting Companies* v. *Vegod Corporation,* 1980).

Hustler Magazine v. Falwell

485 U.S. 46 (1988)

In a recent pronouncement on the law of libel the Court came down more forcefully than ever in protecting freedom of speech and press when the subject of comment is a public figure. *Hustler* magazine, in publishing a parody of Campari liquor advertising, displayed celebrities supposedly sampling Campari for the first time, but with a twist suggesting that the celebrities were discussing their first sexual encounters. In the November 1983 issue the magazine ran what purported to be a Campari ad in which evangelist Jerry Falwell told about his "first time" with his mother in an outhouse. Falwell and his mother were also depicted as drunks. In the table of contents the parody was listed as "Fiction: Ad and Personality Parody" and a disclaimer printed at the bottom of the "ad" read "ad parody—not to be taken seriously." Falwell, however, thought it a serious matter and brought an action against *Hustler* and its publisher Larry Flynt, for libel, invasion of privacy, and intentional infliction of emotional distress. While dismissing the libel charge, the jury accepted the claim of emotional distress and awarded Falwell $200,000 in damages from *Hustler* and from Larry Flynt. It was the first lower-court decision ordering such a payment after the publication had been cleared of libel. In the questions put to the opposing counsel at oral argument, it was clear that the justices were struggling with the question whether the First Amendment permits any limits on political satire.

Chief Justice **Rehnquist** delivered the opinion of the Court.

. . .

This case presents us with a novel question involving First Amendment limitations upon a State's authority to protect its citizens from the intentional infliction of emotional distress. We must decide whether a public figure may recover damages for emotional harm caused by the publication of an ad parody offensive to him, and doubtless gross and repugnant in the eyes of most. Respondent would have us find that a State's interest in protecting public figures from emotional distress is sufficient to deny First Amendment protection to speech that is patently offensive and is intended to inflict emotional injury, even when that speech could not reasonably have been interpreted as stating actual facts about the public figure involved. This we decline to do.

At the heart of the First Amendment is the recognition of the fundamental importance of the free flow of ideas and opinions on matters of public interest and concern. "[T]he freedom to speak one's mind is not only an aspect of individual liberty—and thus a good unto itself—but also is essential to the common quest for truth and the vitality of society as a whole." We have therefore been particularly vigilant to ensure that individual expressions of ideas remain free from governmentally imposed sanctions. The First Amendment recognizes no such thing as a "false" idea. As Justice Holmes wrote, "[W]hen men have realized that time has upset many fighting faiths, they may come to believe even more than they believe the very foundations of their own conduct that the ultimate good desired is better reached by free trade in ideas— that the best test of truth is the power of the thought to get itself accepted in the competition of the market. . . ."

The sort of robust political debate encouraged by the First Amendment is bound to produce speech that is critical of those who hold public office or those public figures who are "intimately involved in the resolution of important public questions or, by reason of their fame, shape events in areas of concern to society at large." Justice Frankfurter put it succinctly in Baumgartner v United States, when he said that "[o]ne of the prerogatives of American citizenship is the right to criticize public men and measures." Such criticism, inevitably, will not always be reasoned or moderate; public figures as well as public officials will be subject to "vehement, caustic, and sometimes unpleasantly sharp attacks." "[T]he candidate who vaunts his spotless record and sterling integrity cannot convincingly cry 'Foul!' when an opponent or an industrious reporter attempts to demonstrate the contrary."

Of course, this does not mean that *any* speech about a public figure is immune from sanction in the form of damages. Since New York Times Co. v Sullivan, we have consistently ruled that a public figure may hold a speaker liable for the damage to reputation caused by publication of a defamatory falsehood, but only if the statement was made "with knowledge that it was false or with reckless disregard of whether it was false or not." False statements of fact are particularly valueless; they interfere with the truth-seeking function of the marketplace of ideas, and they cause damage to an individual's reputation that cannot easily be repaired by counterspeech, however persuasive or effective. But even though falsehoods have little value in and of themselves, they are "nevertheless inevitable in free debate," and a rule

that would impose strict liability on a publisher for false factual assertions would have an undoubted "chilling" effect on speech relating to public figures that does have constitutional value. "Freedoms of expression require "'breathing space.'" This breathing space is provided by a constitutional rule that allows public figures to recover for libel or defamation only when they can prove *both* that the statement was false and that the statement was made with the requisite level of culpability.

Respondent argues, however, that a different standard should apply in this case because here the State seeks to prevent not reputational damage, but the severe emotional distress suffered by the person who is the subject of an offensive publication. In respondent's view, and in the view of the Court of Appeals, so long as the utterance was intended to inflict emotional distress, was outrageous, and did in fact inflict serious emotional distress, it is of no constitutional import whether the statement was a fact or an opinion, or whether it was true or false. It is the intent to cause injury that is the gravamen of the tort, and the State's interest in preventing emotional harm simply outweighs whatever interest a speaker may have in speech of this type.

Generally speaking the law does not regard the intent to inflict emotional distress as one which should receive much solicitude, and it is quite understandable that most if not all jurisdictions have chosen to make it civilly culpable where the conduct in question is sufficiently "outrageous." But in the world of debate about public affairs, many things done with motives that are less than admirable are protected by the First Amendment. In Garrison v. Louisiana, we held that even when a speaker or writer is motivated by hatred or ill-will his expression was protected by the First Amendment:

"Debate on public issues will not be uninhibited if the speaker must run the risk that it will be proved in court that he spoke out of hatred; even if he did speak out of hatred, utterances honestly believed contribute to the free interchange of ideas and the ascertainment of truth."

Thus while such a bad motive may be deemed controlling for purposes of tort liability in other areas of the law, we think the First Amendment prohibits such a result in the area of public debate about public figures.

Were we to hold otherwise, there can be little doubt that political cartoonists and satirists would be subjected to damages awards without any showing that their work falsely defamed its subject. Webster's defines a caricature as "the deliberately distorted picturing or imitating of a person, literary style, etc. by exaggerating features or mannerisms for satirical effect." The appeal of the political cartoon or caricature is often based on exploration of unfortunate physical traits or politically embarrassing events—an exploration often calculated to injure the feelings of the subject of the portrayal. The art of the cartoonist is often not reasoned or even-handed, but slashing and one-sided. One cartoonist expressed the nature of the art in these words:

"The political cartoon is a weapon of attack, of scorn and ridicule and satire; it is least effective when it tries to pat some politician on the back. It is usually as welcome as a bee sting and is always controversial in some quarters."

Several famous examples of this type of intentionally injurious speech were drawn by Thomas Nast, probably the greatest American cartoonist to date, who was associated for many years during the post-Civil War era with Harper's Weekly. In the pages of that publication Nast conducted a graphic vendetta against William M. "Boss" Tweed and his corrupt associates in New York City's "Tweed Ring." It has been described by one historian of the subject as "a sustained attack which in its passion and effectiveness stands alone in the history of American graphic art." Another writer explains that the success of the Nast cartoon was achieved "because of the emotional impact of its presentation. It continuously goes beyond the bounds of good taste and conventional manners."

Despite their sometimes caustic nature, from the early cartoon portraying George Washington as an ass down to the present day, graphic depictions and satirical cartoons have played a prominent role in public and political debate. Nast's castigation of the Tweed Ring, Walt McDougall's characterization of presidential candidate James G. Blaine's banquet with the millionaires at Delmonico's as "The Royal Feast of Belshazzar," and numerous other efforts have undoubtedly had an effect on the course and outcome of contemporaneous debate. Lincoln's tall, gangling posture, Teddy Roosevelt's glasses and teeth, and Franklin D. Roosevelt's jutting jaw and cigarette holder have been memorialized by political cartoons with an effect that could not have been obtained by the photographer or the portrait artist. From the viewpoint of history it is clear that our political discourse would have been considerably poorer without them.

Respondent contends, however, that the caricature in question here was so "outrageous" as to distinguish it from more traditional political cartoons. There is no doubt that the caricature of respondent and his mother published in Hustler is at best a distant cousin of the political cartoons described above, and a rather poor relation at that. If it were possible by laying down a principled standard to separate the one from the other, public discourse would probably suffer little or no harm. But we doubt that there is any such standard, and we are quite sure that the pejorative description "outrageous" does not supply one. "Outrageousness" in the area of political and social discourse has an inherent subjectiveness about it which would allow a jury to impose liability on the basis of the jurors' tastes or views, or perhaps on the basis of their dislike of a particular expression. An "outrageousness" standard thus runs afoul of our longstanding refusal to allow damages to be awarded because the speech in question may have an adverse emotional impact on the audience.

. . .

Admittedly, these oft-repeated First Amendment principles, like other principles, are subject to limitations. We recognized in Pacifica Foundation, that speech that is " 'vulgar,' 'offensive,' and 'shocking' " is "not entitled to absolute constitutional protection under all circumstances." In Choplinsky v. New Hampshire, we held that a state could lawfully punish an individual for the use of insulting " 'fighting' words— those which by their very utterance inflict injury or tend to incite an immediate breach of the peace." These limitations are but recognition of the observation in Dun & Bradstreet, Inc. v Greenmoss Builders, Inc., that this Court has "long recognized that not all speech is of equal First Amendment importance." But the sort of expression involved in this case does not seem to us to be governed by any exception to the general First Amendment principles stated above.

We conclude that public figures and public officials may not recover for the tort of intentional infliction of emotional distress by reason of publications such as the one here at issue without showing in addition that the publication contains a false statement of fact which was made with "actual malice," i.e., with knowledge that the statement was false or with reckless disregard as to whether or not it was true. This is not merely a "blind application" of the New York Times standard, it reflects our considered judgment that such a standard is necessary to give adequate "breathing space" to the freedoms protected by the First Amendment.

Here it is clear that respondent Falwell is a "public figure" for purposes of First Amendment law. The jury found against respondent on his libel claim when it decided that the Hustler ad parody could not "reasonably be understood as describing actual facts about [respondent] or actual events in which [he] participated." The Court of Appeals interpreted the jury's finding to be that the ad parody "was not reasonably believable," and in accordance with our custom we accept this finding. Respondent is thus relegated to his claim for damages awarded by the jury for the intentional infliction of emotional distress by "outrageous" conduct. But for reasons heretofore stated this claim cannot, consistently with the First Amendment, form a basis for the award of damages when the conduct in question is the publication of a caricature such as the ad parody involved here. The judgment of the Court of Appeals is accordingly reversed.

Aftermath of Hustler Magazine *v.* Falwell

Since Falwell proved to the satisfaction of a jury that the magazine's conduct had caused him severe emotional distress and that the publisher admitted knowledge of falsity, why did the Supreme Court reverse the lower courts? It did so by tightening the "actual malice" standard to require more than proof of falsehood or reckless disregard for the truth. In order to collect damages, one must show that the perpetrator of a false statement *intended* to deceive, *intended* to pass off a falsehood as truth. Such was not the case in this instance since the speech involved, in the words of Chief Justice Rehnquist's opinion, "could not reasonably have been interpreted as stating actual facts."

As matters now stand, private persons may collect damages for defamation if they can prove fault or negligence on the part of the press. Public officials and public figures, however, are held to such a rigid standard of proof that the media have an extremely broad, albeit not unlimited, area for critical commentary on the actions of all those who choose to work in the public arena.

First Amendment protection for journalists was narrowed somewhat in 1990 when the Court decided the case of *Milkovich* v. *Lorain Journal Company.* A reporter for an Ohio newspaper, J. Theodore Diadiun, wrote an article in which he implied that Michael Milkovich, a high school wrestling coach, had lied under oath in a judicial proceeding about an incident involving a wrestling match. In part Diadiun's column read: "Anyone who attended the meet . . . knows in his heart that Milkovich . . . lied at the hearing after . . . having given his solemn oath to tell the truth." Milkovich sued the newspaper for libel but lost in the state courts, in part on the ground that the article constituted "opinion," as opposed to fact, and was protected from a defamation suit by the First Amendment. For a majority of seven, Chief Justice Rehnquist reversed the Ohio courts. The upshot of the ruling was that the news media are not exempt from libel suits for expression of opinion and may be subject to a damage award if the opinion can be proved to be false.

Branzburg v. *Hayes*
408 U.S. 665 (1972)

On occasion two or more guarantees of the Bill of Rights are in direct conflict. When this occurs, the Supreme Court must decide which right has the higher value to society and should therefore prevail. One such recurring conflict is between freedom of the press and the right of an accused person to a fair trial. A major purpose of a free press is to inform the public about activities of government officials, to keep the spotlight of publicity trained on the executive, legislative, and judicial branches in order to enlighten the citizen, and to prevent corruption. Clearly, reporters and news commentators must have access to the halls of government if they are to perform their tasks efficiently. On the other hand, the zeal of the press in covering a criminal case may impede the progress of a fair trial. In the case of a reporter's refusal to testify on grounds that such testimony is privileged, a defendant's liberty or even his or her life may be in jeopardy if a jury is denied access to crucial information.

In a series of decisions culminating in the 1982 case of *Globe Newspaper Company* v. *Superior Court*, the Court dealt with access of the press to criminal trials. In 1979, in a 5–4 decision, the Supreme Court upheld the right of a judge to close a preliminary hearing in a murder case in which pretrial publicity might endanger the defendant's case (*Gannett Company* v. *DePasquale*). Following this decision judges began to close their courtrooms for trials as well as for preliminary hearings over strong protests by the press, and in 1980 the Court clarified the rules in *Richmond Newspapers* v. *Virginia*. Declaring that the *Gannett* decision regarding preliminary hearings remained in place, the Court held that a criminal trial was a different matter and that "the First Amendment can be read as protecting the right of everyone to attend trials so as to give meaning to those explicit guarantees." In the course of the opinion the Court emphasized that public access to criminal trials was not an unqualified right, that a judge might bar public attendance, but such closure bore a heavy burden of proof and must be a "last resort" move to ensure the fairness of a trial. In the *Globe* case the Court invalidated a Massachusetts law that *required* trial judges to close a trial in sexual offense cases during testimony of victims under the age of 18. Mandatory closing of a trial, observed the Court, was in violation of the First Amendment's purpose "to protect the free discussion of governmental affairs."

A second conflict of free press-fair trial rights arises when a reporter refuses to testify in a criminal proceeding, claiming the right to remain silent about confidential news sources. Consolidating three cases—*Branzburg* v. *Hayes, In Re Pappas*, and *United States* v. *Caldwell*—the Court attempted to deal with the issue. Branzburg, a reporter for the *Louisville-Courier Journal*, had refused to testify before grand juries about two stories he had written in which he described his observations of young persons synthesizing hashish from marijuana and other details about the use of drugs. In the companion cases reporters from Massachusetts and California refused to appear before grand juries to testify about in-depth interviews they had had with black militant groups.

Opinion of the Court by Mr. Justice **White,** announced by The **Chief Justice.**

The issue in these cases is whether requiring newsmen to appear and testify before state or federal grand juries abridges the freedom of speech and press guaranteed by the First Amendment. We hold that it does not.

. . .

Petitioners Branzburg and Pappas and respondent Caldwell press First Amendment claims that may be simply put: that to gather news it is often necessary to agree either not to identify the source of information published or to publish only part of the facts revealed, or both; that if the reporter is nevertheless forced to reveal these confidences to a grand jury, the source so identified and other confidential sources of other reporters will be measurably deterred from furnishing publishable information, all to the detriment of the free flow of information protected by the First Amendment. Although the newsmen in these cases do not claim an absolute privilege against official interrogation in all circumstances, they assert that the reporter should not be forced either to appear or to testify before a grand jury or at trial until and unless sufficient grounds are shown for believing that the reporter possesses information relevant to a crime the grand jury is investigating, that the information the reporter has is unavailable from other sources, and that the need for the information is sufficiently compelling to override the claimed invasion of First Amendment interests occasioned by the disclosure. Principally relied upon are prior cases emphasizing the importance of the First Amendment guarantees to individual development and to our system of representative government, decisions requiring that official action with adverse impact on First Amendment rights be justified by a public interest that is "compelling" or "paramount," and those precedents establishing the principle that justifiable government goals may not be achieved by unduly broad means having an unnecessary impact on protected rights of speech, press, or association. The heart of the claim is that the burden on news gathering resulting from compelling reporters to disclose confidential information outweighs any public interest in obtaining the information.

We do not question the significance of free speech, press, or assembly to the country's welfare. Nor is it suggested that news gathering does not qualify for First Amendment protection; without some protection for seeking out the news, freedom of the press could be eviscerated. But these cases involve no intrusions upon speech or assembly, no prior restraint or restriction on what the press may publish, and no express or implied command that the press publish what it prefers to withhold. No exaction or tax for the privilege of publishing, and no penalty, civil or criminal, related to the content of published material is at issue here. The use of confidential sources by the press is not forbidden or restricted; reporters remain free to seek news from any source by means within the law. No attempt is made to require the press to publish its sources of information or indiscriminately to disclose them on request.

The sole issue before us is the obligation of reporters to respond to grand jury subpoenas as other citizens do and to answer questions relevant to an investigation into the commission of crime. Citizens generally are not constitutionally immune from grand jury subpoenas; and neither the First Amendment nor any other constitution provision protects the average citizen from disclosing to a grand jury information that he has received in confidence. The claim is, however, that reporters are exempt from these obligations because if forced to respond to subpoenas and identify their sources or disclose other confidences, their informants will refuse or be reluctant to furnish newsworthy information in the future. This asserted burden on news gathering is said to make compelled testimony from newsmen constitutionally suspect and to require a privileged position for them.

It is clear that the First Amendment does not invalidate every incidental burdening of the press that may result from the enforcement of civil or criminal statutes of general applicability. Under prior cases, otherwise valid laws serving substantial public interests may be enforced against the press as against others, despite the possible burden that may be imposed. The Court has emphasized that "[t]he publisher of a newspaper has no special immunity from the application of general laws. He has no special privilege to invade the rights and liberties of others."

. . .

The prevailing view is that the press is not free to publish with impunity everything and anything it desires to publish. Although it may deter or regulate what is said or published, the press may not circulate knowing or reckless falsehoods damaging to private reputation without subjecting itself to liability for damages, including punitive damages, or even criminal prosecution.

. . .

Despite the fact that news gathering may be hampered, the press is regularly excluded from grand jury proceedings, our own conferences, the meetings of other official bodies gathered in executive session, and the meetings of private organizations. Newsmen have no constitutional right of access to the scenes of crime or disaster when the general public is excluded, and they may be prohibited from attending or publishing information about trials if such restrictions are necessary to assure a defendant a fair trial before an impartial tribunal.

It is thus not surprising that the great weight of authority is that newsmen are not exempt from the normal duty of appearing before a grand jury and answering questions relevant to a criminal investigation. At common law, courts consistently refused to recognize the existence of any privilege authorizing a newsman to refuse to reveal confidential information to a grand jury.

. . .

The prevailing constitutional view of the newsman's privilege is very much rooted in the ancient role of the grand jury that has the dual function of determining if there is probable cause to believe that a crime has been committed and of protecting citizens against unfounded criminal prosecutions. Grand jury proceedings are constitutionally mandated for the institution of federal criminal prosecutions for capital or other serious crimes, and "its constitutional prerogatives are rooted in long centuries of Anglo-American history." The Fifth Amendment provides that "[n]o person shall be held to answer for a capital, or otherwise infa-

mous crime, unless on a presentment or indictment of a Grand Jury." The adoption of the grand jury "in our Constitution as the sole method for preferring charges in serious criminal cases shows the high place it held as an instrument of justice." Although state systems of criminal procedure differ greatly among themselves, the grand jury is similarly guaranteed by many state constitutions and plays an important role in fair and effective law enforcement in the overwhelming majority of the States. Because its task is to inquire into the existence of possible criminal conduct and to return only well-founded indictments, its investigative powers are necessarily broad. "It is a grand inquest, a body with powers of investigation and inquisition, the scope of whose inquiries is not to be limited narrowly by questions of propriety or forecasts of the probable result of the investigation, or by doubts whether any particular individual will be found properly subject to an accusation of crime." Hence, the grand jury's authority to subpoena witnesses is not only historic, but essential to its task. Although the powers of the grand jury are not unlimited and are subject to the supervision of a judge, the longstanding principle that "the public . . . has a right to every man's evidence," except for those persons protected by a constitutional, common-law, or statutory privilege.

A number of States have provided newsmen a statutory privilege of varying breadth, but the majority have not done so, and none has been provided by federal statute. Until now the only testimonial privilege for unofficial witnesses that is rooted in the Federal Constitution is the Fifth Amendment privilege against compelled self-incrimination. We are asked to create another by interpreting the First Amendment to grant newsmen a testimonial privilege that other citizens do not enjoy. This we decline to do. Fair and effective law enforcement aimed at providing security for the person and property of the individual is a fundamental function of government, and the grand jury plays an important, constitutionally mandated role in this process. On the records now before us, we perceive no basis for holding that the public interest in law enforcement and in ensuring effective grand jury proceedings is insufficient to override the consequential, but uncertain, burden on news gathering that is said to result from insisting that reporters, like other citizens, respond to relevant questions put to them in the course of a valid grand jury investigation or criminal trial.

This conclusion itself involves no restraint on what newspapers may publish or on the type or quality of information reporters may seek to acquire, nor does it threaten the vast bulk of confidential relationships between reporters and their sources. Grand juries address themselves to the issues of whether crimes have been committed and who committed them. Only where news sources themselves are implicated in crime or possess information relevant to the grand jury's task need they or the reporter be concerned about grand jury subpoenas. Nothing before us indicates that a large number or percentage of *all* confidential news sources fall into either category and would in any way be deterred by our holding that the Constitution does not, as it never has, exempt the newsman from performing the citizen's normal duty of appearing and furnishing information relevant to the grand jury's task.

The preference for anonymity of those confidential informants involved in actual criminal conduct is presumably a product of their desire to escape criminal prosecution, and this preference, while understandable, is hardly deserving of constitutional protection. It would be frivolous to assert—and no one does in these cases—that the First Amendment, in the interest of securing news or otherwise, confers a license on either the reporter or his news sources to violate valid criminal laws. Although stealing documents or private wiretapping could provide newsworthy information, neither reporter nor source is immune from conviction for such conduct, whatever the impact on the flow of news. Neither is immune, on First Amendment grounds, from testifying against the other, before the grand jury or at a criminal trial. The Amendment does not reach so far as to override the interest of the public in ensuring that neither reporter nor source is invading the rights of other citizens through reprehensible conduct forbidden to all other persons. To assert the contrary proposition "is to answer it, since it involves in its very statement the contention that the freedom of the press is the freedom to do wrong with impunity and implies the right to frustrate and defeat the discharge of those governmental duties upon the performance of which the freedom of all, including that of the press, depends. . . . It suffices to say that, however complete is the right of the press to state public things and discuss them, that right, as every other right enjoyed in human society, is subject to the restraints which separate right from wrong-doing."

Thus, we cannot seriously entertain the notion that the First Amendment protects a newsman's agreement to conceal the criminal conduct of his source, or evidence thereof, on the theory that it is better to write about crime than to do something about it. Insofar as any reporter in these cases undertook not to reveal or testify about the crime he witnessed, his claim of privilege under the First Amendment presents no substantial question. The crimes of news sources are no less reprehensible and threatening to the public interest when witnessed by a reporter than when they are not.

There remain those situations where a source is not engaged in criminal conduct but has information suggesting illegal conduct by others. Newsmen frequently receive information from such sources pursuant to a tacit or express agreement to withhold the source's name and suppress any information that the source wishes not published. Such informants presumably desire anonymity in order to avoid being entangled as a witness in a criminal trial or grand jury investigation. They may fear that disclosure will threaten their job security or personal safety or that it will simply result in dishonor or embarrassment.

The argument that the flow of news will be diminished by compelling reporters to aid the grand jury in a criminal investigation is not irrational, nor are the records before us silent on the matter. But we remain unclear how often and to what extent informers are actually deterred from furnishing information when newsmen are forced to testify before a grand jury. The available data indicate that some newsmen rely a great deal on confidential sources and that some informants are particularly sensitive to the threat of exposure and may be silenced if it is held by this Court that, ordinarily, newsmen must testify pursuant to subpoenas, but the evidence fails to demonstrate that there would be a significant constriction of the flow of news to the public if this Court reaffirms the prior common-law and constitutional rule regarding the testimonial obligations of newsmen.

Accepting the fact, however, that an undetermined number of informants not themselves implicated in crime will nevertheless, for whatever reason, refuse to talk to newsmen if they fear identification by a reporter in an official investigation, we cannot accept the argument that the public interest in possible future news about crime from undisclosed, unverified sources must take precedence over the public interest in pursuing and prosecuting those crimes reported to the press by informants and in thus deterring the commission of such crimes in the future.

We note first that the privilege claimed is that of the reporter, not the informant, and that if the authorities independently identify the informant, neither his own reluctance to testify nor the objection of the newsman would shield him from grand jury inquiry, whatever the impact on the flow of news or on his future usefulness as a secret source of information. More important, it is obvious that agreements to conceal information relevant to commission of crime have very little to recommend them from the standpoint of public policy. Historically, the common law recognized a duty to raise the "hue and cry" and report felonies to the authorities. Misprision of a felony—that is, the concealment of a felony . . . was often said to be a common-law crime. The first Congress passed a statute, which is still in effect, defining a federal crime of misprision. . . . It is apparent from this statute, as well as from our history and that of England, that concealment of crime and agreements to do so are not looked upon with favor. Such conduct deserves no encomium, and we decline now to afford it First Amendment protection by denigrating the duty of a citizen, whether reporter or informer, to respond to grand jury subpoena and answer relevant questions put to him.

. . .

We are admonished that refusal to provide a First Amendment reporter's privilege will undermine the freedom of the press to collect and disseminate news. But this is not the lesson history teaches us. As noted previously, the common law recognized no such privilege, and the constitutional argument was not even asserted until 1958. From the beginning of our country the press has operated without constitutional protection for press informants, and the press has flourished. The existing constitutional rules have not been a serious obstacle to either the development or retention of confidential news sources by the press.

. . .

It is said that currently press subpoenas have multiplied, that mutual distrust and tension between press and officialdom have increased, that reporting styles have changed, and that there is now more need for confidential sources, particularly where the press seeks news about minority cultural and political groups or dissident organizations suspicious of the law and public officials. These developments, even if true, are treacherous grounds for a far-reaching interpretation of the First Amendment fastening a nationwide rule on courts, grand juries, and prosecuting officials everywhere. The obligation to testify in response to grand jury subpoenas will not threaten these sources not involved with criminal conduct and without information relevant to grand jury investigations, and we cannot hold that the Constitution places the sources in these two categories either above the law or beyond its reach.

. . .

At the federal level, Congress has freedom to determine whether a statutory newsman's privilege is necessary and desirable and to fashion standards and rules as narrow or broad as deemed necessary to deal with the evil discerned and, equally important, to refashion those rules as experience from time to time may dictate. There is also merit in leaving state legislatures free, within First Amendment limits, to fashion their own standards in light of the conditions and problems with respect to the relations between law enforcement officials and press in their own areas. It goes without saying, of course, that we are powerless to bar state courts from responding in their own way and construing their own constitutions so as to recognize a newsman's privilege, either qualified or absolute.

In addition, there is much force in the pragmatic view that the press has at its disposal powerful mechanisms of communication and is far from helpless to protect itself from harassment or substantial harm. Furthermore, if what the newsmen urged in these cases is true—that law enforcement cannot hope to gain and may suffer from subpoenaing newsmen before grand juries—prosecutors will be loath to risk so much for so little. Thus, at the federal level the Attorney General has already fashioned a set of rules for federal officials in connection with subpoenaing members of the press to testify before grand juries or at criminal trials. These rules are a major step in the direction the reporters herein desire to move. They may prove wholly sufficient to resolve the bulk of disagreements and controversies between press and federal officials.

Finally, as we have earlier indicated, news gathering is not without its First Amendment protections, and grand jury investigations if instituted or conducted other than in good faith, would pose wholly different issues for resolution under the First Amendment. Official harassment of the press undertaken not for purposes of law enforcement but to disrupt a reporter's relationship with his news sources would have no justification. Grand juries are subject to judicial control and subpoenas to motions to quash. We do not expect courts will forget that grand juries must operate within the limits of the First Amendment as well as the Fifth.

. . .

Mr. Justice **Douglas,** dissenting.

It is my view that there is no "compelling need" that can be shown which qualifies the reporter's immunity from appearing or testifying before a grand jury, unless the reporter himself is implicated in a crime. His immunity in my view is therefore quite complete, for, absent his involvement in a crime, the First Amendment protects him against an appearance before a grand jury and if he is involved in

a crime, the Fifth Amendment stands as a barrier. Since in my view there is no area of inquiry not protected by a privilege, the reporter need not appear for the futile purpose of invoking one to each question. And, since in my view a newsman has an absolute right not to appear before a grand jury, it follows for me that a journalist who voluntarily appears before that body may invoke his First Amendment privilege to specific questions. The basic issue is the extent to which the First Amendment (which is applicable to investigating committees, must yield to the Government's asserted need to know a reporter's unprinted information).

. . .

Two principles which follow from this understanding of the First Amendment are at stake here. One is that the people, the ultimate governors, must have absolute freedom of, and therefore privacy of, their individual opinions and beliefs regardless of how suspect or strange they may appear to others. Ancillary to that principle is the conclusion that an individual must also have absolute privacy over whatever information he may generate in the course of testing his opinions and beliefs. In this regard, Caldwell's status as a reporter is less relevant than is his status as a student who affirmatively pursued empirical research to enlarge his own intellectual viewpoint.

The second principle is that effective self-government cannot succeed unless the people are immersed in a steady, robust, unimpeded, and uncensored flow of opinion and reporting which are continuously subjected to critique, rebuttal, and re-examination. In this respect, Caldwell's status as a news gatherer and an integral part of that process becomes critical.

. . .

Today's decision will impede the wide-open and robust dissemination of ideas and counterthought which a free press both fosters and protects and which is essential to the success of intelligent self-government. Forcing a reporter before a grand jury will have two retarding effects upon the ear and the pen of the press. Fear of exposure will cause dissidents to communicate less openly to trusted reporters. And, fear of accountability will cause editors and critics to write with more restrained pens.

I see no way of making mandatory the disclosure of a reporter's confidential source of the information on which he bases his news story.

The press has a preferred position in our constitutional scheme not to enable it to make money, not to set newsmen apart as a favored class, but to bring fulfillment to the public's right to know. The right to know is crucial to the governing powers of the people, to paraphrase Alexander Meiklejohn. Knowledge is essential to informed decisions.

. . .

The people who govern are often far removed from the cabals that threaten the regime; the people are often remote from the sources of truth even though they live in the city where the forces that would undermine society operate. The function of the press is to explore and investigate events, inform the people what is going on, and to expose the harmful as well as the good influences at work. There is no higher function performed under our constitutional regime. Its performance means that the press is often engaged in projects that bring anxiety or even fear to the bureaucracies, departments, or officials of government. The whole weight of government is therefore often brought to bear against a paper or a reporter.

A reporter is no better than his source of information. Unless he has a privilege to withhold the identity of his source, he will be the victim of governmental intrigue or aggression. If he can be summoned to testify in secret before a grand jury, his sources will dry up and the attempted exposure, the effort to enlighten the public, will be ended. If what the Court sanctions today becomes settled law, then the reporter's main function in American society will be to pass on to the public the press releases which the various departments of government issue.

. . .

Today's decision is more than a clog upon news gathering. It is a signal to publishers and editors that they should exercise caution in how they use whatever information they can obtain. Without immunity they may be summoned to account for their criticism. Entrenched officers have been quick to crash their powers down upon unfriendly commentators.

The intrusion of government into this domain is symptomatic of the disease of this society. As the years pass the power of government becomes more and more pervasive. It is a power to suffocate both people and causes. Those in power, whatever their politics, want only to perpetuate it. Now that the fences of the law and the tradition that has protected the press are broken down, the people are the victims. The First Amendment, as I read it, was designed precisely to prevent that tragedy.

. . .

Mr. Justice **Stewart,** with whom Mr. Justice **Brennan** and Mr. Justice **Marshall** join, dissenting.

The Court's crabbed view of the First Amendment reflects a disturbing insensitivity to the critical role of an independent press in our society. The question whether a reporter has a constitutional right to a confidential relationship with his source is of first impression here, but the principles that should guide our decision are as basic as any to be found in the Constitution. While Mr. Justice Powell's enigmatic concurring opinion gives some hope of a more flexible view in the future, the Court in these cases holds that a newsman has no First Amendment right to protect his sources when called before a grand jury. The Court thus invites state and federal authorities to undermine the historic independence of the press by attempting to annex the journalistic profession as an investigative arm of government. Not only will this decision impair performance of the press' constitutionally protected functions, but it will, I am convinced, in the long run harm rather than help the administration of justice.

I respectfully dissent.

Aftermath of Branzburg *v.* Hayes

Following *Branzburg,* over half the states enacted or revised journalists' "shield" laws in which reporters are given qualified protection from testifying in criminal proceedings. Indicative of the inability of the Court to arrive at a satisfactory solution of the problem is a New Jersey case, *In Re Farber* (1978) in which the dilemma was never resolved. M. A. Farber published a series of stories in *The New York Times* that led to a murder indictment and trial of Dr. Mario E. Jascalevich who was alleged to have brought about the deaths of several of his patients by administering the drug curare. A New Jersey court ordered Farber to produce confidential documents which he refused to do, with the *Times'* support. Farber spent 40 days in jail for contempt; the *Times* was fined $100,000. Although the documents were never produced, Governor Brendan Byrne of New Jersey pardoned both the newspaper and Farber in 1982. What may be needed is a national shield law for the federal courts that would serve as a standard and bring some order out of the mishmash of various state laws. So far none has been forthcoming.

Miller v. *California*
413 U.S. 15 (1973)

Commentators on the law of obscenity have referred to it as an "intractable problem," a "quagmire" and a "constitutional disaster area," primarily because the justices have had such difficulty in agreeing upon a definition and standards that could be applied with some semblance of consistency. Historically, the Supreme Court's treatment of the obscenity issue can be divided into three periods: (1) from 1842, when Congress passed a tariff act that included a section barring the importation of indecent and obscene prints, paintings, lithographs, and engravings, to 1957 when the Court decided the *Roth* case; (2) from 1957 to 1973 with the decision in *Miller* v. *California;* (3) from 1973 to the present.

During the early period the Supreme Court initially adopted the "Hicklin rule" which grew out of the 1868 English case of *Queen* v. *Hicklin* and defined obscenity as that which has a tendency to deprave and corrupt those "whose minds are open to such immoral influences, and into whose hands a publication of this sort may fall." In 1886 the Court decided two cases that set the standards for obscenity which remained in place, although they were somewhat eroded in the 1930s, until 1957. In one, *Rosen* v. *United States,* Lew Rosen's conviction under the Comstock Act of 1873 for sending "indecent" pictures of females through the U.S. mails was upheld with reliance on *Hicklin.* In the second, *Swearingen* v. *United States,* the Court overturned the conviction of Dan Swearingen who had mailed a newspaper containing scurrilous material that portrayed a person as a "red headed mental and physical bastard" who would "sell a mother's honor with less hesitancy and for much less silver than Judas betrayed the Savior, and who would pimp and fatten on a sister's shame with as much unction as a buzzard gluts in carrion." According to the Court, obscenity did not embrace words that are simply coarse and vulgar. The rule of the latter case remains unchanged today, but the *Hicklin* rule applied in *Rosen* no longer obtains.

In 1957 the Court combined two cases, *Roth* v. *United States* and *Alberts* v. *California,* into a single opinion. It should be noted that the federal government

attempts to deal with obscenity by prohibiting material from the mails and by excluding it from entry into the country under tariff and customs legislation. On the other hand the states may outlaw whatever they deem obscene under their broad powers to protect public morality. In combining *Roth* and *Alberts* the Court fashioned a rule that would apply to both federal and state jurisdictions. Samuel Roth, a New York bookseller, had been convicted for mailing obscene circulars in violation of the federal Comstock Act. David Alberts had run afoul of a California statute prohibiting the sale of obscene books. In upholding the convictions of both men, the Court ruled that laws against obscenity were constitutional, that obscenity was not essential to the "exposition of ideas" and thus not protected by the First Amendment. But what precisely was obscenity? As stated in the Court's opinion by Justice William Brennan, something is obscene if "to the average person applying contemporary community standards, the dominant theme of the material taken as a whole appeals to prurient interest."

Unfortunately, this definition lacked precision, so much so in fact, that the gates were wide open for a veritable flood of litigation. In attempting to comply with *Roth* while still outlawing the display and distribution of obscene material, state and local governments inevitably encountered the problem of including protected speech within the statutory language, thus placing the issue once again in the hands of the justices. In the 16 years between *Roth* and *Miller* the issue was in disarray as the Court frequently handed down split-plurality decisions in which not even a majority consensus could be reached. Adding to the confusion were new precepts, not agreed upon by a majority but used nevertheless by the opinion writer, to overturn convictions under local laws. In *Manuel Enterprises* v. *Day* (1962) it was held that in order to be obscene, material must be "patently offensive" as well as to appeal to the prurient interest. In *Jacobellis* v. *Ohio* (1964) and *"Memoirs"* v. *Massachusetts* (1966), otherwise known as the *Fanny Hill Case*, material that appeals to the prurient interest and is patently offensive is still not obscene unless it is *utterly* without redeeming social importance or contains some literary and social value. From 1967, when the Court reversed the convictions of a newsstand dealer and two other persons on the basis of the then rather tattered *Roth* standard (*Redrup* v. *New York*), to 1973 when it decided the *Miller* case, 35 more convictions were overturned with simple *per curiam* opinions. Although *Miller* did shore up the obscenity rules, the opinion had the support of a bare majority of five justices.

Marvin Miller had been convicted by a California jury under the state's obscenity statute for disseminating advertising brochures containing explicit sexual illustrations. At the trial the judge had instructed the jury to evaluate the materials in accordance with state rather than national standards. After the California appellate courts sustained Miller's conviction he appealed to the Supreme Court.

Mr. Chief Justice **Burger** delivered the opinion of the Court.

.   .   .

This case involves the application of a State's criminal obscenity statute to a situation in which sexually explicit materials have been thrust by aggressive sales action upon unwilling recipients who had in no way indicated any desire to receive such materials. This Court has recognized that the States have a legitimate interest in prohibiting dissemination or exhibition of obscene material when the mode of dis-semination carries with it a significant danger of offending the sensibilities of unwilling recipients or of exposure to juveniles. . . . It is in this context that we are called on to define the standards which must be used to identify obscene material that a State may regulate without infringing on the First Amendment as applicable to the States through the Fourteenth Amendment.

The dissent of Mr. Justice Brennan reviews the background of the obscenity problem, but since the Court now undertakes to formulate standards more concrete than those in the past, it is useful for us to focus on two of the landmark cases in the somewhat tortured history of the Court's obscenity decisions. In Roth v United States, the Court sustained a conviction under a federal statute punishing the mailing of "obscene, lewd, lascivious or filthy . . ." materials. The key to that holding was the Court's rejection of the claim that obscene materials were protected by the First Amendment. Five Justices joined in the opinion stating:

"All ideas having even the slightest redeeming social importance—unorthodox ideas, controversial ideas, even ideas hateful to the prevailing climate of opinion—have the full protection of the [First Amendment] guaranties, unless excludable because they encroach upon the limited area of more important interests. But implicit in the history of the First Amendment is the rejection of obscenity as utterly without redeeming social importance."

Nine years later, in Memoirs v Massachusetts, the Court veered sharply away from the Roth concept and, with only three Justices in the plurality opinion, articulated a new test of obscenity. The plurality held that under the Roth definition

"as elaborated in subsequent cases, three elements must coalesce: it must be established that (a) the dominant theme of the material taken as a whole appeals to a prurient interest in sex; (b) the material is patently offensive because it affronts contemporary community standards relating to the description or representation of sexual matters; and (c) the material is utterly without redeeming social value."

The sharpness of the break with Roth, represented by the third element of the Memoirs test and emphasized by Mr. Justice White's dissent, was further underscored when the Memoirs plurality went on to state:

"The Supreme Judicial Court erred in holding that a book need not be 'unqualifiedly worthless before it can be deemed obscene.' A book cannot be proscribed unless it is found to be *utterly* without redeeming social value."

While Roth presumed "obscenity" to be "utterly without redeeming social importance," Memoirs required that to prove obscenity it must be affirmatively established that the material is *"utterly* without redeeming social value." Thus, even as they repeated the words of Roth, the Memoirs plurality produced a drastically altered test that called on the prosecution to prove a negative, i.e., that the material was *"utterly* without redeeming social value"—a burden virtually impossible to discharge under our criminal standards of proof. Such considerations caused Mr. Justice Harlan to wonder if the *"utterly* without redeeming social value" test had any meaning at all.

Apart from the initial formulation in the Roth case, no majority of the Court has at any given time been able to agree on a standard to determine what constitutes obscene, pornographic material subject to regulation under the States' police power. We have seen "a variety of views among the members of the Court unmatched in any other course of constitutional adjudication." This is not remarkable, for in the area of freedom of speech and press the courts must always remain sensitive to any infringement of genuinely serious, literary, artistic, political or scientific expression. This is an area in which there are few eternal verities.

The case we now review was tried on the theory that the California Penal Code § 311 approximately incorporates the three-stage Memoirs test. But now the Memoirs test has been abandoned as unworkable by its author, and no Member of the Court today supports the Memoirs formulation. . . .

This much has been categorically settled by the Court, that obscene material is unprotected by the First Amendment. We acknowledge, however, the inherent dangers of undertaking to regulate any form of expression. State statutes designed to regulate obscene materials must be carefully limited. As a result, we now confine the permissible scope of such regulation to works which depict or describe sexual conduct. That conduct must be specifically defined by the applicable state law, as written or authoritatively construed. A state offense must also be limited to works which, taken as a whole, appeal to the prurient interest in sex, which portray sexual conduct in a patently offensive way, and which, taken as a whole, do not have serious literary, artistic, political, or scientific value.

The basic guidelines for the trier of fact must be: (a) whether "the average person, applying contemporary community standards" would find that the work, taken as a whole, appeals to the prurient interest, (b) whether the work depicts or describes, in a patently offensive way, sexual conduct specifically defined by the applicable state law; and (c) whether the work, taken as a whole, lacks serious literary, artistic, political, or scientific value. We do not adopt as a constitutional standard the *"utterly* without redeeming social value" test of Memoirs v Massachusetts, that concept has never commanded the adherence of more than three Justices at one time. If a state law that regulates obscene material is thus limited, as written or construed, the First Amendment values applicable to the States through the Fourteenth Amendment are adequately protected by the ultimate power of appellate courts to conduct an independent review of constitutional claims when necessary.

We emphasize that it is not our function to propose regulatory schemes for the States. That must await their concrete legislative efforts. It is possible, however, to give a few plain examples of what a state statute could define for regulation under part (b) of the standard announced in this opinion, supra:

(a) Patently offensive representations or descriptions of ultimate sexual acts, normal or perverted, actual or simulated.

(b) Patently offensive representations or descriptions of masturbation, excretory functions, and lewd exhibition of the genitals.

Sex and nudity may not be exploited without limit by films or pictures exhibited or sold in places of public accommodation any more than live sex and nudity can be exhibited or sold without limit in such public places. At a minimum, prurient, patently offensive depiction or description of sexual conduct must have serious literary, artistic, political, or scientific value to merit First Amendment protection. For example, medical books for the education of physicians and related personnel necessarily use graphic illustrations and descriptions of human anatomy. In resolving the inevitably sensitive questions of fact and law, we must continue to rely on the jury system, accompanied by the safeguards that judges, rules of evidence, presumption of innocence, and other protective features provide, as we do with rape, murder, and a host of other offenses against society and its individual members.

Mr. Justice Brennan, author of the opinions of the Court, or the plurality opinions, in Roth v United States, Jacobellis v Ohio, Ginzburg v United States, Mishkin v New York, and Memoirs v Massachusetts, has abandoned his former position and now maintains that no formulation of this Court, the Congress, or the States can adequately distinguish obscene material unprotected by the First Amendment from protected expression. Paradoxically, Mr. Justice Brennan indicates that suppression of unprotected obscene material is permissible to avoid exposure to unconsenting adults, as in this case, and to juveniles, although he gives no indication of how the division between protected and nonprotected materials may be drawn with greater precision for these purposes than for regulation of commercial exposure to consenting adults only. Nor does he indicate where in the Constitution he finds the authority to distinguish between a willing "adult" one month past the state law age of majority and a willing "juvenile" one month younger.

Under the holdings announced today, no one will be subject to prosecution for the sale or exposure of obscene materials unless these materials depict or describe patently offensive "hard core" sexual conduct specifically defined by the regulating state law, as written or construed. We are satisfied that these specific prerequisites will provide fair notice to a dealer in such materials that his public and commercial activities may bring prosecution. If the inability to define regulated materials with ultimate, godlike precision altogether removes the power of the States or the Congress to regulate, then "hard core" pornography may be exposed without limit to the juvenile, the passerby, and the consenting adult alike, as, indeed, Mr. Justice Douglas contends. . . .

Mr. Justice Brennan also emphasizes "institutional stress" in justification of his change of view. Noting that "[t]he number of obscenity cases on our docket gives ample testimony to the burden that has been placed upon this

Court," he quite rightly remarks that the examination of contested materials "is hardly a source of edification to the members of this Court." He also notes, and we agree, that "uncertainty of the standards creates a continuing source of tension between state and federal courts. . . ." "The problem is . . . that one cannot say with certainty that material is obscene until at least five members of this Court, applying inevitably obscure standards, have pronounced it so."

It is certainly true that the absence, since Roth, of a single majority view of this Court as to proper standards for testing obscenity has placed a strain on both state and federal courts. But today, for the first time since Roth was decided in 1957, a majority of this Court has agreed on concrete guidelines to isolate "hard core" pornography from expression protected by the First Amendment. Now we may abandon the casual practice of Redrup v New York, and attempt to provide positive guidance to federal and state courts alike.

This may not be an easy road, free from difficulty. But no amount of "fatigue" should lead us to adopt a convenient "institutional" rationale—an absolutist, "anything goes" view of the First Amendment—because it will lighten our burdens. "Such an abnegation of judicial supervision in this field would be inconsistent with our duty to uphold the constitutional guarantees." Nor should we remedy "tension between state and federal courts" by arbitrarily depriving the States of a power reserved to them under the Constitution, a power which they have enjoyed and exercised continuously from before the adoption of the First Amendment to this day. . . .

Under a national Constitution, fundamental First Amendment limitations on the powers of the States do not vary from community to community, but this does not mean that there are, or should or can be, fixed, uniform national standards of precisely what appeals to the "prurient interest" or is "patently offensive." These are essentially questions of fact, and our nation is simply too big and too diverse for this Court to reasonably expect that such standards could be articulated for all 50 States in a single formulation, even assuming the prerequisite

consensus exists. When triers of fact are asked to decide whether "the average person, applying contemporary community standards" would consider certain materials "prurient," it would be unrealistic to require that the answer be based on some abstract formulation. The adversary system, with lay jurors as the usual ultimate factfinders in criminal prosecutions, has historically permitted triers of fact to draw on the standards of their community, guided always by limiting instructions on the law. To require a State to structure obscenity proceedings around evidence of a *national* "community standard" would be an exercise in futility.

As noted before, this case was tried on the theory that the California obscenity statute sought to incorporate the tripartite test of Memoirs. This, a "national" standard of First Amendment protection enumerated by a plurality of this Court, was correctly regarded at the time of trial as limiting state prosecution under the controlling case law. The jury, however, was explicitly instructed that, in determining whether the "dominant theme of the material as a whole . . . appeals to the prurient interest" and in determining whether the material "goes substantially beyond customary limits of candor and affronts contemporary community standards of decency," it was to apply "contemporary community standards of the State of California."

During the trial, both the prosecution and the defense assumed that the relevant "community standards" in making the factual determination of obscenity were those of the State of California, not some hypothetical standard of the entire United States of America. Defense counsel at trial never objected to the testimony of the State's expert on community standards or to the instructions of the trial judge on "statewide" standards. On appeal to the Appellate Department, Superior Court of California, County of Orange, appellant for the first time contended that application of state, rather than national, standards violated the First and Fourteenth Amendments.

We conclude that neither the State's alleged failure to offer evidence of "national standards," nor the trial court's charge that the jury consider state community standards, were constitutional errors. Nothing in the First Amendment requires that a jury must consider hypothetical and unascertainable "national standards" when attempting to determine whether certain materials are obscene as a matter of fact. . . .

It is neither realistic nor constitutionally sound to read the First Amendment as requiring that the people of Maine or Mississippi accept public depiction of conduct found tolerable in Las Vegas, or New York City. . . . People in different States vary in their tastes and attitudes, and this diversity is not to be strangled by the absolutism of imposed uniformity. As the Court made clear in Mishkin v New York the primary concern with requiring a jury to apply the standard of "the average person, applying contemporary community standards" is to be certain that, so far as material is not aimed at a deviant group, it will be judged by its impact on an average person, rather than a particularly susceptible or sensitive person—or indeed a totally insensitive one. We hold that the requirement that the jury evaluate the materials with reference to "contemporary standards of the State of California" serves this protective purpose and is constitutionally adequate.

. . .

The dissenting Justices sound the alarm of repression. But, in our view, to equate the free and robust exchange of ideas and political debate with commercial exploitation of obscene material demeans the grand conception of the First Amendment and its high purposes in the historic struggle for freedom. It is a "misuse of the great guarantees of free speech and free press. . . ." The First Amendment protects works which, taken as a whole, have serious literary, artistic, political, or scientific value, regardless of whether the government or a majority of the people approve of the ideas these works represent. "The protection given speech and press was fashioned to assure unfettered interchange of *ideas* for the bringing about of political and social changes desired by the people." But the public portrayal of hard core sexual conduct for its own sake, and for the ensuing commercial gain, is a different matter.

There is no evidence, empirical or historical,

that the stern 19th century American censorship of public distribution and display of material relating to sex, in any way limited or affected expression of serious literary, artistic, political, or scientific ideas. On the contrary, it is beyond any question that the era following Thomas Jefferson to Theodore Roosevelt was an "extraordinarily vigorous period," not just in economics and politics, but in belles lettres and in "the outlying fields of social and political philosophies." We do not see the harsh hand of censorship of ideas—good or bad, sound or unsound—and "repression" of political liberty lurking in every state regulation of commercial exploitation of human interest in sex.

Mr. Justice Brennan finds "it is hard to see how state-ordered regimentation of our minds can ever be forestalled." These doleful anticipations assume that courts cannot distinguish commerce in ideas, protected by the First Amendment, from commercial exploitation of obscene material. Moreover, state regulation of hard core pornography so as to make it unavailable to nonadults, a regulation which Mr. Justice Brennan finds constitutionally permissible, has all the elements of "censorship" for adults; indeed even more rigid enforcement techniques may be called for with such dichotomy of regulation. One can concede that the "sexual revolution" of recent years may have had useful byproducts in striking layers of prudery from a subject long irrationally kept from needed ventilation. But it does not follow that no regulation of patently offensive "hard core" materials is needed or permissible; civilized people do not allow unregulated access to heroin because it is a derivative of medicinal morphine.

In sum, we (a) reaffirm the Roth holding that obscene material is not protected by the First Amendment; (b) hold that such material can be regulated by the States, subject to the specific safeguards enunciated above without a showing that the material is "*utterly* without redeeming social value"; and (c) hold that obscenity is to be determined by applying "contemporary community standards," not "national standards." . . .

Vacated and remanded.

Aftermath of Miller *v.* California

How does the *Miller* test differ from that of *Roth* and its progeny? All the elements of the earlier case law are present: the material taken as a whole, the average person, contemporary community standards, the prurient interest, patent offensiveness, lack of redeeming social value. However, there are two major alterations in the rule. First, community standards are redefined in terms of local areas rather than national community, and these may differ markedly from place to place. Second, *social* value is defined more precisely as "serious literary, artistic, political or scientific value." Within the framework of the modified standards, state and local governments have been able to deal more effectively with obscenity without abusing First Amendment rights.

On the same day that the Court decided *Miller* it handed down the opinion in *Paris Adult Theater I* v. *Slayton,* a case involving an action to restrain a movie theater from continuing to show an allegedly obscene film. It was the theater's position that since it displayed a sign reading that only consenting adults would be admitted, the showing of the films was constitutionally protected. Not so, said the Court, categorically rejecting that theory and upholding the state's injunction. The Court decided three additional cases in 1973, all upholding state or federal prosecutions for obscenity in some form. In *Kaplan* v. *California,* the proprietor of an "adult" bookstore argued unsuccessfully that only graphic sexual depictions should fall under the legally obscene proscription. Obscenity, said the Court, can manifest itself in written and oral descriptions of conduct as well as in pictorial representations. The second case, *United States* v. *Twelve 200-ft Reels of Super 8-mm Film,* involved a federal law forbidding the importation of sexually explicit materials. Relying on *Stanley* v. *Georgia* (1969), in which the Court held that a person had a privacy right to possess obscene materials in his home, the defendant sought to have the films and photographs returned after they had been confiscated by United States Customs officials. Supporting the government, the Court declared that "*Stanley* does not permit one to go abroad and bring such material into the country for private purposes." Similarly in *United States* v. *Orito,* the Court sustained the application of a federal law prohibiting sexually explicit materials from shipment by common carrier in interstate commerce.

In 1982 the Supreme Court added a new category of unprotected expression, child pornography in which juveniles are employed in the preparation of explicitly sexual materials of a visual nature (*New York* v. *Ferber*). This constraint was needed, declared the Court, in order to safeguard the physical and emotional well-being of minors. Unlike all of the other cases described above there were no dissenting justices in *Ferber* as all agreed that the *Miller* test was not a satisfactory one for dealing with the child pornography problem.

In 1990 in *Osborne* v. *Ohio* the Court went a step further when it made an exception to *Stanley* v. *Georgia* in holding that a state may make it a crime to possess pornographic photographs of children. In a 6–3 ruling upholding an Ohio law similar to those in 18 states, Justice Byron White, speaking for the majority, distinguished the law from that upheld in *Stanley,* arguing that in the Georgia case the state "sought to proscribe the private possession of obscenity because it was concerned that obscenity would poison the minds of its viewers," a paternalistic motive that was impermissible under the First Amendment. By contrast the purpose of the Ohio law was to "protect the victims of child pornography," that is, to destroy a market used to exploit children.

For the minority Justice Brennan argued that the majority was so "disquieted by the possible exploitation of children" that it would tolerate criminal penalties for simple possession of materials. This, he believed, was an improper "balance between the First Amendment and the state's interests." Justice White and his colleagues in the majority, of course, believed otherwise.

Cohen v. *California*

403 U.S. 15 (1971)

Profane or offensive language does not automatically fall into the category of proscribed speech but depends upon the time, place, and manner of its use. Under the common law prior to the adoption of the First Amendment, if speech provoked others to anger, the perpetrator might be punished. In spite of some vacillation, the Supreme Court has in recent years tended to permit a fairly broad range of protection for provocative and abusive language. Cases decided in the 1940s and early 1950s concluded that offensive language addressed to persons in such a way as to incite violence or create a clear and present danger of violence was not protected by the First Amendment. In the landmark case of *Chaplinsky* v. *New Hampshire* (1944) the Court enunciated the "fighting words" doctrine, words "which by their very utterance (1) inflict injury or (2) tend to incite an immediate breach of the peace" and "are of such slight social value as a step to truth that any benefit that may be derived from them is clearly outweighed by the social interest in order and morality." It was not until the 1970s that the Court dealt with a series of "four-letter" words cases in which the *Chaplinsky* doctrine was severely narrowed and words with "slight social value," even though provocative, were given constitutional protection.

Paul Robert Cohen attended a meeting with friends on April 25, 1968, to discuss strategy for demonstrating public opposition to the Vietnam war. During the evening someone wrote the words "Fuck the Draft," "Stop War" and drew a peace symbol on Cohen's jacket. On the following day he wore the jacket in the corridors of the Los Angeles County courthouse where he had gone to observe the proceedings. Cohen said nothing nor did he create a disturbance or make threats, but the words he wore were in plain view as he stood in a courthouse hall. He was arrested, convicted, and sentenced to 30 days in jail for violating a California law prohibiting "maliciously or willfully" disturbing the peace by offensive conduct. His conviction was upheld by the California appellate courts and Cohen appealed to the Supreme Court. His case had the financial and legal support of the Southern California affiliate of the American Civil Liberties Union.

JOHN MARSHALL HARLAN II

Appointed by President Dwight Eisenhower in 1955, John Marshall Harlan, the grandson and namesake of a famous Court justice, served on the Court until 1971. A strong believer in judicial restraint, Harlan became an outspoken dissenter on the Warren Court from decisions altering the constitutional norms in free speech, criminal procedure, and legislative reapportionment cases. He was respected as a judge of great intellect and integrity whose concern with precedent and institutional legitimacy provided a healthy balance to the judicial inventiveness of the Warren Court.

Mr. Justice **Harlan** delivered the opinion of the Court.

This case may seem at first blush too inconsequential to find its way into our books, but the issue it presents is of no small constitutional significance.

. . .

I

In order to lay hands on the precise issue which this case involves, it is useful first to canvass various matters which this record does not present.

The conviction quite clearly rests upon the asserted offensiveness of the *words* Cohen used to convey his message to the public. The only "conduct" which the State sought to punish is the fact of communication. Thus, we deal here with a conviction resting solely upon "speech," not upon any separately identifiable conduct which allegedly was intended by Cohen to be perceived by others as expressive of particular views but which, on its face, does not necessarily convey any message and hence arguably could be regulated without effectively repressing Cohen's ability to express himself. Further, the State certainly lacks power to punish Cohen for the underlying content of the message the inscription conveyed. At least so long as there is no showing of an intent to incite disobedience to or disruption of the draft, Cohen could not, con-

sistently with the First and Fourteenth Amendments, be punished for asserting the evident position on the inutility or immorality of the draft his jacket reflected.

Appellant's conviction, then, rests squarely upon his exercise of the "freedom of speech" protected from arbitrary governmental interference by the Constitution and can be justified, if at all, only a as valid regulation of the manner in which he exercised that freedom, not as a permissible prohibition on the substantive message it conveys. This does not end the inquiry, of course, for the First and Fourteenth Amendments have never been thought to give absolute protection to every individual to speak whenever or wherever he pleases, or to use any form of address in any circumstances that he chooses. In this vein, too, however, we think it important to note that several issues typically associated with such problems are not presented here.

In the first place, Cohen was tried under a statute applicable throughout the entire State. Any attempt to support this conviction on the ground that the statute seeks to preserve an appropriately decorous atmosphere in the courthouse where Cohen was arrested must fail in the absence of any language in the statute that would have put appellant on notice that certain kinds of otherwise permissible speech or conduct would nevertheless, under California law, not be tolerated in certain places. No fair reading of the phrase "offensive conduct" can be said sufficiently to inform the ordinary person that distinctions between certain locations are thereby created.

In the second place, as it comes to us, this case cannot be said to fall within those relatively few categories of instances where prior decisions have established the power of government to deal more comprehensively with certain forms of individual expression simply upon a showing that such a form was employed. This is not, for example, an obscenity case. Whatever else may be necessary to give rise to the States' broader power to prohibit obscene expression, such expression must be, in some significant way, erotic. It cannot plausibly be maintained that this vulgar allusion to the Selective Service System would conjure up such psychic stimulation in anyone likely to be confronted with Cohen's crudely defaced jacket.

This Court has also held that the States are free to ban the simple use, without a demonstration of additional justifying circumstances, of so-called "fighting words," those personally abusive epithets which, when addressed to the ordinary citizen, are, as a matter of common knowledge, inherently likely to provoke violent reaction. While the four-letter word displayed by Cohen in relation to the draft is not uncommonly employed in a personally provocative fashion, in this instance it was clearly not "directed to the person of the hearer." No individual actually or likely to be present could reasonably have regarded the words on appellant's jacket as a direct personal insult. Nor do we have here an instance of the exercise of the State's police power to prevent a speaker from intentionally provoking a given group to hostile reaction. There is, as noted above, no showing that anyone who saw Cohen was in fact violently aroused or that appellant intended such a result.

Finally, in arguments before this Court much has been made of the claim that Cohen's distasteful mode of expression was thrust upon unwilling or unsuspecting viewers, and that the State might therefore legitimately act as it did in order to protect the sensitive from otherwise unavoidable exposure to appellant's crude form of protest. Of course, the mere presumed presence of unwitting listeners or viewers does not serve automatically to justify curtailing all speech capable of giving offense. While this Court has recognized that government may properly act in many situations to prohibit intrusion into the privacy of the home of unwelcome views and ideas which cannot be totally banned from the public dialogue, we have at the same time consistently stressed that "we are often 'captives' outside the sanctuary of the home and subject to objectionable speech." The ability of government, consonant with the Constitution, to shut off discourse solely to protect others from hearing it is, in other words, dependent upon a showing that substantial privacy interests are being invaded in an essentially intolerable manner. Any broader view of this authority would effectively empower a majority to silence dissidents simply as a matter of personal predilections.

In this regard, persons confronted with Cohen's jacket were in a quite different posture than, say, those subjected to the raucous emissions of sound trucks blaring outside their residences. Those in the Los Angeles courthouse could effectively avoid further bombardment of their sensibilities simply by averting their eyes. And, while it may be that one has a more substantial claim to a recognizable privacy interest when walking through a courthouse corridor than, for example, strolling through Central Park, surely it is nothing like the interest in being free from unwanted expression in the confines of one's own home. Given the subtlety and complexity of the factors involved, if Cohen's "speech" was otherwise entitled to constitutional protection, we do not think the fact that some unwilling "listeners" in a public building may have been briefly exposed to it can serve to justify this breach of the peace conviction where, as here, there was no evidence that persons powerless to avoid appellant's conduct did in fact object to it, and where that portion of the statute upon which Cohen's conviction rests evinces no concern, either on its face or as construed by the California courts, with the special plight of the captive auditor, but, instead, indiscriminately sweeps within its prohibitions all "offensive conduct" that disturbs "any neighborhood or person."

II

Against this background, the issue flushed by this case stands out in bold relief. It is whether California can excise, as "offensive conduct," one particular scurrilous epithet from the public discourse, either upon the theory of the court below that its use is inherently likely to cause violent reaction or upon a more general assertion that the States, acting as guardians of public morality, may properly remove this offensive word from the public vocabulary.

The rationale of the California court is plainly untenable. At most it reflects an "undifferentiated fear or apprehension of disturbance [which] is not enough to overcome the right to freedom of expression." Tinker v Des Moines Indep. Community School Dist. (1969). We have been shown no evidence that substantial numbers of citizens are standing ready to strike out physically at whoever may assault their sensibilities with execrations like that uttered by Cohen. There may be some persons about with such lawless and violent proclivities, but that is an insufficient base upon which to erect, consistently with constitutional values, a governmental power to force persons who wish to ventilate their dissident views into avoiding particular forms of expression. The argument amounts to little more than the self-defeating proposition that to avoid physical censorship of one who has not sought to provoke such a response by a hypothetical coterie of the violent and lawless, the States may more appropriately effectuate that censorship themselves.

Admittedly, it is not so obvious that the First and Fourteenth Amendments must be taken to disable the States from punishing public utterance of this unseemly expletive in order to maintain what they regard as a suitable level of discourse within the body politic. We think, however, that examination and reflection will reveal the shortcomings of a contrary viewpoint.

At the outset, we cannot overemphasize that, in our judgment, most situations where the State has a justifiable interest in regulating speech will fall within one or more of the various established exceptions, discussed above but not applicable here, to the usual rule that governmental bodies may not prescribe the form or content of individual expression. Equally important to our conclusion is the constitutional backdrop against which our decision must be made. The constitutional right of free expression is powerful medicine in a society as diverse and populous as ours. It is designed and intended to remove governmental restraints from the arena of public discussion, putting the decision as to what views shall be voiced largely into the hands of each of us, in the hope that use of such freedom will ultimately produce a more capable citizenry and more perfect polity and in the belief that no other approach would comport with the premise of individual dignity and choice upon which our political system rests.

To many, the immediate consequence of this freedom may often appear to be only verbal tumult, discord, and even offensive utterance. These are, however, within established limits, in truth necessary side effects of the broader enduring values which the process of open debate permits us to achieve. That the air may at times seem filled with verbal cacophony is, in this sense not a sign of weakness but of strength. We cannot lose sight of the fact that, in what otherwise might seem a trifling and annoying instance of individual distasteful abuse of a privilege, these fundamental societal values are truly implicated. That is why "[w]holly neutral futilities . . . come under the protection of free speech as fully as do Keats' poems or Donne's sermons," and why "so long as the means are peaceful, the communication need not meet standards of acceptability."

Against this perception of the constitutional policies involved, we discern certain more particularized considerations that peculiarly call for reversal of this conviction. First, the principle contended for by the State seems inherently boundless. How is one to distinguish this from any other offensive word? Surely the State has no right to cleanse public debate to the point where it is grammatically palatable to the most squeamish among us. Yet no readily ascertainable general principle exists for stopping short of that result were we to affirm the judgment below. For, while the particular four-letter word being litigated here is perhaps more distasteful than most others of its genre, it is nevertheless often true that one man's vulgarity is another's lyric. Indeed we think it is largely because governmental officials cannot make principled distinctions in this area that the Constitution leaves matters of taste and style so largely to the individual.

Additionally, we cannot overlook the fact, because it is well illustrated by the episode involved here, that much linguistic expression serves a dual communicative function: it conveys not only ideas capable of relatively precise, detached explication but otherwise inexpressible emotions as well. In fact, words are often chosen as much for their emotive as their cognitive force. We cannot sanction the view that the Constitution, while solicitous of the cognitive content of individual speech, has little or no regard for that emotive function which, practically speaking, may often be the more important element of the overall message sought to be communicated. Indeed, as Mr. Justice Frankfurter has said, "[o]ne of the prerogatives of American citizenship is the right to criticize public men and measures—and that means not only informed and responsible criticism but the freedom to speak foolishly and without moderation."

Finally, and in the same vein, we cannot indulge the facile assumption that one can forbid particular words without also running a substantial risk of suppressing ideas in the process. Indeed, governments might soon seize upon the censorship of particular words as a convenient guise for banning the expression of unpopular views. We have been able, as noted above, to discern little social benefit that might result from running the risk of opening the door to such grave results.

It is, in sum, our judgment that, absent a more particularized and compelling reason for its actions, the State may not, consistently with the First and Fourteenth Amendments, make the simple public display here involved of this single four-letter expletive a criminal offense. Because that is the only arguably sustainable rationale for the conviction here at issue, the judgment below must be

Reversed.

Mr. Justice **Blackmun,** with whom The **Chief Justice** and Mr. Justice **Black** join.

. . . Cohen's absurd and immature antic, in my view, was mainly conduct and little speech. The California Court of Appeal appears so to have described it, and I cannot characterize it otherwise. Further, the case appears to me to be well within the sphere of Chaplinsky v New Hampshire, where Mr. Justice Murphy, a known champion of First Amendment freedoms, wrote for a unanimous bench. As a consequence, this Court's agonizing over First Amendment values seems misplaced and unnecessary.

Aftermath of Cohen v. California

In a series of cases since *Cohen* the Supreme Court has overturned numerous convictions based on the use of offensive language. In 1972 *Gooding* v. *Wilson* grew out of an attempt to stop the process of military recruiting by blocking the entrance to a building in Atlanta. Johnny C. Wilson said to a police officer, "White son of a bitch, I'll kill you" and to another, "You son of a bitch, if you ever put your hands on me again, I'll cut you all to pieces." Wilson was arrested, tried, and convicted under a Georgia statute making it a misdemeanor to use "opprobrious words or abusive language, tending to cause a breach of the peace." Overturning Wilson's conviction, the Court emphasized that "opprobrious words" and "abusive language" must be narrowly defined to avoid the suppression of speech and that the "fighting words" doctrine of *Chaplinsky* was not all-encompassing but was limited to language that had a tendency to cause violence by the person to whom the remark is addressed.

In 1973 the Court reversed three convictions based on the use of offensive language. In *Plummer* v. *Columbus* it struck down a city ordinance outlawing the abuse of another person by "menacing, insulting, slanderous or profane language" when it reversed the conviction of a cab driver who was found to have directed a series of "vulgar, suggestive and abhorrent" sexually oriented statements to a female passenger. Although admitting that such language could be construed as "fighting words," the ordinance could not support a conviction since its overbroad language could be applied to protected expression and was therefore facially unconstitutional. Similarly broad and thus invalid was a Cincinnati ordinance that prohibited behaving in a "noisy, boisterous, rude, insulting or other disorderly manner with intent to annoy or abuse another" (*Norwell* v. *Cincinnati*).

A third case turned not on the application of a vaguely worded ordinance or statute but on action by a state university. Barbara Susan Papish, a student at the University of Missouri, was a member of the staff of a newspaper called the *Free Press Underground* that had distributed an issue on the campus containing (1) a political cartoon depicting policemen raping the Statue of Liberty and the Goddess of Justice; and (2) an article entitled "Motherfucker Acquitted," a reprint from another newspaper which discussed the trial and acquittal of the leader of an organization called "Up Against the Wall, Motherfucker," also known as "The Motherfuckers." As a consequence of distributing the issue containing this material, Barbara Papish was expelled from the university for violating a rule prohibiting "indecent conduct or speech." In ordering the district court to reinstate Papish the Supreme Court ruled that both the cartoon and the article were constitutionally protected speech.

In all of the cases discussed, dissenting justices have argued that protecting vulgar speech contributes nothing to the exchange of ideas, but simply lowers the tone of intellectual discourse and offends the sensibilities of individuals specifically addressed as well as those innocently subjected to it. However, Court majorities have continued to hold that the First Amendment does not permit governments to distinguish between worthwhile and worthless speech. Only when speech is an explicit incitement to unlawful conduct does it lose its constitutional protection.

6 Freedom of Religion

R eligion was apparently not much on the minds of the delegates who gathered at the Philadelphia Convention in 1787. The framers met for 4 months without once reciting public prayers (despite Benjamin Franklin's suggestion at a tense moment in the proceedings that they do so) and produced a document that made no reference to God and only one to religion—the prohibition in Article VI of any religious test for public office. Despite the framers' lack of attention to the subject, questions about the relationship of the new national government to the various churches, and to religion in general, soon became part of the postratification agitation for a Bill of Rights.

When Congress convened in 1789, it voted to include two references to church-state relations in its proposed Bill of Rights. The very first clause of the First Amendment prohibits the Congress from making any "law respecting an establishment of religion." In the parlance of the day, an "establishment of religion" was an arrangement whereby government provided a religious denomination with financial support, a common practice in the American colonies and later in the original states. The next clause of the First Amendment forbids Congress from making any law "prohibiting the free exercise" of religion. At the risk of oversimplification, one might say that the purpose of the establishment clause was to prevent government from being controlled by religion, while the free exercise clause was intended to protect religion from being dominated by government.

The key figure in drafting the religion clauses, and indeed the entire Bill of Rights, was James Madison. Like many of the framers, Madison was a Deist, more committed to the Enlightenment notion of "nature's God" than to the "personal God" of the mainstream churches of the day. Uncomfortable with organized religion and formal worship, Madison strongly opposed mixing religious rituals and public affairs. He believed that conferring official favor on any religion would undermine the principles upon which the new republic had been founded, including its core value, the sovereignty of the individual. While Madison felt that the Constitution as originally drafted would not permit any such action, if there was to be a Bill of Rights he wanted it to contain a provision explicitly denying Congress the power to legislate on religious matters. At the same time, Madison's belief in natural rights compelled him to propose that the Constitution safeguard what he first called the "rights of conscience," a phrase that underwent a series of stylistic changes before emerging as the free exercise clause of the First Amendment.

Madison was no stranger to debates about the proper relationship between government and religion. The establishment and free exercise clauses were a distillation of the ideas in his famous essay, "Memorial and Remonstrance Against Religious Assessments" in which he argued against a proposal introduced in 1785 in the Virginia legislature to support "teachers of the Christian religion" through a general tax assessment. There he contended that religion was a private, voluntary affair that ought to be completely independent of government. Madison's arguments helped defeat the general assessment bill and pave the way for passage of Jefferson's "Virginia Statute of Religious Freedom" which contained both of the principles soon to be embodied in the First Amendment—freedom *of* and freedom *from* religion.

There were also pragmatic concerns underlying adoption of the religion clauses, mainly about the religious strife that might result from too close a connection between government and religion in the new nation. American colonial history had been plagued by sectarian conflicts, but as the eighteenth century progressed, the homogeneous and often intolerant religious groups that had founded the colonies were absorbed into more pluralistic communities where dissenters and the unchurched sometimes outnumbered members of the nominally established religion. At the time the Constitution was ratified, the states which still retained established churches were under increasing pressure to abandon such arrangements. In an era of growing religious diversity and tolerance, it would have been a long step backward for the new United States government to engage in either sponsorship or suppression of religion. The fledgling nation, faced with severe economic problems and military threats from abroad, could hardly afford the kind of internecine political conflict that might result from either course of action.

In sum, the establishment and free exercise clauses reflected a desire on the part of their authors and ratifiers to define distinct spheres of influence for government and religion. Ironically, the long-term effect of this eighteenth-century effort to separate government and religion by constitutional fiat has been to link them inextricably as subjects of twentieth-century constitutional adjudication.

THE ESTABLISHMENT CLAUSE

Although both sides in the current debate over the proper interpretation of the establishment clause claim to represent what the framers themselves intended the clause to mean, they have come to quite opposite conclusions which we will refer to as the separationist and the accommodationist positions. The two sides agree that the framers intended the establishment clause to prohibit the federal government from creating a national religion. After that, however, the separationists and accommodationists quickly part company. Separationists argue that in addition to banning a state church, Madison and his colleagues wanted to stop Congress from taking any action that would support religion in general. By 1790 the only remaining form of state establishment was one in which citizens were assessed a tax for religion but could choose which church would receive their support. Therefore, according to the separationists, when Madison opposed the establishment of religion he was referring to multiple as well as exclusive establishment. Moreover, by adopting language that banned all "laws *respecting* an establishment of religion" [emphasis added], as opposed to an earlier proposal that merely prohibited "establishing any particular denomination of religion in preference to another," the framers clearly intended to deny the federal government *all* power to act with regard to religion. From this the separationists conclude that in the establishment clause the framers intended to erect, in Jefferson's famous phrase, "a wall of separation between church and state."

The accommodationists reply that their opponents have turned what Jefferson intended as a simple metaphor into a constitutional doctrine. They also note that Jefferson was not present when the Bill of Rights was drafted or debated and that his "wall" reference was written many years after the religion clauses were adopted. Accommodationists acknowledge Madison's key role in the drafting process but claim that the separationists overstate his views. When Madison spoke of banning a national religion, they say, he meant to do just that, but not to require the complete neutrality toward religion that the separationists read into the establishment clause.

Accommodationists point to contemporary evidence that Congress felt free to cooperate with religion in a variety of ways despite the establishment clause. Besides moving straightaway to appoint a legislative chaplain for each House, the First Congress also voted to provide assistance for church schools in the Northwest Territory and to designate Thanksgiving as a national holiday devoted to "public thanksgiving and prayer." In sum, accommodationists assert, the establishment clause was meant to require that government not prefer one religion over others, but not to prohibit other actions that might assist *all* religions.

The separationist-accommodationist debate has played itself out in the Supreme Court over the last 40 years, beginning in 1947 with the seminal establishment clause case of *Everson* v. *Board of Education* in 1947 (see edited case in this chapter). The issue before the Court in *Everson*, as in many of the cases that followed it, was whether a particular form of state financial assistance to sectarian schools (usually Roman Catholic, that being the largest church-run school system in the United States) ran afoul of the establishment clause. In *Everson* Justice Black used separationist reasoning but reached an accommodationist result, holding that by paying bus transportation costs for parochial school students the state of New Jersey did not breach the "wall of separation" that the First Amendment had erected between church and state. In retrospect, we can see in Black's *Everson* opinion the same ambivalent feelings toward the establishment clause that the Court as a whole would display over the next 40 years.

After parochial school aid, which will be discussed shortly, the most important establishment clause issue to come before the Court has been the question of religion in the public schools. In such cases the Court has taken a strong separationist position, citing the potential dangers of coercion and political divisiveness that are present in state-run schools. The Court has found any practice in public schools that favors one religion over others or religion generally over nonreligion to be unconstitutional. Since the 1960s the Court has invalidated school-sponsored prayers and Bible readings (see *Engel* v. *Vitale*, excerpted in this chapter); the posting of the Ten Commandments in public school classrooms; a state-mandated "silent moment" intended to encourage students to pray; and a state law requiring that science teachers who discuss the theory of evolution also present the biblical version of creation.

In reviewing other forms of church-state cooperation outside the public school setting the Supreme Court has taken a decidedly more accommodationist stance. In recent years it has upheld two venerable institutions, legislative chaplains (*Marsh* v. *Chambers*, 1983) and government-sponsored nativity scenes (see *Lynch* v. *Donnelly*, excerpted in this chapter), mainly because in the Court's view they have lost much of their religious significance over the years.

It is more difficult to characterize the Court's performance on parochial school aid because it has zigzagged unpredictably between separationist and accommodationist positions. The landmark case on the subject, *Lemon* v. *Kurtzman*, was decided in 1971 (see case excerpted in this chapter). In *Lemon*, the Court abandoned the "child benefit" approach used to decide earlier parochial aid cases and unveiled a more complicated "three pronged" test that has been used, almost without exception, in establishment clause cases ever since. In applying the *Lemon* test to a law that has been challenged on establishment grounds, the Court has asked these three questions: (1) Does the law have a valid secular purpose? (2) Is the primary effect of the law to either advance or inhibit religion? (3) Does the law promote excessive entanglement between government and religion? The first question must be answered affirmatively and the second and third negatively, for the law to be sustained.

In its mixed bag of case outcomes since 1971 the Court has approved the following forms of parochial school aid;

Federal funds for building secular buildings at church-affiliated colleges and universities

State use of its bonding power to help secure less expensive financing of church-affiliated colleges and universities

Annual state subsidies to nonpublic, including church-affiliated, colleges and universities

State aid to parochial secondary and elementary schools for administering and scoring state-mandated standardized tests and for the costs of required attendance record keeping

State-financed off-premises remedial and therapeutic services provided to parochial school students by public school employees

A state income tax deduction available to the parents of all public and private school children for tuition, textbook, and transportation expenses

During the same period, the Court has declared the following forms of governmental assistance unconstitutional:

State reimbursements to parochial schools for teacher salaries and instructional materials

State-funded salary supplements paid to church school teachers who teach secular subjects

State funding for maintaining and repairing parochial school buildings

State income tax credits and deductions for parents of private school students only

State aid for instructional materials used in parochial school classrooms, even if loaned to students and parents

State-subsidized bus transportation for parochial school field trips

State and federally financed on-premise auxiliary services provided after school to parochial school students

To many observers, the Court's decisions in the parochial school-aid cases have been marked by little clarity or consistency. Some have suggested that the *Lemon* test is insufficiently rigorous and should be discarded. Three members of the Court—Chief Justice Rehnquist and Justices Stevens and Kennedy—have explicitly advocated such a course. Two others—Justices O'Connor and Scalia— have suggested that merely sharpening one or more of *Lemon's* "prongs" would lead to better results. Justice O'Connor wishes the Court to consider whether the purpose and effect of a challenged law is to "endorse or disapprove" (rather than to "advance or inhibit") religion. Both blocs can use the test to achieve their desired results in establishment clause cases as long as they can persuade one or two "moderates" to join them.

In fact, the real reason for the Court's wavering path in establishment clause cases is not the *Lemon* test itself, but rather the failure of either the separationist or the accommodationist positions to win consistent support from a solid majority of the justices. For the last 20 years, the balance of power in establishment cases has been held by two or three unaligned justices who have moved back and forth between the two camps depending upon the particular facts before them. Justice Lewis Powell played such a role until his retirement in 1987; in the dozen or so establishment cases decided during his tenure on the Court, encompassing both separationists and accommodationists, Powell was only once on the losing side. In other words, his decision to join one side or the other would usually determine how the case came out. (Powell played this "swing" role on other issues as well.) In recent years Justice O'Connor has occupied a similar middle position. It is ironic that despite all of the attention given to the competing claims of the separationists and the accommodationists, the establishment clause is being given its definitive meaning by justices who are not convinced that either position is entirely correct.

THE FREE EXERCISE CLAUSE

One striking difference between establishment and free exercise cases is the kind of religious organization that tends to be involved in each. As we have seen above, many establishment clause cases feature large mainstream denominations with enough political influence to persuade Congress or state legislatures to provide them with financial support or other considerations. Free exercise litigants, on the other hand, have usually been relatively small, unconventional sects with few friends in the political arena.

In the typical free exercise case an individual or organization is challenging a law that allegedly either requires them to violate their religious principles, or prohibits them from acting in accordance with those principles. Some such laws have been enacted specifically to preclude certain religious practices—for example, prohibitions against snake handling and animal sacrifices. More often, how-

ever, the laws under challenge have secular purposes and were adopted without
any religious group or exercise in mind. Among the religious organizations' practices that have run afoul of state or federal laws are Jehovah's Witnesses, for their
door-to-door evangelism and their refusal to participate in flag salutes; Seventh-
Day Adventists, for their sabbath observances; Christian Scientists, for their
refusal of medical care; Muslims, for their dietary laws; Orthodox Jews, for their
Saturday worship and required religious apparel; Amish, for their early withdrawal of children from school; and nineteenth-century Mormons, for engaging
in the practice of polygamy.

The first free exercise cases came to the Supreme Court in the 1870s and
1880s, when the First Amendment still applied exclusively to the national government. After the Civil War, Congress had passed legislation forbidding polygamy
in the western territories. The statute was aimed at Mormons who had settled in
the Utah Territory and taken up the practice of plural marriage. A Mormon convicted of violating the law appealed to the Supreme Court arguing that the statute
interfered with his religious freedom. In *Reynolds* v. *United States* (1878) the
Supreme Court distinguished between religious *belief,* which it said the First
Amendment protected absolutely, and religious *conduct,* which could be restricted if it violated "social duties or [was] subversive of good order." The anti-
polygamy law was not unconstitutional, the Court concluded, because Congress
had a legitimate interest in preserving social stability through monogamous
marriage.

The Court used this doctrine, which became known as the secular regulation
rule, until well into the twentieth century. In most cases it led to the dismissal of
free exercise claims since the government had to do nothing more than demonstrate that the law had a "reasonable" purpose behind it. However, in *Cantwell* v.
Connecticut (1940) (see edited opinion in this chapter), the Court retired the
belief-conduct distinction, asserting for the first time that the free exercise clause
protected both. Religious conduct remained "subject to regulation for the protection of society," wrote Justice Owen Roberts for the majority, but henceforth government must take care not "unduly to infringe [on] the protected [religious]
freedom." Under this approach, which the Court has used ever since, free exercise cases are decided by balancing society's interests against the value of religious freedom, with the latter given greater weight because of its status as a constitutionally protected right. Of course, the outcome of a given case depends
upon the priorities which individual justices assign to the competing claims.

When a law is challenged today on free exercise grounds, the government is
required to show that the statute serves a "compelling" state interest that could
not be achieved in a less restrictive manner. The government has usually been
more successful in persuading the Court that a law is sufficiently important than
in demonstrating that it would be rendered ineffective if a religious exception
were allowed. Normally it is difficult for the government to prove that granting a
small number of religious exemptions will undermine a law that applies to thousands or even millions of people. Therefore officials usually try to show that one
religious exemption will open a door through which many other claimants will
attempt to enter, and that the administrative costs of processing such applications will be prohibitive.

Although the challenger's burden of proof is much less than the government's,
the claimant must show that the challenge is based on sincere religious principles, and that those principles will be significantly compromised if he or she is

required to obey the law. However, following the Supreme Court's lead, judges have usually declined to conduct theological or psychological inquiries into applicants' religious beliefs, an exercise that would itself seriously violate the spirit of the First Amendment. Therefore courts generally assume the applicant's sincerity unless there is strong evidence to suggest that he or she "got religion" merely to obtain relief from the law. Similarly, the Court has declined to define precisely what constitutes a religion. In recent years the Court has made it clear that it is the substance of one's religious beliefs rather than membership in a particular church that determines the validity of a free exercise claim.

In seeking to determine how seriously a law interferes with the applicant's religion, the Court has sometimes distinguished between "direct" and "indirect" burdens on free exercise. All things being equal, the Court is less likely to invalidate a law that merely inconveniences a religious practice than one which prohibits it outright. The Court has also distinguished between laws that significantly interfere with religious practices and laws that coerce individuals into violating their religious beliefs. The former are constitutional (assuming they serve compelling governmental interests), but the latter are not. This distinction was prominent in two recent free exercise cases involving Native Americans. In *Bowen* v. *Roy* (1986), the Court heard a challenge to a federal statute requiring the states to use social security numbers in administering certain welfare programs. An applicant for benefits under one of these programs contended that the use of numbers would "rob the spirit" of his daughter, preventing "her from attaining greater spiritual power." In *Lyng* v. *Northwest Indian Cemetery Protective Association* (1988), three Native American tribes sought to block a government plan to build roads in a national forest that had historically been used by them for religious rituals and training. Both challenges failed because in neither case did the Court find evidence that individuals were being forced by government to violate their beliefs.

In the 1960s and 1970s the Court was solidly supportive of free exercise claims (see, for example, *Sherbert* v. *Verner* and *Wisconsin* v. *Yoder*, excerpted in this chapter), and in recent cases the Court has narrowly rejected such claims (see *Goldman* v. *Weinberger* and *Employment Division* v. *Smith*, excerpted in this chapter). The present Court is closely divided in its views. As with the establishment clause cases discussed earlier, the balance of power in free exercise cases rests with the justices who approach the issues without strong commitments to either side. It is worth noting that the three members of the Court who have been the strongest separationists in establishment-clause cases—Justices William Brennan, Thurgood Marshall, and Harry Blackmun—have also been most deferential to applicants for religious exemptions in free exercise cases.

Bibliography

ALLEY, ROBERT S. (ed.). *The Supreme Court on Church and State.* New York: Oxford University Press, 1988.

LEVY, LEONARD W. *The Establishment Clause.* New York: Macmillan, 1986.

MORGAN, RICHARD. *The Supreme Court and Religion.* New York: The Free Press, 1972.

OATS, DALLIN H. (ed.). *The Wall Between Church and State.* Chicago: University of Chicago Press, 1963.

SWANSON, WAYNE. *The Christ Child Goes to Court.* Philadelphia: Temple University Press, 1990.

Everson v. Board of Education

330 U.S. 1 (1947)

Whether the federal or state governments can provide financial assistance to church-related schools without running afoul of the establishment clause was a question of no real constitutional significance until the middle of the twentieth century. During the nineteenth century there was little public support for such assistance; on the contrary, public opinion viewed with suspicion and even hostility the desire of Roman Catholics to establish and maintain their own schools. Such feelings were reflected in the "Blaine Amendments" that were written into a number of state constitutions forbidding the use of public money for any religious purpose. These provisions took their name from Congressman James G. Blaine of Maine, who, in the 1870s, nearly succeeded in adding such a proscription to the text of the First Amendment. By the 1930s, however, political circumstances had changed considerably. Many politicians were now solicitous of the financial well-being of Catholic schools, recognizing that should they be forced to close, the public schools would be hard-pressed to accommodate the influx of parochial school students. In addition, Catholic voters, who wielded considerable political power in a number of states, were beginning to demand some relief from the "double tax" they incurred for choosing to send their children to parochial schools.

Responding to these new facts of political life, New York in 1939 amended its constitution to permit the state to subsidize bus transportation for private school students, as it already did for those attending public schools. Two years later, a law was enacted in neighboring New Jersey permitting school districts to decide for themselves whether to pay the costs of transporting students to private schools. The township of Ewing subsequently voted to reimburse all parents for their children's transportation expenses. A Ewing citizen, Arch Everson, filed a lawsuit contending that the state statute and the school board decision violated the First Amendment's prohibition against laws "respecting an establishment of religion." Among those filing *amicus curiae* briefs supporting New Jersey were the attorneys general of Illinois, Indiana, Louisiana, Massachusetts, Michigan, and New York—all states with similar transportation aid statutes on the books. Everson received support from several organizations active on the separationist side of the church-state question, including the American Civil Liberties Union and the General Conference of Seventh-Day-Adventists.

Mr. Justice **Black** delivered the opinion of the Court.

. . .

. . . The New Jersey statute is challenged as a "law respecting an establishment of religion." The First Amendment, as made applicable to the states by the Fourteenth, commands that a state "shall make no law respecting an establishment of religion, or prohibiting the free exercise thereof. . . ." These words of the First Amendment reflected in the minds of early Americans a vivid mental picture of conditions and practices which they fervently wished to stamp out in order to preserve liberty for themselves and for their posterity. Doubtless their goal has not been entirely reached; but so far has the Nation moved toward it that the expression "law respecting an establishment of religion," probably does not so vividly remind present-day Americans of the evils, fears, and political problems that caused that expression to be written into our Bill of Rights. Whether this New Jersey law is one respecting an "establishment of religion" requires an understanding of the meaning of that language, particularly with respect to the imposition of taxes. Once again, therefore, it is not inappropriate briefly to review the background and environment of the period in which that constitutional language was fashioned and adopted.

A large proportion of the early settlers of this country came here from Europe to escape the bondage of laws which compelled them to support and attend government-favored churches. The centuries immediately before and contemporaneous with the colonization of America had been filled with turmoil, civil strife, and persecutions, generated in large part by established sects determined to maintain their absolute political and religious supremacy. With the power of government supporting them, at various times and places, Catholics had persecuted Protestants, Protestants had persecuted Catholics, Protestant sects had persecuted other Protestant sects, Catholics of one shade of belief had persecuted Catholics of another shade of belief, and all of these had from time to time persecuted Jews. In efforts to force loyalty to whatever religious group happened to be on top and in league with the government of a particular time and place, men and women had been fined, cast in jail, cruelly tortured, and killed. Among the offenses for which these punishments had been inflicted were such things as speaking disrespectfully of the views of ministers of government-established churches, nonattendance at those churches, expressions of nonbelief in their doctrines, and failure to pay taxes and tithes to support them.

These practices of the old world were transplanted to and began to thrive in the soil of the new America. The very charters granted by the English Crown to the individuals and companies designated to make the laws which would control the destinies of the colonials authorized these individuals and companies to erect religious establishments which all, whether believers or non-believers, would be required to support and attend. An exercise of this authority was accompanied by a repetition of many of the old-world practices and persecutions. Catholics found themselves hounded and proscribed because of their faith; Quakers who followed their conscience went to jail; Baptists were peculiarly obnoxious to certain dominant Protestant

sects; men and women of varied faiths who happened to be in a minority in a particular locality were persecuted because they steadfastly persisted in worshipping God only as their own consciences dictated. And all of these dissenters were compelled to pay tithes and taxes to support government-sponsored churches whose ministers preached inflammatory sermons designed to strengthen and consolidate the established faith by generating a burning hatred against dissenters.

These practices became so commonplace as to shock the freedom-loving colonials into a feeling of abhorrence. The imposition of taxes to pay ministers' salaries and to build and maintain churches and church property aroused their indignation. It was these feelings which found expression in the First Amendment. No one locality and no one group throughout the Colonies can rightly be given entire credit for having aroused the sentiment that culminated in adoption of the Bill of Rights' provisions embracing religious liberty. But Virginia, where the established church had achieved a dominant influence in political affairs and where many excesses attracted wide public attention, provided a great stimulus and able leadership for the movement. The people there, as elsewhere, reached the conviction that individual religious liberty could be achieved best under a government which was stripped of all power to tax, to support, or otherwise to assist any or all religions, or to interfere with the beliefs of any religious individual or group.

The movement toward this end reached its dramatic climax in Virginia in 1785–86 when the Virginia legislative body was about to renew Virginia's tax levy for the support of the established church. Thomas Jefferson and James Madison led the fight against this tax. Madison wrote his great Memorial and Remonstrance against the law. In it, he eloquently argued that a true religion did not need the support of law; that no person, either believer or non-believer, should be taxed to support a religious institution of any kind; that the best interest of a society required that the minds of men always be wholly free; and that cruel persecutions were the inevitable result of government-established religions. Madison's Remonstrance received strong support throughout Virginia, and the Assembly postponed consideration of the proposed tax measure until its next session. When the proposal came up for consideration at that session, it not only died in committee, but the Assembly enacted the famous "Virginia Bill for Religious Liberty" originally written by Thomas Jefferson. The preamble to that Bill stated among other things that

"Almighty God hath created the mind free; that all attempts to influence it by temporal punishments or burthens, or by civil incapacitations, tend only to beget habits of hypocrisy and meanness, and are a departure from the plan of the Holy author of our religion, who being Lord both of body and mind, yet chose not to propagate it by coercions on either . . . ; that to compel a man to furnish contributions of money for the propagation of opinions which he disbelieves, is sinful and tyrannical; that even the forcing him to support this or that teacher of his own religious persuasion, is depriving him of the comfortable liberty of giving his contributions to the particular pastor, whose morals he would make his pattern. . . ."

And the statute itself enacted

"That no man shall be compelled to frequent or support any religious worship, place, or ministry whatsoever, nor shall be enforced, restrained, molested, or burthened in his body or goods, nor shall otherwise suffer on account of his religious opinions or belief. . . ."

This Court has previously recognized that the provisions of the First Amendment, in the drafting and adoption of which Madison and Jefferson played such leading roles, had the same objective and were intended to provide the same protection against governmental intrusion on religious liberty as the Virginia statute. Prior to the adoption of the Fourteenth Amendment, the First Amendment did not apply as a restraint against the states. Most of them did soon provide similar constitutional protections for religious liberty. But some states persisted for about half a century in imposing restraints upon the free exercise of religion and in discriminating against particular religious groups. In recent years, so far as the provision against the estab-

lishment of a religion is concerned, the question has most frequently arisen in connection with proposed state aid to church schools and efforts to carry on religious teachings in the public schools in accordance with the tenets of a particular sect. Some churches have either sought or accepted state financial support for their schools. Here again the efforts to obtain state aid or acceptance of it have not been limited to any one particular faith. The state courts, in the main, have remained faithful to the language of their own constitutional provisions designed to protect religious freedom and to separate religions and governments. Their decisions, however, show the difficulty in drawing the line between tax legislation which provides funds for the welfare of the general public and that which is designed to support institutions which teach religion.

The meaning and scope of the First Amendment, preventing establishment of religion or prohibiting the free exercise thereof, in the light of its history and the evils it was designed forever to suppress, have been several times elaborated by the decisions of this Court prior to the application of the First Amendment to the states by the Fourteenth. The broad meaning given the Amendment by these earlier cases has been accepted by this Court in its decisions concerning an individual's religious freedom rendered since the Fourteenth Amendment was interpreted to make the prohibitions of the First applicable to state action abridging religious freedom. There is every reason to give the same application and broad interpretation to the "establishment of religion" clause. The interrelation of these complementary clauses was well summarized in a statement of the Court of Appeals of South Carolina, quoted with approval by this Court in *Watson v. Jones:* "The structure of our government has, for the preservation of civil liberty, rescued the temporal institutions from religious interference. On the other hand, it has secured religious liberty from the invasion of the civil authority."

The "establishment of religion" clause of the First Amendment means at least this: Neither a state nor the Federal Government can set up a church. Neither can pass laws which aid one religion, aid all religions, or prefer one religion over another. Neither can force nor influence a person to go to or to remain away from church against his will or force him to profess a belief or disbelief in any religion. No person can be punished for entertaining or professing religious beliefs or disbeliefs, for church attendance or non-attendance. No tax in any amount, large or small, can be levied to support any religious activities or institutions, whatever they may be called, or whatever form they may adopt to teach or practice religion. Neither a state nor the Federal Government can, openly or secretly, participate in the affairs of any religious organizations or groups and *vice versa*. In the words of Jefferson, the clause against establishment of religion by law was intended to erect "a wall of separation between church and State."

We must consider the New Jersey statute in accordance with the foregoing limitations imposed by the First Amendment. But we must not strike that state statute down if it is within the State's constitutional power even though it approaches the verge of that power. New Jersey cannot consistently with the "establishment of religion" clause of the First Amendment contribute tax-raised funds to the support of an institution which teaches the tenets and faith of any church. On the other hand, other language of the amendment commands that New Jersey cannot hamper its citizens in the free exercise of their own religion. Consequently, it cannot exclude individual Catholics, Lutherans, Mohammedans, Baptists, Jews, Methodists, Non-believers, Presbyterians, or the members of any other faith, *because of their faith, or lack of it*, from receiving the benefits of public welfare legislation. While we do not mean to intimate that a state could not provide transportation only to children attending public schools, we must be careful, in protecting the citizens of New Jersey against state-established churches, to be sure that we do not inadvertently prohibit New Jersey from extending its general state law benefits to all its citizens without regard to their religious belief.

Measured by these standards, we cannot say that the First Amendment prohibits New Jersey from spending tax-raised funds to pay the bus fares of parochial school pupils as a part of a general program under which it pays the fares of pupils attending public and other schools. It is undoubtedly true that children are helped to get to church schools. There is even a possibility that some of the children might not be sent to the church schools if the parents were compelled to pay their children's bus fares out of their own pockets when transportation to a public school would have been paid for by the State. The same possibility exists where the state requires a local transit company to provide reduced fares to school children including those attending parochial schools, or where a municipally owned transportation system undertakes to carry all school children free of charge. Moreover, state-paid policemen, detailed to protect children going to and from church schools from the very real hazards of traffic, would serve much the same purpose and accomplish much the same result as state provisions intended to guarantee free transportation of a kind which the state deems to be best for the school children's welfare. And parents might refuse to risk their children to the serious danger of traffic accidents going to and from parochial schools, the approaches to which were not protected by policemen. Similarly, parents might be reluctant to permit their children to attend schools which the state had cut off from such general government services as ordinary police and fire protection, connections for sewage disposal, public highways and sidewalks. Of course, cutting off church schools from these services, so separate and so indisputably marked off from the religious function, would make it far more difficult for the schools to operate. But such is obviously not the purpose of the First Amendment. That Amendment requires the state to be a neutral in its relations with groups of religious believers and non-believers; it does not require the state to be their adversary. State power is no more to be used so as to handicap religions than it is to favor them.

This Court has said that parents may, in the discharge of their duty under state compulsory education laws, send their children to a religious rather than a public school if the school meets the secular educational requirements which the state has power to impose. It appears that these parochial schools meet New Jersey's requirements. The State contributes no money to the schools. It does not support them. Its legislation, as applied, does no more than provide a general program to help parents get their children, regardless of their religion, safely and expeditiously to and from accredited schools.

The First Amendment has erected a wall between church and state. That wall must be kept high and impregnable. We could not approve the slightest breach. New Jersey has not breached it here.

Mr. Justice **Jackson,** dissenting.

I find myself, contrary to first impressions, unable to join in this decision. I have a sympathy, though it is not ideological, with Catholic citizens who are compelled by law to pay taxes for public schools, and also feel constrained by conscience and discipline to support other schools for their own children. Such relief to them as this case involves is not in itself a serious burden to taxpayers and I had assumed it to be as little serious in principle. Study of this case convinces me otherwise. The Court's opinion marshals every argument in favor of state aid and puts the case in its most favorable light, but much of its reasoning confirms my conclusions that there are no good grounds upon which to support the present legislation. In fact, the undertones of the opinion, advocating complete and uncompromising separation of Church from State, seem utterly discordant with its conclusion yielding support to their commingling in educational matters. The case which irresistibly comes to mind as the most fitting precedent is that of Julia who, according to Byron's reports, "whispering 'I will ne'er consent,'—consented."

The Court sustains this legislation by assuming two deviations from the facts of this particular case; first, it assumes a state of facts the record does not support, and secondly, it refuses to consider facts which are inescapable on the record.

The Court concludes that this "legislation, as applied, does no more than provide a general program to help parents get their children, regardless of their religion, safely and expeditiously to and from accredited schools," and it draws a comparison between "state provisions intended to

guarantee free transportation" for school children with services such as police and fire protection, and implies that we are here dealing with "laws authorizing new types of public services. . . ." This hypothesis permeates the opinion. The facts will not bear that construction.

The Township of Ewing is not furnishing transportation to the children in any form; it is not operating school busses itself or contracting for their operation; and it is not performing any public service of any kind with this taxpayer's money. All school children are left to ride as ordinary paying passengers on the regular busses operated by the public transportation system. What the Township does, and what the taxpayer complains of, is at stated intervals to reimburse parents for the fares paid, provided the children attend either public schools or Catholic Church schools. This expenditure of tax funds has no possible effect on the child's safety or expedition in transit. As passengers on the public busses they travel as fast and no faster, and are as safe and no safer, since their parents are reimbursed as before.

In addition to thus assuming a type of service that does not exist, the Court also insists that we must close our eyes to a discrimination which does exist. The resolution which authorizes disbursement of this taxpayer's money limits reimbursement to those who attend public schools and Catholic schools. That is the way the Act is applied to this taxpayer.

. . .

It is of no importance in this situation whether the beneficiary of this expenditure of tax-raised funds is primarily the parochial school and incidentally the pupil, or whether the aid is directly bestowed on the pupil with indirect benefits to the school. The state cannot maintain a Church and it can no more tax its citizens to furnish free carriage to those who attend a Church. The prohibition against establishment of religion cannot be circumvented by a subsidy, bonus or reimbursement of expense to individuals for receiving religious instruction and indoctrination.

The Court, however, compares this to other subsidies and loans to individuals and says, "Nor does it follow that a law has a private rather than a public purpose because it provides that tax-raised funds will be paid to reimburse individuals on account of money spent by them in a way which furthers a public program. Of course, the state may pay out tax-raised funds to relieve pauperism, but it may not under our Constitution do so to induce or reward piety. It may spend funds to secure old age against want, but it may not spend funds to secure religion against skepticism. It may compensate individuals for loss of employment, but it cannot compensate them for adherence to a creed.

It seems to me that the basic fallacy in the Court's reasoning, which accounts for its failure to apply the principles it avows, is in ignoring the essentially religious test by which beneficiaries of this expenditure are selected. A policeman protects a Catholic, of course—but not because he is a Catholic; it is because he is a man and a member of our society. The fireman protects the Church school—but not because it is a Church school; it is because it is property, part of the assets of our society. Neither the fireman nor the policeman has to ask before he renders aid "Is this man or building identified with the Catholic Church?" But before these school authorities draw a check to reimburse for a student's fare they must ask just that question, and if the school is a Catholic one they may render aid because it is such, while if it is of any other faith or is run for profit, the help must be withheld. To consider the converse of the Court's reasoning will best disclose its fallacy. That there is no parallel between police and fire protection and this plan of reimbursement is apparent from the incongruity of the limitation of this Act if applied to police and fire service. Could we sustain an Act that said the police shall protect pupils on the way to or from public schools and Catholic schools but not while going to and coming from other schools, and firemen shall extinguish a blaze in public or Catholic school buildings but shall not put out a blaze in Protestant Church schools or private schools operated for profit? That is the true analogy to

the case we have before us and I should think it pretty plain that such a scheme would not be valid.

The Court's holding is that this taxpayer has no grievance because the state has decided to make the reimbursement a public purpose and therefore we are bound to regard it as such. I agree that this Court has left, and always should leave to each state, great latitude in deciding for itself, in the light of its own conditions, what shall be public purposes in its scheme of things. It may socialize utilities and economic enterpries and make taxpayers' business out of what conventionally had been private business. It may make public business of individual welfare, health, education, entertainment or security. But it cannot make public business of religious worship or instruction, or of attendance at religious institutions of any character. There is no answer to the proposition, more fully expounded by Mr. Justice Rutledge, that the effect of the religious freedom Amendment to our Constitution was to take every form of propagation of religion out of the realm of things which could directly or indirectly be made public business and thereby be supported in whole or in part at taxpayers' expense. That is a difference which the Constitution sets up between religion and almost every other subject matter of legislation, a difference which goes to the very root of religious freedom and which the Court is overlooking today. This freedom was first in the Bill of Rights because it was first in the forefathers' minds; it was set forth in absolute terms, and its strength is its rigidity. It was intended not only to keep the states' hands out of religion, but to keep religion's hands off the state, and, above all, to keep bitter religious controversy out of public life by denying to every denomination any advantage from getting control of public policy or the public purse. Those great ends I cannot but think are immeasurably compromised by today's decision.

. . .

Aftermath of Everson v. Board of Education

Both sides in the *Everson* case claimed victory, but neither side had much reason to celebrate. Separationists were disappointed that the Court, in its first establishment clause case, had countenanced the use of public funds to support, even indirectly, religious schools. Accommodationists were alarmed by the over-all tone of Black's opinion, including his endorsement of the idea that the First Amendment had erected a "wall of separation" between church and state.

Uncertainty on both sides about where the Court would go from there may help explain why the state aid to parochial schools issue lay dormant for nearly 20 years before coming back to the Supreme Court. The next case after *Everson* to address the question involved a 1965 New York law that required local school boards to provide textbooks to all private schools located in their districts. Technically, the books, which were chosen from a state-approved list and were on secular subjects only, were "on loan" to the private schools, although in fact they remained in the private schools' possession until they were no longer used. The law had been supported by Governor Nelson Rockefeller, a strong proponent of state aid to parochial schools. In 1968 the Supreme Court upheld the law against an establishment clause challenge in *Board of Education* v. *Allen*, with Justice White employing the "child benefit theory" that Black had fashioned in *Everson* to argue that the beneficiaries of the textbook loans were students, not the churches whose schools they attended. Justice Black took issue with the application of his *Everson* test, maintaining in his dissent that since books were much more central to the church schools' educational mission than were bus fares, the state through its textbook loans was providing direct assistance to religious institutions in violation of the establishment clause.

Lemon v. *Kurtzman*

403 U.S. 602 (1971)

The Supreme Court's willingness to permit states to assist parochial schools by providing buses and books encouraged state legislatures to develop other financial support schemes. In 1969 Rhode Island, a state with a large Roman Catholic population, passed a law designed to assist its financially pressed Catholic schools in attracting and retaining qualified teachers by supplementing their salaries with state-education funds. The law applied only to teachers who taught secular subjects. Pennsylvania had previously adopted a similar law reimbursing nonpublic schools directly for the costs of secular teachers' salaries, textbooks, and materials. Taxpayers in both states challenged the statutes on establishment clause grounds.

Mr. Chief Justice **Burger** delivered the opinion of the Court.

. . .

In Everson v Board of Education (1947), this Court upheld a state statute which reimbursed the parents of parochial school children for bus transportation expenses. There Mr. Justice Black, writing for the majority, suggested that the decision carried to "the verge" of forbidden territory under the Religion Clauses. Candor compels acknowledgment, moreover, that we can only dimly perceive the lines of demarcation in this extraordinarily sensitive area of constitutional law.

The language of the Religion Clauses of the First Amendment is at best opaque, particularly when compared with other portions of the Amendment. Its authors did not simply prohibit the establishment of a state church or a state religion, an area history shows they regarded as very important and fraught with great dangers. Instead they commanded that there should be "no law *respecting* an establishment of religion." A law may be one "respecting" the forbidden objective while falling short of its total realization. A law "respecting" the proscribed result, that is, the establishment of religion, is not always easily identifiable as one violative of the Clause. A given law might not *establish* a state religion but nevertheless be one "respecting" that end in the sense of being a step that could lead to such establishment and hence offend the First Amendment.

In the absence of precisely stated constitutional prohibitions, we must draw lines with reference to the three main evils against which the Establishment Clause was intended to afford protection: "sponsorship, financial support, and active involvement of the sovereign in religious activity." Walz v Tax Commission (1970).

Every analysis in this area must begin with consideration of the cumulative criteria developed by the Court over many years. Three such tests may be gleaned from our cases. First, the statute must have a secular legislative purpose; second, its principal or primary effect must be one that neither advances nor inhibits religion; finally, the statute must not foster "an excessive government entanglement with religion."

Inquiry into the legislative purposes of the Pennsylvania and Rhode Island statutes affords no basis for a conclusion that the legislative intent was to advance religion. On the contrary, the statutes themselves clearly state that they are intended to enhance the quality of the secular education in all schools covered by the compulsory attendance laws. There is no reason to believe the legislatures meant anything else. A State always has a legitimate concern for maintaining minimum standards in all schools it allows to operate. As in Allen, we find nothing here that undermines the stated legislative intent; it must therefore be accorded appropriate deference.

In Allen the Court acknowledged that secular and religious teachings were not necessarily so intertwined that secular textbooks furnished to students by the State were in fact instrumental in the teaching of religion. The legislatures of Rhode Island and Pennsylvania have concluded that secular and religious education are identifiable and separable. In the abstract we have no quarrel with this conclusion.

The two legislatures, however, have also recognized that church-related elementary and secondary schools have a significant religious mission and that a substantial portion of their activities are religiously oriented. They have therefore sought to create statutory restrictions designed to guarantee the separation between secular and religious educational functions and to ensure that State financial aid supports only the former. All these provisions are precautions taken in candid recognition that these programs approached, even if they did not intrude upon the forbidden areas under the Religion Clauses. We need not decide whether these legislative precautions restrict the principal or primary effect of the programs to the point where they do not offend the Religion Clauses, for we conclude that the cumulative impact of the entire relationship arising under the statutes in each State involves excessive entanglement between government and religion.

In Walz v Tax Commission, the Court upheld state tax exemptions for real property owned by religious organizations and used for religious worship. That holding, however, tended to confine rather than enlarge the area of permissible state involvement with religious institutions by calling for close scrutiny of the degree of entanglement involved in the relationship. The objective is to prevent, as far as possible, the intrusion of either into the precincts of the other.

Our prior holdings do not call for total separation between church and state; total separation is not possible in an absolute sense. Some relationship between government and religious organizations is inevitable. Fire inspections, building and zoning regulations, and state requirements under compulsory school attendance laws are examples of necessary and permissible contacts. Indeed, under the statutory exemption before us in Walz, the State had a continuing burden to ascertain that the exempt property was in fact being used for religious worship. Judicial caveats against entanglement must recognize that the line of separation, far from being a "wall," is a blurred, indistinct and variable barrier depending on all the circumstances of a particular relationship.

This is not to suggest, however, that we are to engage in a legalistic minuet in which precise rules and forms must govern. A true minuet is a matter of pure form and style, the observance of which is itself the substantive end. Here we examine the form of the relationship for the light that it casts on the substance.

In order to determine whether the government entanglement with religion is excessive, we must examine the character and purposes of the institutions which are benefited, the nature of the aid that the State provides, and the resulting relationship between the government and the religious authority. . . .

The church schools involved in the [Rhode Island] program are located close to parish churches. This understandably permits convenient access for religious exercises since instruction in faith and morals is part of the total educational process. The school buildings contain identifying religious symbols such as crosses on the exterior and crucifixes, religious paintings and statues either in the classrooms or hallways. Although only approximately 30 minutes a day are devoted to direct religious instruction, there are religiously oriented extracurricular activities. Approximately two-thirds of the teachers in these schools are nuns of various religious orders. Their dedicated efforts provide an atmosphere in which religious instruction and religious vocations are natural and proper parts of life in such schools.

. . .

The substantial religious character of these church-related schools gives rise to entangling church-state relationships of the kind the Religion Clauses sought to avoid. Although the District Court found that concern for religious values did not inevitably or necessarily intrude into the content of secular subjects, the considerable religious activities of these schools led the legislature to provide for careful governmental controls and surveillance by state authorities in order to ensure that state aid supports only secular education.

The dangers and corresponding entanglements are enhanced by the particular form of aid that the Rhode Island Act provides. Our decisions from Everson to Allen have permitted the States to provide church-related schools with secular, neutral, or non-ideological services, facilities, or materials. Bus transportation, school lunches, public health services, and secular textbooks supplied in common to all students were not thought to offend the Establishment Clause. We note that the dissenters in Allen seemed chiefly concerned with the pragmatic difficulties involved in ensuring the truly secular content of the textbooks provided at state expense.

In Allen the Court refused to make assumptions, on a meager record, about the religious content of the textbooks that the State would be asked to provide. We cannot, however, refuse here to recognize that teachers have a substantially different ideological character than books. In terms of potential for involving some aspect of faith or morals in secular subjects, a textbook's content is ascertainable, but a teacher's handling of a subject is not. We cannot ignore the dangers that a teacher under religious control and discipline poses to the separation of the religious from the purely secular aspects of precollege education. The conflict of functions inheres in the situation.

In our view the record shows these dangers are present to a substantial degree. The Rhode Island Roman Catholic elementary schools are under the general supervision of the Bishop of Providence and his appointed representative, the Diocesan Superintendent of Schools. In most cases, each individual parish, however, assumes the ultimate financial responsibility for the school, with the parish priest authorizing the allocation of parish funds. With only two exceptions, school principals are nuns appointed either by the Superintendent or the Mother Provincial of the order whose members staff the school. By 1969 lay teachers constituted more than a third of all teachers in the parochial elementary schools, and their number is growing. They are first interviewed by the superintendent's office and then by the school principal. The contracts are signed by the parish priest, and he retains some discretion in negotiating salary levels. Religious authority necessarily pervades the school system.

. . .

We need not and do not assume that teachers in parochial schools will be guilty of bad faith or any conscious design to evade the limitations imposed by the statute and the First Amendment. We simply recognize that a dedicated religious person, teaching in a school affiliated with his or her faith and operated to inculcate its tenets, will inevitably experience great difficulty in remaining religiously neutral. Doctrines and faith are not inculcated or advanced by neutrals. With the best of intentions such a teacher would find it hard to make a total separation between secular teaching and religious doctrine. What would appear to some to be essential to good citizenship might well for others border on or constitute instruction in religion. Further difficulties are inherent in the combination of religious discipline and the possibility of disagreement between teacher and religious authorities over the meaning of the statutory restrictions.

We do not assume, however, that parochial school teachers will be unsuccessful in their attempts to segregate their religious beliefs from their secular educational responsibilities. But the potential for impermissible fostering of religion is present. The Rhode Island Legislature has not, and could not, provide state aid on the basis of a mere assumption that secular teachers under religious discipline can avoid conflicts. The State must be certain, given the Religion Clauses, that subsidized teachers do not inculcate religion—indeed the State here has undertaken to do so. To ensure that no trespass occurs, the State has therefore carefully conditioned its aid with pervasive restrictions. An eligible recipient must teach only those courses that are offered in the public schools and use only those texts and materials that are found in the public schools. In addition the teacher must not engage in teaching any course in religion.

A comprehensive, discriminating, and continuing state surveillance will inevitably be required to ensure that these restrictions are obeyed and the First Amendment otherwise respected. Unlike a book, a teacher cannot be inspected once so as to determine the extent and intent of his or her personal beliefs and subjective acceptance of the limitations imposed by the First Amendment. These prophylactic contacts will involve excessive and enduring entanglement between state and church.

There is another area of entanglement in the Rhode Island program that gives concern. The

statute excludes teachers employed by nonpublic schools whose average perpupil expenditures on secular education exceed the comparable figures for public schools. In the event that the total expenditures of an otherwise eligible school exceed this norm, the program requires the government to examine the school's records in order to determine how much of the total expenditures are attributable to secular education and how much to religious activity. This kind of state inspection and evaluation of the religious content of a religious organization is fraught with the sort of entanglement that the Constitution forbids. It is a relationship pregnant with dangers of excessive government direction of church schools and hence of churches. The Court noted "the hazards of government supporting churches" in Walz v Tax Commission, and we cannot ignore here the danger that pervasive modern governmental power will ultimately intrude on religion and thus conflict with the Religion Clauses.

. . .

[The Court examines the Pennsylvania statute and concludes that it contains the same potential for "excessive entanglement" of church and state.]

A broader base of entanglement of yet a different character is presented by the divisive political potential of these state programs. In a community where such a large number of pupils are served by church-related schools, it can be assumed that state assistance will entail considerable political activity. Partisans of parochial schools, understandably concerned with rising costs and sincerely dedicated to both the religious and secular educational missions of their schools, will inevitably champion this cause and promote political action to achieve their goals. Those who oppose state aid, whether for constitutional, religious, or fiscal reasons, will inevitably respond and employ all of the usual political campaign techniques to prevail. Candidates will be forced to declare and voters to choose. It would be unrealistic to ignore the fact that many people confronted with issues of this kind will find their votes aligned with their faith.

Ordinarily political debate and division, however vigorous or even partisan, are normal and healthy manifestations of our democratic system of government, but political division along religious lines was one of the principal evils against which the First Amendment was intended to protect. The potential divisiveness of such conflict is a threat to the normal political process. To have States or communities divide on the issues presented by state aid to parochial schools would tend to confuse and obscure other issues of great urgency. We have an expanding array of vexing issues, local and national, domestic and international, to debate and divide on. It conflicts with our whole history and tradition to permit questions of the Religion Clauses to assume such importance in our legislatures and in our elections that they could divert attention from the myriad issues and problems which confront every level of government. The highways of church and state relationships are not likely to be one-way streets, and the Constitution's authors sought to protect religious worship from the pervasive power of government. The history of many countries attests to the hazards of religion intruding into the political arena or of political power intruding into the legitimate and free exercise of religious belief.

. . .

In Walz it was argued that a tax exemption for places of religious worship would prove to be the first step in an inevitable progression leading to the establishment of state churches and state religion. That claim could not stand up against more than 200 years of virtually universal practice imbedded in our colonial experience and continuing into the present.

The progression argument, however, is more persuasive here. We have no long history of state aid to church-related educational institutions comparable to 200 years of tax exemption for churches. Indeed, the state programs before us today represent something of an innovation. We have already noted that modern governmental programs have self-perpetuating and self-expanding propensities. These internal pressures are only enhanced when the schemes involve institutions whose legitimate needs are growing and whose interests have substantial political support. Nor can we fail to see that in constitu-

tional adjudication some steps, which when taken were thought to approach "the verge," have become the platform for yet further steps. A certain momentum develops in constitutional theory and it can be a "downhill thrust" easily set in motion but difficult to retard or stop. Development by momentum is not invariably bad; indeed, it is the way the Common Law has grown, but it is a force to be recognized and reckoned with. The dangers are increased by the difficulty of perceiving in advance exactly where the "verge" of the precipice lies. As well as constituting an independent evil against which the Religion Clauses were intended to protect, involvement or entanglement between government and religion serves as a warning signal.

Finally, nothing we have said can be construed to disparage the role of church-related elementary and secondary schools in our national life. Their contribution has been and is enormous. Nor do we ignore their economic plight in a period of rising costs and expanding need. Taxpayers generally have been spared vast sums by the maintenance of these educational institutions by religious organizations, largely by the gifts of faithful adherents.

The merit and benefits of these schools, however, are not the issue before us in these cases. The sole question is whether state aid to these schools can be squared with the dictates of the Religion Clauses. Under our system the choice has been made that government is to be entirely excluded from the area of religious instruction and churches excluded from the affairs of government. The Constitution decrees that religion must be a private matter for the individual, the family, and the institutions of private choice, and that while some involvement and entanglement is inevitable, lines must be drawn. . . .

Mr. Justice **White,** dissenting.

It is our good fortune that the States of this country long ago recognized that instruction of the young and old ranks high on the scale of proper governmental functions and not only undertook secular education as a public responsibility but also required compulsory attendance at school by their young. Having recognized the value of educated citizens and assumed the task of educating them, the States now before us assert a right to provide for the secular education of children whether they attend public schools or choose to enter private institutions, even when those institutions are church-related. The Federal Government also asserts that it is entitled, where requested, to contribute to the cost of secular education by furnishing buildings and facilities to all institutions of higher learning, public and private alike. Both the United States and the States urge that if parents choose to have their children receive instruction in the required secular subjects in a school where religion is also taught and a religious atmosphere may prevail, part or all of the cost of such secular instruction may be paid for by governmental grants to the religious institution conducting the school and seeking the grant. Those who challenge this position would bar official contributions to secular education where the family prefers the parochial to both the public and nonsectarian private school.

The issue is fairly joined. It is precisely the kind of issue the Constitution contemplates this Court must ultimately decide. This is true although neither affirmance nor reversal of any of these cases follows automatically from the spare language of the First Amendment, from its history or from the cases of this Court construing it and even though reasonable men can very easily and sensibly differ over the import of that language.

But, while the decision of the Court is legitimate, it is surely quite wrong in overturning the Pennsylvania and Rhode Island statutes on the ground that they amount to an establishment of religion forbidden by the First Amendment.

. . .

Our prior cases have recognized the dual role of parochial schools in American society: they perform both religious and secular functions. Our cases also recognize that legislation having a secular purpose and extending governmental assistance to sectarian schools in the performance of their secular functions do not constitute "law[s] respecting an establishment of religion" forbidden by the First Amendment merely

because a secular program may incidentally benefit a church in fulfilling its religious mission. That religion may indirectly benefit from governmental aid to the secular activities of churches does not convert that aid into an impermissible establishment of religion.

. . .

It is enough for me that the States are financing a separable secular function of overriding importance in order to sustain the legislation here challenged. That religion and private interests other than education may substantially benefit does not convert these laws into impermissible establishments of religion.

. . .

The Court strikes down the Rhode Island statute on its face. No fault is found with the secular purpose of the program; there is no suggestion that the purpose of the program was aid to religion disguised in secular attire. Nor does the Court find that the primary effect of the program is to aid religion rather than to implement secular goals. The Court nevertheless finds that impermissible "entanglement" will result from administration of the program. The reasoning is a curious and mystifying blend, but a critical factor appears to be an unwillingness to accept the District Court's express findings that on the evidence before it none of the teachers here involved mixed religious and secular instruction. Rather the District Court struck down the statute because it concluded that activities outside the secular classroom would probably have a religious content and that support for religious education therefore necessarily resulted from the financial aid to the secular programs, since that aid generally strengthened the parochial schools and increased the number of their students.

. . . Accepting the District Court's observation that education is an integral part of the religious mission of the Catholic church—an observation that should neither surprise nor alarm anyone, especially judges who have already approved substantial aid to parochial schools in various forms—the majority then interposes findings and conclusions that the District Court expressly abjured, namely, that nuns, clerics and dedicated Catholic laymen unavoidably pose a grave risk in that they might not be able to put aside their religion in the secular classroom. Although stopping short of considering them untrustworthy, the Court concludes that for them the difficulties of avoiding teaching religion along with secular subjects would pose intolerable risks and would in any event entail an unacceptable enforcement regime. Thus, the potential for impermissible fostering of religion in secular classrooms—an untested assumption of the Court—paradoxically renders unacceptable the State's efforts at insuring that secular teachers under religious discipline successfully avoid conflicts between the religious mission of the school and the secular purpose of the State's education program.

. . .

The Court thus creates an insoluble paradox for the State and the parochial schools. The State cannot finance secular instruction if it permits religion to be taught in the same classroom; but if it exacts a promise that religion not be so taught—a promise the school and its teachers are quite willing and on this record able to give—and enforces it, it is then entangled in the "no entanglement" aspect of the Court's Establishment Clause jurisprudence.

. . .

Aftermath of Lemon *v.* Kurtzman

The *Lemon* decision was the first major constitutional defeat for advocates of parochial school aid, and it provoked a wave of protest in the Catholic community. Fears that the Court was embarking on a strict separationist path with its "three-pronged" test were hardly allayed by the Court's decision in *Tilton* v. *Richardson,* handed down the same day as *Lemon,* which upheld the use of federal education funds to construct dormitory and classroom buildings at sectarian colleges. The *Tilton* majority argued in part that since college students were less "impressionable" than elementary and secondary pupils, government aid to higher education would not usually be helping to propagate church doctrine. Thus the *Tilton* opinion only served to highlight the concerns that underlay the Court's decision in *Lemon.*

An alternative interpretation of *Tilton* was that the Court might be prepared to be more deferential to federal than to state efforts to assist parochial schools. Accordingly, proposals were made in Congress to allow a federal income tax deduction for the costs of private school tuition. Like another federal initiative that was widely discussed in the 1970s, the "educational voucher plan," the income tax proposal generated strong opposition from public educators, and to date has made little headway in Congress.

Zorach v. *Clauson*

343 U.S. 306 (1952)

Despite the strong sentiment in the nineteenth century against using public funds to assist religious schools, there were many instances of accommodation between church and state where no money was involved. These included prayers at the open-

ing of legislative sessions and on other public occasions and laws requiring businesses to close on Sunday. In the nation's public schools, a quasi-official, predominantly
Protestant "public religion" flourished through the prayers and Bible readings that
regularly began school days.

By the middle of the twentieth century, another accommodationist practice had
developed as well. In a number of states, representatives of religious groups, usually
members of the clergy, were permitted to come into public schools at designated
times to offer instruction and devotional services to children whose parents had
given permission for them to participate. These "released-time" programs were
designed primarily for Catholic students who were unable to attend parochial
schools, but many Protestant and some Jewish clergy took part in them as well. In
the 1940s the school board in Champagne, Illinois, acting pursuant to a state law
permitting local boards to control the use of their school buildings, developed a
released-time program with nearby churches and synagogues. During the weekly
instructional meetings, which took place in the regular public school classrooms,
students who did not choose to participate went into study halls instead. Attendance
was taken in both classrooms and study halls.

Vashti McCollum, the mother of a Champagne high school student, initiated a
lawsuit contending that the released-time program constituted an establishment of
religion in violation of the First Amendment. Her Supreme Court appeal was accompanied by *amicus curiae* briefs written by several prominent separationist groups
including the Synagogue Council of America and the American Civil Liberties Union.
The city of Champagne received support from the Protestant Council of New York
City, an organization which had worked with authorities to establish a program in
which public school students were dismissed from classes to attend off-premises
religious instruction.

The Supreme Court's majority opinion in *McCollum* v. *Board of Education,* written
by Justice Black, followed the reasoning but not the result of the *Everson* decision
handed down the previous year. Champagne's released-time plan was found to be
unconstitutional because it involved the use of public property and the state's
mandatory school-attendance law to support a religious purpose.

For the accommodationists, however, all was not lost. If released time was unconstitutional, the Court might still be persuaded that the dismissed-time variation was
acceptable because it did not make use of public property. Suspecting that this
might be true, and noting the overwhelmingly unfavorable public reaction to the
McCollum decision, many separationists were inclined not to challenge dismissed
time. In the end, however, hotter heads prevailed, and a First Amendment challenge
was mounted against New York City's program. The New York Court of Appeals
upheld its constitutionality. When the case reached the Supreme Court, eight state
attorneys general submitted *amicus curiae* briefs on behalf of dismissed time.

Mr. Justice **Douglas** delivered the opinion of
the Court.

. . .

This "released time" program involves neither
religious instruction in public school classrooms
nor the expenditure of public funds. All costs,
including the application blanks, are paid by the
religious organizations. The case is therefore
unlike *McCollum* v. *Board of Education,* which
involved a "released time" program from Illinois.
In that case the classrooms were turned over to
religious instructors. We accordingly held that

the program violated the First Amendment
which (by reason of the Fourteenth Amendment) prohibits the states from establishing religion or prohibiting its free exercise.

. . .

The briefs and arguments are replete with
data bearing on the merits of this type of
"released time" program. Views *pro* and *con* are
expressed, based on practical experience with
these programs and with their implications. We
do not stop to summarize these materials nor to
burden the opinion with an analysis of them.

For they involve considerations not germane to the narrow constitutional issue presented. They largely concern the wisdom of the system, its efficiency from an educational point of view, and the political considerations which have motivated its adoption or rejection in some communities. Those matters are of no concern here, since our problem reduces itself to whether New York by this system has either prohibited the "free exercise" of religion or has made a law "respecting an establishment of religion" within the meaning of the First Amendment.

It takes obtuse reasoning to inject any issue of the "free exercise" of religion into the present case. No one is forced to go to the religious classroom and no religious exercise or instruction is brought to the classrooms of the public schools. A student need not take religious instruction. He is left to his own desires as to the manner or time of his religious devotions, if any.

There is a suggestion that the system involves the use of coercion to get public school students into religious classrooms. There is no evidence in the record before us that supports that conclusion. The present record indeed tells us that the school authorities are neutral in this regard and do no more than release students whose parents so request. If in fact coercion were used, if it were established that any one or more teachers were using their office to persuade or force students to take the religious instruction, a wholly different case would be presented. Hence we put aside that claim of coercion both as respects the "free exercise" of religion and "an establishment of religion" within the meaning of the First Amendment.

Moreover, apart from that claim of coercion, we do not see how New York by this type of "released time" program has made a law respecting an establishment of religion within the meaning of the First Amendment. There is much talk of the separation of Church and State in the history of the Bill of Rights and in the decisions clustering around the First Amendment. There cannot be the slightest doubt that the First Amendment reflects the philosophy that Church and State should be separated. And so far as interference with the "free exercise" of religion and an "establishment" of religion are concerned, the separation must be complete and unequivocal. The First Amendment within the scope of its coverage permits no exception; the prohibition is absolute. The First Amendment, however, does not say that in every and all respects there shall be a separation of Church and State. Rather, it studiously defines the manner, the specific ways, in which there shall be no concert or union or dependency one on the other. That is the common sense of the matter. Otherwise the state and religion would be aliens to each other—hostile, suspicious, and even unfriendly. Churches could not be required to pay even property taxes. Municipalities would not be permitted to render police or fire protection to religious groups. Policemen who helped parishioners into their places of worship would violate the Constitution. Prayers in our legislative halls; the appeals to the Almighty in the messages of the Chief Executive; the proclamations making Thanksgiving Day a holiday; "so help me God" in our courtroom oaths—these and all other references to the Almighty that run through our laws, our public rituals, our ceremonies would be flouting the First Amendment. A fastidious atheist or agnostic could even object to the supplication with which the Court opens each session: "God save the United States and this Honorable Court."

We would have to press the concept of separation of Church and State to these extremes to condemn the present law on constitutional grounds. The nullification of this law would have wide and profound effects. A Catholic student applies to his teacher for permission to leave the school during hours on a Holy Day of Obligation to attend a mass. A Jewish student asks his teacher for permission to be excused for Yom Kippur. A Protestant wants the afternoon off for a family baptismal ceremony. In each case the teacher requires parental consent in writing. In each case the teacher, in order to make sure the student is not a truant, goes further and requires a report from the priest, the rabbi, or the minister. The teacher in other words cooperates in a religious program to the extent of making it possible for her students to participate in it. Whether she does it occasionally for a few students, regularly for one, or pursuant to a systematized program designed to further the religious needs of all the students does not alter the character of the act.

We are a religious people whose institutions presuppose a Supreme Being. We guarantee the freedom to worship as one chooses. We make room for as wide a variety of beliefs and creeds as the spiritual needs of man deem necessary. We sponsor an attitude on the part of government that shows no partiality to any one group and that lets each flourish according to the zeal of its adherents and the appeal of its dogma. When the state encourages religious instruction or cooperates with religious authorities by adjusting the schedule of public events to sectarian needs, it follows the best of our traditions. For it then respects the religious nature of our people and accommodates the public service to their spiritual needs. To hold that it may not would be to find in the Constitution a requirement that the government show a callous indifference to religious groups. That would be preferring those who believe in no religion over those who do believe. Government may not finance religious groups nor undertake religious instruction nor blend secular and sectarian education nor use secular institutions to force one or some religion on any person. But we find no constitutional requirement which makes it necessary for government to be hostile to religion and to throw its weight against efforts to widen the effective scope of religious influence. The government must be neutral when it comes to competition between sects. It may not thrust any sect on any person. It may not make a religious observance compulsory. It may not coerce anyone to attend church, to observe a religious holiday, or to take religious instruction. But it can close its doors or suspend its operations as to those who want to repair to their religious sanctuary for worship or instruction. No more than that is undertaken here.

This program may be unwise and improvident from an educational or a community viewpoint. That appeal is made to us on a theory, previously advanced, that each case must be decided on the basis of "our own prepossessions." *McCollum* v. *Board of Education.* Our individual preferences, however, are not the constitutional standard. The constitutional standard is the separation of Church and State. The prob-

lem, like many problems in constitutional law, is one of degree.

In the *McCollum* case the classrooms were used for religious instruction and the force of the public school was used to promote that instruction. Here, as we have said, the public schools do no more than accommodate their schedules to a program of outside religious instruction. We follow the *McCollum* case. But we cannot expand it to cover the present released time program unless separation of Church and State means that public institutions can make no adjustments of their schedules to accommodate the religious needs of the people. We cannot read into the Bill of Rights such a philosophy of hostility to religion.

Mr. Justice **Black,** dissenting.

McCollum v. *Board of Education* held invalid as an "establishment of religion" an Illinois system under which school children, compelled by law to go to public schools, were freed from some hours of required school work on condition that they attend special religious classes held in the school buildings. Although the classes were taught by sectarian teachers neither employed nor paid by the state, the state did use its power to further the program by releasing some of the children from regular class work, insisting that those released attend the religious classes, and requiring that those who remained behind do some kind of academic work while the others received their religious training. . . .

I see no significant difference between the invalid Illinois system and that of New York here sustained. Except for the use of the school buildings in Illinois, there is no difference between the systems which I consider even worthy of mention. In the New York program, as in that of Illinois, the school authorities release some of the children on the condition that they attend the religious classes, get reports on whether they attend, and hold the other children in the school building until the religious hour is over. As we attempted to make categorically clear, the *McCollum* decision would have been the same if the religious classes had not been held in the school buildings. . . .

McCollum thus held that Illinois could not

constitutionally manipulate the compelled class-room hours of its compulsory school machinery so as to channel children into sectarian classes. Yet that is exactly what the Court holds New York can do.

I am aware that our *McCollum* decision on separation of Church and State has been subjected to a most searching examination throughout the country. Probably few opinions from this Court in recent years have attracted more attention or stirred wider debate. Our insistence on "a wall between Church and State which must be kept high and impregnable" has seemed to some a correct exposition of the philosophy and a true interpretation of the language of the First Amendment to which we should strictly adhere. With equal conviction and sincerity, others have thought the *McCollum* decision fundamentally wrong and have pledged continuous warfare against it. The opinions in the court below and the briefs here reflect these diverse viewpoints. In dissenting today, I mean to do more than give routine approval to our *McCollum* decision. I mean also to reaffirm my faith in the fundamental philosophy expressed in *McCollum* and *Everson* v. *Board of Education.* That reaffirmance can be brief because of the exhaustive opinions in those recent cases.

Difficulty of decision in the hypothetical situations mentioned by the Court, but not now before us, should not confuse the issues in this case. Here the sole question is whether New York can use its compulsory education laws to help religious sects get attendants presumably too unenthusiastic to go unless moved to do so by the pressure of this state machinery. That this is the plan, purpose, design and consequence of the New York program cannot be denied. The state thus makes religious sects beneficiaries of its power to compel children to attend secular schools. Any use of such coercive power by the state to help or hinder some religious sects or to prefer all religious sects over nonbelievers or vice versa is just what I think the First Amendment forbids. In considering whether a state has entered this forbidden field the question is not whether it has entered too far but whether it has entered at all. New York is manipulating its compulsory education laws to help religious sects get pupils. This is

not separation but combination of Church and State.

The Court's validation of the New York system rests in part on its statement that Americans are "a religious people whose institutions presuppose a Supreme Being." This was at least as true when the First Amendment was adopted; and it was just as true when eight Justices of this Court invalidated the released time system in *McCollum* on the premise that a state can no more "aid all religions" than it can aid one. It was precisely because Eighteenth Century Americans were a religious people divided into many fighting sects that we were given the constitutional mandate to keep Church and State completely separate. Colonial history had already shown that, here as elsewhere zealous sectarians entrusted with governmental power to further their causes would sometimes torture, maim and kill those they branded "heretics," "atheists" or "agnostics." The First Amendment was therefore to insure that no one powerful sect or combination of sects could use political or governmental power to punish dissenters whom they could not convert to their faith. Now as then, it is only by wholly isolating the state from the religious sphere and compelling it to be completely neutral, that the freedom of each and every denomination and of all nonbelievers can be maintained. It is this neutrality the Court abandons today when it treats New York's coercive system as a program which *merely* "encourages religious instruction or cooperates with religious authorities." The abandonment is all the more dangerous to liberty because of the Court's legal exaltation of the orthodox and its derogation of unbelievers.

Under our system of religious freedom, people have gone to their religious sanctuaries not because they feared the law but because they loved their God. The choice of all has been as free as the choice of those who answered the call to worship moved only by the music of the old Sunday morning church bells. The spiritual mind of man has thus been free to believe, disbelieve, or doubt, without repression, great or small, by the heavy hand of government. Statutes authorizing such repression have been stricken. Before today, our judicial opinions have refrained from drawing invidious distinctions between those who believe in no religion and those who do believe. The First Amendment has lost much if the religious follower and the atheist are no longer to be judicially regarded as entitled to equal justice under law.

State help to religion injects political and party prejudices into a holy field. It too often substitutes force for prayer, hate for love, and persecution for persuasion. Government should not be allowed, under cover of the soft euphemism of "co-operation," to steal into the sacred area of religious choice.

Mr. Justice **Frankfurter,** dissenting.

By way of emphasizing my agreement with Mr. Justice Jackson's dissent, I add a few words.

The Court tells us that in the maintenance of its public schools, "[The State government] can close its doors or suspend its operations" so that its citizens may be free for religious devotions or instruction. If that were the issue, it would not rise to the dignity of a constitutional controversy. Of course, a State may provide that the classes in its schools shall be dismissed, for any reason, or no reason, on fixed days, or for special occasions. The essence of this case is that the school system did not "close its doors" and did not "suspend its operations." There is all the difference in the world between letting the children out of school and letting some of them out of school into religious classes. If every one is free to make what use he will of time wholly unconnected from schooling required by law—those who wish sectarian instruction devoting it to that purpose, those who have ethical instruction at home, to that, those who study music, to that—then of course there is no conflict with the Fourteenth Amendment.

The pith of the case is that formalized religious instruction is substituted for other school activity which those who do not participate in the released-time program are compelled to attend. The school system is very much in operation during this kind of released time. If its doors are closed, they are closed upon those students who do not attend the religious instruction, in order to keep them within the school. That is the very thing which raises the constitutional issue. It is not met by disregarding it.

Failure to discuss this issue does not take it out of the case.

. . .

The result in the *McCollum* case was based on principles that received unanimous acceptance by this Court, barring only a single vote. I agree with Mr. Justice Black that those principles are disregarded in reaching the result in this case. Happily they are not disavowed by the Court. From this I draw the hope that in future variations of the problem which are bound to come here, these principles may again be honored in the observance.

The deeply divisive controversy aroused by the attempts to secure public school pupils for sectarian instruction would promptly end if the advocates of such instruction were content to have the school "close its doors or suspend its operations"—that is, dismiss classes in their entirety, without discrimination—instead of seeking to use the public schools as the instrument for securing attendance at denominational classes. The unwillingness of the promoters of this movement to dispense with such use of the public schools betrays a surprising want of confidence in the inherent power of the various faiths to draw children to outside sectarian classes—an attitude that hardly reflects the faith of the greatest religious spirits.

Mr. Justice **Jackson,** dissenting.

This released time program is founded upon a use of the State's power of coercion, which, for me, determines its unconstitutionality. Stripped to its essentials, the plan has two stages: first, that the State compel each student to yield a large part of his time for public secular education; and, second, that some of it be "released" to him on condition that he devote it to sectarian religious purposes.

No one suggests that the Constitution would permit the State directly to require this "released" time to be spent "under the control of a duly constituted religious body." This program accomplishes that forbidden result by indirection. If public education were taking so much of the pupils' time as to injure the public or the students' welfare by encroaching upon their religious opportunity, simply shortening everyone's school day would facilitate voluntary and optional attendance at Church classes. But that suggestion is rejected upon the ground that if they are made free many students will not go to the Church. Hence, they must be deprived of freedom for this period, with Church attendance put to them as one of the two permissible ways of using it.

The greater effectiveness of this system over voluntary attendance after school hours is due to the truant officer who, if the youngster fails to go to the Church school, dogs him back to the public schoolroom. Here schooling is more or less suspended during the "released time" so the nonreligious attendants will not forge ahead of the churchgoing absentees. But it serves as a temporary jail for a pupil who will not go to Church. It takes more subtlety of mind than I possess to deny that this is governmental constraint in support of religion. It is as unconstitutional, in my view, when exerted by indirection as when exercised forthrightly.

As one whose children, as a matter of free choice, have been sent to privately supported Church schools, I may challenge the Court's suggestion that opposition to this plan can only be antireligious, atheistic, or agnostic. My evangelistic brethren confuse an objection to compulsion with an objection to religion. It is possible to hold a faith with enough confidence to believe that what should be rendered to God does not need to be decided and collected by Caesar.

The day that this country ceases to be free for irreligion it will cease to be free for religion—

except for the sect that can win political power. The same epithetical jurisprudence used by the Court today to beat down those who oppose pressuring children into some religion can devise as good epithets tomorrow against those who object to pressuring them into a favored religion. And, after all, if we concede to the State power and wisdom to single out "duly constituted religious" bodies as exclusive alternatives for compulsory secular instruction, it would be logical to also uphold the power and wisdom to choose the true faith among those "duly constituted." We start down a rough road when we begin to mix compulsory public education with compulsory godliness.

A number of Justices just short of a majority of the majority that promulgates today's passionate dialectics joined in answering them in *Illinois ex rel. McCollum* v. *Board of Education*. The distinction attempted between that case and this is trivial, almost to the point of cynicism, magnifying its nonessential details and disparaging compulsion which was the underlying reason for invalidity. A reading of the Court's opinion in that case along with its opinion in this case will show such difference of overtones and undertones as to make clear that the *McCollum* case has passed like a storm in a teacup. The wall which the Court was professing to erect between Church and State has become even more warped and twisted than I expected. Today's judgment will be more interesting to students of psychology and of the judicial processes than to students of constitutional law.

Aftermath of Zorach v. Clauson

With the Court's approval, dismissed time programs proliferated and flourished. Despite suggestions from some separationists that under the subsequently developed *Lemon* test such arrangements might be found unconstitutional, the Supreme Court has declined to revisit the issue. As pleased as accommodationists were with the outcome of *Zorach*, they were even more elated by Justice Douglas's assertion in his majority opinion that "(w)e are a religious people whose institutions presuppose a Supreme Being." Few accommodationist legal briefs fail to quote Douglas in attempting to persuade the Court to approve cooperative arrangements between church and state.

Engel v. Vitale

370 U.S. 421 (1962)

No area of establishment clause law has generated more heated controversy than the issue of school prayer. The Supreme Court took an early and emphatic position on school prayer and has adhered to it over the years with a consistency notably lacking in its other establishment clause cases. However, opponents of that position have apparently never ceased to hope that the Court would eventually reconsider and reverse its stand.

From the first appearance of public schools in the United States in the early nineteenth century, it was common practice for students to begin the school day with a brief religious exercise, usually reciting a prayer or reading biblical verse. Although these rituals were described (and probably thought of) as "nondenominational," in fact such prayers and readings were always Christian and nearly always Protestant in orientation.

In the 1950s the New York Board of Regents, the state's highest authority in matters of education, composed the following prayer for recitation in public school classrooms: "Almighty God, we acknowledge our dependence upon Thee, and we beg Thy blessings upon us, our parents, our teachers, and our Country." Adoption of the Regents' prayer by local school districts was optional, but no other prayer was to be used in its place. Soon after the prayer was introduced in one Long Island school district, it was challenged by the Jewish and Unitarian parents of 10 public school students on the ground that such an official prayer constituted "a law respecting an establishment of religion." By the time the case reached the Supreme Court it had attracted the attention of 21 state attorneys general who filed *amicus curiae* briefs in an effort to protect similar practices in their own states.

Mr. Justice **Black** delivered the opinion of the Court.

The respondent Board of Education of Union Free School District No. 9, New Hyde Park, New York, acting in its official capacity under state law, directed the School District's principal to cause the following prayer to be said aloud by each class in the presence of a teacher at the beginning of each school day:

"Almighty God, we acknowledge our dependence upon Thee, and we beg Thy blessings upon us, our parents, our teachers and our Country."

This daily procedure was adopted on the recommendation of the State Board of Regents, a governmental agency created by the State Constitution to which the New York Legislature has granted broad supervisory, executive, and legislative powers over the State's public school system. These state officials composed the prayer

which they recommended and published as a part of their "Statement on Moral and Spiritual Training in the Schools," saying: "We believe that this Statement will be subscribed to by all men and women of good will, and we call upon all of them to aid in giving life to our program."

. . .

We think that by using its public school system to encourage recitation of the Regents' prayer, the State of New York has adopted a practice wholly inconsistent with the Establishment Clause. There can, of course, be no doubt that New York's program of daily classroom invocation of God's blessings as prescribed in the Regents' prayer is a religious activity. It is a solemn avowal of divine faith and supplication for the blessings of the Almighty. The nature of such a prayer has always been religious, none of the respondents has denied this and the trial court expressly so found. . . .

The petitioners contend among other things that the state laws requiring or permitting use of the Regents' prayer must be struck down as a violation of the Establishment Clause because that prayer was composed by governmental officials as a part of a governmental program to further religious beliefs. For this reason, petitioners argue, the State's use of the Regents' prayer in its public school system breaches the constitutional wall of separation between Church and State. We agree with that contention since we think that the constitutional prohibition against laws respecting an establishment of religion must at least mean that in this country it is no part of the business of government to compose official prayers for any group of the American people to recite as a part of a religious program carried on by government.

It is a matter of history that this very practice of establishing governmentally composed prayers for religious services was one of the reasons which caused many of our early colonists to leave England and seek religious freedom in America. . . .

It is an unfortunate fact of history that when some of the very groups which had most strenuously opposed the established Church of England found themselves sufficiently in control of colonial governments in this country to write their own prayers into law, they passed laws making their own religion the official religion of their respective colonies. Indeed, as late as the time of the Revolutionary War, there were established churches in at least eight of the thirteen former colonies and established religions in at least four of the other five. But the successful Revolution against English political domination was shortly followed by intense opposition to the practice of establishing religion by law. . . .

By the time of the adoption of the Constitution, our history shows that there was a widespread awareness among many Americans of the dangers of a union of Church and State. These people knew, some of them from bitter personal experience, that one of the greatest dangers to the freedom of the individual to worship in his own way lay in the Government's placing its official stamp of approval upon one particular kind of prayer or one particular form of religious services. . . . The Constitution was in-

tended to avert a part of this danger by leaving the government of this country in the hands of the people rather than in the hands of any monarch. But this safeguard was not enough. Our Founders were no more willing to let the content of their prayers and their privilege of praying whenever they pleased be influenced by the ballot box than they were to let these vital matters of personal conscience depend upon the succession of monarchs. The First Amendment was added to the Constitution to stand as a guarantee that neither the power nor the prestige of the Federal Government would be used to control, support or influence the kinds of prayer the American people can say—that the people's religions must not be subjected to the pressures of government for change each time a new political administration is elected to office. Under that Amendment's prohibition against governmental establishment of religion, as reinforced by the provisions of the Fourteenth Amendment, government in this country, be it state or federal, is without power to prescribe by law any particular form of prayer which is to be used as an official prayer in carrying on any program of governmentally sponsored religious activity.

There can be no doubt that New York's state prayer program officially establishes the religious beliefs embodied in the Regents' prayer. The respondents' argument to the contrary, which is largely based upon the contention that the Regents' prayer is "non-denominational" and the fact that the program, as modified and approved by state courts, does not require all pupils to recite the prayer but permits those who wish to do so to remain silent or be excused from the room, ignores the essential nature of the program's constitutional defects. Neither the fact that the prayer may be denominationally neutral nor the fact that its observance on the part of the students is voluntary can serve to free it from the limitations of the Establishment Clause, as it might from the Free Exercise Clause, of the First Amendment, both of which are operative against the States by virtue of the Fourteenth Amendment. Although these two clauses may in certain instances overlap, they forbid two quite different kinds of governmental encroachment upon religious freedom. The Establishment Clause, unlike the Free Exercise

Clause, does not depend upon any showing of direct governmental compulsion and is violated by the enactment of laws which establish an official religion whether those laws operate directly to coerce nonobserving individuals or not. This is not to say, of course, that laws officially prescribing a particular form of religious worship do not involve coercion of such individuals. When the power, prestige and financial support of government is placed behind a particular religious belief, the indirect coercive pressure upon religious minorities to conform to the prevailing officially approved religion is plain. But the purposes underlying the Establishment Clause go much further than that. Its first and most immediate purpose rested on the belief that a union of government and religion tends to destroy government and to degrade religion. The history of governmentally established religion, both in England and in this country, showed that whenever government had allied itself with one particular form of religion, the inevitable result had been that it had incurred the hatred, disrespect and even contempt of those who held contrary beliefs. That same history showed that many people had lost their respect for any religion that had relied upon the support of government to spread its faith. The Establishment Clause thus stands as an expression of principle on the part of the Founders of our Constitution that religion is too personal, too sacred, too holy, to permit its "unhallowed perversion" by a civil magistrate. Another purpose of the Establishment Clause rested upon an awareness of the historical fact that governmentally established religions and religious persecutions go hand in hand. . . .

It has been argued that to apply the Constitution in such a way as to prohibit state laws respecting an establishment of religious services in public schools is to indicate a hostility toward religion or toward prayer. Nothing, of course, could be more wrong. The history of man is inseparable from the history of religion. And perhaps it is not too much to say that since the beginning of that history many people have devoutly believed that "More things are wrought by prayer than this world dreams of." It was doubtless largely due to men who believed this

that there grew up a sentiment that caused men to leave the cross-currents of officially established state religions and religious persecution in Europe and come to this country filled with the hope that they could find a place in which they could pray when they pleased to the God of their faith in the language they chose. And there were men of this same faith in the power of prayer who led the fight for adoption of our Constitution and also for our Bill of Rights with the very guarantees of religious freedom that forbid the sort of governmental activity which New York has attempted here. These men knew that the First Amendment, which tried to put an end to governmental control of religion and of prayer, was not written to destroy either. They knew rather that it was written to quiet well-justified fears which nearly all of them felt arising out of an awareness that governments of the past had shackled men's tongues to make them speak only the religious thoughts that government wanted them to speak and to pray only to the God that government wanted them to pray to. It is neither sacrilegious nor antireligious to say that each separate government in this country should stay out of the business of writing or sanctioning official prayers and leave that purely religious function to the people themselves and to those the people choose to look to for religious guidance.

. . .

The judgment of the Court of Appeals of New York is reversed and the cause remanded for further proceedings not inconsistent with this opinion.

Mr. Justice **Stewart,** dissenting.

A local school board in New York has provided that those pupils who wish to do so may join in a brief prayer at the beginning of each school day, acknowledging their dependence upon God and asking His blessing upon them and upon their parents, their teachers, and their country. The Court today decides that in permitting this brief nondenominational prayer the school board has violated the Constitution of the United States. I think this decision is wrong.

The Court does not hold, nor could it, that New York has interfered with the free exercise of anybody's religion. For the state courts have made clear that those who object to reciting the prayer must be entirely free of any compulsion to do so, including any "embarrassments and pressures." But the Court says that in permitting school children to say this simple prayer, the New York authorities have established "an official religion."

With all respect, I think the Court has misapplied a great constitutional principle. I cannot see how an "official religion" is established by letting those who want to say a prayer say it. On the contrary, I think that to deny the wish of these school children to join in reciting this prayer is to deny them the opportunity of sharing in the spiritual heritage of our Nation.

The Court's historical review of the quarrels over the Book of Common Prayer in England throws no light for me on the issue before us in this case. England had then and has now an established church. Equally unenlightening, I think, is the history of the early establishment and later rejection of an official church in our own States. For we deal here not with the establishment of a state church, which would, of course, be constitutionally impermissible, but with whether school children who want to begin their day by joining in prayer must be prohibited from doing so. Moreover, I think that the Court's task, in this as in all areas of constitutional adjudication, is not responsibly aided by the uncritical invocation of metaphors like the "wall of separation," a phrase nowhere to be found in the Constitution. What is relevant to the issue here is not the history of an established church in sixteenth century England or in eighteenth century America, but the history of the religious traditions of our people, reflected in countless practices of the institutions and officials of our government.

At the opening of each day's Session of this Court we stand, while one of our officials invokes the protection of God. Since the days of John Marshall our Crier has said, "God save the United States and this Honorable Court." Both the Senate and the House of Representatives open their daily Sessions with prayer. Each of our Presidents, from George Washington to John F. Kennedy, has upon assuming his Office asked the protection and help of God.

The Court today says that the state and federal governments are without constitutional power to prescribe any particular form of words to be recited by any group of the American people on any subject touching religion. One of the stanzas of "The Star-Spangled Banner," made our National Anthem by Act of Congress in 1931, contains these verses:

> "Blest with victory and peace, may the heav'n rescued land
> Praise the Pow'r that hath made and preserved us a nation!
> Then conquer we must, when our cause it is just, And this be our motto 'In God is our Trust.'"

In 1954 Congress added a phrase to the Pledge of Allegiance to the Flag so that it now contains the words "one Nation *under* God, indivisible, with liberty and justice for all." In 1952 Congress enacted legislation calling upon the President each year to proclaim a National Day of Prayer. Since 1865 the words "IN GOD WE TRUST" have been impressed on our coins.

Countless similar examples could be listed, but there is no need to belabor the obvious. It was all summed up by this Court just ten years ago in a single sentence: "We are a religious people whose institutions presuppose a Supreme Being."

I do not believe that this Court, or the Congress, or the President has by the actions and practices I have mentioned established an "official religion" in violation of the Constitution. And I do not believe the State of New York has done so in this case. What each has done has been to recognize and to follow the deeply entrenched and highly cherished spiritual traditions of our Nation—traditions which come down to us from those who almost two hundred years ago avowed their "firm Reliance on the Protection of divine Providence" when they proclaimed the freedom and independence of this brave new world.

I dissent.

Aftermath of Engel *v.* Vitale

The *Engel* decision was followed a year later by the cases of *Abington School District* v. *Schempp*, which involved challenges to classroom Bible reading and recitation of the Lord's Prayer. The Court strongly reaffirmed *Engel*, holding that the First Amendment prohibited religious exercises of any kind in public classrooms. In *Schempp* as in *Engel*, Justice Stewart was the lone dissenter.

Public reaction to these decisions was strong and hostile. Predictably, many members of Congress lined up to support a constitutional amendment overturning the Court's decisions. But parliamentary maneuvering prevented a floor vote from occurring until 1966, when the proposal was defeated by the Senate. Many school districts, particularly those in the south, reacted to the decisions in their own way, by simply ignoring them. One survey taken in the early 1970s found that schools in 39 of North Carolina's 100 counties still had regular prayers and Bible readings. In the absence of voluntary compliance, Supreme Court decisions are seldom self-executing. There must be someone willing to press the issue either administratively or, if necessary, in court. In many communities there is simply no one willing to take such action.

The school prayer issue flared again briefly in Congress in 1970 when the Senate approved a motion to attach an amendment permitting school prayer to the proposed equal rights amendment. The school prayer portion of the bill was later rejected in the House. A more serious amendment effort occurred in 1984, led this time by President Ronald Reagan, a persistent and longtime critic of the Supreme Court's school prayer decisions. Armed with polls showing that 81 percent of the public supported prayer in public schools, advocates brought the following proposed constitutional amendment to the Senate floor: "Nothing in this Constitution shall be construed to prohibit individual or group prayer in public schools or other public institutions. No person shall be required by the United States or by any state to participate in prayer. Neither the United States or any state shall compose the words of any prayer to be said in public schools." The last sentence had been added during Senate debate in an effort to attract the votes of senators who might have reservations about a "Regents-type prayer" (some had been offended by that prayer either because the government had written it or because of its lack of theological content) while approving of more traditional prayers. The bill also excluded Bible reading, apparently in hopes of avoiding objections from some non-Christians. After several days of emotional debate, the proposal received 56 votes, 11 shy of the two-thirds vote needed to approve a constitutional amendment.

Even before the amendment was defeated, many supporters of school prayer believed that their best hope for reinstating prayer in public classrooms was through an officially mandated "silent moment" that students could devote to any contemplative purpose, including prayer. To date, however, the only "silent moment" law to be reviewed by the Supreme Court was accompanied by irrefutable evidence in the legislative record that it had been enacted for the sole purpose of encouraging students to pray. Thus the Court in *Wallace* v. *Jaffree* found that the statute failed the first prong of the *Lemon* test and declared it unconstitutional. However, several of the concurring justices made it clear that they might find a more artfully drafted silent moment statute constitutional.

Although the religious right has thus far failed both in court and in Congress to reinstate prayer in public schools, it has been more successful at ensuring that public school facilities be made available for meetings and services sponsored by student religious groups. In 1981 the Supreme Court held that public universities must grant such groups the same access to their facilities enjoyed by other student organizations (*Widmar* v. *Vincent*). However, that ruling left open the question whether younger and presumably more impressionable students would be covered by the same constitutional standards, a loophole that Congress attempted to close in 1984 by passing the Equal Access Law, which guaranteed religious groups the use of facilities in all public secondary schools receiving federal funds. In 1990 the Supreme Court heard a challenge to this law brought by a coalition of separationist organizations including the American Jewish Congress, the American Civil Liberties Union, and People for the American Way. By an 8–1 vote the Court declared the Equal Access Law to be constitutional (*Westside Community Board of Education* v. *Mergens*).

In March of 1991 the Supreme Court announced that it would schedule for argument in the fall a case raising the question whether recitation of a prayer at a public junior high school graduation ceremony is a violation of the establishment clause. Providence, Rhode Island, school officials, with the strong backing of the Bush administration, had appealed a Court of Appeals decision holding that such a prayer is unconstitutional. It is possible that the Supreme Court will use this case to revisit the school prayer issue, or at least to consider seriously a change in the *Lemon* test.

Lynch v. *Donnelly*

465 U.S. 668 (1984)

Two familiar and long-standing examples of accommodation between church and state—state legislative chaplains and government-sponsored nativity scenes—reached the Supreme Court for the first time in the 1980s. In 1983, the Court held in *Marsh* v. *Chambers* that the Nebraska legislature did not violate the establishment clause by having on its payroll a Presbyterian minister whose duties consisted of opening each day's session with a prayer. Writing for the majority, Chief Justice Burger emphasized that legislative chaplaincies had originated with the colonial legislatures and continued uninterrupted to the present. Having "become part of the fabric of our society," he concluded, they pose no threat to the values protected by the establishment clause. *Marsh* is notable for being the only establishment clause decision since 1971 that has not been based, at least nominally, on the three-part *Lemon* test. In his dissent, Justice Brennan conceded that in his concurrence some 20 years earlier in *Abington Township High School* v. *Schempp*, he had come "very close to endorsing" the position that such long-standing arrangements as legislative chaplains did not rise to the level of establishment clause violations. Now, however, he was convinced that both the *Lemon* test and the principles of separation and neutrality upon which the establishment clause is based, rendered the practice unconstitutional.

The second question, whether government-sponsored nativity displays violate the establishment clause, was addressed by the Supreme Court in 1984. The existence of an American "civil religion" has long been attested to by the Christmas displays in front of city halls throughout the land each December. However offensive they might be to strict separationists, such displays have proved difficult to challenge in court.

Because the Christmas season is short, the displays would usually be back in municipal storerooms before the separationists could be heard in court. When nativity-
scene cases were heard, the court usually treated them as *de minimus* accommodations between church and state—that is, too trivial to be worthy of judicial notice.

In the early 1940s the city of Pawtucket, Rhode Island, began erecting a
Christmas display each year in its downtown shopping district. By the 1980s the display included a life-sized crèche with figures depicting Jesus, Mary, and Joseph, as
well as shepherds, wise men, Santa Claus, reindeer, snowmen, carolers, a Christmas
tree, and a banner reading "Season's Greetings." A lawsuit challenging the display
was brought in federal district court by the Rhode Island chapter of the American
Civil Liberties Union, the National Council of Churches, and the American Jewish
Committee. The district court ruled that by including the crèche in the Christmas
display, the city of Pawtucket had "tried to endorse and promulgate religious
beliefs," thus violating the establishment clause. The court issued a permanent
injunction against inclusion of the crèche scene in the Christmas display. That decision was upheld by the Court of Appeals. After the Supreme Court agreed to review
the case, the solicitor general of the United States filed an *amicus curiae* brief on behalf of the city of Pawtucket, arguing that prohibiting display of the crèche was tantamount to "cultural censorship." The brief reflected the commitment of the Reagan
administration to promoting an accommodationist approach to church-state issues.

Chief Justice **Burger** delivered the opinion of
the Court.

. . .

This Court has explained that the purpose of
the Establishment and Free Exercise Clauses of
the First Amendment is

"to prevent, as far as possible, the intrusion of
either [the church or the state] into the precincts
of the other." Lemon v Kurtzman (1971).

At the same time, however, the Court has recognized that

"total separation is not possible in an absolute sense. Some relationship between government and religious organizations is inevitable."

In every Establishment Clause case, we must
reconcile the inescapable tension between the
objective of preventing unnecessary intrusion of
either the church or the state upon the other,
and the reality that, as the Court has so often
noted, total separation of the two is not possible.

The Court has sometimes described the
Religion Clauses as erecting a "wall" between
church and state. The concept of a "wall" of separation is a useful figure of speech probably
deriving from views of Thomas Jefferson. The
metaphor has served as a reminder that the
Establishment Clause forbids an established
church or anything approaching it. But the

metaphor itself is not a wholly accurate description of the practical aspects of the relationship
that in fact exists between church and state.

No significant segment of our society and no
institution within it can exist in a vacuum or in
total or absolute isolation from all the other
parts, much less from government. . . . Nor
does the Constitution require complete separation of church and state; it affirmatively mandates accommodation, not merely tolerance,
of all religions, and forbids hostility toward
any. . . . Anything less would require the "callous indifference" we have said was never
intended by the Establishment Clause. Indeed,
we have observed, such hostility would bring us
into "war with our national tradition as embodied in the First Amendment's guaranty of the
free exercise of religion." McCollum v. Board of
Education (1948).

The Court's interpretation of the Establishment Clause has comported with what history
reveals was the contemporaneous understanding
of its guarantees. A significant example of the
contemporaneous understanding of that Clause
is found in the events of the first week of the
First Session of the First Congress in 1789. In
the very week that Congress approved the Establishment Clause as part of the Bill of Rights for
submission to the states, it enacted legislation
providing for paid chaplains for the House and
Senate. In Marsh v Chambers, (1983), we noted

that seventeen Members of that First Congress had been Delegates to the Constitutional Convention where freedom of speech, press and religion and antagonism toward an established church were subjects of frequent discussion. We saw no conflict with the Establishment Clause when Nebraska employed members of the clergy as official Legislative Chaplains to give opening prayers at sessions of the state legislature.

The interpretation of the Establishment Clause by Congress in 1789 takes on special significance in light of the Court's emphasis that the First Congress

"was a Congress whose constitutional decisions have always been regarded, as they should be regarded, as of the greatest weight in the interpretation of that fundamental instrument," Myers v United States (1926).

It is clear that neither the seventeen draftsmen of the Constitution who were Members of the First Congress, nor the Congress of 1789, saw any establishment problem in the employment of congressional Chaplains to offer daily prayers in the Congress, a practice that has continued for nearly two centuries. It would be difficult to identify a more striking example of the accommodation of religious belief intended by the Framers.

There is an unbroken history of official acknowledgment by all three branches of government of the role of religion in American life from at least 1789. Seldom in our opinions was this more affirmatively expressed than in Justice Douglas' opinion for the Court validating a program allowing release of public school students from classes to attend off-campus religious exercises. Rejecting a claim that the program violated the Establishment Clause, the Court asserted pointedly:

"We are a religious people whose institutions presuppose a Supreme Being."

Our history is replete with official references to the value and invocation of Divine guidance in deliberations and pronouncements of the Founding Fathers and contemporary leaders. Beginning in the early colonial period long before Independence, a day of Thanksgiving was celebrated as a religious holiday to give thanks for the bounties of Nature as gifts from God. President Washington and his successors proclaimed Thanksgiving, with all its religious overtones, a day of national celebration and Congress made it a National Holiday more than a century ago. That holiday has not lost its theme of expressing thanks for Divine aid any more than has Christmas lost its religious significance.

Executive Orders and other official announcements of Presidents and of the Congress have proclaimed both Christmas and Thanksgiving National Holidays in religious terms. And, by Acts of Congress, it has long been the practice that federal employees are released from duties on these National Holidays, while being paid from the same public revenues that provide the compensation of the Chaplains of the Senate and the House and the military services. Thus, it is clear that Government has long recognized—indeed it has subsidized—holidays with religious significance.

Other examples of reference to our religious heritage are found in the statutorily prescribed national motto "In God We Trust," which Congress and the President mandated for our currency, and in the language "One nation under God," as part of the Pledge of Allegiance to the American flag. That pledge is recited by thousands of public school children—and adults—every year.

Art galleries supported by public revenues display religious paintings of the 15th and 16th centuries, predominantly inspired by one religious faith. The National Gallery in Washington, maintained with Government support, for example, has long exhibited masterpieces with religious messages, notably the Last Supper, and paintings depicting the Birth of Christ, the Crucifixion, and the Resurrection, among many others with explicit Christian themes and messages. The very chamber in which oral arguments on this case were heard is decorated with a notable and permanent—not seasonal—symbol of religion: Moses with Ten Commandments. Congress has long provided chapels in the Capitol for religious worship and meditation.

There are countless other illustrations of the Government's acknowledgment of our religious heritage and governmental sponsorship of graphic manifestations of that heritage. Congress has directed the President to proclaim a National Day of Prayer each year "on which [day] the people of the United States may turn to God in prayer and meditation at churches, in groups, and as individuals." Our Presidents have repeatedly issued such Proclamations. Presidential Proclamations and messages have also issued to commemorate Jewish Heritage Week, and the Jewish High Holy Days. One cannot look at even this brief resume without finding that our history is pervaded by expressions of religious beliefs such as are found in Zorach. Equally pervasive is the evidence of accommodation of all faiths and all forms of religious expression, and hostility toward none. Through this accommodation, as Justice Douglas observed, governmental action has "follow[ed] the best of our traditions" and "respect[ed] the religious nature of our people."

This history may help explain why the Court consistently has declined to take a rigid, absolutist view of the Establishment Clause. We have refused "to construe the Religion Clauses with a literalness that would undermine the ultimate constitutional objective *as illuminated by history.*" Walz v Tax Commission (1970) (Emphasis added). In our modern, complex society, whose traditions and constitutional underpinnings rest on and encourage diversity and pluralism in all areas, an absolutist approach in applying the Establishment Clause is simplistic and has been uniformly rejected by the Court.

Rather than mechanically invalidating all governmental conduct or statutes that confer benefits or give special recognition to religion in general or to one faith—as an absolutist approach would dictate—the Court has scrutinized challenged legislation or official conduct to determine whether, in reality, it establishes a religion or religious faith, or tends to do so. . . .

In each case, the inquiry calls for line drawing; no fixed, per se rule can be framed. The Establishment Clause like the Due Process Clauses is not a precise, detailed provision in a legal code capable of ready application. The purpose of the Establishment Clause "was to state an objective, not to write a statute." The line between permissible relationships and those barred by the Clause can no more be straight

and unwavering than due process can be defined in a single stroke or phrase or test. The Clause erects a "blurred, indistinct, and variable barrier depending on all the circumstances of a particular relationship."

In the line-drawing process we have often found it useful to inquire whether the challenged law or conduct has a secular purpose, whether its principal or primary effect is to advance or inhibit religion, and whether it creates an excessive entanglement of government with religion. But, we have repeatedly emphasized our unwillingness to be confined to any single test or criterion in this sensitive area.

In two cases, the Court did not even apply the Lemon "test." We did not, for example, consider that analysis relevant in Marsh. Nor did we find Lemon useful in Larson v Valente (1982), where there was substantial evidence of overt discrimination against a particular church.

In this case, the focus of our inquiry must be on the crèche in the context of the Christmas season. In Stone, for example, we invalidated a state statute requiring the posting of a copy of the Ten Commandments on public classroom walls. But the Court carefully pointed out that the Commandments were posted purely as a religious admonition, not "integrated into the school curriculum, where the Bible may constitutionally be used in an appropriate study of history, civilization, ethics, comparative religion, or the like." Similarly, in Abington, although the Court struck down the practices in two States requiring daily Bible readings in public schools, it specifically noted that nothing in the Court's holding was intended to "indicat[e] that such study of the Bible or of religion, when presented objectively as part of a secular program of education, may not be effected consistently with the First Amendment." Focus exclusively on the religious component of any activity would inevitably lead to its invalidation under the Establishment Clause.

The Court has invalidated legislation or governmental action on the ground that a secular purpose was lacking, but only when it has concluded there was no question that the statute or activity was motivated wholly by religious considerations. . . .

The District Court inferred from the religious

nature of the creche that the City has no secular purpose for the display. In so doing, it rejected the City's claim that its reasons for including the creche are essentially the same as its reasons for sponsoring the display as a whole. The District Court plainly erred by focusing almost exclusively on the creche. When viewed in the proper context of the Christmas Holiday season, it is apparent that, on this record, there is insufficient evidence to establish that the inclusion of the creche is a purposeful or surreptitious effort to express some kind of subtle governmental advocacy of a particular religious message. In a pluralistic society a variety of motives and purposes are implicated. The City, like the Congresses and Presidents, however, has principally taken note of a significant historical religious event long celebrated in the Western World. The creche in the display depicts the historical origins of this traditional event long recognized as a National Holiday.

The narrow question is whether there is a secular purpose for Pawtucket's display of the creche. The display is sponsored by the City to celebrate the Holiday and to depict the origins of that Holiday. These are legitimate secular purposes. The District Court's inference, drawn from the religious nature of the creche, that the City has no secular purpose was, on this record, clearly erroneous.

The District Court found that the primary effect of including the creche is to confer a substantial and impermissible benefit on religion in general and on the Christian faith in particular. Comparisons of the relative benefits to religion of different forms of governmental support are elusive and difficult to make. But to conclude that the primary effect of including the creche is to advance religion in violation of the Establishment Clause would require that we view it as more beneficial to and more an endorsement of religion, for example, than expenditure of large sums of public money for textbooks supplied throughout the country to students attending church-sponsored schools, expenditure of public funds for transportation of students to church-sponsored schools, federal grants for college buildings of church-sponsored institutions of higher education combining secular and religious education, noncategorical grants to church-sponsored colleges and universities, and the tax exemptions for church properties sanctioned in Walz. It would also require that we view it as more of an endorsement of religion than the Sunday Closing Laws upheld in McGowan v Maryland (1961); the release time program for religious training in Zorach, and the legislative prayers upheld in Marsh.

We are unable to discern a greater aid to religion deriving from inclusion of the creche than from these benefits and endorsements previously held not violative of the Establishment Clause. What was said about the legislative prayers in Marsh, and implied about the Sunday Closing Laws in McGowan is true of the City's inclusion of the creche: its "reason or effect merely happens to coincide or harmonize with the tenets of some . . . religions."

. . .

The dissent asserts some observers may perceive that the City has aligned itself with the Christian faith by including a Christian symbol in its display and that this serves to advance religion. We can assume, arguendo, that the display advances religion in a sense; but our precedents plainly contemplate that on occasion some advancement of religion will result from governmental action. The Court has made it abundantly clear, however, that "not every law that confers an 'indirect,' 'remote,' or 'incidental' benefit upon [religion] is, for that reason alone, constitutionally invalid." Here, whatever benefit to one faith or religion or to all religions, is indirect, remote and incidental; display of the creche is no more an advancement or endorsement of religion than the Congressional and Executive recognition of the origins of the Holiday itself as "Christ's Mass," or the exhibition of literally hundreds of religious paintings in governmentally supported museums.

The District Court found that there had been no administrative entanglement between religion and state resulting from the City's ownership and use of the creche. But it went on to hold that some political divisiveness was engendered by this litigation. Coupled with its finding of an impermissible sectarian purpose and effect, this persuaded the court that there was "excessive entanglement." The Court of Appeals expressly declined to accept the District Court's finding that inclusion of the crèche has caused political divisiveness along religious lines, and noted that this Court has never held that political divisiveness alone was sufficient to invalidate government conduct.

Entanglement is a question of kind and degree. In this case, however, there is no reason to disturb the District Court's finding on the absence of administrative entanglement. There is no evidence of contact with church authorities concerning the content or design of the exhibit prior to or since Pawtucket's purchase of the crèche. No expenditures for maintenance of the crèche have been necessary; and since the City owns the crèche, now valued at $200, the tangible material it contributes is de minimis. In many respects the display requires far less ongoing, day-to-day interaction between church and state than religious paintings in public galleries. There is nothing here, of course, like the "comprehensive, discriminating, and continuing state surveillance" or the "enduring entanglement" present in Lemon.

The Court of Appeals correctly observed that this Court has not held that political divisiveness alone can serve to invalidate otherwise permissible conduct. And we decline to so hold today. This case does not involve a direct subsidy to church-sponsored schools or colleges, or other religious institutions, and hence no inquiry into potential political divisiveness is even called for. In any event, apart from this litigation there is no evidence of political friction or divisiveness over the crèche in the 40-year history of Pawtucket's Christmas celebration. The District Court stated that the inclusion of the crèche for the 40 years has been "marked by no apparent dissension" and that the display has had a "calm history." Curiously, it went on to hold that the political divisiveness engendered by this lawsuit was evidence of excessive entanglement. A litigant cannot, by the very act of commencing a lawsuit, however, create the appearance of divisiveness and then exploit it as evidence of entanglement.

We are satisfied that the City has a secular purpose for including the crèche, that the City has not impermissibly advanced religion, and that including the crèche does not create excessive entanglement between religion and government.

Justice Brennan describes the crèche as a "recreation of an event that lies at the heart of Christian faith." The crèche, like a painting, is passive; admittedly it is a reminder of the origins of Christmas. Even the traditional, purely secular displays extant at Christmas, with or without a crèche, would inevitably recall the religious nature of the Holiday. The display engenders a friendly community spirit of good will in keeping with the season. The crèche may well have special meaning to those whose faith includes the celebration of religious masses, but none who sense the origins of the Christmas celebration would fail to be aware of its religious implications. That the display brings people into the central city, and serves commercial interests and benefits merchants and their employees, does not, as the dissent points out, determine the character of the display. That a prayer invoking Divine guidance in Congress is preceded and followed by debate and partisan conflict over taxes, budgets, national defense, and myriad mundane subjects, for example, has never been thought to demean or taint the sacredness of the invocation.

Of course the crèche is identified with one religious faith but no more so than the examples we have set out from prior cases in which we found no conflict with the Establishment Clause. It would be ironic, however, if the inclusion of a single symbol of a particular historic religious event, as part of a celebration acknowledged in the Western World for 20 centuries, and in this country by the people, by the Executive Branch, by the Congress, and the courts for two centuries, would so "taint" the City's exhibit as to render it violative of the Establishment Clause. To forbid the use of this one passive symbol— the crèche—at the very time people are taking note of the season with Christmas hymns and carols in public schools and other public places, and while the Congress and Legislatures open sessions with prayers by paid chaplains would be a stilted over-reaction contrary to our history and to our holdings. If the presence of the crèche in this display violates the Establishment Clause, a host of other forms of taking official note of Christmas, and of our religious heritage, are equally offensive to the Constitution.

The Court has acknowledged that the "fears and political problems" that gave rise to the Religion Clauses in the 18th century are of far less concern today. We are unable to perceive the Archbishop of Canterbury, the Vicar of Rome, or other powerful religious leaders behind every public acknowledgment of the religious heritage long officially recognized by the three constitutional branches of government. Any notion that these symbols pose a real danger of establishment of a state church is far-fetched indeed.

. . .

Justice **Brennan,** with whom Justice **Marshall,** Justice **Blackmun** and Justice **Stevens** join, dissenting.

The principles announced in the compact phrases of the Religion Clauses have, as the Court today reminds us, proven difficult to apply. Faced with that uncertainty, the Court properly looks for guidance to the settled test announced in Lemon v Kurtzman, for assessing whether a challenged governmental practice involves an impermissible step toward the establishment of religion. Applying that test to this case, the Court reaches an essentially narrow result which turns largely upon the particular holiday context in which the City of Pawtucket's nativity scene appeared. The Court's decision implicitly leaves open questions concerning the constitutionality of the public display on public property of a crèche standing alone, or the public display of other distinctively religious symbols such as a cross. Despite the narrow contours of the Court's opinion, our precedents in my view compel the holding that Pawtucket's inclusion of a life-sized display depicting the biblical description of the birth of Christ as part of its annual Christmas celebration is unconstitutional. Nothing in the history of such practices or the setting in which the City's crèche is presented obscures or diminishes the plain fact that Pawtucket's action amounts to an impermissible governmental endorsement of a particular faith.

. . .

Last Term, I expressed the hope that the Court's decision in Marsh v Chambers (1983),

would prove to be only a single, aberrant departure from our settled method of analyzing Establishment Clause cases. That the Court today returns to the settled analysis of our prior cases gratifies that hope. At the same time, the Court's less than vigorous application of the Lemon test suggests that its commitment to those standards may only be superficial. After reviewing the Court's opinion, I am convinced that this case appears hard not because the principles of decision are obscure, but because the Christmas holiday seems so familiar and agreeable. Although the Court's reluctance to disturb a community's chosen method of celebrating such an agreeable holiday is understandable, that cannot justify the Court's departure from controlling precedent. In my view, Pawtucket's maintenance and display at public expense of a symbol as distinctively sectarian as a crèche simply cannot be squared with our prior cases. And it is plainly contrary to the purposes and values of the Establishment Clause to pretend, as the Court does, that the otherwise secular setting of Pawtucket's nativity scene dilutes in some fashion the crèche's singular religiosity, or that the City's annual display reflects nothing more than an "acknowledgement" of our shared national heritage. Neither the character of the Christmas holiday itself, nor our heritage of religious expression supports this result. Indeed, our remarkable and precious religious diversity as a nation, which the Establishment Clause seeks to protect, runs directly counter to today's decision.

. . .

Applying the three-part test to Pawtucket's crèche, I am persuaded that the City's inclusion of the crèche in its Christmas display simply does not reflect a "clearly secular purpose." Unlike the typical case in which the record reveals some contemporaneous expression of a clear purpose to advance religion, conversely, a clear secular purpose, here we have no explicit statement of purpose by Pawtucket's municipal government accompanying its decision to purchase, display and maintain the crèche. Governmental purpose may nevertheless be inferred. For instance, in Stone v Graham (1980), this Court found, despite the state's avowed purpose of reminding schoolchildren of the secular application of the commands of the Decalogue, that the "pre-eminent purpose for posting the Ten Commandments on schoolroom walls is plainly religious in nature." In the present case, the City claims that its purposes were exclusively secular. Pawtucket sought, according to this view, only to participate in the celebration of a national holiday and to attract people to the downtown area in order to promote pre-Christmas retail sales and to help engender the spirit of goodwill and neighborliness commonly associated with the Christmas season.

Despite these assertions, two compelling aspects of this case indicate that our generally prudent "reluctance to attribute unconstitutional motives" to a governmental body should be overcome. First, all of Pawtucket's "valid secular objectives can be readily accomplished by other means." Plainly, the City's interest in celebrating the holiday and in promoting both retail sales and goodwill are fully served by the elaborate display of Santa Claus, reindeer, and wishing wells that are already a part of Pawtucket's annual Christmas display. More importantly, the nativity scene, unlike every other element of the Hodgson Park display, reflects a sectarian exclusivity that the avowed purposes of celebrating the holiday season and promoting retail commerce simply do not encompass. To be found constitutional, Pawtucket's seasonal celebration must at least be non-denominational and not serve to promote religion. The inclusion of a distinctively religious element like the crèche, however, demonstrates that a narrower sectarian purpose lay behind the decision to include a nativity scene. That the crèche retained this religious character for the people and municipal government of Pawtucket is suggested by the Mayor's testimony at trial in which he stated that for him, as well as others in the City, the effort to eliminate the nativity scene from Pawtucket's Christmas celebration "is a step towards establishing another religion, non-religion that it may be." Plainly, the City and its leaders understood that the inclusion of the crèche in its display would serve the wholly religious purpose of "keep[ing] 'Christ in Christmas.'" From this record, therefore, it is impossible to say with the kind of confidence that was

possible in McGowan v Maryland, (1961), that a wholly secular goal predominates.

The "primary effect" of including a nativity scene in the City's display is, as the District Court found, to place the government's imprimatur of approval on the particular religious beliefs exemplified by the crèche. Those who believe in the message of the nativity receive the unique and exclusive benefit of public recognition and approval of their views. For many, the City's decision to include the crèche as part of its extensive and costly efforts to celebrate Christmas can only mean that the prestige of the government has been conferred on the beliefs associated with the crèche, thereby providing "a significant symbolic benefit to religion. . . ." The effect on minority religious groups, as well as on those who may reject all religion, is to convey the message that their views are not similarly worthy of public recognition nor entitled to public support. It was precisely this sort of religious chauvinism that the Establishment Clause was intended forever to prohibit. In this case, as in Engel v Vitale, "[w]hen the power, prestige and financial support of government is placed behind a particular religious belief, the indirect coercive pressure upon religious minorities to conform to the prevailing officially approved religion is plain." Our decision in Widmar v Vincent (1981), rests upon the same principle. There the Court noted that a state university policy of "equal access" for both secular and religious groups would "not confer any imprimatur of State approval" on the religious groups permitted to use the facilities because "a broad spectrum of groups" would be served and there was no evidence that religious groups would dominate the forum. Here, by contrast, Pawtucket itself owns the crèche and instead of extending similar attention to a "broad spectrum" of religious and secular groups, it has singled out Christianity for special treatment.

Finally, it is evident that Pawtucket's inclusion of a crèche as part of its annual Christmas display does pose a significant threat of fostering "excessive entanglement." As the Court notes, the District Court found no administrative entanglement in this case, primarily because the City had been able to administer the annual display without extensive consultation with religious officials. Of course, there is no reason to disturb that finding, but it is worth noting that after today's decision, administrative entanglements may well develop. Jews and other non-Christian groups, prompted perhaps by the Mayor's remark that he will include a Menorah in future displays, can be expected to press government for inclusion of their symbols, and faced with such requests, government will have to become involved in accommodating the various demands. More importantly, although no political divisiveness was apparent in Pawtucket prior to the filing of respondents' lawsuit, that act, as the District Court found, unleashed powerful emotional reactions which divided the City along religious lines. The fact that calm had prevailed prior to this suit does not immediately suggest the absence of any division on the point for, as the District Court observed, the quiéscence of those opposed to the crèche may have reflected nothing more than their sense of futility in opposing the majority. Of course, the Court is correct to note that we have never held that the potential for divisiveness alone is sufficient to invalidate a challenged governmental practice; we have, nevertheless, repeatedly emphasized that "too close a proximity" between religious and civil authorities may represent a "warning signal" that the values embodied in the Establishment Clause are at risk. Furthermore, the Court should not blind itself to the fact that because communities differ in religious composition, the controversy over whether local governments may adopt religious symbols will continue to fester. In many communities, non-Christian groups can be expected to combat practices similar to Pawtucket's; this will be so especially in areas where there are substantial non-Christian minorities.

In sum, considering the District Court's careful findings of fact under the three-part analysis called for by our prior cases, I have no difficulty concluding that Pawtucket's display of the crèche is unconstitutional.

. . .

Although the Court's relaxed application of the Lemon test to Pawtucket's crèche is regrettable, it is at least understandable and properly limited to the particular facts of this case. The Court's opinion, however, also sounds a broader and more troubling theme. Invoking the celebration of Thanksgiving as a public holiday, the legend "In God We Trust" on our coins, and the proclamation "God save the United States and this Honorable Court" at the opening of judicial sessions, the Court asserts, without explanation, that Pawtucket's inclusion of a crèche in its annual Christmas display poses no more a threat to Establishment Clause values than these other official "acknowledgments" of religion.

Intuition tells us that some official "acknowledgment" is inevitable in a religious society if government is not to adopt a stilted indifference to the religious life of the people. It is equally true, however, that if government is to remain scrupulously neutral in matters of religious conscience, as our Constitution requires, then it must avoid those overly broad acknowledgments of religious practices that may imply governmental favoritism toward one set of religious beliefs. This does not mean, of course, that public officials may not take account, when necessary, of the separate existence and significance of the religious institutions and practices in the society they govern. Should government choose to incorporate some arguably religious element into its public ceremonies, that acknowledgment must be impartial; it must not tend to promote one faith or handicap another; and it should not sponsor religion generally over non-religion. Thus, in a series of decisions concerned with such acknowledgments, we have repeatedly held that any active form of public acknowledgment of religion indicating sponsorship or endorsement is forbidden. . . .

Despite this body of case law, the Court has never comprehensively addressed the extent to which government may acknowledge religion by, for example, incorporating religious references into public ceremonies and proclamations, and I do not presume to offer a comprehensive approach. Nevertheless, it appears from our prior decisions that at least three principles—tracing the narrow channels which government acknowledgments must follow to satisfy the Establishment Clause—may be identified.

First, although the government may not be compelled to do so by the Free Exercise Clause, it may, consistently with the Establishment Clause, act to accommodate to some extent the opportunities of individuals to practice their religion. This is the essential meaning, I submit, of this Court's decision in Zorach v Clauson (1952), finding that government does not violate the Establishment Clause when it simply chooses to "close its doors or suspend its operations as to those who want to repair to their religious sanctuary for worship or instruction." And for me that principle would justify government's decision to declare December 25th a public holiday.

Second, our cases recognize that while a particular governmental practice may have derived from religious motivations and retain certain religious connotations, it is nonetheless permissible for the government to pursue the practice when it is continued today solely for secular reasons. As this Court noted with reference to Sunday Closing Laws in McGowan v Maryland, the mere fact that a governmental practice coincides to some extent with certain religious beliefs does not render it unconstitutional. Thanksgiving Day, in my view, fits easily within this principle, for despite its religious antecedents, the current practice of celebrating Thanksgiving is unquestionably secular and patriotic. We all may gather with our families on that day to give thanks both for personal and national good fortune, but we are free, given the secular character of the holiday, to address that gratitude either to a divine beneficence or to such mundane sources as good luck or the country's abundant natural wealth.

Finally, we have noted that government cannot be completely prohibited from recognizing in its public actions the religious beliefs and practices of the American people as an aspect of our national history and culture. While I remain uncertain about these questions, I would suggest that such practices as the designation of "In God We Trust" as our national motto, or the references to God contained in the Pledge of Allegiance can best be understood, in Dean Rostow's apt phrase, as a form of "ceremonial deism"; protected from Establishment Clause scrutiny chiefly because they have lost through rote repetition any significant religious content.

Moreover, these references are uniquely suited to serve such wholly secular purposes as solemnizing public occasions, or inspiring commitment to meet some national challenge in a manner that simply could not be fully served in our culture if government were limited to purely non-religious phrases. The practices by which the government has long acknowledged religion are therefore probably necessary to serve certain secular functions, and that necessity, coupled with their long history, gives those practices an essentially secular meaning.

The crèche fits none of these categories. Inclusion of the crèche is not necessary to accommodate individual religious expression. This is plainly not a case in which individual residents of Pawtucket have claimed the right to place a crèche as part of a wholly private display on public land. Nor is the inclusion of the crèche necessary to serve wholly secular goals; it is clear that the City's secular purposes of celebrating the Christmas holiday and promoting retail commerce can be fully served without the crèche. And the crèche, because of its unique association with Christianity, is clearly more sectarian than those references to God that we accept in ceremonial phrases or in other contexts that assure neutrality. The religious works on display at the National Gallery, Presidential references to God during an Inaugural Address, or the national motto present no risk of establishing religion. To be sure, our understanding of these expressions may begin in contemplation of some religious element, but it does not end there. Their message is dominantly secular. In contrast, the message of the crèche begins and ends with reverence for a particular image of the divine.

By insisting that such a distinctively sectarian message is merely an unobjectionable part of our "religious heritage," the Court takes a long step backwards to the days when Justice Brewer could arrogantly declare for the Court that "this is a Christian nation." Those days, I had thought, were forever put behind us by the Court's decision in Engel v Vitale, in which we rejected a similar argument advanced by the State of New York that its Regent's Prayer was simply an acceptable part of our "spiritual heritage."

. . .

Aftermath of Lynch *v.* Donnelly

Ironically, by the time the *Lynch* decision was handed down, Pawtucket's nativity scene was no longer owned by the city itself. After the district court had enjoined the city from erecting its display while the case was on appeal, Mayor Dennis Lynch organized a private group, the Citizens Committee to Continue Christmas, which bought the display from the city for $300. Later the group decided to put the figures into storage until the issue was settled, at which point a group of downtown merchants, concerned that the lack of a Christmas display would discourage holiday shoppers, purchased and erected their own Christmas display.

Lynch was generally perceived as a victory for the accommodationist position, but just how sweeping a victory it was remained to be seen because the ruling was unclear in some respects. Since Pawtucket's Christmas display had included secular as well as religious symbols, a point given considerable weight by the *Lynch* majority, the status of purely religious displays was left somewhat uncertain. Many cities sought to avoid confusion by transferring their crèches to private organizations. In Nashua, New Hampshire, a federal judge permitted the erection of a crèche provided that a sign was posted beside it making clear that the display was not owned or maintained by the city and stating that "the city of Nashua is prohibited by the U.S. Constitution from endorsing or denying any particular religious belief." New York City's corporation counsel ruled that for the first time since the 1920s a nativity scene could be placed in Central Park, as long as the identity of its private sponsors was displayed on an adjacent sign.

In 1989 the Court further clarified the constitutional status of religious seasonal displays. In *Allegheny County* v. *American Civil Liberties Union*, the Court held, 5–4, that the county had violated the establishment clause by placing a crèche alone in the main stairway of its courthouse in Pittsburgh. However, by a 6–3 vote, the Court found that an 18-foot-high menorah placed outside the courthouse was constitutionally acceptable because it stood beside a Christmas tree and a sign proclaiming liberty. Thus the basic principle of *Lynch* and *Allegheny County* is that religious symbols may be used in official displays as long as they are "neutralized" by secular symbols.

Cantwell v. *Connecticut*

310 U.S. 296 (1940)

In 1940 the Supreme Court handed down two important decisions involving the free exercise clause of the First Amendment, both brought by members of the Jehovah's Witnesses. The Witnesses, formally known as the Watch Tower Bible and Tract Society, were a missionary sect that aroused much public ire in the 1930s because of the zeal with which they spread their anti-Catholic message. The Witnesses moved fearlessly into communities where they were not likely to be warmly received and were quick to challenge the various legal barriers that municipal governments tried to throw in their paths. In the late 1930s the Jehovah's Witnesses' highly skilled legal staff won two Supreme Court cases invalidating city ordinances that required permits to be obtained prior to distributing leaflets and other materials. Both decisions were based on the free speech clause.

The Witnesses also became involved in a celebrated set of cases centering on the conflict between freedom of conscience and the demands of citizenship. In 1935 two children from a family of Jehovah's Witnesses were expelled from school in Minersville, Pennsylvania, for refusing to salute the American flag, a practice they considered contrary to the biblical warning that believers should not "bow down" to a "graven image" of a false God. The children's father sued the school board in federal court claiming that their free exercise rights had been violated. The Witnesses won in both the district court and the court of appeals. However, the Supreme Court reversed the decision in *Minersville School District* v. *Gobitis*, holding that freedom of religion was not an absolute guarantee and did not relieve citizens of discharging their political duties. The *Gobitis* decision was written by Justice Felix Frankfurter, who at the time was better known as a political liberal than as an advocate of judicial restraint. Justice Harlan Stone was the only dissenter.

Gobitis touched off an ugly wave of violence directed at Jehovah's Witnesses that continued unabated for some 2 years. Around the country hundreds of Witnesses were assaulted, threatened, and harassed. A number of the Witnesses' Kingdom Halls were destroyed or damaged by fire. In 1943 the Supreme Court docketed a second compulsory flag salute case with facts almost identical to those in *Gobitis*. In *West Virginia Board of Education* v. *Barnette*, the Court explicitly overruled *Gobitis*, holding that refusal to salute the flag was protected by the free speech clause of the First Amendment.

Cantwell v. *Connecticut*, decided just a few weeks before *Gobitis*, raised less sweeping but equally important First Amendment issues. A Jehovah's Witness, Jesse Cantwell, accompanied by his two sons, had been proselytizing in a heavily Catholic neighborhood of New Haven. They carried with them religious books and pamphlets, a portable phonograph, and a set of records. In addition to knocking on doors and offering their reading materials for sale, the Cantwells also approached people on the street asking for permission to play a record which contained a virulent attack on the Roman Catholic church. Two men who heard the record were offended by it and threatened Jesse Cantwell with physical harm if he did not move on, which he did. The Cantwells were subsequently arrested and charged with violating a Connecticut statute that prohibited religious or charitable solicitation without first obtaining a permit, and with inciting a breach of the peace. All three were convicted on both counts. On appeal to the state supreme court, the three convictions for soliciting were affirmed, the younger Cantwells' breach of the peace convictions were reversed, and their father's was upheld. With the help of the Jehovah's Witnesses' legal staff, the Cantwells then appealed to the Supreme Court, claiming that the soliciting statute and the enforcement of the breach of the peace ordinance had violated their free speech and free exercise rights.

OWEN J. ROBERTS

Owen J. Roberts was a successful Philadelphia corporation lawyer when President Herbert Hoover named him to the Supreme Court in 1930. On the Court Roberts moved back and forth between the liberal and conservative camps in the two major issue areas of the 1930s and 1940s, economic regulation and civil liberties. Given the unpredictability of his views, it is fitting that Roberts is best remembered for making "the switch in time that saved nine," reversing his (as well as the Court's) previous position by upholding a state minimum wage law in 1937 while the Court was under heavy political attack by President Franklin Roosevelt for its economic conservatism.

Mr. Justice **Roberts** delivered the opinion of the Court.

. . .

The statute under which the appellants were charged provides:

"No person shall solicit money, services, subscriptions or any valuable thing for any alleged religious, charitable or philanthropic cause, from other than a member of the organization for whose benefit such person is soliciting or within the county in which such person or organization is located unless such cause shall have been approved by the secretary of the public welfare council. Upon application of any person in behalf of such cause, the secretary shall determine whether such cause is a religious one or is a bona fide object of charity or philanthropy and conforms to reasonable standards of efficiency and integrity, and, if he shall so find, shall approve the same and issue to the authority in charge a certificate to that effect. Such certificate may be revoked at any time. Any person violating any provision of this section shall be fined not more than one hundred dollars or imprisoned not more than thirty days or both."

The appellants claimed that their activities were not within the statute but consisted only of distribution of books, pamphlets, and periodicals. The State Supreme Court construed the finding of the trial court to be that "in addition to the sale of the books and the distribution of the pamphlets the defendants were also soliciting contributions or donations of money for an alleged religious cause, and thereby came within the purview of the statute." It overruled the contention that the Act, as applied to the appellants, offends the due process clause of the Fourteenth Amendment, because it abridges or denies religious freedom and liberty of speech and press. The court stated that it was the solicitation that brought the appellants within the sweep of the Act and not their other activities in the dissemination of literature. It declared the legislation constitutional as an effort by the State to protect the public against fraud and imposition in the solicitation of funds for what purported to be religious, charitable, or philanthropic causes.

. . .

First. We hold that the statute, as construed and applied to the appellants, deprives them of their liberty without due process of law in contravention of the Fourteenth Amendment. The fundamental concept of liberty embodied in that Amendment embraces the liberties guaranteed by the First Amendment. The First Amendment declares that Congress shall make no law respecting an establishment of religion or prohibiting the free exercise thereof. The Fourteenth Amendment has rendered the legislatures of the states as incompetent as Congress to enact such laws. The constitutional inhibition of legislation on the subject of religion has a double aspect. On the one hand, it forestalls compulsion by law of the acceptance of any creed or the practice of any form of worship. Freedom of conscience and freedom to adhere to such religious organization or form of worship as the individual may choose cannot be restricted by law. On the other hand, it safeguards the free exercise of the chosen form of religion. Thus the Amendment embraces two concepts—freedom to believe and freedom to act. The first is absolute but, in the nature of things, the second cannot be. Conduct remains subject to regulation for the protection of society. The freedom to act must have appropriate definition to preserve the enforcement of that protection. In every case the power to regulate must be so exercised as not, in attaining a permissible end, unduly to infringe the protected freedom. No one would contest the proposition that a State may not, by statute, wholly deny the right to preach or to disseminate religious views. Plainly such a previous and absolute restraint would violate the terms of the guarantee. It is equally clear that a State may by general and non-discriminatory legislation regulate the times, the places, and the manner of soliciting upon its streets, and of holding meetings thereon; and may in other respects safeguard the peace, good order and comfort of the community, without unconstitutionally invading the liberties protected by the Fourteenth Amendment. The appellants are right in their insistence that the Act in question is not such a regulation. If a certificate is procured, solicitation is permitted without restraint but, in the absence of a certificate, solicitation is altogether prohibited.

The appellants urge that to require them to obtain a certificate as a condition of soliciting support for their views amounts to a prior restraint on the exercise of their religion within the meaning of the Constitution. The State insists that the Act, as construed by the Supreme Court of Connecticut, imposes no previous restraint upon the dissemination of religious views or teaching but merely safeguards against the perpetration of frauds under the cloak of religion. Conceding that this is so, the question remains whether the method adopted by Connecticut to that end transgresses the liberty safeguarded by the Constitution.

The general regulation, in the public interest, of solicitation, which does not involve any religious test and does not unreasonably obstruct or delay the collection of funds, is not open to any constitutional objection, even though the collection be for a religious purpose. Such regulation would not constitute a prohibited previous restraint on the free exercise of religion or interpose an inadmissible obstacle to its exercise.

It will be noted, however, that the Act requires an application to the secretary of the public welfare council of the State; that he is empowered to determine whether the cause is a religious one, and that the issue of a certificate depends upon his affirmative action. If he finds that the cause is not that of religion, to solicit for it becomes a crime. He is not to issue a certificate as a matter of course. His decision to issue or refuse it involves appraisal of facts, the exercise of judgment, and the formation of an opinion. He is authorized to withhold his approval if he determines that the cause is not a religious one. Such a censorship of religion as the means of determining its right to survive is a denial of liberty protected by the First Amendment and included in the liberty which is within the protection of the Fourteenth.

The State asserts that if the licensing officer acts arbitrarily, capriciously, or corruptly, his action is subject to judicial correction. Counsel refer to the rule prevailing in Connecticut that the decision of a commission or an administrative official will be reviewed upon a claim that "it works material damage to individual or corporate rights, or invades or threatens such rights, or is so unreasonable as to justify judicial intervention, or is not consonant with justice, or that a legal duty has not been performed." It is suggested that the statute is to be read as requiring the officer to issue a certificate unless the cause in question is clearly not a religious one; and that if he violates his duty his action will be corrected by a court.

To this suggestion there are several sufficient answers. The line between a discretionary and a ministerial act is not always easy to mark and the statute has not been construed by the state court to impose a mere ministerial duty on the secretary of the welfare council. Upon his decision as to the nature of the cause, the right to solicit depends. Moreover, the availability of a judicial remedy for abuses in the system of licensing still leaves that system one of previous re-straint which, in the field of free speech and press, we have held inadmissible. A statute authrizing previous restraint upon the exercise of the guaranteed freedom by judicial decision after trial is as obnoxious to the Constitution as one providing for like restraint by administrative action.

Nothing we have said is intended even remotely to imply that, under the cloak of religion, persons may, with impunity, commit frauds upon the public. Certainly penal laws are available to punish such conduct. Even the exercise of religion may be at some slight inconvenience in order that the State may protect its citizens from injury. Without doubt a State may protect its citizens from fraudulent solicitation by requiring a stranger in the community, before permitting him publicly to solicit funds for any purpose, to establish his identity and his authority to act for the cause which he purports to represent. The State is likewise free to regulate the time and manner of solicitation generally, in the interest of public safety, peace, comfort or convenience. But to condition the solicitation of aid for the perpetuation of religious views or systems upon a license, the grant of which rests in the exercise of a determination by state authority as to what is a religious cause, is to lay a forbidden burden upon the exercise of liberty protected by the Constitution.

Second. We hold that, in the circumstances disclosed, the conviction of Jesse Cantwell on the fifth count [inciting others to breach of the peace] must be set aside. Decision as to the lawfulness of the conviction demands the weighing of two conflicting interests. The fundamental law declares the interest of the United States that the free exercise of religion be not prohibited and that freedom to communicate information and opinion be not abridged. The State of Connecticut has an obvious interest in the preservation and protection of peace and good order within her borders. We must determine whether the alleged protection of the State's interest, means to which end would, in the absence of limitation by the Federal Constitution, lie wholly within the State's discretion, has been pressed, in this instance, to a point where it has come into fatal collision with the overriding interest protected by the federal compact.

Conviction on the fifth count was not pursuant to a statute evincing a legislative judgment that street discussion of religious affairs, because of its tendency to provoke disorder, should be regulated, or a judgment that the playing of a phonograph on the streets should in the interest of comfort or privacy be limited or prevented. Violation of an Act exhibiting such a legislative judgment and narrowly drawn to prevent the supposed evil, would pose a question differing from that we must here answer. Such a declaration of the State's policy would weigh heavily in any challenge of the law as infringing constitutional limitations. Here, however, the judgment is based on a common law concept of the most general and undefined nature. The court below has held that the petitioner's conduct constituted the commission of an offense under the state law, and we accept its decision as binding upon us to that extent.

The offense known as breach of the peace embraces a great variety of conduct destroying or menacing public order and tranquility. It includes not only violent acts but acts and words likely to produce violence in others. No one would have the hardihood to suggest that the principle of freedom of speech sanctions incitement to riot or that religious liberty connotes the privilege to exhort others to physical attack upon those belonging to another sect. When clear and present danger of riot, disorder, interference with traffic upon the public streets, or other immediate threat to public safety, peace, or order, appears, the power of the State to prevent or punish is obvious. Equally obvious is it that a State may not unduly suppress free communication of views, religious or other, under the guise of conserving desirable conditions. Here we have a situation analogous to a conviction under a statute sweeping in a great variety of conduct under a general and indefinite characterization, and leaving to the executive and judicial branches too wide a discretion in its application.

Having these considerations in mind, we note that Jesse Cantwell, on April 26, 1938, was upon a public street, where he had a right to be, and where he had a right peacefully to impart his views to others. There is no showing that his deportment was noisy, truculent, overbearing or offensive. He requested of two pedestrians permission to play to them a phonograph record. The permission was granted. It is not claimed that he intended to insult or affront the hearers by playing the record. It is plain that he wished only to interest them in his propaganda. The sound of the phonograph is not shown to have disturbed residents of the street, to have drawn a crowd, or to have impeded traffic. Thus far he had invaded no right or interest of the public or of the men accosted.

The record played by Cantwell embodies a general attack on all organized religious systems as instruments of Satan and injurious to man; it then singles out the Roman Catholic Church for strictures couched in terms which naturally would offend not only persons of that persuasion, but all others who respect the honestly held religious faith of their fellows. The hearers were in fact highly offended. One of them said he felt like hitting Cantwell and the other that he was tempted to throw Cantwell off the street. The one who testified he felt like hitting Cantwell said, in answer to the question "Did you do anything else or have any other reaction?" "No, sir, because he said he would take the Victrola and he went." The other witness testified that he told Cantwell he had better get off the street before something happened to him and that was the end of the matter as Cantwell picked up his books and walked up the street.

Cantwell's conduct, in the view of the court below, considered apart from the effect of his communication upon his hearers, did not amount to a breach of the peace. One may, however, be guilty of the offense if he commit acts or make statements likely to provoke violence and disturbance of good order, even though no such eventuality be intended. Decisions to this effect are many, but examination discloses that, in

practically all, the provocative language which was held to amount to a breach of the peace consisted of profane, indecent, or abusive remarks directed to the person of the hearer. Resort to epithets or personal abuse is not in any proper sense communication of information or opinion safeguarded by the Constitution, and its punishment as a criminal act would raise no question under that instrument.

We find in the instant case no assault or threatening of bodily harm, no truculent bearing, no intentional discourtesy, no personal abuse. On the contrary, we find only an effort to persuade a willing listener to buy a book or to contribute money in the interest of what Cantwell, however misguided others may think him, conceived to be true religion.

In the realm of religious faith, and in that of political belief, sharp differences arise. In both fields the tenets of one man may seem the rankest error to his neighbor. To persuade others to his own point of view, the pleader, as we know, at times, resorts to exaggeration, to vilification of men who have been, or are, prominent in church or state, and even to false statement. But the people of this nation have ordained in the light of history, that, in spite of the probability of excesses and abuses, these liberties are, in the long view, essential to enlightened opinion and right conduct on the part of the citizens of a democracy.

The essential characteristic of these liberties is, that under their shield many types of life, character, opinion and belief can develop unmolested and unobstructed. Nowhere is this shield more necessary than in our own country for a people composed of many races and of many creeds. There are limits to the exercise of these liberties. The danger in these times from the coercive activities of those who in the delusion of racial or religious conceit would incite violence and breaches of the peace in order to deprive others of their equal right to the exercise of their liberties, is emphasized by events familiar to all. These and other transgressions of those limits the States appropriately may punish.

Although the contents of the record not unnaturally aroused animosity, we think that, in the absence of a statute narrowly drawn to define and punish specific conduct as constituting a clear and present danger to a substantial interest of the State, the petitioner's communication, considered in the light of the constitutional guarantees, raised no such clear and present menace to public peace and order as to render him liable to conviction of the common law offense in question.

The judgment affirming the convictions . . . is reversed and the cause is remanded for further proceedings not inconsistent with this opinion.

Aftermath of Cantwell *v.* Connecticut

Cantwell drew its significance from the fact that the Supreme Court for the first time held that the free exercise clause (as well as the establishment clause) was applicable to the states through the Fourteenth Amendment. Henceforth religious groups like the Witnesses would have another constitutional weapon, besides the free speech clause, with which to defend themselves against governmental efforts to restrict their activities. Despite the *Cantwell* decision, the Witnesses continued to encounter resistance in many communities as they went from door to door attempting to spread their message. In 1943 the Supreme Court heard several challenges brought by the Witnesses against municipal ordinances aimed at discouraging the Witnesses' missionary activities. In *Jones* v. *Opelika,* the Court used the free speech and free exercise clauses in tandem to overturn a city ordinance requiring payment of a tax by anyone engaged in selling door to door. In *Martin* v. *Struthers* a city had banned all door-to-door canvassing, a practice which the Court held to violate the free speech clause.

Sherbert v. Verner

374 U.S. 398 (1963)

In 1961 the Supreme Court was faced with an unusual set of companion cases. In *McGowan* v. *Maryland,* a state Sunday closing law was challenged on establishment clause grounds by employees of a department store who had been convicted of violating the law by selling merchandise on Sunday. The Court ruled in *McGowan* that the law was not unconstitutional because despite its undoubtedly religious origins, it now served the secular purpose of providing "a uniform day of rest for all citizens. . . ." In the companion case of *Braunfeld* v. *Brown,* the Court examined the same issue from the standpoint of the free exercise clause. The appellants were a group of Orthodox Jewish merchants in Philadelphia whose religion required them to refrain from doing business on Saturdays. Prior to the enactment of the closing law in 1959, each merchant had done a substantial amount of business on Sunday, partially compensating for their closing on Saturday. The merchants claimed that the law interfered with their religious freedom by forcing them to choose between suffering severe economic hardship and violating a basic religious tenet. The Court held in *Braunfeld* that a distinction must be maintained between laws that seek to outlaw religious practices, and laws like this one that simply make the practice of religion more difficult. Because the closing law placed only an indirect burden on the merchants, it did not violate the free exercise clause.

The Court's next important free exercise case was *Sherbert* v. *Verner* in 1963. Mrs. Sherbert, a member of the Seventh-Day Adventist Church in South Carolina, was discharged from her job in a textile mill when she refused to work on Saturday, her

Sabbath Day. Unable to find any other employment because of her unwillingness to violate her Sabbath, she filed a claim for benefits with the state unemployment commission. The commission denied her claim on the ground that she had, without good cause, failed to accept suitable work. After the commission's decision was sustained by the state supreme court, Sherbert appealed on free exercise grounds to the Supreme Court, which granted *certiorari*.

Mr. Justice **Brennan** delivered the opinion of the Court.

. . .

The door of the Free Exercise Clause stands tightly closed against any governmental regulation of religious *beliefs* as such. Government may neither compel affirmation of a repugnant belief; nor penalize or discriminate against individuals or groups because they hold religious views abhorrent to the authorities; nor employ the taxing power to inhibit the dissemination of particular religious views. On the other hand, the Court has rejected challenges under the Free Exercise Clause to governmental regulation of certain overt acts prompted by religious beliefs or principles, for "even when the action is in accord with one's religious convictions, [it] is not totally free from legislative restrictions." The conduct or actions so regulated have invariably posed some substantial threat to public safety, peace or order.

Plainly enough, appellant's conscientious objection to Saturday work constitutes no conduct prompted by religious principles of a kind within the reach of state legislation. If, therefore, the decision of the South Carolina Supreme Court is to withstand appellant's constitutional challenge, it must be either because her disqualification as a beneficiary represents no infringement by the State of her constitutional rights of free exercise, or because any incidental burden on the free exercise of appellant's religion may be justified by a "compelling state interest in the regulation of a subject within the State's constitutional power to regulate. . . ."

We turn first to the question whether the disqualification for benefits imposes any burden on the free exercise of appellant's religion. We think it is clear that it does. In a sense the consequences of such a disqualification to religious principles and practices may be only an indirect result of welfare legislation within the State's general competence to enact; it is true that no criminal sanctions directly compel appellant to work a six-day week. But this is only the beginning, not the end, of our inquiry. For "[i]f the purpose or effect of a law is to impede the observance of one or all religions or is to discriminate invidiously between religions, that law is constitutionally invalid even though the burden may be characterized as being only indirect." Here not only is it apparent that appellant's declared ineligibility for benefits derives solely from the practice of her religion, but the pressure upon her to forego that practice is unmistakable. The ruling forces her to choose between following the precepts of her religion and forfeiting benefits; on the one hand, and abandoning one of the precepts of her religion in order to accept work, on the other hand. Governmental imposition of such a choice puts the same kind of burden upon the free exercise of religion as would a fine imposed against appellant for her Saturday worship.

. . .

Significantly South Carolina expressly saves the Sunday worshipper from having to make the kind of choice which we here hold infringes the Sabbatarian's religious liberty. When in times of "national emergency" the textile plants are authorized by the State Commissioner of Labor to operate on Sunday, "no employee shall be required to work on Sunday . . . who is conscientiously opposed to Sunday work; and if any employee should refuse to work on Sunday on account of conscientious . . . objections he or she shall not jeopardize his or her seniority by such refusal or be discriminated against in any other manner." S. C. Code, § 64–4. No question of the disqualification of a Sunday worshipper for benefits is likely to arise, since we cannot suppose that an employer will discharge him in violation of this statute. The unconstitutionality of the disqualification of the Sabbatarian is thus compounded by the religious discrimination which South Carolina's general statutory scheme necessarily effects. . . .

We must next consider whether some compelling state interest enforced in the eligibility provisions of the South Carolina statute justifies the substantial infringement of appellant's First Amendment right. It is basic that no showing merely of a rational relationship to some colorable state interest would suffice; in this highly sensitive constitutional area, "[o]nly the gravest abuses, endangering paramount interests, give occasion for permissible limitation." No such abuse or danger has been advanced in the present case. The appellees suggest no more than a possibility that the filing of fraudulent claims by unscrupulous claimants feigning religious objections to Saturday work might not only dilute the unemployment compensation fund but also hinder the scheduling by employers of necessary Saturday work. But that possibility is not apposite here because no such objection appears to have been made before the South Carolina Supreme Court, and we are unwilling to assess the importance of an asserted state interest without the views of the state court. Nor, if the contention had been made below, would the record appear to sustain it; there is no proof whatever to warrant such fears of malingering or deceit as those which the respondents now advance. Even if consideration of such evidence is not foreclosed by the prohibition against judicial inquiry into the truth or falsity of religious beliefs—a question as to which we intimate no view since it is not before us—it is highly doubtful whether such evidence would be sufficient to warrant a substantial infringement of religious liberties. For even if the possibility of spurious claims did threaten to dilute the fund and disrupt the scheduling of work, it would plainly be incumbent upon the appellees to demonstrate that no alternative forms of regulation would combat such abuses without infringing First Amendment rights.

In these respects, then, the state interest asserted in the present case is wholly dissimilar to the interests which were found to justify the less direct burden upon religious practices in *Braunfeld* v. *Brown.* The Court recognized that the Sunday closing law which that decision sustained undoubtedly served "to make the practice of [the Orthodox Jewish merchants'] . . . religious beliefs more expensive." But the statute was nevertheless saved by a countervailing factor which finds no equivalent in the instant case—a strong state interest in providing one uniform day of rest for all workers. That secular objective could be achieved, the Court found, only by declaring Sunday to be that day of rest. Requiring exemptions for Sabbatarians, while theoretically possible, appeared to present an administrative problem of such magnitude, or to afford the exempted class so great a competitive advantage, that such a requirement would have rendered the entire statutory scheme unworkable. In the present case no such justifications underlie the determination of the state court that appellant's religion makes her ineligible to receive benefits.

. . .

In holding as we do, plainly we are not fostering the "establishment" of the Seventh-day Adventist religion in South Carolina, for the extension of unemployment benefits to Sabbatarians in common with Sunday worshippers reflects nothing more than the governmental obligation of neutrality in the face of religious differences, and does not represent that involvement of religious with secular institutions which it is the object of the Establishment Clause to forestall. Nor does the recognition of the appellant's right to unemployment benefits under the state statute serve to abridge any other person's religious liberties. Nor do we, by our decision today, declare the existence of a constitutional right to unemployment benefits on the part of all persons whose religious convictions are the cause of their unemployment. This is not a case in which an employee's religious convictions serve to make him a nonproductive member of society. Finally, nothing we say today constrains the States to adopt any particular form or scheme of unemployment compensation. Our holding today is only that South Carolina may not constitutionally apply the eligibility provisions so as to constrain a worker to abandon his religious convictions respecting the day of rest. This holding but reaffirms a principle that we announced a decade and a half ago, namely that no State may "exclude individual Catholics, Lutherans, Mohammedans, Baptists, Jews, Methodists, Non-believers, Presbyterians, or the members of any other faith, *because of their faith, or lack of it,* from receiving the benefits of public welfare legislation."

In view of the result we have reached under the First and Fourteenth Amendments' guarantee of free exercise of religion, we have no occasion to consider appellant's claim that the denial of benefits also deprived her of the equal protection of the laws in violation of the Fourteenth Amendment.

The judgment of the South Carolina Supreme Court is reversed and the case is remanded for further proceedings not inconsistent with this opinion.

Mr. Justice **Stewart,** concurring in the result.

Although fully agreeing with the result which the Court reaches in this case, I cannot join the Court's opinion. This case presents a double-barreled dilemma, which in all candor I think the Court's opinion has not succeeded in papering over. The dilemma ought to be resolved.

. . .

I am convinced that no liberty is more essential to the continued vitality of the free society which our Constitution guarantees than is the religious liberty protected by the Free Exercise Clause explicit in the First Amendment and imbedded in the Fourteenth. And I regret that on occasion, and specifically in *Braunfeld* v. *Brown,* the Court has shown what has seemed to me a distressing insensitivity to the appropriate demands of this constitutional guarantee. By contrast I think that the Court's approach to the Establishment Clause has on occasion, and specifically in *Engel, Schempp* and *Murray,* been not only insensitive, but positively wooden, and that the Court has accorded to the Establishment Clause a meaning which neither the words, the history, nor the intention of the authors of that specific constitutional provision even remotely suggests.

But my views as to the correctness of the Court's decisions in these cases are beside the point here. The point is that the decisions are on the books. And the result is that there are many situations where legitimate claims under the Free Exercise Clause will run into head-on collision with the Court's insensitive and sterile construction of the Establishment Clause. The controversy now before us is clearly such a case.

Because the appellant refuses to accept available jobs which would require her to work on Saturdays, South Carolina has declined to pay unemployment compensation benefits to her. Her refusal to work on Saturdays is based on the tenets of her religious faith. The Court says that South Carolina cannot under these circumstances declare her to be not "available for work" within the meaning of its statute because to do so would violate her constitutional right to the free exercise of her religion.

Yet what this Court has said about the Establishment Clause must inevitably lead to a diametrically opposite result. If the appellant's refusal to work on Saturdays were based on indolence, or on a compulsive desire to watch the Saturday television programs, no one would say that South Carolina could not hold that she was not "available for work" within the meaning of its statute. That being so, the Establishment Clause as construed by this Court not only *permits* but affirmatively *requires* South Carolina equally to deny the appellant's claim for unemployment compensation when her refusal to work on Saturdays is based upon her religious creed. For, as said in *Everson* v. *Board of Education,* the Establishment Clause bespeaks "a government . . . stripped of all power . . . to support, or otherwise to assist any or all religions . . . ," and no State "can pass laws which aid one religion. . . ." In Mr. Justice Rutledge's words, adopted by the Court today in *Schempp,* the Establishment Clause forbids "every form of public aid or support for religion." In the words of the Court in *Engel* v. *Vitale,* reaffirmed today in the *Schempp* case, the Establishment Clause forbids the "financial support of government" to be "placed behind a particular religious belief."

To require South Carolina to so administer its laws as to pay public money to the appellant under the circumstances of this case is thus clearly to require the State to violate the Establishment Clause as construed by this Court. This poses no problem for me, because I think the Court's mechanistic concept of the Establishment Clause is historically unsound and constitutionally wrong. I think the process of constitutional decision in the area of the relationships between government and religion demands considerably more than the invocation of broadbrushed rhetoric of the kind I have quoted. And I think that the guarantee of religious liberty embodied in the Free Exercise Clause affirmatively requires government to create an atmosphere of hospitality and accommodation to individual belief or disbelief. In short, I think our Constitution commands the positive protection by government of religious freedom—not only for a minority, however small—not only for the majority, however large—but for each of us.

South Carolina would deny unemployment benefits to a mother unavailable for work on Saturdays because she was unable to get a babysitter. Thus, we do not have before us a situation where a State provides unemployment compensation generally, and singles out for disqualification only those persons who are unavailable for work on religious grounds. This is not, in short, a scheme which operates so as to discriminate against religion as such. But the Court nevertheless holds that the State must prefer a religious over a secular ground for being unavailable for work—that state financial support of the appellant's religion is constitutionally required to carry out "the governmental obligation of neutrality in the face of religious differences. . . ."

Yet in cases decided under the Establishment Clause the Court has decreed otherwise. It has decreed that government must blind itself to the differing religious beliefs and traditions of the people. With all respect, I think it is the Court's duty to face up to the dilemma posed by the conflict between the Free Exercise Clause of the Constitution and the Establishment Clause as interpreted by the Court. It is a duty, I submit, which we owe to the people, the States, and the Nation, and a duty which we owe to ourselves. For so long as the resounding but fallacious fundamentalist rhetoric of some of our Establishment Clause opinions remains on our books, to be disregarded at will as in the present case, or to be undiscriminatingly invoked as in the *Schempp* case, so long will the possibility of consistent and perceptive decision in this most difficult and delicate area of constitutional law be impeded and impaired. And so long, I fear,

will the guarantee of true religious freedom in our pluralistic society be uncertain and insecure.

. . .

Mr. Justice **Harlan,** whom Mr. Justice **White** joins, dissenting.

Today's decision is disturbing both in its rejection of existing precedent and in its implications for the future. The significance of the decision can best be understood after an examination of the state law applied in this case.

South Carolina's Unemployment Compensation Law was enacted in 1936 in response to the grave social and economic problems that arose during the depression of that period. . . . [T]he purpose of the legislature was to tide people over, and to avoid social and economic chaos, during periods when *work was unavailable.* But at the same time there was clearly no intent to provide relief for those who for purely personal reasons were or became *unavailable for work.* In accordance with this design, the legislature provided, in § 68–113, that "[a]n unemployed insured worker shall be eligible to receive benefits with respect to any week *only* if the Commission finds that . . . [h]e is able to work and is available for work. . . ." (Emphasis added.)

The South Carolina Supreme Court has uniformly applied this law in conformity with its clearly expressed purpose. It has consistently held that one is not "available for work" if his unemployment has resulted not from the inability of industry to provide a job but rather from personal circumstances, no matter how compelling. The reference to "involuntary unemployment" in the legislative statement of policy, whatever a sociologist, philosopher, or theologian might say, has been interpreted not to embrace such personal circumstances. . . .

In the present case all that the state court has done is to apply these accepted principles. Since virtually all of the mills in the Spartanburg area were operating on a six-day week, the appellant was "unavailable for work," and thus ineligible for benefits, when personal considerations prevented her from accepting employment on a full-time basis in the industry and locality in which she had worked. The fact that these personal considerations sprang from her religious convictions was wholly without relevance to the state court's application of the law. Thus in no proper sense can it be said that the State discriminated against the appellant on the basis of her religious beliefs or that she was denied benefits *because* she was a Seventh-day Adventist. She was denied benefits just as any other claimant would be denied benefits who was not "available for work" for personal reasons.

With this background, this Court's decision comes into clearer focus. What the Court is holding is that if the State chooses to condition unemployment compensation on the applicant's availability for work, it is constitutionally compelled to *carve out an exception*—and to provide benefits—for those whose unavailability is due to their religious convictions. Such a holding has particular significance in two respects.

First, despite the Court's protestations to the contrary, the decision necessarily overrules *Braunfeld* v. *Brown*, which held that it did not offend the "Free Exercise" Clause of the Constitution for a State to forbid a Sabbatarian to do business on Sunday. The secular purpose of the statute before us today is even clearer than that involved in *Braunfeld*. And just as in *Braunfeld*—where exceptions to the Sunday closing laws for Sabbatarians would have been inconsistent with the purpose to achieve a uniform day of rest and would have required case-by-case inquiry into religious beliefs—so here, an exception to the rules of eligibility based on religious convictions would necessitate judicial examination of those convictions and would be at odds with the limited purpose of the statute to smooth out the economy during periods of industrial instability. . . .

Second, the implications of the present decision are far more troublesome than its apparently narrow dimensions would indicate at first glance. The meaning of today's holding, as already noted, is that the State must furnish unemployment benefits to one who is unavailable for work if the unavailability stems from the exercise of religious convictions. The State, in other words, must *single out* for financial assistance those whose behavior is religiously

motivated, even though it denies such assistance to others whose identical behavior (in this case, inability to work on Saturdays) is not religiously motivated.

It has been suggested that such singling out of religious conduct for special treatment may violate the constitutional limitations on state action. My own view, however, is that at least under the circumstances of this case it would be a permissible accommodation of religion for the State, if it *chose* to do so, to create an exception to its eligibility requirements for persons like the appellant. The constitutional obligation of "neutrality" is not so narrow a channel that the slightest deviation from an absolutely straight course leads to condemnation. There are too many instances in which no such course can be charted, too many areas in which the pervasive activities of the State justify some special provision for religion to prevent it from being submerged by an all-embracing secularism. The State violates its obligation of neutrality when, for example, it mandates a daily religious exercise in its public schools, with all the attendant pressures on the school children that such an exercise entails. But there is, I believe, enough flexibility in the Constitution to permit a legislative judgment accommodating an unemployment compensation law to the exercise of religious beliefs such as appellant's.

For very much the same reasons, however, I cannot subscribe to the conclusion that the State is constitutionally *compelled* to carve out an exception to its general rule of eligibility in the present case. Those situations in which the Constitution may require special treatment on account of religion are, in my view, few and far between, and this view is amply supported by the course of constitutional litigation in this area. Such compulsion in the present case is particularly inappropriate in light of the indirect, remote, and insubstantial effect of the decision below on the exercise of appellant's religion and in light of the direct financial assistance to religion that today's decision requires.

For these reasons I respectfully dissent from the opinion and judgment of the Court.

Aftermath of Sherbert *v.* Verner

Although the Court in *Sherbert* tried to downplay its incompatibility with *Braunfeld,* it was clear that the Court was moving in a new direction in free exercise law, and that henceforth much more deference would be shown to individuals claiming religious exemptions from otherwise valid laws. In three subsequent free exercise cases involving unemployment claims the Supreme Court has expanded the scope of its ruling in *Sherbert.* The Court held in 1981 that unemployment compensation must be paid to a factory worker who left his job for religious reasons when the factory began to produce military equipment. Six years later the Court ruled that a person who left a job that required Friday and Saturday work after joining a religion that prohibited work at those times was entitled to unemployment benefits. And in 1989 the Court ruled that benefits could not be withheld from a worker who had refused to work on Sunday, even though he belonged to no organized religion. It is sincere religious belief, said the Court, rather than membership in a particular religious denomination, that qualifies one for protection under the free exercise clause.

In each of these cases, the Court acknowledged that there may be circumstances compelling enough to override an individual's free exercise claim, but concluded that no such showing had been made. The Court found such a showing in a 1988 decision, *Lyng* v. *Northwest Indian Cemetery Protective Association,* in upholding a government decision to develop part of a national forest in California that three Native American tribes regarded as sacred land. In language more reminiscent of *Braunfeld* v. *Brown* than of the Court's more recent free exercise decisions, Justice O'Connor wrote for the majority that the First Amendment prohibits only governmental "coercion or penalties on the free exercise of religion" and does not protect against "the incidental effects of government programs" even if they severely disrupt religious practices.

In a further twist on the issue of Sabbath employment, the Supreme Court ruled in *Thornton* v. *Caldor* in 1985 that a state cannot grant all workers an absolute right to refrain from working on his or her Sabbath. The Court said that such a law violated the establishment clause by advancing a particular religious practice.

Wisconsin v. *Yoder*

406 U.S. 205 (1972)

A question over which many heated free exercise battles have been fought is the extent to which government may restrict parental decisions that are based on religious principles. Some of these disputes have involved the refusal of parents to obtain medical care for their children, and in these cases the courts have generally followed the Supreme Court's lead in holding that states are entitled to protect children from physical harm that may result from their parents' religious convictions.

In cases where not life but life style is at stake, the Supreme Court has been less deferential to the states. The leading case on this point is *Wisconsin* v. *Yoder,* decided in 1972, where a state's interest in enforcing mandatory school attendance laws was weighed against parents' sincere religious beliefs. The case involved three mem-

**bers of the Old Order Amish community in New Glarus, Wisconsin, who were con-
victed of violating the compulsory school attendance law for refusing to send their
14- and 15-year-old children to public high school. The children had completed the
eighth grade in a one-room school located in the Amish settlement, but Wisconsin
law required that children attend classes until the age of 16. The Amish, a largely
self-sufficient religious community devoted to farming, reject materialism, competition, and other aspects of modern life. They believe that sending their children to
high school would threaten the children's salvation and the Amish way of life by
exposing them to values contrary to their own. The Wisconsin Supreme Court overturned the parents' criminal convictions on the ground that the law as applied to the
Amish interfered with their First Amendment right to the free exercise of religion.
The state then appealed to the United States Supreme Court, which granted *certiorari*. The Amish, whose pacifism extended to declining to defend themselves in conflicts with outsiders, were represented in court by an ad hoc group of lawyers, ministers, and educators called the National Committee for Amish Religious Freedom.**

Mr. Chief Justice **Burger** delivered the opinion of the Court.

. . .

There is no doubt as to the power of a State,
having a high responsibility for education of its
citizens, to impose reasonable regulations for
the control and duration of basic education. See,
e. g., Pierce v Society of Sisters (1925). Providing
public schools ranks at the very apex of the function of a State. Yet even this paramount responsibility was, in Pierce, made to yield to the right
of parents to provide an equivalent education in
a privately operated system. There the Court
held that Oregon's statute compelling attendance in a public school from age eight to age 16
unreasonably interfered with the interest of parents in directing the rearing of their offspring
including their education in church-operated
schools. As that case suggests, the values of
parental direction of the religious upbringing
and education of their children in their early
and formative years have a high place in our
society. Thus, a State's interest in universal education, however highly we rank it, is not totally
free from a balancing process when it impinges
on other fundamental rights and interests, such
as those specifically protected by the Free
Exercise Clause of the First Amendment and the
traditional interest of parents with respect to the
religious upbringing of their children so long as
they, in the words of Pierce, "prepare [them] for
additional obligations."

It follows that in order for Wisconsin to compel school attendance beyond the eighth grade

against a claim that such attendance interferes
with the practice of a legitimate religious belief,
it must appear either that the State does not deny
the free exercise of religious belief by its requirement, or that there is a state interest of sufficient
magnitude to override the interest claiming protection under the Free Exercise Clause. Long
before there was general acknowledgment of the
need for universal formal education, the Religion
Clauses had specifically and firmly fixed the
right to free exercise of religious beliefs, and buttressing this fundamental right was an equally
firm, even if less explicit, prohibition against the
establishment of any religion by government.
The values underlying these two provisions
relating to religion have been zealously protected, sometimes even at the expense of other interests of admittedly high social importance. . . .

The essence of all that has been said and written on the subject is that only those interests of
the highest order and those not otherwise served
can overbalance legitimate claims to the free
exercise of religion. We can accept it as settled,
therefore, that however strong the State's interest in universal compulsory education, it is by
no means absolute to the exclusion or subordination of all other interests.

We come then to the quality of the claims of
the respondents concerning the alleged encroachment of Wisconsin's compulsory school
attendance statute on their rights and the rights
of their children to the free exercise of the religious beliefs they and their forebears have
adhered to for almost three centuries. In evaluating those claims we must be careful to deter-

mine whether the Amish religious faith and their mode of life are, as they claim, inseparable and interdependent. A way of life, however virtuous and admirable, may not be interposed as a barrier to reasonable state regulation of education if it is based on purely secular considerations; to have the protection of the Religion Clauses, the claims must be rooted in religious belief. Although a determination of what is a "religious" belief or practice entitled to constitutional protection may present a most delicate question, the very concept of ordered liberty precludes allowing every person to make his own standards on matters of conduct in which society as a whole has important interests. Thus, if the Amish asserted their claims because of their subjective evaluation and rejection of the contemporary secular values accepted by the majority, much as Thoreau rejected the social values of his time and isolated himself at Walden Pond, their claim would not rest on a religious basis. Thoreau's choice was philosophical and personal rather than religious, and such belief does not rise to the demands of the Religion Clause.

Giving no weight to such secular considerations, however, we see that the record in this case abundantly supports the claim that the traditional way of life of the Amish is not merely a matter of personal preference, but one of deep religious conviction, shared by an organized group, and intimately related to daily living. That the Old Order Amish daily life and religious practice stems from their faith is shown by the fact that it is in response to their literal interpretation of the Biblical injunction from the Epistle of Paul to the Romans, "Be not conformed to this world . . . ." This command is fundamental to the Amish faith. Moreover, for the Old Order Amish, religion is not simply a matter of theocratic belief. As the expert witnesses explained, the Old Order Amish religion pervades and determines virtually their entire way of life, regulating it with the detail of the Talmudic diet through the strictly enforced rules of the church community.

The record shows that the respondents' religious beliefs and attitude toward life, family, and home have remained constant—perhaps some would say static—in a period of unparalleled progress in human knowledge generally and great changes in education. The respondents freely concede, and indeed assert as an article of faith, that their religious beliefs and what we would today call "life style" has not altered in fundamentals for centuries. Their way of life in a church-oriented community, separated from the outside world and "worldly" influences, their attachment to nature and the soil, is a way inherently simple and uncomplicated, albeit difficult to preserve against the pressure to conform. Their rejection of telephones, automobiles, radios, and television, their mode of dress, of speech, their habits of manual work do indeed set them apart from much of contemporary society; these customs are both symbolic and practical.

As the society around the Amish has become more populous, urban, industrialized, and complex, particularly in this century, government regulation of human affairs has correspondingly become more detailed and pervasive. The Amish mode of life has thus come into conflict increasingly with requirements of contemporary society exerting a hydraulic insistence on conformity to majoritarian standards. So long as compulsory education laws were confined to eight grades of elementary basic education imparted in a nearby rural schoolhouse, with a large proportion of students of the Amish faith, the Old Order Amish had little basis to fear that school attendance would expose their children to the worldly influence they reject. But modern compulsory secondary education in rural areas is now largely carried on in a consolidated school, often remote from the student's home and alien to his daily home life. As the record so strongly shows, the values and programs of the modern secondary school are in sharp conflict with the fundamental mode of life mandated by the Amish religion; modern laws requiring compulsory secondary education have accordingly engendered great concern and conflict. The conclusion is inescapable that secondary schooling, by exposing Amish children to worldly influences in terms of attitudes, goals and values contrary to beliefs, and by substantially interfering with the religious development of the Amish child and his integration into the way of life of the Amish faith community at the crucial adolescent state of development, contravenes the basic religious tenets and practice of the Amish faith, both as to the parent and the child.

The impact of the compulsory attendance law on respondents' practice of the Amish religion is not only severe, but inescapable, for the Wisconsin law affirmatively compels them, under threat of criminal sanction, to perform acts undeniably at odds with fundamental tenets of their religious beliefs. Nor is the impact of the compulsory attendance law confined to grave interference with important Amish religious tenets from a subjective point of view. It carries with it precisely the kind of objective danger to the free exercise of religion which the First Amendment was designed to prevent. As the record shows, compulsory school attendance to age 16 for Amish children carries with it a very real threat of undermining the Amish community and religious practice as it exists today; they must either abandon belief and be assimilated into society at large, or be forced to migrate to some other and more tolerant region.

. . .

Wisconsin concedes that under the Religion Clauses religious beliefs are absolutely free from the State's control, but it argues that "actions," even though religiously grounded, are outside the protection of the First Amendment. But our decisions have rejected the idea that religiously grounded conduct is always outside the protection of the Free Exercise Clause. It is true that activities of individuals, even when religiously based, are often subject to regulation by the States in the exercise of their undoubted power to promote the health, safety, and general welfare, or the Federal Government in the exercise of its delegated powers. But to agree that religiously grounded conduct must often be subject to the broad police power of the State is not to deny that there are areas of conduct protected by the Free Exercise Clause of the First Amendment and thus beyond the power of the State to control, even under regulations of general applicability. This case, therefore, does not become easier because respondents were convicted for their "actions" in refusing to send their children to the public high school; in this context belief and action cannot be neatly confined in logic-tight compartments.

. . .

We turn, then to the State's broader contention that its interest in its system of compulsory education is so compelling that even the established religious practices of the Amish must give way. Where fundamental claims of religious freedom are at stake, however, we cannot accept such a sweeping claim; despite its admitted validity in the generality of cases, we must searchingly examine the interests which the State seeks to promote by its requirement for compulsory education to age 16, and the impediment to those objectives that would flow from recognizing the claimed Amish exemption.

The State advances two primary arguments in support of its system of compulsory education. It notes, as Thomas Jefferson pointed out early in our history, that some degree of education is necessary to prepare citizens to participate effectively and intelligently in our open political system if we are to preserve freedom and independence. Further, education prepares individuals to be self-reliant and self-sufficient participants in society. We accept these propositions.

However, the evidence adduced by the Amish in this case is persuasively to the effect that an additional one or two years of formal high school for Amish children in place of their long established program of informal vocational education would do little to serve those interests. Respondents' experts testified at trial, without challenge, that the value of all education must be assessed in terms of its capacity to prepare the child for life. It is one thing to say that compulsory education for a year or two beyond the eighth grade may be necessary when its goal is the preparation of the child for life in modern society as the majority live, but it is quite another if the goal of education be viewed as the preparation of the child for life in the separated agrarian community that is the keystone of the Amish faith.

. . .

Insofar as the State's claim rests on the view that a brief additional period of formal education is imperative to enable the Amish to participate effectively and intelligently in our democratic process, it must fall. The Amish alternative to formal secondary school education has enabled them to function effectively in their day-to-day life under self-imposed limitations on relations with the world, and to survive and prosper in contemporary society as a separate, sharply identifiable and highly self-sufficient community for more than 200 years in this country. In itself this is strong evidence that they are capable of fulfilling the social and political responsibilities of citizenship without compelled attendance beyond the eighth grade at the price of jeopardizing their free exercise of religious belief. When Thomas Jefferson emphasized the need for education as a bulwark of a free people against tyranny, there is nothing to indicate he had in mind compulsory education through any fixed age beyond a basic education. Indeed, the Amish communities singularly parallel and reflect many of the virtues of Jefferson's ideal of the "sturdy yeoman" who would form the basis of what he considered as the ideal of a democratic society. Even their idiosyncratic separateness exemplifies the diversity we profess to admire and encourage.

. . .

For the reasons stated we hold, with the Supreme Court of Wisconsin, that the First and Fourteenth Amendments prevent the State from compelling respondents to cause their children to attend formal high school to age 16. Our disposition of this case, however, in no way alters our recognition of the obvious fact that courts are not school boards or legislatures, and are ill-equipped to determine the "necessity" of discrete aspects of a State's program of compulsory education. This should suggest that courts must move with great circumspection in performing the sensitive and delicate task of weighing a State's legitimate social concern when faced with religious claims for exemption from generally applicable educational requirements. It cannot be over-emphasized that we are not dealing with a way of life and mode of education by a group claiming to have recently discovered some "progressive" or more enlightened process for rearing children for modern life.

Aided by a history of three centuries as an identifiable religious sect and a long history as a successful and self-sufficient segment of American society, the Amish in this case have convincingly demonstrated the sincerity of their religious beliefs, the interrelationship of belief with their mode of life, the vital role which belief and daily conduct play in the continued survival of Old Order Amish communities and their religious organization, and the hazards presented by the State's enforcement of a statute generally valid as to others. Beyond this, they have carried the even more difficult burden of demonstrating the adequacy of their alternative mode of continuing informal vocational education in terms of precisely those overall interests that the State advances in support of its program of compulsory high school education. In light of this convincing showing, one which probably few other religious groups or sects could make, and weighing the minimal difference between what the State would require and what the Amish already accept, it was incumbent on the State to show with more particularity how its admittedly strong interest in compulsory education would be adversely affected by granting an exemption to the Amish.

Mr. Justice **Douglas,** dissenting in part.

I agree with the Court that the religious scruples of the Amish are opposed to the education of their children beyond the grade schools, yet I disagree with the Court's conclusion that the matter is within the dispensation of parents alone. The Court's analysis assumes that the only interests at stake in the case are those of the Amish parents on the one hand, and those of the State on the other. The difficulty with this approach is that, despite the Court's claim, the parents are seeking to vindicate not only their own free exercise claims, but also those of their high-school-age children.

. . .

Religion is an individual experience. It is not necessary, nor even appropriate, for every Amish child to express his views on the subject in a prosecution of a single adult. Crucial, however, are the views of the child whose parent is the subject of the suit. Frieda Yoder has in fact testified that her own religious views are opposed to high-school education. I therefore join the judgment of the Court as to respondent Jonas Yoder. But Frieda Yoder's views may not be those of Vernon Yutzy or Barbara Miller. I must dissent, therefore, as to respondents Adin Yutzy and Wallace Miller as their motion to dismiss also raised the question of their children's religious liberty.

This issue has never been squarely presented before today. Our opinions are full of talk about the power of the parents over the child's education. And we have in the past analyzed similar conflicts between parent and State with little regard for the views of the child. Recent cases, however, have clearly held that the children themselves have constitutionally protectible interests.

. . .

On this important and vital matter of education, I think the children should be entitled to be heard. While the parents, absent dissent, normally speak for the entire family, the education of the child is a matter on which the child will often have decided views. He may want to be a pianist or an astronaut or an ocean geographer.

To do so he will have to break from the Amish tradition.

It is the future of the student, not the future of the parents, that is imperilled in today's decision. If a parent keeps his child out of school beyond the grade school, then the child will be forever barred from entry into the new and amazing world of diversity that we have today. The child may decide that that is the preferred course, or he may rebel. It is the student's judgment, not his parent's, that is essential if we are to give full meaning to what we have said about the Bill of Rights and of the right of students to be masters of their own destiny. If he is harnessed to the Amish way of life by those in authority over him and if his education is truncated, his entire life may be stunted and deformed. The child, therefore, should be given an opportunity to be heard before the State gives the exemption which we honor today.

The views of the two children in question were not canvassed by the Wisconsin courts. The matter should be explicitly reserved so that new hearings can be held on remand of the case.

. . .

Aftermath of Wisconsin v. Yoder

Because they had no televisions, radios, or telephones, the Amish heard the news of their Supreme Court victory from newspaper reporters. They reacted with characteristic equanimity, expressing only relief and the desire to get on with their peaceful lives. The Court's heavy reliance in the opinion on the longevity and self-sufficiency of the Amish was clearly meant to discourage other religious groups from making similar demands, and in fact there have been only a few isolated court cases since Yoder involving religious challenges to school attendance laws. However, cases have arisen from time to time in which parents have sought on religious grounds to have their children excused from parts of a required public school curriculum, such as sex education courses. State laws generally allow such exemptions. In one recent New York case, the Plymouth Brethren, a 2000-member fundamentalist sect, refused to send their children to an AIDS prevention class required by the state. The Brethren children had previously been excused from sex education on the understanding that their parents would teach them about how conception occurs. However, the parents would not promise to educate their children about AIDS because it would involve discussions of practices they considered immoral. The Brethren challenged the state's claim of a "compelling interest" in having their children attend such classes. Their own strict religious tenets against sex outside marriage would protect their children against AIDS, they claimed. The state argued that the education was necessary because the Brethren could not be certain that their children would never leave the community. The lower courts found for the state and at this writing the New York Court of Appeals is considering its decision.

Ten years after the *Yoder* decision, the Old Order Amish were involved in another free exercise case in the Supreme Court, this time on the losing side. Edwin Lee, an Amish farmer and carpenter in Pennsylvania who employed several workers, had refused to pay the social security and unemployment taxes required by federal law because he regarded the payment of such taxes as sinful. The Court ruled in *United States* v. *Lee* that the government's compelling interest in maintaining the social security system outweighed the Amish claim to religious freedom, particularly since the Amish were in no way *required* to become employers or engage in commerce. In 1985 the Supreme Court disposed of a more sweeping free exercise claim in *Alamo* v. *Secretary of Labor,* ruling that a religious organization could be required by law to pay its workers the federal minimum wage despite the organization's claim that its workers were engaged in a religious mission and did not wish to accept pay for their labor.

Goldman v. *Weinberger*

475 U.S. 503 (1986)

The Supreme Court has traditionally allowed military authorities much greater discretion than civilian officials in restricting constitutional rights. Chief Justice Earl Warren in a 1962 lecture explained the Court's deference to the military in this way:

> It is indisputable that the tradition of our country, from the time of the Revolution until now, has supported the military establishment's broad power to deal with its own personnel. The most obvious reason is that courts are ill-equipped to determine the impact upon discipline that any particular intrusion upon military authority might have. Many of the problems of the military society are in a sense, alien to the problems with which the judiciary is trained to deal.

Following this approach, the Court has consistently refused to review decisions made by the Court of Military Appeals, and when cases involving military personnel have come on appeal from the federal courts, the Supreme Court has shown great deference to the actions of military authorities. In 1976, for example, the Court upheld regulations at Fort Dix, a United States Army post in New Jersey, that prohibited demonstrations on the base and required the prior approval of military authorities before any publication could be distributed or posted there. The majority held that there is "no generalized constitutional right to make political speeches or distribute leaflets" on a military installation (*Greer* v. *Spock*). In a somewhat different context, the Court in 1981 upheld provisions of the Selective Service Act that required men but not women to register for the draft. The law did not violate due process, said the Court, because Congress has wide authority under the Constitution to act in the area of military affairs (*Rostker* v. *Goldberg*). Earlier the Court had held that the military is entitled to treat male and female officers differently with regard to promotion and discharge (*Schlesinger* v. *Ballard,* 1975).

S. Simich Goldman, an Orthodox Jew and ordained rabbi, received a military scholarship to study for a Ph.D. in psychology. Thereafter he entered the Air Force as a commissioned officer, serving as a clinical psychologist at March Air Force Base in California. Goldman wore a yarmulke while on duty at the mental health clinic on the base. He encountered no difficulty until April 1981 when he appeared in uniform

**as a defense witness in a court-martial proceeding wearing his yarmulke. The oppos-
ing counsel filed a complaint with Goldman's commanding officer, charging that the
practice of wearing a yarmulke violated an Air Force regulation stating that "[h]ead-
gear will not be worn . . . [w]hile indoors except by armed security police in the performance of their duties." Goldman was ordered by the hospital commander not to
wear his yarmulke outside the clinic. After refusing to obey this order, Goldman was
directed not to wear his yarmulke even in the hospital. Following a denial of his
request to work in civilian clothes, Goldman was given an official reprimand and a
negative response to his application to extend the term of his active service.
Goldman then sued the Secretary of Defense, asserting that the regulation interfered
with his First Amendment freedom to practice his religion. A federal district court
upheld Goldman's claim, but was reversed by the Court of Appeals.**

Justice **Rehnquist** delivered the opinion of
the Court.

. . .

Petitioner argues that AFR 35-10, as applied
to him, prohibits religiously motivated conduct
and should therefore be analyzed under the
standard enunciated in Sherbert v Verner. But
we have repeatedly held that "the military is, by
necessity, a specialized society separate from
civilian society."

. . .

Our review of military regulations challenged
on First Amendment grounds is far more deferential than constitutional review of similar laws
or regulations designed for civilian society. The
military need not encourage debate or tolerate
protest to the extent that such tolerance is
required of the civilian state by the First
Amendment; to accomplish its mission the military must foster instinctive obedience, unity,
commitment, and esprit de corps. . . .

These aspects of military life do not, of
course, render entirely nugatory in the military
context the guarantees of the First Amendment.
But "within the military community there is
simply not the same [individual] autonomy as
there is in the larger civilian community." In the
context of the present case, when evaluating
whether military needs justify a particular
restriction on religiously motivated conduct,
courts must give great deference to the professional judgment of military authorities concerning the relative importance of a particular military interest. Not only are courts " 'ill-equipped

to determine the impact upon discipline that any
particular intrusion upon military authority
might have,' " . . . but the military authorities
have been charged by the Executive and Legislative Branches with carrying out our Nation's
military policy. "Judicial deference . . . is at its
apogee when legislative action under the congressional authority to raise and support armies
and make rules and regulations for their governance is challenged."

The considered professional judgment of the
Air Force is that the traditional outfitting of personnel in standardized uniforms encourages the
subordination of personal preferences and iden-
tities in favor of the overall group mission. Uniforms encourage a sense of hierarchical unity by
tending to eliminate outward individual distinctions except for those of rank. The Air Force
considers them as vital during peacetime as during war because its personnel must be ready to
provide an effective defense on a moment's
notice; the necessary habits of discipline and
unity must be developed in advance of trouble.
We have acknowledged that "[t]he inescapable
demands of military discipline and obedience to
orders cannot be taught on battlefields; the habit
of immediate compliance with military procedures and orders must be virtually reflex with no
time for debate or reflection."

To this end, the Air Force promulgated AFR
35-10, a 190-page document, which states that
"Air Force members will wear the Air Force uniform while performing their military duties,
except when authorized to wear civilian clothes
on duty." The rest of the document describes in
minute detail all of the various items of apparel

that must be worn as part of the Air Force uniform. It authorizes a few individualized options with respect to certain pieces of jewelry and hair style, but even these are subject to severe limitations. In general, authorized headgear may be worn only out of doors. Indoors, "[h]eadgear [may] not be worn . . . except by armed security police in the performance of their duties." A narrow exception to this rule exists for headgear worn during indoor religious ceremonies. In addition, military commanders may in their discretion permit visible religious headgear and other such apparel in designated living quarters and nonvisible items generally.

Petitioner Goldman contends that the Free Exercise Clause of the First Amendment requires the Air Force to make an exception to its uniform dress requirements for religious apparel unless the accoutrements create a "clear danger" of undermining discipline and esprit de corps. He asserts that in general, visible but "unobtrusive" apparel will not create such a danger and must therefore be accommodated. He argues that the Air Force failed to prove that a specific exception for his practice of wearing an unobtrusive yarmulke would threaten discipline. He contends that the Air Force's assertion to the contrary is mere ipse dixit, with no support from actual experience or a scientific study in the record, and is contradicted by expert testimony that religious exceptions to AFR 35-10 are in fact desirable and will increase morale by making the Air Force a more humane place.

But whether or not expert witnesses may feel that religious exceptions to AFR 35-10 are desirable is quite beside the point. The desirability of dress regulations in the military is decided by the appropriate military officials, and they are under no constitutional mandate to abandon their considered professional judgment. Quite obviously, to the extent the regulations do not permit the wearing of religious apparel such as a yarmulke, a practice described by petitioner as silent devotion akin to prayer, military life may be more objectionable for petitioner and probably others. But the First Amendment does not require the military to accommodate such practices in the face of its view that they would detract from the uniformity sought by the dress regulations. The Air Force has drawn the line essentially between religious apparel which is visible and that which is not, and we hold that those portions of the regulations challenged here reasonably and evenhandedly regulate dress in the interest of the military's perceived need for uniformity. The First Amendment therefore does not prohibit them from being applied to petitioner even though their effect is to restrict the wearing of the headgear required by his religious beliefs.

The judgment of the Court of Appeals is affirmed.

Justice **Stevens,** with whom Justice **White** and Justice **Powell** join, concurring.

Captain Goldman presents an especially attractive case for an exception from the uniform regulations that are applicable to all other Air Force personnel. His devotion to his faith is readily apparent. The yarmulke is a familiar and accepted sight. In addition to its religious significance for the wearer, the yarmulke may evoke the deepest respect and admiration—the symbol of a distinguished tradition and an eloquent rebuke to the ugliness of anti-Semitism. Captain Goldman's military duties are performed in a setting in which a modest departure from the uniform regulation creates almost no danger of impairment of the Air Force's military mission. Moreover, on the record before us, there is reason to believe that the policy of strict enforcement against Captain Goldman had a retaliatory motive—he had worn his yarmulke while testifying on behalf of a defendant in a court-martial proceeding. Nevertheless, as the case has been argued, I believe we must test the validity of the Air Force's rule not merely as it applies to Captain Goldman but also as it applies to all service personnel who have sincere religious beliefs that may conflict with one or more military commands.

Justice Brennan is unmoved by the Government's concern "that while a yarmulke might not seem obtrusive to a Jew, neither does a turban to a Sikh, a saffron robe to a Satchidananda Ashram-Integral Yogi, nor do dreadlocks to a Rastafarian." He correctly points out that "turbans, saffron robes, and dreadlocks are not before us in this case," and then suggests that other cases may be fairly decided by reference to a reasonable standard based on "functional utility, health and safety considerations, and the goal of a polished, professional appearance." As the Court has explained, this approach attaches no weight to the separate interest in uniformity itself. Because professionals in the military service attach great importance to that plausible interest, it is one that we must recognize as legitimate and rational even though personal experience or admiration for the performance of the "rag-tag band of soldiers" that won us our freedom in the revolutionary war might persuade us that the Government has exaggerated the importance of that interest.

The interest in uniformity, however, has a dimension that is of still greater importance for me. It is the interest in uniform treatment for the members of all religious faiths. The very strength of Captain Goldman's claim creates the danger that a similar claim on behalf of a Sikh or a Rastafarian might readily be dismissed as "so extreme, so unusual, or so faddish an image that public confidence in his ability to perform his duties will be destroyed." If exceptions from dress code regulations are to be granted on the basis of a multifactored test such as that proposed by Justice Brennan, inevitably the decisionmaker's evaluation of the character and the sincerity of the requestor's faith—as well as the probable reaction of the majority to the favored treatment of a member of that faith—will play a critical part in the decision. For the difference between a turban or a dreadlock on the one hand, and a yarmulke on the other, is not merely a difference in "appearance"—it is also the difference between a Sikh or a Rastafarian, on the one hand, and an Orthodox Jew on the other. The Air Force has no business drawing distinctions between such persons when it is enforcing commands of universal application.

As the Court demonstrates, the rule that is challenged in this case is based on a neutral, completely objective standard—visibility. It was not motivated by hostility against, or any special respect for, any religious faith. An exception for yarmulkes would represent a fundamental departure from the true principle of uniformity that supports that rule. For that reason, I join the Court's opinion and its judgment.

Justice **Brennan,** with whom Justice **Marshall** joins, dissenting.

. . .

Dr. Goldman has asserted a substantial First Amendment claim, which is entitled to meaningful review by this Court. The Court, however, evades its responsibility by eliminating, in all but name only, judicial review of military regulations that interfere with the fundamental constitutional rights of service personnel.

Our cases have acknowledged that in order to protect our treasured liberties, the military must be able to command service members to sacrifice a great many of the individual freedoms they enjoyed in the civilian community and to endure certain limitations on the freedoms they retain. Notwithstanding this acknowledgment, we have steadfastly maintained that "'our citizens in uniform may not be stripped of basic rights simply because they have doffed their civilian clothes.'" And, while we have hesitated, due to our lack of expertise concerning military affairs and our respect for the delegated authority of a coordinate branch, to strike down restrictions on individual liberties which could reasonably be justified as necessary to the military's vital function, we have never abdicated our obligation of judicial review.

Today the Court eschews its constitutionally mandated role. It adopts for review of military decisions affecting First Amendment rights a subrational-basis standard—absolute, uncritical "deference to the professional judgment of military authorities." If a branch of the military declares one of its rules sufficiently important to outweigh a service person's constitutional rights, it seems that the Court will accept that conclusion, no matter how absurd or unsupported it may be.

A deferential standard of review, however, need not, and should not, mean that the Court must credit arguments that defy common sense. When a military service burdens the free exercise rights of its members in the name of necessity, it must provide, as an initial matter and at a minimum, a *credible* explanation of how the contested practice is likely to interfere with the proffered military interest. Unabashed ipse dixit cannot outweigh a constitutional right.

. . .

The Government maintains in its brief that discipline is jeopardized whenever exceptions to military regulations are granted. Service personnel must be trained to obey even the most arbitrary command reflexively. Non-Jewish personnel will perceive the wearing of a yarmulke by an Orthodox Jew as an unauthorized departure from the rules and will begin to question the principle of unswerving obedience. Thus shall our fighting forces slip down the treacherous slope toward unkempt appearance, anarchy, and, ultimately, defeat at the hands of our enemies.

The contention that the discipline of the armed forces will be subverted if Orthodox Jews are allowed to wear yarmulkes with their uniforms surpasses belief. It lacks support in the record of this case and the Air Force offers no basis for it as a general proposition. While the perilous slope permits the services arbitrarily to refuse exceptions requested to satisfy mere personal preferences, before the Air Force may burden free exercise rights it must advance, at the *very least*, a rational reason for doing so.

. . .

I find totally implausible the suggestion that the overarching group identity of the Air Force would be threatened if Orthodox Jews were allowed to wear yarmulkes with their uniforms. To the contrary, a yarmulke worn with a United States military uniform is an eloquent reminder that the shared and proud identity of United States serviceman embraces and unites religious and ethnic pluralism.

. . .

The Government dangles before the Court a classic parade of horribles, the specter of a brightly-colored, "rag-tag band of soldiers." Although turbans, saffron robes, and dreadlocks are not before us in this case and must each be

evaluated against the reasons a service branch offers for prohibiting personnel from wearing them while in uniform, a reviewing court could legitimately give deference to dress and grooming rules that have a *reasoned* basis in, for example, functional utility, health and safety considerations, and the goal of a polished, professional appearance. It is the lack of any reasoned basis for prohibiting yarmulkes that is so striking here.

. . .

The Court and the military services have presented patriotic Orthodox Jews with a painful dilemma—the choice between fulfilling a religious obligation and serving their country. Should the draft be reinstated, compulsion will replace choice. Although the pain the services inflict on Orthodox Jewish servicemen is clearly the result of insensitivity rather than design, it is unworthy of our military because it is unnecessary. The Court and the military have refused these servicemen their constitutional rights; we must hope that Congress will correct this wrong.

Justice **O'Connor,** with whom Justice **Marshall** joins, dissenting.

. . .

I believe that the Court should attempt to articulate and apply an appropriate standard for a free exercise claim in the military context, and should examine Captain Goldman's claim in light of that standard.

Like the Court today in this case involving the military, the Court in the past has had some difficulty, even in the civilian context, in articulating a clear standard for evaluating free exercise claims that result from the application of general state laws burdening religious conduct. In Sherbert v Verner (1963), and Thomas v Review Board (1981), the Court required the States to demonstrate that their challenged policies were "the least restrictive means of achieving some compelling state interest" in order to deprive claimants of unemployment benefits when the refusal to work was based on sincere religious beliefs. In Wisconsin v Yoder (1972), the Court noted that "only those interests of the highest order and those not otherwise served can overbalance legitimate claims to the free exercise of religion" in deciding that the Amish were exempt from a State's requirement that children attend school through the age of 16. In United States v Lee (1982), the Court stated that "[t]he State may justify a limitation on religious liberty by showing that it is essential to accomplish an overriding governmental interest," and held that the Amish could not exempt themselves from the Social Security system on religious grounds. . . .

These tests, though similar, are not identical. One can, however, glean at least two consistent themes from this Court's precedents. First, when the government attempts to deny a Free Exercise claim, it must show that an unusually important interest is at stake, whether that interest is denominated "compelling," "of the highest order," or "overriding." Second, the government must show that granting the requested exemption will do substantial harm to that interest, whether by showing that the means adopted is the "least restrictive" or "essential," or that the interest will not "otherwise be served." These two requirements are entirely sensible in the context of the assertion of a free exercise claim. First, because the government is attempting to override an interest specifically protected by the Bill of Rights, the government must show that the opposing interest it asserts is of especial importance before there is any chance that its claim can prevail. Second, since the Bill of Rights is expressly designed to protect the individual against the aggregated and sometimes intolerant powers of the state, the government must show that the interest asserted will in fact be substantially harmed by granting the type of exemption requested by the individual.

There is no reason why these general principles should not apply in the military, as well as the civilian, context. . . .

The first question that the Court should face here, therefore, is whether the interest that the Government asserts against the religiously based claim of the individual is of unusual importance. It is perfectly appropriate at this step of the analysis to take account of the special role of the military. The mission of our armed services is to protect our Nation from those who would destroy all our freedoms. I agree that, in order to fulfill that mission, the military is entitled to take some freedoms from its members. . . . The need for military discipline and esprit de corps is unquestionably an especially important governmental interest.

But the mere presence of such an interest cannot, as the majority implicitly believes, end the analysis of whether a refusal by the Government to honor the free exercise of an individual's religion is constitutionally acceptable. A citizen pursuing even the most noble cause must remain within the bounds of the law. So, too, the Government may, even in pursuing its most compelling interests, be subject to specific restraints in doing so. The second question in the analysis of a Free Exercise claim under this Court's precedents must also be reached here: will granting an exemption of the type requested by the individual do substantial harm to the especially important governmental interest?

I have no doubt that there are many instances in which the unique fragility of military discipline and esprit de corps necessitates rigidity by the Government when similar rigidity to preserve an assertedly analogous interest would not pass constitutional muster in the civilian sphere. Nonetheless, as Justice Brennan persuasively argues, the Government can present no sufficiently convincing proof in *this* case to support an assertion that granting an exemp-tion of the type requested here would do substantial harm to military discipline and esprit de corps.

. . .

In the rare instances where the military has not consistently or plausibly justified its asserted need for rigidity of enforcement, and where the individual seeking the exemption establishes that the assertion by the military of a threat to discipline or esprit de corps is in his or her case completely unfounded, I would hold that the Government's policy of uniformity must yield to the individual's assertion of the right of free exercise of religion. On the facts of this case, therefore, I would require the Government to accommodate the sincere religious belief of Captain Goldman. Napoleon may have been correct to assert that, in the military sphere, morale is to all other factors as three is to one, but contradicted assertions of necessity by the military do not on the scales of justice bear a similarly disproportionate weight to sincere religious beliefs of the individual.

I respectfully dissent.

Aftermath of Goldman *v.* Weinberger

In his dissent in *Goldman* Justice Brennan expressed the "hope that Congress will correct this wrong." Congress responded to this invitation in 1987, voting to attach to the Defense Authorization Act an amendment permitting military personnel to wear religious apparel in uniform if it was "neat and conservative," and did not interfere with the performance of military duties.

Another group of government officials to whom the Court has also shown extra deference in civil liberties cases is prison administrators. In *O'Lone* v. *Estate of Shabazz* (1987) the Court held that New Jersey prison officials had not violated Muslim inmates' free exercise rights by assigning them to work details that precluded their attendance at a weekly congregational service. Prisoners do not forfeit their constitutional rights by reason of their confinement, said the Court, but "limits on the exercise of constitutional rights arise both from the fact of incarceration and from valid penological objectives—including deterrence of crime, rehabilitation of prisoners, and institutional security." As long as a prison regulation is "reasonably related to legitimate penological interests," it is not unconstitutional. Thus in free exercise cases involving prisoners and military personnel, the compelling character of the government function is assumed.

Employment Division, Department of Human Resources of Oregon v. *Smith*

494 U.S. 884 (1990)

Before 1990 the most prominent court decision involving the question of whether drug use could be condoned on First Amendment grounds if it was engaged in for religious purposes was a 1964 California case, *People* v. *Woody*. There the California Supreme Court, following the libertarian lead of the United States Supreme Court in *Sherbert* v. *Verner* (excerpted earlier in this chapter), decided the previous year, held that the state could not constitutionally enforce its criminal statutes against Native Americans who used the hallucinogenic drug peyote in a religious ceremony. Noting that the substance had long been a cornerstone of Navaho religious rituals, the California court found that the state had offered no sufficiently compelling reason for prohibiting a practice so crucial to the religion. That decision was not reviewed by the United States Supreme Court.

Two drug counselors, Galen Black and Alfred Smith, both members of the Native American church, were discharged from their jobs after they used peyote (a cactus containing the illegal drug mescaline) for sacramental purposes at a religious ceremony. Their applications for unemployment benefits were subsequently denied because they had been fired for misconduct related to their work. The Oregon Supreme Court overruled the denial of their claim on free exercise grounds. The United States Supreme Court then took the case, but declined to address the consti-

tutional question because the Oregon court had not decided whether the sacramental use of peyote was a violation of state law. On remand, the Oregon Supreme Court ruled that the statute prohibiting the use of peyote made no exception for religious consumption, thus violating the free exercise clause. The court then reaffirmed its decision that Oregon could not deny the applicants unemployment benefits on such a ground. The state brought another appeal to the United States Supreme Court.

ANTONIN SCALIA

Antonin Scalia was nominated to the Supreme Court by President Ronald Reagan in 1986 after a distinguished academic career at the University of Chicago Law School and a 3-year stint on the Court of Appeals for the District of Columbia. Scalia, the first Italian-American to serve on the Court, quickly confirmed that he would be a solidly conservative vote on such matters as abortion, criminal procedure, and affirmative action. He is also an outspoken critic of judicial activism and, as his dissents in Morrison v. Olson *and* Mistretta v. United States *demonstrate, the Court's strongest proponent of strict separation of powers. One of the most visible and accessible members of the Court, Scalia is known for his witty and intellectually aggressive questioning of lawyers in oral arguments before the Court.*

Justice **Scalia** delivered the opinion of the Court.

This case requires us to decide whether the Free Exercise Clause of the First Amendment permits the State of Oregon to include religiously inspired peyote use within the reach of its general criminal prohibition on use of that drug, and thus permits the State to deny unemployment benefits to persons dismissed from their jobs because of such religiously inspired use.

. . .

The Free Exercise Clause of the First Amendment, which has been made applicable to the States by incorporation into the Fourteenth Amendment, provides that "Congress shall make no law respecting an establishment of religion, or *prohibiting the free exercise thereof.* . . ." The free exercise of religion means, first and foremost, the right to believe and profess whatever

religious doctrine one desires. Thus, the First Amendment obviously excludes all "governmental regulation of religious *beliefs* as such." The government may not compel affirmation of religious belief, punish the expression of religious doctrines it believes to be false, impose special disabilities on the basis of religious views or religious status, or lend its power to one or the other side in controversies over religious authority or dogma. . . .

But the "exercise of religion" often involves not only belief and profession but the performance of (or abstention from) physical acts: assembling with others for a worship service, participating in sacramental use of bread and wine, proselytizing, abstaining from certain foods or certain modes of transportation. It would be true, we think (though no case of ours has involved the point), that a state would be "prohibiting the free exercise [of religion]" if it sought to ban such acts or abstentions only when they are engaged in for religious reasons, or only because of the religious belief that they display. It would doubtless be unconstitutional, for example, to ban the casting of "statues that are to be used for worship purposes," or to prohibit bowing down before a golden calf.

Respondents in the present case, however, seek to carry the meaning of "prohibiting the free exercise [of religion]" one large step further. They contend that their religious motivation for using peyote places them beyond the reach of a criminal law that is not specifically directed at their religious practice, and that is concededly constitutional as applied to those who use the drug for other reasons. They assert, in other words, that "prohibiting the free exercise [of religion]" includes requiring any individual to observe a generally applicable law that requires (or forbids) the performance of an act that his religious belief forbids (or requires). As a textual matter, we do not think the words must be given that meaning. It is no more necessary to regard the collection of a general tax, for example, as "prohibiting the free exercise [of religion]" by those citizens who believe support of organized government to be sinful, than it is to regard the same tax as "abridging the freedom . . . of the press" of those publishing companies that must pay the tax as a condition of staying in business. It is a permissible reading of the text, in the one case as in the other, to say that if prohibiting the exercise of religion (or burdening the activity of printing) is not the object of the tax but merely the incidental effect of a generally applicable and otherwise valid provision, the First Amendment has not been offended.

. . . We have never held that an individual's religious beliefs excuse him from compliance with an otherwise valid law prohibiting conduct that the State is free to regulate. On the contrary, the record of more than a century of our free exercise jurisprudence contradicts that proposition. As described succinctly by Justice Frankfurter in Minersville School Dist. Bd. of Educ. v Gobitis (1940): "Conscientious scruples have not, in the course of the long struggle for religious toleration, relieved the individual from obedience to a general law not aimed at the promotion or restriction of religious beliefs. The mere possession of religious convictions which contradict the relevant concerns of a political society does not relieve the citizen from the discharge of political responsibilities (footnote omitted)." We first had occasion to assert that principle in Reynolds v United States (1878), where we rejected the claim that criminal laws against polygamy could not be constitutionally applied to those whose religion commanded the practice. "Laws," we said, "are made for the government of actions, and while they cannot interfere with mere religious belief and opinions, they may with practices. . . . Can a man excuse his practices to the contrary because of his religious belief? To permit this would be to make the professed doctrines of religious belief superior to the law of the land, and in effect to permit every citizen to become a law unto himself."

Subsequent decisions have consistently held that the right of free exercise does not relieve an individual of the obligation to comply with a "valid and neutral law of general applicability on the ground that the law proscribes (or prescribes) conduct that his religion prescribes (or proscribes)." United States v Lee (1982). In Prince v Massachusetts (1944), we held that a mother could be prosecuted under the child labor laws for using her children to dispense literature in the streets, her religious motivation notwithstanding. We found no constitutional infirmity in "excluding [these children] from doing there what no other children may do." In Braunfield v Brown (1961), we upheld Sunday-closing laws against the claim that they burdened the religious practices of persons whose religions compelled them to refrain from work on other days. In Gillette v United States (1971), we sustained the military selective service system against the claim that it violated free exercise by conscripting persons who opposed a particular war on religious grounds.

Our most recent decision involving a neutral, generally applicable regulatory law that compelled activity forbidden by an individual's religion was United States v Lee. There, an Amish employer, on behalf of himself and his employees, sought exemption from collection and payment of Social Security taxes on the ground that the Amish faith prohibited participation in governmental support programs. We rejected the claim that an exemption was constitutionally required. There would be no way, we observed, to distinguish the Amish believer's objection to Social Security taxes from the religious objections that others might have to the collection or use of other taxes. . . .

The only decisions in which we have held that the First Amendment bars application of a neutral, generally applicable law to religiously motivated action have involved not the Free Exercise Clause alone, but the Free Exercise Clause in conjunction with other constitutional protections, such as freedom of speech and of the press, see Cantwell v Connecticut (1940) (invalidating a licensing system for religious and charitable solicitations under which the administrator had discretion to deny a license to any cause he deemed nonreligious); Murdock v Pennsylvania (1943) (invalidating a flat tax on solicitation as applied to the dissemination of religious ideas); or the right of parents, acknowledged in Pierce v Society of Sisters (1925), to direct the education of their children, see Wisconsin v Yoder (1972) (invalidating compulsory school-attendance laws as applied to Amish parents who refused on religious grounds to send their children to school). Some of our cases prohibiting compelled expression, decided exclusively upon free speech grounds, have also involved freedom of religion, cf. Wooley v Maynard (1977) (invalidating compelled display of a license plate slogan that offended individual religious beliefs); West Virginia Board of Education v Barnette (1943) (invalidating compulsory flag salute statute challenged by religious objectors). And it is easy to envision a case in which a challenge on freedom of association grounds would likewise be reinforced by Free Exercise Clause concerns. . . .

The present case does not present such a hybrid situation, but a free exercise claim unconnected with any communicative activity or parental right. Respondents urge us to hold, quite simply, that when otherwise prohibitable conduct is accompanied by religious convictions, not only the convictions but the conduct itself must be free from governmental regulation. We have never held that, and decline to do so now. There being no contention that Oregon's drug law represents an attempt to regulate religious beliefs, the communication of religious beliefs, or the raising of one's children in those beliefs, the rule to which we have adhered ever since Reynolds plainly controls. . . .

Respondents argue that even though exemption from generally applicable criminal laws need not automatically be extended to religiously motivated actors, at least the claim for a religious exemption must be evaluated under the balancing test set forth in Sherbert v Verner (1963). Under the Sherbert test, governmental actions that substantially burden a religious practice must be justified by a compelling governmental interest. Applying that test we have, on three occasions, invalidated state unemployment compensation rules that conditioned the availability of benefits upon an applicant's willingness to work under conditions forbidden by his religion. See Sherbert v Verner; Thomas v Review Board, Indiana Employment Div. (1981); Hobbie v Unemployment Appeals Comm'n of Florida (1987). We have never invalidated any governmental action on the basis of the Sherbert test except the denial of unemployment compensation. Although we have sometimes purported to apply the Sherbert test in contexts other than that, we have always found the test satisfied. In recent years we have abstained from applying the Sherbert test (outside the unemployment compensation field) at all. In Bowen v Roy (1986), we declined to apply Sherbert analysis to a federal statutory scheme that required benefit applicants and recipients to provide their Social Security numbers. The plaintiffs in that case asserted that it would violate their religious beliefs to obtain and provide a Social Security number for their daughter. We held the statute's application to the plaintiffs valid regardless of whether it was necessary to effectuate a compelling interest. In Lyng v Northwest Indian Cemetery Protective Assn. (1988), we declined to apply Sherbert analysis to the Government's logging and road construction activities on lands used for religious purposes by several Native American Tribes, even though it was undisputed that the activities "could have devastating effects on traditional Indian religious practices." In Goldman v Weinberger, (1986), we rejected application of the Sherbert test to military dress regulations that forbade the wearing of yarmulkes. In O'Lone v Estate of Shabazz

(1987), we sustained, without mentioning the Sherbert test, a prison's refusal to excuse inmates from work requirements to attend worship services.

Even if we were inclined to breathe into Sherbert some life beyond the unemployment compensation field, we would not apply it to require exemptions from a generally applicable criminal law. The Sherbert test, it must be recalled, was developed in a context that lent itself to individualized governmental assessment of the reasons for the relevant conduct. As a plurality of the Court noted in Roy, a distinctive feature of unemployment compensation programs is that their eligibility criteria invite consideration of the particular circumstances behind an applicant's unemployment: "The statutory conditions [in Sherbert and Thomas] provided that a person was not eligible for unemployment compensation benefits if, 'without good cause,' he had quit work or refused available work. The 'good cause' standard created a mechanism for individualized exemptions." . . . As the plurality pointed out in Roy, our decisions in the unemployment cases stand for the proposition that where the State has in place a system of individual exemptions, it may not refuse to extend that system to cases of "religious hardship" without compelling reason.

Whether or not the decisions are that limited, they at least have nothing to do with an across-the-board criminal prohibition on a particular form of conduct. Although, as noted earlier, we have sometimes used the Sherbert test to analyze free exercise challenges to such laws, we have never applied the test to invalidate one. We conclude today that the sounder approach, and the approach in accord with the vast majority of our precedents, is to hold the test inapplicable to such challenges. The government's ability to enforce generally applicable prohibitions of socially harmful conduct, like its ability to carry out other aspects of public policy, "cannot depend on measuring the effects of a governmental action on a religious objector's spiritual development." To make an individual's obligation to obey such a law contingent upon the law's coincidence with his religious beliefs, except where the State's interest is "compelling"—permitting him, by virtue of his

beliefs, "to become a law unto himself," contradicts both constitutional tradition and common sense.

The "compelling government interest" requirement seems benign because it is familiar from other fields. But using it as the standard that must be met before the government may accord different treatment on the basis of race, or before the government may regulate the content of speech, is not remotely comparable to using it for the purpose asserted here. What it produces in those other fields—equality of treatment, and an unrestricted flow of contending speech—are constitutional norms; what it would produce here—a private right to ignore generally applicable laws—is a constitutional anomaly.

Nor is it possible to limit the impact of respondents' proposal by requiring a "compelling state interest" only when the conduct prohibited is "central" to the individual's religion. It is no more appropriate for judges to determine the "centrality" of religious beliefs before applying a "compelling interest" test in the free exercise field, than it would be for them to determine the "importance" of ideas before applying the "compelling interest" test in the free speech field. What principle of law or logic can be brought to bear to contradict a believer's assertion that a particular act is "central" to his personal faith? Judging the centrality of different religious practices is akin to the unacceptable "business of evaluating the relative merits of differing religious claims." . . . Repeatedly and in many different contexts, we have warned that courts must not presume to determine the place of a particular belief in a religion or the plausibility of a religious claim.

If the "compelling interest" test is to be applied at all, then, it must be applied across the board, to all actions thought to be religiously commanded. Moreover, if "compelling interest" really means what it says (and watering it down here would subvert its rigor in the other fields where it is applied), many laws will not meet the test. Any society adopting such a system would be courting anarchy, but that danger increases in direct proportion to the society's diversity of religious beliefs, and its determination to coerce or suppress none of them. Precisely because "we are a cosmopolitan nation made up of people of almost every conceivable religious preference," and precisely because we value and protect that religious divergence, we cannot afford the luxury of deeming *presumptively invalid,* as applied to the religious objector, every regulation of conduct that does not protect an interest of the highest order. The rule respondents favor would open the prospect of constitutionally required religious exemptions from civic obligations of almost every conceivable kind—ranging from compulsory military service, the payment of taxes, to health and safety regulation such as manslaughter and child neglect laws, compulsory vaccination laws, drug laws and traffic laws, to social welfare legislation such as minimum wage laws, child labor laws, animal cruelty laws, environmental protection laws, and laws providing for equality of opportunity for the races. The First Amendment's protection of religious liberty does not require this.

Values that are protected against government interference through enshrinement in the Bill of Rights are not thereby banished from the political process. Just as a society that believes in the negative protection accorded to the press by the First Amendment is likely to enact laws that affirmatively foster the dissemination of the printed word, so also a society that believes in the negative protection accorded to religious belief can be expected to be solicitous of that value in its legislation as well. It is therefore not surprising that a number of States have made an exception to their drug laws for sacramental peyote use. But to say that a nondiscriminatory religious-practice exemption is permitted, or even that it is desirable, is not to say that it is constitutionally required, and that the appropriate occasions for its creation can be discerned by the courts. It may fairly be said that leaving accommodation to the political process will place at a relative disadvantage those religious practices that are not widely engaged in; but that unavoidable consequence of democratic government must be preferred to a system in which each conscience is a law unto itself or in which judges weigh the social importance of all laws against the centrality of all religious beliefs.

Because respondents' ingestion of peyote was prohibited under Oregon law, and because that prohibition is constitutional, Oregon may, consistent with the Free Exercise Clause, deny respondents unemployment compensation when their dismissal results from use of the drug. The decision of the Oregon Supreme Court is accordingly reversed.

It is so ordered.

Justice **O'Connor,** with whom Justice **Brennan,** Justice **Marshall,** and Justice **Blackmun** join as to Parts I and II, concurring in the judgment.

Although I agree with the result the Court reaches in this case, I cannot join its opinion. In my view, today's holding dramatically departs from well-settled First Amendment jurisprudence, appears unnecessary to resolve the question presented, and is incompatible with our Nation's fundamental commitment to individual religious liberty.

. . .

The Court today extracts from our long history of free exercise precedents the single categorical rule that "if prohibiting the exercise of religion . . . is . . . merely the incidental effect of a generally applicable and otherwise valid provision, the First Amendment has not been offended." Indeed, the Court holds that where the law is a generally applicable criminal prohibition, our usual free exercise jurisprudence does not even apply. To reach this sweeping result, however, the Court must not only give a strained reading of the First Amendment but must also disregard our consistent application of free exercise doctrine to cases involving generally applicable regulations that burden religious conduct.

. . .

The Court today . . . interprets the Clause to permit the government to prohibit, without justification, conduct mandated by an individual's religious beliefs, so long as that prohibition is generally applicable. But a law that prohibits certain conduct—conduct that happens to be an act of worship for someone—manifestly does prohibit that person's free exercise of his religion. A person who is barred from engaging in religiously motivated conduct is barred from freely exercising his religion. Moreover, that person is barred from freely exercising his religion regardless of whether the law prohibits the conduct only when engaged in for religious reasons, only by members of that religion, or by all persons. It is difficult to deny that a law that prohibits religiously motivated conduct, even if the law is generally applicable, does not at least implicate First Amendment concerns.

The Court responds that generally applicable laws are "one large step" removed from laws aimed at specific religious practices. The First Amendment, however, does not distinguish between laws that are generally applicable and laws that target particular religious practices. Indeed, few States would be so naive as to enact a law directly prohibiting or burdening a religious practice as such. Our free exercise cases have all concerned generally applicable laws that had the effect of significantly burdening a religious practice. If the First Amendment is to have any vitality, it ought not be construed to cover only the extreme and hypothetical situation in which a State directly targets a religious practice. As we have noted in a slightly different context, " '[s]uch a test has no basis in precedent and relegates a serious First Amendment value to the barest level of minimum scrutiny that the Equal Protection Clause already provides.' " . . .

To say that a person's right to free exercise has been burdened, of course, does not mean that he has an absolute right to engage in the conduct. Under our established First Amendment jurisprudence, we have recognized that the freedom to act, unlike the freedom to believe, cannot be absolute. Instead, we have respected both the First Amendment's express textual mandate and the governmental interest in regulation of conduct by requiring the Government to justify any substantial burden on religiously motivated conduct by a compelling state interest and by means narrowly tailored to achieve that interest. The compelling interest test effectuates the First Amendment's command that religious liberty is an independent liberty, that it occupies a preferred position, and that the Court will not permit encroachments upon this liberty, whether direct or indirect, unless required by

clear and compelling governmental interests "of the highest order."

The Court attempts to support its narrow reading of the Clause by claiming that "[w]e have never held that an individual's religious beliefs excuse him from compliance with an otherwise valid law prohibiting conduct that the State is free to regulate." But as the Court later notes, as it must, in cases such as Cantwell and Yoder we have in fact interpreted the Free Exercise Clause to forbid application of a generally applicable prohibition to religiously motivated conduct. Indeed, in Yoder we expressly rejected the interpretation the Court now adopts. . . .

The Court endeavors to escape from our decisions in Cantwell and Yoder by labeling them "hybrid" decisions, but there is no denying that both cases expressly relied on the Free Exercise Clause, and that we have consistently regarded those cases as part of the mainstream of our free exercise jurisprudence. Moreover, in each of the other cases cited by the Court to support its categorical rule, we rejected the particular constitutional claims before us only after carefully weighing the competing interests. . . . That we rejected the free exercise claims in those cases hardly calls into question the applicability of First Amendment doctrine in the first place. Indeed, it is surely unusual to judge the vitality of a constitutional doctrine by looking to the win-loss record of the plaintiffs who happen to come before us.

· · ·

The Court today gives no convincing reason to depart from settled First Amendment jurisprudence. There is nothing talismanic about neutral laws of general applicability or general criminal prohibitions, for laws neutral toward religion can coerce a person to violate his religious conscience or intrude upon his religious duties just as effectively as laws aimed at religion. Although the Court suggests that the compelling interest test, as applied to generally applicable laws, would result in a "constitutional anomaly," the First Amendment unequivocally makes freedom of religion, like freedom from race discrimination and freedom of speech, a "constitutional nor[m]," not an "anomaly." Nor would application of our established free exercise doctrine to this case necessarily be incompatible with our equal protection cases. . . . We have in any event recognized that the Free Exercise Clause protects values distinct from those protected by the Equal Protection Clause. As the language of the Clause itself makes clear, an individual's free exercise of religion is a preferred constitutional activity. A law that makes criminal such an activity therefore triggers constitutional concern—and heightened judicial scrutiny—even if it does not target the particular religious conduct at issue. Our free speech cases similarly recognize that neutral regulations that affect free speech values are subject to a balancing, rather than categorical, approach. . . . The Court's parade of horribles not only fails as a reason for discarding the compelling interest test, it instead demonstrates just the opposite: that courts have been quite capable of applying our free exercise jurisprudence to strike sensible balances between religious liberty and competing state interests.

. . .

The Court's holding today not only misreads settled First Amendment precedent; it appears to be unnecessary to this case. I would reach the same result applying our established free exercise jurisprudence.

. . .

. . . [T]he critical question in this case is whether exempting respondents from the State's general criminal prohibition "will unduly interfere with fulfillment of the governmental interest." Although the question is close, I would conclude that uniform application of Oregon's criminal prohibition is "essential to accomplish" its overriding interest in preventing the physical harm caused by the use of a Schedule I controlled substance. Oregon's criminal prohibition represents that State's judgment that the possession and use of controlled substances, even by only one person, is inherently harmful and dangerous. Because the health effects caused by the use of controlled substances exist regardless of the motivation of the user, the use of such sub-

stances, even for religious purposes, violates the very purpose of the laws that prohibit them. Moreover, in view of the societal interest in preventing trafficking in controlled substances, uniform application of the criminal prohibition at issue is essential to the effectiveness of Oregon's stated interest in preventing any possession of peyote.

For these reasons, I believe that granting a selective exemption in this case would seriously impair Oregon's compelling interest in prohibiting possession of peyote by its citizens. Under such circumstances, the Free Exercise Clause does not require the State to accommodate respondents' religiously motivated conduct. Unlike in Yoder, where we noted that "[t]he record strongly indicates that accommodating the religious objections of the Amish by forgoing one, or at most two, additional years of compulsory education will not impair the physical or mental health of the child, or result in an inability to be self-supporting or to discharge the duties and responsibilities of citizenship, or in any other way materially detract from the welfare of society," a religious exemption in this case would be incompatible with the State's interest in controlling use and possession of illegal drugs.

. . .

I would therefore adhere to our established free exercise jurisprudence and hold that the State in this case has a compelling interest in regulating peyote use by its citizens and that accommodating respondents' religiously motivated conduct "will unduly interfere with fulfillment of the governmental interest." Accordingly, I concur in the judgment of the Court.

Justice **Blackmun,** with whom Justice **Brennan** and Justice **Marshall** join, dissenting.

This Court over the years painstakingly has developed a consistent and exacting standard to test the constitutionality of a state statute that burdens the free exercise of religion. Such a statute may stand only if the law in general, and the State's refusal to allow a religious exemption in particular, are justified by a compelling interest that cannot be served by less restrictive means.

Until today, I thought this was a settled and inviolate principle of this Court's First Amendment jurisprudence. The majority, however, perfunctorily dismisses it as a "constitutional anomaly." As carefully detailed in Justice O'Connor's concurring opinion, the majority is able to arrive at this view only by mischaracterizing this Court's precedents. The Court discards leading free exercise cases such as Cantwell v Connecticut (1972) and Wisconsin v Yoder (1972) as "hybrid." The Court views traditional free exercise analysis as somehow inapplicable to criminal prohibitions (as opposed to conditions on the receipt of benefits), and to state laws of general applicability (as opposed, presumably, to laws that expressly single out religious practices). The Court cites cases in which, due to various exceptional circumstances, we found strict scrutiny inapposite, to hint that the Court has repudiated that standard altogether. In short, it effectuates a wholesale overturning of settled law concerning the Religion Clauses of our Constitution. One hopes that the Court is aware of the consequences, and that its result is not a product of overreaction to the serious problems the country's drug crisis has generated.

This distorted view of our precedents leads the majority to conclude that strict scrutiny of a state law burdening the free exercise of religion is a "luxury" that a well-ordered society cannot afford, and that the repression of minority religions is an "unavoidable consequence of democratic government." I do not believe the Founders thought their dearly bought freedom from religious persecution a "luxury," but an essential element of liberty—and they could not have thought religious intolerance "unavoidable," for they drafted the Religion Clauses precisely in order to avoid that intolerance.

For these reasons, I agree with Justice O'Connor's analysis of the applicable free exercise doctrine, and I join parts I and II of her opinion. As she points out, "the critical question in this case is whether exempting respondents from the State's general criminal prohibition 'will unduly interfere with fulfillment of the gov-

ernmental interest.'" I do disagree, however, with her specific answer to that question.

. . .

In weighing respondents' clear interest in the free exercise of their religion against Oregon's asserted interest in enforcing its drug laws, it is important to articulate in precise terms the state interest involved. It is not the State's broad interest in fighting the critical "war on drugs" that must be weighed against respondents' claim, but the State's narrow interest in refusing to make an exception for the religious, ceremonial use of peyote. . . . Failure to reduce the competing interests to the same plane of generality tends to distort the weighing process in the State's favor. . . .

The State's interest in enforcing its prohibition, in order to be sufficiently compelling to outweigh a free exercise claim, cannot be merely abstract or symbolic. The State cannot plausibly assert that unbending application of a criminal prohibition is essential to fulfill any compelling interest, if it does not, in fact, attempt to enforce that prohibition. In this case, the State actually has not evinced any concrete interest in enforcing its drug laws against religious users of peyote. Oregon has never sought to prosecute respondents, and does not claim that it has made significant enforcement efforts against other religious users of peyote. The State's asserted interest thus amounts only to the symbolic preservation of an unenforced prohibition. But a government interest in "symbolism, even symbolism for so worthy a cause as the abolition of unlawful drugs," cannot suffice to abrogate the constitutional rights of individuals.

. . .

The State proclaims an interest in protecting the health and safety of its citizens from the dangers of unlawful drugs. It offers, however, no evidence that the religious use of peyote has ever harmed anyone. The factual findings of other courts cast doubt on the State's assumption that religious use of peyote is harmful. . . .

The fact that peyote is classified as a Schedule I controlled substance does not, by itself, show that any and all uses of peyote, in any circumstance, are inherently harmful and dangerous. The Federal Government, which created the classifications of unlawful drugs from which Oregon's drug laws are derived, apparently does not find peyote so dangerous as to preclude an exemption for religious use. Moreover, other Schedule I drugs have lawful uses.

The carefully circumscribed ritual context in which respondents used peyote is far removed from the irresponsible and unrestricted recreational use of unlawful drugs. The Native American Church's internal restrictions on, and supervision of, its members' use of peyote substantially obviate the State's health and safety concerns. . . .

Moreover, just as in Yoder, the values and interests of those seeking a religious exemption in this case are congruent, to a great degree, with those the State seeks to promote through its drug laws. . . . Not only does the Church's doctrine forbid nonreligious use of peyote; it also generally advocates self-reliance, familial responsibility, and abstinence from alcohol. . . . There is considerable evidence that the spiritual and social support provided by the Church has been effective in combatting the tragic effects of alcoholism on the Native American population. Two noted experts on peyotism, Dr. Omer C. Stewart and Dr. Robert Bergman, testified by affidavit to this effect on behalf of respondent Smith before the Employment Appeal Board. (Research by Dr. Bergman suggests "that the religious use of peyote seemed to be directed in an ego-strengthening direction with an emphasis on interpersonal relationships where each individual is assured of his own significance as well as the support of the group"; many people have "'come through difficult crises with the help of this religion. . . . It provides real help in seeing themselves not as people whose place and way in the world is gone, but as people whose way can be strong enough to change and meet new challenges.'") . . . Far from promoting the lawless and irresponsible use of drugs, Native American Church members' spiritual code exemplifies values that Oregon's drug laws are presumably intended to foster.

The State also seeks to support its refusal to make an exception for religious use of peyote by invoking its interest in abolishing drug trafficking. There is, however, practically no illegal traffic in peyote. . . . Peyote simply is not a popular drug; its distribution for use in religious rituals has nothing to do with the vast and violent traffic in illegal narcotics that plagues this country.

Finally, the State argues that granting an exception for religious peyote use would erode its interest in the uniform, fair, and certain enforcement of its drug laws. The State fears that, if it grants an exemption for religious peyote use, a flood of other claims to religious exemptions will follow. It would then be placed in a dilemma, it says, between allowing a patchwork of exemptions that would hinder its law enforcement efforts, and risking a violation of the Establishment Clause by arbitrarily limiting its religious exemptions. This argument, however, could be made in almost any free exercise case. . . . This Court, however, consistently has rejected similar arguments in past free exercise cases, and it should do so here as well. . . .

The State's apprehension of a flood of other religious claims is purely speculative. Almost half the States, and the Federal Government, have maintained an exemption for religious peyote use for many years, and apparently have not found themselves overwhelmed by claims to other religious exemptions. Allowing an exemption for religious peyote use would not necessarily oblige the State to grant a similar exemption to other religious groups. The unusual circumstances that make the religious use of peyote compatible with the State's interests in health and safety and in preventing drug trafficking would not apply to other religious claims. Some religions, for example, might not restrict drug use to a limited ceremonial context, as does the Native American Church. Some religious claims involve drugs such as marijuana and heroin, in which there is significant illegal traffic, with its attendant greed and violence, so that it would be difficult to grant a religious exemption without seriously compromising law enforcement efforts. That the State might grant an exemption for religious peyote use, but deny other religious claims arising in different circumstances, would not violate the Establishment Clause. Though the State must treat all religions equally, and not favor one over another, this obligation is fulfilled by the uniform application of the "compelling interest" *test* to all free exercise claims, not by reaching uniform *results* as to all claims. A showing that religious peyote use does not unduly interfere with the State's interests is "one that probably few other religious groups or sects could make."

. . .

For these reasons, I conclude that Oregon's interest in enforcing its drug laws against religious use of peyote is not sufficiently compelling to outweigh respondents' right to the free exercise of their religion. Since the State could not constitutionally enforce its criminal prohibition against respondents, the interests underlying the State's drug laws cannot justify its denial of unemployment benefits. Absent such justification, the State's regulatory interest in denying benefits for religiously motivated "misconduct," is indistinguishable from the state interests this Court has rejected in Frazee, Hobbie, Thomas, and Sherbert. The State of Oregon cannot, consistently with the Free Exercise Clause, deny respondents unemployment benefits.

I dissent.

Aftermath of Employment Division, Department of Human Resources of Oregon *v.* Smith

Justice Scalia's opinion for the Court in *Employment Division* v. *Smith* may mark a turning point in First Amendment law, since it appears to reject much of the basis for a half-century of free exercise clause decisions beginning with *Cantwell* v. *Connecticut* (excerpted earlier in this chapter). It remains to be seen whether Scalia's fragile majority will adhere in future free exercise cases involving less volatile issues than drug use. Will the Court continue to treat criminal laws of general application as sufficiently compelling on their face to be considered invulnerable to free exercise challenges?

One week after its *Employment Division* ruling the Supreme Court ordered the Minnesota Supreme Court to reconsider its decision that members of the Old Order Amish were exempt from a state law requiring reflecting triangles on their horse-drawn buggies (*Minnesota* v. *Hershberger*). The Amish had claimed that complying with the law would indicate a lack of trust in God. Interestingly, the Minnesota Civil Liberties Union sided with the state in its argument that such an exemption would go so far in accommodating the Amish that it would amount to an unconstitutional establishment of religion. However, the unsettled nature of the Court's decision making is illustrated by the fact that all three of the *Employment Division* dissenters—Justices Brennan, Marshall, and Blackmun—voted with the majority, while Justices O'Connor and Stevens, who had concurred in the *Employment Division* decision, filed dissents.

7   Equal Protection of the Laws

O n July 28, 1868, Secretary of State William H. Seward formally proclaimed the Fourteenth Amendment to the Constitution to be in force. Initially proposed on June 13, 1866, the measure encountered long and tortuous debates in Congress and in the state conventions prior to its formal ratification. As the discussion of due process in Chapter 4 made clear, the amendment initiated a revolution in American constitutional law, the reverberations of which are still with us well over a century later. In addition to due process, the amendment contains other clauses: the privileges and immunities clause which was intended to guarantee full rights of citizenship to former slaves; and the equal protection clause—"nor shall any state deprive any person within its jurisdiction the equal protection of the laws"—which guarantees equality before the law. Taken together, these clauses of the Fourteenth Amendment were intended to guarantee equal status for blacks in the body politic by preventing state governments from treating blacks unfairly either by law or by administrative practice. The words "race," "Negro," or "black" do not appear in the amendment's language, and over the years the Supreme Court has given those rather vague phrases, "due process of law" and "equal protection of the laws," an expanded meaning that goes far beyond an exclusive application to racial minorities.

What specifically did the men who fashioned the equal protection clause and those legislators in both Congress and the state legislatures who supported it believe the clause to mean? In theory at least, the clause hung on those twin hooks of democracy, liberty and equality, especially the latter. Its purpose was to make certain that the states would frame legislation in a manner that at a minimum would not disadvantage black people or give special privileges to any person or group based on skin color. Equality as an abstract concept was a moving force in American political thought from the nation's early beginning, originating in natural law and natural rights theory and given classic expression in the words of the Declaration of Independence that "all men are created equal." John A. Bingham, representative from Ohio and author of the first section of the Fourteenth Amendment including the equal protection clause, expressed the general sentiment of the clause's supporters when he proclaimed that in adopting the amendment, the American people would "declare their purpose to stand by the foundation principle of their own institutions, the *absolute equality* of all citizens of the United States politically and civilly before their own laws." Even the amendment's opponents never questioned the principle of equality. However, there was and still remains a considerable disparity among those who sincerely profess a belief in equality, as to what it means in practice. The Supreme Court justices themselves have been unable to agree on a precise meaning of equality as they have attempted to validate the promise and the constitutional mandate of the equal protection clause.

EQUAL PROTECTION AND CLASSIFICATION

Law by its very nature involves classification; that is, it applies rules to certain groups based on criteria ranging from age, sex, and residency to citizenship, legitimacy, and income level. Did the equal protection clause mean that a legislature might no longer classify people into legal categories for any purpose whatsoever? If that were the case it would be impossible for the government to function efficiently and rationally. It would mean, for example, that a state might not fix a minimum age for obtaining a driver's license or for the purchase of alcoholic beverages. Nor could it make distinctions between citizens and aliens for the purpose of voting, since the clause speaks only of "persons," a term that encompasses aliens and citizens alike. In its role as interpreter of the Constitution the Supreme Court has given "equal protection of the laws" a judicial gloss that has become an amalgam of literal meaning softened by doctrines creatively applied to evolving controversies.

It should be emphasized that the clause does not require that all persons be treated identically, but that they be treated "equally." Thus, the first rule a legislature must follow in framing a statute is that all persons "similarly situated" must be treated in the same way, or to phrase it differently, equals must be treated equally. For example, it would be a violation of equal protection if a state were to fix 18 as the requisite age for males to vote, and 20 as the age for females. The principle is not that males and females may not be treated differently for a certain purpose, but that as a condition of voting, sex is not a rational basis for making such distinctions, which brings us to a second rule. When a state does discriminate among groups, it must show that the discrimination has a reasonable relationship to a legitimate state purpose. In the hypothetical example cited above, it would be impossible to fathom a legitimate purpose in fixing an age differential in men and women as a qualification for voting, and a court would invalidate such a law without even moving to analyze the "reasonable relationship" requirement. However, in *Craig* v. *Boren* (1976) in which the state of Oklahoma had prohibited the sale of 3.2 percent beer to males under 21 and females under 18, the state contended that the law was aimed at preventing motor vehicle accidents, certainly a legitimate state purpose. Yet the Court decided that despite statistics showing that male arrests for drunken driving in the 18- to 20-year-old group exceeded those for females of the same age, the relationship between gender and traffic safety was so tenuous as not to be rationally related to the state's objective.

Fundamental to the Court's analysis of state legislation in cases like *Craig* are two key words: reasonableness and fairness. Legislation that classifies groups for the purpose of protecting health, safety, morals, and the general welfare may differentiate, may discriminate, may place burdens on some and grant benefits to others, but in doing so, it must not be arbitrary, capricious, or unreasonable. Under a natural law–natural rights theory it is assumed that rational human beings would agree on what is arbitrary or unreasonable. However, given the predominance of a relativist philosophy in contemporary American society, rational persons do not necessarily agree on a precise, automatic meaning for these terms. Thus the Court has fashioned a set of complex rules to determine with some degree of predictability when a statute is unfair or unreasonable.

Other problems surface when a statute as written passes the constitutional tests, but is unfairly administered or has unintended, unfair consequences. As early as 1880 the Court held in *Strauder* v. *West Virginia* that a law excluding blacks from juries at a trial of a black defendant was a denial of equal protection. Subsequently, West Virginia and states with similar laws respecting jury duty repealed all racial references to service on juries, but exclusion of blacks by practice continued. In *Avery* v. *Georgia* (1953), however, the Court held that even if the law was free of racial discrimination, overt practice of racial exclusion was also unconstitutional. In this instance prospective jurors who were white had their names printed on white tickets, blacks on yellow tickets. A judge drew the jury from a box in which all tickets were placed and black names never appeared on the final list. In the *Avery* case not a single black was selected from a panel of 60. There are, of course, more subtle means of unfair administrative discrimination but, if discovered, any such invidious practice will be held to deny equal protection of the laws.

Another early case, *Yick Wo* v. *Hopkins* (1886), further emphasizes the rule that a law may not be unfairly administered. An ordinance enacted by the city of San Francisco provided that no one could engage in the laundry business without first obtaining the consent of the board of supervisors, and that the business must be located in a building constructed of brick or stone. On its face this appeared to be a reasonable regulatory safety measure. At the time the ordinance was passed most of the laundries in San Francisco were owned and operated by Chinese, some 240 out of a total of 320. Yick Wo, a city resident who had been operating a laundry for 22 years, applied for a license under the new law and was refused even though the fire wardens and health officer had certified his premises to be safe and sanitary. Continuing to do business despite the lack of a license, Yick Wo was arrested and jailed, then petitioned for a writ of *habeas corpus* which eventually afforded him a hearing in the United States Supreme Court. Yick Wo's attorney pointed out that all Chinese applicants were refused a license—some 150 having been arrested—while non-Chinese in all but one instance were granted permission to carry on their businesses. In holding the application of the law violative of the equal protection clause the Supreme Court observed:

> Though the law itself be fair on its face and impartial in appearance, yet, if it is applied and administered by public authority with an evil eye and an unequal hand, so as practically to make unjust and illegal discriminations between persons in similar circumstances, material to their rights, the denial of equal justice is still within the prohibition of the Constitution . . . .

More difficult to decide than the obvious unfair administration of the laws in *Strauder* and *Yick Wo* are those cases in which the law is neutral in its language, and its legislative history shows no "discriminatory purpose," where at least the record indicates that a legislative body had neither selected nor reaffirmed a policy because of its adverse effects upon an identifiable class. In several cases the Court has upheld facially neutral laws, the effect of which was to have a disparate impact on blacks. In *Washington* v. *Davis* (1976) unsuccessful black candidates for positions as police officers in the District of Columbia contended that some of the written tests had a discriminatory racial impact since four times as many blacks as whites failed the test. Rejecting the argument, the Supreme Court held that no proof existed that the test was adopted with a racially discriminatory purpose. Similarly, in *Village of Arlington Heights* v. *Metropolitan Development Corporation* (1977) the Court upheld a zoning board decision that tended to perpetuate racially segregated housing patterns since, apart from its effects, the board's decision was simply an application of a constitutionally neutral zoning policy. In a case involving alleged gender discrimination, *Personnel Administrator of Massachusetts* v. *Feeney* (1979), the Court addressed the question whether Massachusetts, in granting military veterans preferences in civil service jobs, discriminated against women. Although of some 47,000 state employees 57 percent were men and 43 percent were women, and only 2 percent of the women compared to 54 percent of the men were veterans, the Court found no intent on the part of the Massachusetts legislature to discriminate against women. What these cases illustrate is that the equal protection clause guarantees equal laws, not equal results.

Is it ever possible, however, that unintended consequences of a neutral law, nondiscriminatory in intent, may still violate the equal protection clause? The Court has not answered the question directly, but in cases in which it was asked to construe Title VII of the Civil Rights Act of 1964, it has clearly held that in some instances the fact of unequal result outweighs the lack of discriminatory intent. In *Griggs* v. *Duke Power Company* (1971) the Court upheld the claim of a black employee of the Duke Power Company that the intelligence test given by the company to determine hiring and promotion had the effect of discriminating against blacks since a disproportionate number of them failed the test. Later in a challenge under Title VII by a woman to height and weight requirements for prison guards that had the effect of eliminating females, the Court again upheld the principle of unintentional de facto discrimination (*Dothard* v. *Rawlinson*, 1977). More recently, in *Watson* v. *Fort Worth Bank and Trust* (1988), the rule in *Griggs* was extended to subjective criteria as well as to standardized written tests. Clara Watson, an employee of a Fort Worth bank, had been rejected for promotion on four occasions in favor of white candidates. Under the bank's procedures, promotion depended not upon any written tests but upon the judgment of supervisory personnel who were familiar with the work of the applicants. In this instance the administrative officers who had denied the promotions to Watson were white. Relying on the rationale of the *Griggs* case, Justice Sandra Day O'Connor vacated the judgment and remanded the case for a new hearing. In stating the rule for this type of situation, Justice O'Connor declared that the plaintiff (Watson) need not necessarily prove intentional discrimination in order to establish that an employer has violated the law, concluding that "subjective or discretionary employment practices may be analyzed under the disparate impact approach in appropriate cases." Thus, it is possible that a claimant may successfully argue a denial of equal protection under the principle of "disparate impact analysis" even though there is no discriminatory intent in the law or deliberate unfairness in its administration. However, the impact of *Griggs* has recently been undercut by a 1989 case, *Wards Cove Packing Company, Inc.* v. *Atonio*, in which a more conservative Supreme Court ruled 5–4 that the burden of proof is now on persons making such claims to show that an allegedly discriminatory hiring or promotion practice is unrelated to the job. Previously the employer had had the burden of justifying the practice by showing that it was necessary to the job.

Further complicating the issue is the exception the Court has made for seniority systems which have been upheld in spite of the possibility of discriminatory impact, since it cannot be shown that they were adopted with a discriminatory purpose. Are seniority systems fair? Generally they are, but they may have an exclusionary effect on minorities who have recently come to public agencies such as police and fire departments where promotions and salary increases are heavily weighted toward seniority.

NEW STANDARDS SINCE THE 1950s

Until the decision in *Brown* v. *Board of Education* in 1954, cases involving allegations of a denial of equal protection were decided by courts asking the questions: Did the legislation at issue contain a reasonable classification and not unfairly burden members of a particular group? Was the law an appropriate means to effect a legitimate state objective? Was the law administered fairly? Within the confines of these criteria the Supreme Court invalidated very few laws under the equal protection clause. Adhering to the framework of the separate but equal doctrine announced in *Plessy* v. *Ferguson* in 1896, the Court generally upheld racial distinctions as well as differentiations involving sex. With the exception of voting rights and, in some instances, property rights such as those at stake in *Yick Wo* v. *Hopkins*, complainants won few cases in the courts on the basis of an alleged denial of equal protection of the laws. All of this changed radically in the 1950s and 1960s.

As the number of lawsuits mushroomed in which the constitutionality of classifications was attacked, the Supreme Court developed what is known as the three-tiered approach to equal protection cases: strict scrutiny, moderate or intermediate scrutiny, and minimum scrutiny. The strictest scrutiny is applied to "suspect classifications" in which the Court presumes that the statute or ordinance under review is unfairly discriminatory. Similar to the "presumption of invalidity" doctrine in free speech cases, the state carries the burden of proving the law valid by showing first, that the classification furthers a "compelling" state interest and second, that any other course of action would be even more disadvantageous to both the differentiated groups and to the state. Until now the Court has placed only three classifications in the suspect category subject to strict scrutiny: those based on race, national origin, and alienage. Race for obvious reasons is the prototype of the suspect classification since it is so easily identifiable through physical characteristics. Yet gender, which is not subject to strict scrutiny, can also be physically identified. Thus with race, other criteria are taken into account, particularly the history of slavery, racial prejudice, and the lack of political power to protect black Americans from unfair treatment. Black people are, in Justice Harlan Stone's famous phrase, a "discrete and insular minority" and deserve special judicial consideration. Although it is rare that any governmental action based on race, statutory or administrative, can pass constitutional muster, valid racial separation is not inconceivable under unusual circumstances. For example, during a prison riot caused by racial tension blacks and whites might be segregated in order to secure the safety of all, a legitimate and compelling state purpose.

Minimum scrutiny at the bottom of the tier is simply the traditional equal protection test. Is the law a reasonable classification rationally related to a legitimate state purpose? Most laws are upheld under this test. For those classifications that fall somewhere in between the two extremes is the middle tier of moderate scrutiny under which classifications are viewed with mild suspicion. Under this test laws must further an "important" state purpose as opposed to a "compelling" (strict-scrutiny) or "legitimate" (minimum-scrutiny) purpose. Falling into this category are laws dealing with illegitimacy, that is, statutes that treat illegitimate offspring differently from legitimate children for purpose of inheritance or other possible benefits. Some of these laws may be patently unfair; others may be defended as furthering an "important" state purpose such as the goal of preventing illegitimacy in the first place, if putative parents are aware of the disadvantages to the child.

In determining the particular standard to be followed in an alleged denial of equal protection, the initial choice of a category—strict, moderate, or minimum—is usually the key to the outcome of the litigation. As with many areas of constitutional law, the justices do not always agree on the rules for equal protection cases. Once litigation moves beyond race, alienage, and national origin, the Court's opinions tend to be split, frequently to the point of producing a plurality rather than a clear majority in any given case. Some of the justices, for example, would place sex discrimination in the suspect strict-scrutiny category, but a majority has opted for the middle tier which in practice permits some legal distinctions based on sex and forbids others. In recent years alleged denial of equal protection has resulted in lawsuits brought by senior citizens, illegal aliens, prisoners, handicapped persons, and homosexuals. Where each of these groups falls among the judicial tiers depends on various factors, all of which involve compromises between majority rule and minority rights, compromises which are always imperfect and never satisfactory to everyone.

A complicating factor in equal protection litigation is the problem of where to draw the somewhat hazy line between public discrimination (by law or government practice) and private discrimination (by individuals in their private associations). In this respect the Fourteenth Amendment appears to speak in clear, unequivocal language, namely, that it prohibits the *state government* from denying anyone equal protection or due process. But the extent to which a state is a party to unfair discrimination is not always facially obvious. When a private club restricts its membership to white males, such action would appear to be outside the ambit of equal protection strictures since the state is not involved in any discriminatory unfairness either by law or administrative practice. Yet, is the state completely free of involvement? It can be argued that if the club has a charter of incorporation, sells its members liquor under a state license, uses public utilities such as water and electricity, its connections to the state, though tenuous, are such that the state government is a party to any discriminatory practice. This argument was made in *Moose Lodge* v. *Irvis* (1972) when K. Leroy Irvis, a black male who accompanied a white friend to a Moose Lodge chapter in Harrisburg, Pennsylvania, was refused food and drink because of the lodge's restrictions to white male membership. Irvis brought suit but did not convince the Supreme Court that the state of Pennsylvania had denied him equal protection of the laws. It was the Court's view that since there was no intention on the part of

Pennsylvania to use its liquor code to discriminate on a racial basis, the state itself did not "foster or encourage racial discrimination."

Carried to a logical extreme, if *any* connection with the state would bring the Fourteenth Amendment into play, even the individual in his or her home would be caught in the net since one's home is subject to myriad state regulations beginning with the building code, and encompassing such matters as fire regulations and property taxes. At what point then is the constitutional line between public and private crossed? If the state attempts to enforce discrimination through its policy or, more likely, its courts (see *Shelley* v. *Kraemer*, excerpted in this chapter), state involvement is clear enough to warrant judicial intervention and validation of one's rights under the equal protection clause. If the link between public and private is more subtle and the state action less intrusive, an aggrieved litigant must show that state involvement is "significant" and "explicit," and that the state must have intended to make an unfair distinction. This rather severe test tends to keep a relatively small but important sphere of privacy beyond government intervention. Were the Court to permit further state encroachment on private action, another constitutional right, that of freedom of association guaranteed by the First Amendment, would be endangered.

Given the judicial rules that now govern the equal protection clause, the web of protection against action by the states that would be harmful to any minority group is comprehensive in scope and neutral in application. Still, neutrality and objectivity in the laws have not necessarily produced an equitable result, particularly with respect to blacks, although women and ethnic minorities also contend that neutrality in the law is not enough. As a result of sustained pressures based upon the proposition that special positive remedies are needed to rectify centuries of wrongs, a new concept, affirmative action, has come into vogue. Under its rubric schools have been ordered to move beyond segregation and to racially integrate pupils through various means, including busing across district lines. Colleges and universities have been under government pressures, including court orders, to admit more black students and to hire more black, Hispanic, and female faculty members. Similarly state and municipal agencies, especially police and fire departments, have been ordered to admit more minorities and women to their ranks. Noble as this goal may be, it has spawned a backlash from white males who now argue that to be disadvantaged or displaced by minorities and women solely on the basis of race or gender is, in traditional constitutional language, "unfair discrimination and a denial of equal protection." This issue has not been resolved, as the Supreme Court in wrestling with it has yet to arrive at a satisfactory doctrine that permits race and gender to be the basis for receiving preferential treatment when the avowed purpose of constitutional equal protection was the exact opposite. It was quite obvious in the many involved opinions in the *Regents of University of California* v. *Bakke* case (excerpted in this chapter) that the justices cannot even agree on whether affirmative action is commanded or prohibited by the Fourteenth Amendment.

Bibliography

BONNICKSEN, ANDREA L. *Civil Rights and Liberties.* Palo Alto: Mayfield Publishing Company, 1982.

FUNSTON, RICHARD Y. *Constitutional Counter-Revolution.* New York: Wiley, 1977.

HARRIS, ROBERT J. *The Quest for Equality.* Baton Rouge: Louisiana State University Press, 1960.

HYMAN, HAROLD M. and WIECEK, WILLIAM M. *Equal Justice Under Law: Constitutional Develop-*

ment, 1835–1875. New York: Harper & Row, 1982.

KIRK, DAVID L. *Just Schools: The Idea of Racial Equality in American Education.* Berkeley: University of California Press, 1982.

KLUGER, RICHARD. *Simple Justice.* New York: Knopf, 1976.

NELSON, WILLIAM E. *The Fourteenth Amendment.* Cambridge: Harvard University Press, 1988.

WILKINSON, J. HARVIE III. *From Brown to Bakke.* New York: Oxford University Press, 1976.

Brown v. Board of Education

347 U.S. 483 (1954)

The Supreme Court has been justly acclaimed for its leadership in dismantling legal segregation. In fact, the Court's role in outlawing Jim Crow has been so important that it has almost erased the memory of the part that the Court played in erecting that system in the first place.

In the *Civil Rights Cases* (1883) the Supreme Court declared unconstitutional sections of the Civil Rights Act of 1875 that had guaranteed access to public accommodations for all citizens regardless of race or color. Having thus legitimized private discrimination, the Court then gave its blessing to state-sponsored segregation in *Plessy* v. *Ferguson* (1896) by upholding a Louisiana law that required blacks and whites to ride in separate railroad cars. In ruling that the state had not acted unreasonably in regulating race relations in this fashion, the Court gave the states carte blanche to maintain "separate but equal" facilities for blacks and whites. Although this term was merely a euphemism because the facilities for blacks were always inferior to those used by whites—in Louisiana, for instance, black train passengers rode in cattle cars—in *Plessy*, the Court chose to look at the rhetoric, not the reality, of separate but equal.

Over the next half-century the National Association for the Advancement of Colored People (NAACP) worked tirelessly to undermine the system of legal segregation. After concluding that the Supreme Court was not likely to reverse *Plessy* outright, the NAACP's legal team, led by future Supreme Court Justice Thurgood Marshall, instead sought to focus the Court's attention on the states' systematic neglect of the "equal" part of the separate but equal doctrine. One of the NAACP's principal targets in this regard was public education, which was racially segregated by law from top to bottom throughout the southern and border states. Two cases brought to the Supreme Court by the NAACP, both involving segregated law schools, illustrate the organization's legal strategy and the Court's response to it.

In 1938 the NAACP appealed to the Supreme Court on behalf of Lloyd Gaines, a black man who had sought admission to the University of Missouri's law school. Gaines's application was rejected on racial grounds and he was told that he should either apply to Lincoln University, the state-supported black college, where a makeshift legal curriculum would be developed for him, or attend an out-of-state law school, for which Missouri would pay the tuition costs in excess of those at its own law school. This was not good enough, argued the NAACP. If the state chose to deny blacks entrance to its law school, then it was obliged to offer them an equal educational opportunity within the state. The Supreme Court agreed (*Missouri ex rel Gaines* v. *Canada*), and in doing so for the first time treated the separate but equal principle as something more than a subterfuge that allowed the states to ignore the needs of their black citizens.

In 1950 the Supreme Court heard another case involving a state's refusal to admit a black applicant to its university law school and, prodded by the NAACP, cut a bit deeper into the roots of the separate but equal doctrine. Texas had set up a "law school" for blacks in the basement of an Austin office building, equipped it with a library of 10,000 cast-off volumes and hired three part-time faculty members. As in the earlier Missouri case, the NAACP in *Sweatt* v. *Painter* did not ask the Court to rule segregated education unconstitutional per se, but did ask it to acknowledge that segregation as practiced by Texas denied blacks the equal protection of the laws. This the Court did, stressing that even if the physical facilities Texas had provided black law students had been the equal of those at the university's law school—which they decidedly were not—the intangible qualities that make a law school what it is— "reputation of the faculty, experience of the administration . . . standing in the community, traditions and prestige"—all would be lacking at the black school. Hence Texas had not, and probably could not, conform to the Fourteenth Amendment if it continued to segregate law students on the basis of race.

Having made those inroads against Jim Crow in higher education, the NAACP turned its attention to segregation in elementary and secondary schools. Thurgood Marshall and his colleagues hoped to build on the Court's discussion of "intangibles" in *Sweatt*, by showing that school segregation itself imposed such burdens on black children that their whole lives were adversely affected. Unless they were permitted to attend the same schools as whites they would be denied the equal protection of the laws.

For help in making this case Marshall turned to Dr. Kenneth Clark, a psychology professor at City College of New York. Clark had done clinical tests with young children, both black and white, to measure their self-esteem. In one experiment children were shown pink-skinned and brown-skinned dolls, and then asked to identify the "bad" doll, the "nice" doll, the "pretty" doll, and the "ugly" doll. By large margins, children of both races preferred the "white" dolls to the "black" ones. Based on the results of this and other tests, Clark concluded that from an early age black children were aware of their racial identity and formed negative conclusions about themselves because of it. The NAACP hoped to persuade the Court that the negative effects of "separate but equal" public education were so pervasive that only the total elimination of separate schools would guarantee black children the equal protection of the laws.

This was a conclusion that at least some members of the Court were still reluctant to reach. In 1952 the Court docketed a group of five cases—four from states, one from the District of Columbia—involving challenges to legally separated schools. The lead case, *Brown* v. *Board of Education of Topeka, Kansas,* had been brought by Oliver Brown, a railroad worker and part-time minister, on behalf of his daughter Linda. Topeka had integrated its junior high and high schools in the 1940s, but still maintained separate black and white elementary schools. Linda Brown attended a grade school about 1 mile from her home. The case began when Oliver Brown tried to register Linda at a white school closer to their home.

A few months after *Brown* and its companion cases were heard in December of 1952, the Supreme Court took the unusual step of asking for rearguments the following term, with special emphasis on whether or not the framers and ratifiers of the Fourteenth Amendment had intended the amendment to abolish segregation in public schools. At this time several justices were apparently still reluctant to overturn *Plessy.* Before the reargument occurred in December 1953, Chief Justice Fred Vinson—one of those who supported *Plessy*—died suddenly and was succeeded by Earl Warren, the popular Republican governor of California who had sought his party's presidential nomination in 1952 before yielding to the Eisenhower juggernaut. After the *Brown* reargument, Warren made it clear to his brethren that he wanted to declare public school segregation unconstitutional. He also expressed his hope that the Court would agree on a single unanimous opinion supporting such a

position. Over the next few months Warren used his considerable persuasive talent to marshal the Court behind an opinion that would be, in his words, "short, readable by the lay public, non-rhetorical, unemotional and, above all, non-accusatory." On May 17, 1954, the momentous decision was announced. Justice Robert Jackson, who had been recuperating from a serious heart attack, left his hospital bed to be on the bench when the Chief Justice delivered the Court's unanimous judgment.

EARL WARREN

Earl Warren served several successful terms as Republican governor of California before being appointed Chief Justice by President Dwight Eisenhower in 1953. Neither an exceptional lawyer nor a great legal scholar, Warren was an extraordinary leader, and he infused the Supreme Court with a new spirit that manifested itself in bold judicial innovation and constitutional reform. Particularly significant are his opinions on school desegregation, criminal procedure, and reapportionment, which emphasized equality and fairness, and changed the course of American public law.

Mr. Chief Justice **Warren** delivered the opinion of the Court.

These cases come to us from the States of Kansas, South Carolina, Virginia, and Delaware. They are premised on different facts and different local conditions, but a common legal question justifies their consideration together in this consolidated opinion.

In each of the cases, minors of the Negro race, through their legal representatives, seek the aid of the courts in obtaining admission to the public schools of their community on a non-segregated basis. In each instance, they had been denied admission to schools attended by white children under laws requiring or permitting segregation according to race. This segregation was alleged to deprive the plaintiffs of the equal protection of the laws under the Fourteenth Amendment. In each of the cases other than the Delaware case, a three-judge federal district court denied relief to the plaintiffs on the so-called "separate but equal" doctrine announced by this Court in *Plessy* v. *Ferguson.* Under that doctrine, equality of treatment is accorded when the races are provided substan-

tially equal facilities, even though these facilities be separate. In the Delaware case, the Supreme Court of Delaware adhered to that doctrine, but ordered that the plaintiffs be admitted to the white schools because of their superiority to the Negro schools.

The plaintiffs contend that segregated public schools are not "equal" and cannot be made "equal," and that hence they are deprived of the equal protection of the laws. Because of the obvious importance of the question presented, the Court took jurisdiction. Argument was heard in the 1952 Term, and reargument was heard this Term on certain questions propounded by the Court.

Reargument was largely devoted to the circumstances surrounding the adoption of the Fourteenth Amendment in 1868. It covered exhaustively consideration of the Amendment in Congress, ratification by the states, then existing practices in racial segregation, and the views of proponents and opponents of the Amendment. This discussion and our own investigation convince us that, although these sources cast some light, it is not enough to resolve the problem with which we are faced. At best, they are inconclusive. The most avid proponents of the post-War Amendments undoubtedly intended them to remove all legal distinctions among "all persons born or naturalized in the United States." Their opponents, just as certainly, were antagonistic to both the letter and the spirit of the Amendments and wished them to have the most limited effect. What others in Congress and the state legislatures had in mind cannot be determined with any degree of certainty.

An additional reason for the inconclusive nature of the Amendment's history, with respect to segregated schools, is the status of public education at that time. In the South, the movement toward free common schools, supported by general taxation, had not yet taken hold. Education of white children was largely in the hands of private groups. Education of Negroes was almost nonexistent, and practically all of the race were illiterate. In fact, any education of Negroes was forbidden by law in some states. Today, in contrast, many Negroes have achieved outstanding success in the arts and sciences as well as in the business and professional world. It is true that public school education at the time of the Amendment had advanced further in the North, but the effect of the Amendment on Northern States was generally ignored in the congressional debates. Even in the North, the conditions of public education did not approximate those existing today. The curriculum was usually rudimentary; ungraded schools were common in rural areas; the school term was but three months a year in many states; and compulsory school attendance was virtually unknown. As a consequence, it is not surprising that there should be so little in the history of the Fourteenth Amendment relating to its intended effect on public education.

In the first cases in this Court construing the Fourteenth Amendment, decided shortly after its adoption, the Court interpreted it as proscribing all state-imposed discriminations against the Negro race. The doctrine of "separate but equal" did not make its appearance in this Court until 1896 in the case of *Plessy* v. *Ferguson*, involving not education but transportation. American courts have since labored with the doctrine for over half a century. In this Court, there have been six cases involving the "separate but equal"

doctrine in the field of public education. In *Cumming* v. *County Board of Education*, and *Gong Lum* v. *Rice*, the validity of the doctrine itself was not challenged. In more recent cases, all on the graduate school level, inequality was found in that specific benefits enjoyed by white students were denied to Negro students of the same educational qualifications. In none of these cases was it necessary to re-examine the doctrine to grant relief to the Negro plaintiff. And in *Sweatt* v. *Painter*, the Court expressly reserved decision on the question whether *Plessy* v. *Ferguson* should be held inapplicable to public education.

In the instant cases, that question is directly presented. Here, unlike *Sweatt* v. *Painter*, there are findings below that the Negro and white schools involved have been equalized, or are being equalized, with respect to buildings, curricula, qualifications and salaries of teachers, and other "tangible" factors. Our decision, therefore, cannot turn on merely a comparison of these tangible factors in the Negro and white schools involved in each of the cases. We must look instead to the effect of segregation itself on public education.

In approaching this problem, we cannot turn the clock back to 1868 when the Amendment was adopted, or even to 1896 when *Plessy* v. *Ferguson* was written. We must consider public education in the light of its full development and its present place in American life throughout the Nation. Only in this way can it be determined if segregation in public schools deprives these plaintiffs of the equal protection of the laws.

Today, education is perhaps the most important function of state and local governments. Compulsory school attendance laws and the great expenditures for education both demonstrate our recognition of the importance of education to our democratic society. It is required in the performance of our most basic public responsibilities, even service in the armed forces. It is the very foundation of good citizenship. Today it is a principal instrument in awakening the child to cultural values, in preparing him for later professional training, and in helping him to adjust normally to his environment. In these days, it is doubtful that any child may reasonably be expected to succeed in life if he is denied the opportunity of an education. Such an opportunity, where the state has undertaken to provide it, is a right which must be made available to all on equal terms.

We come then to the question presented: Does segregation of children in public schools solely on the basis of race, even though the physical facilities and other "tangible" factors may be equal, deprive the children of the minority group of equal educational opportunities? We believe that it does.

In *Sweatt* v. *Painter*, in finding that a segregated law school for Negroes could not provide them equal educational opportunities, this Court relied in large part on "those qualities which are incapable of objective measurement but which make for greatness in a law school." In *McLaurin* v. *Oklahoma State Regents*, the Court, in requiring that a Negro admitted to a white graduate school be treated like all other students, again resorted to intangible considerations: ". . . his ability to study, to engage in discussions and exchange views with other students, and, in general, to learn his profession." Such considerations apply with added force to children in grade and high schools. To separate them from others of similar age and qualifications solely because of their race generates a feeling of inferiority as to their status in the community that may affect their hearts and minds in a way unlikely ever to be undone. The effect of this separation on their educational opportunities was well stated by a finding in the Kansas case by a court which nevertheless felt compelled to rule against the Negro plaintiffs:

"Segregation of white and colored children in public schools has a detrimental effect upon the colored children. The impact is greater when it has the sanction of the law; for the policy of separating the races is usually interpreted as denoting the inferiority of the Negro group. A sense of inferiority affects the motivation of a child to learn. Segregation with the sanction of law, therefore, has a tendency to [retard] the educational and mental development of Negro children and to deprive them of some of the benefits they would receive in a racial[ly] integrated school system."

Whatever may have been the extent of psychological knowledge at the time of *Plessy* v. *Ferguson*, this finding is amply supported by modern authority. Any language in *Plessy* v. *Ferguson* contrary to this finding is rejected.

We conclude that in the field of public education the doctrine of "separate but equal" has no place. Separate educational facilities are inherently unequal. Therefore, we hold that the plaintiffs and others similarly situated for whom the actions have been brought are, by reason of the segregation complained of, deprived of the equal protection of the laws guaranteed by the Fourteenth Amendment. This disposition makes unnecessary any discussion whether such segregation also violates the Due Process Clause of the Fourteenth Amendment.

Because these are class actions, because of the wide applicability of this decision, and because of the great variety of local conditions, the formulation of decrees in these cases presents problems of considerable complexity. On reargument, the consideration of appropriate relief was necessarily subordinated to the primary question—the constitutionality of segregation in public education. We have now announced that such segregation is a denial of the equal protection of the laws. In order that we may have the full assistance of the parties in formulating decrees, the cases will be restored to the docket, and the parties are requested to present further argument on Questions 4 and 5 previously propounded by the Court for the reargument this Term. The Attorney General of the United States is again invited to participate. The Attorneys General of the states requiring or permitting segregation in public education will also be permitted to appear as *amici curiae* upon request to do so by September 15, 1954, and submission of briefs by October 1, 1954.

It is so ordered.

Aftermath of Brown *v.* Board of Education

The non-accusatory tone of the *Brown* opinion did nothing to temper the outraged reaction which followed the Court's announcement. A few liberal southern whites urged their fellow citizens to accept the end of school segregation as an opportunity for peaceful progress in race relations, but in general the response fell into three categories: outright defiance, evasion, and delay. An opinion poll taken among white public officials in Florida shortly after *Brown* was handed down indicated that three-quarters of those surveyed disagreed with the *Brown* decision—30 percent "violently"—and that only 13 percent of the police officers polled intended to enforce attendance laws at integrated schools. The tone of defiance was most dramatically conveyed in the Southern Manifesto, a statement signed by 101 members of Congress (not including Senators Lyndon Johnson of Texas and Estes Kefauver and Albert Gore of Tennessee) calling *Brown* a "clear abuse of judicial power" and promising "to use all lawful means to bring about a reversal of this decision which is contrary to the Constitution." Some did not draw the line at "lawful means" in expressing their disapproval of Brown; a number of prominent blacks were killed and many blacks who tried to initiate lawsuits to integrate local schools were physically intimidated. In 1957 the violence that attended the integration of Central High School in Little Rock, Arkansas, forced President Dwight Eisenhower, whose lack of enthusiasm for the *Brown* decision was quite apparent, to send federal troops to protect the black students seeking to register for classes.

In *Brown* the Court deliberately avoided the issue of implementation; instead the parties were to return to the Court the following term to make suggestions as to how such a sweeping decision could best be carried out. The NAACP urged the Court to fix a definite deadline—September 1956 at the latest—for southern school districts to integrate themselves. The states wanted implementation left completely open-ended, with local school officials given wide discretion in deciding when and how to comply with *Brown*. The federal government, which had participated in the *Brown* arguments as *amicus curiae* in support of the NAACP, suggested a compromise position, which the Court adopted in its implementation decision issued the following year. In the decision known as *Brown II*, the Court announced that federal judges would be responsible for issuing the actual school desegregation decrees for their districts. These decrees should require that school officials make a "prompt and reasonable start" toward full compliance with *Brown*, and that integration should then proceed "with all deliberate speed." This approach, with its reliance on the good faith of local officials, proved to be an invitation to evasion and delay. Since school officials were under no legal obligation to begin desegregating their schools until they were sued by black parents, there was little incentive for voluntary compliance. Even after a school board had been ordered to desegregate, it was possible to put the day of reckoning off until well into the future by devising a process that occurred only one grade at a time. The opportunities for delay were such that by the early 1960s, as the nation looked forward to the tenth anniversary of the *Brown* decision, only about one-third of the public schools in the south had been substantially desegregated. In fact, neither Linda Brown nor any of the other children involved as plaintiffs in the school segregation cases ever attended a public school desegregated by the *Brown* decision.

Swann v. Charlotte-Mecklenburg Board of Education

402 U.S. 1 (1971)

After issuing *Brown II* in 1955, the Supreme Court had nothing more to say about the pace and progress of desegregation for the remainder of the decade, with the exception of one pronouncement in 1958. A few months after nine black students had entered Little Rock's Central High School in the fall of 1957 under the protection of federalized National Guard troops, the city's school board went to court asking that they be withdrawn and reassigned to black schools, and that the process of desegregation be postponed for 2¹/₂ years. The school board's lawyers persuaded the district judge that the presence of the black students had caused such tumult within the high school that education was being disrupted. On appeal, however, the Court of Appeals reversed. The case then went to the Supreme Court which flatly denied Little Rock's request for a postponement, emphasizing that the black students' constitutional rights could not be compromised by the "violence and disorder which have followed upon the actions of the Governor and Legislature" (*Cooper v. Aaron*, 1958). Having resoundingly restated its support for desegregation, the Court stepped back and let the political processes ensure that desegregation would proceed at a snail's pace. Not until 1964 did the Court issue another significant desegregation decision, this one in a case involving one of the more egregious efforts by a school district to avoid compliance with *Brown*. Prince Edward County in Virginia, the defendant in one of *Brown's* companion cases, had managed through various ploys to delay desegregation until 1959. Then, faced with a court order to desegregate its public schools, the county closed them down instead. White children quickly shifted to private schools that were set up with the help of state and local authorities, assistance which included tuition grants and tax credits. Blacks were offered similar help in establishing their own schools, but their leaders declined it and undertook a legal battle to reopen the public schools on a desegregated basis. For 4 years most black children in Prince Edward County received no formal education. In *Griffin v. County School Board* (1964) the Supreme Court held that the school closures had deprived black children of equal protection of the laws. The state was enjoined from further supporting the private schools and ordered to ensure that Prince Edward County officials reopened desegregated schools. When they finally did so their student body consisted of 1600 blacks and 4 whites.

As of the early 1960s, then, there was still relatively little progress to show for nearly a decade of desegregation. The situation began to change very rapidly, however, after passage of the Civil Rights Act of 1964. One provision of the act declared that school boards could qualify for federal education funds only after their desegregation plans had been approved by the Department of Health, Education and Welfare. In practice, this put HEW into the business of drawing up plans which were then submitted by local boards to the federal courts. Most of these plans required that children be shifted from one school to another to overcome the effects of residential segregation, a process that inevitably involved transporting children by bus to schools some distance from their homes. Although only a tiny fraction of the millions of children who rode buses to school were doing so for purposes of desegregation, by the late 1960s "busing" had become a code word symbolizing government intervention in decisions that had previously been left to local and parental discretion. Many whites resented the fact that their children were seemingly being made to "pay" for a problem they had had no part in creating. Moreover, in an era of increasing black militancy there was a backlash against some of the time-honored assump-

tions of the civil rights movement. While the overwhelming majority of blacks continued to support desegregation, whatever it cost, more than a few were offended by the idea, elevated by *Brown* to the level of constitutional principle, that black children could realize their full potential only through integration with whites.

In the midst of these crosscurrents of public opinion the Supreme Court in 1970 agreed to review a case involving school desegregation in Charlotte, North Carolina, and surrounding Mecklenburg County. The school district's considerable size necessitated extensive use of cross-town busing to redistribute the student population to ensure that no school was racially segregated and that, in certain areas, the racial mix of each school approximated that of the population-at-large. In the 1950s North Carolina had advertised itself as "the school busingest state in the Union," but there was considerable resistance in Charlotte to the court-ordered desegregation plan which went into effect in 1970. A group of citizens sought to delay its implementation on the ground that the amount of busing involved in the plan was excessive.

Mr. Chief Justice **Burger** delivered the opinion of the Court.

We granted certiorari in this case to review important issues as to the duties of school authorities and the scope of powers of federal courts under this Court's mandates to eliminate racially separate public schools established and maintained by state action. This case and those argued with it arose in states having a long history of maintaining two sets of schools in a single school system deliberately operated to carry out a governmental policy to separate pupils in schools solely on the basis of race. That was what Brown v Board of Education was all about. These cases present us with the problem of defining in more precise terms than heretofore the scope of the duty of school authorities and district courts in implementing Brown I and the mandate to eliminate dual systems and establish unitary systems at once. Meanwhile district courts and courts of appeals have struggled in hundreds of cases with a multitude and variety of problems under this Court's general directive. Understandably, in an area of evolving remedies, those courts had to improvise and experiment without detailed or specific guidelines. This Court, in Brown I, appropriately dealt with the large constitutional principles; other federal courts had to grapple with the flinty, intractable realities of day-to-day implementation of those constitutional commands. Their efforts, of necessity, embraced a process of "trial and error," and our effort to formulate guidelines must take into account their experience.

. . .

Over the 15 years since Brown II, many difficulties were encountered in implementation of the basic constitutional requirement that the State not discriminate between public school children on the basis of their race. Nothing in our national experience prior to 1955 prepared anyone for dealing with changes and adjustments of the magnitude and complexity encountered since then. Deliberate resistance of some to the Court's mandates has impeded the good-faith efforts of others to bring school systems into compliance. The detail and nature of these dilatory tactics have been noted frequently by this Court and other courts.

By the time the Court considered Green v County School Board, in 1968, very little progress had been made in many areas where dual school systems had historically been maintained by operation of state laws. In Green, the Court was confronted with a record of a freedom-of-choice program that the District Court had found to operate in fact to preserve a dual system more than a decade after Brown II. While acknowledging that a freedom-of-choice concept could be a valid remedial measure in some circumstances, its failure to be effective in Green required that

"The burden on a school board today is to come forward with a plan that promises realistically to work . . . *now* . . . until it is clear that state-imposed segregation has been completely removed."

This was plain language, yet the 1969 Term of Court brought fresh evidence of the dilatory tactics of many school authorities. Alexander v Holmes County Board of Education restated the basic obligation asserted in Griffin v School Board (1964), and Green that the remedy must be implemented *forthwith*.

The problems encountered by the district courts and courts of appeals make plain that we should now try to amplify guidelines, however incomplete and imperfect, for the assistance of school authorities and courts. The failure of local authorities to meet their constitutional obligations aggravated the massive problem of converting from the state-enforced discrimination of racially separate school systems. This process has been rendered more difficult by changes since 1954 in the structure and patterns of communities, the growth of student population, movement of families, and other changes, some of which had marked impact on school planning, sometimes neutralizing or negating remedial action before it was fully implemented. Rural areas accustomed for half a century to the consolidated school systems implemented by bus transportation could make adjustments more readily than metropolitan areas with dense and shifting population, numerous schools, congested and complex traffic patterns.

. . .

The central issue in this case is that of student assignment, and there are essentially four problem areas:

(1) to what extent racial balance or racial quotas may be used as an implement in a remedial order to correct a previously segregated system;

(2) whether every all-Negro and all-white school must be eliminated as an indispensable part of a remedial process of desegregation;

(3) what are the limits, if any, on the rearrangement of school districts and attendance zones, as a remedial measure; and

(4) what are the limits, if any, on the use of transportation facilities to correct state-enforced racial school segregation.

(1) *Racial Balances or Racial Quotas.*

. . .

In this case it is urged that the District Court has imposed a racial balance requirement of 71%–29% on individual schools. The fact that no such objective was actually achieved—and would appear to be impossible—tends to blunt that claim, yet in the opinion and order of the District Court of December 1, 1969, we find that court directing: "that efforts should be made to reach a 71–29 ratio in the various schools so that there will be no basis for contending that one school is racially different from the others . . . , that no school [should] be operated with an all-black or predominantly black student body, [and] that pupils of all grades [should] be assigned in such a way that as nearly as practicable the various schools at various grade levels have about the same proportion of black and white students."

The District Judge went on to acknowledge that variation "from that norm may be unavoidable." This contains intimations that the "norm" is a fixed mathematical racial balance reflecting the pupil constituency of the system. If we were to read the holding of the District Court to require, as a matter of substantive constitutional right, any particular degree of racial balance or mixing, that approach would be disapproved and we would be obliged to reverse. The constitutional command to desegregate schools does not mean that every school in every community must always reflect the racial composition of the school system as a whole.

As the voluminous record in this case shows, the predicate for the District Court's use of the 71%–29% ratio was twofold: first, its express finding, approved by the Court of Appeals and not challenged here, that a dual school system had been maintained by the school authorities at least until 1969; second, its finding, also approved by the Court of Appeals, that the school board had totally defaulted in its acknowledged duty to come forward with an acceptable plan of its own, notwithstanding the patient efforts of the District Judge who, on at least three occasions, urged the board to submit plans. As the statement of facts shows, these findings are abundantly supported by the record. It was because of this total failure of the school board that the District Court was obliged to turn to other qualified sources, and Dr. Finger was designated to assist the District Court to do what the board should have done.

We see therefore that the use made of mathematical ratios was no more than a starting point in the process of shaping a remedy, rather than an inflexible requirement. From that starting point the District Court proceeded to frame a decree that was within its discretionary powers, an equitable remedy for the particular circumstances. As we said in Green, a school authority's remedial plan or a district court's remedial decree is to be judged by its effectiveness. Awareness of the racial composition of the whole school system is likely to be a useful starting point in shaping a remedy to correct past constitutional violations. In sum, the very limited use made of mathematical ratios was within the equitable remedial discretion of the District Court.

(2) One-Race Schools.

The record in this case reveals the familiar phenomenon that in metropolitan areas minority groups are often found concentrated in one part of the city. In some circumstances certain schools may remain all or largely of one race until new schools can be provided or neighborhood patterns change. Schools all or predominately of one race in a district of mixed population will require close scrutiny to determine that school assignments are not part of state-enforced segregation.

In light of the above, it should be clear that the existence of some small number of one-race, or virtually one-race, schools within a district is not in and of itself the mark of a system which still practices segregation by law. The district judge or school authorities should make every effort to achieve the greatest possible degree of actual desegregation and will thus necessarily be concerned with the elimination of one-race schools. No per se rule can adequately embrace all the difficulties of reconciling the competing interests involved; but in a system with a history of segregation the need for remedial criteria of sufficient specificity to assure a school authority's compliance with its constitutional duty warrants a presumption against schools that are substantially disproportionate in their racial composition. Where the school authority's proposed plan for conversion from a dual to a uni-

tary system contemplates the continued existence of some schools that are all or predominately of one race, they have the burden of showing that such school assignments are genuinely nondiscriminatory. The court should scrutinize such schools, and the burden upon the school authorities will be to satisfy the court that their racial composition is not the result of present or past discriminatory action on their part.

An optional majority-to-minority transfer provision has long been recognized as a useful part of every desegregation plan. Provision for optional transfer of those in the majority racial group of a particular school to other schools where they will be in the minority is an indispensable remedy for those students willing to transfer to other schools in order to lessen the impact on them of the state-imposed stigma of segregation. In order to be effective, such a transfer arrangement must grant the transferring student free transportation and space must be made available in the school to which he desires to move. The court orders in this and the companion Davis case now provide such an option.

(3) Remedial Altering of Attendance Zones.

The maps submitted in these cases graphically demonstrate that one of the principal tools employed by school planners and by courts to break up the dual school system has been a frank—and sometimes drastic—gerrymandering of school districts and attendance zones. An additional step was pairing, "clustering," or "grouping" of schools with attendance assignments made deliberately to accomplish the transfer of Negro students out of formerly segregated Negro schools and transfer of white students to formerly all-Negro schools. More often than not, these zones are neither compact nor contiguous; indeed they may be on opposite ends of the city. As an interim corrective measure, this cannot be said to be beyond the broad remedial powers of a court.

Absent a constitutional violation there would be no basis for judicially ordering assignment of students on a racial basis. All things being equal, with no history of discrimination, it might well be desirable to assign pupils to schools nearest their homes. But all things are not equal in a system that has been deliberately constructed and maintained to enforce racial segregation. The remedy for such segregation may be administratively awkward, inconvenient and even bizarre in some situations and may impose burdens on some; but all awkwardness and inconvenience cannot be avoided in the interim period when remedial adjustments are being made to eliminate the dual school systems.

. . .

We hold that the pairing and grouping of non-contiguous school zones is a permissible tool and such action is to be considered in light of the objectives sought. Judicial steps in shaping such zones going beyond combinations of contiguous areas should be examined in light of what is said in subdivisions (1), (2), and (3) of this opinion concerning the objectives to be sought. Maps do not tell the whole story since non-contiguous school zones may be more accessible to each other in terms of the critical travel time, because of traffic patterns and good highways, than schools geographically closer together. Conditions in different localities will vary so widely that no rigid rules can be laid down to govern all situations.

(4) Transportation of Students.

The scope of permissible transportation of students as an implement of a remedial decree has never been defined by this Court and by the very nature of the problem it cannot be defined with precision. No rigid guidelines as to student transportation can be given for application to the infinite variety of problems presented in thousands of situations. Bus transportation has been an integral part of the public education system for years, and was perhaps the single most important factor in the transition from the one-room schoolhouse to the consolidated school. Eighteen million of the nation's public school children, approximately 39%, were transported to their schools by bus in 1969–1970 in all parts of the country.

The importance of bus transportation as a normal and accepted tool of educational policy is readily discernible in this and the companion case. The Charlotte school authorities did not purport to assign students on the basis of geographically drawn zones until 1965 and then they allowed almost unlimited transfer privileges. The District Court's conclusion that assignment of children to the school nearest their home serving their grade would not produce an effective dismantling of the dual system is supported by the record.

Thus the remedial techniques used in the District Court's order were within that court's power to provide equitable relief; implementation of the decree is well within the capacity of the school authority.

The decree provided that the buses used to implement the plan would operate on direct routes. Students would be picked up at schools near their homes and transported to the schools they were to attend. The trips for elementary school pupils average about seven miles and the District Court found that they would take "not over 35 minutes at the most." This system compares favorably with the transportation plan previously operated in Charlotte under which each day 23,600 students on all grade levels were transported an average of 15 miles one way for an average trip requiring over an hour. In these circumstances, we find no basis for holding that the local school authorities may not be required to employ bus transportation as one tool of school desegregation. Desegregation plans cannot be limited to the walk-in school.

An objection to transportation of students may have validity when the time or distance of travel is so great as to risk either the health of the children or significantly impinge on the educational process. District courts must weigh the soundness of any transportation plan in light of what is said in subdivisions (1), (2), and (3) above. It hardly needs stating that the limits on time of travel will vary with many factors, but probably with none more than the age of the students. The reconciliation of competing values in a desegregation case is, of course, a difficult task with many sensitive facets but fundamentally no more so than remedial measures courts of equity have traditionally employed.

The Court of Appeals, searching for a term to define the equitable remedial power of the district courts, used the term "reasonableness." In Green, this Court used the term "feasible" and by implication, "workable," "effective," and "realistic" in the mandate to develop "a plan that promises realistically to work, and . . . to work *now.*" On the facts of this case, we are unable to conclude that the order of the District Court is not reasonable, feasible and workable. However, in seeking to define the scope of remedial power or the limits on remedial power of courts in an area as sensitive as we deal with here, words are poor instruments to convey the sense of basic fairness inherent in equity. Substance, not semantics, must govern, and we have sought to suggest the nature of limitations without frustrating the appropriate scope of equity.

At some point, these school authorities and others like them should have achieved full compliance with this Court's decision in Brown I. The systems will then be "unitary" in the sense required by our decisions in Green and Alexander.

It does not follow that the communities served by such systems will remain demographically stable, for in a growing, mobile society, few will do so. Neither school authorities nor district courts are constitutionally required to make year-by-year adjustments of the racial composition of student bodies once the affirmative duty to desegregate has been accomplished and racial discrimination through official action is eliminated from the system. This does not mean that federal courts are without power to deal with future problems; but in the absence of a showing that either the school authorities or some other agency of the State has deliberately attempted to fix or alter demographic patterns to affect the racial composition of the schools, further intervention by a district court should not be necessary.

. . .

Aftermath of Swann *v.* Charlotte-Mecklenburg Board of Education

Shortly after the Court's *Swann* decision was announced, the office of Julius Chambers, a civil rights lawyer who had helped James Swann and others bring the lawsuit that led to Charlotte's desegregation plan, was destroyed by a firebomb. The district's schools experienced a period of extreme racial tension which led many white parents to withdraw their children from public schools and send them to the private "academies" that opened up in large numbers after desegregation. By 1973 10,000 students—one of every six white children in the area—attended such schools. An interracial committee, the Citizens Advisory Group, was formed to work with Judge James McMillan to develop a new busing plan that would eliminate some of the larger inequities and inconveniences caused by the judge's 1970 order. The new plan, which went into effect in 1974, guaranteed nearly every student at least three consecutive years in a neighborhood school. At the same time Judge McMillan removed the *Swann* case from his active docket, saying that the desegregation process was proceeding so smoothly that his day-to-day supervision was no longer needed. Five years later Judge McMillan and attorney Chambers were honored by the Charlotte chapter of the National Conference of Christians and Jews for their work improving race relations in the city.

Milliken v. *Bradley*

418 U.S. 717 (1974)

At the end of the 1970s virtually every school system that had ever practiced *de jure* racial segregation (based on law) was operating under the watchful eye of a federal judge with the responsibility of ensuring that desegregation proceeded apace. In addition, many cities in the north and west that had never operated legally segregated schools were also carrying out desegregation orders because courts had found evidence of official actions that had contributed to racially segregated schools. The Supreme Court made it clear in *Keyes* v. *School District No. 1* (1973) that if apparently de facto (based on residential patterns) school segregation could be attributed even in part to such acts, the principles and remedies of *Brown I* and *Brown II* must be applied. In *Keyes* the Court accepted the lower courts' findings that the city of Denver had, among other things, situated new schools and altered school attendance zones to keep certain schools all white. School officials had also set up mobile classrooms at overcrowded black schools rather than reassigning black students to available spaces in white schools. While these actions had affected racial patterns in only a few schools, the Court held that once any official discrimination had been established, the remedial desegregation plan could cover the entire school district, which meant that it would almost certainly require citywide busing. In the following decade school systems in the cities of Boston, Indianapolis, Omaha, Cleveland, and Chicago, and many others, came under federal court desegregation orders.

Federal judges overseeing school desegregation in the north and west (and increasingly in the south as well) soon came face to face with a stark fact of urban life: in many cities there simply were not enough white students in the public schools to produce meaningful desegregation regardless of how they were redistributed around the city. This was partly the result of "white flight"—the movement of white families from cities to suburbs—and partly because many of the white students whose families had remained in the cities were enrolled in private schools. In 1972, 84 percent of the black students in New York City attended schools that were more than half black. In Los Angeles, Chicago, Philadelphia, and Detroit the figures were all above 90 percent. In developing desegregation plans some federal judges began looking at the white suburbs ringing the black cities. Since most of these suburbs had never had any appreciable numbers of black families, they were not likely to have engaged in the sorts of discriminatory practices that had brought the cities under desegregation orders. But towns and cities are agents of the state, and some judges reasoned that if evidence could be found that the state itself had helped foster school segregation, the appropriate remedy could therefore include its suburban as well as its urban school districts.

This was essentially the approach adopted by Federal District Judge Stephen Roth of Detroit in the early 1970s. Having found that both the city of Detroit and the state of Michigan had contributed to a racially segregated school system in Detroit, Roth fashioned a desegregation order that combined 53 suburban districts along with Detroit into a single metropolitan school district containing some 780,000 students. Under the judge's plan, about 310,000 of these students would be transported in or out of the city of Detroit each day. Roth's findings and order were affirmed by the Sixth Circuit Court of Appeals. The Supreme Court granted *certiorari* and issued its decision in 1974.

Mr. Chief Justice **Burger** delivered the opinion of the Court.

. . .

Ever since Brown v Board of Education (1954), judicial consideration of school desegregation cases has begun with the standard that:

"[I]n the field of public education the doctrine of 'separate but equal' has no place. Separate educational facilities are inherently unequal."

This has been reaffirmed time and again as the meaning of the Constitution and the controlling rule of law.

The target of the Brown holding was clear and forthright: the elimination of state mandated or deliberately maintained dual school systems with certain schools for Negro pupils and others for white pupils. This duality and racial segregation was held to violate the Constitution in the cases subsequent to 1954.

The Swann case, of course, dealt

"with the problem of defining in more precise terms than heretofore the scope of the duty of school authorities and district courts in implementing Brown I and the mandate to eliminate dual systems and establish unitary systems at once."

In Brown v Board of Education, (1955) (Brown II), the Court's first encounter with the problem of remedies in school desegregation cases, the Court noted that:

"In fashioning and effectuating the decrees, the courts will be guided by equitable principles. Traditionally, equity has been characterized by a practical flexibility in shaping its remedies and by a facility for adjusting and reconciling public and private needs."

In further refining the remedial process, Swann held, the task is to correct, by a balancing of the individual and collective interests, "the condition that offends the Constitution." A federal remedial power may be exercised "only on the basis of a constitutional violation" and, "[a]s with any equity case, the nature of the violation determines the scope of the remedy."

Proceeding from these basic principles, we first note that in the District Court the complainants sought a remedy aimed at the *condition* alleged to offend the Constitution—the segregation within the Detroit City school district. The court acted on this theory of the case and in its initial ruling on the "Desegregation Area" stated:

"The task before this court, therefore, is now, and . . . has always been, how to desegregate the Detroit public schools."

Thereafter, however, the District Court abruptly rejected the proposed Detroit-only plans on the ground that "while it would provide a racial mix more in keeping with the Black-White proportions of the student population, [it] would accentuate the racial identifiability of the [Detroit] district as a Black school system, and would not accomplish desegregation." "[T]he racial composition of the student body is such," said the court, "that the plan's implementation would clearly make the entire Detroit public school system racially identifiable" "leav[ing] many of its schools 75 to 90 percent Black." Consequently, the court reasoned, it was imperative to "look beyond the limits of the Detroit school district for a solution to the problem of segregation in the Detroit schools . . ." since "school district lines are simply matters of political convenience and may not be used to deny constitutional rights." Accordingly, the District Court proceeded to redefine the relevant area to include areas of predominantly white pupil population in order to ensure that "upon implementation, no school, grade or classroom [would be] substantially disproportionate to the overall racial composition" of the entire metropolitan area.

While specifically acknowledging that the District Court's findings of a condition of segregation were limited to Detroit, the Court of Appeals approved the use of a metropolitan remedy largely on the grounds that it is:

"impossible to declare 'clearly erroneous' the District Judge's conclusion that any Detroit only segregation plan will lead directly to a single segregated Detroit school district overwhelmingly black in all of its schools, surrounded by a ring of suburbs and suburban school districts overwhelmingly white in composition in a state in which the racial composition is 87 percent white and 13 percent black."

Viewing the record as a whole, it seems clear that the District Court and the Court of Appeals shifted the primary focus from a Detroit remedy to the metropolitan area only because of their conclusion that total desegregation of Detroit would not produce the racial balance which they perceived as desirable. Both courts proceeded on an assumption that the Detroit schools could not be truly desegregated—in their view of what constituted desegregation—unless the racial composition of the student body of each school substantially reflected the racial composition of the population of the metropolitan area as a whole. The metropolitan area was then defined as Detroit plus 53 of the outlying school districts.

. . .

Here the District Court's approach to what constituted "actual desegregation" raises the fundamental question, not presented in Swann, as to the circumstances in which a federal court may order desegregation relief that embraces more than a single school district. The court's analytical starting point was its conclusion that school district lines are no more than arbitrary lines on a map "drawn for political convenience." Boundary lines may be bridged where there has been a constitutional violation calling for inter-district relief, but, the notion that school district lines may be casually ignored or treated as a mere administrative convenience is contrary to the history of public education in our country. No single tradition in public education is more deeply rooted than local control over the operation of schools; local autonomy has long been thought essential both to the maintenance of community concern and support for public schools and to quality of the educational process. Thus, in San Antonio School District v Rodriguez, we observed that local control over the educational process affords citizens an opportunity to participate in decision-making, permits the structuring of school programs to fit local needs, and encourages "experimentation, innovation and a healthy competition for educational excellence."

The Michigan educational structure involved in this case, in common with most States, provides for a large measure of local control and a review of the scope and character of these local powers indicates the extent to which the inter-district remedy approved by the two courts could disrupt and alter the structure of public education in Michigan. The metropolitan remedy would require, in effect, consolidation of 54 independent school districts historically administered as separate units into a vast new super school district. Entirely apart from the logistical and other serious problems attending large-scale transportation of students, the consolidation would give rise to an array of other problems in financing and operating this new school system. Some of the more obvious questions would be: What would be the status and authority of the present popularly elected school boards? Would the children of Detroit be within the jurisdiction and operating control of a school board elected by the parents and residents of other districts? What board or boards would levy taxes for school operations in these 54 districts constituting the consolidated metropolitan area? What provisions could be made for assuring substantial equality in tax levies among the 54 districts, if this were deemed requisite? What provisions would be made for financing? Would the validity of long-term bonds be jeopardized unless approved by all of the component districts as well as the State? What body would determine that portion of the curricula now left to the discretion of local school boards? Who would establish attendance zones, purchase school equipment, locate and construct new schools, and indeed attend to all the myriad day-to-day decisions that are necessary to school operations affecting potentially more than three quarters of a million pupils?

It may be suggested that all of these vital operational problems are yet to be resolved by the District Court, and that this is the purpose of the Court of Appeals' proposed remand. But it is obvious from the scope of the inter-district remedy itself that absent a complete restructuring of the laws of Michigan relating to school districts the District Court will become first, a de facto "legislative authority" to resolve these complex questions, and then the "school superintendent" for the entire area. This is a task which few, if any, judges are qualified to perform and one which would deprive the people of control of schools through their elected representatives.

Of course, no state law is above the Constitution. School district lines and the present laws with respect to local control, are not sacrosanct and if they conflict with the Fourteenth Amendment federal courts have a duty to prescribe appropriate remedies. But our prior holdings have been confined to violations and remedies within a single school district. We therefore turn to address, for the first time, the validity of a remedy mandating cross-district or inter-district consolidation to remedy a condition of segregation found to exist in only one district.

The controlling principle consistently expounded in our holdings is that the scope of the remedy is determined by the nature and extent of the constitutional violation. Before the boundaries of separate and autonomous school districts may be set aside by consolidating the separate units for remedial purposes or by imposing a cross-district remedy, it must first be shown that there has been a constitutional violation within one district that produces a significant segregative effect in another district. Specifically it must be shown that racially discriminatory acts of the state or local school districts, or of a single school district have been a substantial cause of inter-district segregation. Thus an inter-district remedy might be in order where the racially discriminatory acts of one or more school districts caused racial segregation in an adjacent district, or where district lines have been deliberately drawn on the basis of race. In such circumstances an inter-district remedy would be appropriate to eliminate the inter-district segregation directly caused by the constitutional violation. Conversely, without an inter-district violation and inter-district effect, there is no constitutional wrong calling for an inter-district remedy.

The record before us, voluminous as it is, contains evidence of de jure segregated conditions only in the Detroit schools; indeed, that was the theory on which the litigation was initially based and on which the District Court took evidence. With no showing of significant violation by the 53 outlying school districts and no evidence of any inter-district violation or effect, the court went beyond the original theory of the case as framed by the pleadings and mandated a metropolitan area remedy. To approve the reme-

dy ordered by the court would impose on the outlying districts, not shown to have committed any constitutional violation, a wholly impermissible remedy based on a standard not hinted at in Brown I and II or any holding of this Court.

. . .

We conclude that the relief ordered by the District Court and affirmed by the Court of Appeals was based upon an erroneous standard and was unsupported by record evidence that acts of the outlying districts affected the discrimination found to exist in the schools of Detroit. Accordingly, the judgment of the Court of Appeals is reversed and the case is remanded for further proceedings consistent with this opinion leading to prompt formulation of a decree directed to eliminating the segregation found to exist in Detroit city schools, a remedy which has been delayed since 1970.

Reversed and remanded.

Mr. Justice **Marshall,** with whom Mr. Justice **Douglas,** Mr. Justice **Brennan,** and Mr. Justice **White** join, dissenting.

In Brown v Board of Education, this Court held that segregation of children in public schools on the basis of race deprives minority group children of equal educational opportunities and therefore denies them the equal protection of the laws under the Fourteenth Amendment. This Court recognized then that remedying decades of segregation in public education would not be an easy task. Subsequent events, unfortunately, have seen that prediction bear bitter fruit. But however imbedded old ways, however ingrained old prejudices, this Court has not been diverted from its appointed task of making "a living truth" of our constitutional ideal of equal justice under law.

After 20 years of small, often difficult steps toward that great end, the Court today takes a giant step backwards. Notwithstanding a record showing widespread and pervasive racial segregation in the educational system provided by the State of Michigan for children in Detroit, this Court holds that the District Court was powerless to require the State to remedy its constitutional violation in any meaningful fashion.

Ironically purporting to base its result on the principle that the scope of the remedy in a desegregation case should be determined by the nature and the extent of the constitutional violation, the Court's answer is to provide no remedy at all for the violation proved in this case, thereby guaranteeing that Negro children in Detroit will receive the same separate and inherently unequal education in the future as they have been unconstitutionally afforded in the past.

I cannot subscribe to this emasculation of our constitutional guarantee of equal protection of the laws and must respectfully dissent. Our precedents, in my view, firmly establish that where, as here, state-imposed segregation has been demonstrated, it becomes the duty of the State to eliminate root and branch all vestiges of racial discrimination and to achieve the greatest possible degree of actual desegregation. I agree with both the District Court and the Court of Appeals that, under the facts of this case, this duty cannot be fulfilled unless the State of Michigan involves outlying metropolitan area school districts in its desegregation remedy. Furthermore, I perceive no basis either in law or in the practicalities of the situation justifying the State's interposition of school district boundaries as absolute barriers to the implementation of an effective desegregation remedy. Under established and frequently used Michigan procedures, school district lines are both flexible and permeable for a wide variety of purposes, and there is no reason why they must now stand in the way of meaningful desegregation relief.

The rights at issue in the case are too fundamental to be abridged on grounds as superficial as those relied on by the majority today. We deal here with the right of all of our children, whatever their race, to an equal start in life and to an equal opportunity to reach their full potential as citizens. Those children who have been denied that right in the past deserve better than to see fences thrown up to deny them that right in the future. Our Nation, I fear, will be ill-served by the Court's refusal to remedy separate and unequal education, for unless our children begin to learn together, there is little hope that our people will ever learn to live together.

. . .

Having found a de jure segregated public school system in operation in the city of Detroit, the District Court turned next to consider which officials and agencies should be assigned the affirmative obligation to cure the constitutional violation. The court concluded that responsibility for the segregation in the Detroit city schools rested not only with the Detroit Board of Education, but belonged to the State of Michigan itself and the state defendants in this case—that is, the Governor of Michigan, the Attorney General, the State Board of Education, and the State Superintendent of Public Instruction. While the validity of this conclusion will merit more extensive analysis below, suffice it for now to say that it was based on three considerations. First, the evidence at trial showed that the State itself had taken actions contributing to the segregation within the Detroit schools. Second, since the Detroit Board of Education was an agency of the State of Michigan, its acts of racial discrimination were acts of the State for purposes of the Fourteenth Amendment. Finally, the District Court found that under Michigan law and practice, the system of education was in fact a *state* school system, characterized by relatively little local control and a large degree of centralized state regulation, with respect to both educational policy and the structure and operation of school districts.

. . .

To begin with, the record amply supports the District Court's findings that the State of Michigan, through state officers and state agencies, had engaged in purposeful acts which created or aggravated segregation in the Detroit schools. The State Board of Education, for example, prior to 1962, exercised its authority to supervise local school site selection in a manner which contributed to segregation. Furthermore, the State's continuing authority, after 1962, to approve school building construction plans had intertwined the State with site selection decisions of the Detroit Board of Education which had the purpose and effect of maintaining segregation.

The State had also stood in the way of past efforts to desegregate the Detroit city schools. In 1970, for example, the Detroit School Board had begun implementation of its own desegregation plan for its high schools, despite considerable public and official resistance. The State Legislature intervened by enacting Act 48 of the Public Acts of 1970, specifically prohibiting implementation of the desegregation plan and thereby continuing the growing segregation of the Detroit school system. Adequate desegregation of the Detroit system was also hampered by discriminatory restrictions placed by the State on the use of transportation within Detroit. While state aid for transportation was provided by statute for suburban districts, many of which were highly urbanized, aid for intra-city transportation was excepted. One of the effects of this restriction was to encourage the construction of small walk-in neighborhood schools in Detroit, thereby lending aid to the intentional policy of creating a school system which reflected, to the greatest extent feasible, extensive residential segregation. Indeed, that one of the purposes of the transportation restriction was to impede desegregation was evidenced when the Michigan Legislature amended the State Transportation Aid Act to cover intra-city transportation but expressly prohibited the allocation of funds for cross busing of students within a school district to achieve racial balance.

. . .

Under Michigan law "a school district is an agency of the State government." It is "a legal division of territory, created by the State for educational purposes, to which the State has granted such powers as are deemed necessary to permit the district to function as a State agency." Racial discrimination by the school district, an agency of the State, is therefore racial discrimination by the State itself, forbidden by the Fourteenth Amendment.

. . .

Vesting responsibility with the State of Michigan for Detroit's segregated schools is particularly appropriate as Michigan, unlike some other States, operates a single statewide system of education rather than several separate and independent local school systems. The majority's emphasis on local governmental control and local autonomy of school districts in Michigan

will come as a surprise to those with any familiarity with that State's system of education. School districts are not separate and distinct sovereign entities under Michigan law, but rather are "auxiliaries of the State," subject to its "absolute power." The courts of the State have repeatedly emphasized that education in Michigan is not a local governmental concern, but a state function.

. . .

What action, then, could the District Court require the State to take in order to cure Detroit's condition of segregation? Our prior cases have not minced words as to what steps responsible officials and agencies must take in order to remedy segregation in the public schools. Not only must distinctions on the basis of race be terminated for the future, but school officials are also "clearly charged with the affirmative duty to take whatever steps might be necessary to convert to a unitary system in which racial discrimination would be eliminated root and branch."

. . .

Because of the already high and rapidly increasing percentage of Negro students in the Detroit system, as well as the prospect of white flight, a Detroit-only plan simply has no hope of achieving actual desegregation. Under such a plan white and Negro students will not go to school together. Instead, Negro children will continue to attend all-Negro schools. The very evil that Brown I was aimed at will not be cured, but will be perpetuated for the future.

. . .

Under a Detroit-only decree, Detroit's schools will clearly remain racially identifiable in comparison with neighboring schools in the metropolitan community. Schools with 65% and more Negro students will stand in sharp and obvious contrast to schools in neighboring districts with less than 2% Negro enrollment. Negro students will continue to perceive their schools as segregated educational facilities and this perception will only be increased when whites react to a Detroit-only decree by fleeing to the suburbs to avoid integration. School district lines, however innocently drawn, will surely be perceived as fences to separate the races when, under a Detroit-only decree, white parents withdraw their children from the Detroit city schools and move to the suburbs in order to continue them in all-white schools. The message of this action will not escape the Negro children in the city of Detroit. It will be of scant significance to Negro children who have for years been confined by de jure acts of segregation to a growing core of all-Negro schools surrounded by a ring of all-white schools that the new dividing line between the races is the school district boundary.

Nor can it be said that the State is free from any responsibility for the disparity between the racial makeup of Detroit and its surrounding suburbs. The State's creation, through de jure acts of segregation, of a growing core of all-Negro schools inevitably acted as a magnet to attract Negroes to the areas served by such schools and to deter them from settling either in other areas of the city or in the suburbs. By the same token, the growing core of all-Negro schools inevitably helped drive whites to other areas of the city or to the suburbs. As we recognized in Swann,

"People gravitate toward school facilities, just as schools are located in response to the needs of people. The location of schools may thus influence the patterns of residential development of a metropolitan area and have important impact on composition of inner-city neighborhoods. . . . [Action taken] to maintain the separation of the races with a minimum departure from the formal principles of 'neighborhood zoning' . . . does more than simply influence the short-run composition of the student body. . . . It may well promote segregated residential patterns which, when combined with 'neighborhood zoning,' further lock the school system into the mold of separation of the races. Upon a proper showing a district court may consider this in fashioning a remedy."

The rippling effects on residential patterns caused by purposeful acts of segregation do not automatically subside at the school district border. With rare exceptions, these effects naturally spread through all the residential neighborhoods within a metropolitan area.

The State must also bear part of the blame for the white flight to the suburbs which would be forthcoming from a Detroit-only decree and would render such a remedy ineffective. Having created a system where whites and Negroes were intentionally kept apart so that they could not become accustomed to learning together, the State is responsible for the fact that many whites will react to the dismantling of that segregated system by attempting to flee to the suburbs. Indeed, by limiting the District Court to a Detroit-only remedy and allowing that flight to the suburbs to succeed, the Court today allows the State to profit from its own wrong and to perpetuate for years to come the separation of the races it achieved in the past by purposeful state action.

. . .

It is the State, after all, which bears the responsibility under Brown of affording a nondiscriminatory system of education. The State, of course, is ordinarily free to choose any decentralized framework for education it wishes, so long as it fulfills that Fourteenth Amendment obligation. But the State should no more be allowed to hide behind its delegation and compartmentalization of school districts to avoid its constitutional obligations to its children than it could hide behind its political subdivisions to avoid its obligations to its voters.

It is a hollow remedy indeed where "after supposed 'desegregation' the schools are segregated in fact." We must do better than "substitute . . . one segregated school system for another segregated school system." To suggest, as does the majority, that a Detroit-only plan somehow remedies the effects of de jure segregation of the races is, in my view, to make a solemn mockery of Brown I's holding that separate educational facilities are inherently unequal and of Swann's unequivocal mandate that the answer to de jure segregation is the greatest possible degree of actual desegregation.

. . .

Desegregation is not and was never expected to be an easy task. Racial attitudes ingrained in our Nation's childhood and adolescence are not quickly thrown aside in its middle years. But just as the inconvenience of some cannot be allowed to stand in the way of the rights of others, so public opposition, no matter how strident, cannot be permitted to divert this Court from the enforcement of the constitutional principles at issue in this case. Today's holding, I fear, is more a reflection of a perceived public mood that we have gone far enough in enforcing the Constitution's guarantee of equal justice than it is the product of neutral principles of law. In the short run, it may seem to be the easier course to allow our great metropolitan areas to be divided up each into two cities—one white, the other black—but it is a course, I predict, our people will ultimately regret. I dissent.

Aftermath of Milliken *v.* Bradley

With the Court's rejection of metropolitan desegregation as an appropriate remedy for racial discrimination that had occurred only within a city, busing receded somewhat as a political issue. However, at the end of the 1980s about two-thirds of the nation's black children still attended predominantly black schools—a proportion unchanged since 1972—and some federal judges continued to look for ways to promote desegregation in overwhelmingly black urban districts. There has been a tendency in recent years to adopt plans that allow higher levels of school-to-school segregation in exchange for potentially greater system-wide desegregation. These plans make use of "magnet" schools and enriched curricula as well as upgraded physical facilities in an effort to attract white students from suburban and private schools. Some judges have gone so far as to order significant increases in property taxes to pay for such improvements, which has generated resistance from citizens and public officials. In *Missouri* v. *Jenkins* (1990) the Supreme Court dealt with the vexing question whether judicially ordered taxation is constitutionally acceptable. The Court upheld the principle that the lower federal courts may direct a local government body to levy taxes in order to obtain adequate funds to maintain a public school system without racial discrimination. In its opinion the Court emphasized the distinction between a court imposing a tax increase to fund a remedy, which is impermissible, and a court directing a government institution to obtain the necessary funds to remedy the deprivation of constitutional rights. It is a rather technical distinction since in either case a local government body is under a judicial order to raise money, but as the law stands, the local agency has considerable discretion as to the means of securing funding.

As the 1980s drew to a close another significant development was a movement to dismiss some of the desegregation cases that had been before the courts for decades. With the encouragement of the United States Department of Justice under Presidents Ronald Reagan and George Bush, federal judges began terminating desegregation plans after concluding that districts had achieved and maintained school systems that were free of the vestiges of legal segregation. In most cases this did not mean that the systems themselves had been desegregated, but only that the segregation that now existed was truly de facto in character. In 1991 the Supreme Court expressed cautious approval of this trend by holding in *Board of Education* v. *Dowell* that formerly segregated school districts could be released from desegregation orders once they have taken all "practicable" steps to eliminate the effects of segregation. However, the Court provided no firm guidelines for the lower courts to use in deciding when the vestiges of segregation have been eliminated or what constitutes all "practicable" steps. Thus it is highly likely that the Court will be called upon to give clearer guidance in future cases.

One of the school boards that still remains under a desegregation order is in Topeka, Kansas. In 1989 the Tenth Circuit Court of Appeals refused to dismiss a lawsuit brought against the school board ten years earlier by a group of Topeka residents which included Linda Brown Buckner, the plaintiff in the 1954 *Brown* case. The appeals court found that "Topeka has not sufficiently countered the effects of both the momentum of its pre-*Brown* segregation and its subsequent segregation act in the 1960s. . . . For the most part, the Topeka school district has exercised a form of benign neglect. The duty imposed by the Constitution, and articulated in numerous cases by the highest Court in this land, requires more."

Shelley v. Kraemer
334 U.S. 1 (1948)

The Fourteenth Amendment, like other provisions of the Constitution, is concerned with defining and limiting the powers of government, not with regulating the actions of private individuals, a task reserved for legislatures at the national, state, and local levels. The Fourteenth Amendment explicitly authorized Congress to take such action as it deemed necessary to enforce the amendment's commands. Even before the Fourteenth Amendment was ratified Congress had passed civil rights legislation in 1866 outlawing the "Black Codes" which the southern states had passed immediately after the Civil War relegating former slaves to second-class citizenship. Realizing that black citizens faced private as well as official discrimination, Congress in 1875 passed another Civil Rights Act, this one guaranteeing equal access to public accommodations (restaurants, hotels, and transportation) to all persons regardless of race or color. However, 8 years later, in the *Civil Rights Cases*, the Supreme Court essentially gutted the law, declaring that neither the Thirteenth nor the Fourteenth Amendment granted Congress the power to prohibit acts of private racial discrimination.

One of the ways in which private parties could thwart public policy was through the use of restrictive racial covenants, legally binding agreements signed by residents of a neighborhood pledging not to sell or rent their property to blacks. Restrictive covenants were widely used in the north as well as the south during the first half of the twentieth century to enforce residential segregation. Thus, although the Civil Rights Act of 1866 guaranteed blacks the right to buy and sell property, and a 1917 Supreme Court decision had struck down municipal laws which prevented blacks from purchasing or occupying property in "white" areas, many blacks were unable to purchase the homes of their choice.

In 1946 a black couple named J. D. and Ethel Lee Shelley, after living for several years with their six children in a small ghetto apartment in St. Louis, bought a duplex house in the residential neighborhood of Grande Prairie. Within a few days Louis and Fern Kraemer, a white couple who lived on the same street some ten blocks away, filed a suit in state court demanding the Shelleys' eviction because their new house was covered by a restrictive covenant signed in 1911 by a previous owner agreeing not to sell or rent the property to "people of the Negro or Mongoloid race." Thirty of the thirty-nine homeowners on the block had signed the agreement which was supposedly binding on all future property owners for fifty years. The Kraemers were supported by the neighborhood association that had drawn up the racial covenant. The Shelleys were defended by a prominent black lawyer, George Vaughan, a leader of the NAACP and of the Democratic party in St. Louis. The trial judge refused to enforce the restrictive covenant on the ground that it had not been signed by all homeowners on the street. That decision was reversed by the Missouri

Supreme Court. Meanwhile, the NAACP, under the leadership of its special counsel Thurgood Marshall, had been trying for some time to persuade the Supreme Court to review a restrictive covenant case. The decision of the United States government to file an *amicus curiae* brief supporting the NAACP position may have helped persuade the Court to hear the Shelleys' case. A few months earlier the President's commission on civil rights had issued a report pointing to the difficulties created by restrictive covenants for federal agencies involved in slum clearance.

Only six members of the Supreme Court heard the *Shelley* v. *Kraemer* case in January 1948. Although justices seldom give their reasons for "recusing" (excusing) themselves from cases, it was widely assumed that Justices Robert Jackson, Stanley Reed, and Wiley Rutledge did so because they themselves owned property that was covered by restrictive convenants.

Mr. Chief Justice **Vinson** delivered the opinion of the Court.

. . .

Whether the equal protection clause of the Fourteenth Amendment inhibits judicial enforcement by state courts of restrictive covenants based on race or color is a question which this Court has not heretofore been called upon to consider. . . .

It is well, at the outset, to scrutinize the terms of the restrictive agreements involved in these cases. In the Missouri case, the covenant declares that no part of the affected property shall be "occupied by any person not of the Caucasian race, it being intended hereby to restrict the use of said property . . . against the occupancy as owners or tenants of any portion of said property for resident or other purpose by people of the Negro or Mongolian Race." Not only does the restriction seek to proscribe use and occupancy of the affected properties by members of the excluded class, but as construed by the Missouri courts, the agreement requires that title of any person who uses his property in violation of the restriction shall be divested. The restriction of the covenant in the Michigan case seeks to bar occupancy by persons of the excluded class. It provides that "This property shall not be used or occupied by any person or persons except those of the Caucasian race."

It should be observed that these covenants do not seek to proscribe any particular use of the affected properties. Use of the properties for residential occupancy, as such, is not forbidden. The restrictions of these agreements, rather, are directed toward a designated class of persons and seek to determine who may and who may

not own or make use of the properties for residential purposes. The excluded class is defined wholly in terms of race or color; "simply that and nothing more."

It cannot be doubted that among the civil rights intended to be protected from discriminatory state action by the Fourteenth Amendment are the rights to acquire, enjoy, own and dispose of property. Equality in the enjoyment of property rights was regarded by the framers of that Amendment as an essential pre-condition to the realization of other basic civil rights and liberties which the Amendment was intended to guarantee. Thus, § 1978 of the Revised Statutes, derived from § 1 of the Civil Rights Act of 1866 which was enacted by Congress while the Fourteenth Amendment was also under consideration, provides:

"All citizens of the United States shall have the same right, in every State and Territory, as is enjoyed by white citizens thereof to inherit, purchase, lease, sell, hold, and convey real and personal property."

This Court has given specific recognition to the same principle.

It is likewise clear that restrictions on the right of occupancy of the sort sought to be created by the private agreements in these cases could not be squared with the requirements of the Fourteenth Amendment if imposed by state statute or local ordinance. We do not understand respondents to urge the contrary. In the case of *Buchanan* v. *Warley*, a unanimous Court declared unconstitutional the provisions of a city ordinance which denied to colored persons the right to occupy houses in blocks in which the greater number of houses were occupied by white persons, and imposed similar restrictions on white persons with respect to blocks in which the greater number of houses were occupied by colored persons. During the course of the opinion in that case, this Court stated: "The Fourteenth Amendment and these statutes enacted in furtherance of its purpose operate to qualify and entitle a colored man to acquire property without state legislation discriminating against him solely because of color."

In *Harmon* v. *Tyler* (1927), a unanimous court, on the authority of *Buchanan* v. *Warley,* declared invalid an ordinance which forbade any Negro to establish a home on any property in a white community or any white person to establish a home in a Negro community, "except on the written consent of a majority of the persons of the opposite race inhabiting such community or portion of the City to be affected."

The precise question before this Court in both the *Buchanan* and *Harmon* cases involved the rights of white sellers to dispose of their properties free from restrictions as to potential purchasers based on considerations of race or color. But that such legislation is also offensive to the rights of those desiring to acquire and occupy property and barred on grounds of race or color is clear, not only from the language of the opinion in *Buchanan* v. *Warley,* but from this Court's disposition of the case of *Richmond* v. *Deans* (1930). There, a Negro, barred from the occupancy of certain property by the terms of an ordinance similar to that in the *Buchanan* case, sought injunctive relief in the federal courts to enjoin the enforcement of the ordinance on the grounds that its provisions violated the terms of the Fourteenth Amendment. Such relief was granted, and this Court affirmed, finding the citation of *Buchanan* v. *Warley* and *Harmon* v. *Tyler* sufficient to support its judgment.

But the present cases, unlike those just discussed, do not involve action by state legislatures or city councils. Here the particular patterns of discrimination and the areas in which the restrictions are to operate, are determined, in the first instance, by the terms of agreements among private individuals. Participation of the State consists in the enforcement of the restrictions so defined. The crucial issue with which we are here confronted is whether this distinction removes

these cases from the operation of the prohibitory provisions of the Fourteenth Amendment.

Since the decision of this Court in the *Civil Rights Cases* (1883), the principle has become firmly embedded in our constitutional law that the action inhibited by the first section of the Fourteenth Amendment is only such action as may fairly be said to be that of the States. That Amendment erects no shield against merely private conduct, however discriminatory or wrongful.

We conclude, therefore, that the restrictive agreements standing alone cannot be regarded as violative of any rights guaranteed to petitioners by the Fourteenth Amendment. So long as the purposes of those agreements are effectuated by voluntary adherence to their terms, it would appear clear that there has been no action by the State and the provisions of the Amendment have not been violated.

But here there was more. These are cases in which the purposes of the agreements were secured only by judicial enforcement by state courts of the restrictive terms of the agreements. The respondents urge that judicial enforcement of private agreements does not amount to state action; or, in any event, the participation of the State is so attenuated in character as not to amount to state action within the meaning of the Fourteenth Amendment. Finally, it is suggested, even if the States in these cases may be deemed to have acted in the constitutional sense, their action did not deprive petitioners of rights guaranteed by the Fourteenth Amendment. We move to a consideration of these matters.

That the action of state courts and judicial officers in their official capacities is to be regarded as action of the State within the meaning of the Fourteenth Amendment, is a proposition which has long been established by decisions of this Court. That principle was given expression in the earliest cases involving the construction of the terms of the Fourteenth Amendment. Thus, in *Virginia* v. *Rives* (1880), this Court stated: "It is doubtless true that a State may act through different agencies,—either by its legislative, its executive, or its judicial authorities; and the prohibitions of the amendment extend to all action of the State denying equal protection of the laws, whether it be action by one of these agencies or by another." In *Ex parte Virginia* (1880), the Court observed: "A State acts by its legislative, its executive, or its judicial authorities. It can act in no other way." In the *Civil Rights Cases* (1883), this Court pointed out that the Amendment makes void "State action of every kind" which is inconsistent with the guaranties therein contained, and extends to manifestations of "State authority in the shape of laws, customs, or judicial or executive proceedings." Language to like effect is employed no less than eighteen times during the course of that opinion.

Similar expressions, giving specific recognition to the fact that judicial action is to be regarded as action of the State for the purposes of the Fourteenth Amendment, are to be found in numerous cases which have been more recently decided. . . .

In numerous cases, this Court has reversed criminal convictions in state courts for failure of those courts to provide the essential ingredients of a fair hearing. Thus it has been held that convictions obtained in state courts under the domination of a mob are void. . . . Convictions obtained by coerced confessions, by the use of perjured testimony known by the prosecution to be such, or without the effective assistance of counsel, have also been held to be exertions of state authority in conflict with the fundamental rights protected by the Fourteenth Amendment.

But the examples of state judicial action which have been held by this Court to violate the Amendment's commands are not restricted to situations in which the judicial proceedings were found in some manner to be procedurally unfair. It has been recognized that the action of state courts in enforcing a substantive common-law rule formulated by those courts, may result in the denial of rights guaranteed by the Fourteenth Amendment, even though the judicial proceedings in such cases may have been in complete accord with the most rigorous conceptions of procedural due process. . . .

The short of the matter is that from the time of the adoption of the Fourteenth Amendment until the present, it has been the consistent ruling of this Court that the action of the States to which the Amendment has reference includes action of state courts and state judicial officials. Although, in construing the terms of the Fourteenth Amendment, differences have from time to time been expressed as to whether particular types of state action may be said to offend the Amendment's prohibitory provisions, it has never been suggested that state court action is immunized from the operation of those provisions simply because the act is that of the judicial branch of the state government.

. . .

Against this background of judicial construction, extending over a period of some three-quarters of a century, we are called upon to consider whether enforcement by state courts of the restrictive agreements in these cases may be deemed to be the acts of those States; and, if so, whether that action has denied these petitioners the equal protection of the laws which the Amendment was intended to insure.

We have no doubt that there has been state action in these cases in the full and complete sense of the phrase. The undisputed facts disclose that petitioners were willing purchasers of properties upon which they desired to establish homes. The owners of the properties were willing sellers; and contracts of sale were accordingly consummated. It is clear that but for the active intervention of the state courts, supported by the full panoply of state power, petitioners would have been free to occupy the properties in question without restraint.

These are not cases, as has been suggested, in which the States have merely abstained from action, leaving private individuals free to impose such discriminations as they see fit. Rather, these are cases in which the States have made available to such individuals the full coercive power of government to deny to petitioners, on the grounds of race or color, the enjoyment of property rights in premises which petitioners are willing and financially able to acquire and which the grantors are willing to sell. The difference between judicial enforcement and nonenforcement of the restrictive covenants is the difference to petitioners between being denied rights of property available to other members of the community and being accorded full enjoyment of those rights on an equal footing.

The enforcement of the restrictive agreements by the state courts in these cases was directed pursuant to the common-law policy of the States as formulated by those courts in earlier decisions. In the Missouri case, enforcement of the covenant was directed in the first instance by the highest court of the State after the trial court had determined the agreement to be invalid for want of the requisite number of signatures. In the Michigan case, the order of enforcement by the trial court was affirmed by the highest state court. The judicial action in each case bears the clear and unmistakable imprimatur of the State. We have noted that previous decisions of this Court have established the proposition that judicial action is not immunized from the operation of the Fourteenth Amendment simply because it is taken pursuant to the state's common-law policy. Nor is the Amendment ineffective simply because the particular pattern of discrimination, which the State has enforced, was defined initially by the terms of a private agreement. State action, as that phrase is understood for the purposes of the Fourteenth Amendment, refers to exertions of state power in all forms. And when the effect of that action is to deny rights subject to the protection of the Fourteenth Amendment, it is the obligation of this Court to enforce the constitutional commands.

We hold that in granting judicial enforcement of the restrictive agreements in these cases, the States have denied petitioners the equal protection of the laws and that, therefore, the action of the state courts cannot stand. We have noted that freedom from discrimination by the States in the enjoyment of property rights was among the basic objectives sought to be effectuated by the framers of the Fourteenth Amendment. That such discrimination has occurred in these cases is clear. Because of the race or color of these petitioners they have been denied rights of ownership or occupancy enjoyed as a matter of course by other citizens of different race or color. The Fourteenth Amendment declares "that all persons, whether colored or white, shall stand equal before the laws of the States, and, in regard to the colored race, for whose protection the amendment was primarily designed, that no discrimination shall be made against them by law because of their color." Only recently this Court had occasion to declare that a state law

which denied equal enjoyment of property rights to a designated class of citizens of specified race and ancestry, was not a legitimate exercise of the state's police power but violated the guaranty of the equal protection of the laws. *Oyama* v. *California* (1948). Nor may the discriminations imposed by the state courts in these cases be justified as proper exertions of state police power.

. . .

The problem of defining the scope of the restrictions which the Federal Constitution imposes upon exertions of power by the States has given rise to many of the most persistent and fundamental issues which this Court has been called upon to consider. That problem was foremost in the minds of the framers of the Constitution, and, since that early day, has arisen in a multitude of forms. The task of determining whether the action of a State offends constitutional provisions is one which may not be undertaken lightly. Where, however, it is clear that the action of the State violates the terms of the fundamental charter, it is the obligation of this Court so to declare.

The historical context in which the Fourteenth Amendment became a part of the Constitution should not be forgotten. Whatever else the framers sought to achieve, it is clear that the matter of primary concern was the establishment of equality in the enjoyment of basic civil and political rights and the preservation of those rights from discriminatory action on the part of the States based on considerations of race or color. Seventy-five years ago this Court announced that the provisions of the Amendment are to be construed with this fundamental purpose in mind. Upon full consideration, we have concluded that in these cases the States have acted to deny petitioners the equal protection of the laws guaranteed by the Fourteenth Amendment. Having so decided, we find it unnecessary to consider whether petitioners have also been deprived of property without due process of law or denied privileges and immunities of citizens of the United States.

For the reasons stated, the judgment of the Supreme Court of Missouri and the judgment of the Supreme Court of Michigan must be reversed.

Aftermath of Shelley *v.* Kraemer

The Shelleys remained in their home for about ten years before moving a few blocks away. The Grande Prairie neighborhood of St. Louis is now predominantly black.

The effective demise of restrictive covenants did not, of course, signal an end to racial segregation in housing. Housing is, in fact, the one area in which there is today more rather than less segregation than a generation ago. Despite a federal fair housing statute and a host of anti-discrimination laws at the state and local levels, people live where they can afford to live, and as long as significant differences persist in the income levels of blacks and whites (median black family income in 1981 was only 56 percent of the white median), there is little likelihood that America's neighborhoods (or its public schools) will be substantially integrated. Moreover, there is little evidence that the United States government has put a high priority on ending residential segregation in deciding on locations for public housing built with federal funds.

Regents of University of California v. *Bakke*
438 U.S. 265 (1978)

In its difficult early days the civil rights movement was driven in large part by faith that once black Americans had achieved equality under the law, social and economic equality would inevitably follow. By the end of the 1960s, however, it was increasingly plain that racial progress would not be achieved so smoothly. Equal access to public schools and polling places had not brought blacks jobs, houses, or social acceptance to any significant degree, nor was there any prospect that it would soon do so. Blacks had won the right to compete as equals, but the vestiges of slavery and segregation were so burdensome that they could seldom hope to win. This was particularly true in higher education, one of the key entry points to status and success in the United States. With tens of thousands of well-prepared students applying for scarce positions at elite institutions, blacks from disadvantaged backgrounds stood little chance of being admitted on the basis of purely academic criteria.

In keeping with the politically liberal ethos of the day, many colleges and universities in the 1960s began to treat race as a factor in their admissions decisions in much the same way as athletic ability, family ties, geographical background, and other nonacademic criteria had traditionally been taken into account in the interest of achieving a diverse, well-rounded student body. Public school desegregation had long since introduced the paradox that the long-term goal of achieving a color-blind society might require a heightened level of race consciousness in the shorter run.

Universities handled this process—known to its supporters as "affirmative action," to its critics as "reverse discrimination"—in two basic ways. Some treated race informally in making admissions decisions, usually with an eye toward meeting a certain "target" percentage of minority students in their entire classes. Other institutions went about achieving the same goal in a more structured way, by establishing precise "quotas" of black or other minority students to be admitted in each class. In 1971 the medical school at the University of California at Davis adopted the latter approach, designating 16 places in its entering class of 100 for black, Mexican-American, and Asian-American students, at least some of whom would not have been admitted under the objective criteria used to judge nonminority applicants. The first class of 50 students admitted to the Davis medical school in 1968 had had three Asian-Americans, no Mexican-Americans, and no blacks. It was this situation that the special admissions program was developed to rectify.

Allan Bakke, an aerospace engineer with degrees from the University of Minnesota and Stanford, decided in his late twenties that he wanted to become a doctor. At the age of 33, after completing premed college courses, Bakke applied to a dozen medical schools, all of which turned him down. Two schools indicated that Bakke was rejected because of his age. The following year Bakke tried again at the University of California at Davis, which again rejected his application. When Bakke learned of Davis's special program for minorities and ascertained that his grade-point and aptitude test averages were higher than those of the 16 students admitted through that program, he filed a lawsuit in California, alleging that Davis had denied him entrance to its medical school solely on account of his race, thus depriving him of his rights to equal protection of the laws under the California and United States constitutions. Bakke also cited Title VI of the Civil Rights Act of 1964, which prohibits racial discrimination in any program receiving federal financial assistance, as the Davis Medical School did.

The Superior Court found the University to have violated the federal and state constitutions and the Civil Rights Act by discriminating in its admissions on the basis of race. However, it refused to order Bakke's admission because he had not proven that he would have been admitted had it not been for the special minority program. On appeal, the California Supreme Court held that it was the university's duty to show that Bakke would not have been admitted even without the special program. Since it had not done so, Bakke was ordered admitted to the medical school. Davis then appealed to the United States Supreme Court, which granted *certiorari* in 1977.

The *Bakke* case generated an enormous amount of public interest and controversy. A record 58 *amicus curiae* briefs were filed (a number since surpassed in the 1989 *Webster* abortion case). Among the parties weighing in on the university's side were the United States Department of Justice, the American Civil Liberties Union, the National Education Association, the American Bar Association, and the NAACP Legal Defense and Educational Fund. Supporting Allan Bakke's position were a number of Jewish organizations that traditionally opposed the use of racial and ethnic quotas. The central issue before the Supreme Court was whether the equal protection clause of the Fourteenth Amendment, which had been adopted to protect black citizens from discrimination by the states, could now be used by a white citizen to protect himself from the racially discriminatory effects of state action intended to overcome the effects of past injustices.

Mr. Justice **Powell** announced the judgment of the Court.

This case presents a challenge to the special admissions program of the petitioner, the Medical School of the University of California at Davis, which is designed to assure the admission of a specified number of students from certain minority groups. The Superior Court of California sustained respondent's challenge, holding that petitioner's program violated the California Constitution, Title VI of the Civil Rights Act of 1964 [42 USCS § 2000d], and the Equal Protection Clause of the Fourteenth Amend-

ment. The court enjoined petitioner from considering respondent's race or the race of any other applicant in making admissions decisions. It refused, however, to order respondent's admission to the Medical School, holding that he had not carried his burden of proving that he would have been admitted but for the constitutional and statutory violations. The Supreme Court of California affirmed those portions of the trial court's judgment declaring the special admissions program unlawful and enjoining petitioner from considering the race of any applicant. It modified that portion of the judgment denying respondent's requested injunction and directed the trial court to order his admission.

For the reasons stated in the following opinion, I believe that so much of the judgment of the California court as holds petitioner's special admissions program unlawful and directs that respondent be admitted to the Medical School must be affirmed. For the reasons expressed in a separate opinion, my Brothers The Chief Justice, Mr. Justice Stewart, Mr. Justice Rehnquist, and Mr. Justice Stevens concur in this judgment.

I also conclude for the reasons stated in the following opinion that the portion of the court's judgment enjoining petitioner from according any consideration to race in its admissions process must be reversed. For reasons expressed in separate opinions, my Brothers Mr. Justice Brennan, Mr. Justice White, Mr. Justice Marshall, and Mr. Justice Blackmun concur in this judgment.

Affirmed in part and reversed in part.

. . .

[The Court finds it unnecessary to discuss the applicability of Title VI of the Civil Rights Act since the law prohibits the same racial classifications as the equal protection clause.]

Petitioner does not deny that decisions based on race or ethnic origin by faculties and administrations of state universities are reviewable under the Fourteenth Amendment. For his part, respondent does not argue that all racial or ethnic classifications are per se invalid. The parties do disagree as to the level of judicial scrutiny to be applied to the special admissions program. Petitioner argues that the court below erred in applying strict scrutiny, as this inexact term has been applied in our cases. That level of review, petitioner asserts, should be reserved for classifications that disadvantage "discrete and insular minorities." Respondent, on the other hand, contends that the California court correctly rejected the notion that the degree of judicial scrutiny accorded a particular racial or ethnic classification hinges upon membership in a discrete and insular minority and duly recognized that the "rights established [by the Fourteenth

Amendment] are personal rights." Shelley v Kraemer, (1948).

En route to this crucial battle over the scope of judicial review, the parties fight a sharp preliminary action over the proper characterization of the special admissions program. Petitioner prefers to view it as establishing a "goal" of minority representation in the medical school. Respondent, echoing the courts below, labels it a racial quota.

This semantic distinction is beside the point; the special admissions program is undeniably a classification based on race and ethnic background. To the extent that there existed a pool of at least minimally qualified minority applicants to fill the 16 special admissions seats, white applicants could compete only for 84 seats in the entering class, rather than the 100 open to minority applicants. Whether this limitation is described as a quota or a goal, it is a line drawn on the basis of race and ethnic status.

The guarantees of the Fourteenth Amendment extend to persons. Its language is explicit: "No state shall . . . deny to any person within its jurisdiction the equal protection of the laws." It is settled beyond question that the "rights created by the first section of the Fourteenth Amendment are, by its terms, guaranteed to the individual. They are personal rights," Shelley v Kraemer. The guarantee of equal protection cannot mean one thing when applied to one individual and something else when applied to a person of another color. If both are not accorded the same protection, then it is not equal.

Nevertheless, petitioner argues that the court below erred in applying strict scrutiny to the special admissions programs because white males, such as respondent, are not a "discrete and insular minority" requiring extraordinary protection from the majoritarian political process. This rationale, however, has never been invoked in our decisions as a prerequisite to subjecting racial or ethnic distinctions to strict scrutiny. Nor has this Court held that discreteness and insularity constitute necessary preconditions to a holding that a particular classification is invidious. These characteristics may be relevant in deciding whether or not to add new types of classifications to the list of "suspect" categories or whether a particular classification survives close examination. Racial and ethnic classifications, however, are subject to stringent examination without regard to these additional characteristics. . . . Racial and ethnic distinctions of any sort are inherently suspect and thus call for the most exacting judicial examination.

. . .

Although many of the Framers of the Fourteenth Amendment conceived of its primary function as bridging the vast distance between members of the Negro race and the white "majority," the Amendment itself was framed in universal terms, without reference to color, ethnic origin, or condition of prior servitude. As this Court recently remarked in interpreting the 1866 Civil Rights Act to extend to claims of racial discrimination against white persons, "the 39th Congress was intent upon establishing in federal law a broader principle than would have been necessary to meet the particular and immediate plight of the newly freed Negro slaves." And that legislation was specifically broadened in 1870 to ensure that "all persons," not merely "citizens," would enjoy equal rights under the law. Indeed, it is not unlikely that among the Framers were many who would have applauded a reading of the Equal Protection Clause which states a principle of universal application and is responsive to the racial, ethnic and cultural diversity of the Nation.

Over the past 30 years, this Court has embarked upon the crucial mission of interpreting the Equal Protection Clause with the view of assuring to all persons "the protection of equal laws," in a Nation confronting a legacy of slavery and racial discrimination. Because the landmark decisions in this area arose in response to the continued exclusion of Negroes from the mainstream of American society, they could be characterized as involving discrimination by the "majority" white race against the Negro minority. But they need not be read as depending upon that characterization for their results. It suffices to say that "[o]ver the years, this Court consistently repudiated '[d]istinctions between citizens solely because of their ancestry' as being 'odious

to a free people whose institutions are founded upon the doctrine of equality.' "

Petitioner urges us to adopt for the first time a more restrictive view of the Equal Protection Clause and hold that discrimination against members of the white "majority" cannot be suspect if its purpose can be characterized as "benign." The clock of our liberties, however, cannot be turned back to 1868. It is far too late to argue that the guarantee of equal protection to *all* persons permits the recognition of special wards entitled to a degree of protection greater than that accorded others. "The Fourteenth Amendment is not directed solely against discrimination due to a 'two-class theory'—that is, based upon differences between 'white' and Negro."

Once the artificial line of a "two-class theory" of the Fourteenth Amendment is put aside, the difficulties entailed in varying the level of judicial review according to a perceived "preferred" status of a particular racial or ethnic minority are intractable. The concepts of "majority" and "minority" necessarily reflect temporary arrangements and political judgments. As observed above, the white "majority" itself is composed of various minority groups, most of which can lay claim to a history of prior discrimination at the hands of the state and private individuals. Not all of these groups can receive preferential treatment and corresponding judicial tolerance of distinctions drawn in terms of race and nationality, for then the only "majority" left would be a new minority of White Anglo-Saxon Protestants. There is no principled basis for deciding which groups would merit "heightened judicial solicitude" and which would not. Courts would be asked to evaluate the extent of the prejudice and consequent harm suffered by various minority groups. Those whose societal injury is thought to exceed some arbitrary level of tolerability then would be entitled to preferential classifications at the expense of individuals belonging to other groups. Those classifications would be free from exacting judicial scrutiny. As these preferences began to have their desired effect, and the consequences of past discrimination were undone, new judicial rankings would be necessary. The kind of variable sociological and political analysis necessary to produce such rankings simply does not lie within the judicial competence—even if they otherwise were politically feasible and socially desirable.

. . .

If it is the individual who is entitled to judicial protection against classifications based upon his racial or ethnic background because such distinctions impinge upon personal rights, rather than the individual only because of his membership in a particular group, then constitutional standards may be applied consistently. Political judgments regarding the necessity for the particular classification may be weighed in the constitutional balance, but the standard of justification will remain constant. This is as it should be, since those political judgments are the product of rough compromise struck by contending groups within the democratic process. When they touch upon an individual's race or ethnic background, he is entitled to a judicial determination that the burden he is asked to bear on that basis is precisely tailored to serve a compelling governmental interest. The Constitution guarantees that right to every person regardless of his background.

. . .

We have held that in "order to justify the use of a suspect classification, a State must show that its purpose or interest is both constitutionally permissible and substantial, and that its use of the classification is 'necessary . . . to the accomplishment' of its purpose or the safeguarding of its interest." The special admissions program purports to serve the purposes of: (i) "reducing the historic deficit of traditionally disfavored minorities in medical schools and the medical profession," (ii) countering the effects of societal discrimination; (iii) increasing the number of physicians who will practice in communities currently underserved; and (iv) obtaining the educational benefits that flow from an ethnically diverse student body. It is necessary to decide which, if any, of these purposes is substantial enough to support the use of a suspect classification.

If petitioner's purpose is to assure within its student body some specified percentage of a particular group merely because of its race or ethnic origin, such a preferential purpose must be rejected not as insubstantial but as facially invalid. Preferring members of any one group for no reason other than race or ethnic origin is discrimination for its own sake. This the Constitution forbids.

The State certainly has a legitimate and substantial interest in ameliorating, or eliminating where feasible, the disabling effects of identified discrimination. The line of school desegregation cases, commencing with Brown, attests to the importance of this state goal and the commitment of the judiciary to affirm all lawful means towards its attainment. In the school cases, the States were required by court order to redress the wrongs worked by specific instances of racial discrimination. That goal was far more focused than the remedying of the effects of "societal discrimination," an amorphous concept of injury that may be ageless in its reach into the past.

We have never approved a classification that aids persons perceived as members of relatively victimized groups at the expense of other innocent individuals in the absence of judicial, legislative, or administrative findings of constitutional or statutory violations. After such findings have been made, the governmental interest in preferring members of the injured groups at the expense of others is substantial, since the legal rights of the victims must be vindicated. In such a case, the extent of the injury and the consequent remedy will have been judicially, legislatively, or administratively defined. Also, the remedial action usually remains subject to continuing oversight to assure that it will work the least harm possible to other innocent persons competing for the benefit. Without such findings of constitutional or statutory violations, it cannot be said that the government has any greater interest in helping one individual than in refraining from harming another. Thus, the government has no compelling justification for inflicting such harm.

Petitioner does not purport to have made, and is in no position to make, such findings. Its broad mission is education, not the formulation of any legislative policy or the adjudication of particular claims of illegality. . . .

Hence, the purpose of helping certain groups

whom the faculty of the Davis Medical School perceived as victims of "societal discrimination" does not justify a classification that imposes disadvantages upon persons like respondent, who bear no responsibility for whatever harm the beneficiaries of the special admissions program are thought to have suffered. To hold otherwise would be to convert a remedy heretofore reserved for violations of legal rights into a privilege that all institutions throughout the Nation could grant at their pleasure to whatever groups are perceived as victims of societal discrimination. That is a step we have never approved.

Petitioner identifies, as another purpose of its program, improving the delivery of health care services to communities currently underserved. It may be assumed that in some situations a State's interest in facilitating the health care of its citizens is sufficiently compelling to support the use of a suspect classification. But there is virtually no evidence in the record indicating that petitioner's special admissions program is either needed or geared to promote that goal.

. . .

The fourth goal asserted by petitioner is the attainment of a diverse student body. This clearly is a constitutionally permissible goal for an institution of higher education. Academic freedom, though not a specifically enumerated constitutional right, long has been viewed as a special concern of the First Amendment. The freedom of a university to make its own judgments as to education includes the selection of its student body.

. . .

Ethnic diversity, however, is only one element in a range of factors a university properly may consider in attaining the goal of a heterogeneous student body. Although a university must have wide discretion in making the sensitive judgments as to who should be admitted, constitutional limitations protecting individual rights may not be disregarded. Respondent urges—and the courts below have held—that petitioner's dual admissions program is a racial classification that impermissibly infringes his rights under the Fourteenth Amendment. As the inter-est of diversity is compelling in the context of a university's admissions program, the question remains whether the program's racial classification is necessary to promote this interest.

It may be assumed that the reservation of a specified number of seats in each class for individuals from the preferred ethnic groups would contribute to the attainment of considerable ethnic diversity in the student body. But petitioner's argument that this is the only effective means of serving the interest of diversity is seriously flawed. In a most fundamental sense the argument misconceives the nature of the state interest that would justify consideration of race or ethnic background. It is not an interest in simple ethnic diversity, in which a specified percentage of the student body is in effect guaranteed to be members of selected ethnic groups, with the remaining percentage an undifferentiated aggregation of students. The diversity that furthers a compelling state interest encompasses a far broader array of qualifications and characteristics of which racial or ethnic origin is but a single though important element. Petitioner's special admissions program, focused *solely* on ethnic diversity, would hinder rather than further attainment of genuine diversity.

Nor would the state interest in genuine diversity be served by expanding petitioner's two-track system into a multitrack program with a prescribed number of seats set aside for each identifiable category of applicants. Indeed, it is inconceivable that a university would thus pursue the logic of petitioner's two-track program to the illogical end of insulating each category of applicants with certain desired qualifications from competition with all other applicants.

The experience of other university admissions programs, which take race into account in achieving the educational diversity valued by the First Amendment, demonstrates that the assignment of a fixed number of places to a minority group is not a necessary means toward that end. An illuminating example is found in the Harvard College program:

"In recent years Harvard College has expanded the concept of diversity to include students from disadvantaged economic, racial and ethnic groups. Harvard College now recruits not only

Californians or Louisianans but also blacks and Chicanos and other minority students.

. . .

"In practice, this new definition of diversity has meant that race has been a factor in some admission decisions. When the Committee on Admissions reviews the large middle group of applicants who are 'admissible' and deemed capable of doing good work in their courses, the race of an applicant may tip the balance in his favor just as geographic origin or a life spent on a farm may tip the balance in other candidates' cases. A farm boy from Idaho can bring something to Harvard College that a Bostonian cannot offer. Similarly, a black student can usually bring something that a white person cannot offer."

. . .

"In Harvard College admissions the Committee has not set target-quotas for the number of blacks, or of musicians, football players, physicists or Californians to be admitted in a given year. . . . But that awareness [of the necessity of including more than a token number of black students] does not mean that the Committee sets the minimum number of blacks or of people from west of the Mississippi who are to be admitted. It means only that in choosing among thousands of applicants who are not only 'admissible' academically but have other strong qualities, the Committee, with a number of criteria in mind, pays some attention to distribution among many types and categories of students."

In such an admissions program race or ethnic background may be deemed a "plus" in a particular applicant's file, yet it does not insulate the individual from comparison with all other candidates for the available seats. The file of a particular black applicant may be examined for his potential contribution to diversity without the factor of race being decisive when compared, for example, with that of an applicant identified as an Italian-American if the latter is thought to exhibit qualities more likely to promote beneficial educational pluralism. Such qualities could include exceptional personal talents, unique work or service experience, leadership

potential, maturity, demonstrated compassion, a history of overcoming disadvantage, ability to communicate with the poor, or other qualifications deemed important. In short, an admissions program operated in this way is flexible enough to consider all pertinent elements of diversity in light of the particular qualifications of each applicant, and to place them on the same footing for consideration, although not necessarily according them the same weight. Indeed, the weight attributed to a particular quality may vary from year to year depending upon the "mix" both of the student body and the applicants for the incoming class.

This kind of program treats each applicant as an individual in the admissions process. The applicant who loses out on the last available seat to another candidate receiving a "plus" on the basis of ethnic background will not have been foreclosed from all consideration for that seat simply because he was not the right color or had the wrong surname. It would mean only that his combined qualifications, which may have included similar nonobjective factors, did not outweigh those of the other applicant. His qualifications would have been weighed fairly and competitively, and he would have no basis to complain of unequal treatment under the Fourteenth Amendment.

It has been suggested that an admissions program which considers race only as one factor is simply a subtle and more sophisticated—but no less effective—means of according racial preference than the Davis program. A facial intent to discriminate, however, is evident in petitioner's preference program and not denied in this case. No such facial infirmity exists in an admissions program where race or ethnic background is simply one element—to be weighed fairly against other elements—in the selection process. "A boundary line," as Mr. Justice Frankfurter remarked in another connection, "is none the worse for being narrow." And a Court would not assume that a university, professing to employ a facially nondiscriminatory admissions policy, would operate it as a cover for the functional equivalent of a quota system. In short, good faith would be presumed in the absence of a showing to the contrary in the manner permitted by our cases.

In summary, it is evident that the Davis special admissions program involves the use of an explicit racial classification never before countenanced by this Court. It tells applicants who are not Negro, Asian, or "Chicano" that they are totally excluded from a specific percentage of the seats in an entering class. No matter how strong their qualifications, quantitative and extracurricular, including their own potential for contribution to educational diversity, they are never afforded the chance to compete with applicants from the preferred groups for the special admission seats. At the same time, the preferred applicants have the opportunity to compete for every seat in the class.

The fatal flaw in petitioner's preferential program is its disregard of individual rights as guaranteed by the Fourteenth Amendment. Such rights are not absolute. But when a State's distribution of benefits or imposition of burdens hinges on the color of a person's skin or ancestry, that individual is entitled to a demonstration that the challenged classification is necessary to promote a substantial state interest. Petitioner has failed to carry this burden. For this reason, that portion of the California court's judgment holding petitioner's special admissions program invalid under the Fourteenth Amendment must be affirmed.

In enjoining petitioner from ever considering the race of any applicant, however, the courts below failed to recognize that the State has a substantial interest that legitimately may be served by a properly devised admissions program involving the competitive consideration of race and ethnic origin. For this reason, so much of the California court's judgment as enjoins petitioner from any consideration of the race of any applicant must be reversed.

With respect to respondent's entitlement to an injunction directing his admission to the Medical School, petitioner has conceded that it could not carry its burden of proving that, but for the existence of its unlawful special admissions program, respondent still would not have been admitted. Hence, respondent is entitled to the injunction, and that portion of the judgment must be affirmed.

Opinion of Mr. Justice **Brennan,** Mr. Justice

White, Mr. Justice **Marshall,** and Mr. Justice **Blackmun,** concurring in the judgment in part and dissenting.

The Court today, in reversing in part the judgment of the Supreme Court of California, affirms the constitutional power of Federal and State Government to act affirmatively to achieve equal opportunity for all. The difficulty of the issue presented—whether Government may use race-conscious programs to redress the continuing effects of past discrimination—and the mature consideration which each of our Brethren has brought to it have resulted in many opinions, no single one speaking for the Court. But this should not and must not mask the central meaning of today's opinions: Government may take race into account when it acts not to demean or insult any racial group, but to remedy disadvantages cast on minorities by past racial prejudice, at least when appropriate findings have been made by judicial, legislative, or administrative bodies with competence to act in this area.

The Chief Justice and our Brothers Stewart, Rehnquist, and Stevens, have concluded that Title VI of the Civil Rights Act of 1964 prohibits programs such as that at the Davis Medical School. On this statutory theory alone, they would hold that respondent Allan Bakke's rights have been violated and that he must, therefore, be admitted to the Medical School. Our Brother Powell, reaching the Constitution, concludes that, although race may be taken into account in university admissions, the particular special admissions program used by petitioner, which resulted in the exclusion of respondent Bakke, was not shown to be necessary to achieve petitioner's stated goals. Accordingly, these Members of the Court form a majority of five affirming the judgment of the Supreme Court of California insofar as it holds that respondent Bakke "is entitled to an order that he be admitted to the University."

We agree with Mr. Justice Powell that, as applied to the case before us, Title VI goes no further in prohibiting the use of race than the Equal Protection Clause of the Fourteenth Amendment itself. We also agree that the effect of the California Supreme Court's affirmance of the judgment of the Superior Court of California would be to prohibit the University from establishing in the future affirmative action programs that take race into account. Since we conclude that the affirmative admissions program at the Davis Medical School is constitutional, we would reverse the judgment below in all respects. Mr. Justice Powell agrees that some uses of race in university admissions are permissible and, therefore, he joins with us to make five votes reversing the judgment below insofar as it prohibits the University from establishing race-conscious programs in the future.

. . .

The assertion of human equality is closely associated with the proposition that differences in color or creed, birth or status, are neither significant nor relevant to the way in which persons should be treated. Nonetheless, the position that such factors must be "[c]onstitutionally an irrelevance," summed up by the shorthand phrase "[o]ur Constitution is color-blind," has never been adopted by this Court as the proper meaning of the Equal Protection Clause. Indeed, we have expressly rejected this proposition on a number of occasions.

Our cases have always implied that an "overriding statutory purpose" could be found that would justify racial classifications. More recently, in McDaniel v Barresi (1971), this Court unanimously reversed the Georgia Supreme Court which had held that a desegregation plan voluntarily adopted by a local school board, which assigned students on the basis of race, was per se invalid because it was not colorblind. And in North Carolina State Board of Ed. v Swann (1971), we held, again unanimously, that a statute mandating colorblind school assignment plans could not stand "against the background of segregation," since such a limit on remedies would "render illusory the promise of Brown."

We conclude, therefore, that racial classifications are not per se invalid under the Fourteenth Amendment. Accordingly, we turn to the problem of articulating what our role should be in reviewing state action that expressly classifies by race.

Respondent argues that racial classifications are always suspect and, consequently, that this Court should weigh the importance of the objectives served by Davis' special admissions program to see if they are compelling. In addition, he asserts that this Court must inquire whether, in its judgment, there are alternatives to racial classifications which would suit Davis' purposes. Petitioner, on the other hand, states that our proper role is simply to accept petitioner's determination that the racial classifications used by its program are reasonably related to what it tells us are its benign purposes. We reject petitioner's view, but, because our prior cases are in many respects inapposite to that before us now, we find it necessary to define with precision the meaning of that inexact term, "strict scrutiny."

Unquestionably we have held that a government practice or statute which restricts "fundamental rights" or which contains "suspect classifications" is to be subjected to "strict scrutiny" and can be justified only if it furthers a compelling government purpose and, even then, only if no less restrictive alternative is available. But no fundamental right is involved here. Nor do whites as a class have any of the "traditional indicia of suspectness: the class is not saddled with such disabilities, or subjected to such a history of purposeful unequal treatment, or relegated to such a position of political powerlessness as to command extraordinary protection from the majoritarian political process."

On the other hand, the fact that this case does not fit neatly into our prior analytic framework for race cases does not mean that it should be analyzed by applying the very loose rational-basis standard of review that is the very least that is always applied in equal protection cases. . . . Instead, a number of considerations—developed in gender discrimination cases but which carry even more force when applied to racial classifications—lead us to conclude that racial classifications designed to further remedial purposes " 'must serve important governmental objectives and must be substantially related to achievement of those objectives.' "

. . .

In sum, because of the significant risk that racial classifications established for ostensibly benign purposes can be misused, causing effects not unlike those created by invidious classifications, it is inappropriate to inquire only whether there is any conceivable basis that might sustain such a classification. Instead, to justify such a classification an important and articulated purpose for its use must be shown. In addition, any statute must be stricken that stigmatizes any group or that singles out those least well represented in the political process to bear the brunt of a benign program. Thus our review under the Fourteenth Amendment should be strict—not "'strict' in theory and fatal in fact," because it is stigma that causes fatality—but strict and searching nonetheless.

. . .

Properly construed . . . our prior cases unequivocally show that a state government may adopt race-conscious programs if the purpose of such programs is to remove the disparate racial impact its actions might otherwise have and if there is reason to believe that the disparate impact is itself the product of past discrimination, whether its own or that of society at large. There is no question that Davis' program is valid under this test.

Certainly, on the basis of the undisputed factual submissions before this Court, Davis had a sound basis for believing that the problem of underrepresentation of minorities was substantial and chronic and that the problem was attributable to handicaps imposed on minority applicants by past and present racial discrimination. Until at least 1973, the practice of medicine in this country was, in fact, if not in law, largely the prerogative of whites. In 1950, for example, while Negroes comprised 10% of the total population, Negro physicians constituted only 2.2% of the total number of physicians. The overwhelming majority of these, moreover, were educated in two predominantly Negro medical schools, Howard and Meharry. By 1970, the gap between the proportion of Negroes in medicine and their proportion in the population had widened: The number of Negroes employed in medicine remained frozen at 2.2% while the Negro population had increased to 11.1%. The number of Negro admittees to predominantly white medical schools, moreover, had declined

in absolute numbers during the years 1955 to 1964.

. . .

The second prong of our test—whether the Davis program stigmatizes any discrete group or individual and whether race is reasonably used in light of the program's objectives—is clearly satisfied by the Davis program.

It is not even claimed that Davis' program in any way operates to stigmatize or single out any discrete and insular, or even any identifiable, nonminority group. Nor will harm comparable to that imposed upon racial minorities by exclusion or separation on grounds of race be the likely result of the program. It does not, for example, establish an exclusive preserve for minority students apart from and exclusive of whites. Rather, its purpose is to overcome the effects of segregation by bringing the races together. True, whites are excluded from participation in the special admissions program, but this fact only operates to reduce the number of whites to be admitted in the regular admissions program in order to permit admission of a reasonable percentage—less than their proportion of the California population—of otherwise underrepresented qualified minority applicants.

. . .

We disagree with the lower courts' conclusion that the Davis program's use of race was unreasonable in light of its objectives. First, as petitioner argues, there are no practical means by which it could achieve its ends in the foreseeable future without the use of race-conscious measures. With respect to any factor (such as poverty or family educational background) that may be used as a substitute for race as an indicator of past discrimination, whites greatly outnumber racial minorities simply because whites make up a far larger percentage of the total population and therefore far outnumber minorities in absolute terms at every socioeconomic level. . . .

Second, the Davis admissions program does not simply equate minority status with disadvantage. Rather, Davis considers on an individual basis each applicant's personal history to determine whether he or she has likely been disadvantaged by racial discrimination. The record makes clear that only minority applicants likely to have been isolated from the mainstream of American life are considered in the special program; other minority applicants are eligible only through the regular admissions program. . . .

Finally, Davis' special admissions program cannot be said to violate the Constitution simply because it has set aside a predetermined number of places for qualified minority applicants rather than using minority status as a positive factor to be considered in evaluating the applications of disadvantaged minority applicants. For purposes of constitutional adjudication, there is no difference between the two approaches. In any admissions program which accords special consideration to disadvantaged racial minorities, a determination of the degree of preference to be given is unavoidable, and any given preference that results in the exclusion of a white candidate is no more or less constitutionally acceptable than a program such as that at Davis. . . .

The "Harvard" program, as those employing it readily concede, openly and successfully employs a racial criterion for the purpose of ensuring that some of the scarce places in institutions of higher education are allocated to disadvantaged minority students. That the Harvard approach does not also make public the extent of the preference and the precise workings of the system while the Davis program employs a specific, openly stated number, does not condemn the latter plan for purposes of Fourteenth Amendment adjudication. It may be that the Harvard plan is more acceptable to the public than is the Davis "quota." If it is, any State, including California, is free to adopt it in preference to a less acceptable alternative, just as it is generally free, as far as the Constitution is concerned, to abjure granting any racial preferences in its admissions program. But there is no basis for preferring a particular preference program simply because in achieving the same goals that the Davis Medical School is pursuing, it proceeds in a manner that is not immediately apparent to the public.

Accordingly, we would reverse the judgment of the Supreme Court of California holding the Medical School's special admissions program unconstitutional and directing respondent's admission, as well as that portion of the judgment enjoining the Medical School from according any consideration to race in the admissions process.

Mr. Justice **Stevens,** with whom The **Chief Justice,** Mr. Justice **Stewart,** and Mr. Justice **Rehnquist** join, concurring in the judgment in part and dissenting in part.

. . .

Both petitioner and respondent have asked us to determine the legality of the University's special admissions program by reference to the Constitution. Our settled practice, however, is to avoid the decision of a constitutional issue if a case can be fairly decided on a statutory ground. . . . The more important the issue, the more force there is to this doctrine. In this case, we are presented with a constitutional question of undoubted and unusual importance. Since, however, a dispositive statutory claim was raised at the very inception of this case, and squarely decided in the portion of the trial court judgment affirmed by the California Supreme Court, it is our plain duty to confront it. Only if petitioner should prevail on the statutory issue would it be necessary to decide whether the University's admissions program violated the Equal Protection Clause of the Fourteenth Amendment.

Section 601 of the Civil Rights Act of 1964 provides:

"No person in the United States shall, on the ground of race, color, or national origin, be excluded from participation in, be denied the benefits of, or be subjected to discrimination under any program or activity receiving Federal financial assistance."

The University, through its special admissions policy, excluded Bakke from participation in its program of medical education because of his race. The University also acknowledges that it was, and still is, receiving federal financial assistance. The plain language of the statute therefore requires affirmance of the judgment below. A different result cannot be justified unless that language misstates the actual intent of the Congress that enacted the statute. . . .

Title VI is an integral part of the far-reaching Civil Rights Act of 1964. No doubt, when this legislation was being debated, Congress was not directly concerned with the legality of "reverse discrimination" or "affirmative action" programs. Its attention was focused on the problem at hand, "the glaring . . . discrimination against Negroes which exists throughout our Nation," and, with respect to Title VI, the federal funding of segregated facilities. The genesis of the legislation, however, did not limit the breadth of the solution adopted. Just as Congress responded to the problem of employment discrimination by enacting a provision that protects all races, so too its answer to the problem of federal funding of segregated facilities stands as a broad prohibition against the exclusion of *any* individual from a federally funded program "on the ground of race." In the words of the House Report, Title VI stands for "the general principle that *no person* . . . be excluded from participation . . . on the ground of race, color or national origin under any program or activity receiving Federal financial assistance." This same broad view of Title VI and § 601 was echoed throughout the congressional debate and was stressed by every one of the major spokesmen for the Act.

. . .

The legislative history reinforces this reading. The only suggestion that § 601 would allow exclusion of nonminority applicants came from opponents of the legislation and then only by way of a discussion of the meaning of the word "discrimination." The opponents feared that the term "discrimination" would be read as mandating racial quotas and "racially balanced" colleges and universities, and they pressed for a specific definition of the term in order to avoid this possibility. In response, the proponents of the legislation gave repeated assurances that the Act would be "colorblind" in its application. Senator Humphrey, the Senate floor manager for the Act, expressed this position as follows:

"[T]he word 'discrimination' has been used in many a court case. What it really means in the bill is a distinction in treatment . . . given to different individuals because of their different race, religion or national origin. . . .

"The answer to this question [what was meant by 'discrimination'] is that if race is not a factor, we do not have to worry about discrimination because of race. . . . The Internal Revenue Code does not provide that colored people do not have to pay taxes, or that they can pay their taxes 6 months later than everybody else."

"[I]f we started to treat Americans as Americans, not as fat ones, short ones, tall ones, brown ones, green ones, yellow ones or white ones, but as Americans. If we did that we would not need to worry about discrimination."

. . .

In short, nothing in the legislative history justifies the conclusion that the broad language of § 601 should not be given its natural meaning. We are dealing with a distinct statutory prohibition, enacted at a particular time with particular concerns in mind; neither its language nor any prior interpretation suggests that its place in the Civil Rights Act, won after long debate, is simply that of a constitutional appendage. In unmistakable terms the Act prohibits the exclusion of individuals from federally funded programs because of their race. As succinctly phrased during the Senate debate, under Title VI it is not "permissible to say 'yes' to one person, but to say 'no' to another person, only because of the color of his skin."

. . .

The University's special admissions program violated Title VI of the Civil Rights Act of 1964 by excluding Bakke from the medical school because of his race. It is therefore our duty to affirm the judgment ordering Bakke admitted to the University.

Accordingly, I concur in the Court's judgment insofar as it affirms the judgment of the Supreme Court of California. To the extent that it purports to do anything else, I respectfully dissent.

Aftermath of Regents of University of California *v.* Bakke

Allan Bakke was admitted to the Davis Medical School in 1978 and graduated 4 years later. He now practices anesthesiology in Rochester, Minnesota.

After *Bakke* was announced, most civil rights organizations expressed fears that the Court's decision would discourage universities and graduate schools from maintaining effective affirmative action programs. The post-*Bakke* record in this regard is mixed. In 1978, about 6 percent of medical students were black. Ten years later the figure was still 6 percent. During the same period the figure for blacks in law schools also remained constant at 5 percent. The number of minority undergraduates has dropped slightly since the 1970s, however, and some critics attribute this decline to *Bakke's* "chilling effect" on colleges and universities which are afraid of being sued by rejected white applicants. At the same time, it is clear that institutions firmly committed to affirmative action have found in Justice Powell's opinion ample support for the concept in general, as well as quite specific guidelines about how affirmative action can be pursued without violating the Fourteenth Amendment.

Since *Bakke*, the focus of the national debate over affirmative action has shifted from education to employment. The Court's decisions in this area have continued to reflect the same ambivalence found in *Bakke*—support for the goals of affirmative action programs, but doubts about the constitutionality of some of the means adopted to achieve them. For example, in *Fullilove* v. *Klutznick* (1980) the Court upheld an act of Congress which provided that at least 10 percent of the federal funds to support local public works projects be earmarked for "minority business enterprises." But the Court divided on the reasons for its decision and issued no majority opinion, leaving the constitutional status of minority "set-aside" programs somewhat unclear.

The Court's most significant pronouncement on affirmative action since *Bakke* came in 1989. The city of Richmond, Virginia, intending to guarantee blacks and other minorities a larger share of the city's construction contracts, adopted an ordinance setting aside 30 percent of its municipal construction budget for minority-owned businesses. Similar set-aside programs were in use in 36 states and some 200 local governments. In *Richmond* v. *Croson Co.,* the Court held 6–3 that the city had not proved a level of past discrimination that would justify its set-aside rule. In her majority opinion Justice O'Connor ruled that since race-conscious programs were subject to "strict scrutiny," the government must show a compelling interest in redressing "identified discrimination." However the Court did not adopt the position urged on it by the Reagan Justice Department, that if such discrimination were identified the remedy must be limited specifically to those who had been its victims. As in the aftermath of *Bakke,* many state and city officials expressed confidence that their set-aside programs would not be affected by the *Richmond* decision because, unlike Richmond, they established "goals" rather than "quotas" for minority contracts. It remains to be seen, however, whether the "strict scrutiny" with which lower courts will now examine the justifications for set-aside quotas will result in others being found unconstitutional.

Metro Broadcasting, Inc. v. Federal Communications Commission

497 U.S.____(1990)

Under the Federal Communications Act of 1934 Congress assigned to the Commission (FCC) exclusive authority to grant licenses based on "public convenience, interest or necessity" to persons wishing to construct and operate radio and television stations in the United States. While minorities constitute one-fifth of the nation's population, they own only a small number of broadcasting stations. Among the 12,000 radio licenses and 1200 television licenses, 182 radio and 17 television stations are licensed to 110 companies owned by blacks. Hispanics and Asians have an even smaller presence in the industry. Recognizing this discrepancy, the FCC pledged to consider minority ownership as a factor in comparative proceedings for a new license and outlined a plan to increase minority opportunities to receive reassigned and transferred licenses through a so-called distress sale policy. This latter policy allowed a broadcaster whose license had been designated to a revocation or renewal hearing to assign the license to an FCC-approved minority enterprise. Both policies are challenged in the present case.

Several applicants including Metro Broadcasting and Rainbow Broadcasting were involved in a comparative proceeding to select a new UHF television station in the Orlando, Florida, metropolitan area. Ultimately the FCC awarded the application to Rainbow, asserting it was 90 percent Hispanic-owned whereas Metro had only one minority partner who owned 19.8 percent of the enterprise. Metro then challenged the award and the commission's policy of granting preference to minority owners.

Decided simultaneously was a companion case, *Astroline Communications Company* v. *Shurberg Broadcasting of Hartford* in which Shurberg challenged an FCC order approving a distress sale of its television license by Faith Center, Inc., to Astroline Communications, a minority-owned enterprise. Both Metro and Shurberg alleged a denial of equal protection of the laws.

Justice **Brennan** delivered the opinion of the Court.

The issue in these cases, consolidated for decision today, is whether certain minority preference policies of the Federal Communications Commission violate the equal protection component of the Fifth Amendment. The policies in question are (1) a program awarding an enhancement for minority ownership in comparative proceedings for new licenses, and (2) the minority "distress sale" program, which permits a limited category of existing radio and television broadcast stations to be transferred only to minority-controlled firms. We hold that these policies do not violate equal protection principles.

. . .

It is of overriding significance in these cases that the FCC's minority ownership programs

have been specifically approved—indeed, mandated—by Congress. In *Fullilove* v. *Klutznick*, Chief Justice Burger, writing for himself and two other Justices, observed that although "[a] program that employs racial or ethnic criteria . . . calls for close examination," when a program employing a benign racial classification is adopted by an administrative agency at the explicit direction of Congress, we are "bound to approach our task with appropriate deference to the Congress, a co-equal branch charged by the Constitution with the power to 'provide for the . . . general Welfare of the United States' and 'to enforce, by appropriate legislation,' the equal protection guarantees of the Fourteenth Amendment."

. . .

A majority of the Court in *Fullilove* did not apply strict scrutiny to the race-based classification at issue. Three Members inquired "whether the *objectives* of th[e] legislation are within the power of Congress" and "whether the limited use of racial and ethnic criteria . . . is a constitutionally permissible *means* for achieving the congressional objectives." Three other Members would have upheld benign racial classifications that "serve important governmental objectives and are substantially related to achievement of those objectives." We apply that standard today. We hold that benign race-conscious measures mandated by Congress—even if those measures are not "remedial" in the sense of being designed to compensate victims of past governmental or societal discrimination—are constitutionally permissible to the extent that they serve important governmental objectives within the power of Congress and are substantially related to achievement of those objectives.

Our decision last Term in *Richmond* v. *J. A. Croson Co.*, concerning a minority set-aside program adopted by a municipality, does not prescribe the level of scrutiny to be applied to a benign racial classification employed by Congress. As Justice Kennedy noted, the question of congressional action was not before the Court, and so *Croson* cannot be read to undermine our decision in *Fullilove*. In fact, much of the language and reasoning in *Croson* reaffirmed the lesson of *Fullilove* that race-conscious classifications adopted by Congress to address racial and ethnic discrimination are subject to a different standard than such classifications prescribed by state and local governments. For example, Justice O'Connor, joined by two other Members of this Court, noted that "Congress may identify and redress the effects of society-wide discrimination," and that Congress "need not make specific findings of discrimination to engage in race-conscious relief." Echoing *Fullilove's* emphasis on Congress as a national legislature that stands above factional politics, Justice Scalia argued that as a matter of "social reality and governmental theory," the Federal Government is unlikely to be captured by minority racial or ethnic groups and used as an instrument of discrimination. Justice Scalia explained that "[t]he struggle for racial justice has historically been a struggle by the national society against oppres-

sion in the individual States," because of the "heightened danger of oppression from political factions in small, rather than large, political units."

We hold that the FCC minority ownership policies pass muster under the test we announce today. First, we find that they serve the important governmental objective of broadcast diversity. Second, we conclude that they are substantially related to the achievement of that objective.

. . .

Congress found that "the effects of past inequities stemming from racial and ethnic discrimination have resulted in a severe underrepresentation of minorities in the media of mass communications." Congress and the Commission do not justify the minority ownership policies strictly as remedies for victims of this discrimination, however. Rather, Congress and the FCC have selected the minority ownership policies primarily to promote programming diversity, and they urge that such diversity is an important governmental objective that can serve as a constitutional basis for the preference policies. We agree.

We have long recognized that "[b]ecause of the scarcity of [electromagnetic] frequencies, the Government is permitted to put restraints on licensees in favor of others whose views should be expressed on this unique medium." *Red Lion Broadcasting Co.* v. *FCC*. The Government's role in distributing the limited number of broadcast licenses is not merely that of a "traffic officer," *National Broadcasting Co.* v. *United States;* rather, it is axiomatic that broadcasting may be regulated in light of the rights of the viewing and listening audience and that "the widest possible dissemination of information from diverse and antagonistic sources is essential to the welfare of the public." *Associated Press* v. *United States.* Safeguarding the public's right to receive a diversity of views and information over the airwaves is therefore an integral component of the FCC's mission. We have observed that "'the "public interest" standard necessarily invites reference to First Amendment principles,'" *FCC* v. *National Citizens Committee for Broadcasting,* quoting *Columbia Broadcasting System, Inc.* v.

Democratic National Committee, and that the Communications Act has designated broadcasters as "fiduciaries for the public." *FCC* v. *League of Women Voters of California.* "[T]he people as a whole retain their interest in free speech by radio [and other forms of broadcast] and their collective right to have the medium function consistently with the ends and purposes of the First Amendment," and "[i]t is the right of the viewers and listeners, not the right of broadcasters, which is paramount." "Congress may . . . seek to assure that the public receives through this medium a balanced presentation of information on issues of public importance that otherwise might not be addressed if control of the medium were left entirely in the hands of those who own and operate broadcasting stations."

Against this background, we conclude that the interest in enhancing broadcast diversity is, at the very least, an important governmental objective and is therefore a sufficient basis for the Commission's minority ownership policies. Just as a "diverse student body" contributing to a "'robust exchange of ideas'" is a "constitutionally permissible goal" on which a race-conscious university admissions program may be predicated, the diversity of views and information on the airwaves serves important First Amendment values. The benefits of such diversity are not limited to the members of minority groups who gain access to the broadcasting industry by virtue of the ownership policies; rather, the benefits redound to all members of the viewing and listening audience. As Congress found, "the American public will benefit by having access to a wider diversity of information sources."

. . .

We also find that the minority ownership policies are substantially related to the achievement of the Government's interest. One component of this inquiry concerns the relationship between expanded minority ownership and greater broadcast diversity; both the FCC and Congress have determined that such a relationship exists. Although we do not " 'defer' to the judgment of the Congress and the Commission on a constitutional question," and would not "hesitate to invoke the Constitution should we determine that the Commission has not fulfilled

its task with appropriate sensitivity" to equal protection principles, we must pay close attention to the expertise of the Commission and the factfinding of Congress when analyzing the nexus between minority ownership and programming diversity. With respect to this "complex" empirical question, we are required to give "great weight to the decisions of Congress and the experience of the Commission."

. . .

The FCC has determined that increased minority participation in broadcasting promotes programming diversity. As the Commission observed in its 1978 Statement of Policy on Minority Ownership of Broadcasting Facilities, "ownership of broadcasting facilities by minorities is [a] significant way of fostering the inclusion of minority views in the area of programming" and "[f]ull minority participation in the ownership and management of broadcast facilities results in a more diverse selection of programming." Four years later, the FCC explained that it had taken "steps to enhance the ownership and participation of minorities in the media" in order to "increas[e] the diversity in the control of the media and thus diversity in the selection of available programming, benefitting the public and serving the principle of the First Amendment." ("[T]here is a critical underrepresentation of minorities in broadcast ownership, and full minority participation in the ownership and management of broadcast facilities is essential to realize the fundamental goals of programming diversity and diversification of ownership'") (citation omitted). The FCC's conclusion that there is an empirical nexus between minority ownership and broadcasting diversity is a product of its expertise, and we accord its judgment deference.

Furthermore, the FCC's reasoning with respect to the minority ownership policies is consistent with longstanding practice under the Communications Act. From its inception, public regulation of broadcasting has been premised on the assumption that diversification of ownership will broaden the range of programming available to the broadcast audience. Thus, "it is upon *ownership* that public policy places primary reliance with respect to diversification of content, and that historically has proved to be significantly influential with respect to editorial comment and the presentation of news." The Commission has never relied on the market alone to ensure that the needs of the audience are met. Indeed, one of the FCC's elementary regulatory assumptions is that broadcast content is not purely market-driven; if it were, there would be little need for consideration in licensing decisions of such factors as integration of ownership and management, local residence, and civic participation. In this vein, the FCC has compared minority preferences to local residence and other integration credits:

"[B]oth local residence and minority ownership are fundamental considerations in our licensing scheme. Both policies complement our concern with diversification of control of broadcast ownership. Moreover, similar assumptions underlie both policies. We award enhancement credit for local residence because . . . [i]t is expected that [an] increased knowledge of the community of license will be reflected in a station's programming. Likewise, credit for minority ownership and participation is awarded in a comparative proceeding [because] 'minority ownership is likely to increase diversity of content, especially of opinion and viewpoint.'"

. . .

Congress also has made clear its view that the minority ownership policies advance the goal of diverse programming. In recent years, Congress has specifically required the Commission, through appropriations legislation, to maintain the minority ownership policies without alteration. We would be remiss, however, if we ignored the long history of congressional support for those policies prior to the passage of the appropriations acts because, for the past two decades, Congress has consistently recognized the barriers encountered by minorities in entering the broadcast industry and has expressed emphatic support for the Commission's attempts to promote programming diversity by increasing minority ownership. Limiting our analysis to the immediate legislative history of the appropriations acts in question "would erect an artificial barrier to [a] full understanding of the legislative

process." The "special attribute [of Congress] as a legislative body lies in its broader mission to investigate and consider all facts and opinions that may be relevant to the resolution of an issue. One appropriate source is the information and expertise that Congress acquires in the consideration and enactment of earlier legislation. After Congress has legislated repeatedly in an area of national concern, its Members gain experience that may reduce the need for fresh hearings or prolonged debate when Congress again considers action in that area."

. . .

The judgment that there is a link between expanded minority ownership and broadcast diversity does not rest on impermissible stereotyping. Congressional policy does not assume that in every case minority ownership and management will lead to more minority-oriented programming or to the expression of a discrete "minority viewpoint" on the airwaves. Neither does it pretend that all programming that appeals to minority audiences can be labeled "minority programming" or that programming that might be described as "minority" does not appeal to nonminorities. Rather, both Congress and the FCC maintain simply that expanded minority ownership of broadcast outlets will, in the aggregate, result in greater broadcast diversity. A broadcasting industry with representative minority participation will produce more variation and diversity than will one whose ownership is drawn from a single racially and ethnically homogeneous group. The predictive judgment about the overall result of minority entry into broadcasting is not a rigid assumption about how minority owners will behave in every case but rather is akin to Justice Powell's conclusion in *Bakke* that greater admission of minorities would contribute, on average, "to the 'robust exchange of ideas.'" To be sure, there is no ironclad guarantee that each minority owner will contribute to diversity. But neither was there an assurance in *Bakke* that minority students would interact with nonminority students or that the particular minority students admitted would have typical or distinct "minority" viewpoints.

Although all station owners are guided to some extent by market demand in their programming decisions, Congress and the Commission have determined that there may be important differences between the broadcasting practices of minority owners and those of their nonminority counterparts. This judgment—and the conclusion that there is a nexus between minority ownership and broadcasting diversity—is corroborated by a host of empirical evidence. Evidence suggests that an owner's minority status influences the selection of topics for news coverage and the presentation of editorial viewpoint, especially on matters of particular concern to minorities. "[M]inority ownership does appear to have specific impact on the presentation of minority images in local news," inasmuch as minority-owned stations tend to devote more news time to topics of minority interest and to avoid racial and ethnic stereotypes in portraying minorities. In addition, studies show that a minority owner is more likely to employ minorities in managerial and other important roles where they can have an impact on station policies. If the FCC's equal employment policies "ensure that . . . licensees' programming fairly reflects the tastes and viewpoints of minority groups," it is difficult to deny that minority-owned stations that follow such employment policies on their own will also contribute to diversity. While we are under no illusion that members of a particular minority group share some cohesive, collective viewpoint, we believe it a legitimate inference for Congress and the Commission to draw that as more minorities gain ownership and policymaking roles in the media, varying perspectives will be more fairly represented on the airwaves. The policies are thus a product of "'analysis'" rather than a "'stereotyped reaction'" based on "'[h]abit.'"

Our cases demonstrate that the reasoning employed by the Commission and Congress is permissible. We have recognized, for example, that the fair cross-section requirement of the Sixth Amendment forbids the exclusion of groups on the basis of such characteristics as race and gender from a jury venire because "[w]ithout that requirement, the State could draw up jury lists in such manner as to produce a pool of prospective jurors disproportionately ill disposed towards one or all classes of defendants, and thus more likely to yield petit juries with similar disposition." It is a small step from this logic to the conclusion that including minorities in the electromagnetic spectrum will be more likely to produce a "fair cross section" of diverse content. In addition, many of our voting rights cases operate on the assumption that minorities have particular viewpoints and interests worthy of protection. We have held, for example, that in safeguarding the "'effective exercise of the electoral franchise'" by racial minorities, "[t]he permissible use of racial criteria is not confined to eliminating the effects of past discriminatory districting or apportionment." Rather, a State subject to § 5 of the Voting Rights Act of 1965, 79 Stat. 439, as amended, 42 U. S. C. § 1973c, may "deliberately creat[e] or preserv[e] black majorities in particular districts in order to ensure that its reapportionment plan complies with § 5"; "neither the Fourteenth nor the Fifteenth Amendment mandates any *per se* rule against using racial factors in districting and apportionment."

. . .

In short, the Commission established minority ownership preferences only after long experience demonstrated that race-neutral means could not produce adequate broadcasting diversity. The FCC did not act precipitately in devising the programs we uphold today; to the contrary, the Commission undertook thorough evaluations of its policies *three* times—in 1960, 1971, and 1978—before adopting the minority ownership programs. In endorsing the minority ownership preferences, Congress agreed with the Commission's assessment that race-neutral alternatives had failed to achieve the necessary programming diversity.

. . .

The minority ownership policies, furthermore, are aimed directly at the barriers that minorities face in entering the broadcasting industry. The Commission's Task Force identified as key factors hampering the growth of minority ownership a lack of adequate financing, paucity of information regarding license availability, and broadcast inexperience. The Commission assigned a preference to minority status in the comparative licensing proceeding, reasoning that such an enhancement might help to compensate for a dearth of broadcasting experience. Most license acquisitions, however, are by necessity purchases of existing stations, because only a limited number of new stations are available, and those are often in less desirable markets or on less profitable portions of spectrum, such as the UHF band. Congress and the FCC therefore found a need for the minority distress sale policy, which helps to overcome the problem of inadequate access to capital by lowering the sale price and the problem of lack of information by providing existing licensees with an incentive to seek out minority buyers. The Commission's choice of minority ownership policies thus addressed the very factors it had isolated as being responsible for minority underrepresentation in the broadcast industry.

The minority ownership policies are "appropriately limited in extent and duration, and subject to reassessment and reevaluation by the Congress prior to any extension or re-enactment." Although it has underscored emphatically its support for the minority ownership policies, Congress has manifested that support through a series of appropriations acts of finite duration, thereby ensuring future reevaluations of the need for the minority ownership program as the number of minority broadcasters increases. In addition, Congress has continued to hold hearings on the subject of minority ownership. The FCC has noted with respect to the minority preferences contained in the lottery statute, that Congress instructed the Commission to "report annually on the effect of the preference system and whether it is serving the purposes intended. Congress will be able to further tailor the program based on that information, and may eliminate the preferences when appropriate." Furthermore, there is provision for administrative and judicial review of all Commission decisions, which guarantees both that the minority ownership policies are applied correctly in individual cases, and that there will be frequent opportunities to revisit the merits of those policies. Congress and the Commission have adopted a policy of minority ownership not as an end in itself, but rather as a means of achieving greater programming diversity. Such a goal carries its own natural limit, for there will be no need for further minority preferences once sufficient diversity has been achieved. The FCC's plan, like the Harvard admissions program discussed in *Bakke*, contains the seed of its own termination.

Finally, we do not believe that the minority ownership policies at issue impose impermissible burdens on nonminorities. Although the nonminority challengers in these cases concede that they have not suffered the loss of an already-awarded broadcast license, they claim that they have been handicapped in their ability to obtain one in the first instance. But just as we have determined that "[a]s part of this Nation's dedication to eradicating racial discrimination, innocent persons may be called upon to bear some of the burden of the remedy," we similarly find that a congressionally mandated benign race-conscious program that is substantially related to the achievement of an important governmental interest is consistent with equal protection principles so long as it does not impose *undue* burdens on nonminorities.

. . .

The Commission's minority ownership policies bear the imprimatur of longstanding congressional support and direction and are substantially related to the achievement of the important governmental objective of broadcast diversity. The judgment in No. 89–453 is affirmed, the judgment in No. 89–700 is reversed, and the cases are remanded for proceedings consistent with this opinion.

It is so ordered.

Justice **Stevens,** concurring.

Today the Court squarely rejects the proposition that a governmental decision that rests on a racial classification is never permissible except as a remedy for a past wrong. I endorse this focus on the future benefit, rather than the remedial justification, of such decisions.

I remain convinced, of course, that racial or ethnic characteristics provide a relevant basis for disparate treatment only in extremely rare situations and that it is therefore "especially important that the reasons for any such classification be clearly identified and unquestionably legitimate." *Fullilove* v. *Klutznick.*

The Court's opinion explains how both elements of that standard are satisfied. Specifically, the reason for the classification—the recognized interest in broadcast diversity—is clearly identified and does not imply any judgment concerning the abilities of owners of different races or the merits of different kinds of programming. Neither the favored nor the disfavored class is stigmatized in any way. In addition, the Court demonstrates that this case falls within the extremely narrow category of governmental decisions for which racial or ethnic heritage may provide a rational basis for differential treatment. The public interest in broadcast diversity—like the interest in an integrated police force, diversity in the composition of a public school faculty or diversity in the student body of a professional school—is in my view unquestionably legitimate.

Therefore, I join both the opinion and the judgment of the Court.

Aftermath of Metro Broadcasting, Inc. *v.* Federal Communications Commission

It is too soon to assess the impact of the *Metro Broadcasting* decision on FCC licensing practices, or on other instances of government decision making based on racial classifications. However, it is worth noting that the author of the majority opinion, Justice William Brennan, retired from the Supreme Court shortly after the 5–4 decision was announced. His successor, Justice David Souter, is widely assumed to be more politically conservative than Brennan, and thus it is possible that the Court may soon reconsider its decision upholding the FCC's minority ownership preference policy.

Reed v. *Reed*

404 U.S. 71 (1971)

Until very recently American law has reflected the paternalistic cultural norm that defines a man's place as the world and a woman's place as the home. In the nineteenth century women were prohibited by law from voting, entering certain professions, and even buying and selling property. In the early twentieth century, as economic necessity brought large numbers of women into the workplace, legal paternalism took a different form, as special "protective" legislation was enacted to regulate working conditions for women in some industries.

Gender-based statutes began to come under challenge soon after the Fourteenth Amendment was ratified, but court decisions, including those of the Supreme Court, consistently upheld both the laws and the sexual stereotypes on which they were based. For example, in *Bradwell* v. *Illinois* (1873), a woman who had been certified by examiners as qualified to practice law was denied admission to the bar by the state supreme court. The United States Supreme Court found no constitutional defect in such a decision since, as Justice Bradley put it in his concurrence, "the paramount destiny and mission of women are to fulfill the noble and benign offices of wife and mother. This is the law of the Creator."

Bradwell was followed by an unbroken string of decisions in which the Court upheld state laws that either discriminated against women or enacted special protections for them. Two years after *Bradwell* the Court ruled that a Missouri law pro-

hibiting women from voting did not violate the privileges and immunities clause of the Fourteenth Amendment.

In 1908, in *Muller* v. *Oregon*, the Court upheld against a due process challenge a state law restricting women from working more than 10 hours a day, noting that longer hours would threaten the well-being of women as wives and mothers. In 1948 the Court held constitutional a Michigan statute prohibiting a woman from working as a bartender unless she was the wife or daughter of a male bar owner. Justice Frankfurter's majority opinion contained joking references to "sprightly and ribald" Shakespearean alewives practicing a "historic calling," but held that given contemporary concerns for women's welfare, the Michigan law was not unreasonable and hence did not violate the equal protection clause (*Goesaert* v. *Cleary*). The Court once again employed the reasonableness standard in 1961 when it rejected an equal protection challenge to a Florida law which provided that no woman could serve on a state jury unless she visited the courthouse personally and asked to be put on the jury list. Justice Harlan concluded that since "a woman is still regarded as the center of home and family life," it was not unreasonable for a state to relieve her from jury duty "unless she herself determines that such service is consistent with her own special responsibilities" (*Hoyt* v. *Florida*).

Such was the state of equal protection law when the Supreme Court heard the case of *Reed* v. *Reed* in 1971. After the death of an adopted son, Sally Reed, who was separated from her husband Cecil Reed, petitioned the county probate court to be named administratrix of her son's estate. Cecil Reed then filed a competing petition seeking appointment as administrator. Under the Idaho Probate Code, males were to be given preference over females when two persons of equal entitlement applied for appointment as administrator of an estate. Under the terms of that law, Cecil Reed was then appointed administrator. That decision was overturned in state district court but reinstated by the state supreme court.

Mr. Chief Justice **Burger** delivered the opinion of the Court.

. . .

Section 15–312 designates the persons who are entitled to administer the estate of one who dies intestate. In making these designations, that section lists 11 classes of persons who are so entitled and provides, in substance, that the order in which those classes are listed in the section shall be determinative of the relative rights of competing applicants for letters of administration. One of the 11 classes so enumerated is "[t]he father or mother" of the person dying intestate. Under this section, then, appellant and appellee, being members of the same entitlement class, would seem to have been equally entitled to administer their son's estate. Section 15–314 provides, however, that "[o]f several persons claiming and equally entitled [under § 15–312] to administer, males must be preferred to females, and relatives of the whole to those of the half blood."

In issuing its order, the probate court implicitly recognized the equality of entitlement of the two applicants under § 15–312 and noted that neither of the applicants was under any legal disability; the court ruled, however, that appellee, being a male, was to be preferred to the female appellant "by reason of Section 15–314 of the Idaho Code." In stating this conclusion, the probate judge gave no indication that he had attempted to determine the relative capabilities of the competing applicants to perform the functions incident to the administration of an estate. It seems clear the probate judge considered himself bound by statute to give preference to the male candidate over the female, each being otherwise "equally entitled."

. . .

Idaho does not, of course, deny letters of administration to women altogether. Indeed, under § 15–312, a woman whose spouse dies intestate has a preference over a son, father, brother, or any other male relative of the decedent. Moreover, we can judicially notice that in this country, presumably due to the greater longevity of women, a large proportion of estates, both intestate and under wills of decedents, are administered by surviving widows.

Section 15–314 is restricted in its operation to those situations where competing applications for letters of administration have been filed by both male and female members of the same entitlement class established by § 15–312. In such situations, § 15–314 provides that different treatment be accorded to the applicants on the basis of their sex; it thus establishes a classification subject to scrutiny under the Equal Protection Clause.

In applying that clause, this Court has consistently recognized that the Fourteenth Amendment does not deny to States the power to treat different classes of persons in different ways. The Equal Protection Clause of that Amendment does, however, deny to States the power to legislate that different treatment be accorded to persons placed by a statute into different classes on the basis of criteria wholly unrelated to the objective of that statute. A classification "must be reasonable, not arbitrary, and must rest upon some ground of difference having a fair and substantial relation to the object of the legislation, so that all persons similarly circumstanced shall be treated alike." The question presented by this case, then, is whether a difference in the sex of competing applicants for letters of administration bears a rational relationship to a state objective that is sought to be advanced by the operation of §§ 15–312 and 15–314.

In upholding the latter section, the Idaho Supreme Court concluded that its objective was to eliminate one area of controversy when two or more persons, equally entitled under § 15–312, seek letters of administration and there-by present the probate court "with the issue of which one should be named." The court also concluded that where such persons are not of the same sex, the elimination of females from consideration "is neither an illogical nor arbitrary method devised by the legislature to resolve an issue that would otherwise require a hearing as to the relative merits . . . of the two or more petitioning relatives. . . ."

Clearly the objective of reducing the workload on probate courts by eliminating one class of contests is not without some legitimacy. The crucial question, however, is whether § 15–314 advances that objective in a manner consistent with the command of the Equal Protection Clause. We hold that it does not. To give a mandatory preference to members of either sex over members of the other, merely to accomplish the elimination of hearings on the merits, is to make the very kind of arbitrary legislative choice forbidden by the Equal Protection Clause of the Fourteenth Amendment; and whatever may be said as to the positive values of avoiding intrafamily controversy, the choice in this context may not lawfully be mandated solely on the basis of sex.

We note finally that if § 15–314 is viewed merely as a modifying appendage to § 15–312 and as aimed at the same objective, its constitutionality is not thereby saved. The objective of § 15–312 clearly is to establish degrees of entitlement of various classes of persons in accordance with their varying degrees and kinds of relationship to the intestate. Regardless of their sex, persons within any one of the enumerated classes of that section are similarly situated with respect to that objective. By providing dissimilar treatment for men and women who are thus similarly situated, the challenged section violates the Equal Protection Clause.

. . .

Aftermath of Reed *v.* Reed

Despite its brevity and absence of rhetorical flourishes, *Reed* was a revolutionary decision because it marked the first time the Court had ruled a gender-based law unconstitutional on equal protection grounds. A century of deference to state legislatures was apparently at an end. However, because the relationship between the Idaho law and the stated purpose of lessening the probate court's work load was so attenuated, the Supreme Court spent little time in *Reed* discussing the standard that it intended to use in the future to evaluate such laws.

Frontiero v. Richardson

411 U.S. 677 (1973)

An important question left unanswered by *Reed* v. *Reed* in 1971 was whether the Supreme Court would henceforth treat a legal distinction based on gender as a "suspect classification" similar to one based on race. If so, such laws would be subject to the Court's "strict scrutiny," requiring a showing by the state that they were necessary to achieve a compelling governmental objective. This is a considerably more demanding standard than the "rational basis" test that courts have traditionally applied to most government classifications. Although an answer was not long in coming, when it arrived it was hardly definitive. Indeed, the inability of the Supreme Court to settle on a single, clearly articulated test for gender-based classifications, a problem first apparent in *Frontiero* v. *Richardson* in 1973, persists to this day.

This case involved a challenge to a federal law that treated males and females differently in determining the benefits available to dependents of military personnel. Sharron Frontiero was an Air Force lieutenant and her husband Joseph was a veteran attending college full time on the GI bill. Under the law, male military personnel automatically received an extra housing allowance and medical benefits if they were married. However, a married servicewoman received those benefits only if she could prove that she paid more than one-half of her husband's living costs, a standard that Sharron Frontiero did not meet. The Frontieros based their challenge not on the equal protection clause of the Fourteenth Amendment, which applies only to the states, but on the Fifth Amendment's due process clause, which the Court had held in 1954 to embrace the principle of equal protection (*Bolling* v. *Sharpe*). The constitutionality of the law was upheld by a divided three-judge federal district court. The Frontieros then appealed to the Supreme Court.

Mr. Justice **Brennan** announced the judgment of the Court and an opinion in which Mr. Justice **Douglas,** Mr. Justice **White,** and Mr. Justice **Marshall** join.

. . .

At the outset, appellants contend that classifications based upon sex, like classifications based upon race, alienage, and national origin, are inherently suspect and must therefore be subjected to close judicial scrutiny. We agree and, indeed, find at least implicit support for such an approach in our unanimous decision only last Term in *Reed* v. *Reed* (1971).

In *Reed*, the Court considered the constitutionality of an Idaho statute providing that, when two individuals are otherwise equally entitled to appointment as administrator of an estate, the male applicant must be preferred to the female. Appellant, the mother of the deceased, and appellee, the father, filed competing petitions for appointment as administrator of their son's estate. Since the parties, as parents of the deceased, were members of the same entitlement class, the statutory preference was invoked and the father's petition was therefore granted. Appellant claimed that this statute, by giving a mandatory preference to males over females without regard to their individual qualifications, violated the Equal Protection Clause of the Fourteenth Amendment.

The Court noted that the Idaho statute "provides that different treatment be accorded to the applicants on the basis of their sex; it thus establishes a classification subject to scrutiny under the Equal Protection Clause." Under "traditional" equal protection analysis, a legislative classification must be sustained unless it is "patently arbitrary" and bears no rational relationship to a legitimate governmental interest.

In an effort to meet this standard, appellee contended that the statutory scheme was a reasonable measure designed to reduce the workload on probate courts by eliminating one class of contests. Moreover, appellee argued that the mandatory preference for male applicants was in itself reasonable since "men [are] as a rule more conversant with business affairs than . . . women." Indeed, appellee maintained that "it is a matter of common knowledge, that women still are not engaged in politics, the professions, business or industry to the extent that men are." And the Idaho Supreme Court, in upholding the constitutionality of this statute, suggested that the Idaho Legislature might reasonably have "concluded that in general men are better qualified to act as an administrator than are women."

Despite these contentions, however, the Court held the statutory preference for male applicants unconstitutional. In reaching this result, the Court implicitly rejected appellee's apparently rational explanation of the statutory scheme, and concluded that, by ignoring the individual qualifications of particular applicants, the challenged statute provided "dissimilar treatment for men and women who are . . . similarly situated." The Court therefore held that, even though the State's interest in achieving administrative efficiency "is not without some legitimacy," "[t]o give a mandatory preference to members of either sex over members of the other, merely to accomplish the elimination of hearings on the merits, is to make the very kind of arbitrary legislative choice forbidden by the [Constitution]. . . ." This departure from "traditional" rational-basis analysis with respect to sex-based classifications is clearly justified.

There can be no doubt that our Nation has had a long and unfortunate history of sex discrimination. Traditionally, such discrimination was rationalized by an attitude of "romantic paternalism" which, in practical effect, put women, not on a pedestal, but in a cage. Indeed, this paternalistic attitude became so firmly rooted in our national consciousness that, 100 years ago, a distinguished Member of this Court was able to proclaim:

"Man is, or should be, woman's protector and defender. The natural and proper timidity and delicacy which belongs to the female sex evidently unfits it for many of the occupations of civil life. The constitution of the family organization, which is founded in the divine ordinance, as well as in the nature of things, indicates the domestic sphere as that which properly belongs to the domain and functions of womanhood. The harmony, not to say identity, of interests and views which belong, or should belong, to the family institution is repugnant to the idea of a woman adopting a distinct and independent career from that of her husband. . . .

". . . The paramount destiny and mission of woman are to fulfil the noble and benign offices of wife and mother. This is the law of the Creator." *Bradwell* v. *State* (1873) (Bradley, J., concurring).

As a result of notions such as these, our statute books gradually became laden with gross, stereotyped distinctions between the sexes and, indeed, throughout much of the 19th century the position of women in our society was, in many respects, comparable to that of blacks under the pre-Civil War slave codes. Neither slaves nor women could hold office, serve on juries, or bring suit in their own names, and married women traditionally were denied the legal capacity to hold or convey property or to serve as legal guardians of their own children. And although blacks were guaranteed the right to vote in 1870, women were denied even that right—which is itself "preservative of other basic civil and political rights"—until adoption of the Nineteenth Amendment half a century later.

It is true, of course, that the position of

women in America has improved markedly in recent decades. Nevertheless, it can hardly be doubted that, in part because of the high visibility of the sex characteristic, women still face pervasive, although at times more subtle, discrimination in our educational institutions, in the job market and, perhaps most conspicuously, in the political arena.

Moreover, since sex, like race and national origin, is an immutable characteristic determined solely by the accident of birth, the imposition of special disabilities upon the members of a particular sex because of their sex would seem to violate "the basic concept of our system that legal burdens should bear some relationship to individual responsibility. . . ." And what differentiates sex from such nonsuspect statuses as intelligence or physical disability, and aligns it with the recognized suspect criteria, is that the sex characteristic frequently bears no relation to ability to perform or contribute to society. As a result, statutory distinctions between the sexes often have the effect of invidiously relegating the entire class of females to inferior legal status without regard to the actual capabilities of its individual members.

We might also note that, over the past decade, Congress has itself manifested an increasing sensitivity to sex-based classifications. In Tit. VII of the Civil Rights Act of 1964, for example, Congress expressly declared that no employer, labor union, or other organization subject to the provisions of the Act shall discriminate against any individual on the basis of "race, color, religion, *sex*, or national origin." Similarly, the Equal Pay Act of 1963 provides that no employer covered by the Act "shall discriminate . . . between employees on the basis of *sex*." And § 1 of the Equal Rights Amendment, passed by Congress on March 22, 1972, and submitted to the legislatures of the States for ratification, declares that "[e]quality of rights under the law shall not be denied or abridged by the United States or by any State on account of sex." Thus, Congress itself has concluded that classifications based upon sex are inherently invidious, and this conclusion of a coequal branch of Government is not without significance to the question presently under consideration.

With these considerations in mind, we can only conclude that classifications based upon sex, like classifications based upon race, alienage, or national origin, are inherently suspect, and must therefore be subjected to strict judicial scrutiny. Applying the analysis mandated by that stricter standard of review, it is clear that the statutory scheme now before us is constitutionally invalid.

. . .

The sole basis of the classification established in the challenged statutes is the sex of the individuals involved. Thus, under 37 U. S. C. §§ 401, 403, and 10 U. S. C. §§ 1072, 1076, a female member of the uniformed services seeking to obtain housing and medical benefits for her spouse must prove his dependency in fact, whereas no such burden is imposed upon male members. In addition, the statutes operate so as to deny benefits to a female member, such as appellant Sharron Frontiero, who provides less than one-half of her spouse's support, while at the same time granting such benefits to a male member who likewise provides less than one-half of his spouse's support. Thus, to this extent at least, it may fairly be said that these statutes command "dissimilar treatment for men and women who are . . . similarly situated."

Moreover, the Government concedes that the differential treatment accorded men and women under these statutes serves no purpose other than mere "administrative convenience." In essence, the Government maintains that, as an empirical matter, wives in our society frequently are dependent upon their husbands, while husbands rarely are dependent upon their wives. Thus, the Government argues that Congress might reasonably have concluded that it would be both cheaper and easier simply conclusively to presume that wives of male members are financially dependent upon their husbands, while burdening female members with the task of establishing dependency in fact.

The Government offers no concrete evidence, however, tending to support its view that such differential treatment in fact saves the Government any money. In order to satisfy the demands of strict judicial scrutiny, the Government must demonstrate, for example, that it is actually cheaper to grant increased benefits with respect to *all* male members, than it is to determine which male members are in fact entitled to such benefits and to grant increased benefits only to those members whose wives actually meet the dependency requirement. Here, however, there is substantial evidence that, if put to the test, many of the wives of male members would fail to qualify for benefits. And in light of the fact that the dependency determination with respect to the husbands of female members is presently made solely on the basis of affidavits, rather than through the more costly hearing process, the Government's explanation of the statutory scheme is, to say the least, questionable.

In any case, our prior decisions make clear that, although efficacious administration of governmental programs is not without some importance, "the Constitution recognizes higher values than speed and efficiency." And when we enter the realm of "strict judicial scrutiny," there can be no doubt that "administrative convenience" is not a shibboleth, the mere recitation of which dictates constitutionality. On the contrary, any statutory scheme which draws a sharp line between the sexes, *solely* for the purpose of achieving administrative convenience, necessarily commands "dissimilar treatment for men and women who are . . . similarly situated," and therefore involves the "very kind of arbitrary legislative choice forbidden by the [Constitution]. . . ." We therefore conclude that, by according differential treatment to male and female members of the uniformed services for the sole purpose of achieving administrative convenience, the challenged statutes violate the Due Process Clause of the Fifth Amendment insofar as they require a female member to prove the dependency of her husband.

Reversed.

Mr. Justice **Powell,** with whom The **Chief Justice** and Mr. Justice **Blackmun** join, concurring in the judgment.

I agree that the challenged statutes constitute an unconstitutional discrimination against servicewomen in violation of the Due Process Clause of the Fifth Amendment, but I cannot join the opinion of Mr. Justice Brennan, which would hold that all classifications based upon sex, "like classifications based upon race, alienage, and national origin," are "inherently suspect and must therefore be subjected to close judicial scrutiny." It is unnecessary for the Court in this case to characterize sex as a suspect classification, with all of the far-reaching implications of such a holding. *Reed* v. *Reed* (1971), which abundantly supports our decision today, did not add sex to the narrowly limited group of classifications which are inherently suspect. In my view, we can and should decide this case on the authority of *Reed* and reserve for the future any expansion of its rationale.

There is another, and I find compelling, reason for deferring a general categorizing of sex classifications as invoking the strictest test of judicial scrutiny. The Equal Rights Amendment, which if adopted will resolve the substance of this precise question, has been approved by the Congress and submitted for ratification by the States. If this Amendment is duly adopted, it will represent the will of the people accomplished in the manner prescribed by the Constitution. By acting prematurely and unnecessarily, as I view it, the Court has assumed a decisional responsibility at the very time when state legislatures, functioning within the traditional democratic process, are debating the proposed Amendment. It seems to me that this reaching out to preempt by judicial action a major political decision which is currently in process of resolution does not reflect appropriate respect for duly prescribed legislative processes.

There are times when this Court, under our system, cannot avoid a constitutional decision on issues which normally should be resolved by the elected representatives of the people. But democratic institutions are weakened, and confidence in the restraint of the Court is impaired, when we appear unnecessarily to decide sensitive issues of broad social and political importance at the very time they are under consideration within the prescribed constitutional processes.

Aftermath of Frontiero v. Richardson

In his concurring opinion in *Frontiero*, Justice Powell explained that his unwillingness to apply "strict scrutiny" to gender classifications was based partly on the fact that the Equal Rights Amendment, which presumably would give gender the same constitutional status as race, was still in the process of ratification by the states. The amendment had been passed by Congress and submitted to the states the previous year. Its text read as follows: "Equality of rights under the law shall not be denied or abridged by the United States or by any state on account of sex. The Congress shall have the power to enforce by appropriate legislation, the provisions of this article. The amendment shall take effect two years after the date of ratification." Since 30 of the required 38 states had already approved the amendment by the end of 1973, when *Frontiero* was decided, there was every reason to believe that the Equal Rights Amendment would soon be part of the Constitution.

It was not to be. After 1973, only five more states approved the proposed amendment, despite a 3-year extension in 1979 of the original 7-year ratification period. The reasons for the ERA's defeat have been extensively analyzed. Although the proposal had broad popular support, its opponents were effective in mobilizing fears that the amendment would remove some of the "privileges" women now enjoy—exemption from the military draft was one frequently cited—without providing any substantial benefits that could not be obtained through specific legislation or through litigation under the Fourteenth Amendment. At bottom, ERA advocates were never able to dispel the perception in some quarters that their purpose was to negate constitutionally the biological differences between men and women.

Using various combinations of tests—strict scrutiny (is the law necessary to a compelling objective?); intermediate scrutiny (is the law substantially related to important governmental interests?); and even the traditional rational basis approach (is the law reasonably related to a legitimate governmental objective?)—the Supreme Court during the 1970s and 1980s struck down several gender-conscious laws that clearly worked to the disadvantage of women. In 1975 a Utah law requiring a parent to support a son until age 21 but a daughter only until she became 18 was declared unconstitutional (*Stanton* v. *Stanton*), and in *Kirchberg* v. *Feenstra* (1981) a statute allowing a husband unilaterally to dispose of property jointly owned with his wife met the same fate. But the Court has accorded much gentler treatment to laws where the discriminatory impact against women was only incidental to their intended purposes. A state law excluding disability benefits for pregnancy and childbirth (*Geduldig* v. *Aiello*, 1974) and a statute giving veterans absolute preference in public employment (*Personnel Administrator of Massachusetts* v. *Feeney*, 1975) were both upheld when the Court determined from their legislative histories that they had clear purposes other than gender classifications.

Both *Reed* v. *Reed* and *Frontiero* v. *Richardson* involved statutes that created disadvantages for women relative to men. Another category of equal protection cases involves laws that have a prejudicial impact against men. Like Allan Bakke and other whites who have challenged affirmative action programs, men have charged that such laws discriminate unconstitutionally against them. And like Allan Bakke, some of these male plaintiffs have found the Supreme Court willing to use the Fourteenth Amendment to vindicate their claims. In *Weinberger* v.

Wiesenfeld (1975) the Court unanimously overturned a provision of the Social Security Act that provided benefits to the mother of a deceased wage-earner's child, but not to the father. Although the government claimed that the law had a compensatory purpose—"to offset the adverse economic situation of women"—the Court found no such purpose reflected in the law's legislative history and declared it unconstitutional. In the same year, however, the Court upheld a naval regulation permitting female officers more time in rank than male officers before being discharged for nonpromotion, because the rule was intended to compensate for earlier discrimination suffered by women in the military (*Schlesinger* v. *Ballard*).

In 1976, in *Craig* v. *Boren*, the Court reviewed an Oklahoma law that permitted females to purchase 3.2 percent beer at age 18, but prohibited its sale to males until age 21. A suit had been filed against the law by an underage male and a licensed vendor of alcohol. The Court held the law unconstitutional, finding that the state had not established "that sex represents a legitimate, accurate proxy for the regulation of drinking and driving." As in *Frontiero* and most of the cases that followed it, the majority in *Craig* was unable to agree on a single standard for evaluating gender-based statutes. Justices Brennan, Marshall, White, and Blackmun endorsed the strict scrutiny test, Justice Powell preferred intermediate scrutiny, and Justice Stevens expressed dissatisfaction with the multitiered approach to equal protection analysis. Post-*Craig* cases have brought mixed results. In two 1981 decisions the Court employed a combination of intermediate scrutiny and rational basis to find laws constitutional despite their prejudicial impact on men. In *Michael M.* v. *Superior Court* the majority upheld a law punishing males but not females for statutory rape, finding the law's stated purpose, the prevention of teenage pregnancy, to be legitimate. In *Rostker* v. *Goldberg* the Court upheld the males-only selective service registration law, showing its usual deference to the decisions of Congress in military matters. Both opinions were written by Justice Rehnquist, the member of the Court who during this period showed the least sympathy for Fourteenth Amendment challenges to sex classifications.

A number of the Court's decisions have gone the other way. Without being able to agree on its reasons for doing so, the Court in 1977 invalidated social security regulations extending automatic survivors' benefits to widows, whereas widowers received benefits only after showing that their wives had supplied three-quarters of the couple's support (*Califano* v. *Goldfarb*). Two years later the Court struck down a statute requiring husbands but never wives to pay alimony after divorce (*Orr* v. *Orr*), and another law permitting an unwed mother but not the unwed father to halt the adoption of their child (*Caban* v. *Mohammed*). And in 1982 the Supreme Court overturned Mississippi's policy of refusing to admit males to one of its state universities (*Mississippi University for Women* v. *Hogan*). This opinion was issued one day after the extended deadline for ratification of the Equal Rights Amendment had expired. It was written by Justice O'Connor, who a century earlier could have been constitutionally barred from the practice of law, and who, after graduating from Stanford Law School near the top of her class in the 1950s, had been unable to find work except as a legal secretary.

Reynolds v. *Sims*

377 U.S. 533 (1964)

When the American colonies originally worked out arrangements for determining how their representative assemblies would be constituted, they almost unanimously used population as the guiding standard. All towns might be given a seat in the assembly, but the more populous towns received a larger number. When the states were formed they too adopted population as the basis of representation in both houses of their bicameral legislatures. (The national government, of course, had a different arrangement, the result of a compromise at the Constitutional Convention between the large and small states.)

American population patterns began to undergo significant change in the late-nineteenth century as people began leaving farms for the cities, which were also attracting large numbers of immigrants from Europe. In 1790 the ratio of farmers to city dwellers in the United States was 19 to 1. By the middle of the twentieth century, farmers comprised less than one-twelfth of the American population. Today more than two-thirds of the American people live in urban areas; 70 percent of the population lives on about 1 percent of the land.

If legislative representation had continued to be based on equality it should have reflected these population changes, and power in state legislatures should have shifted overwhelmingly to the cities. But that did not occur because rural legislators, unwilling to lose their jobs, simply refused to reapportion themselves according to the new population patterns. Despite provisions in state constitutions that provided for reapportionment every 10 years based upon the most recent census figures, most states ignored that requirement after 1900. Some states also amended their constitutions so that one house of the legislature would be based on another standard besides population. In 1928, H. L. Mencken complained that in his native Maryland "the vote of a malarious peasant on the lower Eastern Shore counts as much as the votes of twelve Baltimoreans." In other states even more dramatic disparities could be found. A Vermont town of 38 people had the same representation in the state legislature as the state's largest city, with 35,000 inhabitants. In Connecticut a town of 383 had two state representatives, as did Hartford, with 162,000 residents. In California, Los Angeles County had one state senator for six million citizens, while another senate district had only 14,000 people. In a number of states, less than 20 percent of the inhabitants could elect a majority of the legislature.

In the 1940s three voters in Illinois brought a suit in federal court claiming that malapportionment in the state's congressional districts had deprived them of equal protection of the laws. After each decennial census Congress reapportions its 435 seats to reflect shifts in population among the states. It is then up to each state to work out its own congressional district lines. Illinois had neglected to redraw its congressional districts since 1901, to the detriment of voters in the city of Chicago, where one city district had over 900,000 residents while rural districts downstate typically had populations of less than 100,000. In *Colegrove* v. *Green* (1946), Justice Frankfurter wrote a majority opinion dismissing the plaintiffs' equal protection argument and emphasizing that courts were ill-equipped to enter the "political thicket" of legislative apportionment because they lacked meaningful standards to determine what constituted equality with regard to voting. This opinion was widely but incorrectly interpreted to mean that the federal courts lacked jurisdiction in such cases. What Frankfurter actually said was not that the courts had no authority to hear reapportionment cases, but that as a matter of judicial policy they should not do so.

Matters remained in this rather confused state until 1962, when the Supreme Court accepted a case from Tennessee alleging a violation of equal protection because of the state legislature's failure to reapportion itself since 1901. In *Baker* v. *Carr* the Court made it clear that reapportionment cases, since they arose under the Constitution, were within the jurisdiction of the federal courts, and remanded the case to the district court (where it had been dismissed for lack of jurisdiction) for consideration on its merits.

In 1964 the Court decided a case involving the same questions it had declined to address in *Colegrove* nearly 20 years earlier. Voters from Georgia's fifth congressional district, which had a population in excess of 800,000—about twice that of the average for the state's 10 congressional districts—argued that they had been denied equal protection because their votes were worth less than those of other voters. In *Wesberry* v. *Sanders* the Supreme Court agreed that the Constitution required that congressional districts had to have substantially equal populations, but based its ruling not on the Fourteenth Amendment but rather on Article I, Section II, which says that congressional representatives shall be chosen "by the people of the several states."

Soon after *Wesberry*, the Court heard a set of six cases from different states under the heading of *Reynolds* v. *Sims*. All involved alleged malapportionment in state legislatures. Alabama, the defendant in *Reynolds*, intended to reapportion its House of Representatives according to a plan that would distribute only 39 of the 106 seats on a population basis and under which each of the state's 67 counties would elect one senator regardless of its population. The plan was rejected by the federal district court on equal protection grounds.

Mr. Chief Justice **Warren** delivered the opinion of the Court.

. . .

Undeniably the Constitution of the United States protects the right of all qualified citizens to vote, in state as well as in federal elections. A consistent line of decisions by this Court in cases involving attempts to deny or restrict the right of suffrage has made this indelibly clear. It has been repeatedly recognized that all qualified voters have a constitutionally protected right to vote and to have their votes counted. . . . The right to vote can neither be denied outright, nor destroyed by alteration of ballots, nor diluted by ballot-box stuffing. . . . Racially based gerrymandering, and the conducting of white primaries, both of which result in denying to some citizens their right to vote, have been held to be constitutionally impermissible. And history has seen a continuing expansion of the scope of the right of suffrage in this country. The right to vote freely for the candidate of one's choice is of the essence of a democratic society, and any restrictions on that right strike at the heart of representative government. And the right of suffrage can be denied by a debasement or dilution of the weight of a citizen's vote just as effectively as by wholly prohibiting the free exercise of the franchise.

In *Baker* v. *Carr,* we held that a claim asserted under the Equal Protection Clause challenging the constitutionality of a State's apportionment of seats in its legislature, on the ground that the right to vote of certain citizens was effectively impaired since debased and diluted, in effect presented a justiciable controversy subject to adjudication by federal courts. The spate of similar cases filed and decided by lower courts since our decision in *Baker* amply shows that the problem of state legislative malapportionment is one that is perceived to exist in a large number of the States. In *Baker,* a suit involving an attack on the apportionment of seats in the Tennessee Legislature, we remanded to the District Court, which had dismissed the action, for consideration on the merits. We intimated no view as to the proper constitutional standards for evaluating the validity of a state legislative apportionment scheme. Nor did we give any consideration to the question of appropriate remedies. Rather, we simply stated:

"Beyond noting that we have no cause at this stage to doubt the District Court will be able to fashion relief if violations of constitutional rights are found, it is improper now to consider what remedy would be most appropriate if appellants prevail at the trial."

We indicated in *Baker,* however, that the Equal Protection Clause provides discoverable and manageable standards for use by lower courts in determining the constitutionality of a state legislative apportionment scheme, and we stated:

"Nor need the appellants, in order to succeed in this action, ask the Court to enter upon policy determinations for which judicially manageable standards are lacking. Judicial standards under the Equal Protection Clause are well developed and familiar, and it has been open to courts since the enactment of the Fourteenth Amendment to determine, if on the particular facts they must, that a discrimination reflects *no* policy, but simply arbitrary and capricious action."

Subsequent to *Baker,* we remanded several cases to the courts below for reconsideration in light of that decision.

. . .

A predominant consideration in determining whether a State's legislative apportionment scheme constitutes an invidious discrimination violative of rights asserted under the Equal Protection Clause is that the rights allegedly impaired are individual and personal in nature. As stated by the Court in *United States* v. *Bathgate,* "[t]he right to vote is personal. . . ." While the result of a court decision in a state legislative apportionment controversy may be to require the restructuring of the geographical distribution of seats in a state legislature, the judicial focus must be concentrated upon ascertaining whether there has been any discrimination against certain of the State's citizens which constitutes an impermissible impairment of their constitutionally protected right to vote. Like *Skinner* v. *Oklahoma,* such a case "touches a sensitive and important area of human rights," and "involves one of the basic civil rights of man," presenting questions of alleged "invidious discriminations . . . against groups or types of individuals in violation of the constitutional guaranty of just and equal laws." Undoubtedly, the right of suffrage is a fundamental matter in a free and democratic society. Especially since the right to exercise the franchise in a free and unimpaired manner is preservative of other basic civil and political rights, any alleged infringement of the right of citizens to vote must be carefully and meticulously scrutinized. Almost a century ago, in *Yick Wo* v. *Hopkins,* the Court referred to "the political franchise of voting" as "a fundamental political right, because preservative of all rights."

Legislators represent people, not trees or acres. Legislators are elected by voters, not farms or cities or economic interests. As long as ours is a representative form of government, and our legislatures are those instruments of government elected directly by and directly representative of the people, the right to elect legislators in a free and unimpaired fashion is a bedrock of our political system. It could hardly be gainsaid that a constitutional claim had been asserted by an allegation that certain otherwise qualified voters had been entirely prohibited from voting for members of their state legislature. And, if a State should provide that the votes of citizens in one part of the State should be given two times, or five times, or 10 times the weight of votes of citizens in another part of the State, it could hardly be contended that the right to vote of those residing in the disfavored areas had not been effectively diluted. It would appear extraordinary to suggest that a State could be constitutionally permitted to enact a law providing that certain of the State's voters could vote two, five, or 10 times for their legislative representatives, while voters living elsewhere could vote only once. And it is inconceivable that a state law to the effect that, in counting votes for legislators, the votes of citizens in one part of the State would be multiplied by two, five, or 10, while the votes of persons in another area would be counted only at face value, could be constitutionally sustainable. Of course, the effect of state legislative districting schemes which give the same number of representatives to unequal numbers of constituents is identical. Overweighting and overvaluation of the votes of those living here has the certain effect of dilution and undervaluation of the votes of those living there. The resulting discrimination against those individual voters living in disfavored areas is easily demonstrable mathematically. Their right to vote is simply not the same right to vote as that of those living in a favored part of the State. Two, five, or 10 of them must vote before the effect of their voting is equivalent to that of their favored neighbor. Weighting the votes of citizens differently, by any method or means, merely because of where they happen to reside, hardly seems justifiable. One must be ever aware that the Constitution forbids "sophisticated as well as simple-minded modes of discrimination." As we stated in *Wesberry* v. *Sanders:*

"We do not believe that the Framers of the Constitution intended to permit the same vote-diluting discrimination to be accomplished through the device of districts containing widely varied numbers of inhabitants. To say that a vote is worth more in one district than in another would . . . run counter to our fundamental ideas of democratic government. . . ."

State legislatures are, historically, the fountainhead of representative government in this country. A number of them have their roots in colonial times, and substantially antedate the creation of our Nation and our Federal Government. In fact, the first formal stirrings of American political independence are to be found, in large part, in the views and actions of several of the colonial legislative bodies. With the birth of our National Government, and the adoption and ratification of the Federal Constitution, state legislatures retained a most important place in our Nation's governmental structure. But representative government is in essence self-government through the medium of elected representatives of the people, and each and every citizen has an inalienable right to full and effective participation in the political processes of his State's legislative bodies. Most citizens can achieve this participation only as qualified voters through the election of legislators to represent them. Full and effective participation by all citizens in state government requires, therefore, that each citizen have an equally effective voice in the election of members of his state legislature. Modern and

viable state government needs, and the Constitution demands, no less.

Logically, in a society ostensibly grounded on representative government, it would seem reasonable that a majority of the people of a State could elect a majority of that State's legislators. To conclude differently, and to sanction minority control of state legislative bodies, would appear to deny majority rights in a way that far surpasses any possible denial of minority rights that might otherwise be thought to result. Since legislatures are responsible for enacting laws by which all citizens are to be governed, they should be bodies which are collectively responsive to the popular will. And the concept of equal protection has been traditionally viewed as requiring the uniform treatment of persons standing in the same relation to the governmental action questioned or challenged. With respect to the allocation of legislative representation, all voters, as citizens of a State, stand in the same relation regardless of where they live. Any suggested criteria for the differentiation of citizens are insufficient to justify any discrimination, as to the weight of their votes, unless relevant to the permissible purposes of legislative apportionment. Since the achieving of fair and effective representation for all citizens is concededly the basic aim of legislative apportionment, we conclude that the Equal Protection Clause guarantees the opportunity for equal participation by all voters in the election of state legislators. Diluting the weight of votes because of place of residence impairs basic constitutional rights under the Fourteenth Amendment just as much as invidious discriminations based upon factors such as race or economic status. Our constitutional system amply provides for the protection of minorities by means other than giving them majority control of state legislatures. And the democratic ideals of equality and majority rule, which have served this Nation so well in the past, are hardly of any less significance for the present and the future.

We are told that the matter of apportioning representation in a state legislature is a complex and many-faceted one. We are advised that States can rationally consider factors other than population in apportioning legislative representation. We are admonished not to restrict the power of the States to impose differing views as to political philosophy on their citizens. We are cautioned about the dangers of entering into political thickets and mathematical quagmires. Our answer is this: a denial of constitutionally protected rights demands judicial protection; our oath and our office require no less of us. As stated in *Gomillion* v. *Lightfoot:*

"When a State exercises power wholly within the domain of state interest, it is insulated from federal judicial review. But such insulation is not carried over when state power is used as an instrument for circumventing a federally protected right."

To the extent that a citizen's right to vote is debased, he is that much less a citizen. The fact that an individual lives here or there is not a legitimate reason for overweighting or diluting the efficacy of his vote. The complexions of societies and civilizations change, often with amazing rapidity. A nation once primarily rural in character becomes predominantly urban. Representation schemes once fair and equitable become archaic and outdated. But the basic principle of representative government remains, and must remain, unchanged—the weight of a citizen's vote cannot be made to depend on where he lives. Population is, of necessity, the starting point for consideration and the controlling criterion for judgment in legislative apportionment controversies. A citizen, a qualified voter, is no more nor no less so because he lives in the city or on the farm. This is the clear and strong command of our Constitution's Equal Protection Clause. This is an essential part of the concept of a government of laws and not men. This is at the heart of Lincoln's vision of "government of the people, by the people, [and] for the people." The Equal Protection Clause demands no less than substantially equal state legislative representation for all citizens, of all places as well as of all races.

We hold that, as a basic constitutional standard, the Equal Protection Clause requires that the seats in both houses of a bicameral state legislature must be apportioned on a population basis. Simply stated, an individual's right to vote for state legislators is unconstitutionally impaired when its weight is in a substantial fashion diluted when compared with votes of citizens living in other parts of the State. Since, under neither the existing apportionment provisions nor either of the proposed plans was either of the houses of the Alabama Legislature apportioned on a population basis, the District Court correctly held that all three of these schemes were constitutionally invalid.

. . .

By holding that as a federal constitutional requisite both houses of a state legislature must be apportioned on a population basis, we mean that the Equal Protection Clause requires that a State make an honest and good faith effort to construct districts, in both houses of its legislature, as nearly of equal population as is practicable. We realize that it is a practical impossibility to arrange legislative districts so that each one has an identical number of residents, or citizens, or voters. Mathematical exactness or precision is hardly a workable constitutional requirement.

In *Wesberry* v. *Sanders*, the Court stated that congressional representation must be based on population as nearly as is practicable. In implementing the basic constitutional principle of representative government as enunciated by the Court in *Wesberry*—equality of population among districts—some distinctions may well be made between congressional and state legislative representation. Since, almost invariably, there is a significantly larger number of seats in state legislative bodies to be distributed within a State than congressional seats, it may be feasible to use political subdivision lines to a greater extent in establishing state legislative districts than in congressional districting while still affording adequate representation to all parts of the State. To do so would be constitutionally valid, so long as the resulting apportionment was one based substantially on population and the equal-population principle was not diluted in any significant way. Somewhat more flexibility may therefore be constitutionally permissible with respect to state legislative apportionment than in congressional districting. Lower courts can and assuredly will work out more concrete and specific standards for evaluating state legislative apportionment schemes in the context of actual litigation. For the present, we deem it expedient not to attempt to spell out any precise constitutional tests. What is marginally permissible in one State may be unsatisfactory in another, depending on the particular circumstances of the case. Developing a body of doctrine on a case-by-case basis appears to us to provide the most satisfactory means of arriving at detailed constitutional requirements in the area of state legislative apportionment. Thus, we proceed to state here only a few rather general considerations which appear to us to be relevant.

A State may legitimately desire to maintain the integrity of various political subdivisions, insofar as possible, and provide for compact districts of contiguous territory in designing a legislative apportionment scheme. Valid considerations may underlie such aims. Indiscriminate districting, without any regard for political subdivision or natural or historical boundary lines, may be little more than an open invitation to partisan gerrymandering. Single-member districts may be the rule in one State, while another State might desire to achieve some flexibility by creating multimember or floterial districts. Whatever the means of accomplishment, the overriding objective must be substantial equality of population among the various districts, so that the vote of any citizen is approximately equal in weight to that of any other citizen in the State.

History indicates, however, that many States have deviated, to a greater or lesser degree, from the equal-population principle in the apportionment of seats in at least one house of their legislatures. So long as the divergences from a strict population standard are based on legitimate considerations incident to the effectuation of a rational state policy, some deviations from the equal-population principle are constitutionally permissible with respect to the apportionment of seats in either or both of the two houses of a bicameral state legislature. But neither history alone, nor economic or other sorts of group interests, are permissible factors in attempting to justify disparities from population-based representation. Citizens, not history or economic interests, cast votes. Considerations of area alone provide an insufficient justification for deviations from the equal-population principle. Again, people, not land or trees or pastures, vote. Modern

developments and improvements in transportation and communications make rather hollow, in the mid-1960's, most claims that deviations from population-based representation can validly be based solely on geographical considerations. Arguments for allowing such deviations in order to insure effective representation for sparsely settled areas and to prevent legislative districts from becoming so large that the availability of access of citizens to their representatives is impaired are today, for the most part, unconvincing.

A consideration that appears to be of more substance in justifying some deviations from population-based representation in state legislatures is that of insuring some voice to political subdivisions, as political subdivisions. Several factors make more than insubstantial claims that a State can rationally consider according political subdivisions some independent representation in at least one body of the state legislature, as long as the basic standard of equality of population among districts is maintained. Local governmental entities are frequently charged with various responsibilities incident to the operation of state government. In many States much of the legislature's activity involves the enactment of so-called local legislation, directed only to the concerns of particular political subdivisions. And a State may legitimately desire to construct districts along political subdivision lines to deter the possibilities of gerrymandering. However, permitting deviations from population-based representation does not mean that each local governmental unit or political subdivision can be given separate representation, regardless of population. Carried too far, a scheme of giving at least one seat in one house to each political subdivision (for example, to each county) could easily result, in many States, in a total subversion of the equal-population principle in that legislative body. This would be especially true in a State where the number of counties is large and many of them are sparsely populated, and the number of seats in the legislative body being apportioned does not significantly exceed the number of counties. Such a result, we conclude, would be constitutionally impermissible. And careful judicial scrutiny must of course be given, in evaluating state apportionment schemes, to the character as well as the degree of deviations from a strict population basis. But if, even as a result of a clearly rational state policy of according some legislative representation to political subdivisions, population is submerged as the controlling consideration in the apportionment of seats in the particular legislative body, then the right of all of the State's citizens to cast an effective and adequately weighted vote would be unconstitutionally impaired.

. . .

Mr. Justice **Harlan,** dissenting.

In these cases the Court holds that seats in the legislatures of six States are apportioned in ways that violate the Federal Constitution. Under the Court's ruling it is bound to follow that the legislatures in all but a few of the other 44 States will meet the same fate. These decisions, with *Wesberry* v. *Sanders,* involving congressional districting by the States, and *Gray* v. *Sanders,* relating to elections for statewide office, have the effect of placing basic aspects of state political systems under the pervasive overlordship of the federal judiciary. Once again, I must register my protest.

PRELIMINARY STATEMENT.

Today's holding is that the Equal Protection Clause of the Fourteenth Amendment requires every State to structure its legislature so that all the members of each house represent substantially the same number of people; other factors may be given play only to the extent that they do not significantly encroach on this basic "population" principle. Whatever may be thought of this holding as a piece of political ideology—and even on that score the political history and practices of this country from its earliest beginnings leave wide room for debate (see the dissenting opinion of Frankfurter, J., in *Baker* v. *Carr*)—I think it demonstrable that the Fourteenth Amendment does not impose this political tenet on the States or authorize this Court to do so.

The Court's constitutional discussion . . . is remarkable . . . for its failure to address itself at all to the Fourteenth Amendment as a whole or to the legislative history of the Amendment pertinent to the matter at hand. Stripped of aphorisms, the Court's argument boils down to the assertion that appellees' right to vote has been invidiously "debased" or "diluted" by systems of apportionment which entitle them to vote for fewer legislators than other voters, an assertion which is tied to the Equal Protection Clause only by the constitutionally frail tautology that "equal" means "equal."

Had the Court paused to probe more deeply into the matter, it would have found that the Equal Protection Clause was never intended to inhibit the States in choosing any democratic method they pleased for the apportionment of their legislatures. This is shown by the language of the Fourteenth Amendment taken as a whole, by the understanding of those who proposed and ratified it, and by the political practices of the States at the time the Amendment was adopted. It is confirmed by numerous state and congressional actions since the adoption of the Fourteenth Amendment, and by the common understanding of the Amendment as evidenced by subsequent constitutional amendments and decisions of this Court before *Baker* v. *Carr* made an abrupt break with the past in 1962.

The failure of the Court to consider any of these matters cannot be excused or explained by any concept of "developing" constitutionalism. It is meaningless to speak of constitutional "development" when both the language and history of the controlling provisions of the Constitution are wholly ignored. Since it can, I think, be shown beyond doubt that state legislative apportionments, as such, are wholly free of constitutional limitations, save such as may be imposed by the Republican Form of Government Clause (Const., Art. IV, § 4), the Court's action now bringing them within the purview of the Fourteenth Amendment amounts to nothing less than an exercise of the amending power by this Court.

So far as the Federal Constitution is concerned, the complaints in these cases should all have been dismissed below for failure to state a cause of action, because what has been alleged or proved shows no violation of any constitutional right.

. . .

A. *The Language of the Fourteenth Amendment.*

The Court relies exclusively on that portion of § 1 of the Fourteenth Amendment which provides that no State shall "deny to any person within its jurisdiction the equal protection of the laws," and disregards entirely the significance of § 2, which reads:

"Representatives shall be apportioned among the several States according to their respective numbers, counting the whole number of persons in each State, excluding Indians not taxed. *But when the right to vote at any election for* the choice of electors for President and Vice President of the United States, Representatives in Congress, *the Executive and Judicial officers of a State, or the members of the Legislature thereof, is denied* to any of the male inhabitants of such State, being twenty-one years of age, and citizens of the United States, *or in any way abridged,* except for participation in rebellion, or other crime, the basis of representation therein shall be reduced in the proportion which the number of such male citizens shall bear to the whole number of male citizens twenty-one years of age in such State." (Emphasis added.)

The Amendment is a single text. It was introduced and discussed as such in the Reconstruction Committee, which reported it to the Congress. It was discussed as a unit in Congress and proposed as a unit to the States, which ratified it as a unit. A proposal to split up the Amendment and submit each section to the States as a separate amendment was rejected by the Senate. Whatever one might take to be the application to these cases of the Equal Protection Clause if it stood alone, I am unable to understand the Court's utter disregard of the second section which expressly recognizes the States' power to deny "or in any way" abridge the right of their inhabitants to vote for "the members of the [State] Legislature," and its express provision of a remedy for such denial or abridgment. The comprehensive scope of the second section and its particular reference to the state legislatures preclude the suggestion that the first section was intended to have the result

reached by the Court today. If indeed the words of the Fourteenth Amendment speak for themselves, as the majority's disregard of history seems to imply, they speak as clearly as may be against the construction which the majority puts on them. But we are not limited to the language of the Amendment itself.

B. *Proposal and Ratification of the Amendment.*

The history of the adoption of the Fourteenth Amendment provides conclusive evidence that neither those who proposed nor those who ratified the Amendment believed that the Equal Protection Clause limited the power of the States to apportion their legislatures as they saw fit. Moreover, the history demonstrates that the intention to leave this power undisturbed was deliberate and was widely believed to be essential to the adoption of the Amendment.

. . .

The facts . . . show beyond any possible doubt:

(1) that Congress, with full awareness of and attention to the possibility that the States would not afford full equality in voting rights to all their citizens, nevertheless deliberately chose not to interfere with the States' plenary power in this regard when it proposed the Fourteenth Amendment;

(2) that Congress did not include in the Fourteenth Amendment restrictions on the States' power to control voting rights because it believed that if such restrictions were included, the Amendment would not be adopted; and

(3) that at least a substantial majority, if not all, of the States which ratified the Fourteenth Amendment did not consider that in so doing, they were accepting limitations on their freedom, never before questioned, to regulate voting rights as they chose.

Even if one were to accept the majority's belief that it is proper entirely to disregard the unmistakable implications of the second section of the Amendment in construing the first section, one is confounded by its disregard of all this history. There is here none of the difficulty which may attend the application of basic principles to situations not contemplated or understood when the principles were framed. The problems which concern the Court now were problems when the Amendment was adopted. By the deliberate choice of those responsible for the Amendment, it left those problems untouched.

C. After 1868.

The years following 1868, far from indicating a developing awareness of the applicability of the Fourteenth Amendment to problems of apportionment, demonstrate precisely the reverse: that the States retained and exercised the power independently to apportion their legislatures. . . .

D. Today.

Since the Court now invalidates the legislative apportionments in six States, and has so far upheld the apportionment in none, it is scarcely necessary to comment on the situation in the States today, which is, of course, as fully contrary to the Court's decision as is the record of every prior period in this Nation's history. As of 1961, the Constitutions of all but 11 States, roughly 20% of the total, recognized bases of apportionment other than geographic spread of population, and to some extent favored sparsely populated areas by a variety of devices, ranging from straight area representation or guaranteed minimum area representation to complicated schemes of the kind exemplified by the provisions of New York's Constitution of 1894, still in effect until struck down by the Court today.

. . .

I have tried to make the catalogue complete, yet to keep it within the manageable limits of a judicial opinion. In my judgment, today's decisions are refuted by the language of the Amendment which they construe and by the inference fairly to be drawn from subsequently enacted Amendments. They are unequivocally refuted by

history and by consistent theory and practice from the time of the adoption of the Fourteenth Amendment until today.

. . .

It should by now be obvious that these cases do not mark the end of reapportionment problems in the courts. Predictions once made that the courts would never have to face the problem of actually working out an apportionment have proved false. This Court, however, continues to avoid the consequences of its decisions, simply assuring us that the lower courts "can and . . . will work out more concrete and specific standards." Deeming it "expedient" not to spell out "precise constitutional tests," the Court contents itself with stating "only a few rather general considerations."

Generalities cannot obscure the cold truth that cases of this type are not amenable to the development of judicial standards. No set of standards can guide a court which has to decide how many legislative districts a State shall have, or what the shape of the districts shall be, or where to draw a particular district line. No judicially manageable standard can determine whether a State should have single-member districts or multimember districts or some combination of both. No such standard can control the balance between keeping up with population shifts and having stable districts. In all these respects, the courts will be called upon to make particular decisions with respect to which a principle of equally populated districts will be of no assistance whatsoever. Quite obviously, there are limitless possibilities for districting consistent with such a principle. Nor can these problems be avoided by judicial reliance on legislative judgments so far as possible. Reshaping or combining one or two districts, or modifying just a few district lines, is no less a matter of choosing among many possible solutions, with varying political consequences, than reapportionment broadside.

The Court ignores all this, saying only that "what is marginally permissible in one State may be unsatisfactory in another, depending on the particular circumstances of the case." It is well to remember that the product of today's decisions will not be readjustment of a few districts in a few States which most glaringly depart from the principle of equally populated districts. It will be a redetermination, extensive in many cases, of legislative districts in all but a few States.

. . .

CONCLUSION.

With these cases the Court approaches the end of the third round set in motion by the complaint filed in *Baker* v. *Carr*. What is done today deepens my conviction that judicial entry into this realm is profoundly ill-advised and constitutionally impermissible. As I have said before, I believe that the vitality of our political system, on which in the last analysis all else depends, is weakened by reliance on the judiciary for political reform; in time a complacent body politic may result.

These decisions also cut deeply into the fabric of our federalism. What must follow from them may eventually appear to be the product of state legislatures. Nevertheless, no thinking person can fail to recognize that the aftermath of these cases, however desirable it may be thought in itself, will have been achieved at the cost of a radical alteration in the relationship between the States and the Federal Government, more particularly the Federal Judiciary. Only one who

has an overbearing impatience with the federal system and its political processes will believe that that cost was not too high or was inevitable.

Finally, these decisions give support to a current mistaken view of the Constitution and the constitutional function of this Court. This view, in a nutshell, is that every major social ill in this country can find its cure in some constitutional "principle," and that this Court should "take the lead" in promoting reform when other branches of government fail to act. The Constitution is not a panacea for every blot upon the public welfare, nor should this Court, ordained as a judicial body, be thought of as a general haven for reform movements. The Constitution is an instrument of government, fundamental to which is the premise that in a diffusion of governmental authority lies the greatest promise that this Nation will realize liberty for all its citizens. This Court, limited in function in accordance with that premise, does not serve its high purpose when it exceeds its authority, even to satisfy justified impatience with the slow workings of the political process. For when, in the name of constitutional interpretation, the Court *adds* something to the Constitution that was deliberately excluded from it, the Court in reality substitutes its view of what should be so for the amending process.

. . .

Aftermath of Reynolds *v.* Sims

Chief Justice Earl Warren considered *Reynolds* v. *Sims,* known as the "one-person, one-vote" decision, the most important opinion he ever wrote. He was referring to its potential for revolutionizing representative democracy in the United States. Although polls showed that the ruling was popular with the public, politicians—who after all had the most to fear from reapportionment—were strongly opposed. The Republican leader in the United States Senate, Everett Dirksen of Illinois, assumed leadership of a movement to amend the Constitution to limit the Supreme Court's jurisdiction in the area of legislative apportionment. Thirty-two state legislatures petitioned for a constitutional convention to consider the issue, but without broad public support the effort eventually lost its momentum and died.

Since the *Reynolds* case was decided the Supreme Court has reviewed dozens of cases involving legislative and congressional district reapportionment plans, as well as other lawsuits seeking to extend the one-person, one-vote principle to other levels of government. In the early post-*Reynolds* years the major question before the Court was how much variation in district populations the Court would

allow before finding a constitutional violation. While refusing to establish a precise mathematical standard, the Court has said that variations of more than 10
percent between the largest and smallest districts require the state to show that a
rational state policy is being advanced by the districting plan. In 1983 the Court
rejected a New Jersey congressional districting plan with a maximum population
deviation of only 0.7 percent, because other plans with lower population differences were available and the state had not explained why its chosen plan was
preferable to them. Thus the state had not made a "good faith effort to achieve
precise mathematical equality" (*Karcher* v. *Daggett*). In general, the Court has
taken a more relaxed view of state legislative district variations, treating a state's
history and geography as factors in deciding whether districting plans are constitutional. On the same day as the *Karcher* decision was announced the Court
upheld a Wyoming legislative redistricting plan with a maximum deviation of 89
percent because, since statehood, Wyoming's constitution had guaranteed each
county at least one senator and one representative (*Brown* v. *Thomson*).

The Court has applied the one-person, one-vote principle to local government
as well, holding that the standard must be adhered to by all bodies performing
general functions that elect their members from single districts (as opposed to at-
large) (*Avery* v. *Midland County*, 1968). However, the Court has drawn the line at
special-purpose governmental units like water districts, ruling that they may elect
their members through weighted schemes that, for example, reflect the value of
voters' land holdings (*Salyer Land Co.* v. *Tulare Water District*, 1973.)

In 1989 the Court unanimously declared New York City's powerful Board of
Estimate unconstitutional because each of the five borough presidents, represent-
ing areas with widely varying populations, had one vote on the board (*Board of
Estimate* v. *Morris*). The decision forced a fundamental restructuring of New
York's municipal government in which most of the board's powers were given to
an expanded city council.

APPENDIX 1
How to Read United States Supreme Court Opinions

United States Supreme Court opinions often contain examples of creative, reasonable, and eloquent writing about complex legal, political, and social problems. They also contain a fair share of unimaginative, pedestrian, and downright muddy thinking expressed in prose that is sometimes less than sparkling. You will be reading a substantial number of opinions and you will no doubt be expected to discuss them intelligently in class. Some will be a pleasure to read and others will be rather hard going, but all will be important in developing an understanding of judicial policy-making in the United States. These brief paragraphs are designed to help you extract the maximum possible benefit from each of them.

Get into the habit of taking notes on each opinion you read. Read the opinion through once, jotting down main ideas as you go. Then read it again, expanding on your notes and organizing them into a coherent framework. No opinion can be adequately evaluated until it has been read through at least twice. It will prove helpful to organize your notes for each case under the following five headings: facts, rule of law, reasoning, concurrences, and dissents.

FACTS

Usually the important facts of a case can be gleaned from the majority opinion. What was the conflict that produced this legal confrontation in the first place? What was the "travel" of the case (i.e., where did the case originate and how was it acted upon before coming to the Supreme Court?)? Is it a state or a federal case? What are the issues being raised on appeal by the petitioner? What, specifically, is the Supreme Court being asked by the petitioner to do—to overrule a previous decision, to reiterate a previously stated rule, to distinguish this case from earlier precedents, or to carve out a new interpretation where no constitutional guidelines previously existed? On what particular constitutional or statutory ground is the petitioner basing the claim? On what ground does the respondent rest the case?

RULE OF LAW

Your primary concern is with the rule of law announced by the Court in its majority opinion. (Occasionally there is no majority opinion per se, and you will be required to piece together the rule of law from the separate concurrences.) Generally the rule will be fairly explicitly stated, and will contain a reference to a particular constitutional or statutory provision as it applies to the case at hand. Usually the Court will decide that the Constitution or the statute in question either permits or prohibits a particular action whose legitimacy is being disputed by the litigants. Aim for precision *and* comprehensiveness in your statement of the rule of law—even if the Court has not. In other words, you may have to state the rule in your own language, but without changing the Court's essential meaning. Some hints for identifying the rule of law: Ask yourself how the Court has answered the petitioner's request for relief. Has it been granted, denied, or some of both? Or perhaps the Court has gone beyond the petitioner's request, enunciating a more comprehensive rule or principle than it was asked to (this happens only rarely, but you should be prepared to recognize it when it does). Does the Court specifically exclude certain issues from the ruling (e.g., "We do not discuss today the following questions . . .")? Does the Court fail to discuss some issue(s) at all? Does the Court appear to be inviting further litigation before it attempts to refine its rule of law? In other words, how extensive is the rule which the Court has stated?

REASONING

You should be prepared to explain how the majority arrived at and justified its decision. Is the rule of law based on constitutional or statutory interpretation? Is the decision based on previous cases which point in a particular direction, or does the Court explicitly depart from earlier rules by overruling or distinguishing them? Or does the majority depart from precedent altogether and instead justify its decision on extra-legal (e.g., sociological, moral, economic) grounds? Does the Court consider the opposing arguments in any detail in its majority opinion? Does it seem to be trying at any point to placate potential critics of the decision? Are there conflicting points of view built into the majority's reasoning? How are these conflicts resolved, if indeed they are resolved? Are any important issues left unexplained? Finally, how persuasive do you find the Court's reasoning?

CONCURRENCES

Careful consideration of the concurring opinion(s) will usually help you to understand better the majority's rule of law and the reasoning that supports it. Ask yourself why the concurring justice(s) feel obliged to speak separately. Is there something in the Court's reasoning processes that the concurring justices find objectionable? How would the majority have had to modify its rule or its reasoning in order to include the concurrers? Why was this not done? Do the concurring justices speak with one voice or are there significant differences among them?

DISSENTS

Finally, you should look closely at the dissenting opinions. What are the dissenters' criticisms of the majority opinion? Do they object to the rule, the reasoning, or both? Do they agree with the majority's interpretation of past decisions? If they object to the rule of law, is it because of practical problems they feel might arise from the decision? Do the dissenters write detailed analyses of the Court's opinion, or do they confine themselves to general critical remarks? Are the dissenters themselves in agreement, or are there significant differences among them? What would it have taken to get each of the dissenters to concur with the majority?

APPENDIX 2
The Constitution of the United States

We the People of the United States, in Order to form a more perfect Union, establish Justice, insure domestic Tranquility, provide for the common defence, promote the general Welfare, and secure the Blessings of Liberty to ourselves and our Posterity, do ordain and establish this Constitution for the United States of America.

ARTICLE 1

Section 1.   All legislative Powers herein granted shall be vested in a Congress of the United States, which shall consist of a Senate and House of Representatives.

Section 2.   The House of Representatives shall be composed of Members chosen every second Year by the People of the several States, and the Electors in each State shall have the Qualifications requisite for Electors of the most numerous Branch of the State Legislature.

No Person shall be a Representative who shall not have attained to the Age of twenty five Years, and been seven Years a Citizen of the United States, and who shall not, when elected, be an Inhabitant of that State in which he shall be chosen.

Representatives and direct Taxes shall be apportioned among the several States which may be included within this Union, according to their respective Numbers, which shall be determined by adding to the whole Number of free Persons, including those bound to Service for a Term of Years, and excluding Indians not taxed, three fifths of all other Persons. The actual Enumeration shall be made within three Years after the first Meeting of the Congress of the United States, and within every subsequent Term of ten Years, in such Manner as they shall by Law direct. The Number of Representatives shall not exceed one for every thirty Thousand, but each State shall have at Least one Representative; and until such enumerations shall be made, the State of New Hampshire shall be entitled to chuse three, Massachusetts eight, Rhode-Island and Providence Plantations one, Connecticut five, New-York six, New Jersey four, Pennsylvania eight, Delaware one, Maryland six, Virginia ten, North Carolina five, South Carolina five, and Georgia three.

When vacancies happen in the Representation from any State, the Executive Authority thereof shall issue Writs of Election to fill such Vacancies.

The House of Representatives shall chuse their speaker and other Officers; and shall have the sole Power of Impeachment.

Section 3.   The Senate of the United States shall be composed of two Senators from each State, chosen by the Legislature thereof, for six Years; and each Senator shall have one Vote.

Immediately after they shall be assembled in Consequence of the first Election, they shall be divided as equally as may be into three Classes. The Seats of the Senators of the first Class shall be vacated at the Expiration of the second Year, of the second Class at the Expiration of the fourth Year, and of the third Class at the Expiration of the sixth Year, so that one third may be chosen every second Year; and if Vacancies happen by Resignation, or otherwise, during the Recess of the Legislature of any State, the Executive thereof may make temporary Appointments until the next Meeting of the Legislature, which shall then fill such Vacancies.

No Person shall be a Senator who shall not have attained to the Age of thirty Years, and been nine Years a Citizen of the United States, and who shall not, when elected, be an Inhabitant of that State for which he shall be chosen.

The Vice President of the United States shall be President of the Senate, but shall have no Vote, unless they be equally divided.

The Senate shall chuse their other Officers, and also a President pro tempore, in the Absence of the Vice President, or when he shall exercise the Office of President of the United States.

The Senate shall have the sole Power to try all Impeachments. When sitting for that Purpose, they shall be on Oath or Affirmation. When the President of the United States is tried, the Chief Justice shall preside: And no Person shall be convicted without the concurrence of two thirds of the Members present. Judgment in Cases of Impeachment shall not extend further than to removal from Office, and disqualification to hold and enjoy any Office of honor, Trust or Profit under the United States: but the Party convicted shall nevertheless be liable and subject to Indictment, Trial, Judgment and Punishment, according to law.

Section 4.   The Times, Places and Manner of holding Elections for Senators and Representatives, shall be prescribed in each State by the Legislature thereof; but the Congress may at any time by Law make or alter such Regulations, except as to the Places of chusing Senators.

The Congress shall assemble at least once in every Year, and such Meeting shall be on the first Monday in December, unless they shall by Law appoint a different Day.

Section 5.   Each House shall be the Judge of the Elections, Returns and Qualifications of its own Members, and a Majority of each shall constitute a Quorum to do business; but a smaller Number may adjourn from day to day, and may be authorized to compel the Attendance of absent Members, in such Manner, and under such Penalties as each House may provide.

Each House may determine the Rules of its Proceedings, punish its Members for disorderly Behaviour, and, with the Concurrence of two thirds, expel a Member.

Each House shall keep a Journal of its Proceedings, and from time to time publish the same, excepting such Parts as may in their Judgment require Secrecy; and the yeas and Nays of the Members of either House on any question shall, at the Desire of one fifth of those Present, be entered on the Journal.

Neither House, during the Session of Congress, shall, without the Consent of the other, adjourn for more than three days, nor to any other place than that in which the two Houses shall be sitting.

Section 6.   The Senators and Representatives shall receive a Compensation for their Services, to be ascertained by Law, and paid out of the Treasury of the United States. They shall in all Cases, except Treason, Felony and Breach of the Peace, be privileged from Arrest during their Attendance at the Session of their respective Houses, and in going to and returning from the same; and for any Speech or Debate in either House, they shall not be questioned in any other Place.

No Senator or Representative shall, during the Time for which he was elected, be appointed to any civil Office under the Authority of the United States, which shall have been created, or the Emoluments whereof shall have been encreased during such time; and no Person holding any Office under the United States, shall be a Member of either House during his Continuance in Office.

Section 7.   All Bills for raising Revenue shall originate in the House of Representatives; but the Senate may propose or concur with Amendments as on other Bills.

Every Bill which shall have passed the House of Representatives and the Senate, shall, before it become a Law, be presented to the President of the United States; If he approve he shall sign it, but if not he shall return it, with his Objections to that House in which it shall have originated, who shall enter the Objections at large on their Journal, and proceed to reconsider it. If after such Reconsideration two thirds of that House shall agree to pass the Bill, it shall be sent, together with the Objections, to the other House, by which it shall likewise be reconsidered, and if approved by two thirds of that House, it shall become a Law. But in all such Cases the Votes of both Houses shall be determined by yeas and Nays, and the Names of the Persons voting for and against the Bill shall be entered on the Journal of each House respectively. If any Bill shall not be returned by the President within ten Days (Sundays excepted) after it shall have been presented to him, the Same shall be a Law, in like Manner as if he had signed it, unless the Congress by their Adjournment prevent its Return, in which Case it shall not be a Law.

Every Order, Resolution, or Vote to which the Concurrence of the Senate and House of Representatives may be necessary (except on a question of Adjournment) shall be presented to the President of the United States; and before the Same shall take Effect, shall be approved by him, or being disapproved by him, shall be repassed by two thirds of the Senate and House of Representatives, according to the Rules and Limitations prescribed in the Case of a Bill.

Section 8.   The Congress shall have Power To lay and collect Taxes, Duties, Imposts and Excises, to pay the Debts and provide for the common Defence and general Welfare of the United States; but all duties, Imposts and Excises shall be uniform throughout the United States;

To borrow Money on the Credit of the United States;

To regulate Commerce with foreign Nations, and among the several States, and with the Indian Tribes;

To establish an uniform Rule of Naturalization, and uniform Laws on the subject of Bankruptcies throughout the United States;

To coin Money, regulate the Value thereof, and of foreign Coin, and fix the Standard of Weights and Measures;

To provide for the Punishment of counterfeiting the Securities and current Coin of the United States;

To establish Post Offices and post Roads;

To promote the Progress of Science and useful Arts, by securing for limited Times to Authors and Inventors exclusive Right to their respective Writings and Discoveries;

To constitute Tribunals inferior to the supreme Court;

To define and punish Piracies and Felonies committed on the high Seas, and Offences against the Law of Nations;

To declare War, grant Letters of Marque and Reprisal, and make rules concerning Captures on Land and Water;

To raise and support Armies, but no Appropriation of Money to that Use shall be for a longer Term than two Years;

To provide and maintain a Navy;

To make rules for the Government and Regulation of the land and naval Forces;

To provide for calling forth the Militia to execute the Laws of the Union, suppress Insurrections and repel Invasions;

To provide for organizing, arming, and disciplining, the Militia, and for governing such Part of them as may be employed in the Service of the United States, reserving to the States respectively, the Appointment of the Officers, and the Authority of training the Militia according to the discipline prescribed by Congress;

To exercise exclusive Legislation in all Cases whatsoever, over such District (not exceeding ten Miles square), as may, by Cession of particular States, and the Acceptance of Congress, become the Seat of the Government of the United States, and to exercise like Authority over all Places purchased by the Consent of the Legislature of the State in which the Same shall be for the Erection of Forts, Magazines, Arsenals, dock-Yards, and other needful Buildings;—And

To make all Laws which shall be necessary and proper for carrying into Execution the foregoing Powers, and all other Powers vested by this Constitution in the Government of the United States, or in any Department or Officer thereof.

Section 9.   The Migration or Importation of such Persons as any of the States now existing shall think proper to admit, shall not be prohibited by the Congress prior to the Year one thousand eight hundred and eight, but a Tax or duty may be imposed on such Importation, not exceeding ten dollars for each Person.

The Privilege of the Writ of Habeas Corpus shall not be suspended, unless when in Cases of Rebellion or Invasion the public Safety may require it.

No Bill of Attainder or ex post facto Law shall be passed.

No Capitation, or other direct, Tax shall be laid, unless in Proportion to the Census or Enumeration herein before directed to be taken.

No Tax or Duty shall be laid on Articles exported from any State.

No Preference shall be given by any Regulation of Commerce or Revenue to the Ports of one State over those of another: nor shall Vessels bound to, or from, one State, be obliged to enter, clear, or pay Duties in another.

No money shall be drawn from the Treasury, but in Consequence of Appropriations made by Law; and a regular Statement and Account of the Receipts and Expenditures of all public Money shall be published from time to time.

No Title of Nobility shall be granted by the United States: And no Person holding any Office of Profit or Trust under them, shall, without the Consent of the Congress, accept of any present, Emolument, Office, or Title, of any kind whatever, from any King, Prince, or foreign State.

Section 10.   No State shall enter into any Treaty, Alliance, or Confederation; grant Letters of Marque and Reprisal; coin Money; emit Bills of Credit; make any Thing but gold and silver Coin a Tender in Payment of Debts; pass any Bill of Attainder, ex post facto Law, or Law impairing the Obligation of Contracts, or grant any Title of Nobility.

No State shall, without the Consent of the Congress, lay any Imposts or Duties on Imports or Exports, except what may be absolutely necessary for executing it's inspection Laws: and the net Produce of all Duties and Imposts, laid by any State on Imports or Exports, shall be for the Use of the Treasury of the United States; and all such Laws shall be subject to the Revision and Controul of the Congress.

No State shall, without the Consent of Congress, lay any Duty of Tonnage, keep Troops, or Ships of War in time of Peace, enter into any Agreement or Compact with another State, or with a foreign Power, or engage in War, unless actually invaded, or in such imminent Danger as will not admit of delay.

ARTICLE II

Section 1.   The executive Power shall be vested in a President of the United States of America. He shall hold his Office during the Term of four Years, and, together with the Vice President, chosen for the same term, be elected, as follows

Each State shall appoint, in such Manner as the Legislature thereof may direct, a Number of Electors, equal to the whole Number of Senators and Representatives to which the State may be entitled in the Congress: but no Senator or Representative, or Person holding an Office of Trust or Profit under the United States, shall be appointed an Elector.

The Electors shall meet in their respective States, and vote by Ballot for two Persons, of whom one at least shall not be an Inhabitant of the same State with themselves. And they shall make a List of all the Persons voted for, and of the Number of Votes for each; which List they shall sign and certify, and transmit sealed to the Seat of the Government of the United States, directed to the President of the Senate. The President of the Senate shall, in the Presence of the Senate and House of Representatives, open all the Certificates, and the Votes shall then be counted. The Person having the greatest Number of Votes shall be the President, if such Number be a Majority of the whole Number of Electors appointed; and if there be more than one who have such Majority, and have an equal Number of Votes, then the House of Representatives shall immediately chuse by Ballot one of them for President: and if no Person have a Majority, then from the five highest on the List the said House shall in like Manner chuse the President. But in chusing the President, the Votes shall be taken by States, the Representation from each State having one Vote; A quorum for this Purpose shall consist of a Member or Members from two thirds of the States, and a Majority of all the States shall be necessary to a Choice. In every Case, after the Choice of the President, the Person having the greatest Number of Votes of the Electors shall be the Vice President. But if there should remain two or more who have equal Votes, the Senate shall chuse from them by Ballot the Vice President.

The Congress may determine the Time of chusing the Electors, and the Day on which they shall give their Votes; which Day shall be the same throughout the United States.

No Person except a natural born Citizen, or a Citizen of the United States, at the time of the Adoption of this Constitution, shall be eligible to the Office of President; neither shall any Person be eligible to that Office who shall not have attained to the Age of thirty five Years, and been fourteen Years a Resident within the United States.

In Case of the Removal of the President from Office, or of his Death, Resignation, or Inability to discharge the Powers and Duties of the said Office, the Same shall devolve on the Vice President, and the Congress may by Law provide for the Case of Removal, Death, Resignation or Inability, both of the President and Vice President, declaring what Officer shall then act as President, and such Officer shall act accordingly, until the Disability be removed, or a President shall be elected.

The President shall, at stated Times, receive for his Services, a Compensation, which shall neither be encreased nor diminished during the Period for which he shall have been elected, and he shall not receive within that Period any other Emolument from the United States, or any of them.

Before he enter on the Execution of his Office, he shall take the following Oath or Affirmation:—"I do solemnly swear (or affirm) that I will faithfully execute the Office of President of the United States, and will to the best of my Ability, preserve, protect and defend the Constitution of the United States."

Section 2.   The President shall be Commander in Chief of the Army and Navy of the United States, and of the Militia of the several States, when called into the actual Service of the United States; he may require the Opinion, in writing, of the principal Officer in each of the executive Departments, upon any Subject relating to the Duties of their respective Offices, and he shall have Power to grant Reprieves and Pardons for Offences against the United States, except in Cases of Impeachment.

He shall have Power, by and with the Advice and Consent of the Senate, to make Treaties, provided two thirds of the Senators present concur; and he shall nominate, and by and with the Advice and Consent of the Senate, shall appoint Ambassadors, other public Ministers and Consuls, Judges of the supreme Court, and all other Officers of the United States, whose Appointments are not herein otherwise provided for, and which shall be established by Law: but the Congress may by Law vest the Appointment of such inferior Officers, as they think proper, in the President alone, in the Courts of Law, or in the Heads of Departments.

The President shall have Power to fill up all Vacancies that may happen during the Recess of the Senate, by granting Commissions which shall expire at the End of their next Session.

Section 3.   He shall from time to time give to the Congress Information of the State of the Union, and recommend to their Consideration such Measures as he shall judge necessary and expedient; he may, on extraordinary Occasions, convene both Houses, or either of them, and in Case of Disagreement between them, with Respect to the Time of Adjournment, he may adjourn them to such Time as he shall think proper; he shall receive Ambassadors and other public Ministers; he shall take Care that the Laws be faithfully executed, and shall Commission all the Officers of the United States.

Section 4.   The President, Vice President and all civil Officers of the United States, shall be removed from Office on Impeachment for, and Conviction of, Treason, Bribery, or other High Crimes and Misdemeanors.

ARTICLE III

Section 1.   The judicial Power of the United States, shall be vested in one supreme Court, and in such inferior Courts as the Congress may from time to time ordain and establish. The Judges, both of the supreme and inferior Courts, shall hold their Offices during good Behaviour, and shall, at stated Times, receive for their Services, a Compensation, which shall not be diminished during their Continuance in Office.

Section 2.   The judicial Power shall extend to all Cases, in Law and Equity, arising under this Constitution, the Laws of the United States, and Treaties made, or which shall be made, under their Authority;—to all Cases affecting Ambassadors, other public Ministers and Consuls;—to all Cases of admiralty and maritime Jurisdiction;—to Controversies to which the United States shall be a Party;—to Controversies between two or more States; between a State and Citizens of another State;—between Citizens of different States;—between Citizens of the same State claiming Lands under Grants of different States, and between a State, or the Citizens thereof, and foreign States, Citizens or Subjects.

In all Cases affecting Ambassadors, other public Ministers and Consuls, and those in which a State shall be Party, the supreme Court shall have original Jurisdiction. In all the other Cases before mentioned, the supreme Court shall have appellate Jurisdiction, both as to Law and Fact, with such Exceptions, and under such Regulations as the Congress shall make.

The Trial of all Crimes, except in Cases of Impeachment, shall be by Jury; and such Trial shall be held in the State where the said Crimes shall have been committed; but when not committed within any State, the Trial shall be at such Place or Places as the Congress may by Law have directed.

Section 3.   Treason against the United States, shall consist only in levying War against them, or in adhering to their Enemies, giving them Aid and Comfort. No Person shall be convicted of Treason unless on the Testimony of two Witnesses to the same overt Act, or on Confession in open Court.

The Congress shall have Power to declare the Punishment of Treason, but no Attainder of Treason shall work Corruption of Blood, or Forfeiture except during the Life of the Person attainted.

ARTICLE IV

Section 1.   Full Faith and Credit shall be given in each State to the public Acts, Records, and judicial Proceedings of every other State. And the Congress may by general Laws prescribe the Manner in which such Acts, Records and Proceedings shall be proved, and the Effect thereof.

Section 2.   The Citizens of each State shall be entitled to all Privileges and Immunities of Citizens in the several States.

A Person charged in any State with Treason, Felony, or other Crime, who shall flee from Justice, and be found in another State, shall on Demand of the executive Authority of the State from which he fled, be delivered up, to be removed to the State having Jurisdiction of the Crime.

No person held to Service or Labour in one State, under the Laws thereof, escaping into another, shall, in Consequence of any Law or Regulation therein, be discharged from such Service or Labour, but shall be delivered up on Claim of the Party to whom such Service or Labour may be due.

Section 3.   New States may be admitted by the Congress into this Union; but no new State shall be formed or erected within the Jurisdiction of any other State; nor any State be formed by the Junction of two or more States, or Parts of States, without the Consent of the Legislatures of the States concerned as well as of the Congress.

The Congress shall have Power to dispose of and make all needful Rules and Regulations respecting the Territory or other Property belonging to the United States; and nothing in this Constitution shall be so construed as to Prejudice any Claims of the United States, or of any particular State.

Section 4.   The United States shall guarantee to every State in this Union a Republican Form of Government, and shall protect each of them against Invasion; and on Application of the Legislature, or of the Executive (when the Legislature cannot be convened) against domestic Violence.

ARTICLE V

The Congress, whenever two thirds of both Houses shall deem it necessary, shall propose Amendments to this Constitution, or, on the Application of the Legislatures of two thirds of the several States, shall call a Convention for proposing Amendments, which, in either Case, shall be valid to all Intents and Purposes, as Part of this Constitution, when ratified by the Legislatures of three fourths of the several States, or by Conventions in three fourths thereof, as the one or the other Mode of Ratification may be proposed by the Congress; Provided that no Amendment which may be made prior to the Year One thousand eight hundred and eight shall in any Manner affect the first and fourth Clauses in the Ninth Section of the first Article; and that no State, without its Consent, shall be deprived of its equal Suffrage in the Senate.

ARTICLE VI

All Debts contracted and Engagements entered into, before the Adoption of this Constitution, shall be as valid against the United States under this Constitution, as under the Confederation.

This Constitution, and the Laws of the United States which shall be made in Pursuance thereof; and all Treaties made, or which shall be made, under the Authority of the United States, shall be the supreme Law of the Land; and the Judges in every State shall be bound thereby, any Thing in the Constitution or Laws of any State to the Contrary notwithstanding.

The Senators and Representatives before mentioned, and the Members of the several State Legislatures, and all executive and judicial Officers, both of the United States and of the several States, shall be bound by Oath or Affirmation, to support this Constitution; but no religious Test shall ever be required as a Qualification to any Office or public Trust under the United States.

ARTICLE VII

The Ratification of the Conventions of nine States, shall be sufficient for the Establishment of this Constitution between the States so ratifying the Same.

AMENDMENTS

(The first 10 Amendments were ratified December 15, 1791, and form what is known as the "Bill of Rights.")

AMENDMENT 1

Congress shall make no law respecting an establishment of religion, or prohibiting the free exercise thereof; or abridging the freedom of speech, or of the press; or the right of the people peaceably to assemble, and to petition the Government for a redress of grievances.

AMENDMENT 2

A well regulated Militia, being necessary to the security of a free State, the right of the people to keep and bear Arms, shall not be infringed.

AMENDMENT 3

No Soldier shall, in time of peace be quartered in any house, without the consent of the Owner, nor in time of war, but in a manner to be prescribed by law.

AMENDMENT 4

The right of the people to be secure in their persons, houses, papers, and effects, against unreasonable searches and seizures, shall not be violated, and no Warrants shall issue, but upon probable cause, supported by Oath or affirmation, and particularly describing the place to be searched, and the persons or things to be seized.

AMENDMENT 5

No person shall be held to answer for a capital, or otherwise infamous crime, unless on a presentment or indictment of a Grand Jury, except in cases arising in the land or naval forces, or in the Militia, when in actual service in time of War or public danger; nor shall any person be subject for the same offence to be twice put in jeopardy of life or limb; nor shall be compelled in any criminal case to be a witness against himself, nor be deprived of life, liberty, or property, without due process of law; nor shall private property be taken for public use, without just compensation.

AMENDMENT 6

In all criminal prosecutions, the accused shall enjoy the right to a speedy and public trial, by an impartial jury of the State and district wherein the crime shall have been committed, which district shall have been previously ascertained by law, and to be informed of the nature and cause of the accusation; to be confronted with the witnesses against him; to have compulsory process for obtaining witnesses in his favor, and to have the Assistance of Counsel for his defence.

AMENDMENT 7

In Suits at common law, where the value in controversy shall exceed twenty dollars, the right of trial by jury shall be preserved, and no fact tried by a jury, shall be otherwise re-examined in any Court of the United States, than according to the rules of the common law.

AMENDMENT 8

Excessive bail shall not be required, nor excessive fines imposed, nor cruel and unusual punishments inflicted.

AMENDMENT 9

The enumeration in the Constitution, of certain rights, shall not be construed to deny or disparage others retained by the people.

AMENDMENT 10

The powers not delegated to the United States by the Constitution, nor prohibited by it to the States, are reserved to the States respectively, or to the people.

AMENDMENT 11

(Ratified February 7, 1795)

The Judicial power of the United States shall not be construed to extend to any suit in law or equity, commenced or prosecuted against one of the United States by Citizens of another State, or by Citizens or Subjects of any Foreign State.

AMENDMENT 12

(Ratified July 27, 1804)

The Electors shall meet in their respective states and vote by ballot for President and Vice-President, one of whom, at least, shall not be an inhabitant of the same state with themselves; they shall name in their ballots the person voted for as President, and in distinct ballots the person voted for as Vice-President, and they shall make distinct lists of all persons voted for as President, and of all persons voted for as Vice-President, and of the number of votes for each, which lists they shall sign and certify, and transmit sealed to the seat of the government of the United States, directed to the President of the Senate;—The President of the Senate shall, in the presence of the Senate and House of Representatives, open all the certificates and the votes shall then be counted;—The person having the greatest number of votes for President, shall be the President, if such number be a majority of the whole number of Electors appointed; and if no person have such majority, then from the persons having the highest numbers not exceeding three on the list of those voted for as President, the House of Representatives shall choose immediately, by ballot, the President. But in choosing the President, the votes shall be taken by states, the representation from each state having one vote; a quorum for this purpose shall consist of a member or members from two-thirds of the states, and a majority of all the states shall be necessary to a choice. And if the House of Representatives shall not choose a President whenever the right of choice shall devolve upon them, before the fourth day of March next following, then the Vice-President shall act as President, as in the case of the death or other constitutional disability of the President.—The person having the greatest number of votes as Vice-President, shall be the Vice-President, if such number be a majority of the whole number of Electors appointed, and if no person have a majority, then from the two highest numbers on the list, the Senate shall choose the Vice-President; a quorum for the purpose shall consist of two-thirds of the whole number of Senators, and a majority of the whole number shall be necessary to a choice. But no person constitutionally ineligible to the office of President shall be eligible to that of Vice-President of the United States.

AMENDMENT 13

(Ratified December 6, 1865)

Section 1.   Neither slavery nor involuntary servitude, except as a punishment for crime whereof the party shall have been duly convicted, shall exist within the United States, or any place subject to their jurisdiction.

Section 2.   Congress shall have power to enforce this article by appropriate legislation.

AMENDMENT 14

(Ratified July 9, 1868)

Section 1.   All persons born or naturalized in the United States, and subject to the jurisdiction thereof, are citizens of the United States and of the State wherein they reside. No State shall make or enforce any law which shall abridge the privileges or immunities of citizens of the United States; nor shall any State deprive any person of life, liberty, or property, without due process of law; nor deny to any person within its jurisdiction the equal protection of the laws.

Section 2.   Representatives shall be apportioned among the several States according to their respective numbers, counting the whole number of persons in each State, excluding Indians not taxed. But when the right to vote at any election for the choice of electors for President and Vice President of the United States, Representatives in Congress, the Executive and Judicial officers of a State, or the members of the Legislature thereof, is denied to any of the male inhabitants of such State, being twenty-one years of age, and citizens of the United States, or in any way abridged, except for participation in rebellion, or other crime, the basis of representation therein shall be reduced in the proportion which the number of such male citizens shall bear to the whole number of male citizens twenty-one years of age in such State.

Section 3.   No person shall be a Senator or Representative in Congress, or elector of President and Vice President, or hold any office, civil or military, under the United States, or under any State, who, having previously taken an oath, as a member of Congress, or as an officer of the United States, or as a member of any State legislature, or as an executive or judicial officer of any State, to support the Constitution of the United States, shall have engaged in insurrection or rebellion against the same, or given aid or comfort to the enemies thereof. But Congress may by a vote of two-thirds of each House, remove such disability.

Section 4.   The validity of the public debt of the United States, authorized by law, including debts incurred for payment of pensions and bounties for services in suppressing insurrection or rebellion, shall not be questioned. But neither the United States nor any State shall assume or pay any debt or obligation incurred in aid of insurrection or rebellion against the United States, or any claim for the loss or emancipation of any slave; but all such debts, obligations and claims shall be held illegal and void.

Section 5.   The Congress shall have power to enforce, by appropriate legislation, the provisions of this article.

AMENDMENT 15

(Ratified February 3, 1870)

Section 1.   The right of citizens of the United States to vote shall not be denied or abridged by the United States or by any State on account of race, color, or previous condition of servitude.

Section 2.   The Congress shall have power to enforce this article by appropriate legislation.

AMENDMENT 16

(Ratified February 3, 1913)

The Congress shall have power to lay and collect taxes on incomes, from whatever source derived, without apportionment among the several States, and without regard to any census or enumeration.

AMENDMENT 17

(Ratified April 8, 1913)

The Senate of the United States shall be composed of two Senators from each State, elected by the people thereof for six years; and each Senator shall have one vote. The electors in each State shall have the qualifications requisite for electors of the most numerous branch of the State legislatures.

When vacancies happen in the representation of any State in the Senate, the executive authority of such State shall issue writs of election to fill such vacancies: *Provided,* That the legislature of any State may empower the executive thereof to make temporary appointments until the people fill the vacancies by election as the legislature may direct.

This amendment shall not be so construed as to affect the election or term of any Senator chosen before it becomes valid as part of the Constitution.

AMENDMENT 18

(Ratified January 16, 1919. Repealed December 5, 1933 by Amendment 21)

Section 1.   After one year from the ratification of this article the manufacture, sale, or transportation of intoxicating liquors within, the importation thereof into, or the exportation thereof from the United States and all territory subject to the jurisdiction thereof for beverage purposes is hereby prohibited.

Section 2.   The Congress and the several States shall have concurrent power to enforce this article by appropriate legislation.

Section 3.   This article shall be inoperative unless it shall have been ratified as an amendment to the Constitution by the legislatures of the several States as provided in the Constitution, within seven years from the date of the submission hereof to the States by the Congress.

AMENDMENT 19

(Ratified August 18, 1920)

The right of citizens of the United States to vote shall not be denied or abridged by the United States or by any State on account of sex.
    Congress shall have power to enforce this article by appropriate legislation.

AMENDMENT 20

(Ratified January 23, 1933)

Section 1.   The terms of the President and Vice President shall end at noon on the 20th day of January, and the terms of Senators and Representatives at noon on the 3d day of January, of the years in which such terms would have ended if this article had not been ratified; and the terms of their successors shall then begin.

Section 2.   The Congress shall assemble at least once in every year, and such meeting shall begin at noon on the 3d day of January, unless they shall by law appoint a different day.

Section 3.   If, at the time fixed for the beginning of the term of the President, the President elect shall have died, the Vice President elect shall become President. If a President shall not have been chosen before the time fixed for the beginning of his term, or if the President elect shall have failed to qualify, then the Vice President elect shall act as President until a President shall have qualified; and the Congress may by law provide for the case wherein neither a President elect nor a Vice President elect shall have qualified, declaring who shall then act as President, or the manner in which one who is to act shall be selected, and such person shall act accordingly until a President or Vice President shall have qualified.

Section 4.   The Congress may by law provide for the case of the death of any of the persons from whom the House of Representatives may choose a President whenever the right of choice shall have devolved upon them, and for the case of the death of any of the persons from whom the Senate may choose a Vice President whenever the right of choice shall have devolved upon them.

Section 5.   Sections 1 and 2 shall take effect on the 15th day of October following the ratification of this article.

Section 6.   This article shall be inoperative unless it shall have been ratified as an amendment to the Constitution by the legislatures of three-fourths of the several States within seven years from the date of its submission.

AMENDMENT 21

(Ratified December 5, 1933)

Section 1.   The eighteenth article of amendment to the Constitution of the United States is hereby repealed.

Section 2.   The transportation or importation into any State, Territory, or possession of the United States for delivery or use therein of intoxicating liquors, in violation of the laws thereof, is hereby prohibited.

Section 3.   This article shall be inoperative unless it shall have been ratified as an amendment to the Constitution by conventions in the several States, as provided in the Constitution, within seven years from the date of the submission hereof to the States by the Congress.

AMENDMENT 22

(Ratified February 27, 1951)

Section 1.   No person shall be elected to the office of the President more than twice, and no person who has held the office of President, or acted as President, for more than two years of a term to which some other person was elected President shall be elected to the office of the President more than once. But this Article shall not apply to any person holding the office of President when this Article was proposed by the Congress, and shall not prevent any person who may be holding the office of President, or acting as President, during the term within which this Article becomes operative from holding the office of President or acting as President during the remainder of such term.

Section 2.   This article shall be inoperative unless it shall have been ratified as an amendment to the Constitution by the legislatures of three-fourths of the several States within seven years from the date of its submission to the States by the Congress.

AMENDMENT 23

(Ratified March 29, 1961)

Section 1.   The District constituting the seat of Government of the United States shall appoint in such manner as the Congress may direct:

A number of electors of President and Vice President equal to the whole number of Senators and Representatives in Congress to which the District would be entitled if it were a State, but in no event more than the least populous State; they shall be in addition to those appointed by the States, but they shall be considered, for the purposes of the election of President and Vice President, to be electors appointed by a State; and they shall meet in the District and perform such duties as provided by the twelfth article of amendment.

Section 2.   The Congress shall have power to enforce this article by appropriate legislation.

AMENDMENT 24

(Ratified January 23, 1964)

Section 1.   The right of citizens of the United States to vote in any primary or other election for President or Vice President, for electors for President or Vice President, or for Senator or Representative in Congress, shall not be denied or abridged by the United States or any State by reason of failure to pay any poll tax or other tax.

Section 2.   The Congress shall have power to enforce this article by appropriate legislation.

AMENDMENT 25

(Ratified February 10, 1967)

Section 1.   In case of the removal of the President from office or of his death or resignation, the Vice President shall become President.

Section 2.   Whenever there is a vacancy in the office of the Vice President, the President shall nominate a Vice President who shall take office upon confirmation by a majority vote of both Houses of Congress.

Section 3.   Whenever the President transmits to the President pro tempore of the Senate and the Speaker of the House of Representatives his written declaration that he is unable to discharge the powers and duties of his office, and until he transmits to them a written declaration to the contrary, such powers and duties shall be discharged by the Vice President as Acting President.

Section 4.   Whenever the Vice President and a majority of either the principal officers of the executive departments or of such other body as Congress may by law provide, transmit to the President pro tempore of the Senate and the Speaker of the House of Representatives their written declaration that the President is unable to discharge the powers and duties of his office, the Vice President shall immediately assume the powers and duties of the office as Acting President.

Thereafter, when the President transmits to the President pro tempore of the Senate and the Speaker of the House of Representatives his written declaration that no inability exists, he shall resume the powers and duties of his office unless the Vice President and a majority of either the principal officers of the executive department or of such other body as Congress may by law provide, transmit within four days to the President pro tempore of the Senate and the Speaker of the House of Representatives their written declaration that the President is unable to discharge the powers and duties of his office. Thereupon Congress shall decide the issue, assembling within forty-eight hours for that purpose if not in session. If the Congress, within twenty-one days after receipt of the latter written declaration, or, if Congress is not in session, within twenty-one days after Congress is required to assemble, determines by two-thirds vote of both Houses that the President is unable to discharge the powers and duties of his office, the Vice President shall continue to discharge the same as Acting President; otherwise, the President shall resume the powers and duties of his office.

AMENDMENT 26

(Ratified July 1, 1971)

Section 1.   The right of citizens of the United States, who are eighteen years of age or older, to vote shall not be denied or abridged by the United States or by any State on account of age.

Section 2.   The Congress shall have the power to enforce this article by appropriate legislation.

APPENDIX 3
Table of Cases*

*Cases excerpted in the text are indicated by **boldface.**

INDEX